Janie's Journal

VOLUME 1

1984-1987

Also by Janie Tippett

Four Lines a Day

Anthology Appearances

Talking On Paper: An Anthology
of Oregon Letters and Diaries

Crazy Woman Creek:
Women Rewrite the American West

Janie's Journal

VOLUME 1

1984-1987

Janie Tippett

Lucky Marmot Press

www.luckymarmotpress.com

Wallowa, Oregon

For Virgil Rupp

Acknowledgements

First of all, I would like to give credit to my mother, Blanche Bachman (Frenaye), who always encouraged my writing, and who insisted I keep a record of my columns from the beginning.

Next, my father, Matthew Bachman, who along with my mother offered unconditional love, no matter how many mistakes I made in life. It was after my father's death in 1984 that I began to write these columns, and I continued to do so for 31 years.

I credit Agri-Times N.W. Editor Virgil Rupp, who believed in me and taught me journalism, as well as the support offered by the Agri-Times' current editor, Sterling Allen.

I thank Wallowa County's Fishtrap for providing the only college I ever attended.

I am in-debted to Jenner Hanni, whom I met at Fishtrap's Outpost writing workshop on the Zumwalt Prairie in 2017. He has made these compilations of my columns possible.

Above all, I am most grateful for the vast readership of Janie's Journal, as published in the newspaper Agri-Times, North West.

Janie Tippett,
Alder Slope, Oregon, 2021

The Country Auction

In 1984, the agricultural newspaper Agri-Times N.W. sent a free copy of its first issue to rural mailboxes. Janie Tippett read and really liked her copy, "thought it was all really positive stuff." She and her husband Doug trailed their cattle to summer pasture in the hills that morning, then spent the afternoon at a country auction of the estate of a family they had known. When she got home, something moved Janie to write up what she had seen at the auction, and something else made her send the essay in to the publication. In the quickest time a letter could possibly take to arrive, Virgil Rupp was on the phone. "We loved your piece and we want to publish it," he said. "We want you to be a columnist." As Janie recalls, she said, "Gee, I keep a journal every day. I can write about ranch life," to which he replied, "You're in!" This is that first essay.

The last of the yearlings filed into the hill pasture at Butte Creek. It was the last day of March, and we had trailed three hundred head of cows and yearlings to the hills from the ranch on upper Prairie Creek. A two-day's drive, and nearly thirty miles, we had ridden the long road, gazing at the fields of buttercups amid the last of winter's snowbanks. Now on this Saturday we headed for the valley to attend the auction.

We drove into the ranch setting to find the auction already in progress. This spot was situated in the beautiful Wallowa Valley, near the small town of Joseph. Cars were parked everywhere. The day warm and lovely with periods of sunshine. Crowds of people mingled around the fifty-year accumulation of this family's life, and it was with pathos, nostalgia and empathy that I viewed the proceedings of this auction.

Widowed and alone, the ranch woman sat in a chair in her run-down yard. The vacant house stood nearby. The yard fence sagging, all the furniture sitting out in the March sunshine. Everything... including a HomeComfort wood-cooking stove of grey enamel. The stove, appearing to have been used until just recently, was in good condition.

Some months ago, the woman, living alone, had gone into Joseph to help a neighbor and friend clean house, had slipped on the winter's ice and broken a hip. It had mended sufficiently to allow her to walk with the aid of a walker. She had been brought to the auction by a daughter. As a result, however, she had made the decision to leave her beloved home and now resides in an apartment out of the area.

So here she sat...watching her treasured belongings and personal items, many of which were of antique value, being purchased by all these people, to be scattered to the winds of time. I could not but think of the memories and feelings she must be experiencing as each item sold.

I walked around, looking at the old furniture, then entered a root cellar. The shelves were still lined with jars of fruit and vegetables. I gazed down at the barn lot at the many kinds of old farm machinery. Presently, I sat down next to the woman, and visited with her. We talked about how this morning we had driven the cattle to the hills. How, at the spot we loaded up our horses for the return trip, I had learned from one of the cowboys, that on this same spot lay the homestead of her deceased husband's parents! The same cowboy, an old-timer himself, born in these hills, had related to me a little about her life.

We talked about where she was born, which was just down the canyon from there, and how she was a school marm at the now-crumbling Dry Salmon Creek School. She had boarded with the family and ultimately married a son, while teaching at this remote school. I could picture her in my mind's eye, riding her horse to school.

"Yes," she replied. "I packed water for the school's needs and taught grades one through eight in that one-room school."

I didn't have any further opportunity to talk to her, because her daughter was helping her up to leave.

This Wallowa County woman, her hands calloused and worn from ranch work, the cooking, cleaning, canning, and raising of a family. Her eyes reflected the wisdom of time spent in the Wallowa country, the hard winters and the busy summers and falls. Now the milk cow is gone, along with the butter churn and cream separator. The baby chicks she used to raise each spring no longer "cheep, cheep" in the barn and the worn feeders and waterers are being sold today. The hoes, rakes, and garden tools are lined up along the fence, the garden she so faithfully tended no longer there.

The auctioneer was chanting and talking about each item...a copper boiler, a butter churn, an old Griswold waffle iron for a wood stove. Children and dogs ran around and over the furniture. A food concession wagon was doing a land office business feeding the crowds of people. Wallowa County loves a country auction! The warm afternoon became clouded up, and a brisk, chill wind began to blow. The nearby Wallowa mountains were wreathed in swirling mists and a spring snow storm became evident very quickly. All manner of harness, shop tools, milk cans, old wagons, relics of the past, lined up to be sold to the highest bidder.

"Better step right up and bid now, folks, they don't make these anymore," chanted the auctioneer. People bought the old wagons just to get the wagon wheels. The cold became more intense and the crowd thinned. The last wagon loaded with junk sold. The people loaded up their wares and left. The woman had left earlier, aided by her daughter. She had given a long, sad look at a part of her life that would never be again. She climbed into her car and never looked back. I could see that she had tears in her eyes. I did, too...

I glanced at the house as a breeze sent a light sifting of snow downward. The pretty day ending in a cold spring storm. March going out like both the proverbial lion and lamb! The close-by mountains, a sight the woman must have loved, looked down on the near-deserted scene. The lonely house, devoid of its contents, stood forlorn, old...the outbuildings in need of repair. Once well-tended and loved, now stood vacant and sad-looking. Life is so short. Old age so full of hurt and pain. Memories are what the woman has left, and the satisfaction of having lived in an era which could have been one of the best. Time will tell.

The gate hanging from broken hinges in the yard banged in the wind. The plastic around the windows, to keep out the winter cold, fluttered and tore itself in each new gust of wind. The ghosts of the past played in the barn. All was still as we drove out of the yard to our own ranch, to tend to our chores, build a fire, and find food and warmth in our home.

Sunday morning, my husband and I baked sourdough waffles on our wood cook stove. We thought them especially good. They had been made an with old Griswold waffle iron! One that my son Todd had purchased for me at yesterday's auction...

Two Wallowa County cowboys and their dogs trail cattle to the hills along the Crow Creek Road. The last snowbanks remain on the hillsides.

1984

May 1—Turnout time.

The annual exodus to the hills has begun. The cattle, tired of being hayed the long winter months, are on the go to grass. Grass…the most important ingredient in cattle ranching.

The native, nutritious bunch grass of the Wallowa County hill country beckons. The cattle graze the first succulent shoots along the way to their summer ranges. Little calves tag behind, having to be prodded along by the riders on horseback. Sometimes it is easier to walk and lead the horse as we push the small ones along.

It is a slow journey, and long. The 450 head of yearlings, fall calves, cows and calves in this drive will cover 30 miles in two days. Some of the small calves are hauled in a truck.

In May, the weather is not always warm in Wallowa County. On this drive they experienced cold rain, winds, sleet, snow squalls and brief periods of sun.

We camped out with the cattle on Crow Creek, where the thermometer dipped low by morning, causing ice to cover the puddles. The cowboys, clad in longjohns, slickers and warm gloves, urge the cattle on and cover the long miles to the summer pastures on Salmon Creek.

Bluebelles, yellowbelles and buttercups gladden the hearts of the riders. Hawks fly lazily in their air currents. Mallard ducks and Hungarian partridge are "paired up."

The snow banks have mostly disappeared. The stock ponds are full and the ground contains sufficient moisture for growing grass—we just need some warm temperatures. The grass is later in coming this year.

May First is the traditional "Turnout Time" in Wallowa County. It will be considerably later at the higher elevation summer ranges.

The hay piles have disappeared. It has been a long winter in our high mountain valley.

May 18—As the dawn light appears, birdsong awakens us here on Prairie Creek. It is four a.m. A lovely day begins, clear with sunny blue skies. The grass turns the valley into brilliant hues of green, a sight for sore eyes after our long winter. I spent yesterday cooking and baking—a potato salad, two raspberry pies, a large loaf of sourdough bread, three fried chickens, and a pot of beans.

After a hearty breakfast of sourdough hot cakes, bacon and eggs, we load up our gear and "head for the hills." For today is branding day, and it is a 30-mile drive to our ranch headquarters on Wet Salmon Creek. Along the Crow Creek road we pass the old log buildings of the Church Dorrance place; nostalgic reminders of a bygone era. I stop to photograph (in this perfect morning light) the lovely, old log structures.

Out on the lonely reaches of Salmon Creek, the cowboys soon have cows and calves gathered up and corralled. They are sorted and penned separately. A cacophony of sound fills the air; cows bawling for their calves and calves calling mamma!

Our sheepherder stove is burning. Pots of coffee and beans send delicious aromas into the fresh morning air.

The irons are soon red hot in the branding fire. Dust and smoke mingle with the sounds of the cattle. Everyone has a job. Vaccinating, branding, castrating, working the chute gate, and flesh marking. My job is pushing, three by three, the calves up a long, muddy, wooden chute.

At noon, we spread the picnic out upon the green grass and eat. Food never tasted so good! The horses, dogs and cowboys rest. Then back at 'em, until the last calf goes through the chute. The cows are then put through to be vaccinated and some have their ear tags changed.

The afternoon wears on, the sun sinks low. The cows and calves, reunited once more, are turned out to their summer range. The cows will milk good now on the native bunch grass, and the calves will grow sleek and fat.

We unsaddle the horses, pack up the picnic and leave for the valley ranch where our nightly chores await. As I gather the eggs, milk the cow and clean the mountain oysters, I reflect on this day. How lucky we are to be healthy enough to do a good day's work and live in such a beautiful country.

My father, who passed away in March of this year, had a clipping pinned up on his wall. After his death, I kept it. On closer inspection, I see it was torn from an old recipe book. It is entitled: "Take time for 10 Things."

During these busy spring days, I am reminded of this simple message. How we should all take note of these "things."

Daddy always brought this clipping to the attention of his children and grandchildren. He was a dairyman, was close to the good earth and lived by this code—so should we all.

Todd Nash and Doug and Ben Tippett brand calves on Wet Salmon Creek.

A loaf of sourdough bread comes out of the Dutch oven

TAKE TIME FOR 10 THINGS

1. Take time to Work— It is the price of success.

2. Take time to Think— it is the source of power.

3. Take time to Play— it is the secret of youth.

4. Take time to Read— it is the foundation of knowledge.

5. Take time to Worship— it is the highway of reverence and washes the dust of earth from our eyes.

6. Take time to Help and Enjoy Friends— it is the source of happiness.

7. Take time to Love— it is the one sacrament of life.

8. Take time to Laugh— it is the singing that helps with life's loads.

10. Take time to Plan— it is the secret of being able to have time to take for the first nine things.

For some unknown reason the 9th Thing is missing. Perhaps it could be: Take time to take care of yourself, eat well, exercise and rest. For you must feel good and healthy to accomplish any of the above.

June 9—We are saddling up the horses on Salmon Creek by 7:30 on this cool, cloudy morning. We've driven the 30 miles to the hill ranch after arising early to fix breakfast, lunches and do chores.

The four horses caught and saddled, we mount up and ride off into the Deadman pasture to gather up the fall calving cows. These cows have put on weight since March 30 when they were trailed out to this hill range. Our "cowboys" for this three-day ride are Jennifer and Jeanette (my visiting nieces), husband Doug and myself. These cows will be driven 40 miles to our leased pasture land on the east moraine of Wallowa Lake.

The green rolling hills, covered with a lush growth of bunch grass, carpets of wildflowers, their scent hanging in the morning air, and the happy song of the meadowlark fill our senses. We gather up the scattered cows and let them out onto the gravel road. Jeanette rides in the lead, Jennifer and I bring up the rear.

We pass the Dry Salmon Creek School house, and down Dorrance Grade. These girls are good hands. My husband catches up with us at the Dorrance place where we let the cows rest and eat our lunch.

It is cold now, with a chill wind blowing, threatening black clouds loom ahead of us. We are warmly clad and carry slickers.

AGRI-TIMES NORTHWEST, Friday, June 29, 1984 Page 7

Ranch hands are, from left, Todd Nash, Jennifer Bachmann, Steve Tippett, and Jeanette Bachmann.

The weather does everything to us as we cover the long miles. It rains and sleets, the wind blows in furious gusts. Then the sun comes out, only to disappear again behind a dark cloud.

The girls, 22-year-old twins, are visiting from California. They shiver in the cold, but don't complain.

My husband has driven back to the valley ranch, leaving us in charge of the herd. We are told to drive the cattle to Circle M Ranch, then let the cows graze the road side until six o'clock. When they had their fill, we were to corral them for the night. We trailed into Circle M at 3:30 p.m. and began the long wait, "holding" the cows in the road.

The wind increased, a cold rain began. Even in down jackets, slickers and gloves, we were chilled to the bone.

I knew there was a small wood stove in a nearby scale house, so started up a fire. Pack rats were in evidence and the shack was dusty and small. We took turns warming ourselves by the fire, sitting on chunks of wood while rain pelted down on the scale house's tin roof.

At 5:30 p.m. we made the decision to corral the cows. I opened the gate and we drove them in. The girls and I tied up our horses and fled again to the fire.

Our "boss" showed up after six. We unsaddled, left the horses in a corral and headed to the valley.

June 10—We were back at the corrals just after sunup Sunday morning. A nicer day, coolish, but no wind or rain, yet. The three of us trailed the herd to the valley; 30 miles over with, the final leg tomorrow.

June 11—Monday morning, we were saddled up and had the cattle heading up toward the moraine before seven. A lovely morning with snow-clad mountains so close, green fields and meadows, June just "Busting out all over!"

These fall calvers will graze the steep mountain pastures and start calving in the middle of August. They are of many colors from the Simmental cross-breeding.

As we headed back to the main ranch, we felt as if these last three days were indeed an experience. Just our everyday life in the country, but almost 40 miles of riding for the twins. They grew up on a ranch in the northern California foothill country, riding in high school rodeos, but this was their first taste of a working Oregon cattle ranch, a trip they may remember all their lives.

It is a pity more young people cannot experience these events. It would make for less problems in some of our modern youth. Enduring a few discomforts, sticking with a job, and seeing it through is a learning experience that many young people never do learn.

June 26—Star is as natural a part of my daily life here on Prairie Creek as eating and sleeping. She is a ritual, a chore, a task that I perform twice a day seven days a week. Is it any wonder that this big black and white Holstein cow and I are on the same wavelength? She needs me and I need her.

Star is a link with my childhood. Being reared on a purebred Guernsey dairy ranch, I formed an early love for the milk cow, a love that has endured for over 45 years.

My father taught me to milk when I was only five. Perched on a small wooden one-legged stool, I struggled with the large teats until finally I managed to squeeze out the first drops of milk.

My father was consumed by the raising and breeding of fine registered Guernsey cattle. I therefore shared this intense love for these wonderful cows.

Guernseys were my favored 4-H projects and I delighted in showing them at local and state fairs. While raising my own family, it seemed only natural to own a family milk cow. I became proficient at grafting orphan calves on several other dairy cows we owned.

Now, here on Prairie Creek, I have the "run" so to speak, of the milk cow herd! My herd consists of three milk cows of various mixed

"Star doesn't like men."

lineage, and their offspring heifers (future replacements). Each has a name—Daisy, Liza, May, and Star.

Star is the one who has stolen my heart. This Holstein matron has not only produced milk for our family these last six years, but raised 15 calves as well. In addition to raising her own yearly calf, she is the one I graft orphan or rejected calves on.

She gives gallons of milk. The overflow goes to raise other "adopted" calves and also feed an assortment of barn cats, cowdogs, and chickens. Her wholesome milk has nourished our bodies and given us strength to do our daily work. Since I am the one who sees her the most, I've become tuned in to her moods.

Only once did she appear sick. The veterinarian was summoned. The diagnosis... Hardware! Star was taken to the vet's, operated on and allowed to come home.

I'll never forget the look she gave me when she returned. She had survived the operation, but somehow some of her former dignity was missing—her tail was a bloody stub. It had been caught in the chute gate! Our vet apologized. But I must say that, although the stub of her tail has long since healed, I think of that vet every time she whacks me in the face with that hard nub of a tail.

Like daddy taught me, a tail is the tail and the "switch" is the coarse hairy part attached to the tail.

Always before, I could slip the switch between my knees, thus eliminating a swoosh in the face during fly time. Now the switch is missing and I am left to deal with the dull thwack or thud of the tail stump.

Star doesn't like men, no doubt due to previous unpleasant incidents, plus the chute gate episode. She does like me, and there is something gratifying about this. I treat her with respect and ditto her with me.

We have this mutual understanding. Milk cow behavior has been written about for years, but this cow is very special. I remember all the cold winter days I have tended to her.

Some mornings in January, she would walk into the barn sheathed in ice, other times covered with snow. The blobs of white soft snow would melt and fall onto the barn floor.

Star is a creature of habit. If I don't show up at the appointed hour she lets me know by loud moos.

In all seasons, in all moods, our daily lives are entwined. When Star has to leave us, I hope it is to where sweet clover, shade, no flies and everlasting springtime will fill her days...

Now, I must stop pounding on this typewriter. Star is bawling at the barn door!

July 18—Hin-mah-too-yah-lat-kekht is said to mean "Thunder-rolling-in-the-mountains." It is the name given to young Chief Joseph, the famous Nez Perce Indian. Chief Joseph and his band lived in the Wallowa Valley before the advent of the white man. It was their ancestral home.

On this hot and humid July afternoon, all that remains of the Nez Perce in the valley is the "Thunder-rolling-in-the-mountains." As I write, huge rolling thunder heads romp and play, creating a resounding roar over the Wallowas.

The snow-melt has been tumbling down the canyons to join the creeks and rivers. The Imnaha, Snake, Minam, Lostine, and Wallowa rivers are full of rushing white water.

On the valley ranches, haying is in full swing. Over 20 days of blue skies, sunshine and dry weather has enabled the farmers to put up their hay in record time.

Here on Prairie Creek, my men have deep tans, look continually tired, are covered with hay dust, and eat three big meals a day. This necessitates cooking in a hot kitchen for many hours. It also means dishes, washing work clothes and a running battle to keep hay, dirt and whatever down to a minimum on the floors. It is a frantically busy time. Our brief, beautiful summer will end all too soon. Summertime means

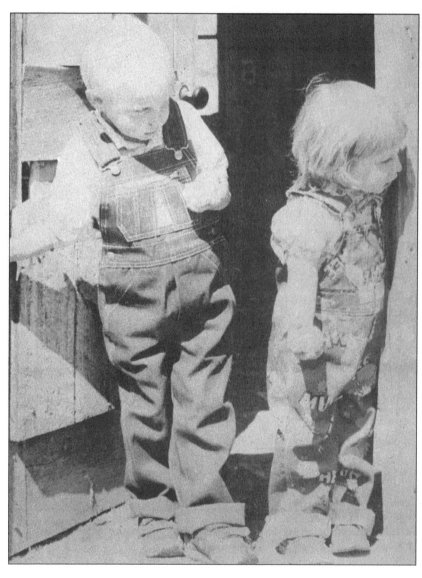

Grandchildren Buck and Mona Lee Matthews gather eggs from a chicken house built by a pioneer on Prairie Creek.

a garden to water, weed, hoe, and pick; a yard and flowers to care for; strawberries, raspberries, and gooseberries to pick.

It is also a time for summer visitors. I love our house guests, especially family from out of state. It is fun to watch them as they awaken into a golden-green morning and stare in awe at our valley with its snow-clad mountains. It is like experiencing these wonders anew.

Grandchildren visit often. How I love mine—all ten of them! They delight in simple pleasures...gathering eggs, helping me milk the cow, baking cookies or going for long walks. I am a child again when they are here.

We eat outside in the yard on these long golden evenings, then listen to the "chunk-thump" of the baler as the men keep working into the dark. The full moon Friday the 13th was spectacular, as it rose over the rolling hill land to the east.

Last night a persimmon sunset glowed over Prairie Creek. My men had quit for the night to rest. A hawk circled into the glowing, westering sun—our reward for a 14 or 15-hour day; and what a reward. How very lucky we are.

July 27—Once a year, our normally calm hometown of Joseph is transformed into a bustling city that resembles an early frontier metropolis. Overnight, the population soars to unreal proportions.

The reason for all this "Hoopty do" is the annual Chief Joseph Days celebration.

A carnival appears, lending a gaudy, noisy air of confusion to the once quiet town. The young people love it. This is their yearly chance to ride the "scary" rides, toss dimes for the girl friend's teddy bear, or just walk around and visit.

Four big rodeos draw crowds, as do cowboy breakfasts, parades, and even a muzzleloaders shoot. There is something for everyone.

However, this celebration falls during the valley rancher's busiest time. We are winding up the haying, changing sprinkler pipes, working cattle, roguing potatoes, weeding gardens, picking berries and amid all this we have houses full of company.

Returning children, some between jobs, waiting for college or "whatever", visiting kinfolk, all converge at once. The house here is Grand Central Station. The already groaning dinner table must accommodate more settings. The cook, cow milker, housekeeper, 4-H leader, mother, grandmother, photo journalist's nerves become a bit frazzled.

This summer all eligible or prospective brides decided to take the plunge. Wedding invitations cover my desk.

The Sourdough Shutterbugs 4-H club shows off their prize-winning float.

Because our summers are so short, all manner of social functions plaster our calendar. Tours, field days, luncheons, get-togethers of every description. On any given day, we can pick and choose from at least three conflicting invitations.

This year, as always, grandma became "involved" in the Kiddie Parade. "Involved" meant halter breaking two of my sex-sal-link pullets! Actually we managed very successfully with fishing leader secured to their feet.

The docile nature of this particular breed of chicken contributed to the success of my grandchildren's parade entry. Buck pedaled a tricycle with a wagon attachment down Main Street. Riding in the back, appearing to enjoy the parade, was one pullet. Little two-year-old Mona Lee pulled a wagon which transported another chicken. The result was hilarious, and drew comments from the crowds along the parade route. We managed to arrive home safely on this hot day with "none the worse for wear" chickens.

The next day they laid their first small brown eggs.

Grandma did not fare so well. The next day was the big parade. Yours truly rode a riding mule and led a pack mule to promote our local CowBelle Bar-B-Ques. She also organized a 4-H float, which consisted of members making sourdough bread. Halfway down the street, a "flour fight" ensued and sourdough "balls" fell to the sidewalk. Smoke poured from the sheepherder stove and they won first place.

Meanwhile, in the weather department, thunderheads built up and Saturday night saw one of the worst flash floods in history. Cowboys, cowgirls, carnival and Chief Joseph Days were drenched in a deluge that dumped two inches of rain.

Here on Prairie Creek, I watched the hail and downpour pound my garden. Chief Joseph had the last word on this celebration in his honor.

Sunday dawned clear, sunny and calm. The garden picked itself up, refreshed in the tropical warmth and continued to produce.

The final rodeo was terrific, the carnival "folded" and left for the next town, and another Chief Joseph Days bit the dust... er',... mud!

As I write, I gaze longingly up toward our beautiful mountains. Somehow, I seem to draw strength from them during these hectic days. It is only a dream, but, I think of how wonderful it would be to escape and unwind in their solitude.

August 8—Sometime last week, August appeared on the calendar. So did our annual Wallowa County Fair. The summer season rolls on, like a parade, with one after another of scheduled events. I find myself caught in the "daze" of activities.

It is time for the valley residents to show their stuff. "A family affair" states the premium list.

Cloverleaf Hall at the fairgrounds is transformed into a creative collage of garden produce, homemade quilts, luscious jams, jellies, homemade bread, photography, paintings, flowers, plus arts and crafts of many mediums.

Out in the livestock barns you are apt to see most anything—a runaway steer with an FFA'er or 4-H'er in hot pursuit, followed by two or three husky dads! The steer is eventually caught, but creates havoc in its wake.

Fat lambs are groomed to perfection. They fairly shine and even their noses are wiped.

I had three of my grandchildren in tow. While they carried my camera equipment, I photographed the fair. We wandered around among kids and animals. Rowdy, Chad and Chelsie were enthralled with poultry and

Two of Wallowa County's real cowboys ride in the parade—from left, Dick Hammond of Enterprise, and Jess Early, 81, of Imnaha.

rabbit grooming. Especially interesting was watching a large goose flap and honk, while being held to clean his toe nails.

Wednesday evening was beautiful at the fairgrounds. The weather perfect: the mountains, serene, calm and almost devoid of snow, looked down on the scene.

A pit barbecue dinner served by the FFA members at 5:30 was followed by the lady's lead sheep contest.

"Make it yourself with wool" contestants paraded in their outfits and led their prize sheep. A very impressive presentation. A 4-H fashion show was next; then the annual 4-H and FFA fat stock sale.

A time for parting—small girls with tears spilling down their cheeks, hugged their lambs and steers goodbye. At Cloverleaf Hall, I joined other exhibitors and took down my photographs. I will add these ribbons to my collection. We said goodbye to another fair and look forward to a bigger and better one next year.

August 9—Meanwhile back at the ranch, I avert my eyes as I walk past the raspberry patch. The zucchini are multiplying like flies, strawberries hang heavy on the plants, and all manner of vegetables in my garden are ready.

Deana Mallon shows off her registered Suffolk lamb at the Wallowa County Fair. She was a contestant in the lady's lead sheep contest and made her own outfit, as well as the sheep's.

The cow still needs milking and small brown eggs appear in the chicken house nest. The 17 Sex-Sal-Link pullets are almost into full production. There is still a family to feed, and chores to do. But for a few days we were in a "daze"…a wonderful "fair-time" feeling that comes once a year. Somehow, however, here in the valley, summer seems already over. As I write this morning, there is a chill in the air. Fall is already calling.

Monday, August 20—Here is me at 5 a.m. on a chilly morning, parked in our mini-motorhome. Doug is antelope hunting and we are somewhere out in the "boonies" between the small community of Unity and near Ironside.

We spent last night at a campground in the nearby mountains. Pulled in at 9:30 p.m. to a grassy spot near a gurgling stream. Through tall pines, we could see the stars from our bed.

We had eaten supper on a lonely spur road, surrounded by sage brush and just at the edge of Eastern Oregon-type mountains. A lovely vista below unfolded ridge after ridge in the pink glows of evening.

While Doug hunted, I cooked supper (fresh produce from our garden, and steak). We didn't see a single antelope, so asked some locals about the prospects; were told the antelope were scarce here this year.

Doug's tag was for the Beulah area, which extends down toward Vale, Juntura and Ontario. The people we talked to advised us to drive in that direction and be there for the early morning hunting.

Beat, after a long day of preparing to go on this hunt, the drive from Wallowa County, and a previous week of frenzied activity on the ranch, we crashed early.

Before daylight, Doug got up and took off down the road to the promised herds of antelope! Me, snug in my bed. Lurching along in a motorhome isn't what you'd call conducive to restful sleep. So, I soon got up. As first light appeared, and the sagebrush hills near Ironside turned pink and lavender, we sped past alfalfa fields ready for their second cuttings.

Ranches dotted the landscape on this lonely road. Dusty places, dry, with ranch-like settings, bleached skulls nailed over corrals. Cattle grazed among the sagebrush hills and draws. The Oregon desert has its own kind of beauty and it grows on one.

Suddenly I hollered whoa! Grazing in an alfalfa field was a small band of antelope. In the middle of the bunch, rearing his impressive head, was ol' Silvertip himself!

What a sight in the early pink light of an Eastern Oregon morning. They lifted their heads from grazing, looked at us and fled. We watched through binoculars until they came to the edge of the alfalfa, then milled around and stayed there. We drove to the nearest ranch headquarters to ask permission to hunt. The area wasn't posted, but thought it better to ask anyway.

The antelope by this time had started up a sagebrush-strewn draw. The golden sun broke over an eastern hill as morning appeared. The white rumps of the antelope made a startling picture. They grazed and wandered up the draw, the fawns jumping and playing in the golden light.

As I write, my husband has left on foot to circle around and "sneak up on" his wily buck. On this chilly high desert morning, with a slight breeze moving the tall mature grasses along the road, I can look up in the direction from whence my man has disappeared.

At 7 a.m., still no sign from husband hunter. With an old army packboard on his back, his hunting knife and rifle at the ready, he was last seen going over a distant hill.

7:30 a.m.

Doug is back! And on his packboard is ol' Silvertip! Blood on Doug's shirt and a smile on his face. At the mountain campground, I cook up breakfast while Doug skins the buck. After a leisurely breakfast, we almost feel like tourists on vacation instead of busy ranchers with myriad projects to carry on with back at the ranch.

The antelope is placed in a game bag and put up on top of our motorhome. He will "chill out" nicely on the return trip. The day is coolish, which will help.

Over Dooley Mountain, to Baker and down into La Grande, and through Minam Canyon into Wallowa County once more.

A brief, successful hunt and a respite from the ranch work. Back to sprinkler pipes, second cutting, shipping cattle, roguing seed potatoes, raspberry jam, canning, CowBelles, ad infinitum!

These last few precious days of summer will soon end and the fall harvest time will be upon us. This winter we will enjoy antelope meat and remember the hunt.

August 25—This gorgeous day, we are climbing up a steep, switch-back trail into the Wallowas. "We" consists of five members of my Sourdough Shutterbugs 4-H Club, a young woman leading a llama, plus two volunteer guides. I am riding my Appaloosa mare and leading our pack mule, Maud.

Doug Tippett and his antelope.

Traveling with Cupcake

The llama also carries a pack outfit. The 4-H'ers and other members of our contingent are all back-packing. We make quite a picture, as we climb higher and higher into the heart of the Eagle Cap Wilderness. Our selected camping spot is the Thorp Creek Basin. Nestled under the protective east face of Sacajawea, this pristine meadow is stilled in beauty.

Thorp Creek runs clear and pure at the edge of the basin. The last of the snow banks hug Sacajawea's rocky clefts and the riverlets of melting snow gleam in the afternoon sunlight. Yellow cinquefoil and myriad alpine wildflowers cover the area. Lovely evergreens fringe the meadow. We are surrounded by high, loose, rocky inclines. Over one ridge lies Ice Lake. Looking northwest, we can see the colorful rock formations of the Hurricane Divide.

The llama, "Cupcake," is staked in the meadow. The 4-H'ers are in heaven, gathering firewood, preparing their evening meal, setting up their tents. The weather remains perfect. Smoke from our cooking fire drifts upward, the golden light turns the Hurricane Divide to fire as evening descends. Only a tip of light on Sacajawea's summit.

As the stars come out one by one, we roast marshmallows and pop popcorn. This night, the last warm one in the high country, is breathtaking. Crawling into my sleeping bag, I can barely make out the outline of Sacajawea's slopes. This mountain is the highest in the Wallowa chain. The Milky Way arches across the sky; the glittering stars so close.

There is no wind, only the murmur of Thorp Creek.

August 26—I awake to a mountain morning, not a drop of dew on the meadow. I slept on a cinquefoil mattress next to the ground. Refreshed in the pure air, I gaze up at the pink light of dawn on Sacajawea's face. Scrambling up a rock slide, I later film the surrounding area in the morning's first light.

The 4-H'ers awaken, cook breakfast, and break camp. They don't want to leave. None of us does. Sunshine spills over the eastern ridge into our meadow. The llama, Cupcake, adds interest to our venture. As the 4-H'ers pack up their gear, I load up my pack mule and saddle my mare.

The long trail down is steep. We stop often to adjust packs. Riding along the bottom trail that borders Hurricane Creek, a wind comes up, wispy "mare's tails" clouds appear. Weather is changing. The 4-H'ers are tired but happy that they have accomplished this trip.

We look back to Sacajawea before she disappears from sight, and say goodbye to summer.

August 31—The first new snowfall covers the Wallowas today and there are four baby kittens in the cow barn manger. Back to pickled beets, sauerkraut and apple sauce!

September 22—Autumn begins, says our calendar. The signs are everywhere: corn stalks in the garden, withered and dull, showing evidence of the first killing frost.

Crookneck and Zucchini squash blossoms contrast with the frosted plant's dying leaves. The huge sunflowers defy the cold. Like tall sentinels, they continue to turn their heavy, golden heads toward the sun.

Down along the creek, I can see the first yellowing of the cottonwoods.

Star, the milk cow, needs no coaxing to leave the pasture and come into the barn now. She can "taste" her grain before she is locked into her stanchion. Cooler weather has sharpened her appetite.

Another sign of colder weather, the Bag Balm is firmer now as I apply it to Star's teats. By mid-December, it will be hard as a rock. So the Bag Balm is a thermometer of sorts!

Mama kitty meows for her dish of warm milk, her four kittens demanding and hungry.

The appetites of our ranch crew have also increased. Endless loaves of sourdough bread, apple pies, and hearty meat dishes appear on our table. It is a time of plenty. The wondrous garden continues to supply a daily feast. The last of the sweet corn is picked, a final batch of green beans. How I love my garden.

My oldest daughter, Ramona, embroidered a sampler for me. It hangs on the wall behind our wood cook stove. The simple message sums up the feeling I have for my yearly labor of love: REAP RICH HARVEST THAT LOVE HAS SOWN.

We are blessed with beautiful fertile soil here in parts of Wallowa County. Even though the seasons are short and the weather completely unpredictable, I shall always have a garden. I plant too much, says my husband, but half the fun and satisfaction is being able to give some of the bountiful harvest to friends and relatives.

A garden is a place to meditate, to be alone, to see and appreciate beauty, to be in touch with the soil.

Pierre Van Paassen once wrote: "Half of our misery and weakness derives from the fact that we have broken with the soil and that we have allowed the roots that bound us to the earth to rot. We have become detached from the earth, we have abandoned her. And a man who abandons nature, has begun to abandon himself."

In this age of mechanization and sophisticated agri-business operations, the simple family garden plot continues to be an integral part of our lives. What a satisfaction to be able to "pick" your own meal each day, knowing that the nutritious vegetables will keep your family strong and healthy.

The canning cupboard shelves are lined with a rainbow of colorful produce, preserving a bit of summer in a jar. The freezer contains berries for winter pies and cobblers. The sauerkraut ferments in the crock. We'll eat better this winter because of the garden.

Often times as I milk my cow, pull weeds in the garden and tend to my chickens, I think of the pioneer women who helped settle this lovely area. Did they enjoy the life as much as I do? Or was it all just hard work? Somehow, I don't think their lives were as complicated as our modern-day ones.

September 23—A snowfall covers the valley this morning. Sunflowers droop under the weight. The new little fall calves run around in the pasture, wondering what all this white stuff is. Added now to my chores is wood chopping. The wood cook stove pops merrily as I cook breakfast, and gulps the split tamarack almost as fast as I can pack it from the woodshed. They say wood warms you twice: once while you are splitting it and again while it burns.

September 24—Another snowfall during the night. Our new "used" potato harvester arrived today; soon be time to dig the seed potatoes, go deer hunting and trail the cattle in from the hills.

September 27—On a ranch we roll with the seasons and now welcome Indian Summer. Picked apples last evening in a neighbor's yard. Buckets of them, three varieties. This morning we are headed to the Imnaha canyon to press apple cider. The gorgeous thirty mile drive follows Little Sheep Creek. Elderberries hang in dark purple clusters and the red sumac is bright on this clear fall day.

At the Upper Imnaha River ranch, we are greeted by Pam, who gets us started on the pressing. This old press has been lovingly restored by Pam's husband, Skip. As the fragrant apple juice flows into our containers, we can hardly wait for a refreshing first drink. The wonderful freshly pressed apple juice captures the very essence of autumn.

Towering rimrocks around us and the Imnaha flowing past makes for a very pleasant outdoor task.

Pam's fall garden was overflowing with huge orange pumpkins, yellowing cornstalks, tomatoes, and squash. In a nearby pen four bronze turkeys were being fattened.

After a delicious lunch of homemade cornbread and chili, served up by Pam, we headed home with our jugs of juice, one more item to pack into our loaded freezers against the winter.

September 29—Shortly after daylight this morning found us deer hunting. Doug shot his buck, had it gutted out and packed to the road by the time I drove the truck around to pick him up.

This afternoon we checked the cattle in the hills. When we returned to the ranch, son Steve and his college friend Shane also had their bucks.

Hunter success is lower this year, so guess we lucked out.

We spent the night at Cayuse Flat Cow Camp with daughter Jackie, son-in-law Bill and their children Buck and Mona Lee. Bill had packed out a nice five-point buck from the canyons. Using pack mule and horses they had packed the deer a long way.

September 30—Returned to the ranch chores and rested up a bit, as we start harvesting seed potatoes soon. Another son, Todd, also got his buck this weekend. Buck deer season lasts only five days this year, due to the heavy winter losses caused by our previous severe winter in Eastern Oregon.

October 2—We started digging our seed potatoes today. This means breakfast on the table by no later than 6 a.m. or 6:30, all through the harvest. Lunches to make, cow and chickens to tend to and yours truly in the field by eight.

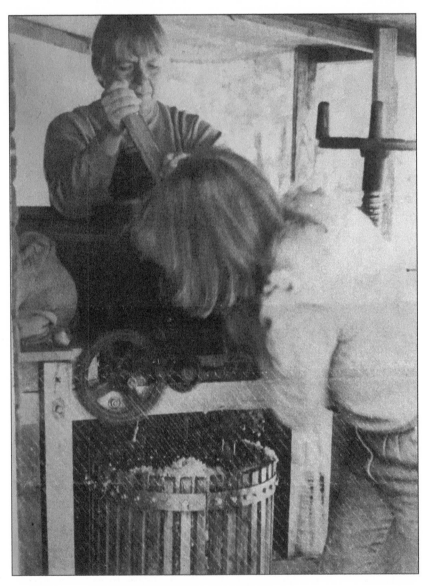

Doris pokes apples into the grinder while Pam Royes turns the crank of the old apple press, to release the juice.

Harvesting seed potatoes in Wallowa County, working from dawn to dusk.

The weather cooperates. Warm fall days pass in succession, as we women pick out dirt clods, rocks, weeds and vines to throw into the trash eliminator. The moving chain in front of us is full of freshly dug Russetts. The big potato harvester creaks, clanks and groans while we work.

As we pause to catch our breath at the ends of the rows, we notice the first yellowing of the tamarack groves high up on the mountain sides.

October 6—We are privileged to have two foreign-born women working on our harvest crew: Una, from England, and Scotty, from Scotland. We are constantly entertained by them. Today, we had "tea time" instead of a coffee break. Right in the field, Scotty set up a lace-cloth covered table, complete with matching service. In addition to hot tea, she treated us to homemade muffins, cookies, bread, butter and strawberry jam! Truck drivers and field workers did a double take at the sight.

Today was also the 15th wedding anniversary of a pair of our employees. As I hurriedly left the house this morning, I fashioned a corsage from some of the last flowers in the garden. Doris beamed like a new bride today, as she proudly wore her flowers. Although wearing overalls and covered with dust, it didn't seem to matter.

The news around the world continues bleak, acts of violence, political issues go on and on. But I am here to report that in rural America, the unsung heroes who bring food to the world's tables warm our hearts while they work. Mankind will be the richer for their very existence.

October 8—After a long day in the field, we watched the harvest moon appear this evening. A big, glowing, orange moonrise, flanked by the purple-hued Seven Devils mountain range in Idaho. There are advantages to working on the digger.

October 21—Although the first day of winter isn't until Dec. 21, we in Wallowa County can attest to the fact that it is already here! This morning, our thermometer registered a mere 15 degrees.

Heavy frost covers all. We have been working all this weekend to get all of our seed potatoes harvested. We can't begin to dig until noon, when the frost goes out of the ground.

So far the potatoes remain firm and unfrozen, but it is critical that we work fast now, in the time left. Two full crews on two harvesters, plus a cellar crew, altogether around 25 of us working this Sunday. In addition, we have seven truck drivers, who must ferry the laden potato trucks to our big insulated cellar. The potatoes are then sorted, picked through and unloaded into huge bays, where they will spend the winter in a controlled temperature situation until they are shipped out of the county early next year.

Some of us gals on the digger (we call ourselves the "Over the Hill Gang"; as we are in the minority middle-aged work force), decided to add a little diversity to our weekend. Since we didn't have to work on the digger until noon, we decided to go on a hike. This meant arising early, in order to tend to breakfast, milk cow, etc., in order to be ready to play. We drove to a nearby lake, parked the car, and on this crisp, clear, frozen morning, took a wonderful hike.

The Wallowas, snow-covered, provided constant scenery from the top of the hill. We walked down along a trail to a meadow, crunched across it to an abandoned log building. A creek alongside was almost stilled in ice. We could hear a faint gurgling underneath. We climbed a steep path that led back to the lake. Swimming in the lake were migrating Canadian honkers. They took off in flight at our approach, their haunting clamor giving us a thrill. A flock of mallards skimmed along the water, making large V's on the surface. Deer and elk tracks were visible on the trail; also, signs that coyote had been in the vicinity.

It has turned cold so quickly this year that we are not experiencing the gorgeous, colorful splendor of recent autumns. A few quaking aspen trees near the old homestead site had just begun to turn when they were frozen in the process. It is an unusual year. When, normally, most of the yellow leaves have peaked in color around the middle of October, this year finds them mostly still green. Due to this recent cold, they will merely turn brown and wither away.

The wild rose hips have turned a brilliant red as usual, and the canyon's sumac is lovely to see in bright sunshine. But the cottonwoods, aspen and willows just aren't yellowing in our part of the world this year. We photography bugs took some pictures. Then we drove to the sleepy Sunday morning atmosphere of Joseph, found a tiny eatery open, called "Back to Basics," and enjoyed a bowl of hearty soup and bread.

Thus fortified, we headed for the field to spend the day, and evening, tossing rocks, dirt clods, and weeds on the big, rattling, clanging digger. We are so bundled up against the cold, we can scarcely climb aboard the harvester. We load seven trucks in six hours, not bad.

At six o'clock, we are working with the lights turned on overhead, the sun having long since disappeared over the mountains. A bitter chill sets in. We must work fast to keep warm.

The last load of the day rumbles off across the field to the cellar. Dirty, cold and tired, we trudge to our cars and head home. A long day, but a good one.

The barn chores beckon, supper to fix and a hot bath. Phone calls from grandchildren, all's well with the family. Blissful sleep, so as to be up and at 'em in the morning.

We have a new little cow dog, a Border Collie puppy. We named him "Spud," natch! Why not? Since everything lately is coming up potatoes!

October 27—As the snowline creeps closer, we see it has covered the range grasses on the moraine pasture. Time to bring home the fall calving cows and their babies. They fairly run home to the valley ranch, smelling already the hayed-over ground that will sustain them until it is time to feed hay.

The calves born in late August and September are husky and growing well. All over the valley, the sound of bawling cows and calves, it is weaning time for the spring calves. The sounds of fall.

October 28—After chores this morning, we drove out of our snow-covered valley to the 30-mile distant, canyon community of Imnaha.

We attended a church service held in the Imnaha School House. Inside, fellowship, warmth, caring neighbors and friends. The school room was decorated with fall, country decoration: cornstalks, pumpkins, asters, colorful leaves and baskets of fall fruits and gourds.

Outside, towering rimrocks reign supreme, the Imnaha River gleaming in the bright October sunshine. Inside, the simple service (the last conducted by a departing pastor) was delivered to a full house. Tables were set up in the same room and there appeared from the kitchen a potluck that defies description. Imnaha cooks are among the best.

A local family by the name of Boswell sang for us, harmonizing in a refreshing style, the mother at the piano, brother and sister and dad all joining in. We were also entertained by local musicians on the fiddle, guitar and mandolin. The mandolin and guitar were made by one of the players.

On the way home up the canyon road this Sunday, we feel a bit better about the world after witnessing such positive goings-on in this tiny, remote community.

October 30—The men branded, castrated, vaccinated and worked the fall calves out on Salmon Creek today. It is cold, and the ground doesn't thaw much these days.

Picked up all the sprinkler pipes and stored for the winter. Also rescued the last garden cabbage; frozen a little outside, but crisp and sweet inside.

October 31—We have been invaded all week by elk hunters, the vanguard having arrived last week, followed by a steady stream of campers, RV's, horse trailers, trucks, and four-wheel drive vehicles of every description.

The first hunt began today. We will hunt in the second hunt this year. It takes real concentration to decipher the game rules these days, road closures, different hunts, special tag permits, to name a few. Trying to keep everyone happy is a monumental job. The elk continue to thrive in spite of all the varied "management" practices.

I drove to La Grande (sixty miles distant) to meet the Greyhound and my mother this evening. She will spend November with us.

In the Minam canyon, grazing contentedly on a hillside, was a herd of elk. Even on this first day of elk season, no one had yet bothered them.

November 1—The wind began to blow today, coming slowly at first, then with unrelenting fury. Every remaining leaf was stripped from the branches by a howling, keening wind that lasted without let-up until the next morning.

Our electricity went out about 9:30 p.m. We lit the kerosene lantern and had the wood stove for warmth. We were without power all night and it wasn't restored until around 10 a.m. the next morning. We heard later that the storm created havoc all over the valley.

November 5—Yesterday was mostly fair, so took a hike up on the neighboring hill, the view from on top was lovely and the walk refreshing.

This morning it is a cold 20 degrees, ground frozen and a dull cloud layer above. As I walked in from the barn with my pailful of milk, I heard them! Waving strands of wild geese filled the skies, as their southern migration continues.

It is a somehow sad and lonely feeling to see and hear the honkers. Spring seems so far away. Hanging on my kitchen wall is a saying I am trying to adhere to this season: "Be like the sun and the meadow, which are not in the least concerned about the coming winter." Bernard Shaw said that. Maybe I'll give it a try.

November 6—While Ronald Reagan was being elected to a second term in the White House, we were still digging seed potatoes.

It was as if we were on a ship a sail on the "Sea of Potato," with the wind buffeting the tarp and a light rain falling in the early darkness.

Home to change from muddy clothes, then in to vote before the polls closed.

November 7—Cloudy. Just enough rain fell to keep us out of the field today. I prepared a lunch of antelope steak, baked potatoes, sourdough bread, salad and pumpkin pie. We were joined by our P.C.A. man. He has been here all morning preparing our '85 ranch operating budget.

November 9—Spent all day cooking for our annual harvest dinner tonight. A huge bowl of potato salad, forty pounds of roast beef, six loaves of sourdough bread, pies were baked in the wood stove and electric ovens. A big kettle of ham hocks and beans simmered all day on the wood range.

The men cleaned out our big shop, built a fire in the wood stove and we gals decorated picnic tables with Indian corn, fall leaves and potatoes. Although the harvest isn't over, we decided to go ahead with the dinner.

Around 60 appetites were satiated as our employees and their families enjoyed our way of saying thanks.

November 10—Opening morning of the second bull elk season. The men were out hunting all day. By nightfall a nice spike bull is skinned, quartered and now chills in the cold night air.

Son-in-law and grandson from California are visiting, and get in on the elk hunt. Didn't have to cook for a few days, had left-overs from the harvest dinner.

November 12—Hooray! We worked all day and finished the potato digging. You could hear our whoops for miles.

November 14—Left at noon for Portland, to attend the annual cattleman's convention. Enjoyed traveling down the Columbia Gorge as a spectacular sunset flared red in the westering sun. Mt. Hood, clad in snow, put on a show for us before nightfall.

We entered the busy city atmosphere, hurtling along with the traffic.

In our entire county there is not one traffic light, so it is always a miracle of sorts to arrive safely after the rigors of city traffic. I breathed a sigh of relief, as we exited into the Red Lion/Lloyd Center.

Here we were to relax in a world of creature comforts, far removed from our humble surroundings in Wallowa County.

November 15—Awoke before dawn to a clear morning, watched a flaming sunrise flanked by Mt. Hood. Could also see the peakless dome of Mt. St. Helens from our sliding glass doors 12 stories up.

I locate my partner for the CowBelles annual school blitz and together we drive to the Mt. Tabor school, me reading a map and my partner doing the driving. We arrive at the school and do our thing. This consists of putting on a beef cooking demonstration involving the students, answering questions about all phases of agriculture, and talking about our lives on the ranch. I brought along pictures depicting our ranch operations, which proved to be of great interest to the students.

We presented the same program to three classes, about 90 students. The girls and boys ate every crumb of the food that was prepared. We felt that the country to city contacts would help bridge the gap between producers and consumers.

November 17—Heading home after three enjoyable days at the convention. No chores, no meals to prepare, living in luxury—it was fun for a while but the challenges of ranch life beckon once more. It is always nice to make new friendships and exchange ideas with people from other parts of the country.

It is pouring down rain and a fierce wind blows as we head up the gorge. We glimpse waterfalls and notice that the fall colors are still in evidence here. As we near Eastern Oregon and leave the coastal region, the rain ceases. It is good to be home.

November 19—It feels good to work hard again. Good to cook and "do" for my family. I think we must remove ourselves once in awhile to a totally different environment to more fully appreciate what we have at home.

As I grocery shop for the Thanksgiving turkey, I note the absence of the elk hunters and tourists. Only cow elk season left before the valley belongs to us again, at least for the winter. The people I meet are familiar faces, those who will share a common bond through the long winter.

We in the Wallowa Valley have much to be thankful for this Thanksgiving season.

November 21—Snow covers everything now, all the dog bones in the yard, transforming ordinary junk into objects of beauty. We shipped a huge load of heifers and steers to the C&B feedlot in Hermiston this morning. These animals will never know Wallowa County again.

Such is their lot in life.

Whole cranberries pop in their red juice, as the sauce simmers on the wood range. My kitchen is full of pre-Thanksgiving smells. Mincemeat and pumpkin pies bake in the oven.

Made up a batch of refrigerator roll dough for tomorrow's big meal.

November 22—Thanksgiving Day dawns cold and frosty, with snow everywhere. The 20-pound turkey, brown and moist, is carefully lifted from the wood stove oven. Steaming bowls of dressing, gravy, mashed potatoes, candied yams and a luscious platter of turkey is served up with fruit salad, relishes, hot dinner rolls and cranberry sauce. Thirteen around our table enjoy the food and give thanks this day for our many blessings.

As nightfall descends, quiet reigns again, relatives gone home, college young ones off to other events. We are reduced to the three of us again. Grandma gathers the eggs and I do the barn chores.

November 25—My friend Doris has a cow elk tag, so this morning we will hunt the lake hill. Bundled against the cold we hike through deep snow up to a meadow and into some woods. We come to an old mill site and have thus far only encountered deer and snowshoe rabbit tracks, no elk sign. We keep going, the snow is deeper now, then up a forested path to an old road. Just up from us is the Moraine of Wallowa Lake. We decide to take a look-see from on top.

On the windswept ridge we see where elk have recently bedded down. Exposed grasses provide elk feed here and also a high vantage point to watch out for us! The tracks led off up the mountain side. The snow along this route was very deep and the day disappearing, so we opted to turn back and give it another try tomorrow.

November 26—Got an earlier start this morning, drove to Wallowa Lake, where we began our hike. We followed an old road up until we came to a game trail that zig-zagged up the steep lake hill. Sometimes we were on our hands and knees, but we made it to the place where we had seen the elk beds of the previous day.

Down on the lake a huge band of wild geese took off, honking across the top of us. Sneaking up to within a few yards of the top, we couldn't see any elk. We decided to follow the tracks that headed up toward Mt. Howard. To make a long story short, we had a most invigorating hike, but didn't intercept the wily elk herd.

We did see cougar tracks and had the pleasure of being outdoors on a beautiful clear day. The snow-covered landscape was incredible with winter scenery of all types.

And we did manage to work off some of that Thanksgiving dinner.

November 27—We are weaning the spring calves today. They are being trucked into the valley from the Salmon Creek ranch. It is a real blizzard outside, with 60 mile an hour winds blowing snow into drifts and limiting visibility to only a few feet. It is very cold and the wind takes our breath away.

I look out from the warmth of our living room to see our horses and mule head-to-tailed with their backs to the stinging wind-swept snow. I decide to photograph them through the picture window using a flash.

It works! This picture is worth a thousand words.

November 28—Interviewed a Prairie Creek rancher's wife and neighbor this afternoon. While visiting her a snow storm developed. A quiet, soft snowfall fell outside, while inside her warm ranch kitchen I enjoyed talking to this most talented lady about her writing career. She is our "Poet of Prairie Creek," Betty Cornwell, and we are all very proud of her.

November 29—Preg-tested cows in the hills today. Also finished hauling in more calves to be weaned. Our barn lot is a cacophony of sound. At least we can't hear the mammas answering out on lonely Salmon Creek.

I have dried Star up, giving her a rest before she calves. I weaned her latest foster calves—and the barn cats are mad at me for not having their accustomed milk these mornings. Leftover sourdough hotcakes and mice will have to suffice.

November 30—Christmas bazaars put on by the local granges and churches are held in town today, but it is icy on the roads. Followed my husband into town so we could leave a truck to be repaired. Seven cars were off in the ditch or straddling the road. We had to take an alternate route, where even yours truly went off the road. The surfaces had an icy glaze that people couldn't even stand upright on, so gave up on going in.

Horses and a mule, backs to the wind, endure winter's lash as a storm sweeps through the Prairie Creek country of Wallowa County.

December 1—December makes its appearance on a clear, crisp, cold day. It is the day for the Stockgrowers' annual pre-conditioned calf sale. We attend with grandma and the grandchildren. My husband purchases a bunch of good calves that we will feed out here this winter.

December 2—The men worked and branded our newly purchased calves while we drove grandma to La Grande to catch the bus. The house seems strangely quiet now with just the two of us. We will miss her.

Christmas looms ahead, busy days of baking, sewing, CowBelle activities and company. The days are cold—been below zero for the last few mornings—but no wind and the snow sparkles both in the sunlight and the moonlight.

December 7—A pink, dawn sky backgrounds a blue and white landscape, as a cold, white moon slips over the mountains. It is a typical December morning, with the temperature hovering around zero. Not a breath of wind.

Misty vapors rise above the warmer waters of the creeks and rivers, smaller waterways are frozen over. We keep the wood cook stove and fireplace both burning these days. Coyotes slink through the neighbor's cattle, hoping to catch mice or rodents that have escaped the cold. As the first light appears, they disappear over the hillside. Often, their pre-dawn yipping comes to us on the cold air.

This is the best time of day, when all starts anew, a time to enjoy a cup of ovaltine and read a book, or simply watch the colors change in the sky, the pink light's touch on the highest peaks in the Wallowas.

The horses paw through the snow to the last of the grass beneath. The cattle huddle in bunches waiting for their daily feeding of hay. The leafless branches of the willows move gently to a dawn breeze. The rooster in the hen house crows and the fire crackles on a country morning in winter.

At four o'clock in the afternoon, a full moon rises over the eastern hills! A few pink clouds surround this phenomenon that glows in a pale, cold light that lends a surreal quality to the winter landscape. Tomorrow night will be the Immaculate Conception full moon.

December 9—Today a friend and I hiked up to the snowy woods and cut our Christmas trees. Knee-deep in snow, we looked for just the "right" tree.

We lucked out and found two trees that were part of forked trees. Selecting the straightest ones, we were able to leave behind a tree that looked undestroyed and would perhaps supply a Christmas tree next year. As we slid the trees over the snow, thick flakes of soft snow fell from a layer of misty clouds that obscured the mountains.

December 11—The glistening starburst of the sunrise was a nice welcome to the day, as seen from my kitchen window.

We drove out to the hills today to check on the cattle, the blue and white hills of winter. Weeds, teasels and grasses are transformed into objects of beauty as they droop under their covering of snow. We broke the ice on the pond for the cattle to drink, sprinkling some salt around the area to keep it free of more ice.

We put out some protein blocks to supplement the winter grasses. A few ridges were free of snow allowing the animals to graze, but we noted that the snow was becoming deeper and it would soon be time to trail the cattle to the valley. The cattle remain in good shape, however, but because the roads could drift shut, we must bring them in soon.

We note that the old crumbling Dry Salmon Creek School has burned down. Another landmark fades into memory. As we drive home dark clouds move in and a wind stirs and sifts around that vast, lonely country.

A deep winter chill sets in as the sun is obscured. It is 10 degrees when we arrive back at the valley ranch. The reflected lights of our Christmas tree cast a cheery glow on the snow. 'Tis the season to be jolly.

December 16—The cattle arrived at the ranch here in the valley about 1:30. I think they could smell the hay for miles; not so cold today.

December 21—It has warmed up on this first day of winter. The winter solstice, the time in the Northern Hemisphere when the sun is farthest south of the equator.

The temperature is at six above zero and a south wind is blowing. The drifts grow into interesting shapes, as the wind-driven snow piles ever higher and deeper. The every morning chore of feeding cattle continues. Long lines of cattle strung out across the snowy pastures eating up their daily ration of hay.

Children are for Christmas and Christmas is for children. They remind us not to lose our sense of wonder. It is the sad and lonely people who do.

Went cross-country skiing between feeding cattle and people today. City friends often ask, "What do you do in the winter?" To which I reply that it is a time to catch our breath from the pace of spring, summer and fall, a time for introspection, a time to read a good book and mostly go cross-country skiing! How I love this sport. Gliding down a snowy hill in the pure, white, glistening snow, breathing the fresh air and enjoying the camaraderie of friends is my idea of really living.

Delivered baked Christmas breads (Stollens) to friends and relatives today. One friend lives up a snowy lane just at the foot of the mountains. Really in the spirit of Christmas today!

A hay-covered wagon drawn by a wonderful team of Clydesdales was seen driving up and down the snowy streets of the small town of Joseph today, delivering the annual Christmas baskets to the needy. Strains of "Oh, Little Town of Bethlehem" drift out over the cold air. Brightly colored lights decorate the store fronts and tiny, cold crystals float in the air. Wallowa County has kept alive the true spirit of Christmas. The steam from the big draft horses' breath hangs in the frosty air and their harness bells ring.

December 23—The icy, cold deep-freeze has relaxed its grip; it is 32 degrees this morning. The drifts settle and thaw a little, the cattle perk up and the little fall calves run around and play. The sky is a dark purple and a snow storm obscures the Wallowas. Magpies, crows and hawks fly around the snowscape in search of food. A number of wild mallard ducks have decided to winter here, and can be seen among the feeding cattle, pecking at bits of grain and cured hay seeds.

We took a drive to Imnaha for a visit with relatives and to look at bare ground amid grassy canyons. The high rims were wearing a dusting of snow. The quiet, little settlement was going about its business, loaded hay trucks were going up-river to haul winter feed for the cattle.

Lacey Jo, 1-and-a-half-year-old granddaughter from Wyoming.

We noted on the way down that the ice was breaking up in Little Sheep Creek. In places the ice had blocked the flow of the water and it had spilled out onto some of the meadows where it had frozen completely over. It was creating a giant skating rink as it spread over the low, flat places adjacent to the creek.

December 24—What a wonderful Christmas Eve we had tonight, all children and grandchildren present except for the California daughter and her family. Excited children, beautiful Christmas tree, wrappings strewn all over good food and family everywhere.

The Imnaha bunch left, as they had to be back to feed cattle on Christmas day. The Alder Slope family went home and we went to bed. Visions of stuffing the turkey and cooking filled my head as I slept.

December 25—Merry Christmas from Prairie Creek! I gave the cows at the barn just a little more hay and took some goodies to the barn cats. Fed the horses and chickens and began to cook. Stuffed the 21-pound turkey, baked the rolls and worked up an appetite for the big meal.

After dinner the family began to break up and leave. First, the Wyoming one; it just won't be the same around here without Lacey Jo's friendly little banter and active presence. One by one they all left, save for one college son. What a let-down, but such a nice Christmas, and I am left with enough food so I won't have to cook for a few days.

December 30—Tenderfoot Valley Road is all drifted over this Sunday morning as a result of wind and blowing snow. A kind neighbor made an opening down one side with his tractor and blade. It is an "experience" to drive our country roads these days, even in a four-wheel drive.

Often here on Prairie Creek we must negotiate large drifts to make it to the main roads. Did manage to get out and do some cross-country skiing after the chores were finished.

December 31—A beautiful, clear day with the purest of blue skies. Cold, down near zero again. Having company over this New Year's Eve. Couldn't stand being in the house, finished chores and loaded up the skis, headed up to Alder Slope with a friend. We skied up old roads, over bridges, across snow covered fields, over fences, past frozen ponds to a friend's cabin.

The hard crust on the snow made it a delightful trip. Also the sparkling winter landscape all around us. The still, quiet, cold and the vigorous exercise stirs up our blood. Being alive to our surroundings is important to our well-being. Skied until 12:30, then home to cook, sweep, dust and prepare for an informal evening.

Built a fire in the fireplace and cooked on the wood cookstove. Home-made pizzas and snack foods with good friends, we played hearts and Uno until the New Year was ushered in by a bright, cold moonlit night. To make all dairy farmers happy we toasted the New Year with a glass of milk and some of Scotty's famous shortbread.

1984 will never be again. Do we live each day or waste the precious hours? My New Year's resolution: "If it is to be, it is up to me." Heard that on an early morning farm show on TV a few weeks ago.

This is a typical winter scene in Wallowa County. Cattle feed on their daily ration of hay in zero weather. That's Mt. Joseph filling the horizon.

Inside, a pot of beans and ham hocks simmers on the stove.

1985

January 1—Twenty degrees and partially overcast; the frost building up around the window panes has melted. A cloud layer remains poised over the peaks to create a beautiful sight on this first day of the New Year. As the sun hits the high snowy ramparts of the Wallowas, they alone are illumined by a golden light. Cattle, horses, chickens, dogs, cats fed; house warm and cozy. We take down the Christmas tree this morning, putting the bright baubles in their boxes for next season.

A resident covey of Hungarian partridge are scratching around in the hay near where the horses are eating. Most mornings, they can be seen fluffed up in the cold around my chicken pen. Pheasants up by our neighbor's also feed near the animals. An enormous flock of wild mallard ducks circles and lands to feed among Allison's Longhorn, Watusi cattle. The grain hay provides good food for them too. During the long, cold winters here in Wallowa County, man and beast must help each other to survive.

May 1985 be the year you: Mend a quarrel, seek out a forgotten friend, share some treasure, give a soft answer, encourage youth, keep a promise, find the time, forego a grudge, apologize if you're wrong, be kind, be gentle, think first of someone else, gladden the heart of a child, go to church, examine your demands on others, welcome a stranger, laugh a little more, try to understand, speak your love.

January 23—These past two weeks my husband and I took our yearly trek to California to visit relatives. Yes, ranchers do take vacations!

January is the only month we can leave, for it will soon be time to ship the seed potatoes. We are fortunate in having dependable and knowledgeable employees to leave in charge of the ranching operations.

So, we head toward warmer climes. The roads were a bit icy leaving Wallowa County, but we soon left the deep snow and bitter cold behind.

As we sped through the Oregon high desert regions, we noted an absence of snow. Cattle in most areas were being fed hay, but as we crossed over into Nevada, the cattle remained in good shape grazing the grassy sagebrush areas that stretch across that arid land for miles.

We stayed in Winnemucca the first night. Woke up to a soft, wet snowfall covering everything. On the highway to Reno, it had already melted and was gone entirely by the next day.

Crossing the Sierra was lovely and we thought often about the ill-fated Donner party as we looked down on Donner Lake and crossed that high Sierra pass.

Down into the Golden state…a land of foothills, oak trees, manzanita, Gold Rush history, fruit trees, green grass, and my roots.

We passed through towns Auburn, Gold Hill, Ophir, Virginia Town and finally Mt. Pleasant, all early day diggings, built up now as people flee from the cities to relocate in rural settings. They now commute to the Sacramento area for their jobs. Vast freeway systems connect the old, winding, narrow rural roads.

In between the urban sprawl still exist woodsy areas where the bubbling waters of the streams glide over bits of gold left over from the 49'ers gold diggings.

Dredge piles are in evidence all over Placer County. As we reach our destination in the Mt. Pleasant District, memories of my growing-up years come flooding back. Of the original 240-acre ranch, 69 still remain intact. Here we were to enjoy ourselves in a quiet atmosphere among relatives and friends.

One day we ate outside on the patio. Over 70 degrees in bright sunshine. Another time we visited my father's burial place at the old pioneer Manzanita cemetery. I sprinkled a packet of wildflower seeds over the grave. The engraving of a cow on his granite head stone brought a lump to my throat. How he loved his cows!

I spent several days spading up my mother's garden and planting onions, swiss chard, beets, and spinach. The earth was so friable due to daddy's composting all those years. The granite soil was enriched with the nutritious mulch deep down and was a pleasure to spade.

We spent a little of every day panning for gold in the creek. We were able to bring home a jar with "hard-won" gold finds. One nugget was worth all the effort, found in the first panning. We had "gold fever" from then on.

We built a fire by the stream and in the quiet oak woods, panned for gold. If we had to survive on this occupation, we would be on a "beans" diet, but it was fun.

We spent two days visiting in the South Lake Tahoe area. We were surprised to see coyotes roaming near the big airport. More memories of my girlhood—the airport covers the former Sierra House headquarters, part of a ranching operation conducted by my cousins years ago.

The Scott place situated in a huge meadow by the Little Truckee River is now a golf course. I could envision the bunkhouse where I spent my 14 and 15-year-old summers.

The mountain known as Tallac remains unchanged. Here we trailed cattle for summer grazing. A metropolis has grown around the South Shore. Casinos now dominate the horizon and the cattleman has gone.

We arrived home to a foggy, frozen, snow-covered world last evening. It was as if we had never left.

The cows, barn cats, chickens and horses are glad to see me and the wood stove is begging for wood. January is almost gone and February is near.

January 24—Back in the swing of Wallowa County living. The days are foggy and cold. The trees, power lines, cattle and fences are covered with a layer of frozen fog.

The temperature, not far from zero in the mornings, warms up to the teens, then dips back to the deep freeze chill by late afternoon. The sun tries to shine, but with no wind to stir the fog around, it remains obscured. The snow that began falling in November remains, the drifts have settled a little and a new powdering of snow from a week ago covers all. Caught up on housework and baked bread, the inactive sourdough soon came to life as we had waffles for breakfast.

January 25—Went cross-country skiing after chores here on the ranch. Our hills are great and the old ski trails were still there. Made tamale pie for lunch and invited three gals who skied with me to join us.

My husband and I had an appointment with our accountant to go over our '84 tax returns. Got that job over with for another year. Husband has spent hours at his desk working on that yearly headache that produces more forms each year to fill out. Ranchers and farmers anymore have to be good bookkeepers or they would surely sink in these times.

After supper I made a batch of potato candy to take to the potato conference next week. It is an old pioneer recipe and makes a conversation piece for our booth at the conference.

January 26—Woke up to a clear, bright dawn light. The sun came up and we have had a glorious sunny day, no fog, clouds or wind. Hurried through chores and met a friend up on Alder Slope to cross-country ski.

Scotty and I skied all day. What fun we had. We put ski poles up on our sloping downhill course and skiing without poles did a slalom of sorts. The magnificent view of the close-by mountains, the town below and the hills beyond was something else. It was so clear we could see the Seven Devil Range in Idaho.

Home in the late afternoon to bake a sourdough chocolate cake for my little granddaughter's birthday dinner here tomorrow. This cake is a tradition for birthdays at our house.

College son Steve and girlfriend home to visit when I arrive. Gathered the eggs, pullets laying the nice big brown eggs in spite of the cold winter. The fresh eggs make such a difference in baking and cooking. I am spoiled.

January 27—The fog with us again this morning, but miraculously it cleared here on Prairie Creek, while all around us it appeared to hang around the edges.

Happy third birthday, little Mona Lee! My precious little grand-daughter is three years old today. When the family arrived from Imnaha after church she came running up to me, throwing her arms about my neck and giving me a big hug. This is what life is all about. Seeing the excitement as she opened her present was worth all the effort I had put into a handmade doll. Using scraps of material at hand, I had made the 27-inch doll from a pattern in the Oregon Farmer.

Big brother Buck got his treat of the day also, as I had rented little kiddie skis for him. After we ate, I put on the clumsy paraphernalia that accompanies skiing. He trudged up the hill, I clamped on the little skis and he was off. The little tow-headed 4-year-old was gliding down the ski trail like a pro. At the bottom of the hill he crashed into some soft snow. After being helped up, mom and grandma pulled him by ski poles back up, then he was off again. What fun and thrills for a small country boy.

Seeing the light and joy in Mona Lee's eyes at the birthday cake was another treat for grandma. We enjoyed cake and ice cream and relaxed. Grandma was a bit weary by this time.

After the family left for the canyon country and we reflected on a perfect day, we realize how family get-togethers hold our families and communities together. It seems they are vital to the well-being of our youth by providing a sense of continuity and that feeling of belonging, so important in these times.

January 28—My husband and I left for Portland this morning to attend the annual Oregon Potato Conference. As we drove along the Minam Canyon, we spotted a bald eagle winging low over the frigid waters of the river. Deer and elk were scrounging for food along the exposed canyon sides. It will be a long time 'til spring for the wildlife.

A gray day with clouds interspersed with high fog. Absolutely still air hung over the gorge and the Columbia River was like glass! The reflections of hills, bridges and clouds was rather spectacular. Had it been convenient to stop on that fast freeway, I would have liked to photograph many areas that unusual day. We saw hundreds of wild mallard ducks and Canadian Honkers in the river. They must have a grain supply nearby to feed that many.

At the Red Lion we were ensconced in our fifth floor room and made comfortable.

January 29—Since the conference this year was not geared to the wives, we womenfolk left our potato-oriented husbands to their meetings and for three days toured Portland's antique shops. Today was a cold day, but blue and full of sunshine. Bundled to the teeth, we "did" the shops.

In the Sellwood area we wandered in and out of a maze of shops, some in older homes, which were interesting in themselves. Signs that read "Second Hand Rose," "Country Collectibles," "The Den of Antiquity" and "The Salt Box" adorned the entrances to these charming places. We climbed up into attics and poked around old, dusty basements.

For whole days we lived in a wonderful world of old lace, vintage clothing, rhinestone jewelry, cast iron ware, ruby glass, blue granite and gorgeous oak furniture. Never had we seen such furniture. The grand old, round oak tables, china closets and beautiful desks.

We found the proprietors friendly, courteous and very involved in their businesses. We ate lunch at little "hole in the wall" eateries, like "Jerry's Place." Collectibles from around the world decorate the walls of this charming place that could only accommodate about 10 people at a time. The food, prepared simply and deliciously, was reasonably priced, and the soups in these tiny places were simply wonderful; hitting the spot during this cold snap.

On the third day we visited the Multnomah area. Both sides of the streets were lined with tempting wares that defy description.

Donna collects miniature doll furniture and old rhinestone jewelry. Eileen was on the look-out for anything old that she can stock her soon-to-open antique shop in Joseph this spring. I have a weakness for blue granite-ware and cast iron pots and pans. If those husbands of ours knew how dangerous it was to let us loose in Portland with all these temptations they would personally plan something for the women at the conference, I am sure.

Anyway, before our buying "spree" got out of hand the conference ended. We could have opened our own shop in the lobby of the Red Lion and done quite well. I found some excellent pieces of blue granite and an old corn stick cast ironware piece by Griswold. Each evening we returned with our wares to the hotel, feeling just a little guilty (not much) about our husbands attending all those meetings.

We Wallowa County wives set up the booth at the trade show. It featured a soft-sculpture potato created by Eileen and Donna that goes by the name of "Nuclear Nell." I put out the potato candy that I'd made along with brochures about our county's seed potato industry. We gave away as door-prizes two potato clocks (run by the energy from two potatoes)!

At our evening meals we got together with other potato growers and their wives and ate at fascinating places like "The Old Spaghetti Factory" and "The Oyster Bar." Country bumpkins like us were always agape at the big city sights. It was fun, but a steady diet of it we couldn't take and our pocketbooks couldn't either. My "egg" money was all spent.

Woke up to a Portland snowfall! All the schools closed and traffic at a snail's pace. Fender-benders at every stop light. Here at home we have lived with snow since November and this city is paralyzed at a two-inch snowfall! As we drove up the gorge, the storm increased and by the time we reached Boardman the flakes were big, fat and falling thickly. Visibility was reduced to near zero. To keep my mind off the treacherous driving conditions, I sat in the back seat and embroidered three squares of my State Flower quilt. We had another passenger along on the return trip, so it didn't look like I had a chauffeur. Works great, gals. Eliminated any back seat driving.

Incredibly, as we neared the Blue Mountains the roads cleared and the snow stopped. The rest of the trip was pleasant. At home we have more new snow on our already high drifts. As usual, it is great to be home.

February 2—That little ground hog crept out of his den and saw his shadow here in Wallowa County, so guess we still have plenty of winter left. The last of the carrots that didn't get dug from my fall garden are now under an enormous drift of snow. Am sure the insulation will keep them just fine, and come spring we will eat sweet carrots!

My lucky day! Our local KWVR radio station sponsored a ground hog promotion involving local businesses. If you entered a store and asked the question "Is this the den of the KWVR ground hog?" you would win $5. As my Sex-Sal-Link pullets were in need of laying mash,

I walked into the Wallowa County Grain Growers feed store, recited the above and won the $5. The little wooden ground hog had indeed just moved to the feed store! Went cross-country skiing to work off the Spaghetti Factory and the Oyster Bar!

Back to organizing my 16-member Sourdough Shutterbug 4-H Club. A moon out this evening and 10 degrees when I chore.

February 4—Ten below zero this morning on our carport! It is much colder on other parts of the ranch. Our local radio station reports 24 below in Joseph and 26 below in Enterprise.

I bundle up: down vest, insulated overalls, wool hat and a scarf, lined mittens and snow boots. I feel like a polar bear! The minute the porch door bangs shut, the horses nicker, the cows moo, and the barn cats run to join me. This apparition in winter-clothing will wield a pitchfork to throw the cows and horses their breakfast and take warm water mixed with dog food to the cats.

Next I haul a bucket of water to the chickens and scatter wheat on the floor for them. I contend that chickens locked in on these cold, snowy days need something to keep them from getting cabin, 'er, Chicken House Fever. They happily scratch and cluck contentedly, gossiping like so many women at a "hen party." The resemblance is striking.

The coziness of our warm house with the wood stove popping merrily, and the lingering smell of the breakfast bacon is like a haven after being out on such a morning. It is clear, however, and from "inside" looking out, it resembles a wonderland.

I put a pot of beans and ham hocks on the wood cook stove. After they come to the boil, I push them to the back and let them simmer all day.

After evening chores I baked corn sticks in my new antique, Griswold corn stick pan. What an accompaniment to the beans!

February 5—Much warmer, only around zero, with tiny flakes of snow falling this morning. My Imnaha grandchildren here with me all day, while mom did her monthly shopping. I let everything go and just played with the children. We had a fun day, even went outside all bundled up and built snow caves and snowmen. My house was awash with snowy mittens, dripping boots, and wet clothing. A few cups of hot chocolate later, we were snug and warm. The children and mom spent the night, which was nice, as husband is off to another potato meeting. I elected to stay home this time, and keep the home-fires burning.

Outside, the drifts pile higher, and a border collie pup stands on a drift to peer in the window.

February 6—The lovely waning moon made a startling picture for early risers here on Prairie Creek this morning. Just before dawn's pink light hit the high peaks, the pale yellow moon was visible over the Wallowas. I ran for the camera, but by the time I got set up, a cloud layer had obscured the sight.

After the children left I dug into the house-cleaning, cleaned out drawers and straightened up after the holiday rush. At day's end I felt good about my labors. Relaxed and embroidered on the state flower quilt.

A wind began out of the south; picking up speed, it blew all night.

February 7—Knew before I looked outside what I would see. Huge drifts everywhere, our road drifted in, the horses head-to-tail against the stinging snow.

Our radio announcing some school bus routes closed. One of them being the Crow Creek Road. I could envision that lonely country virtually isolated until some snow removal equipment could get through.

It was an "experience" to chore this morning, through waist-high drifts to the chicken pen. My cows were "plastered" with the wind-driven snow all night, like someone had thrown meringue at them. Our hired man had to park at the main road and walk in, as our lane is drifted in. The cattle wait for their hay like it is the very meaning of their existence, as indeed it is. We are feeding the "Ag Bag" silage now in addition to the hay. The smell carries in the cold air, reminding me of summer.

By 7:30 the wind abates and the snow begins falling thickly. It soon adds more height to the already deep drifts. Another day to stay close to home.

Only 12 above this morning, still not exactly what you would call warm. I shovel a path to the wood shed and the chicken house. The hired men work on reopening drifted-in gates and breaking ice in the creek to open water for the cattle.

February 9—The drifts cover our fences and the cattle walk over the top. A neighbor returned one of our wandering bulls today.

The stock water problem has become acute, with drifted ditches, the water diverted above our ranch, and no water to dig down to. We hired a man with a big backhoe to break open the ditch. The cattle, without water for three days, were thirsty.

This problem exists over most of the Prairie Creek area. The high wind and blowing snow continues.

After chores I pitted some frozen pie cherries. By letting them partially thaw, they were easy to pit.

Memories of picking this bright red fruit from a friend's tree last summer made the pitting go faster. The pie was worth the effort and February is definitely a time to bake cherry pies.

Husband is out with the tractor unplugging drifts again. I am becoming adjusted to choring in these conditions, but what a breeze it will be to go outside with no bulky clothing and walk on ground.

At the barn I am greeted by four pregnant milk cows. They, too, will be glad to see green grass. I can foresee a busy spring grafting calves on these cows.

February 10—Barely made it in to the Stallion Service Auction today. Our county roads here are so badly drifted. Just gunned the motor and kept going. Did some photo-journalism and made it home the same way.

February 11—High wind all last night, drifts well over our heads around the house. It is unreal. The hired man comes to work riding a tractor, the only way he can get through.

Sunk to my waist going to the chicken pen, had to shovel out again. Our radio reports all roads out of La Grande closed. The bigger drifts have been re-arranged and formed taller shapes.

All available hands are digging out around gates to get to the cattle. The wind blew all day again here on Prairie Creek, plugging our road completely now.

Most all the ranchers are snowed in. The isolated canyon community of Imnaha is really shut off from the rest of the world, as the Sheep Creek Highway is closed by huge drifts.

We neighbors call each other and compare notes. All agree that this has been some winter.

Some ranchers are starting to calve already and dealing with that also. It is a daily chore just to get to the cattle and attend to their needs.

The weather is warming, however, and the banty rooster flew to the top of the chicken pen fence, peered over at the drifts and flew back into the chicken house. Even though the warmer air and sun spell the end of winter, my rooster decided to wait a bit longer to venture forth.

February 12—With a local pilot, my husband flew over our Salmon Creek property out in the hills today. They spotted our mule "Maud" and the young Appaloosa mare.

They appeared in fine shape, although surrounded by unbelievable drifts. The wind-swept ridges had exposed bunch grass to sustain them.

He will soon go out on a snowmobile and open more gates so they will have access to more feed.

February 13—Beautiful, clear, sunny day. The roads are finally plowed out. Our county road crews work long and hard doing a fine job of keeping the roads clear. This winter has really been a challenge.

Went cross-country skiing on Alder Slope; the fresh air and incredible view buoyed my spirit.

Attended a fifth grade "college bowl" competition at Joseph High School in which a grandson of mine participated. Amazing what our young people are learning these days. I have a newer appreciation for our school system after watching this event.

February 14—Valentine's Day dawns cold (eight above) and foggy. Made valentines for my 10 grandchildren this morning, by cutting up old greeting cards and using red construction paper. It was fun to create special ones for each child. Husband and I exchanged cards; nice to be remembered.

Planted onion seeds today in peat pots. In June, I will set the plants out in the garden's soil.

Wanting to get out of the fog, Scotty and I drove up Tucker Down Road, parked our rig and skied down a still drifted-in road to neighbor Betty Cornwell's.

The skiing was excellent and we were in bright sunshine there on upper Prairie Creek. Here, too, the snow covered the fences, so we skied

High winds and drifting snow marooned the Gardner Locke Ranch, pictured here, on Tenderfoot Valley Road in Wallowa County. Many other ranches were snowbound until they could be dug out.

back and forth across them. We delivered a borrowed book to Betty and visited with her and her husband Ken. The snow along Tucker Down Road piled so high we couldn't see over it.

Home to prepare lunch, then off to a CowBelle meeting. We are planning a Food Fair in March. Sun out, clear, cold and thank goodness no wind! Maybe we'll stay "dug out" for awhile.

February 15—We spotted four coyotes this morning in our neighbor's field. One ventured within range of my husband's rifle, so he fired, wounding it in the leg.

The coyote ran off some distance and laid down. While doing the breakfast dishes, I glimpsed him occasionally as he limped off toward the hills.

After chores, Scotty and I had planned to cross-country ski. Feeling sorry for the coyote, she and I made the decision to ski out to the suffering animal and put him out of his misery.

With my .243 rifle slung over my shoulder and mounted on my cross-country skis, I took off across the flat, frozen, snow covered field. Scotty trailed behind, pulling a sled to bring back our quarry.

Halfway across the field I spotted the coyote and he spotted me. He took off; I positioned myself as firmly as I could and shot. He went down, dying instantly.

I skied over to where he lay, having mixed feelings about killing this wild thing. Then I thought about the coyotes eating the calf being born to a heifer on our neighbor's hill and about all the deer they are pulling down this winter.

Survival of the fittest is the law of nature, but the coyote population has gotten out of hand and they say the fawn crop is in jeopardy this spring. I could see where the coyote had been hunting mice under the snow tunnels, but they are scarce and Mr. Coyote isn't getting enough to eat this cold winter.

We lashed him to the sled and skied home to give him to a young fellow who can possibly sell the pelt. Luckily, there wasn't much traffic on our road this morning or passers by would surely think these two women a bit daffy.

February 16—Beautiful, clear morning and only three coyotes out on the flat at dawn. They were sniffing around, marking the area where their comrade had met his demise. After chores, I put on my skis and skied out to where they had been. Tracks were everywhere and the coyotes had long since departed with the sunup over their hill.

This big, flat area, which lies near the eastern boundary of Prairie Creek, provides great "Slide and Glide" skiing. The harsh winter winds that have buffeted it for so long, coupled with the zero temps, have created a smooth frozen surface to ski on. It is good exercise and really gets the old blood going. I can then come home, bake, clean house and write.

My husband took me to the Sweetheart Ball tonight at the local Elks lodge. After a great meal with friends, we danced our legs off to music of the '60s until midnight. Home to sleeping Prairie Creek, lying cold and still under a canopy of stars.

February 17—Gorgeous, clear, sunny, crispy cold. Photographed upper Prairie Creek. The drifts wear a hard, frozen crust and have settled somewhat. During the day it thaws and the snow piled along the roads is something to see, like driving through carved roofless tunnels.

After chores, we drove to Imnaha to get out of the snow and visit the grandchildren. It's a different world down there in the canyon country. Little calves frolicking around on BARE ground amid unfolding canyon vistas that go on forever. The high rims wear their snow, but the lower areas are completely devoid of the white stuff.

Scotty helped move Mr. Coyote. Note the snow drifted over the fence posts.

We picked pussy willows along Little Sheep Creek. The colors were changing in the brushes along the creek; reds, browns and yellows, as the sap begins to rise. Spring is coming to the lower climes. We were invited to attend the Imnaha Fellowship Sweetheart dinner at the little school house at the bridge.

Planned by the young women of the community, it was a wonderful affair. The small schoolhouse was overflowing with canyon residents, some of whom had driven over 20 miles from up and down river to attend.

Good food, singing, guitar and fiddle playing filled the evening. Everyone in a good mood, as Spring is in the air. These people are the salt of the earth. They work hard, but always have time to help their neighbors or enjoy a special evening.

We drove the 30 miles up that winding canyon road to our snow covered valley, as always, feeling better about the world in general.

February 18—Did my chores this morning while it was still dark. My chickens wondered who was invading the hen house at that ungodly hour. The horses were pleased to receive their hay that early and began chomping down their breakfast. By 6:30 I was on my way with friends to the Anthony Lakes ski area for a day of skiing.

The lift lines were long, but the chair ride up was breath-taking on this beautiful day. On top we viewed the world. In the heart of the Elkhorn Range at an altitude of well over 6,000 feet, we had a view of the Blue Mountains, plus miles of vistas devoid of civilization.

Doris and I, who are strictly amateurs at downhill skiing, had some rather humorous experiences when it came to climbing aboard and exiting the chair lift. We stopped in La Grande for pizza and made it home by 8 p.m. A fun day, but we agreed cross-country skiing was more our speed.

February 19—We are back to the cold, foggy days again. Fog dissipated and was replaced by a snowfall.

Decided to bake Adobe bread from a recipe I'd brought home from Sutter's Fort in Sacramento. The recipe calls for whole wheat flour. The smell of it baking cheered us up on this cold day. Fixed elk steaks for supper and the bread turned out great. We'll make it through winter yet!

February 20—Hurried into Joseph after supper to organize my Sourdough Shutterbug 4-H Club. We planned our field trips and camp-outs for the 4-H year. A busy time ahead! We hope to visit and photograph new and never visited before (by us) places in this vast county of ours.

February 21—Doris came out this morning and we skied on Coyote Flats while it was still frozen. Since the good cross-country skiing days are numbered, both from the standpoint of snow conditions and time to do so, we must make the most of this winter sport.

The onion seeds all sprouted and are growing nicely. By June, I will have healthy plants to set out.

Ordered 50 Cornish-Cross baby chicks this morning from our local Grain Growers feed store. They will arrive in April and hopefully be in the freezer by the first of June.

We are busy here on the ranch preparing for our annual Bull Sale. Also we are lining up dates to start shipping the seed potatoes soon. A busy season just around the corner.

The still present drifts of snow evaporate ever so slowly, it will surely be a mess around here when all this frost goes out of the ground.

The Wallowa Valley Arts Council and their dedicated members see to it that we in the county are not culturally deprived. They sponsored a showing of the movie version of the opera "Carmen." Doris and I attended tonight at our local OK Theater in Enterprise. A fantastic performance!

We were transported to Seville and the pageantry of a bull fight. A bit gory perhaps, but a colorful segment of the opera. The film shot in the Spanish countryside contains superb photography. The wonderful songs of Carmen resounded in our little theater. What a treat! A night we shall always remember.

February 22—We've already celebrated your birthday, George, but best wishes just the same!

Went about my chores this morning singing the Toreador Song from Carmen. The animals seemed to enjoy the music. It is a drippy, warm morning. Gone is the hard freeze. The hay I fork to the horses is wet, not frozen to the next bale. The coyotes (still hungry) sing plaintively on the eastern hill. Hawks wait patiently for mice to emerge, and the birds in the willows sing of spring.

February 23—After chores Scotty and I cross-country skied, following an old snow mobile track. We were heading toward the woods that flank the eastern side of the Wallowa Lake Moraine.

After we left the track we sank at each step in deep, drifted snow. We finally made our way to the woods. Here we scooped out of the snow a pit and built a cozy fire to dry our soaked selves. The days are changing and the word is "melt." We brewed some "burnt tea" by melting snow in a small frypan. Those who camp out in the winter will know what burnt tea is.

February 24—Partly cloudy and still thawing. On this Sunday, Scotty and I decided to cross-country ski and pack the snow shoes in case the snow gave way again. What a day we had. We skied up on Alder Slope to a friend's cabin found out the hill was great skiing for awhile until it began to thaw and we began to sink.

We put on our snow shoes and trudged with those cumbersome things on until we became used to them (after a fashion). We snow-shoed down to a partially frozen pond. Here our friend caught us some trout. We had a great time, that is until we decided to ski back down the slope to the car.

Scotty elected to ski down the road, while I stuck to the field. Our old ski trail seemed firm enough until I sunk out of sight. Picture yours truly collapsed in the snow, a daypack of fish on her back (not to mention the snow shoes slung on the pack), floundering around looking for a buried ski pole.

About that time a neighbor's son came by and helped me over the fence whereupon I skied down the road. The road was icy, but the slope not too steep, and we made it without mishap to the car. Talk about embarrassing.

Naturally, when I returned home, husband had no sympathy whatsoever.

Oh well, I still contend that if you live in Wallowa County, you should enjoy the outdoors (especially in winter) or resort to being cooped up inside for over half of the year. Not for me! Besides, grandmas have to have something to tell their grandchildren.

The trout, served with hot cornsticks for supper, was worth it all.

February 25—We are receiving a load of seed potatoes at our cellars this morning. Also a semi-load of hay that is being trucked in from Union County.

Due to the long, cold winter, we've fed more hay than usual. Here in Wallowa County, the hay stacks are dwindling daily and there is no available hay left to be purchased

Yesterday's slush is frozen this morning, and the weather is cold.

February 26—The drippings of daytime meltings are stilled in icicles. Our drifts are hardened from the thawing and re-freezing. They resemble icebergs. Our house is surrounded by them. The largest one covers the garden fence. The grandchildren love to walk over this big drift and into the garden. They play among the high chunks of snow, the puppy ever at their heels.

My husband used the crawler tractor to open up paths in the fields, so the cows will have a place to calve. Received more seed potatoes today.

February 27—Today was sale day at our local livestock auction. Met husband for lunch there and then did my weekly grocery shopping. This morning, early, I had an appointment with an interesting, round barn near Lostine. I wanted to photograph this unusual structure and find out some of its history. Coming home I spotted eight groundhogs, sunning themselves on some rocks. I read somewhere that the males are the first to emerge from their dens, so perhaps these were all males.

All over the valley little calves are being born, sometimes in snowbanks. They appear healthy and can stand the cold as long as their tummies are full of Mom's milk. Only eight above this morning; the thawing and re-freezing continues.

February 28—Up early to fix breakfast and pick husband up at our feedlot, as he had driven a truck there for the hired man to feed with.

A hectic day on this last day of the shortest month. Was a "gopher" for husband, running errands, paying bills, and feeding two sons who are washing and clipping our sale bulls. Cooked a big chicken dinner at noon with homemade whole wheat rolls and a lemon pie.

Wrote an article for Agri-Times and did some dark room work. Met at the Bookloft this evening with our Wallowa County history group. An interesting meeting with interesting people.

March 2—March crept into Prairie Creek with the soft footsteps of a light snowfall. The snow let up and the thawing continued until evening when it began snowing again. I had the grandchildren all day. Little Buck and Mona were fascinated with the grooming and washing of the sale bulls.

The bulls received a warm water washing, followed by brushing and clipping. The steam created by their baths made our calving shed feel like a sauna as the warm water hit the cold air. Another semi-load of hay arrived today and had to be unloaded by our crew.

We are off over the "Mountain" to Hermiston to attend the annual C&B Livestock Production Sale. We see our bald eagle again along the banks of the Minam River, this time with his mate. Snowing as we left Wallowa County.

At C&B's sale area, a large crowd was already viewing the animals, which included some Brahman and Saler cattle in addition to the popular

Simmentals. A long line quickly formed for Jane Baker's famous brunch of bar-b-cued steak, eggs, biscuits and honey.

The sale began after the meal, with the lively bidding until all the animals were sold. The sun appeared and even though it was cold, we enjoyed the absence of snow-scapes for awhile. After my husband purchased a Simmental-cross bull, we left for the Tri-Cities to spend the night with a sister-in-law.

March 3—Beautiful, clear morning, as we head up the Yakima River to Sunnyside, Washington, to attend a farm equipment auction. Arriving at the auction we viewed all manner of older farm vehicles, tractors and implements; everything except the truck bed we had come to purchase. On the way back to Kennewick, we spotted a Barn Sale sign.

My husband got bit by the "antique bug" and we came away with several treasures to add to our own treasures at home. We both admit we must have our own barn sale one of these days.

I had fun purchasing an old set of custard cups and an antique soap dish. The sunshine and fun of browsing around the old items made for a pleasurable afternoon. Near Prosser, we lunched at the Red Barn (a restored barn turned restaurant). As we headed back over the Blue Mountains and entered again our snowy world, we thought about all the busy days ahead. A clear moon-lit night guided us home.

Meanwhile, back at the ranch. We walked into our back porch and a new-born calf blinked at us from a rug he was lying on. Ben had put him there to warm the little fellow up. The thermometer was hovering in the low teens. Guess he had gotten chilled down.

Woke up to baby calf's bawling on the porch. We loaded him into the back of a pickup (me astraddle the calf, to hold him down). When we left him with mamma cow, the pair were glad to be reunited.

The bulls in the barn look so nice, all groomed and bedded in straw. In the morning we will haul them into the sale. Snowing again today. Prospective buyers here to look at the bulls.

Star, the milk cow, is approaching her calving date. Guess I better limber up my "milking" hands soon.

March 5—On this cold, foggy morning, Star the milk cow laid down under an old willow tree in the lower pasture and gave birth to a bouncing heifer calf. Since Star was bred to a black baldy Simmental-cross bull, this baby has a white mask on her face, and she looks at me "goggle-eyed." And of all mornings to be born. Today is our bull sale. Since the door to the milking section of our barn is frozen shut, we had to put mom and baby in the calving shed.

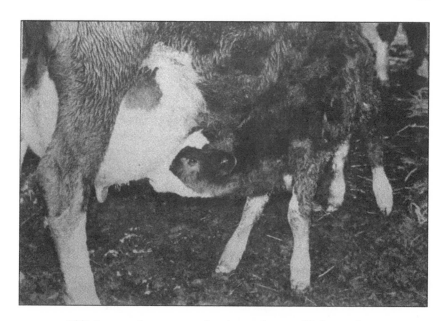

Oblivious to the camera, Star's newborn calf chows down.

We got through the bull sale in good shape. The auction ring and stands were warmed by a space heater, thank goodness. Home to chore and milk out Star. Goodness, the milk this cow has. I carefully saved the colostrum milk and froze it in plastic containers. Now we will have this life-saver ingredient for any problem calves.

March 6—Four above zero this morning. Just heard on the radio that our area was among the coldest in the state this morning.

The hungry coyotes wail on the opposite hill from us.

As spring approaches, the tempo quickens. It was felt when Star calved and it will continue until the work's all done this fall. The temperatures remain cold, but the calendar (now marked up with springtime events) marches toward a busy season. Gone are the slower paced days of winter. Upon arising now, each day is preplanned, and the moments for leisure must be stolen.

Star's calf drinks her fill, then I milk...the bucket overflows. The hungry cats finally satiate their thirst for warm milk. The dogs lap up the stuff, and the chickens are in heaven with all this excess.

Met at our local radio station this afternoon to make a recording that will advertise our forthcoming Food Fair. Three other ranch wives met with us; all busy, with lambing and calving season in full swing. Hopefully we will have another calf to put on Star soon.

Am doctoring a pneumonia calf today. Gave him some of Star's milk and a shot of antibiotic.

March 7—Clear and cold, the sun feels so good. Have been milking Star by putting a rope around her neck and tying it to a post. This morning I ran her into a chute, thus simplifying my chore considerably. Although he is having difficulty breathing, the sick calf is still with us this morning. Made an apple pie and worked on recipes to prepare for our potato booth at the Food Fair.

March 8—Cleaned house, got a case of "spring fever." A beautiful, sunny day. The T.L.C. given to the ailing calf paid off and it is all better and back with mamma. I always hate to lose a calf. My husband and I plus some friends attended a Neil Simon play tonight at the OK Theatre. It was a hilarious musical comedy put on by the Montana Repertory Theatre. Another effort of our Wallowa Valley Arts Council. Our theatre is undergoing extensive stage and lighting changes, and the play was presented well.

It used to be that show business was considered frivolous, yet people traveled hundreds of miles to see a live play. Now small, professional theatre companies travel hundreds of miles to bring live performances to the "provinces," much as in Shakespeare's day. Show business today is considered a respectable business. The director of the Montana Repertory states, "Where else can you have the very personal experience of traveling to another time and another place, and sharing the lives of exciting characters for a short time? It is positively rejuvenating."

How true this is, I thought, and the play was well received by a packed house here in our remote area. Tonight I am contemplating the fact that here in our rather isolated valley, we can be tending to a new-born calf one minute and enjoying live theatre the next.

March 9—Doesn't seem possible that my father passed away a year ago today. How often we think of him. Ironic that I have been enjoying the best of two worlds... those that daddy also enjoyed... music and cows! A pity that only the cows were the audience for his beautiful voice, or was it? His children heard and remember.

Another beautiful, clear day. The snow banks recede day by day. The birdsong becomes more intense, the sun has more strength and the days are noticeably longer.

A first calf heifer died of blood poisoning and left a nice three-day-old heifer calf as an orphan. Now I have an upcoming adoption for Star.

Interviewed and photographed at a local rabbitry this afternoon.

Helen Stonebrink plays the fiddle and sings "Springtime in the Rockies."
A recent get-to-gether of the Blue Mountain Fiddlers drew fiddle-players
from all over the Northwest. Don Foster, Enterprise, had a unique vocal
accompaniment to his fiddle playing—his small dog sat up near the mi-
crophone and "sang." An enthusiastic audience filled Cloverleaf Hall in
Enterprise. Accompanying Helen, from left, are Bob Dunn (guitar), Joe
Colvin (bass fiddle), Clarence Stonebrink (guitar), Burl Morris (banjo), and
champion fiddle player Charles Trump (guitar). Don Norton of Imnaha
was the master of ceremonies.

Enjoyed visiting with the wife, Ruth Proctor, in her country kitchen.
Over a cup of tea, we talked about their rabbits and about their lives. A
hard-working, interesting gal.

Home to find son Steve and fiancée here. They joined us along with
son Todd and girlfriend for dinner in town tonight. We also attended a
Blue Mountain Fiddler's get-to-gether. A real hoe-down. We listened to
the toe-tapping, hand-clapping fiddle tunes until almost 11 p.m.

Home to bed, dreaming of Star's big udder and all that milk. The
orphan calf is most welcome.

March 10—Clear and beautiful this Sunday morning, and the orphan
calf nursed Star! Am I glad to have help with all this milk. Another
lactation begins for this grand old cow. She contentedly munches her
grain, while at her side, wagging their tails, are two happy calves.

After chores I baked a raspberry pie (from frozen berries in freezer). I also thawed out and fried some chicken. We will drive to Imnaha today and picnic along the river at a spot where a daughter's family is in the process of moving. As we leave for the canyon country, we check our calving cows. Little calves sleeping in the sun, while mammas are eating their morning hay between the snow banks.

We had a fun day at our family get-together. Two more sons joined us and grandchildren ran everywhere. We enjoyed the good potluck meal, the sunshine in the yard and the sweeping views of the Imnaha's canyons, river, and blue skies. The children were drawn to the river, where they played along the bank. The age-old lure of watery places draws children like a magnet. Up a little creek they all got into a water fight. What fun, after the long winter of trying to keep warm, to be able at last to enjoy the outdoors and the sun's warmth.

March 11—Spotted the first pair of returning robins from my kitchen window on this bright, crisp morning, their feathers puffed up in the cold. I could imagine the thoughts going through their heads as they viewed the still present, awesome drifts beneath them while they perched in the bare-limbed apple tree.

This week, until Wednesday, most of my energies will be directed to the Food Fair. Delivered potatoes to a neighbor (potato wife), so she can prepare potato toppers for the Food Fair potato booth. Really warm today, even let the fire go out in the stove.

Another member of my milk cow herd calved today. Liza delivered a nice, big bull calf. Even though the snow banks remain, patches of ground appear and we now have MUD.

On this clear, cold, starry night, husband and I attended a computer fair at our local Joseph High School.

We have been experiencing a succession of clear, warm, sunny days, a real deviation from most Wallowa County Marches, when mother nature usually delivers a final blow of blizzards just in time for calving.

Since we finally got the milk barn door unstuck and the floor partially thawed out, we moved Star back over to her quarters this morning. Son Todd hog-tied her calf in the back of the pickup and mom followed behind. My milk barn is filling up. Two cows and three calves are brought in each morning and night. One first-calf heifer is due any day.

Scrubbed 75 pounds of potatoes for door prizes at the food fair this morning. Made a batch of potato candy, for potato booth. Put an elk roast in the dutch oven for supper. Let the fire go out again today.

As the ice and snow melts, riverlets of water run down the middle of our driveway from the snowy fields above. A great pool of water has formed next to my cow feeder; we dig a trench to drain it. Our crew preg-tested 70 head of heifers today.

March 13—We started shipping out the seed potatoes today; also, the crew unloaded another big truckload of hay from Union County.

This has been a most incredible day. Future days such as this will become commonplace as spring accelerates and we get "in shape," so to speak. This type of day tests the patience, versatility, endurance and stamina of us Wallowa County ranch women. Let me recount the events briefly:

6:30 a.m. Cook breakfast, do dishes, housework.

7:30 a.m. Out to barn where I run Liza in to be nursed by her calf and the orphan. Run Star in, let her calf nurse and milk my house milk. Hay the horses, feed and water chickens, strain milk.

9 a.m. Do a wash, assemble utensils for food fair, also materials for the potato booth. Phone rings 10 times in succession...potato people, wanting to have their seed shipped; typical answering service, I fetch husband (when available) from shop to phone.

10 a.m. Load car with food fair materials. Gas up car, pick up a CowBelle to help, pick up husband at potato cellar, bring him home (he had driven a truck in and needed a ride back to ranch). Stop at another CowBelle's for more utensils for fair.

11 a.m. Arrive Cloverleaf Hall, assemble potato booth, help put together trays for tonight, eat lunch in town, back to hall, stuff gift-pack bags.

2:30 p.m. Take Doris home. Arrive at ranch.

May, a first-calf Guernsey heifer, calving. Change into overalls and boots; calf half out, hip locked, tongue turning blue. Sit on ground and pull with each contraction. Heifer very tired...me too. Calf same. One final pull, the big heifer calf slithers onto a patch of bare ground in a mass of amniotic fluid. Baby gasps for air; me too. I clear mucous from calf's mouth and nose. Exhausted mamma just lays prone...finally up and tends calf.

Husband drives in. All available men were working in the potatoes or unloading hay. Oh well. By now I smell like corral #2. Clean up, assemble last minute details, phone continues to ring.

4:30 p.m. Gather eggs, repeat procedure at barn (same as morning). In house to wash off corral #2.

Off to food fair by 5:30 p.m. Doors open at 6. Begin to photograph for publicity pictures.

Over 500 people pack our Cloverleaf Hall. A huge success. The farm and ranch gals have done it again. Home to bed by midnight. Tired but happy…a day spent really living.

That is, if I can survive.

March 14—Another gorgeous day. We are loading more seed potatoes to be shipped out of the county. Around five baby calves a day are being born in the lower pasture now.

The drifts melt like glaciers by day and by night the resulting run-off freezes. It will be weeks before I can see ground in the garden. Somewhere under all that snow, my carrots remain, hopefully insulated by their protective cover. Day by day the snow drifts retreat, as the sun's warmth brings the ooze and mud to the bare spots. The burning barrel has surfaced! Also the top of the garden fence and the raspberry patch.

Made a pot of soup for lunch and then attended our monthly Cow-Belle meeting. A busy group planning more events that will help fill the calendar.

March 15—It is 9:30 before I finish at the barn and chores; worth it, as calves and mammas all doing so well. Only one more cow to calve, Daisy.

A Bluebird Day! Clear, blue sky and melting snow. Bright sunlight glares off the snowfields of the Wallowas.

A friend called to tell me about a pair of bluebirds that has just returned to scout out their nesting site. Nothing provides such a thrill as seeing these bright, beautiful birds as they dart around in a flash of blue.

A few people have built and set out bird houses to encourage these lovely birds to multiply. Sometimes joy comes in small packages.

Loaded three semis of seed potatoes today at the cellars near Joseph. While we were eating our lunches, three mule deer does wandered in and around the trucks and go-betweens, munching spilled potatoes. I was able to photograph them near the potato machinery.

Took a birthday present up to Alder Slope to granddaughter, Chelsie, who will be six tomorrow. Chores are becoming easier now. However, I feel like I'm running a dairy; need two more calves.

March 16—Another beautiful day, a record for so many nice ones in a row, and in March! In our local paper the headlines for the Imnaha column have to do with the discovery of buttercups. How refreshing to see such headlines as these. Compared to the daily national news, which is most always grim. The article states that Kid and Mary Marks found buttercups on Summit Creek. Love it.

Three curious mule deer does inspect the seed potato trucks.

Jim Blankenship delivers the mail three times a week.

Pools of water form adjacent to the snow banks as the melting continues. Made a blueberry crumb cake this afternoon.

March 17—Clear and sunny again on this St. Patrick's Day. Awakened this Sunday morning by Star, Liza and May mooing at the barn door. No sleeping in for the milk maid.

I notice the greening of the primroses, protected alongside the house. A close inspection of the snapdragons reveals tiny, green leaves near the base of the plants.

It is always a miracle of sorts to think that any plant could survive our cold winters. Soon the grape hyacinths, given to me by a neighbor last fall, will emerge and bloom. I can't wait to see my tulips and daffodils.

We drove to Imnaha this afternoon to treat the grandchildren to ice cream at the Riverside Cafe. Also visited "old-timer" Jim Dorrance while there. On the way home we visited Max and Dorothy Gorsline, who were opening up their log cabin on Little Sheep Creek, and invited them for dinner Tuesday night.

Five calves were born in our absence. Late to tending my cows; they were waiting at the door again. Let the calves nurse and milked with the aid of the barn light, as it was dark by this time.

There is a different "feel" to the air tonight. I noticed it while walking back to the house with a pail of milk…the wet, spring-like smell of the awakening earth. The starlight and warmer air mingle with a freshness that produces the phenomenon of SPRING!

March 18—A friend called to tell me that they had seen buttercups on the lake moraine. These are the kinds of friends to have, they make your day. We, too, spied the first, golden, waxy buttercups on Sheep Creek Hill, as we drove to Imnaha yesterday.

The sun came up over the eastern hill across from our house at 6:30 this Monday morning. A few cirrus, or maybe cumulus, clouds float on the horizon; been days since we've seen a cloud in the sky. Cleared up and another clear day ensued. The snowbanks and drifts evaporate a little more each day.

March 19—One more beautiful, clear day on this last day of winter. Fixed an antelope roast, sourdough biscuits and apple pie for dinner tonight. Enjoyed the company of Max and Dorothy. Max has made a clapper for the old school bell that Doug is restoring.

The fresh excess milk that is mixed with barley to feed my laying hens has boosted egg production. Seventeen pullets laid 17 eggs today.

Spring makes its appearance in Joseph. Patches of snow still remained on much of the landscape late in March, but the ice had gone out of the creeks.

March 20—In the dark of early morning a change occurred. Those of us who live close to the earth notice. The vernal equinox marks the official beginning of spring. This annual recurrence makes us aware again of the forces of nature that places all of mankind's inventions in their proper perspective. How do the buttercups know when to bloom?

As if on cue, the weather changes, cloudy, cold with snow predicted. After chores I go into the cellars to help sort and load seed potatoes. Loaded three semis of seed. Home to work on the Simmental registering applications. Dark, ominous snow clouds hover in the distance and over the mountains. Doug working out in the shop tonight on his antique school bell. The smell of snow is in the air.

March 21—All the bare ground of yesterday covered by a fresh snowfall this morning…the soft, wet snow of Spring.

After fixing lunch, I was off to our local county extension office where I answered the phone and filled in for the secretary, who is attending a computer school.

Home after 5 p.m. to start supper, chore and be ready to attend a 7:30 meeting of our local history group. A great evening, as we were transported into summer via the beautiful slides shown by Bill George, a local photographer.

While it was spitting snow outside, we were visiting the high, beautiful places, where pristine lakes gleam in the August sunlight, and alpine wildflowers dance to the summer breeze. Bill enlightened us on local geology and other points of historic interest in this vast county of ours.

March 22—Acquired another orphan calf. A neighbor on Alder Slope had one for sale, am grafting the little bull on May.

Daisy, due to calve any day…need two more calves! Cold and the ground frozen this morning. Husband has been working on restoring an old, rusty school bell. With a rancher's hands, he has created his own "work of art." He made a new stand, put in a clapper and gave all a new paint job. It is truly magnificent.

Wood stove feels good again. Caught up on some darkroom work.

Out to chore, found the new calf dead as a doornail. Don't know what the little fellow died of. Seemed all right this morning when he nursed the cow. Back to milking again.

March 23—Windy, cold and threatening snow while our crew braves the elements to load out more seed potatoes.

After chores I worked at the writing and darkroom work. Baked sourdough bread, put some corned beef on to simmer. Made a gooseberry pie from our freezer. So nice to enjoy the summertime berries all winter.

We had company for supper. Fixed cabbage, potatoes and carrots to go with the corned beef. An enjoyable evening with friends. There is a warm Chinook wind blowing out over the valley tonight.

Husband worked late in the shop to complete the bell. Around 11 p.m. the sound of an old school bell rang out in the darkness and resounded over Prairie Creek. The wind has calmed down. Wonder if it will snow tonight.

March 24—Woke up on this Sunday morning to four inches of new snow. Still snowing heavily, covering the bare ground once again.

While I was choring, the sound of the lovely, old bell pealed forth. Husband is enjoying his old relic. Silent for so long, the bell lives again. Hopefully, future generations can share in the joy of hearing this sound of a bygone era.

Big globs of snow slide off the milk cows, some down my neck. Got a line on a new calf this afternoon. Soft, wet snow piling up on everything. The canyons need the moisture; we don't. The melting snow penetrates the ground here in the valley.

Was successful in purchasing the new calf and coaxing him to nurse one of my cows.

Clearing and very cold tonight. Husband spreads straw in the calving field for the new babies.

Weather map showed Eastern Oregon the coldest spot in the nation this morning. Here it is zero degrees. What happened to Spring? A frozen baby calf by our fire this morning.

I was needed at the cellars this morning to help load potatoes. Before I left, I warmed up some colostrum for the little calf thawing out. The barn floor had frozen muck on it again. So slippery, I had to chop at it so the cows wouldn't slip and fall.

We loaded two semi's of potatoes. On our feet all day in the cold. Ten head of mule deer walked into the cellar looking for potatoes to chew on. Cloudy and snowing over the mountains. Home by 5:00 to chore and fix supper on the wood cook stove.

Attended the annual meeting of the Alder Slope Pipeline Association tonight on Alder Slope.

Husband up, on and off checking the calving cows on this cold night. Baby calf on porch up and around, so went back to mamma. Crashed into bed by 10 p.m.

March 26—Cloudy, with a chill wind blowing. Everything all frozen again. We've had some of this same snow since the 26th of October.

Two Wallowa County cowboys and their dogs trail a bunch of cattle to the hills along the Crow Creek Road. Last of the snowbanks remain on the hillsides. Recent moisture and warm temperatures have made the native bunch grass come on earlier than usual.

Husband off to the cellars on this typical March day. The cold wind is blowing the new, soft snow into new drifts atop the old ones. Hopefully, Daisy will hold off calving until the weather warms. Spring, elusive spring, where have you gone? The snow "banners" swirl around the high peaks of the Wallowas as I watch from my kitchen window.

Used some of my canned plums in a cobbler. Split some wood for the stove. Crew and husband loading more seed spuds today. Ben and Todd to the daily feeding of all these cattles. Located another orphan calf today, had him hauled to the barn where I immediately put him on a cow. More help for the milk maid.

Looking out the living room picture window, I spotted a robin on the front steps. He was bracing himself against the wind. He had been hovering near the house for protection. A gust of wind hurled him aloft and he was swept away. Hang in there, my feathered friend. Spring will come.

March 27—All six calves nursed out three cows this morning...for the first time I didn't have to milk a cow. The barometer plunges downward, a big storm brewing and the wind has died down to a dull roar.

Yesterday the UPS man reported two of our neighbors were drifted in by the high wind and blowing snow. Again? This is getting old.

Down to the calving shed at 8 on this cold night to feed some colostrum to a weak calf. Afterwards he wanted to follow me. I am mother to these unfortunates and the T.L.C. is often better administered by the woman of the household. As I walked back to the house, a soft wind was blowing the stars around. Like the words from a song.

March 28—Another snowfall during the night. Temps in the teens, a foggy mist hanging around the mountains, partially clear by mid-morning, but a bone-chilling cold. Finished chores, then into the cellars to load and sort more spuds. Another long day...I'm either going to get in shape or fall apart. The days are never long enough to do all that needs doing.

We didn't get a final semi loaded today, so we invited the driver out to the ranch for supper and to spend the night.

My 4-H'ers are calling about a field trip tomorrow. Slept fitfully, dreaming of potatoes going by on a conveyor belt.

March 29—Partly clear with huge, billowy clouds. Hurried through the chores, made sourdough waffles for breakfast with bacon and eggs to feed us and the potato truck driver. Made lunches and off to Imnaha with my Sourdough Shutterbug 4-H members. It was lovely in the canyons. We walked on an old road that follows the Imnaha River. We took many nice shots of canyons, river and pretty clouds. We ate our lunches in the warm sunshine along the river. The buds on the trees and bushes are just ready to burst open any minute. We photographed around the small town of Imnaha on the way home. A very picturesque community, with its store front, small post office and wooden Indians amid the towering canyons.

We watched Ben's two young sons slug it out at a benefit boxing smoker tonight in Enterprise. Home to the calving cows.

March 30—Did chores in the cold, with threatening rain clouds approaching. More seed spuds shipped out today. Our faithful crew working in all kinds of weather.

Doris and I attended a brunch at the Cloud 9 Bakery in Enterprise this morning. It was put on by the Wallowa Valley Arts Council. They are planning a "Western Art in Eastern Oregon" Art Festival in April. Very enjoyable and a break from the ranch.

Meanwhile, back at the ranch, a first-calf heifer starting to calve. No men around again. Decided to bake an applesauce cake. While mixing up the cake, I occasionally looked through the binoculars to watch the progress of the heifer. No progress. After three trips to the field, I decided to pull the calf. Armed with the pulling chains, I once more trudged out to the field where the heifer lay. A mixed wind and rain storm materialized as I bent to my task.

Thoughts of my warm country kitchen and the fragrant aroma of spicy applesauce cake came to me. I wished to be back inside, but the calf looked defeated and the heifer distraught. I pulled with all I had and the calf was born. Mother got up and tended to baby while I left the scene.

Son Steve home on college break. Crew loaded two semi loads of seed spuds today.

March 31—March is going out like a lamb. It is mild, warm, overcast with patches of blue, no wind, or frost, or ice.

The barnlot is muddy, manurey and yuk. Typical for this time of year. As the snowbanks recede, the flotsam and jetsam of winter's accumulation is exposed in all its ugly glory. The yard is a clutter of limbs and baling twine, bones and dog manure, due in part to our puppy. A prelude to the miracle of spring, when green will cover the landscape and like the snow, transforms it into a thing of beauty. But for the time being everything is devoid of color.

Made Kristen Tallman's Nantucket blueberry muffins for breakfast on this Sunday morning, using a recipe from the March 22nd issue of the Agri-Times. Highly recommend them, they were excellent. Of course they were baked in the Monarch wood range.

Alongside the house, purple, pink and yellow primroses are in bloom. Tulips emerge there also, as well as the daffodils.

We drove to Imnaha this morning and left the refurbished school bell at the Bridge School. What a surprise to the congregation when the services let out, to find that grand old bell sitting in the school yard with a poem taped to it.

A new church (Imnaha's first) will be built and the bell is my husband's gift to the new building. Lovely day on the river, trees budding, green grass, and the Imnaha River sparkling in the sunlight. Visited daughter and family, then home to the calving cows.

Into Joseph for dinner with friends. After an excellent meal, we viewed slides of Arizona and Baja, California. A world far removed from Wallowa County. A cloudy sky, illumined by a moon tonight as the last hours of March 1985 fade into history.

April 1—Daisy obligingly calved on this gorgeous, warm morning. An April Fool bull calf. Two mornings in a row now without frost. The first time it has been above freezing…a long winter.

If I can find one more calf to graft on Daisy, I'll have it made with eight calves on four cows.

Opened all windows and doors, gave the house a good "airing." So good to have the fresh air circulate through the rooms. An occasional cloud floats in the sky and a fresh spring breeze makes the curtains move. Hung clothes on the line. How I love the smell of clean clothes, dried in the fresh air. Did some spring cleaning.

The cellar crew, their spirits lifted by the spring-like weather, are loading trucks again. The temperature got into the 60s before noon. Our warmest day yet.

A neighbor down the road lost a cow last night, so I found an orphan for Daisy.

Enjoyed the grandchildren this afternoon, while mom did her monthly shopping. The new calf took right to Daisy. Snow really disappearing and yesterday's clear streams are running chocolate-colored today with all the run-off. Balmy, moonlight, and warm tonight as April begins.

April 2—A lovely, clear, warm, sunny day. In the 70s. The remaining snowbanks don't stand a chance now; they evaporate before our eyes.

Busy at the barn with the eight calves and four cows. My "herd" all calved out. Picked up junk around the yard that has been exposed by the melting snow. The newborn calves soaking up the sun's warmth.

Cellar crew working again. All the cattle here on the ranch search for old grass to graze; they are becoming tired of hay.

Husband out to the hills to check conditions there. Could only make it to the top of Dorrance Grade. Drifts still cover the roads from there to our place on Salmon Creek. We need to think about trailing some cattle out soon. There is plenty of old bunch grass out there and with this warm spell, the grass should start to come.

Turned May out with her two calves and all is well.

April 3—North wind blowing, cold and cloudy. Angry storm clouds sweep cross Prairie Creek. A light rain falling.

Wrote up a story on a local girl who is a guide and packer.

I can walk from the house to the chicken pen now without climbing up and over a big snow bank.

My husband shows up with a truckload of cull potatoes for the cattle; they come a-running when they hear the approaching truck. Have the quarters ready for the baby chicks: fresh straw, heat lamp, scrubbed out the feeders and waterers. All set to receive 50 baby chicks any day now.

This old school bell has been restored by Wallowa County rancher Doug Tippett. The bell, with a poem taped to it, was found by the congregation of the Imnaha fellowship as they walked outside from the worship service.

I am a Bell
I love to ring
will anybody have me?

by Doug Tippett

There is to be a new church
Built with loving care
Where all the people of Imnaha
Can come to say a prayer.

Every church should have a bell
To call the community together
One to ring both loud and clear
To announce every joint endeavor.

I once had a ringing job
So many years ago
I called the children to their class
And loved to watch them grow.

Now I have no place to ring
But I would love it so,
If someone would take me in
That would surely make me glow.

If you would like to hear my chime
From off the rims above
I would be happy for all time
And perhaps I could win your love.

From under your steeple
I'll greet all the people.

April 3, continued—The great snow drift in the garden has retreated enough to expose the row of carrots. Dug some for supper, sweet, firm and delicious. I notice the sage is still alive. Insulated by months of snow, it surfaces looking like it did last October.

The red, green, curly shoots of the rhubarb have just emerged. The pain of winter (like childbirth) is soon forgotten when spring arrives. For with all of its harshness, there will be summer days when the clover blossom scent floats across the valley and the shining mountains stand boldly against the purest of blue skies. It is for these reasons we live and endure all seasons here in the valley.

April 4—May's two calves escaped somehow through the fence last night, and were all mixed up with the main herd in the calving pasture. I caught May and led her down among the cows and calves. Finally got them paired up and they followed us back to their pasture. I fixed a "bluff" repair job where I suspected they got out.

April 5—Calves in lower field again, repeated yesterday's procedure. This time son Todd put in a new post and repaired the fence.

It was "Chick Day" at our local feed store. The air was filled with the peeping of hundreds of day-old chicks. A beautiful day, nice to bring the chicks home in.

The hills are beginning to show the first tinges of green, the snow banks mostly gone except on the norths.

Enjoyed a free lunch I'd won in a drawing, at the "Country Place" in Enterprise.

The county road crew is opening up the Salmon Creek road today.

Baby chicks all comfy under their heat lamp, brings back memories of my eight years as feed store clerk at Wallowa County Grain Growers.

Eighteen eggs from my 17 hens today. Can't figure this one out. Did the Banty rooster lay one?

A big, full moon illumines the snow-covered mountains on this Good Friday night.

April 6—Another nice day. Helped son Todd run a heifer (having trouble calving) into the calving shed. Assisted as he pulled the calf. My job...holding her head down. Everything came out ok.

Decided to make colored Easter eggs. Using an old method of food coloring, vinegar and salt, they turned out very pretty. Baked a big loaf of Easter bread and made a macaroni salad for tomorrow's get-together at Imnaha.

Had an invitation to go trout fishing at a friend's pond. Couldn't resist that. Dug worms, called another friend, and stole away for an hour or so to relax and fish. Caught two nice Eastern Brook trout for supper.

April 7—Easter Sunday dawns clear, sunny and incredibly warm. Put a chicken to roast in the oven, did chores, then left for Imnaha where I attended the Easter Sunday service of the Imnaha fellowship at the Bridge School. Three-year-old-granddaughter, Mona Lee, crawled up into my lap and fell asleep.

The Sarvisberry a-bloom up the draws. Yellow Forsythia, weeping willows, daffodils and violets everywhere. The apricot trees all in bloom.

The old bell rang out the call to worship at the school on this Easter Sunday.

The Imnaha River running a little muddied up due to warm days and snow melt from above.

Had a great family get-together at daughter Jackie's. Nice walk along the river, pretty cloud formations creating interesting shadows on the canyons.

Grandma "Easter Bunny" left special treats in the little one's nests.

Home to chores on this warm, still evening. A wind rises and a big, dark cloud races across from the mountains, a curtain of rain rushes toward us—a baptism from heaven—a warm rain to melt the last snow and green up the grass.

April 8—Gorgeous, warm morning, you can SEE the grass grow. Turned Daisy out with her two calves, only have Liza and Star to drive in and let calves nurse now.

Won a battle with the scours; all of the calves came down with it at once. Have been "pilling" for a week. This warm air and sunshine is really the best medicine.

Found some frozen apricots in the freezer and made a big, deep dish pie. Tasted like freshly picked Imnaha apricots. We discovered that our Nuclear seed, planted in isolation on Alder Slope, has come through the winter without freezing.

We didn't dig them last fall, as winter closed in before we got the job done. The long winter's coverlet of snow insulated them, they remained in good condition and can now be dug.

Ben and Todd a-horseback separating newborn calves and mammas from the rest of the "expectant" bunch of cows. Ben is making sure all the horses are shod in readiness for trailing cattle to the hills.

Remains of an April snowfall on the Wallowa Lake moraine make a striking background for a barn on Mike Brennan's ranch. The Brennan brand is painted on the barn. Mike is the son of the late, famous Walter Brennan. He and his wife, Florence, run this ranch, which is just out of the small town of Joseph, Oregon, on upper Prairie Creek.

April 9—We start a bunch of yearlings to the hills today. Actually driving them is easy compared to getting ready to go. I do chores at 5 a.m., husband fixes breakfast while I make lunches. By 7, we have the yearlings out on the road headed for the hills.

It is warm and beautiful. We see hillsides covered with buttercups, melting snowbanks, and are serenaded by the song of the meadow lark. It is in the 70s, the cattle still wearing their winter coats, get a little warm. We make it to the Dorrance place where we corral them for the night, feed the cattle hay, unsaddle our horses and head back to town with Todd in the truck. Am I sore. The first ride since fall, am not in shape. A hot shower does wonders and I revive enough to chore and fix supper.

To bed for this cowgirl before 7 p.m. All day in the saddle and I can't keep my eyes open.

April 10—Up at 4:30, husband fixing sourdough waffles on the wood cook stove, while I tended to cows, calves, horses and chickens. In house to eat breakfast and make lunches. A half-moon hangs in the sky at this hour.

We drive the 20 miles to Dorrance Corrals, saddle up and start the cattle up the grade. A fresh, morning breeze blows; another great, clear day. The yearlings move easily, the smell of the grass being tromped beside the road in our nostrils.

The bunch grass is greening, huge drifts on the norths melting, with riverlets of water flowing down through patches of buttercups. Hawks, ground hogs, and an occasional pair of mallards keep us entertained.

Made it to the Johnson pasture where we sorted in the lane, the yearlings and two-year-olds. I took the one bunch to the Butte Creek place and the others were turned into the Johnson pasture. Ben and Doug check fences.

Another long day, drive the 30 miles back home...do two days' accumulation of dishes, a washing, some housework. The house shows that the maid has been "buck-a-rooing" for two days now.

Not so tired today, but have a sunburned neck and a bit saddle sore. One more day of riding and I'd be in shape, offers husband.

April 11—Rained during the night, a warm, "grass-growing" rain. The entire valley is greening before our eyes, and the last snowbank has melted in the yard. Can't believe this.

Two semis to load at the cellars today. A CowBelle meeting at Marilyn Johnson's in Wallowa. Enjoyed the drive to the lower valley, seeing daffodils in bloom and the Lostine River running full as its turbulent waters pour down from the melting snows above.

April 12—Up at 5 a.m., so as to be able to photograph on Alder Slope early on this sunny morning. Interviewed a local potter and his wife. Enjoyed the interview, while sitting on the couple's deck and looking over toward the Seven Devil Range in Idaho. Left the spell of Alder Slope in the springtime and headed home to the ranch.

Pruned the raspberries. The crew working late at the cellars. Ben and Todd repairing fences. The heavy, winter snows have raised havoc with fences everywhere. The eight calves healthy and growing like weeds. Baby chicks getting their wing feathers and are rapidly turning into the big MOUTH. The feed they consume!

April 13—After chores, breakfast, and making lunches, into the cellar to help out on this Saturday. It was actually hot today. The view's so gorgeous of the mountains. However, we had to keep our heads bent to sorting potatoes and didn't have much time for sightseeing.

Left at 3 p.m. with Doris to attend a reception at the Bookloft in Enterprise for Mike Straw, a local photographer, who has some of his work displayed at the Skylight Gallery. Enjoyed the relaxed atmosphere and listening to the guitar music accompanied by a vocalist and a saxophone. Mike, the photographer, is also the guitarist. Mike's black and white photographs were taken in the canyon country and were very good.

Home to chores and to fix supper. Another late night for the crew; it was 8:30 before we ate. Warm, hazy and overcast sky tonight. Can't believe this weather.

April 14—Another warm morning. Found some wild huckleberries in the freezer, so made some yummy hot cakes on this Sunday morning. Doug to cellar to meet a potato buyer who is flying into the Joseph airport; also due to meet with a potato specialist who is coming over.

Actually got hot during chores; can't believe this.

The grass continues to grow and the willows are showing the first faint tinge of green. The sunlight and open windows reveal a dusty house, so remedied that. Dusted and cleaned all morning. Todd here to feed all the cattle. Luther Fitch with his wife and mother-in-law here for a brief visit.

April 15—Overcast and warm. Raspberries beginning to bud. Apple tree's new leaves emerging. Sure hope we don't get a cold snap now. The rhubarb has bolted and huge blooms appear at the base of the plants.

Todd and Ben saddled up the horses, rounded up the fall calvers and their calves. There is much bawling and confusion at the chutes and corrals as they ear tag, spray, vaccinate, dehorn and wean the calves.

Still loading out spuds at the cellars. Phone rings off the hook. We had a phone installed at the potato cellar, which helps. I can now direct calls there. A high wind materialized, black clouds from direction of Hat Point and over the mountains came sweeping down over the valley. Our electricity went out, called PP&L and it was soon restored. A sheet of rain pelted us as we caught the edge of a passing thunderstorm.

If we didn't have insulated walls so the sounds of the bawling cows and calves were muffled in our bedroom, we couldn't have slept a wink all night.

April 16—Cloudy and cool, mist blowing over the prairie and mountains. Better pack the ol' slicker behind the saddle today. The wood stove felt good this morning, as I fixed a sourdough pancake breakfast on the iron griddle. We must eat good, for it will be many miles down the Crow Creek road before we stop to eat our lunches. As I chored, the bawling became intense, cows, low and sonorous, the calves high pitched sopranos, some becoming a bit hoarse.

Dan, Ben, Todd and I drive the unwilling cows from the corral, which is next to their calves. They kept running back to the bawling calves. We finally got them on the road where we soon left the bawling behind. On our way to the quiet of the hill country. After a few miles the cows forgot about motherhood completely and all they could think about was the hill pastures with their sweet grasses, ponds, fresh air and freedom.

The cattle traveled well on this cool morning. Perfect weather to trail cattle. They moved right along. Most of these cows know the way and can't wait to get there.

We made a lunch stop along the roadside. Someone had shot a porcupine in a willow tree and it hung upside down on a branch. Even crumpled-up warm sandwiches that had been jostled around in our saddle bags tasted mighty good.

Doug appeared with more grub, in case we didn't have enough for all the hands. The fresh, cold water was especially welcome. I went back in with him, leaving Todd to lead my mare, since the cattle were moving so good, they didn't need me. Doug back to the cellars. I gathered eggs, loaded up grain for our horses, and drove the pickup (with hay bales for the cows) back out to the trailing herd. They were almost to the night stop at Circle M Ranch.

We penned the cattle for the night in a holding area that contained a pond, and fed hay. Unsaddled and turned the horses into a corral, fed their grain and hay, all settled for the night. We then headed to the valley. Back to the bawling.

April 17—Up before 5 a.m., went directly outside to chore, feed horses, let the calves nurse the cows, tend to baby chicks, laying hens.

In house to do last night's dishes, make lunches for crew, breakfast, whew. Off to the hills to find our penned cattle ready to be on the road.

Beautiful morning. Clouds casting shadows on the greening hills, sunshine and shade, buttercups, pink clarkia, yellow belles and birdbills were scattered among the roadside grasses. The first greening of the aspen outlined against the snowbanks, which clung high in the draws.

Old abandoned homesteads, the Dorrance Place with its picturesque log buildings. Crow Creek gurgling full and happy among the willows, chokecherry and thornbrush thickets. Everything awakening to the call of spring. Meadowlarks, hawks and mallard ducks in the swamps.

Had to hold the cattle back several times as another rancher was trailing a bunch of yearlings ahead of us.

Up we rode over Dorrance Grade. What a sight, as we looked back over our horses, the cattle filing up the winding grade, the greening hills, the Wallowas in the distance, framed by a blue sky and billowy, white clouds.

We riders: Dan, Carol, Ben and I enjoying this day. We wind our way through the Dry Salmon Creek country, where mile after mile of rolling bunch grass pastures stretch before us. A cattleman's heaven. "Cow Country." The cattle have waited all winter for this and pick up their pace.

We turn the cows into the Johnson pasture, dismount, and eat our lunches as it is now 1 p.m. The truck with Todd does not show. We decide to ride back down to the Dorrance corrals and wait there. Unbeknown to us Todd is having trouble with a first-calf heifer. Had to have the vet out and many complications. He finally drives up; we load up and head for home.

Daughter Jackie here in my absence, left a spray of Imnaha flowers: Sarvisberry, lilacs and apple blossoms. Potato crew loaded two more semis today. Husband and I off to attend the Enterprise FFA banquet by 7 p.m. Always have renewed faith in our "future farmers" after attending these functions. These young people stand tall, poised and knowledgeable about agriculture.

April 18—Cloudy, cool and raining lightly…good, the valley and canyons can stand a warm rain to bring on the grass, which already has a fine start. Using the wood stove to cook breakfast again, as there is a chill in the air. Ben and Todd hauling the bulls to the hills, the weaned, fall calves finally quit bawling and went to eating.

Still shipping the seed spuds. Hopefully we'll be through calving soon, only a few cows left. Two were born this morning.

Spent afternoon readying two photographs for entries in our Wallowa Valley Arts Festival Show. Grocery shopped and took a birthday present to grandson Chad, who is eleven today.

Tonight I attended the Wallowa County History Group meeting. The time fairly flew, as we were entertained by Cressie Green, who brought her collection of old barn pictures. Cressie, a native, has a terrific recall of old-timers and early Wallowa County history. Her wealth of historical information is incredible.

Grace Bartlett, our local historian and museum curator, is also extremely well-versed on early history. Always a fun evening, as well as educational for us history buffs. We meet monthly at the Bookloft in Enterprise. Many of Cressie's old photographs depict buildings that have now crumbled or gone by the wayside. Her pictures will eventually go into the museum for safe-keeping.

Home after 10 p.m. The rain had changed to snow, wind blowing snow against my windshield all the way home. Prairie Creek covered with the white stuff.

April 19—Awoke to see everything blanketed with a light, spring snow. A cold wind blowing. Thank goodness we aren't trailing cattle to the hills today. Wood stove in use again.

The snow sifted through the cracks in my old barn door this morning while I milked Star. The calves at their "Calf-a-teria" had a keen appetite due to the cold. Their mouths foam and drip as they partake of their warm milkshakes. The baby chicks comfy under their heat lamp.

Prepared a meat loaf, potatoes and gravy, biscuits, fresh asparagus dinner at noon for my men. They need fuel when working hard on this cold day. Worked til late on photography entries for the Art Festival.

This morning I helped other CowBelles serve the senior services dinner in Joseph. The snow flurries outside melted on contact with the paved streets. Mountain-born, these small "mini blizzards" sweep down on us, then continue on their merry way. Steam from the ground's warmth mingles with the flurries of snow. Sometimes a bit of sunshine will come through.

April 20—Down to 15 degrees! Ice in the puddles, some snow left from yesterday's storm, contrasts with green grass.

More small blizzards from over the mountains this morning. It is a mix of sun, blue sky, storm clouds, snow falling and frozen ground. You name it, we have it.

Old-timers hereabouts say, "Only fools and newcomers predict the weather," and "if you don't like it, wait 10 minutes and it will change."

Bundled up to chore, as if it were in the middle of winter. Physical exertion of choring always warms me up, and then am too warm.

Oblivious to the cold, the feathered-out chicks are thriving in their warm quarters. They are really putting away the feed these days.

Husband to potato cellar, then to an auction in La Grande. I deliver my photos to the Art show at Cloverleaf Hall.

The robins have returned in full force. Counted 20 in the old apple tree. Snow squalls all afternoon.

April 21—Another light snowfall during night. Dark snow clouds and periods of clearing, warmer this morning.

Breakfast, chores, then off by 9:30 to Imnaha where we drove up-river to look at a used feeder bed for our truck. Canyons unbelievably beautiful, with balsamroot appearing on sunny ledges, the bright, yellow blooms, gay against the greening canyon sides.

Huge gnarled, old apple trees, perhaps planted by early homesteaders, showed off white clouds of blooms. It would snow, the cooler, unsettled, spring-like weather causing the sunlit flakes to fall. Apple blossoms and snow flakes. A phenomenon...or real? The river ran full with snowmelt.

Back down to the Riverside Cafe, where we visited Jim Dorrance and ate lunch, later joined by daughter Jackie and family.

At 2 p.m. we attended a benefit pie and ice-cream social at the Bridge School to honor and remember Jack and Harriette Finch, two former members of Imnaha who left an impact on the entire community. They were former school teachers at the small, two-room school. Homemade pies of every mouthwatering description were served up with hand-cranked ice cream to over 200 people.

The tiny community drew an impressive gathering to pay tribute to a fine couple. A scholarship established, perpetuates their memory.

April 22—Big, fat flakes of snow falling. Can't complain. We need the moisture whatever form it takes. As it melts, the grass takes on a brilliant green, almost as if the snow contained some magical ingredient.

The men harrowing the fields today. Tulips ready to bloom. Ham hocks and beans on wood stove. Made an apple pie from some canned apples in my canning cupboard. Cold, brisk wind outside.

Attended the Joseph FFA banquet, where we enjoyed a roast beef dinner. The CowBelles donated beef certificates to help pay for the beef. Tim Kiesecker, the talented young FFA member, played for us on his fiddle, banjo, and mandolin. A very nice, well organized banquet.

Old homestead buildings on the upper Imnaha River in Northeastern Oregon's Wallowa County. It was snowing in the background (farther down the canyon) on this April morning. Note the hand-hewn log barn in the center.

April 23—Began to snow and stick around 6 a.m., but melted by noon. Cold wind, clouds and sunshine, March weather in April.

The wind and cold has chapped the teats on my milk cow's udders. "Bag Balmed" them all this morning.

Husband off to Hermiston with seed potato samples for the OSU Experiment Station's seed trials. Our newly harrowed fields have a "groomed" look to them. The grass that has started came to a standstill again in this cold spell.

A mini blizzard materialized out of a gray cloud, swirling snow flakes engulfing me as I chored this evening. All over in minutes as the final snow sifted down between shafts of sunlight.

While cooking supper, I heard a thud on the kitchen window. The strange lighting outside caused a small bird to fly into the pane. Tiny gray feathers clung to the glass. Outside I picked up the little bird, his heart fluttered in a frenzy of beats, a pretty little Brewer's Sparrow. It seemed to be having difficulty breathing. I brought it indoors and laid it gently in an old cowboy hat. It lived for about an hour, then its little heart stopped beating. The small feet and wings relaxed, I felt badly that this tiny wild thing would never enjoy the spring.

Another blizzard around 7 p.m.

Pinkish, gray clouds reflected the sunset on Prairie Creek, the clouds opened up and dusted us with feather-like flakes, that resembled those of the dead sparrow. Clearing by nightfall, with a new moon in the sky.

April 24—Have a touch of the flu today. Didn't do much except read, feed the fire and chore. Spring blizzards came and went all day. Still shipping seed spuds.

April 25—Good thing I "rested" up yesterday. Didn't have time to be under the weather today. Up early to fix breakfast, chore and be ready to help drive all the steers and heifers from the feedlot (about five miles) to the ranch.

Felt sorry for our cowboys, Bud, Ben and Todd. It was freezing weather, intermittent snow squalls, icy wind and just plain cold. Not much relief from the cold a-horseback. My job was to drive a pickup and block up holes (stand in front of open gates and roads) and turn the cattle in the right direction.

Rushed home, stoked up the wood cook stove, had fresh coffee, hot chili beans, cornbread and sourdough rolls ready for the cold, hungry cowboys. Apple pie for dessert.

Spent rest of day and on into the night (between errands in town and chores) typing up material for the art auction this Saturday night. Finished at midnight. A long day. Ben and Todd worked at the chutes, worming, vaccinating, dehorning etc. until 8:30 p.m. Half done, will finish tomorrow. Snowed off and on all day.

April 26—Slept in 'till 6:30. Clear skies and warmer, but cloudy by noon. Ben and Todd finishing up the yearlings at the chutes. Fixed a good hot elk roast, biscuits and salad meal at noon for the working men. Eileen picked up the art auction material I had typed last night.

My chicks are outgrowing their quarters, will have to move them soon. The cellars are cleaned out now. Only some semis to load tomorrow and we'll be all finished with shipping. Maybe a breather before planting.

April 27—Blue skies, sunny and warm. Beautiful clouds float over the Wallowas. Ran up on our hill at 6 a.m. to capture the sight on film.

After chores, into Cloverleaf Hall to view the Art Show. What a display of art. The visual arts, in all medias, sculpture, ceramics, pottery, wood-working, oils, pen and ink, watercolor, photography, and textiles. An incredible array of pieces. Most of them reflected the feelings and inspirations of our great Northwest. Especially east of the Cascades. How proud I am to be part of this great show, "Western Art in Eastern Oregon."

*Eileen Thiel and Eva Slinker, charman of the Wallowa Valley Arts Festival,
pose atop an old buggy used to welcome crowds attending the event at the
Cloverleaf Hall in Enterprise.*

Bales of straw, old wagons, buggies, horse collars and mounted wild
animal heads adorned our Cloverleaf Hall. Very nicely laid out and
displayed. Some pictures depicted life in agriculture, with wildlife scenes
dominant.

Home to clean house, write and chore. Into Cloverleaf Hall for the
big night. CowBelles served a pit-barbecue beef dinner. There was an art
auction and entertainment. Informal western atmosphere welcomed the
sell-out crowd who came to view the art work. Local color was reflected
in many of the ranch scenes.

The prize winner was truly impressive. It was entitled "The Nap,"
and it was a painting of a farmer taking a nap in his reclining chair. His
face reflected the hard life that could not let him entirely relax, even in
sleep. Off in the distance were his fields, tractors and farm.

All of us who are married to men of the soil can identify with this
piece of work. Many of the works displayed at the show will forever
portray the interesting life-styles of people in our part of the Northwest. This art captures the "Moment in Time" and records for history
our present era. The canyon cowboys, the wildlife and the working
agriculturists.

These young Cornish-cross fryer chicks enjoy the fresh air and sunshine.

We were entertained by a charming pair who played the fiddle, guitar, harmonica, bones, wash board, Jew's Harp, mandolin and many more folk instruments. Much to the merriment of the crowd, the audience participated in the playing of some of these old-time instruments.

Eva Slinker, who was chairman of this event, is to be commended for her efforts to put together such an outstanding show.

April 28—A warm, sunny day. Slept in until 7:30. Goodness! Did my chores, while husband fixed breakfast. Todd here to feed the cattle on this Sunday morning.

We moved the fryer chicks up to the chicken house. Quite an undertaking. Husband helped by cleaning out the chicken house yesterday, a yearly undesirable job. He hauled the manure to the garden, to be tilled in later.

The chicks, happy to be out in the sunlight and fresh air, are really growing fast. Their Cornish ancestry causes the heavy bodies to grow so quickly that their legs can't support the weight. Some have crooked legs. They look so clumsy as they walk, mostly from feeder to waterer. Gaining each day at an incredible rate.

Soon be time to butcher them.

Picked the first, tender shoots of rhubarb, combined them with strawberries from the freezer and made a cobbler. Clouded up by 4 p.m. Looks like rain and do we need it.

Husband poisoning gophers with the gopher machine in the hay field. The fields are all harrowed and fertilized now.

April 29—Up at 5 a.m., in the saddle 'til very late, we are moving the cows and little calves out to the hills. A L-O-N-G day. Too tired to write about it.

May 1—Up at daylight, another long day, hot and sultry, cattle got tired and hot going up Dorrance Grade. One cow turned back looking for her calf when we were almost to the top. Todd chased her all the way down to Crow Creek, where he penned her in a corral. Waiting for him to return, I ate my lunch at the top of the hill and enjoyed a breeze while the cattle rested. I caught a few winks, lying in the grass with my hat over my face to keep out the sun's glare. We caught up eventually with the faster bunch and made it safely to the Deadman pasture.

The cattle were turned out to grass and were they happy.

On the road near Dry Salmon Creek, one of our cows had gotten her head caught in an old, rusty 55-gallon barrel. What a sight, and to see that cow running around with a barrel on her head. It finally dislodged and she hurled it off in the ditch.

Yellow belles, pink and white Birdbills, Blue Bells and many varieties of wild flowers coming out more each day. We saw a few mule deer up near the snowbanks. The mule Maud and my Appaloosa filly greeted us at Salmon Creek. They survived the winter none the worse for wear. They were so happy to see us. They ran around bucking and playing. After their long winter of isolation in this vast lonely hill country, I could understand why.

Unsaddled our horses. Over 30 miles in two days of slow travel. The little calves got pretty tired, and so did the cowboys who had to prod them along.

Doug picked up the errant cow in the Dorrance corrals and delivered a neighbor's calf that joined the drive along the way. Homeward, the long dusty miles, chores, fixed rib steaks for supper and crashed.

Warm on this first day of May. A real grass growing night. A cow across the field from us bawled all night for her calf. From our open window, I could hear it plainly. So tired even my bones ache.

May 2—Up to a warm, muggy morning. Just need rain and the grass will leap up. Sapped of energy this morning as I fixed breakfast and chored. Just did the bare minimum of housework and tried to rest up. The tulips and daffodils are all in full bloom. It cheers me up.

Ben and Todd working the weaned fall calves today. Calvin running the gopher machine on the Alder Slope rented property. Doris "kidnapped" me and we went mushrooming up in the woods. No morels up yet. Need a warm rain.

Doug treated 17 of us to dinner at Vali's Delicatessen at Wallowa Lake tonight. His way of saying thanks for a job well done by our potato shipping crew. The menu, steak and potatoes, natch. An enjoyable evening and everyone glad the shipping is over. Calvin and Doris presented Doug with an award for the "Traveling Dirt Clod." It is a memento to all the hundreds of dirt clods thrown out by the crew these past weeks.

May 3—My rancher-farmer husband is directing his energies to farming now. The potatoes are shipped and most of the cattle turned out to grass. Upon arising every morning, he taps the barometer and turns on the TV for the satellite weather map.

From now on we will be "ruled" by the whims of Wallowa County weather. Our fava beans must be planted and that holds precedence over all today.

On the one hand we need moisture and on the other, we need to get the crop in. Husband takes off on tractor to haul a drill over to the rented field where we'll plant the fava beans to use in our Ag Bag silage operation. I leave for Wallowa, where I have an appointment to interview a family who are leaving for Inner Mongolia.

They are branding yearlings as a cold wind blows down off the mountain. Home to find note from husband: "Pick me up at noon in bean field."

At the top of the hilly plowed field, I can see an impressive storm approaching. Suddenly snow swirls around me and a full-blown blizzard wipes out all visibility. We decide to park the truck (loaded with bean seed) in a shed until the storm abates. I suddenly remember my young fryers, who will be outside when this storm hits Prairie Creek.

We drive home and I catch 50 fryers and place them in the safety of the chicken house just as the storm hits. They were all bunched in a pile in a corner of their pen. Now nearly 2 p.m., fix lunch.

Todd and Ben hauled nine truckloads of our feedlot yearlings to the rented pasture up the Lostine River Canyon.

One thing about this weather: it is the only opportunity a farmer has to rest. Husband sacked out in his recliner chair where he takes a much needed nap. Meanwhile the blizzard rages outside on this third day of May. Our needed moisture, coming in the form of snow.

May 4—Another blizzard! Huge snowflakes fall from above. After chores, the snow suddenly ceased, so I drove up on Alder Slope to photograph; misty clouds obscure the brilliance of the snowy mountains.

Snow quickly melts and sinks into the green grass, which is of a bright green in the morning sun.

Steam from the black loam of Alder Slope's rich soil rises from the newly plowed fields. The sight is like a surreal painting...the clouds move and change position to reveal patches of the mountains's snowy ramparts. A breathtaking sight.

Calvin is running the gopher machine on some of our rented alfalfa field on Alder Slope, while his wife, Doris, rides along enjoying the view.

Got some good shots with my camera. On the way home, stopped at the Grain Growers to buy barley for my milk cows. Sold some more ads for our CowBelle cookbook.

Home to lunch, then worked on the photo-journalism all afternoon. Husband home late from the "bean field."

May 5—Small cylindrical pieces of ice sputtered out on the ground from the garden hose as I watered my chicks this morning. The tulips drooped to the ground, their red blossoms closed tightly in the cold. Frost covers everything, fair and sunny, warming to above freezing by 9 a.m., when a chill breeze began to blow.

Make huckleberry muffins, sausage and eggs for this Sunday breakfast.

Not many cattle left here now. Just bulls, my "herd," the hospital pen, two horses, the tail end calvers and the weaned fall calves.

Husband feeds all but my charges and leaves for the bean field to finish planting; the crew has today off.

Purchased my combination fishing and hunting license yesterday while at Bud's Hardware in Joseph. Does this mean I'll go fishing? Am reminded of Thoreau as trout season nears. He wrote: "Time is but the stream I go a-fishing in. I drink at it; but while I drink, I see the sandy bottom and detect how shallow it is. Its thin current slides away, but eternity remains."

Years ago I committed this to memory and to this day think of it as our busy season keeps us so caught up in work, that as Thoreau said, eternity remains, whether we go fishing or not. Maybe now in our "rushed" generation we need to take heed of this solitary man's musings on "Time," and leave a sign out on the door once in awhile, "Gone fishin'."

Put a rope calf halter on Star's heifer this morning and left her tied to the fence for her first lesson in leading.

Calvin Woempner drives a tractor that is pulling a gopher machine in a
hay field on Roger Nedrow's ranch on Alder Slope in Oregon's Wallowa
County. Wife, Doris, rides along.

My gray mamma kitty "Barn Cat" is delivering another litter of
kittens. Right in the middle of the process (between births) she appeared
for her morning bowl of warm milk. Two were born and her protruding
tummy made me suspect more were only minutes from delivery. My
assumption was right.

Roto-tilled the strawberry patch this morning. The freshly turned
earth made the beds look so neat and tidy. Our small "pony" tiller is great
for a woman to manage. Sometimes it hits a rock, bucks and takes off,
but usually it goes right down the row spewing forth earth and weeds.
Nice to get this job done before the weeds get ahead of me.

I mowed our large lawn and tilled the raspberry patch as well as a
portion of the garden. Did chores, fixed a chicken casserole for supper.

Was very tired tonight, all the physical work. Husband in bean field
until 5 p.m.

May 6—No rest for the wicked.

After chores met some photo journalism deadlines, fixed lunch, then
Doris and I walked up and down Joseph's main street selling ads for our
soon-to-be-published CowBelle Chuckwagon Cookbook.

On the way to a meeting of the Wallowa Valley Arts Council tonight,

I left husband off at the bean field so he could drive the tractor home. The view from those high rolling hills in the evening light was gorgeous, the sprouting grain fields in three hues of green.

Attended an evaluation meeting concerning the recent Wallowa Valley Arts Festival. Home by 10 p.m.

May 7—Another hectic, but enjoyable day. After chores took husband to bean field to drive home another rig. Drove up near Hurricane Creek and did an interview with Stanlynn Daugherty. I photographed her pack llamas amid the beautiful setting of the ranch headquarters.

Times like these make my job as country correspondent most enjoyable. Home to fix lunch and write up my article.

Fixed Hawaiian spareribs and rice for supper, did chores and attended a 4-H meeting with my Sourdough 4-H members. We viewed a film about Yellowstone Park. The photography was superb.

Husband to a planning commission meeting to obtain a permit to build a new potato storage. Spring is definitely here; the pace quickens. Can we keep up?

May 8—Daughter Jackie and two children spent the night. Was accompanied on my round of chores by two cheerful grandchildren who "helped."

Cloudy and cool, woodstove going most of day. Ben and Todd cleaning up around the ranch, burning trash and hauling junk to the dump. A spring shower around 5 p.m., followed by a shot of sunshine and May's first rainbow. What a sight as the vivid colors arched over Prairie Creek. We sure need more rain, as the ground dries out more each day.

May 9—CowBelle meeting day. Imnaha-bound, six of us go in my car upriver to the neat, tidy home of Barbara Warnock.

Barbara's love of gardening shows in her well-kept yard and garden. Daffodils, tulips, and lilacs bloomed in profusion along their river front home. In addition to raising a family, being a cattle rancher's wife, Barbara drives the Imnaha school bus and cleans the school house, as well as yard maintenance for the school yard. She had freshly made rolls just out of the oven to go with our potluck.

An enjoyable day. To bed early tonight. We work cattle in the hills tomorrow. Raining lightly, hope it keeps up.

May 10—A busy day ahead, I go directly to the barn to chore, milk Star and tend to my charges. While I strain milk and make lunches, husband fixes sourdough hot cakes. Soon we are off to the hills. Overcast with big storm clouds being tossed around by a light wind.

Barbara Warnock, rancher's wife, mother of three sons, school bus driver, CowBelle and expert gardener, poses amid daffodils in her yard.

Buck, 4, son of Bill and Jackie Matthews, rides his pony, Cricket.

A cow that died shortly after our last trail drive is reduced to a bony skeleton. Four Golden eagles, one coyote and numerous crows fly and run off at the approach of our truck. Nature's way. The scavengers have just about finished the dead animal off. It is interesting to note that the eagle holds sway, with the coyote snatching bits as he can then slinking to the background. The raucous crows get what is left, after the others eat their fill.

We run the horses into the corral, catch, saddle them and take off over the hill to drive in the cows and calves. Some yearlings are mixed with them. These yearlings create a problem when they approach the carcass. Curious, they smell around the skeletal remains.

We yell and wave, to no avail. They mill around and keep running away from the main herd to investigate their fallen member. We finally get them gathered up and with the main bunch. When everything is corraled, we sort out the yearlings and some cows that we will haul back to the valley to inseminate.

Lunch break at 11:30, then Todd and I bring in 69 yearlings from a large pasture. These hill pastures go on seemingly forever. You ride over one rise or hill, no cattle; over another and another, until the yearlings are all accounted for. Miles of grass, sprinkled here and there with wildflowers. This is quiet, lonely country. Clouds, sky, me and my horse. This vast country grows on one. The stillness, peace, far-reaching vistas and solitude will forever be imprinted on my mind's eye.

While we drive the yearlings in, Doug and Ben round up the bulls to be moved to the Red Barn pasture. The yearlings are sorted, heifers one way, steers another. A section of fence torn down by marauding elk is given a temporary repair job. We load up the dead mamma cow's orphan calf along with the other cows to be inseminated, and head the 30 miles home.

Chores and supper. Threatening rain, but not doing it. We could sure use some. The grass in the hills has such a good start. Cold this evening.

May 11—The snow line is right at upper Prairie Creek this morning. Looking out my kitchen window, I see the frosted slopes of the mountains. Fixed lunches for Doug and Todd and they left for the hills to repair the elk damaged fence where the bulls got out.

Brisk, cold wind and frost everywhere. My once lush delphiniums are drooping and frozen. They will survive.

Today I purchased an authentic old Sheepherder's Wagon. I have wanted one for so long. It comes complete with a little stove. Our Sourdough 4-H Club will use it for bake sales, parades and campouts.

Mona Lee Matthews, 3, can ride, too.

Worked in Joseph collecting ad money for new CowBelle Cookbook. Am roasting a turkey and making cranberry sauce for a get-to-gether at Imnaha for Mother's Day tomorrow. Clear and sunny with an icy breeze.

A lovely fresh cut flower bouquet appeared at my door from our local florists this afternoon, a Mother's Day remembrance from daughter Lori and family in far-off Wyoming. Planted some irises and garlic in the garden. Husband treated "Mom" to pizza at the local Pizzaria tonight. A treat, relaxing, delicious—and no dishes.

May 12—Mother's Day dawns clear and cold, 18 degrees. The tulips and daffodil blooms frozen in their prime. Made sourdough hotcakes for breakfast. A lovely day, but we need rain so badly, the ground is the driest I can remember in May. Husband gave me a beautiful Mother's Day card and a children's book by James Herriot to read to my grandchildren. He is tilling up my garden with the tractor and tiller, the best present yet.

Loaded up the turkey and cranberry sauce, and headed for Imnaha. What a great day. Relaxed with family. Buck and Mona Lee rode their pony, while proud grandparents and parents watched. Doug hooked up the water supply for their garden. He added more hose to a spring, gravity flow water system. I read to the children. The sound of the river put us to sleep.

We enjoyed the turkey sandwiches and Jackie's apricot pie. We note the apricots have already set on the trees in the yard. Daughter and family gave me a lovely basket made by a local girl from pine needles. A great Mother's Day and I feel loved by all my children. A most gratifying feeling.

May 13—Yesterday the official low in the nation was West Yellowstone at 18 degrees. That was also us. Quite often we have that distinction. Today: another clear, sunny day, no rain in sight. The grain and crops need moisture desperately, as do the grasslands. I water plants in the yard. Twenty-one degrees this morning, with ice on the chicken's water.

Todd and Ben branding the tail-end calves here today. Doug winds up the harrowing. I made a cherry pie from frozen pie cherries. One of the cows out in the hills has dried up, so I have another orphan for Star and Liza. Now five calves will have to "share." Plenty of milk, so should be no problem.

The vet came out to vaccinate 68 head of heifers today. Doug cultivating the potato field, soon be time to plant the spuds. I planted my red potato seed in the garden this afternoon. Warming up to the 70s. Weeded some in the strawberry patch.

A rising wind and storm clouds appear. Rain??? Husband brought in three large wild bird eggs from the field. They are blue and brown speckled, very unusual, couldn't identify them in the bird book.

May 14—Blessed rain. A warm one, until around 8 a.m., when it became mixed with sleet.

Success in getting the orphan to nurse Star.

This morning Star provided milk for mamma kitty, three calves and one gallon for our house milk. Snowing heavily by 9 a.m.

Concentrated on turkey left-overs, simmered carcass for soup, made gravy for future meals and left a meal for Todd while Doris and I collected the final ad commitments for the CowBelle Cook Book. We treated ourselves to lunch at the "Country Place."

Doris and I attended a live theatre production tonight at our local OK Theatre. The play was entitled "Wild Oats," an 18th century play, set in Hampshire England in the 1790s, and presented by the Eastern Oregon State College Players. Home to bed and rest. We brand in the hills tomorrow.

May 15—Up early to get ready to go branding in the hills. Made sourdough hot cakes, did last night's dishes, chores, fixed lunches and finally off to the hills.

Rain during night had stopped. Glistening droplets of water shone in the sunlight on every bush and tree. The hills all green now with only a few scattered snowbanks left.

Different varieties of wildflowers carpet the hills, as the procession of wildings continues with the spring. Larkspur, lupine and balsamroot provide blues and golds. "Noxious weeds," comments husband. The rain-washed blue sky wears a few clouds, making the day neither too warm, nor too cool.

We saddle up on Salmon Creek, drive the cows and calves in, sort some cows, and work until 3 p.m. to finish half the job. We spray the cows. The newly branded calves run around sporting their new x quarter circle brand. We drive the cows and calves to a farther pasture, unsaddle the horses and make the long drive home.

Long daylight hours enable us to do even more today. Doug and Calvin to the potato field to continue cultivating. I do my chores, then make a batch of homemade noodles to go with leftover turkey and broth. I boil eggs for sandwiches tomorrow, and clean the mountain oysters. On a ranch always something to do.

In the event some readers would like to try a delicacy that is strictly "Western," I will give you a recipe from the Wallowa County CowBelle Cook Book. It was one of my contributions:

Mountain Oysters

Clean oysters and chill overnight in cold water in refrigerator. Drain well on paper towels. Dip oysters in mixture of beaten egg and top milk. Roll in freshly-rolled cracker crumbs. Have oil hot in electric frypan. Fry until golden brown. Serve hot with lemon wedges, sourdough bread and tossed salad.

Mountain oysters may be found growing in hill pastures in Wallowa County. They are in season during spring branding time. They grow in clusters under bull calves. Use a sharp knife when picking them. This recipe is good for a laugh, but seriously it is a gourmet delight. The "oysters" should be kept cool in a pail of water during branding, and the tough membrane removed when you get home. They can also be frozen successfully. We have gotten many city friends "hooked" on this treat. Most didn't know what they were eating.

Ben and Todd stayed out in the hills to drive in a heifer that needed attention for a sore foot. A long day for all the cowboys. Up and at 'em again in the morning. My day didn't end until I developed some film,

A freshly branded Simmental-crossbred calf looks none the worse for wear.

caught up on my country correspondent job and picked up husband at 8:30 p.m. in the potato field. Crashed shortly after.

May 16—A small bird's persistent loud chirp in the lilac bush woke me at 5 a.m. Through the open bedroom window the sound was quite close. Warm all night and a clear, beautiful day. Cooked sourdough hot cakes and mountain oysters with scrambled eggs on the wood stove. A hearty breakfast for another big day. Milked the cow, made egg sandwiches and we were off to the hills once more. Ben and Todd left earlier so as to have cows and calves corraled before we got there.

Doug off to potato field to get the hired man started on the cultivating. We hope to start planting potato seed Monday.

Turned very warm, in the 70s as we began the branding. Ben's two young sons helping push calves up the chute, so I photographed, using color slide film. Tried to capture a picture story on film of this day. From my vantage point on a nearby hill, I could photograph the entire scene. Although this scene is duplicated all over Eastern Oregon, there are many areas where the cowboy and old-time brandings are no more.

I note that the weathered, old long barn and rugged corrals show the effects of time and harsh winters. The grays and browns are most interesting to photograph.

The two boys become tired, so yours truly gets her job back. The branding fire's scorched hair, smoke, dust, heat, and the cacophony of bawling cows and calves filled the air.

We finished after spraying the cows. The mother cows, reunited with their freshly branded calves, were turned out to the bunch grass pastures once more. The bawling subsides and fades away.

Dark thunder headers loom in the direction of Hat Point and the Wallowas. As we headed home, ragged streaks of lightning zig-zagged across the sky. A free show all the way home.

It began to rain on Crow Creek road. Did my chores at 6 p.m. amid the crashing of thunder and a real cloudburst.

Took a hot shower, fixed supper and left to grocery shop for more lunch supplies. We'll need lunches for three more days.

Attended our local history group meeting at the Bookloft tonight. Lloyd Coffman, author of the recently published "5200 Thursdays in the Wallowas," presented an interesting program.

May 17—Awakened to the birdsong out the bedroom window. The sun comes over the eastern hills in a blaze of warmth. Fixed breakfast and lunch for Ben and husband, who says I will receive a reprieve today. I need to catch up here on the ranch.

He and Ben head for the hills to drive the fall calving cows to the Salmon Creek corrals, where a vet will preg-test them today. The "drys" will be left out there, and tomorrow we will drive the others here to the valley, a three-day trek to end at Wallowa Lake moraine. Many hours in the saddle ahead, over 40 miles.

I finished chores, the five calves thriving on the two cows. My fryers are within a week of butchering. Made two loaves of sourdough bread for a 4-H bake sale tomorrow. Caught up on housework and darkroom work.

Thunderheads form from out of the blue. I decided to plant my peas, chard, and spinach before it rained again. Baked a batch of sourdough biscuits to go with a Spanish casserole for supper.

After reading "What's Up With Rupp" concerning Morel mushroom hunting, we gave it a try. We visited our old haunts, within earshot of a brook, in an old burn area where sun and shadow meet, between 3,000 and 4,000 feet.

After this warm rain, conditions were just right and we found 'em—bags full of them. The woodsy, spring smell of the evening was wonderful.

We spied a porcupine ambling along for a stroll about dark, a coyote hunting two gophers, and a white tail deer. The morels were just a bonus.

Home to ready the mushrooms for the freezer. Soaked in salt water, drained, dried, rolled in flour, browned in butter, and frozen individually on cookie sheets, the mushrooms can then be stored in plastic bags in the freezer. They can be taken out of the freezer as needed and reheated in a frypan and they will taste just like fresh. Of course one has to sample a few when preparing them.

To bed by 10 p.m.; up early in the morning to start the fall calvers to the valley. Long days in the saddle ahead.

May 18—Up at first light, chores, breakfast, make lunches and out to Salmon Creek.

I catch my horse, head off over the hills to the Johnson pasture, where I gather up the fall calvers. Ben, in the meantime, is rounding up some heifers to move. Doug bringing son Ken, his two sons (Rowdy and Chad) and their horses. I have the cows mostly into one bunch when they appear over the hill. We drive the cows onto the gravel road and begin the long drive to the holding pasture on Crow Creek.

My two young grandsons, 7 and 11, enjoying buckarooing. A gorgeous day, warmed up into the 70s. Wildflowers at their peak now. We make the 15 miles by 3:30. Ride our horses to Circle M corrals and leave them there for the night. I take Ken home and keep the two grandsons. They will spend the night. Together we chored and fixed supper.

Doug and Ben back by 6:30 from shifting cattle from Butte Creek and sorting more cows to go with different bulls. A long day for all of us.

The two boys climbed trees and hunted robin nests. Hot shower and blissful sleep. Warm out tonight.

A thunderstorm appeared while we finished the end of our ride today. We got a little wet, but it felt good with the warmth of the trail dust. We are always entertained along the ride. Today we saw six baby ground hogs, one coyote, numerous hawks nesting and mallard ducks.

May 19—Up and at 'em again. Milked the cow, did chores, fixed lunches while Doug made breakfast for all of us. Ken here for breakfast also. Off to the hills on another beautiful morning to round up the cows and start the second lap of our 40-mile drive. Warm, and the cows travel slowly. Rowdy spies a garter snake, catches it and it bites him. Boys will be boys. They are enjoying riding with their dad and grandma.

The long miles disappear behind us as we near the valley. We eat our lunches out in the sunshine. No relief from the sun; no trees.

Met another trailing herd, brother Biden's bunch; had to turn back onto the Crow Creek road and wait for them to pass. Made it to the main ranch around 3 p.m., tired, hot and dusty. One more lap to go and the cows will be on the lake hill until fall, where they will calve out and fatten on the high country grasses.

Doug takes Ken and the boys home. I rest up then do a wash, chores, and fix supper. A long day on this Sunday. Proud of my two grandsons, who made the 30 miles without complaint and were good help.

May 20—Off a-horseback again, this time in the rain. Clad in slickers, Doug and Bud, Ben and I head the cows up the final trail to their high summer pastures. We split the herd. Doug and I drove one bunch up the steep side of the moraine to a separate pasture. As we rode up on top, we were engulfed by a misty cloud. What a sight we made. The bright yellow slickers stood out in the mist. Everything else was muted. The cattle, steaming bodies climbing upward to their high pasture. Visibility was limited to only a few feet. We drove them through a gate and left them by a pond.

We rode down to the truck, loaded the horses and joined the other trailing bunch. Horseback again, we helped Ben and Bud push the cattle up a timbered ridge and up on top of the moraine. Fine, misty rain as our horses wound around the forested areas that skirt the Wallowa Lake moraine. We could see hundreds of purple woods violets, and the False Hellebore (skunk cabbage) was popping up all around. We even saw morel mushrooms, due to the warm rain. Sarvisberry bushes, white with blossoms, wild strawberry plants blooming underfoot and lots of elk sign, as we were in back of the big elk fence. We drove the cows up and over the top, and down the west side to their salt grounds.

Wallowa Lake, a sheer drop off below, was invisible due to the clouds and mist. An eerie feeling riding along and seeing a misty void below.

We left the cattle and rode back to the truck. At a lower meadow we ran into a white tail doe, wagging her flag behind her, as she bobbed along in the way peculiar to the White Tail.

Home to fix lunch for us "cowboys."

Daughter Jackie and children out from the canyon. We attended an Inspirational Dance put on by a local troupe. Granddaughter Chelsie performed in two of the numbers. Good entertainment at our OK Theatre.

May 21—Slept in for the first time in five days. Till 6:15 anyway.

Granddaughter Mona and grandson Buck "helped" me chore. Cloudy and warm, the lawn has bolted. So have the weeds in the strawberry patch and garden.

Feathers fly amid the dandelions as Doris and Scotty pluck chickens.

Caught up on writing and darkroom work. Did some weeding. What a lushness in the valley now. after this warm rain. The crops are all up and a brilliant green carpets our county.

Husband and crew preparing to cut potato seed and start planting. We are also building a new potato storage facility. It will be a monolithic design.

Ran errands in town, treated myself to lunch at the "Country Place." Purchased my bedding plants, petunias, cosmos, tomatoes, cabbages.

Home to set them out before the next thunderstorm. Lawn is a "hayfield." Mowed and "stacked" it. Worked outside 'til after dark. Yard looked nice in the evening light.

May 22—Up early to haul lawn "hay" to chickens, chore, breakfast and go mush-rooming. Warmth and recent thunderstorms brought up a new crop of morels. Scotty, Doris and I tromped through timbered slopes all morning. What a wonderful time we had. The woodsy smell, tiny wild orchids, and morels everywhere. The water running in the brooks from the snow melt.

We saw a white tail deer and a snowshoe rabbit (with his white coat now changed to brown). We enjoyed seeing yellow and purple violets, Indian Paint Brush and many more wildflowers. We were far from reality in this wild area. Returned at noon with buckets of morels and some nettles to cook for supper.

Baked an apple pie this afternoon, made a tossed rice salad, sourdough rolls, mountain oysters, browned morels, asparagus and nettles.

Invited six people to dinner. It was so warm we ate outside on this May evening. Husband and crew readying the fields for planting spuds. Hot today. Nice relaxing evening. Lightning flashes in the eastern sky. A new moon in the west. All windows open all night.

May 23—Up early, chicken plucking day has arrived. Scotty, Doris and I attack the fryers. I chop off heads, scald them and we begin to pluck. Feathers fly and we soon have some beautiful birds in the freezer. We joke and laugh to make light of this task. I gut them outside; the fresh air helps curtail the smell. There was a time when I couldn't do this, but time has changed me. And of course any job is easier when shared with friends.

May 23, evening—Bad news—granddaughter Lacey in the hospital in Wyoming with a lung infection, son Todd kicked in the leg by a horse. Our California daughter's family is moving up to the Sierra Valley where her husband will take a new job. Some good news, some bad.

Children are a constant concern, a threat of worry all our lives, but they are forever, and thank God for that.

My radishes, lettuce and chard all up in the garden, am irrigating already this morning. We start planting the seed potatoes today.

Worked out in the yard until after dark, then clipped the laying hens' wings; some of them have been flying over their fence and scratching around in the strawberry patch. Husband off to a stockgrowers meeting. Daughter called from Imnaha, grandson saw a big rattlesnake today. Another worry!

May 24—Hurried through breakfast and chores, put water on to heat in a big kettle. My two "chicken plucker" friends, Doris and Scotty, here at 8 a.m. to butcher more fryers. We set up shop out under a tree in the yard. I chopped off 10 heads, scalded the birds and we began to pick. Hot scalding feathers flew everywhere. I gutted the plump birds and we laughed and joked, trying to make this task fun. We packaged the 10 for the freezer, then had a tea break, then did more. 28 fryers in the freezer.

We all three took off to run errands in town, and I treated the "pluckers" to salads at "The Country Place." We ate outside and watched the pond: baby ducks cavorting, two white and two black swans diving, and huge trout swimming lazily by.

Relaxed with the neat day. Spectacular thunder clouds built up all over the valley, and it was cooler today, in the 70s. Yesterday it got up to 80 and above in some areas.

Our crew planting potatoes today. Another crew setting out our sprinkler pipes in the hay fields.

So lush are the grasses now, that the cows have to be driven in from pasture to the milk barn. Usually, they are waiting at the barn door for me. Rain showers this morning, accompanied by loud claps of thunder, as storm after storm sweeps over the valley. Warm, beautiful, growing weather.

A beautiful rainbow arched over the valley in a rare "Ross light" this evening. Was busy typing and missed most of it. Spent the evening working on local historical research.

May 25—Warm and misty over the mountains, rained during the night, ground warm and steaming. Almost tropical growing conditions.

After chores, I planted my cabbage, the variety is Copenhagen. Jimmy Weaver on Alder Slope claims this variety is best for sauerkraut. I planted it last year and made the best sauerkraut. I also set out some red cabbage plants. I broke an early 20-year precedent by planting my garden before June 1st. Three factors influenced the deviation from former tradition:

1. Husband had my garden tilled,
2. The soil is warm and friable, ready to receive the seed, and
3. We've been experiencing warm nights lately (a must for sprouting seeds) and mostly because it is not snowing today.

Attacked the weeding of the strawberry patch. Broke a hoe on some Button weed and discovered a potato roguing tool worked better.

The remaining fryers doing better. Less competition. Will let the pullets grow a while longer. The six-week old cockerels averaged four lbs dressed, with a few going five.

Potato crew cutting seed at the cellar, with the planting crew going great guns in the field this morning. Summer is just around the corner and the sprinklers are shooting out jets of water in the hay fields. Summer...how brief it will be, and so busy will we be, that it will be gone before we know it. Each day so precious that it must not be wasted.

May 26—Was planning a hike up Murray Gap, but large thunderheads cover the mountain tops and there are "whiskers" on the mountains. An old timer I once knew said that meant rain.

After chores, I met Calvin and Doris on Alder Slope where we attended the Llama Ranch's open house. Across the field from the ranch stood my newly purchased sheepherder wagon, so we hauled it home. This old wagon came originally from Twin Falls, Idaho.

Sheepherder's Wagon is hauled home from Alder Slope, to be used for 4-H club's camp outs and a parade entry.

Michael, Patrick, and Sharon Brennan, great-grandchildren of late actor Walter Brennan, grandfather Mike Brennan this summer on upper Prairie Creek. Here they pick up rocks in a hayfield.

Husband, along with another hired man, are planting seed spuds on this Sunday. The rest of the crew have the day off.

Scotty came out and we tackled the cleaning of the sheepherder wagon. Mouse droppings, chewings, cobwebs, old junk tossed to the dump. I scrubbed out the boxes and utensils, cleaned the little stove. What fun. Afterwards we saddled two horses and went for a ride up the road. It threatened rain all the way, but we had a pleasant ride.

Husband home by 4 p.m., took a nap then up to the moraine to put salt out for the cows. Then he changed pipes. A long day for a rancher, but just another day.

Son Steve appeared with a load of furniture from college, accompanied by a roommate. They spent the night.

Fried one of our fresh fryers on this Sunday evening. Delicious!

May 27—A beautiful morning this Memorial Day. Our crew still going strong—planting seed potatoes. We must get the crop in while weather cooperates.

Fixed sourdough waffles for breakfast for the four of us. The boys helped change pipes before heading back to Pendleton.

Armed with pinesol and soapy water, I began the all-day job of scrubbing out the sheepherder wagon. My memorial to the Basque sheep herders who have spent many lonely days and nights in this old relic of the west.

I scrubbed the cupboards, put all utensils and pots and pans through the dishwasher, lined the cupboards with contact and even hung some blue - print curtains. By nightfall, it looked comfy and cozy. Stocked now with matches, candles, wood, newspaper, kindling and staples, it is ready to use. We will plan an overnight campout with the 4-H club soon.

By 8:00 p.m., I was fatigued. Never scrubbed so long and hard in my life.

Chores, supper to fix and a tired husband in from the fields. Huge thunderheads appear and lightning lights up the sky. I go down to the sheepherder wagon at dark, light a fire in the little stove and by candle light watch the storm.

I can imagine how lonely the life of the sheepherder must be, but on the other hand, how nice, quiet and nostalgic.

I savor the peace. No humming of electric appliances, no phone, T.V. blaring, radio. Just the night sounds of Prairie Creek and the retreating storm, the little flicker of my candle, the occasional popping of the fire, and me.

May 28—Cloudy and cool. Planting again today, as it isn't raining—yet. Our thunderstorms, though threatening, haven't been providing appreciable moisture. We are still flood irrigating and running the sprinklers.

Grocery shopped, planted more petunias in old pots and pans. Relics collected from the hills. Checked on son Todd, who is laid up with a badly swollen leg due to the horse-kicking incident. He improves slowly.

Rained some, shower and thunderstorms, followed by a lovely, brilliantly-hued rainbow.

May 29—The steady drum of rain on the roof, which began in the middle of the night, continues on through the day. The hills will really benefit from this warm soaking rain. How we needed it.

Our cellar crew hand cutting (tuber uniting) potato seed. Field planting is halted.

The wood stove crackles merrily and I decide to bake a chocolate cake. It is called a "Too Good Chocolate Cake," a recipe from my family's side, taken from the Wilson family cookbook. A quick, delicious cake, a favorite of Aunt Lindy's. Only trouble is, it's too good, and doesn't last long.

As I was mixing up the cake, I looked out the kitchen window to see rain and snow mixed. It has turned colder. We have over an inch of rain in the rain gauge. Did my chores in a pouring rain and snow mixture. Fixed supper of elk steak, morels, coleslaw and potatoes. The chocolate cake was a special treat.

Doug cracking butternuts (found under a tree at daughter Jackie's on Imnaha). These nuts resemble English walnuts and have a crinkled, hard, outer shell. At first we thought them to be black walnuts, but research proved that they were butternuts. The enormous tree they grew on, appears very old, probably planted by some of Imnaha's first settlers. I will save the cracked nuts for a special recipe.

Went to sleep listening to the sound of rain on the roof.

May 30—Our rain gauge emptied out two inches during the past 24 hours. A startling sight greeted us as we looked out the window this morning. The sun shone briefly on the slopes, which were covered with a new snowfall. The "frosted" appearance of the trees and gleaming mountains contrasted sharply with the bright spring green of Prairie Creek's grasses. It was over in minutes and a mist-layered cloud formation covered the Wallowas with "whiskers." More storms in the forecast.

Our cellar crew cutting the tuber unit seed, all done by hand.

The five calves on the two cows, Star and Liza, had voracious appetites this morning. They are all doing well. Daisy and May's calves growing so fast I can scarcely recognize them. The succulent grass has boosted all four cows' production. What factories these wonderful cows are, to be able to convert their forage into such quantities of milk. Their calves fairly "bloom."

Visited Guy and Reatha McCormack, my Alder Slope neighbors, this morning. They have a very large, wonderful, old English elm tree in their yard. Reatha tells me it was planted in the late 1800s.

Guy McCormack's grandfather, William McCormack, was the first white man to settle in the Wallowa Valley, making his home on Alder Slope. The old town-site of Alder, just down the road from the McCormack home, existed before Enterprise was established.

Reatha gave me some comfrey plants, I will give some of the leaves to son Todd for his bruised leg. Comfrey has been used for its healing qualities for years and goes back to old folk remedies. Made into a poultice, it aids in healing of bruises.

Briefly visited Ted Juve, the potter of Alder Slope, then on to Dan and Carol Jarvis, where I photographed their historical, old dairy barn.

As I talked this morning, I realized it is interesting souls such as these that make Wallowa County unique. "Real people," sincere, living here by choice, because they love the valley.

My next stop was at Wallowa Lake where I had an appointment to take pictures. I noticed our cows grazing the steep slopes of the moraine.

Worked in the garden this afternoon. Radishes, spinach, peas, lettuce, chard, and sweet peas all up.

May 31—Planted my Early Sunglow corn seed last evening and this morning a little frost is evident on this final day of May. Not enough to damage anything.

Spent morning running errands and preparing the Sheepherder Wagon for our weekend camp out. 4-H'ers and I will spend the night out in the boondocks, fishing, camping, hiking and outdoor cooking, as well as picture taking. Hope the weather cooperates.

June 1—My friend Scotty ran in a seven-mile race today, at age 63. She finished in 1 hour and 16 minutes. The running was all done in a pouring rain. No wind, just incessant rain drops. The rain gauge filling up again. Needless to say our campout canceled. Grandson Rowdy most disappointed of all, so decided to take him fishing anyway. Had promised to, rain or shine, anyway. A treat for a birthday present.

So, Rowdy and I, clad in slickers, boots, and hats, fished the sodden shores of Kinney Lake. We were the only fishermen about on this rainy Saturday. It was rather peaceful with raindrops falling on the surface of the lake, wildflowers and Sarvisberry blooms drooped under their moisture laden petals.

Although we caught no fish, we fished, then ate our fried chicken lunch in the warmth of the pickup. We drove to another spot near a meadow, found a swampy area where water pooled and found it contained poly wogs. This soon-to-be-eight-year-old grandson was in heaven. Memories of my own spring-time excursions to collect poly wogs came back to me.

We found an old jar and caught many wiggly tadpoles, some with legs beginning to appear. The rain slackened somewhat and we enjoyed the tramping around, grandma and grandson spending quality time together. The children grow all too quickly; if we don't give them memories, even on rainy days, the time goes by and soon it is too late.

Husband to Hermiston to pick up some Simmental semen and look at a truck bed. Rowdy and I chore, then start a fire in the Sheepherder Wagon stove. We will sleep in the old wagon tonight, and pretend we are camping. The poly wogs swim in their jar atop my kitchen sink. The rain has temporarily ceased. A beautiful, cloudy evening. Potato planting has come to a halt, as has the irrigating.

Cozy and comfy in the Sheepherder Wagon, we light a kerosene lamp and pretend we are out herding sheep. The little creek murmurs outside the wagon and the ranch sounds lull us to sleep.

June 2—Bright, beautiful sunshine. We slept well in our cozy nest. Up to chore and breakfast. Huge clouds cover the Wallowas, but it is warm. Rowdy and I mow the lawn and do some yard work. Delivered Rowdy and his jar of tadpoles back to his family.

Planted the remainder of my vegetable garden. Beans, carrots, beets, dill, and Sunflowers; now mother nature can take over. the soil, warm, friable and moist, accepts the seed.

Husband returned from Hermiston. Relaxed on this Sunday, read all afternoon.

After evening chores, we headed to Wallowa Lake, rented a small boat and went kokanee fishing. A gorgeous evening on the lake, the views of the mountains spectacular. We both caught equal amounts of the land-locked salmon. Got our limits before dark. As we clean the fish in the kitchen sink, a full moon illumines Prairie Creek.

June 3—An absolutely gorgeous day. Warm and sunny, with every-thing growing so fast, a person must step back or the growth will engulf him. An exaggeration, but the short, fast growing season is upon us.

Son Todd back to work today, his leg still a bit stiff and lame. He and Ben branding the last of the calves today. Potato planters hard at it again. We turn the milk cows out in the machinery yard each night now to graze down the tall grass. Each morning they must be rounded up and driven back to their quarters.

Feeling domestic this morning, washing clothes, hanging them out in the fresh, sunshiney air. Picked some succulent red rhubarb and made a pie. The delicious "pie plant," sometimes known as a spring tonic. Swept floors, and picked a bouquet of wildflowers for the kitchen table.

Grandson Rowdy 8 years old today. Grandchildren Mona and Buck here with me today, so the two little ones and I fished the creek on the ranch, they walking with me through the chin-high hayfield. We made it, sat on the bank below the big poplar trees, and fished with night crawlers. Four and a half-year-old Buck caught a rainbow trout right off, then three-year-old Mona caught one. Two excited kids. It was so peaceful by the creek. A perfect June day.

Had a kokanee fish fry tonight for supper. The two grandchildren and I spent the night once more in the Sheepherder Wagon. I exhausted my repertoire of fairy tales. Finally at 9:30 they went to sleep.

I awoke at 3:30 a.m. to the cows rubbing against the side of the wagon. We were swaying and the CowBelle (dinner bell) was ringing. The children slept through it. Rain showers pit-patted on the roof most of the night.

June 4—I crept out of the wagon and left the sleeping children to drive the cows into their pasture. Had been awakened at 5:30 with more violent shaking, as Liza rubbed her neck on the wagon. The children helped me chore and Buck led Star's heifer around the yard all morning. The grandchildren left with their mom, taking their fish home to show daddy. Crew planting again, not enough rain to slow the field crew down.

Planted some blue Lobelia in some of my granite-ware pots and pans.

Helped Todd run a cow into the chute to inseminate this evening. Had a loaf of sourdough bread in the oven at the time and it was well done by the time I got back into the house.

June 5—Rained off and on all night. The good, warm June rain. Doug left at 5:30 a.m. to attend a potato storage seminar in Pasco. Before leaving, he gave me a run-down on a list of instructions for the day. Field crew rained out.

After chores, I run errands for the ranch. I then drove a repaired car to daughter Jackie's at Imnaha. The canyons were a sight, with the scent of "Mock Orange," from the wild syringa blossoms everywhere. Wild roses, their delicate pinks profuse and in bloom everywhere. Red climbing roses in daughter Jackie's yard. The river running muddied due to rain storm last night.

Helped Jackie load up her pickup to leave for Cayuse Flat. She will join husband Bill at the cow camp there, and spend the remainder of the week at that remote spot. With the mouser cat under one arm and the sourdough jug under the other, she loaded the two children and they were off up the winding, steep, rough road to Cayuse Flat.

I visited and had lunch at the Riverside Cafe, where I caught a ride back out "on top." These rains have turned the valley into a verdant, almost tropical paradise, everything is green and growing. The cold, whiteness of the long winter months only a dream now.

The zucchini is up. One of my favorite and my husband's least favorite vegetables. Jokes about zucchini run rampant around here in the summer.

Todd inseminated another cow. We have a "spotter" steer running with the cows we want to inseminate to different bulls. He wears a harness that marks the cows with paint, so we know which ones are in heat.

Husband back late from Pasco, had a good meeting. We start building our new potato storage in about two weeks.

June 6—Rained on and off all night. Blustery, warm winds and rain squalls. The garden just "jumping" up. Soon the cabbages will be enormous and the squash prolific. Green gooseberries hang thickly on the bushes already. Muddy at the barn lot this morning. Mamma kitty has hidden her kittens from the dogs so well, I can't find them.

Made a gooseberry pie from frozen gooseberries. Working on the planning of two outdoor catering cooking jobs. One is a ranch wedding, and another lunch is for the state vo-ag teachers' meeting.

Son Ken and his family here for lunch, fixed pocket bread, hamburger filling sandwiches. Wonder how the little family is doing up on Cayuse Flat this stormy morning. Son-in-law Bill has done a beautiful pen and ink drawing for our anniversary present. It is of a cowboy with his saddle slung over his shoulder. An artist in the family, Bill is a dyed-in-the-wool cowboy himself, so he knows of what he draws.

Ben, Todd and Kirk building a new irrigation box, worked until 6:30 this evening on the project.

June 7—After chores, Scotty and I butchered and dressed eight more fryers. They have grown so, I could scarcely squeeze them into gallon-size plastic bags. A violent wind storm all morning. A tree blew down over a power line and our electricity out until 3 p.m. Had managed to cook a stew for lunch before it went out. The wind was a prelude to a steady, dripping rain that began around 3:30. Our crew planting spuds again during the wind storm, then halted by the drenching rain. The "irrigation box" crew continues to operate backhoe and work in the rain. Doug along with Doris and Calvin fished for kokanee on Wallowa Lake tonight. I elected to stay home, feeling tired tonight.

June 8—Potato crew will attempt to plant, only 20 acres to go. After chores, I followed mamma kitty to the calving shed where I discovered the kittens in their hiding place, way down a hole in the straw stack. Very safe from the dogs. My calves have grown so, I can't fit them all in the milking parlour, so must bring one cow in at a time. Since everyone else on the ranch is working, I got in and cleaned house on this Saturday; mopped and waxed floors, dusted, and vacuumed. The house looks much better.

We ate out tonight at Vali's Delicatessen at Wallowa Lake. Good food, good friends and a good time. We noticed the kokanee fishermen out in full force on the lake. Boats of all shapes and colors make a pretty sight in the evening light.

June 9—Between storm fronts this morning, no potato crew planting on this Sunday. Baby robins emerge from their nests, while nervous mothers call and bring them endless supplies of worms. Our lilacs are finally blooming.

Nice afternoon visit with kinfolk, Janet and Jim of Kennewick stopped by. Doug back to cellar to transfer seed to a local seed grower.

Made a raspberry cobbler and took some pictures with a loaned camera. To bed early.

June 10—Scotty and I finished the fryers this morning. Had them all in the freezer before noon.

The Raleigh man making his rounds today. We always know it is spring when he makes his appearance. The Raleigh man is a tradition and his extracts and spices are used by many rural housewives.

June 11—Had granddaughter Chelsie with me all day. We went fishing in our irrigation ditch and caught a 14-inch rainbow trout. This ditch flows from Wallowa Lake and occasionally some nice trout find their way downstream.

Bill Matthews, an Imnaha cowboy, did this sketch in pen and ink.

Chelsie Nash shows off 14-inch rainbow.

Chelsie quite excited about catching the big trout. Grandma, with no net, had to wade down into the stream to grab the fish. Chelsie held the pole, a steep embankment kept us from horsing the fish out. We would have lost him for sure. It was a perfect hiding place for the trout—a back water eddy formed below some riffles, the water swirled around and under an old stump that hung over a steep bank.

We let the night crawler sit in the pool and wham! The fish took the entire hook in his mouth, then took off down stream. Things were pretty exciting for awhile. Grandma covered with mud and wet. We trudged home through the high hayfield, Chelsie proudly carrying her prize.

Grandma and Chelsie spent the night make believe camping in the old Sheepherder Wagon. Eventually I suppose all the grandchildren will want to sleep here. Once again I was awakened by the milk cows and their rubbing on the outside of the wagon. A remnant of a moon appeared through the willow trees in the early morning hours.

June 12—Chelsie slept in while I chored and fixed breakfast.

We finished planting potato seed today. Took Chelsie home. She so enjoyed her stay. Spending time alone with one child at a time is time well spent. At these impressionable ages is the important time.

Haying time is near. My garden is all up and growing at an incredible rate. Summer is just around the corner.

June 13—Drove to Imnaha today to show off the canyon country to some visiting friends. We stopped to admire an immaculately cared-for garden along Sheep Creek.

A woman motioned for us to drive on in, we did and they gave us a grand tour of their beautiful place. These two older people, husband and wife, winter in Arizona and summer on this parcel near Imnaha, living in a trailer.

To occupy their time they have, through the years, built up this incredible garden of flowers, vegetables, lawns, shrubs and even a small orchard. Not a weed could we see.

Before we left they gave us bags of red leaf lettuce, white radishes and onions. Their yard was a blaze of color from Zinnias, marigolds, petunias, sunflowers and many other flowers. Red, ripe strawberries lay among the healthy plants and Sheep Creek, full of trout, splashed past the garden. A high deer-proof fence enclosed the area. The gentleman was a retired farmer, and his wife went along with his dream of building this retirement place. His knowledge of the soil, coupled with his love of growing things, really showed in this well-kept yard.

Next, we visited daughter Jackie and family, they ate lunch with us at the Imnaha Store. Large wooden Indians grace the entrance to this neat old store, which has wooden booths to dine in.

On the way home, we stopped to gather armloads of wild Syringa, in full bloom now. Their cloying sweetness fills the canyons this time of year. We could have surrendered to the canyon's charm and spent a week there.

June 14—Busy preparing for our 4-H Kinney Lake campout tonight.

Son Steve home from college with his furniture and belongings. Loading up the Sheepherder Wagon with supplies for our trip. Made sourdough rolls and fried chicken for husband's dinner tonight. I also did the evening chores before leaving. Excited boys and girls converged on the ranch around 5 p.m.

Armed with sleeping bags, tents, fishing gear and other paraphernalia, the 4-H'ers helped load up the wagon. We left, me driving a pickup pulling the Sheepherder Wagon. Twelve 4-H'ers cheering from the back of the pickup.

At the lake, tents sprang up and camp chores occupied the 4-H'ers time. Most members fished before we cooked our supper. Willow sticks were used to roast marshmallows over glowing coals. The kids fished, took pictures, went for hikes and generally enjoyed the camping experience. Are there children who do not enjoy this? Seven boys and five girls, ranging in age from 8 to 14, two of my grandsons included.

Yours truly very weary by 10:00, when the Sourdough Shutterbugs were just getting their second wind. The sourdough bubbled in the crock, and finally—much later—the talking ceased and all was quiet.

June 15—Woke up to a meadow lark singing and a brilliant sunrise. The Wallowas, so close, were lovely in the morning light. Wildflowers of all descriptions in full bloom among the lush passes. The lake serene, fish jumping.

I started a fire, mixed the enormous bowl of sourdough hot cake batter, and put the large cast iron griddle on to heat. The kids and I fried bacon and eggs, then began cooking hotcakes. The children outdid themselves and the champion hot cake eater was Landon Moore, who consumed 12 large hot cakes, in addition to two eggs and bacon. Not to mention hot chocolate.

Sourdough was made for the outdoors; in its element here on a hot griddle over a grate on an open fire.

We left reluctantly, after one more hike and more fishing.

Meanwhile, back at the ranch, my cows waited at the barn door.

June 16—Father's Day! Spent the day hoeing in the gardens and strawberry patch. Doug and I enjoyed a chicken dinner at the Chief Joseph Hotel, then fished for kokanee on Wallowa Lake this evening. We limited out and enjoyed the quiet peacefulness of the lake.

June 17—Our wedding anniversary! Am busy roasting 30 pounds of beef for barbecued sandwiches tomorrow. The irrigating of the lawns and fields continues. Boiled potatoes for a salad to feed 100 people for the State Vo-Ag convention in Joseph tomorrow.

Felt like I was running a bake shop-made cobblers for the desserts tomorrow: gooseberry, apple, raspberry, apricot and cherry. Doris, Scotty and Annie came out to help make barbecue sauce and potato salad.

Invited to dinner tonight at Doris and Calvin's. What a treat after cooking all day. Almost fell asleep at the table.

June 18—The big day. Cooked breakfast for the men. Baked one more rhubarb-strawberry cobbler, did the chores, then loaded the car with food and catering supplies. Scotty, Doris and Annie helped me at the meal site, the Joseph City Park.

A warm day, but a stream, shade, and green lawns with a mountain view made the meal pleasant. We placed the food on the picnic tables and served the 100 vo-ag teachers.

The meat came out just right, and I had a few left-overs on everything else. Had a few anxious moments upon arriving, when the outlet I plugged the meat roaster pan into blew a fuse. These fellows really had appetites and the food disappeared.

At home, I unloaded all the dirty pots, pans and utensils. Very hot today. Crashed for a brief rest, then into Enterprise to grocery shop for my household. At 6 p.m., I finished the clean-up…the unfun part of catering. Worked in the garden after it cooled off. Men changing sprinklers until after 8 p.m. We didn't eat until late. I fixed the kokanee. Worked in darkroom until after 10, then blissful sleep.

June 19—Another hot day; the endless irrigating goes on. The hay is ripening and maturing faster this year. Soon be time to swath. After chores I photographed the new monolithic construction going on at our cellars—quite impressive.

A circular concrete foundation has already been laid and they are putting rebars in today. An interesting project to watch.

Also did some color photography at the "Country Place" in Enterprise, a quaint little eatery. Was able to photograph the swans, and huge trout swimming in the pond.

The Sourdough Shutterbugs 4-H club camped out recently at Kinney Lake in the Wallowa Valley. Seven boys and five girls dedicated to fishing, hiking, picture taking and outdoor cooking camped overnight with the help of this old sheepherder wagon, brought along to carry supplies.

Home to fix lunch for the three men. Had a 7 p.m. appointment for dinner at Fern and Bill Wolfe's in Wallowa. After a great meal prepared by Fern of creamed new Hermiston potatoes, steak, and green beans, Bill drove us out into their pasture so I could photograph their Gelbvieh cattle. The bull I wanted to photograph was more interested in pursuing the girl (heifer) of his dreams than posing for a picture. I managed to click off a few shots as he passed.

The lower valley looked lush and green, lovely in the evening light. I enjoyed my visit with the Wolfes in their comfortable home that commands a view of cattle grazing against a mountain backdrop.

June 20—Photographed the continuing construction of the monolithic dome. Much to my amazement, I found that the bubble-like balloon dome was already up. Looking like a giant puffball mushroom, it rose against the sky. Foam insulation was being blown inside to coat the structure.

Spent the day baking bread, writing and developing film. A little cooler today, but things are really drying out. Men irrigating from early until late each day.

Attended a benefit show for the Chief Joseph Summer Seminars at the OK Theatre tonight. A showing of a film made in 1937 in Enterprise was really interesting.

Although filmed during the Great Depression, one would never know times were hard. Smiling faces, happy people, small town America with its hard-working, honest citizens—each doing their jobs as if all the world were fine.

The intent of the film was to encourage support of local merchants during hard times. I enjoyed it immensely, a glimpse of another era, brought to life on a movie screen.

One special scene showed small boys herding cows in for the evening milking, right in town. Many old buildings still stand in Enterprise, scattered in and among the newer structures, mute testimony to another time.

In one scene, August Staub posed in his cheese factory, standing beside one of his wonderful wheels of Swiss cheese. This cheese was processed from milk from local dairies that were numerous around the county at the time.

My evening was made especially memorable due to my being seated beside Goldie (Day) Perren. She was born in Wallowa County, her grandfather having settled on Whiskey Creek. She married Henry Perren, who had immigrated from Switzerland and herded sheep in Wallowa County when he married Goldie. Henry is gone now, but Goldie filled me in on life as it was in the 30s.

Curious as to how Whiskey Creek got its name, I asked Goldie. She replied that moonshiners heard revenuers were coming, so they threw the whiskey into the creek. Rumors of "drunken" fish and inebriated roosters (they drank the mash) ran rampant at the time. The story, like whiskey, gets better with age.

Goldie related to me how once her husband warmed up some "boiled" coffee in sheep camp one morning. It tasted terrible. Henry looked into the pot and found he had boiled a chipmunk that had crawled into the pot during the night.

June 21—Cooled off during the night. Another clear, sunny day. Started baking sourdough bread for a wedding reception I will cater on the 29th.

Our fall and winter Montgomery Ward catalog came today. It is just now officially summer. As I leaf through the pages, seeing the emaciated women models, I wonder how long they could stand up under our typical days on the ranch. If our livestock were that thin, we'd be in trouble.

On the other hand, their jobs aren't all that easy either, in the scheme of things. I cannot imagine myself in these ultra-slim modern creations. Think I'll stick to jeans and an occasional pretty skirt and blouse.

The hairstyles some of the models wear resemble the wind-blown effect we on the ranch attain after a day in the saddle—and they pay people to style it that way.

Made a raspberry pie for the annual Grass Tour tomorrow. The calendar is filling up for the summer rush.

June 21—Am constantly amazed at how we ranch wives become almost expert at "holding" a meal, sometimes for hours, depending on pipe changing schedules or other ranch activities. Eggs, for instance, can be broken into a frypan and simmered for quite some time. I refer to this as my half-hour eggs.

The toast popped down in the toaster when the sound of a Honda motor can be heard. Or if you are lucky enough to see the sprinklers come on from your kitchen window you can proceed with the last minute details. We are all adept at thawing hamburger and serving it in 100 ways inside an hour, or less. Stretching a two-man meal to an eight-man dinner at a moment's notice is commonplace. Left-overs are never a problem on a ranch. They are in fact welcome for a quick meal.

Today is the first day of summer. Bees make honey, couples are getting married and due to the fact that this moon doesn't rise as high as the others, our atmosphere gives it a golden amber color.

The moon wanes, as does the honeymoon, first love fades, but can be kept full and long lasting by working at it.

June 22—Caught the bus at Cloverleaf Hall to attend the annual Grass Tour. Spent the day at my photo journalism, taking pictures and notes along the way. We drove to upper Prairie Creek to view the elk fence, then the hydro-electric project at McCully Creek. From there we drove to Elk Creek where we viewed efforts of the fish and wildlife people to restore spawning habitat for returning steelhead.

Despite all the hoopla about this area, which has been a watering and grazing place for some of Wallowa County's fine cattle, the stream continues to flow and looks relatively the same as it has for years. Early day logging had changed the area as far as cover and protection from trees, but damage by cattle did not appear to be such a problem to most of us. Oh well, this is life, we are always faced with a newer generation's approach to things.

Willow trees are being planted along the riparian areas to restore shade, that will hopefully lower the water temperature, so as to be favorable for steelhead spawning. Time will tell if this idea will work.

The total absence of willows along that creek made us wonder how they would withstand the winters, but some plantings had withstood last winter, and that was a test. Maybe in future years the willows will so choke the banks and creek itself that it will become a series of springs and bogs. Who knows. One thing for sure, the willows that are being planted there are not native to the area and look a little out of place with the native flora. But then think of all that deer and elk browse.

So the battle between man and the environment goes on. Each generation trying to decide what is best for the overall plan of the future. An awesome responsibility when you really give it serious thought. I personally would hope there will be streams for future generations to graze their cattle along and provide shade for a hot summer's day, and also provide a trout or two for a small child many years down the road.

We then drove out nine miles on Day Ridge, clear out to the Harvey Gilworth's ranch, where Harvey and Ginger Gilworth hosted us for lunch. The hamburgers fried on a grill soon had hungry tour members thinking about food. Salads, cold drinks and an array of desserts made the trip worthwhile.

Harvey had built a new outhouse out of "old" lumber for the occasion, and the ranchers enjoyed resting and eating in a cool shady area, surrounded by tall pines and meadows. On either side stood the remains of two of Wallowa County's early day homesteads; the Morris homestead on on and the Bryant buildings on the other.

We stopped along the north highway to view two bands of sheep owned by the Krebs family. The scene was colorful, as we could see the herder, his sheepherder's wagon, his horse and his dog. The herder was mounting his horse to tend to the sheep, his dog following behind. The sheep were contentedly grazing the lush meadow grasses. A very pleasant day spent with ranchers and seeing yet another part of our vast county.

June 23—Enjoyed my grandchildren today. Baked a rhubarb pie. Fixed a fried chicken dinner. The irrigating goes on, as does the hot weather.

June 24—Thirty degrees! My garden got nipped. Green beans look especially bad, supposed to get cold again tonight. Just when we thought summer was here. Oh well, this is Wallowa County, and we shouldn't be surprised. Baking sourdough bread all day for the country wedding reception. Fixed an elk roast for supper; never know when pipe changers will be ready to eat.

Wish we could bottle the sweet clover scent that fills the air now. How I love the smell.

June 25—Worked until 11 p.m. in the darkroom last night, then turned the garden sprinkler on, as it was already approaching 30 degrees. By morning the temperature had warmed and it didn't freeze after all. Twenty-nine degrees at Hurricane Creek, according to our local radio, the coldest spot in 48 states.

Haying is under way on Prairie Creek. We started swathing this morning. Mike Brennan was one of the first to get his hay baled and off the field. Threatening rain clouds put on a show overhead, while below farmers hurry, hurry to put up their precious hay. Very unusual to get dry hay up by the 25th.

Baking more sourdough bread today, a very busy time. Three men to feed a hot meal at noon these days. Fuel for the haying crew is as important as fuel for the machinery they operate. Son Steve running the swather, irrigating goes on and on.

Preparing to plant our generation 1 seed. Crew hand-cutting the potatoes at the cellars.

My kitchen smells like a bakery and the sourdough bubbles in its crock with all this use. Hopefully, by Saturday I'll have 20 loaves baked. I make the big "Sheepherder" round loaves, and others are huge and oblong.

Found the little kittens this morning. They finally appeared after being hidden by mamma for three weeks. They are ready to wean and two grandchildren want one, if I can catch the wild things.

Our potato rougers are attending a rouging school in Hermiston today. The OSU Experiment Station will show the results of our seed trials this afternoon. Always important to the growers, as the results greatly affect our seed business.

June 26—Baked four more loaves of sourdough bread. Spent the day cooking for the boys, doing dishes (which seem to multiply before my eyes), and keeping up with the endless irrigating of the garden and yards.

Husband home by evening with the good news. Results of the seed lot trials were favorable. We can now proceed with the planting of the Nuclear seed (dug this spring) that will become our generation 1 seed.

June 27—Warm morning, with a slight breeze. Neighbors were baling hay until late last night. Can't believe the weather holding dry for this time of year. Normally when Melvin Brink cuts his hay, it rains.

Definitely a different year. All over the valley the haystacks grow. The snow has gone off the mountains so quickly this summer. The high patches melt more each day.

After milking my cow, I looked through a knot-hole in the barn wall, hoping to glimpse the wild kittens. There they were. I set down the milk pail and pursued them. A small gray one and a striped gray one scurried into a large flexible irrigation hose, just ahead of my reach. I blocked both ends and had Steve help me flush them out. They came flying out one end into my waiting box. One bit me on the finger.

We put them into a gunny sack. Later I put them into a large box and brought them into the house. They gentled down quickly and drank some milk. Now the grandchildren can finish the taming of these cute kittens.

Our strawberries are ripening. Fixed strawberry shortcake for dessert tonight.

Never have I seen such a crop of gooseberries that hang thickly on the bushes in my garden.

A hot, dry wind blowing to speed up the curing of the hay. Six women ride our potato planter today, planting the generation 1 seed.

Into town to pick up the 130 pounds of beef I ordered for the wedding reception on Saturday. Also picked up my photographs for a coming show at the Skylight Gallery. The photography show and wedding reception will coincide.

Doris and I drove down in the cool of evening to Imnaha to pick cherries. What a neat experience. The trees were loaded with the bright red fruit and the views of canyons and river in summertime dress were most impressive and relaxing. Home late to freeze the cherries.

June 28—Scotty, Doris and I made potato salad for 300, salad dressing for a lot of tossed salad, barbecue sauce and worked like beavers in general, readying the food for the reception tomorrow at the Butterfield Ranch.

Made two more loaves of sourdough bread. At noon Doris and I took our photography into the Skylight Gallery to be hung for a month-long exhibit. Scotty held down the fort at home and finished peeling spuds.

This morning I pulled the sheepherder wagon over to the reception site with the pickup.

Finished planting the generation 1 seed and haying is going full-throttle here on the ranch. The new potato storage facility is nearly complete.

We cleaned up the kitchen, then Doris and I actually made it to a reception in our honor at the Skylight Gallery by 5 p.m. Three other local photographers were also feted: Bill George, Jack Teese and Dave Jensen.

Doug came in later, then took me to dinner, a real treat after a hectic day. Home to lug cast-iron dutch ovens from bunkhouse to house in readiness for the big day tomorrow. Doug to the field, where he baled hay by moonlight until 1:30 in the morning. I could hear the "thump, chunk" of the baler through the open bedroom window and smell the fragrant hay on this summer's night.

June 29—All hands on deck early, Doug over to supervise the fire in the pit at Butterfields. Meanwhile I placed the marinated meat in the cast-iron dutch ovens. Doug placed the kettles in the bed of coals, making sure coals covered the top and sides as well. A sheet of galvanized tin over the coals, then dirt over all. "Beef in the ground" for 300 people under control.

Meanwhile, back at our ranch, Scotty, Doris and I continued on. I did chores while Scotty picked three varieties of lettuce from my garden. We also picked radishes and onions for a huge tossed salad. I made two more loaves of bread. Earlier I had put on a humongus kettle of beans and hamhocks to simmer.

Later, we moved my catering operation over to the wedding reception site on Butterfield's lawn. Here we worked to finish the tossed salad, relish tray and myriads of details.

By 2:30 we were ready to serve. Doug shoveled the dirt off the pit and with a long hook, lifted the pots of steaming beef from the ground.

The meat, done to perfection, simmered in its juices. Doug carved the roasts at a long table, where my crew served the beans, bread, potato salad, tossed salad, relishes and coffee. Punch was served from a 10-gallon milk can with a granite-ware ladle.

Such a crowd, in a beautiful setting on the Butterfield Ranch. The showy mountains forming their ever-present backdrop and peaceful Prairie Creek farm land surrounding all.

A hot breeze sprang up, which didn't seem to bother too much, as there was plenty of yard shade. We used the sheepherder wagon for supplies. It lended a colorful note to the setting.

Presently, the bride and groom appeared. Not in an ordinary vehicle, but in an old fashioned buggy pulled by a pair of matching mules.

The radiant bride in her long white dress and the handsome groom, complete with western hat and attire, stepped down to join the well-wishers and family. People had come from miles around to honor them. A "Just Married" sign hung from the rear of the buggy. All in all it was a western wedding and fun.

Around 6 p.m., a weary me gathered up my kettles and left. Home to bawling cows, eggs to gather and a turned-upside-down-house. Doris and Scotty had washed up the dishes, bless them.

Company. Daughter Jackie's family here to spend the night. While Doug baled until after midnight, I labored at the cleaning of the dutch ovens, which had to be specially cleaned and greased for storage. Couldn't relax enough to sleep, but felt good about the reception. It was worthwhile.

June 30—Hurried through chores and breakfast, packed a sandwich, put my camera in the daypack and met other photographers on Alder Slope. Drove to the quarry road, then hiked up the mountain side to photograph and hunt fossils. A delightful, relaxing day. Warm, with deer flies out in the timber. A large slice of Walla Walla Sweet onion in my roast beef sandwich seemed to work as a repellent for these flies. They hovered around but didn't bite.

June is normally one of our wet months; I've never seen the woods so dry.

We saw many alpine flowers: Penstemons, Indian Paint Brush, the delicate twin flower, wild geranium and the wonderful blue Alpine Forget-Me-Nots. We came upon the remains of a gigantic avalanche left in a chute, high up on the mountain-side. Tree roots, limbs and fir boughs were all mixed up in the snow as it had halted in its tracks.

Some of the waterways already dried up, others trickling down in refreshing green glades.

We hunted fossils and found several nice specimens. A most enjoyable day, far removed from the maddening crowd. The view on this Sunday from mountain to valley below was spectacular. A pleasant way to end June and welcome July.

July 1—Haying in full swing all over the valley, as stack after stack appears. The hot weather continues. Irrigating gardens, lawns, flowers and berries almost a full-time job in itself.

Cooked steaks at intervals for returning men as they appeared from haying or irrigating. Todd in from raking hay at 9:30 p.m., whereupon he ate supper and headed for home. A gorgeous full moon glows over the hay field tonight. Hot, sultry and not cooling off much.

July 2—Hot and humid. The haying goes on. Irrigating becomes the number one priority, as we have had so many days without rain.

The crew looking continually weary and warm. I make gallons of sun tea and keep food available at all hours.

Picked strawberries and rhubarb this morning and made a pie from them. While putting the pie together I could watch Doug bale. I guess there's no prettier sight than the newly baled hay lying in the field. Hay, such an important ingredient in cattle ranching, the sustaining force that will support our cattle all the long winter. Winter is like a dream now on this hot, dry day.

In a bold mood this morning, I turned Liza's calf out with her. My milking parlour was just too small for five calves and two cows. Was afraid we'd all be trampled sooner or later. Am weaning two calves and putting them on grain, letting Star come in to nurse the other two. This way I'll have my house milk when I need it and if we choose to be gone, I can turn the two calves out with Star.

July 3—Another hot day in a succession of hot days. The prolonged heat wave is making berries and everything in general ripen faster.

July 4—I attended the Lostine Flea Market this morning. An annual "happening" in the small, friendly community of Lostine. This normally quiet town is where the "action" is today.

Vendors with every item imaginable spread their wares on tables and spaces that line the entire main street of Lostine. The heat, even more intense today, doesn't seem to deter the crowds of people. The runners appear, coming down main street from the Lostine Canyon road when I arrive, the perspiration streaming down their faces. The Lostine River Run is a 10-kilometer run and my friend Scotty completes it on this blistering, hot morning.

I photographed the colorful array of vendors. My friend Ted Juve setting up his beautiful pottery in front of Crow's General Store.

I found a shady bench outside an antique shop and sat down to visit some friends. A slight breeze floated down the canyon and I enjoyed watching people and visiting. Barbecued beef smells wafted up the street, so I partook of a good sandwich. Sunburned children, "hot" dogs on leashes, popcorn vendors, tired children, humanity in all shapes and sizes.

On the drive home I noted the ranchers still in their fields, still haying frantically despite the fact that it is a national holiday. No matter to the agriculturalist, one day is like the next when a job must be done. Rural

America, celebrating **their** independence by choice. My husband among them, still baling hay.

At home, I baked a large round loaf of sourdough bread and barbecued a chicken for my working men. "Picked" a salad from the garden and had a good 4th of July meal for them tonight.

Have been reading the book "Wild Horse Rider," by Rick Steber, the story of Lew Minor, the 1912 world saddle bronc champion. Very interesting, a great book and good reading. Lew was born in the Wallowa Valley in a log cabin, lived to be 93 and passed away in 1978. One of the all-time great bronc riders. His big moment was when he won the world championship at the Pendleton Round-Up.

Mowed the lawn this evening. Husband in from the field at 9:30 p.m. I slept under the stars tonight, on the lawn. Far off in the distance; I could hear the pop-pop-pop of firecrackers on this Fourth of July night. A chunk of a moon appeared over the eastern hills and cast a golden glow over Prairie Creek's hayfields for the remainder of the night. A cool, quiet and peaceful night.

July 5—Raked the lawn before it got too hot. Moved Liza and her calf down with the other cows. My chores are simplified considerably. Hot, dry weather continues on and on. We are swathing up on Alder Slope, as all the hay here is baled and stacked. Picked and froze two buckets of gooseberries today.

July 6—Steve and Tod swathing and raking, then Doug bales on Alder Slope.

We attended a 50th wedding anniversary celebration for Ted and Mary Howerton at the Edelweiss Inn, an old log building at Wallowa Lake this evening. We were late for the potluck because of haying and irrigating. Everyone having a good time, old-time music and fiddle playing with children dancing along with grandmas and grandpas. A warm evening with a few clouds floating over the mountains.

July 7—Another hot, Sunday morning. Fixed breakfast for the pipe changers, did chores, fixed a lunch for my daypack and loaded up my camera. Met Scotty at Wallowa Lake and we began the eight-mile hike to Ice Lake.

Cool on the lower trail that leaves the lake. Before we arrived at the wilderness boundary, we startled a doe and twin fawns. The cute little fawns, covered with white spots, trotted alongside mamma ahead of us. All at once they melted into the timber alongside the trail.

This three-week-old Shetland pony horse colt, "Thunder," weighed in at 22 pounds at birth (he was weighed in a feed sack hung on a scales.) His mother is in the pony rides at the Wallowa Lake Corrals at Wallowa Lake. Owner Ben Banks also provides, with regular horses, day rides to Aneroid, Ice and Frazier Lakes.

We made the three-mile mark at the Ice Lake sign, then turned right to go down across the rushing West Fork of the Wallowa River. A wooden bridge spanned the waters that tumble down in a white froth and disappear into blue-green pools.

We began the very steep ascent to Ice Lake. Five more miles. The heat glared off the rocks, but a small breeze kicked up its heels and kept following us up and up. Thundering waterfalls appeared and the trail is never far from the roar of these magnificent falls.

As we wound around and around the five miles of switchbacks, a new sight greeted us at every bend. Entire slopes covered with Alpine Forget-Me-Nots, Indian Paint Brush, Penstemons and Cinquefoil to name a few. Clusters of Mountain Bluebells appeared around water seeping over moss-covered rocks.

As we climbed higher, clouds appeared. Scurrying along so swiftly, they would be gone in minutes. As they floated overhead, a shadow would appear below. Lovely light effects on the mountain sides. The trail continued to follow roaring waterfalls, which tumbled down to join the river. White, frothy, foamy, wild water, falling seemingly from the sky. Looking up, we could see the thin, distant line of white water flowing from Ice Lake.

After interminable miles, we met several backpackers who informed us it was tough going and we were only half way. We wound through a high Alpine meadow, trembling Aspen groves shimmering in the breeze, huge talus slopes, chutes where avalanches had sent whole trees crushing down upon the area below. Uprooted, they lay in a disheveled upheaval alongside these flash flood chutes. Huge boulders lay strewn around these loose rock areas.

We climbed higher, determined now to complete the hike. I got some terrific shots of waterfalls. We ate lunch high on a bend in the trail. Water trickled down from melting snowbanks, or appeared gushing from under rocks, ice cold and delicious. We drank our fill and replenished our water bottles.

We traversed a long switchback that took us into an Alpine coolness. Then when we thought we couldn't take another step, the lake appeared. Ice Lake, sparkling in pristine beauty, flanked by talus slopes still covered with patches of snow. Due to our unseasonally warm summer, we encountered no snow in the trail. Only a few patches remained around the shore of this 7,900-foot elevation lake. Many early Julys find Ice Lake still frozen over and the trail impassable.

Scotty and I donned swimming suits and stepped gingerly into the frigid waters of the lake. The water so cold that our limbs turned blue. It revived our tired feet and we took pictures to prove we actually did go into the lake.

We started a small fire at the end of the lake and brewed a cup of tea.

At 3:30, we decided to start back, eight miles. We enjoyed a different view going back. A passing thunderstorm sprinkled us with a welcome rain and the thunder reverberated off the high peaks.

Sunshot raindrops appeared before us as a burst of sun shone between clouds. Mother Nature put on a show for us. Tired and weary, we made it back to Wallowa Lake by 7 p.m.

Home to chores and supper. My husband informed me he had a much more "productive" day…but somehow as I grow older this trip will mean more and the sights we saw today were so incredibly lovely, they will be forever imprinted on my mind's eye. Only wish more people would make the effort to go to these places. They would be better for it.

July 8—Will try to "catch up" on my journal, so will skip a few days and describe briefly some of our busy, HOT July.

These days are spent rouging potatoes, irrigating, haying and working cattle. The skies were sometimes hazy with smoke from Idaho's fires; ignited by lightning, they burned for days. Our hill country, normally still green, is drying up and looking withered. The feed remains good however, and the water in the stock ponds is sufficient.

July 9—Our history group, accompanied by local artists and this photographer, made a trip to the Day Ridge Homesteads. We spent the morning recording history for our coming centennial project, which consists of paintings, photographs and notes that will form a permanent record of our early settlers and historic landmarks in the county. A hot day, but pleasant and interesting nevertheless.

The days melted into each other. Trying to keep up with the ripening strawberries, 4-H meetings, a CowBelle meeting here in July, I made a strawberry trifle, a fancy dessert for refreshments. It was a hit.

My heart goes out to my husband, who puts in such long hours on these hot days, it seems he puts in the longest hours of anyone on the ranch. After everyone is through, he is still chasing water around with a shovel.

July 12—I accompanied the no-till field day tour and completed the photo journalism assignment for our local paper. Another scorcher of a day. Later that day, I drove to La Grande to meet my mother on the bus. It was 9 p.m. when I did my chores tonight. Star wondering where I was.

July 13—Our neighbors across the road, the Houghs, are putting up the "bread loaf" haystacks. Fascinating to watch and a pretty sight in the field.

Dug new potatoes from my garden and fixed creamed potatoes and peas for supper. What a long, awaited treat.

Doug changing pipes in the potato field, as our foreman has the flu. Haying still going on up on Alder Slope. We are trying to catch up on the ranch work so we can take a brief vacation in the motor home to Wyoming, for a visit with daughter Lori and family. Getting away will be hard to do.

July 15—The heat continues, potato roguers in the field by 6 a.m.

The mountains are almost devoid of snow, except at the very highest elevations. The raspberries are ripening.

The motor home is parked in the driveway and I am cleaning it out. Does this mean we can actually leave tomorrow?

Grandma, at 75, mowed the lawn. Hope I, too, can mow at 75.

Grandma will stay here in our absence, watering and caring for the garden and yards. She is glad to be out of the 106-degree California heat wave.

July 16—We actually got away around 9 this morning. The haying is almost done. I turned Star out with two calves and we left. We drove up to Salt Creek Summit, took the road to Halfway, then turned onto the road that follows Oxbow and Brownlee dams. We came out at Cambridge, Idaho.

Up in the coolness of the mountains, we stopped by a shady stream and fixed our lunch in the motor home. We rested for the first time in days, away from the ranch. We proceeded to Indian Valley, then took a long, dusty road to Ola, Idaho. Ola, a tiny 100-degree spot in the road. I took a picture of a quaint little church when we stopped to have a cold drink.

We passed through Sweet, Horseshoe Bend, Gardena and stopped in Lowman to buy a one day Idaho fishing license. We followed the South Fork of the Payette River, a lovely drive along a beautiful river, with fishing spots everywhere. Soon we came in sight of the beautiful Sawtooth mountain range, just as the sky turned pink with evening light.

We pulled over to a campground and ate our supper along the river. I drove until dark, which took us into the primitive area near the quiet, peaceful Stanley Basin. We could glimpse the rustic log fences along both sides of the road as dusk descended. I pulled into a campground in the Challis National Forest, where we spent the first night. A light rain began to fall during the night, the first rain we had experienced in days.

July 17—Awoke to the sounds of cranes calling in a nearby meadow. Miles of wooden rail fences fringed Stanley Basin's meadows. The beautiful Sawtooths' jagged formations were a sight to behold in the morning light. Stopped in Stanley, elevation 6,200, to purchase bacon, then drove up the Salmon River to fish for our breakfast. Doug soon caught enough, so in view of the Sawtooths, I cooked fish, bacon, eggs and toast. We didn't eat until 10. What a switch from the ranch schedule.

A lovely drive to Challis, following the Salmon River. Floaters everywhere in colorful orange rafts, fly fishermen in hip boots in the river. Rest stop near Challis, napped while Doug caught three more trout. We noted the cattle grazing the Stanley basin and were told that they winter near Challis, where the ranchers raise hay in fertile bottom lands.

Many newer log homes contrasted with old log cabins in this area. The country doesn't appear to have changed much in many years.

Passed Yankee Fork, where that river runs into the Salmon. Lots of gold dredging history, according to the historical markers; beaver were plentiful here in the early days, when the Hudson Bay Company Fur Trading was a big business.

We followed the beautiful, clear Salmon River to Salmon, Idaho, then turned south on 28 to Baker, following the historical Lewis and Clark Trail.

At Tendoy, we turned away from the Lemhi River, still following Lewis and Clark, onto a dirt (seldom used) road that would take us over Lemhi Pass.

We drove by Chief Tendoy's grave, then up a narrow, winding steep grade. I was driving, and so steep was the grade, I began to lose power. No place to stop, so kept chugging along until I could. Doug took over and we made the top. Am sure we were among only a few who chose to negotiate that road in a motorhome.

A sign at the beginning of the road had recommended that no buses or vehicles over 25 feet long travel this way over the pass. Good thing our motorhome is a mini version. At Lemhi Pass, elevation 7,373, we could look down on the route taken by the Lewis and Clark party. We would now enter into the Beaverhead Country of Montana, as we had just crossed over the Continental Divide safely. Whew!

We wound down a gentle switchback dirt road to the Clark's Canyon Reservoir, driving near the spot where Sacajawea met her brother Cameahwait of the Shoshone tribe. An important event in the journey, as this young, Indian girl guide's brother then was able to lead the Corps of Discovery across the mountains. We were re-living history here, and the sense of adventure was exhilarating.

It was fun to see the old Beaver Slide haying equipment, turning gray with age, still parked in the lush fields where newer methods were now being employed. In the nearby Big Hole Valley, the Beaverslide is still used, as are horses for much of the ranch work.

The Beaverhead Valley ranchers were busy putting up their hay in much the same way we do in the Wallowa Valley, some using the round bales, or the "bread loaf" haystacks.

It was quite a sight at this 6,000-foot elevation, seeing the haying season unfold in valley after valley as we drove along.

We drove onto Highway 91 and headed south toward Dubois. We passed through Kidd, and dusk found us at Dell. I drove into this small town and parked in front of a place that defies description.

July 17—The sign over the door read, "CALF-A." Relics of Montana's past hung over, around and on everything.

The structure itself was an old school house and had been operated as such for 60 years, we were told by the proprietor.

We walked around an adjacent antique shed that joined the school house. Never had we seen such an array of old things.

There were collections of barb wire, mower seats, wood cookstoves, horse collars, harness bells, cast iron cookware, butterchurns, and rare, old items too numerous to describe. A congenial, old gentleman welcomed us and showed us around. He had welded many of the old pieces of equipment together to make chairs, tables and whatnots.

We walked into the school house, which had been turned into a family restaurant in 1978, and seated ourselves at a long oak dining table, already occupied by some other people. A red checked tablecloth was spread on the table and we noticed the guests helping themselves from steaming bowls of mashed potatoes, gravy, corn-on-the-cob, salad, homemade rolls and chicken fried steak. Family-style and all you could eat, including milk, coffee and dessert for $4.

We were soon partaking of the same fare with gusto, as it was late and we had come many miles since the Stanley Basin country.

As we enjoyed our meal, we noticed the old blackboard still in place. Instead of class assignments, it now displayed the menu, printed in chalk.

Early primers, such as the "Dick and Jane" books, lined the bookshelves, the original old heating stove occupied one wall and the teacher's desk, overflowing with paper, served as the "office."

An old carved-oak piano stood in one corner and the walls were adorned with dated pictures of another time. The place was packed. The establishment's reputation had evidently spread, as cars from many states were parked out front.

Since it was dark when we finished eating, we drove the motor home to a vacant lot across the street from the CALF-A, and as Dell, Montana, population 25, settled in for the night, so did we.

A lonely train whistled in the dark, and soon the train rumbled on into the Montana night; then all was quiet, we slept well.

July 18—We were up by 5:30, the temperature was 49 degrees. After days of 80s and 90s, it felt good.

We watched the mist rising over the Red Rock River as we proceeded down 91. Antelope feeding in the morning light alongside the road. Sagebrush country, miles and miles of rolling hills and an occasional hay field. Numerous range cattle in places.

Turned off at Spencer, gassed up the motorhome and purchased some fixin's for lunch plus two more Idaho day fishing licenses. We drove over some railroad tracks onto a gravel road that led to Kilgore. Sagebrush soon gave way to a green valley, more ranchers putting up hay. Evidence of yesterday's thunderstorm everywhere. A clean morning smell on this seldom-traveled road. We saw more cranes feeding in the hay fields and found out later they were whooping cranes. We drove alongside a covey of sharp-tailed grouse, the first we had ever seen. After miles and miles of open country, we finally reached Kilgore and turned back on a dirt road toward the Targhee National Forest.

We now entered into a lovely area of Aspen groves, fishing creeks, meadows and the blazing bright pink of the Fireweed in full bloom. Indian Paint brush was everywhere.

We selected a spot near West Camas Creek to fish, pulled our motor home over into an Aspen fringed meadow and began to fish.

The mosquitos were out in full force, but we did manage to catch some trout. We also fixed and ate our breakfast here in this quiet place. Idaho has so many unpeopled places. A few clouds formed and the breeze made the green aspen leaves tremble. The sound of the birds in the willows bordering West Camas Creek, the only sound to be heard. What a life.

We left the coolness of the creek and headed back toward Kilgore, stopping along the way so I could photograph an enormous pink patch of fireweed. Walking out to the site, I was overwhelmed by a hoard of deer flies. They clung to my skin and got caught in my hair. I managed to endure these pesky insects until I got my pictures.

We drove into Antelope Valley, a beautiful, big area of grassy meadows with cattle grazing everywhere. We entered into an area of more Aspen thickets, skunk cabbage, and sagebrush, and finally came out onto a paved road. In the Targhee National Forest, we stopped to fix lunch at a campground near Henry's Fork of the Snake River. We discovered a flat tire on the motorhome, which Doug quickly changed. I fished from the dock with no success, although people next to me were pulling in 13-inchers.

More thunderheads formed and a cool breeze sprang up. We came out at Island Park and onto Highway 20; on our way now to West Yellowstone.

As we sped through Henry's Lake Flat, it began to rain. We were saddened to see so many of the big cattle ranches for sale. We encountered the first traffic on the trip as we neared the entrance to West Yellowstone.

Climbing up and over Targhee Pass, we stopped to read a historical marker that told about Chief Joseph's retreat from General Howard over this same pass.

The traffic wasn't as bad as we had anticipated in the park, and we drove around and enjoyed seeing herds of elk and other wildlife, including a bear. I was able to photograph elk in some beautiful settings.

I drove now toward the east entrance. A furious storm developed, and wind, rain, then hail dashed against the windshield. Whipped by the wind, the motor home swayed a bit. The steep downgrade in the canyon was an "experience," as a boulder, loosened by the rain, rolled across in front of me, barely missing my front tires.

Minutes later a grouse, confused in the storm, flew up and crashed against my windshield. Needless to say, I was glad to reach the bottom and drive on level road again. We exited at the east entrance to the park. The lightning flashes were so brilliant, even in daylight I was almost blinded. My husband had slept through the whole thing.

I pulled off at a spot along the Shoshone River in the Shoshone National Park. Here in view of precipitous cliffs and red rock formations, I cooked the Camas Creek trout. The storm continued, with thunder and lightning, followed by a pouring rain.

We elected to continue on down the road to Cody, where we would spend the night in a motel and take hot showers. Deer came out in the twilight to feed and the storm eased. Millions of newly hatched moth millars filled the air and converged on our windshield as we turned off into Cody, Wyoming, Cody of Buffalo Bill fame. Home of the fabulous Buffalo Bill Museum, a worthwhile stop.

In our room, we relaxed and watched T.V. We saw on the local station that cattle rustling was a big problem in Wyoming. A program of nose tattooing was being implemented. The commentator reflected on an early-day cattle rustler, by the name of "Cattle Kate," a gal who had been "collecting" cattle for some time. No problem in those days, as Kate was eventually lynched by local ranchers.

July 19—Awoke refreshed after a night in the Stagestop motel. A clear, rain-washed day in bustling Cody. New homes are springing up on the surrounding countryside, on canyon-cliff-like-settings. Some fancy new ones were perched on incredible rock formations, which looked down on the Shoshone River.

We breakfasted and read the newspaper, noting that three people had been gored by Yellowstone's buffalo. Photographers. The Billings Gazette reported over 2 and a half inches of rain had fallen in a short time, and warned people to stay out of the gullies.

Heading now for Meetetsee, then our destination: Thermopolis.

July 19, later—Meeteetse, elevation 5,797, located in northwestern Wyoming's Big Horn Basin, is known as the biggest, small western town. Settled by cattle ranchers in the late 1870s, Meeteetse is one of the oldest settlements in the Basin. The present community's economy still stems from the Greybull and Wood River valley ranches.

Curious as to what the name Meeteetse meant, I read in a local paper that it was an Indian word meaning "the meeting place."

According to the 1980 census, "Meeteetse is 512 cordial, hard-working, fun-loving, salt of the earth human beings."

Today it is interesting to note that in addition to ranching, the economy is based on oil-related services and production, as well as small businesses. Tourism plays an insignificant role in the economy of Meeteetse.

The fun of traveling is delving into the local history of a place like this. We could hardly wait to reach the next point of interest.

We crossed the Greybull River and traveled through sagebrush hills; antelope grazed unconcerned along the road. We noticed lots of hayland, fields of oats, Charlois cattle and red rock formations as we approached Thermopolis.

Thermopolis (thermal metropolis), home of the world's largest hot springs. Each year in early August the Shoshone Indians gather to honor the Big Springs, known to them as "Bah-que-wana" or Smoking Waters.

The spring is so large that the Shoshone called it the biggest spring in the four corners of their world. According to Herman St. Clair, Chief of Shoshones, the four corners of the world are symbolized by the yellow flying bird for the north, the green tree of the east, the red buffalo of the south and the white circle of purity for the west.

Much religious significance is attached to these symbols and the yearly gathering of the Shoshones for the Gift of the Water Pageant is very colorful.

Over 27 minerals are found in the water and today people from all over converge on the Hot Springs. It is thought to have healing powers for many ills, including arthritis. We turned onto the road to Worland and Lucerne along the Big Horn River to daughter Lori's. Cloudy and cool, thank goodness, as this place can get really hot.

After arriving in Thermopolis, I had locked the keys inside the motor home. A local locksmith had obligingly extricated it to the tune of $10.50. We had met our family while waiting for the break-in of our motorhome. Lori, Tom and Lacey led us toward Worland and their home, about 10 miles out.

After lunch, we walked down with Tom to change irrigation water in a lower pasture, and enjoyed seeing a young red fox. A litter of them comes out of the nearby den to play each day, says Tom. The mosquitos were out in full force and the weather was hot and muggy.

We could see thunderstorms over in the direction of Ten Sleep, and the Big Horn Mountains. We noted that the Big Horn River was running RED, muddy from the flash floods up in the mountains. Never before had we seen such a red color in a running river.

So good to see granddaughter Lacey, such a jabber box and full of fun. Enjoyed a spectacular sunset tonight and a new moon appeared in the sky. Even the moon was red in the Wyoming sunset.

July 20—Slept in the motorhome, listened to sounds of horses grazing outside the window and the sounds of the Bighorn River. A very warm night.

I arose at 6 a.m. to fix sourdough hotcakes from the batter I had stirred up the night before. Three mule deer were feeding in the alfalfa near the dining room window.

All of us off to Worland for a women's softball tournament that Lori was playing in. Very hot day.

July 21—Doug and I up at first light on this Sunday morning. We take off on a back road near Cottonwood Creek. Miles of sagebrush, dirt roads, cotton-tails, doe antelope and their fawns. Oil wells pumping

Granddaughter Lacey Jo sits astride her horse under daddy's watchful eye. The horse had a fat summer along the Big Horn River near Thermopolis, Wyoming.

silently in an arid, hot land. We drove by a hot springs with steam rising from the water. This water flowed into another creek. There were many dry stream beds and sunlight glared off rock formations of every shape, size and color.

Doug hunting for rattlesnakes. Wants a big one to skin. Thank goodness we didn't find one.

We took a wrong turn and drove for miles on a bumpy, gravel road that finally connected with a main paved road to Worland. Ranchers were putting up hay and harvesting their oats. Interesting to note that they swathed the oats first, then came back to combine it. Many sugar beet fields here, as there is a White Satin Sugar refinery in Worland. We had fixed our breakfast out in the middle of nowhere and eaten with the cottontails and the antelope. We donated some left-over sourdough hot-cakes to the resident wildlife of the area on that lonely road.

We finally arrived in Worland for another hot day of viewing daughter Lori's softball tournament. That afternoon Lori's team lost a game, thus eliminating them from state competition. Softball apparently a big thing here in the summer.

Driving back to Thermopolis, we napped under a shade tree in the state park, then drove around the buffalo herd which is located in the park. We had had enough softball and sun to last a long time. I noticed in local gardens that the zucchini was ripening and I wondered about my own far-away one.

July 22—Left Thermopolis, tearful goodbyes to granddaughter Lacey, daughter Lori, and son-in-law Tom. We drove up the Wind River Canyon. Old strata shown in rock formations, millions of years old. Signs told of different periods and kinds of rock. A beautiful drive in an awesome canyon.

We stopped to fill our larder in Riverton, Wyoming, a thriving metropolis. Here we were surprised to purchase Walla Walla Sweet onions at a local store.

We drove on by the Wind River Indian Reservation. Shoshone Country. We gazed out over in the direction of where Sacajawea is supposed to have been buried in 1884. Near here, also lies the great chief of the Shoshone, Washakie.

We headed for the Tetons and left the snow-covered Wind River Mountains behind. It begins to cool off as we near the mountains. We pass by alfalfa and corn fields, and see many horses. This is definitely horse country. Off in the distance, we glimpse the Tetons, covered with dark thunderheads.

In Dubois, we call home. All is well and the crew had finished haying. Still very hot there, reports grandma.

Up and over Togwotee Pass, elevation 9,658 feet. We said a final goodbye to the Wind River country and hello to the Tetons. Down a steep grade into the Teton National Park, while it hailed, rained and the wind blew furiously. The Tetons stood majestic against their stormy backdrop.

We proceeded through Jackson Hole and Jackson (tourist trap), then up the steep pass, 9,000 feet again to where we could glimpse the sight below.

Now we dropped down into Pierre's Hole to spend the night.

July 22—Now here is me tending a campfire in the middle of Pierre's Hole. Around here, "hole" is the term used for valley.

Pierre's Hole was a rendezvous for trappers and early day mountain men. I suppose Pierre or Sublett may have camped here. Doug is fishing and his wife is cooking supper.

This enormous valley is rimmed on one side by the jagged crest of the Teton range and to the west opens out toward the big Idaho country.

Gathered firewood and after letting my fire burn to coals, buried potatoes and roasting ears. While they cooked, I went fishing too: lots of white fish jumping, only caught one trout. I returned to grill the steaks on the fire.

As dusk descended, it was like being in the middle of a wildlife sanctuary. We listened to the haunting cries of some loons, then from the willow marshes came the sounds of ducks, sagehens, Canadian honkers and cranes.

Enjoyed our delicious repast that had been cooked on a simple fire. It was as if the moment in time stood still and we were the early day inhabitants of the hole this evening. We could see no human habitation or hear any sounds, save the wildlife that mingled with distant thunder off in the mountains. However, when it began to rain, we were glad for the snug motor home instead of Pierre's tent.

At 10 p.m. we were awakened by a violent thunder and lightning storm. The flashes of lightning illumined our home on wheels like day. The storm, over quickly, retreated and was followed by a steady downpour of rain that lasted throughout the night.

July 23—Up at 6:30. Mists curling up and around the mountain peaks, still raining. The wild fowl silent this morning.

We drove up toward Victor in the Targhee National Forest and pulled in beside a creek named Moose Creek. The sourdough bubbling in its crock was in its element here, having been mixed last night with spring water from Dubois. Fixed hotcakes while Doug fished. The rain curtailed that, but we enjoyed our sourdoughs.

We heard on the local station that a grizzly was raising havoc with sheep, had killed 16 head. Local ranchers were setting snares and traps in the hope of catching the bear.

Read on a historical marker that Pierre's Hole was discovered in 1808 by John Colter, as he had come from the Teton Valley. With a 30-pound pack and his gun, he had set out to find good beaver country. Colter also discovered Yellowstone, known earlier as "Colter's Hell."

We drove by miles of seed potato fields around Tetonia. Ranchers' hay laying in the fields soaked up the rain. We noted that there were many dairies and bees. Portable sawmills were also numerous.

Near Tetonia, population 191, we passed by a small cemetery that lay in the middle of a big valley. A new grave, laden with flowers, still fresh in the misty rain, caught my eye. The Teton Range, said to be still rising, was shrouded in rain clouds. We fished briefly in the Teton River; no luck.

Around Rexburg, we began to see the monolithic type construction. We stopped at one, which was a grocery store, and purchased a few items.

We located Mike Hunter near Idaho Falls and he took us to lunch after showing us around his offices, all housed in the "dome." These are the people who built our new potato storage facility.

Mike drove us into Idaho Falls to the Mill Wheel First Street Restaurant, where an old mill wheel was going around in a mill pond, right inside the place. Antiques and rustic decor gave the establishment a homey atmosphere. I ordered fajitas, to help promote beef for our Cow-Belles.

From Idaho Falls, we drove to Pocatello, bought a loaf of sheepherders bread at a Buttrey's Food Store. What a store. One could purchase live lobsters, swimming in a tank. I was amazed at the convenience foods ready for the shopper to take home and serve.

I drove from Pocatello to American Falls, the long miles across the state of Idaho, heading toward Twin Falls, then onward to Boise.

We drove alongside the mighty Snake, where great scars in the earth revealed new and wider highways being constructed. Miles and miles of Idaho's famous potatoes, acres of irrigated farm land, hay, corn, beans. It's 7:30 p.m., and 80 more miles before we arrive in Boise.

The sun slipped over the horizon in a red ball, just as we pulled into Boise. After eating a bite, we headed up toward Lucky Peak Dam. Wind and spray covered the road with water. We drove on up the mountain and camped near the Lucky Peak Reservoir's marina. A good night's rest in a quiet place.

July 24—We headed up More's Creek on a beautiful canyon road, then 20 miles farther to Canyon City. Gold seekers came to this place in 1864, whereupon the settlement became the largest town in the Northwest.

In 1862, gold was discovered in Grimes Creek, where we now pulled alongside to fix breakfast and fish. The fellow, Grimes, who had discovered the gold, was killed by Indians. This strike started the Boise Basin Gold Rush. Doug did a little panning while I fixed breakfast. He didn't start another Gold Rush but had fun.

As I fixed breakfast I could "feel" the history along this creek. I felt it in the early morning sun as it spilled down through aspen covered draws, in the murmur of the creek, and in the mountain-morning smells that mingled with frying bacon.

The creek ran pure and clear over rocks that shone in the morning sunlight. While Doug fished, I reflected on Grimes, poor fellow, buried by his comrades in a mining test hole.

We drove into the sleepy Wednesday morning atmosphere of Idaho City. The once bustling gold-mining community. Most of the old stores weren't open until 10 or 11 a.m., so we walked up and down the quiet boardwalk streets, imagining how it must have been in 1865 when the city was in its heyday.

One of two establishments open was the Idaho World Newspaper office. The huge, old printing press was still there. The paper, published weekly, boasts of being Idaho's oldest newspaper. We purchased a copy and enjoyed visiting with the editors.

We wandered into the Boise Basin Mercantile, an old establishment that still survives to do business in 1985. When the museum finally opened, we toured its contents. Very interesting.

We learned that when the town was booming, it burned down. The population at the time was 7,000. Amazingly, the place was rebuilt, as the "gold fever" couldn't keep people away long.

In the museum we learned how huge fires were built along the creek to provide light throughout the nights, while miners worked to free the gold from the surrounding soil and rocks. Miles of dredger piles remain, mute evidence of former feverish activity.

Placer mining was the type employed, and Chinese came in by the hundreds, reworking the areas abandoned by the white miners. Killings were so common, more residents died of lead poisoning than from natural causes. No law to speak of. The Chinese operated laundries and restaurants, earning more "gold" this way than did some of the miners.

Saloons like Calamity Jane's lined the streets. Gold dust must have sifted down through cracks in the wooden floors, as the legal tender of the times. Idaho City today is referred to as "the city that refused to die," and has permanent, year-round residents.

July 24—During our walk around Idaho City we came upon the jail and "pest house." People who had communicable diseases were kept in confinement here, as were the few who were ever jailed.

We stopped to investigate an old miner's cabin and some of the mining equipment.

The day warmed up, so back on Main Street, we wandered into a sarsaparilla, ice-cream shop and refreshed ourselves with a homemade ice-cream cone.

The young girl working in the ice-cream parlour said she traveled 40 miles to Boise on a school bus to attend high school. Idaho City has a grade school, post office, city hall and a few businesses.

Everyone is cordial and the locals are in no hurry. Dogs lazily sun themselves on the boardwalks and neighbors chat leisurely on the street corners. The "Idaho World" keeps the citizenry abreast of the "outside" via its printed pages and the tourists provide a source of income, like us, passing through in all manner of R.V.'s.

Left Idaho City behind and headed up a dirt road to Placerville, an older ghost town.

We drove up near the ghost town of New Centerville and parked off the road, in the shade, fixed lunch and napped. Doug did some panning in a creek, which we discovered to be the same Grimes Creek where we had breakfasted. He discovered some fool's gold (mica) in quartz rocks and a good fishin' hole.

The fish weren't biting, but the fresh waters of the creek running over sun-warmed rocks was a wonderful place to swim. Swim we did, out in the middle of nowhere. Doug finally found color in scoops of sand brought up from the streambed. The forests here are tinder-dry, apparently didn't receive the drenching rains that fell on us near the Tetons. In fact we were lucky to be there, as, according to the Idaho World, all off-road camping, chainsaw use, etc. would be prohibited as of July 27.

Because it was late in the afternoon and we had yet to find a way out to civilization before dark, we decided to leave.

As we pulled out onto the dusty road, I noticed an upside down sign which read Violet Gulch! After a few miles we drove into another ghost town by the name of Pioneerville. Someone peered out a window at us. A few rickety old shacks and hand-hewn log structures were all that remained of the town. The person peering through parted curtains at us was perhaps wondering what a motor home was doing out in these parts. We then realized we hadn't passed any type of vehicle in miles.

In fact the map was rather vague about the road ahead. Hopes of finding the main road that joined near the South Fork of the Payette River dimmed at each turn.

Bumpy, dirt roads led us to an old mine and cabins, where some people lived. Curious, the inhabitants walked out to greet us with: "Lost in God's Country, are you?" We found out they were owner-operators of this mine that enabled them to eke out a living. One miner said we had taken a wrong turn where the road forked a mile or so back. We turned around and eventually found the right turn in that powdery, dusty road.

According to our map, we were heading upward to Grimes Pass.

Presently the summit appeared, and we nosed up over the top.

An old, weathered sign proclaimed that the ill-fated Grimes had been reburied at the top of this unbelievable pass.

I'll never forget the sight spread out below us. The evening sun glinted off the winding waters of the South Fork of the Payette River.

I don't know the elevation drop from the summit to the highway below, but it was mind-boggling. We looked down to Garden Valley and the road we had to travel to reach it.

We started down this incredible grade. In low gear, we braked as we dropped straight down, then twisted around ourselves in a hairpin turn. Straight down again and another hairpin. Doug was munching on cashews and acting unconcerned.

Growing up on canyon roads posed no threat to him. I too have many times driven the Dug Bar and Hat Point roads, not to mention other Wallowa County roads, but this one was a thriller.

Most Wallowa County roads have a few level spots to catch one's breath; not so this one.

Because it was a single vehicle road, with incredible steepness, coupled with the narrowness, I prayed we wouldn't meet anyone. After what seemed like hours, we reached the bottom. My fingernails were permanently embedded in the door handle. I had been ready to jump.

Doug remarked that the person who constructed the road must have started at the top with a cat and just bulldozed his way down the mountain.

We were now on a dirt road that followed the river. Around the first bend we ran smack dab into a young bull buffalo. He grunted and scampered off to join a milk cow and some calves.

Now we could see the main highway, but couldn't cross the river to get on it.

After what seemed like miles, we crossed an old wooden bridge that spanned the South Fork of the Payette and emerged onto the highway to Garden Valley. We turned up the Middle Fork and selected a camping spot in a cow pasture near Crouch.

July 25—Up early to leave this pretty valley, we headed up the North Fork of the Payette to Smith's Ferry. We ate breakfast at a log kitchen along the river. Morning mists clung to the surface of the river and many wild geese swam across to reach the opposite bank to feed. I ordered huckleberry pancakes and they were excellent.

Stopped to fish and met a couple who knew people we knew in Joseph.

Continued along Highway 55 to McCall.

We were held up by the construction of a new bridge. As we waited, I couldn't help but ponder the fact that their biggest obstacle here was removing the old bridge. The earlier construction was solid and reinforced well, not to mention the pleasing old design.

Huge jackhammers were at work to tear the lovely, old bridge down. It would be replaced by one not so attractive, but I suppose able to accommodate heavier traffic.

We passed through McCall, a pretty place, then on down to New Meadows and Tamarack. We fixed our lunch while parked in the shade of an old, abandoned one-room school house near Cambridge, Idaho.

Back where we began our journey, we now headed toward Brownlee, Oxbow and home. Forest fires were now raging in the Payette forests and a smoky haze filled the air. We stopped to pick apricots from a tree that grew out of the canyonside near Brownlee. As we neared the upper reaches of the Imnaha, we checked out the huckleberries. Finding a ripe patch, we stopped to pick some.

Back on the Sheep Creek highway and down Sheep Creek hill to our own valley.

Nice to be home, but the sights we have seen will enrich our lives and provide fond memories. Meanwhile, back at the ranch all was well, the crew had continued on and grandma had kept the garden and yard in good shape despite the sweltering heat in our absence. I immediately got to work organizing my 4-H'ers for the Chief Joseph Days float.

A Nez Perce Indian girl waits for the Chief Joseph Days parade to start. Thousands of spectators lined the streets of Joseph for the annual celebration.

July 26—We arrived back to see our home-town in the "throes" of Chief Joseph Days. This morning was the children's parade down Main Street. This year grandma and I sat on the sidelines and watched the parade, letting the younger generation do the work. The grandchildren did just fine.

The county is drying up. The mountains, devoid of snow, look like it is the end of August.

July 27—Hitched up the sheepherder wagon and drove it into Joseph for the big parade. People three-deep lined the parade route to view the long procession of horses, mules, floats and visiting Indians. Our Sourdough Shutterbugs entry brought up the rear.

Home to lay out a dinner on our picnic table outside on the shady side of the lawn. We feasted on corn on the cob, fried chicken and all the wonderful vegetables that our garden is now producing.

July 27—Grandma and I attended the rodeo tonight. A great show, the highlight being the trained sheep dog, a border collie, penning a bunch of sheep with a "cowboy" monkey on his back.

July 28—Am becoming spoiled. Star still turned out with her calves and I am vacationing from the daily milking job.

Attended the rodeo finals this afternoon. Especially enjoyed the exciting wild horse race and businessman's cow milking events. The carnival is pulling up stakes and leaving Joseph with the refuse of many people. The cowboys have flown off to another rodeo, and the horses and horse trailers have evacuated every vacant lot in town. The Indian tepees will come down as the curtain falls on another Chief Joseph Days.

Picked the strawberries tonight. We came home to a burgeoning garden—raspberries ripening and the zucchini has gone mad.

July 29—Back to normal this morning, whatever that term implies. Grandma accompanied me on my photo journalism rounds. We visited a friend who gave us some crisp, red rhubarb for a pie.

Home to fix a garden dinner. Dug new red potatoes, picked three varieties of squash, onions and lettuce. Had a full table at noon, then grandma and daughter Linda left; Grandma California-bound, Linda back to Pendleton. The house is strangely quiet this afternoon.

A big storm approached and the temperature fell for the first time in weeks. Strong winds blew my corn over, and thunder and lightning played around the mountains. I made a juicy rhubarb pie.

Just before grandma left, she gathered the eggs. I haven't seen my hens in almost three weeks, as she had so faithfully tended to their needs.

It began to rain this evening, a fresh, cool wind blew over the valley, clearing the air for the first time in this long, dry summer.

Potato inspector out in the seed potato fields today.

July 30—Cool and nice, very refreshing. After breakfast, I milked Star for the first time in almost three weeks. So good to have fresh milk again.

Really missing grandma. She did so many things to help out and was always cheerful.

The county fair nears. Must organize my 4-H photography group. Raspberries and strawberries ready for a second picking.

A patch of wildflowers that I seeded in a corner of the garden is adding a gay patch of color these days, and the sweet peas are in bloom. Four-H'ers here on and off all day, preparing their photographs for the fair. From Chief Joseph Days directly to the fair. No time for a breather.

At 9:30, the last 4-H'er finished mounting her prints and I took her home on upper Prairie Creek. Still pouring rain.

August 1—Summer, just begun, is heading down the home stretch. Our hot days have been replaced by cool (even cold) mornings, followed by cloudy days; at least the fire danger is over. All second cutting haying has come to a halt, and the woods opened up to logging again.

August 2—Set two batches of sourdough bread to rise, one loaf for the fair and another on a new cutting board, for a wedding present. Milked my cow, put bread in to bake, picked zucchini, peas, summer squash and some of my cosmos to enter in the fair. Had everything loaded in the car by 9:30 and made it to Cloverleaf Hall by 10 a.m., the deadline for entries.

Ended up clerking for the 4-H entries, didn't get back to the ranch until late afternoon. Made a batch of apricot-pineapple jam. Hung clothes on the line, as it has completely cleared off.

Son Todd packed into the mountains with horses for a few days of fishing at one of the high lakes.

August 3—Got down to 38 degrees on this beautiful, rain-washed, clear-sky morning. My chores lessened due to the rain. Didn't realize how much time was spent irrigating. Made a loaf of sourdough bread for us. Made a luscious strawberry cream pie. Just finished cleaning house when company drove in.

Shelled the peas and froze them. Family from Kennewick here with more fresh vegetables; eggplant, cucumbers, broccoli and watermelon. I roasted a chicken, made creamed new potatoes and peas, a big garden salad and we feasted. Twelve of us ate outside on the picnic table.

Enjoyed our company and the children fished the creek. The youngsters followed me to do the barn chores. I always feel like the Pied Piper with them trailing after me. I saddled up the horse for a special treat and let the children take turns riding my mare.

August 4—Fixed sourdough waffles for breakfast, which we enjoyed outside. Attended a family reunion-meeting of the Tippett Clan at brother Biden's in Enterprise. Enjoyed seeing the relatives and partaking of a delicious luncheon prepared by Betty Tippett.

August 5—Delivered the pies to the fair, met daughter Jackie and children, brought the grandchildren home, as mom had jury duty.

More relatives for dinner tonight: Wayne and Diane Tippett and children, Jim and Dinah. Jim, the fisherman, fished the same creek that his granddad Jidge fished with his dad, years ago. He brought back six nice trout.

August 6—Jackie picked the raspberries and I made two more batches of jam for the freezer. Moving cattle today. Been giving zucchini to all the neighbors and using it 100 ways. Baked six more pies for the fair booth.

Brent Zollman practices on "Pumpkin," a fat lamb, for the Pee Wee Showman class at the Wallowa County Fair. This is the first year for the pre-4-H'ers to have a club.

August 7—After delivering the pies, picked bush cherries in Joseph, home to make jelly.

Moved cattle again today.

Attended a pit barbecue this evening at the fair, put on by the FFA chapters. Watched the fat stock auction, and Doug purchased a hog and a steer to help support the young people.

August 8—Into the fair to pick up my entries; seven blue ribbons on my photography, flowers and vegetables.

The men are off to the hills today. Hauling some cattle out and bringing some calvy ones in.

August 9—Frost in the low places, but the garden escaped.

Up early to make breakfast and lunches for the three cowboys. They left with the saddle horses to gather up and trail the yearlings to the Dorrance Corrals, where the big trucks will be waiting to load them. They will be shipped to a Washington feedlot. The drys will be hauled in to sell at the auction. Feed in the hills is still plentiful and, in spite of our long dry spell, the stock ponds are in good shape.

The cowboys reported seeing elk, nine buck deer and three coyotes today.

I would rather have been cowboying too, but the lawn needed mowing and a dessert had to be made for a potato meeting here tonight.

August 10—This day has been like participating in a marathon, only with different obstacles and courses.

Since Ben and his family are on a much needed vacation, I started the morning off by doing their chores; let the calves in to nurse the milk cow, fed the chickens, and watered the dog. Home to do likewise for my own menagerie.

The menfolk off earlier to attend the Stockgrowers annual breakfast meeting, which began at 7:30. I actually made it by 8, having already eaten a quick bite. Armed with my camera, I took the required publicity pictures. Was very pleased to meet Fred Kerr, who was introduced as a cartoonist, nutritionist.

Home at 10 to do a few more chores, then back into Enterprise at noon to attend the annual CowBelles luncheon and meeting.

Home to catch up and do Ben's chores and mine, then be ready for the annual Stockgrowers dinner-dance at Cloverleaf Hall.

Here we enjoyed a barbecued steak dinner and danced until midnight. A once-a-year shindig that brings the cowboys out from the hills, canyons and valleys. Lots of boot stompin' music, while visiting old friends and new acquaintances. Cattlemen and their wives whirl around the dance floor with seemingly unlimited energy.

Fun to watch Mack and Marion Birkmaier, who live over 30 miles out on Crow Creek, enjoy this special night. This couple has raised a family and operates a cattle ranch out on a "picture pretty" place that makes do without electricity or many modern conveniences. The hard work and lack of frills must agree with Mack and Marion, as they always have that young sparkle about them.

August 11—Slept in 'til 8. After doing Ben's and my chores, Scotty and I decided to go on a hike up Bear Creek. As a misty cloud layer lifted, she and I could see the first snowfall of the season had fallen during the night. The high mountains were wearing a dusting of snow, and it is only August.

We drove to Wallowa and began our walk at the Boundary Campground. Huge, fluffy, white clouds sailed overhead all day, but it didn't rain. A wonderful fall smell in the air already. We nibbled on bright red Thimble berries and wild raspberries that grew along the trail.

This seldom-used trail follows the splashing waters of Bear Creek. Toadstools appeared all around, due to recent rains. We hiked nearly to Goat Creek, where we ate our lunch. Scotty's little stove had water boiling for chicken soup to go with our sandwiches. Wish we had brought fishing poles, many good holes in the creek.

Home to chores at 6. Tired, but a day well spent. There is something refreshing and renewing about being in the wilderness... it is virtually free for all to use; a pity that so many times we choose to be housebound, never realizing that housework will wait, and be done better when our spirits have been lifted by a refreshing walk.

Worked in the darkroom until late, catching up on deadlines.

August 12—The busy days continue without let-up. Our fall calves are beginning to arrive.

Still doing Ben's chores. I watch a convoy of cattle trucks pull out of our ranch driven by Kirk, Todd and Steve. They will be hauling cattle from Lostine to Enterprise to meet a semi that will ship them to a feedlot.

Made a "soup bone soup," adding half the garden to it, even zucchini. Made sourdough bread, and an apple pie from some transparent apples. Feeling more like fall everyday.

August 13—Ben's cow is becoming attached to me. Milked Star, then made freezer strawberry jam. The raspberries and peas need picking again.

Washed a week's worth of dirty jeans and accumulated work clothes, amazes me how so much cow manure, grease and grime can actually come clean in the washer.

Starting to ready the equipment for Ag Bagging. A beautiful, clear day with just a hint of fall.

The garden is wonderful, I thaw out some meat, then go there to "pick" supper. Such a variety.

August 14—I have breakfast ready by 6:30, so Doug, Todd and Steve can leave for the hills to haul some drys to the sale and bring in some two-year-old heiferettes.

Spent most of the day picking and shelling peas, for freezing. There is much to contemplate while shelling peas. The very act itself teaches patience and perseverance. One can count the peas in the pods, (in mine, I found seven to be the most common number). Or, one can reflect on what a short time it took for the peas to mature. I think about the good meals this winter with peas in the freezer. And I mentally planned what I would fix for supper tonight. I pulled up some good beets, cooked them in a huge kettle, then made pickled beets to can. The spicy-sweet vinegar smell fills the kitchen, and the sealing jars go pop.

We in Wallowa County spend our summers preparing for winter, whether it be putting hay up for the cattle or preserving food for ourselves. On this beautiful day, the peas, beets, strawberries, and raspberries are temporarily under control.

The men have begun working in the fava bean field, chopping the crop to be stored in the sealed Ag Bags. The days shorten noticeably, and it is dark by 8 instead of 9 now.

The blackbirds gather in large numbers, sometimes covering the entire fence rows with their bodies. Another sign of fall. We started up the wood cookstove this morning and I fixed our breakfast on the old Monarch range. It takes the chill away in the morning, and feels good.

We are getting the second cutting, on the rented land on Alder Slope, up today. Lots of hay around the valley this summer.

August 15—Spent all afternoon cooking for company tonight. Eight of us at the table, visitors from Missouri. Had baked another strawberry pie, sourdough bread, three pans of manicotti (which I added grated zucchini to the meat filling of). Tricky way to get Doug to eat that vegetable. We enjoyed corn-on-the-cob, fresh garden salad, pickled beets and sliced, fresh tomatoes. We also celebrated Todd's 23rd birthday, which was yesterday.

After dishes, I showed slides of our recent four-state trip.

August 16—Everyone putting up second cutting hay. Our neighbors, the Lockes, creating a loose hay stack that grows each day, a pleasing sight from my kitchen window. The smell of roasting beef fills my kitchen, as I prepare a roast for tomorrow's potato tour.

Busy planning a 4-H hike into Red's Horse Ranch and a history group trip to the old Maxville town-site. On the phone "arranging" most of the morning.

Made a chocolate zucchini cake; Doug says I can really disguise that stuff.

A mobile slaughter unit came to butcher the crippled steer today. Why is it that we ranchers always get to eat the rejects or cripples?

The butcher presented me with an enormous kettle-full of heart, tongue, and liver. I simmered the tongue with bay leaves, peppercorns and onions, we will use it for sandwiches.

Looking at this year's crop of seed potatoes in Jim Dawson's field on the annual Wallowa County Seed Potato Tour are, from left, Doug Tippett, John Wampler and Arleigh Isley, Wallowa County extension agent.

Interviewed the Ketscher family on Alder Slope this afternoon, a truly all-American family. They were in the middle of their second cutting also. This hard-working family is doing a great job of managing their ranches and I enjoyed the interview.

August 17—Made a zucchini salad for the potato tour lunch this morning, with shrimp, fresh herbs, and garden lettuce. Mixed with a tangy dressing, it was a hit.

Luther Fitch and wife, Joyce, drove in from Hermiston to attend our potato tour. As they drove up, I could see cats, many cats, looking out from the back seat. Luther and Joyce thought I needed some barn cats, two families of them in all colors. Apparently the cat population at the Fitch household had gotten out of hand, and this seemed the logical solution. We unloaded the transplanted cat families in the barn, where they immediately made themselves at home in the hay. The mice won't stand a chance now and Star's fresh milk will keep the cats around.

Luther was also laden with some good Hermiston watermelons and fresh sweet corn from Bryan Wolfe's.

We potato growers' wives laid out the spread for lunch at the Butter-field ranch. This was followed by a tour of local seed potato fields. In the evening we hosted our out-of-town tour members to a steak feed at Wallowa Lake. A beautiful evening at the lake, and everyone enjoyed the steaks, fresh corn-on-the-cob and "taste-testing" Luther's watermelons, some of which were new varieties.

August 18—Today is grandson Buck's fifth birthday. Usually, Buck is up at Monument Ridge Cow Camp during his birthday. Then grandma must drive on remote roads, bearing the traditional sourdough chocolate cake. Like the mail, grandma always comes through, regardless of bad roads or inclement weather.

But this year, he was on the Imnaha, so we celebrated the event there on this bright beautiful Sunday. Buck's party was attended by the young population of Imnaha. Since it was after church, his parents had invited most of the congregation. We enjoyed potato toppers and of course the birthday cake, which was served up with handcranked ice cream. Grandma and Buck fished off the bridge, whereupon grandson skunked me again and caught two nice trout, while I pulled out one squawfish.

Todd, Doug and Steve finished the haying on Alder Slope today.

August 19—Started ag bagging the fava beans today.

Made the barn cats happy this morning, presented them with a large squawfish caught in the Imnaha River.

August 20—A couple from England visited us today. I took them on a tour of our ranching operation, which included the fava bean field, the potato cellar (monolithic dome) and our cattle. They will be back in the morning to ride a "western" horse. Started to rain this evening, with thunder and lightning playing around in the mountains.

August 21—Beautiful and clear, with more powdery new snow sprin-kled on the high peaks. The English couple enjoyed riding my cowhorse. It was amusing to watch them "posting" English style on my cow pony.

Assembled my back pack for our 4-H club's trip to Red's Horse Ranch in the morning. All the 4-H'ers excited, as am I.

August 22—We left at 6 a.m. and drove to Cove, in Union County. From Cove we wound up a steep gravel road to Moss Springs Camp-ground, our jumping-off place. I scouted out several trails that offered

different choices, none of which had a sign that read "Red's Horse Ranch."
Having been on this trail horse back on several occasions in the past, I
had remembered such a sign. Choosing a trail that said "Little Minam
River," we began our hike. Since the trail to Red's does follow the Little
Minam River, then crosses it, I figured we couldn't go wrong. But go
wrong we did, four miles wrong.

The worst part for me was knowing immediately after we started
down the trail it wasn't right, but I kept hoping it would intercept the
right trail farther down the canyon. Naturally, I had left my map in the
car. Luckily one of the 4-H'ers produced one. Since we were now heading
the wrong direction toward the upper reaches of the Little Minam River
country, I could see by the map that the trail would eventually join the
Minam River Trail, about 15 or 20 miles out of our way.

All along I kept thinking I should turn back, but kept hoping we'd
come upon a trail junction. So, we trudged back up that four miles and
began at the beginning, this time on the Minam River Trail. We had
already done eight miles, with packs on; eight more to go. Fortunately,
this trail was mostly downhill and it did follow the Little Minam, which
was lovely on this nice day. Kurt couldn't stand passing by all the
tempting fishing holes, so tried his luck and limited out in less than 15
minutes. The day was perfect. We were heading into the vast Minam
Wilderness. Tired as we were, it was still adventure.

We finally approached the wooden bridge that crossed the Little
Minam, and presently came out onto a ridge. It was nearing 5 p.m. From
the ridge top, we began descending a long, switchback trail that allowed
us an occasional glimpse of the meadow and ranch buildings far below.
We were finally going to make it, after 16 weary miles. By 6 p.m., the last
of us walked across the meadow and up to the lodge-dining log building.
The young cook, a good-natured girl, and the ranch crew said they were
expecting us, and supper was ready.

A place never looked or smelled so good. Red's Horse Ranch, pri-
vately owned, is situated in the heart of the Minam Wilderness. A
generator started up and suddenly lights came on. After resting our
trail-weary feet, we washed up for supper. What a meal. Barbecued
country pork ribs, cauliflower, broccoli and fresh cabbage coleslaw from
the ranch garden, heavenly homemade rolls, and apple crisp, still warm
from the oven.

The hearty fare revived us and since we had previously arranged to
sleep in the hay barn, we were told we could bed down next to the horse
stalls.

The still, quiet beauty of the Minam River on a late August morning near Red's Horse Ranch.

August 23—We awoke to the sound of horses' hooves thundering past us. The wrangler was driving them into the corral from the landing-strip meadow. Off in the distance, we could hear the drone of a light plane. Frost covered the meadow and had nipped the green beans in the garden. Presently the small plane landed, and three fellows alighted. They had flown in to eat breakfast.

We tumbled out of our hay-covered sleeping bags and went to warm ourselves by the huge, roaring fire in the dining lodge.

The sun spilled over a ridge and turned the ranch into a photographer's dream. We photographed, then enjoyed a wonderful ranch-style breakfast of hot cakes, eggs, bacon, blueberry kutchen, melons, apricots, and juice. The 4-H'ers had really worked up an appetite in this mountain air and made quick work of the meal.

Landon had developed blisters on his blisters, and was running in his stocking feet. We toured the ranch, looking at the log cabins and the nearby Minam River, wishing we didn't have to leave. The place brought back fond memories for me, as I had cooked there at the ranch and also 19 miles upriver at Elk Creek during elk season. In those days, I rode horseback, a far cry from backpacking in.

Reluctantly we left by 10 a.m. Landon hiked the entire way out in his socks. Quite a testimony to the manufacturer of that brand of wool socks, as they had nary a hole in them after eight miles of trail. We climbed the last of the steep, mountain trail to Moss Springs in the heat of the day. We were very glad to see the campground. It was 4 p.m.

Kurt had limited out again, catching more of the beautiful dolly varden trout at each tempting hole along the trail. We stopped in Cove, where Kurt "iced" his fish and we treated ourselves to a popsicle.

It had been a steep hike out, as the elevation at Red's is 3,600 feet and one climbs exactly a mile upward in elevation to reach Moss Springs. However, tired as we were we agreed it had been a trip we'd always remember. The sense of satisfaction that accompanies such adventuresome feats, more than compensates for the discomforts.

August 24—Up early to fix sourdough waffles for breakfast. Daughter Jackie and family here to spend the night.

No time to recover from my 24-mile hike to Red's yesterday, as I was to meet the local history group in Enterprise by 7:30. This day, we would tour the old townsite of Maxville, remains of some of the old logging railroad routes, and hopefully, the Grossman, Noregard areas.

A large group of enthusiastic history buffs, writers and photographers turned out. We car-pooled; I rode with Grace Bartlett. Our group included

Cressie Green and Irene Barklow, both interesting people to ride with. All of us share an interest in Wallowa County's early history, as well as a spirit of adventure.

We drove to Wallowa, where we added more people to our caravan, including Wallowa rancher Reid Johnson, who would "guide" us through the "tracked" wilderness of the Grossman area.

Earlier, I had procured a key from the Department of Fish and Wildlife by obtaining permission to go beyond the road closure in the Grossman unit. This was necessary, as the area we wished to tour was inside the huge Boise Cascade timber management area and locked up for Bow season, which began this morning.

As our caravan climbed out of the lower Wallowa Valley, Reid called a stop on a high point overlooking the valley below. Quite a sight greeted us. Reid pointed out different landmarks and gave us a brief rundown on how his own forefathers came to the Wallowa Valley and settled here.

We traveled the dusty, gravel road to the old townsite of Maxville. It was most interesting to walk among the ruins of this once booming logging town. Today, all that remains is a log structure that once housed the executive offices of the logging operation-based town.

Reid pointed out where the hotel had been, and explained that many of the buildings were moved in later years to the town of Wallowa. He said some of the original structures can still be seen today. Many have been remodeled or added onto.

We walked down through a meadow and discovered old, faint, but unmistakable remains of the railroad. We could see visible evidence of the roundhouse.

A breeze stirred the golden grasses on this late August day. A splendid day for an outing. The area around the old townsite was peaceful and calm. We were reflecting on how it must have been in those days, when sturdy loggers, Swedes and Negroes built the town of Maxville by the sweat of their trade.

We drove on, stopping to view remains of an old railroad trestle. It was hard to imagine the work involved in constructing and operating that railroad system, which carried thousands of logs over miles of wilderness tracks to the ills in Wallowa.

Presently, we came to the road closure and unlocked the gate to enter the vast Grossman compartment. This area, under the jurisdiction of Boise Cascade, contains a network of roads defying description. A maze of logging roads that sometimes connect, sometimes dead-end, cross a creek, are not numbered, and all look alike. Somehow, Reid got us to the Noregard place.

We ate our lunch here, and afterward, some of us did some investigating up a draw, and found an old hand-hewn log cabin; very old, but still hanging in there.

We were told that the old Noregard homestead was about a half-mile up a draw from the Joe Clay homestead. We eventually found the spot, after driving around some more. Cressie spotted it through a group of trees.

It was fun photographing the huge, old barn and walking among the foundations of other buildings that comprised the early-day homestead. These places were so far out. No wonder our ancestors were so self-sufficient; they had to be.

Even though it was a hot, dusty drive, our group was congenial. and continued congenial, as we tried in vain to find our way out of the area to our next point of interest, which was the site of Camp 5.

Our capable guide finally led us down the right road to Camp 5. He remarked that it would have been easier to head across country on horseback than to figure out the roads. After driving on several wrong roads we found the right one.

At Camp 5, we were amazed at the remains of an old building used to repair the engines and flat cars. We saw an enormous, rusty spark arrestor from a steam engine. Walking up a nearby hill, we viewed what was left of the meat house at Camp 5. We had been told that the homesteaders would butcher a beef and haul it to the camp on a horse-drawn wagon, where it would be sold to the loggers.

The customer would simply take a knife and hack off a hunk of meat. The meat house was the only place to keep meat cool. Only as much meat as could be consumed in a few days was purchased, due to lack of adequate refrigeration.

Soon, we were on the road to Smith Mountain, where we eventually wound down into the valley via a descending road that offered a breathtaking view of the lower Wallowa Valley. Reid's father had viewed the valley for the first time from this point long ago. He had paused to study the panorama, with the Wallowa River winding through green meadows and the Wallowa range in the background.

"Right over there," he said, "will be my home," and home it became, and now as we gazed down in awe at the scene below, we knew how Mr. Johnson must have felt.

Even though we were all covered with dust, we had enjoyed our day immensely.

Meanwhile, back at the ranch, the men came in to shower, covered with the black grime from ag bagging.

We were invited to dinner at the lake tonight; Aunt Amey had cooked us a delicious meal in her cabin. A nice way to end a perfect day.

August 25—The men all in the fava bean field, then home at intervals for a noon meal. I decided to defrost the refrigerator, an enormous undertaking that took me all morning. A ranch kitchen's refrigerator must not only store an immense amount of foodstuffs, but cattle vaccine, allergy medication, and even cans of Copenhagen.

Nothing is ever thrown out until it either develops mold or turns a blue color. Like Erma Bombeck says, "There is no known navy blue food." I've found this a good rule to follow. It was nice to have a sparkling clean refrigerator, which I can now fill up with the odds and ends again, like I always do.

Doug decided to take a break from the ranch on this Sunday afternoon, so headed to Imnaha to "look for a fish, a blackberry, and maybe a rattlesnake." He returned after dark with trout, four gallons of blackberries, and rattlesnake rattles. The Imnaha had provided all three.

August 26—A little cooler today, the drifting clouds reminding me of fall again. The men repairing breakdowns on ag bagging equipment.

The two calves that have been turned out with Star are protesting loudly this morning down near the barn. I shut them away from her last night, eliminating their constant milk supply. They must share with my pail and the kitty's dish, and drink only at night and morning once again. A procession of hungry cats follows me to the barn; seeing the milk pail means warm milk in their dish.

Made a blackberry cobbler as per Doug's instructions: a thick crust over bubbling juicy berries. Nothing finer.

A spectacular display of nature's fireworks this evening. Jagged, white lightning, edged in pink, zig-zagged across the sky. Had a good view from the picture window. Thunder, sounding like cymbals, crashed and echoed across the mountains and rent the skies above with a deafening roar. Fun to watch, but it definitely places man in his proper perspective.

Pouring rain, hail and wind accompanied the passing storm, which swept on by and left a calm, cool, washed sky.

I picked the strawberry patch and watched the brilliant sunset fade. Even the berries took on the hues of the sky.

August 27—It is time to make sauerkraut. The cabbages that have grown to gigantic sizes wait to be cut. Doris and I set up shop out on the lawn and begin shredding the cabbage with a kraut cutter. The firm, crisp, sweet heads of the Copenhagen variety will make wonderful kraut. I carried the large crocks up from the basement and began layering the shredded cabbage with salt. It was a pleasant day to make sauerkraut.

By noon we were finished and I had a taco dinner ready for four men, thanks to Doris' good help with the shredding.

Doug presented me with a small calf that he had found on the moraine. A twin that had been rejected by mom. Wild as a little fawn at first, it was soon following me around.

Mowed our large lawn and made a zucchini frittata for supper.

August 28—Doris, Scotty and I picked Early transparent apples from a tree in Joseph this morning. We picked up the windfalls and shook the tree until we had buckets of them. We took the apples to Doris' where we peeled and sliced until 12:30. We layered the apple slices with sugar. Left over night the juices will come out of the apples and provide the liquid to can them in. An excellent way to preserve apples for those delicious winter pies, and most of the work is already done.

Wallowa County is richly blessed with so many foods to preserve. During these late summer days, pickling, canning, drying, and root cellaring is going on in most households.

Made a batch of applesauce with some left-over apples. Dug potatoes and carrots from the garden to put around an elk roast for supper. A fresh head of cabbage made a wonderful coleslaw. Must enjoy the garden while we can.

August 29—The men finished ag bagging today and moved to a neighbor's field to chop some hay for them. I picked and froze the green beans.

August 30—After a hectic day of getting ready to go grouse hunting, would you believe we finally drove out of the yard at 9:30 p.m? At 9 this morning, a neighbor showed up to purchase two orphans I had at the barn. I was able to turn Star out with her calves, thus eliminating that chore.

When we finally escaped, Doug drove the motor home and I followed driving our four-wheel drive pickup in the wake of his dust. It was a cold, clear, moonlit night out on the Crow Creek road.

We turned up Chesnimnus Creek, which was a ribbon of moonlight, as glimpsed through the trees. Since it was so late, we didn't drive all the way out to Cold Springs Ridge, but pulled off at Vigne Campground, where we spent the night.

Using an old kraut cutter purchased in an antique shop, Doris shreds cabbage that will be placed with salt in the crock. After fermentation, sauerkraut will be ready to can.

August 31—Up at dawn, we drove to Cold Springs Ridge. The sun was just coming over the canyon country when we parked our rigs. Taking the small four-wheel drive, we went for an opening morning hunt. The birds were scarce, but we did get a shot at two near an old log watering trough near Road Gulch. "Probably two, old, tough ones," commented husband. "Just as well we missed."

We fixed a good breakfast out on the ridge in the comfort of the motor home, then drove around some of the many roads in the area. We visited the Cold Springs cow camp, where Doug's family had summered cattle when the children were growing up. The old house is still standing.

After a day of hunting (no luck) we drove out on Grasshopper in the early evening. Beautiful views, and not a soul did we see.

We hiked around, noticing elk and deer signs, but not one grouse. We made our camp near the Frog Pond and were joined by Doris and Calvin, who had arranged to meet us there this evening. A big, beautiful moon appeared over the canyon while we barbecued steaks, enjoyed a campfire and said goodbye to August.

September 1—A lone range bull had bellowed off and on during the night, as he investigated our camp. A warm morning. We were all up early, me photographing the canyon vistas, which are pretty spectacular out on Cold Springs Ridge.

We went for a morning hunt and were startled to see five cow elk with one huge six-point bull. We watched them for some time, until the cow went one direction and the bull split off into the timber. We did finally jump some grouse; I downed one that had flown off into a tree.

Back to camp to fix a sourdough hot cake breakfast, which we enjoyed outside in the sunshine. After packing a picnic lunch we took off in the four-wheel drive down Horse Creek, stopping above Downey Saddle to view the scene before us. Miles of canyons unfolded, separating into different tones and hues in the morning light. Soft shadows covered this vast area of unpeopled places.

On down Horse Creek, we stopped to pick blackcaps and wild black-berries. We arrived at Joseph Creek and entered Asotin County, Washington. We passed by the cave where Chief Joseph is supposed to have been born. Doug also pointed out the old Tippett Ranch (now owned by the Game Commission), Doug's one-room school house, the Joseph Creek School.

Presently we came to where Joseph Creek joins the Grande Ronde, then followed that river the Snake. We stopped to rest at Heller Bar and enjoyed the views of the Snake River as it flowed past.

We picked more blackberries along Joseph Creek and picnicked near an old apple tree on the way up Horse Creek. When we arrived back up on Cold Springs Ridge, the wind had come up and a storm was moving in.

We decided to go on home rather than spend another night. Driving home by way of Red Hill, we saw many herds of elk feeding that evening.

What a perfect day, and what miles of country we had seen. The grouse, blackberries and wild apples were another bonus. After all sometimes grouse hunting is just an excuse to get away from it all, right?

September 2—Picked the first sweet corn in the garden today. Another first, a ripe tomato, an accomplishment on Prairie Creek.

We CowBelles served hundreds of steak dinners at the big feeder sale in Enterprise today. The weather cooperated and as usual the affair was a success.

September 4—Caught up on housework. Spent an hour in the "pea patch" picking peas. It was rather pleasant there in the midst of my flourishing garden, surrounded by corn stalks, enormous squash plants and all manner of bearing vegetables. And the smells, aromatic mixtures of dill, sage, onions and flowering sweet peas.

Towering above all were the giant sunflowers, drooping under their own weight. The wildflower patch is a blaze of color; my favorites are the golden California poppies. In the evening these blooms fold up, opening again in the morning sunshine. The garden's days are numbered, and any night now can bring the killing frost.

The ag bagging crew having problems in the field; the silage too dry and more breakdowns. Difficult on the workers, who put in long hours as it is.

September 5—Scotty, Doris and I converged on the canyons of the Imnaha today. Armed with picking buckets and boxes, we headed first to daughter Jackie's, where we picked red, ripe tomatoes, the wonderful Imnaha tomatoes. You haven't lived until you've tasted an Imnaha tomato. The lower elevation and warmer climate is ideal for growing them.

While we were there next to the river, my five-year-old grandson, Buck, caught a nice rainbow trout and proudly presented it to grandma.

We drove downriver to Inez Meyer's peach orchard and picked peaches. Naturally, we had to sample a few. Back at Inez's pretty little place, we weighed the fruit. This amazing older woman continues to grow an abundant garden and tends to the many flowers that grace her neat yard. Inez, who has been widowed for some time, always has a smile and a good outlook on life. We ended up purchasing our pickling cucumbers from Inez also, as they needed picking. Our pickup was now looking like a traveling produce stand.

We stopped at the Imnaha Store to relax, then drove on up the Sheep Creek highway to patch of blackberries. Homeward bound with our colorful harvest of fruit and vegetables. We had fun gathering the food, now to begin preserving it for winter. I immediately set to canning the tomatoes, made a batch of peach jam and started the pickles in the crocks; one batch of sweet, another of dill.

September 6—Rained during the night. A warm rain, refreshing. The garden perked up. An occasional burst of sun slants downward from a patch of blue sky, illuminating strips of Prairie Creek.

My kitchen smells of dill, vinegar and garlic this morning, as I can the dill pickles. Men working in the shop, having been rained out of the field. Cleaned out one of our freezers; our cut and wrapped locker beef is ready. Canned sauerkraut today. Jars of canned tomatoes, pickles and sauerkraut brighten up my kitchen. Made a spicy applesauce cake. Fragrances from country kitchens during harvest should be bottled.

September 7—Raining. The mountain tops appear briefly through clouds, and we glimpse another new snowfall. Sourdough hot cakes bake on the cast-iron griddle atop the wood cookstove, warming the house up against the chill.

I drove into Enterprise to photograph the Mule Days parade. Enjoyed watching the variety of mules and especially seeing Jess Earl and Clara Hearing, two old-timers who were the grand marshals. The rain stopped long enough for the parade, but resumed shortly afterward.

I treated my husband to a birthday dinner at Vali's Delicatessen at the lake tonight. A wonderful meal served up by Mike and Maggie Vali. The lake was cloaked in a misty coverlet. There will be more new snow on the mountains come morning.

September 8—Doris had us to dinner to celebrate three birthdays; Doug's, today; mine, tomorrow, and Calvin's the 10th. She fixed a delicious Mexican dinner, which included chili rellenos.

September 9—A rainy, drippy day on this birthday, which happens to be my 52nd. Phone calls, with small voices at the other end, singing "Happy Birthday" grandma, the best gifts of all. Doug took me to dinner at Toma's in Enterprise for a special evening.

Not so bad being 52 after all.

Each day the snow line creeps lower. Hurricane Creek is in the middle canyon, Le Gore Lake near the twin peaks. These cattle are grazing on Prairie Creek on the Doug Tippett ranch.

September 10—The clouds parted at dawn to reveal snowy mountain tops wearing a pink blush. Still no frost to end the garden.

The chore of wood chopping and hauling has replaced the irrigating of the garden and yard. The potato cellar crew is building huge bays to store the potatoes in our new "dome." Continued rainy weather has halted the ag bagging altogether now.

September 11—More rain.

September 12—I took a carload of CowBelles to Wallowa for our monthly meeting, held at Laidee Ann Wolfe's. Nice day, good meeting. Fixed chicken and dumplings for supper. Son Steve left for the Pendleton Round-Up. Wouldn't mind going myself…maybe someday.

September 14—I decided to take Scotty and Doris for a short hike up Hurricane Creek this morning. Hiking to Falls Creek, I led them on a seldom-used trail that led to the old LeGore Mine. As we climbed higher, we were treated to views of the mountain, Sacajawea, the highest in the Wallowa chain. Soon swirling mists engulfed the canyon below us.

Across from us, as we climbed higher, we could see snowfields gleaming in intermittent shafts of sunlight.

It appeared to be snowing above us in the direction of Twin Peaks and LeGore Lake. It had been nearly 10 years since I had been on this trail and I so wanted to continue on, at least to the mine. I kept telling my two friends it wasn't too far, and since we'd come clear up here we may as well go for it.

We came to a hillside covered with mountain mahogany, startled deer, that scrambled up rock slides at our approach. The trail was very steep in places and Scotty and Doris thought I was leading them on a wild goose chase into the clouds.

The chokecherry was beginning to turn red and the golden haze of fall color was just beginning to show itself up the steep draws. It began to rain, mist and sleet, but would be replaced by a patch of clear sky and a shot of sun. So we kept on. Just when Scotty and Doris were about to quit me, we came to the old mine.

"Just a little ways further, and there is LeGore's cabin," I announced. My hiking companions, by this time were afraid of that term "just a ways further," but did follow me to the cabin. What a treat we were in for.

As we gathered some dry tinder in the trees to start a small fire and brew some soup and tea, the awesome panorama across and below us was brightened in sunlight. The old rough-hewn, moss-covered cabin stood in the foreground of this magnificent view. That spell of weather was short-lived and another cloud passed over and it began to snow and sleet. The temperature dropped very quickly and our breath hung in the cold air.

We warmed ourselves by the fire and enjoyed the hot tea and soup. The cloud passed and I decided to take them still higher to where I used to camp on my way to LeGore Lake. They actually followed me, mumbling something about me being a mountain goat. The high cirque where I had camped 10 years ago brought back fond memories...I pointed out the route to LeGore Lake, which goes over a massive rockslide and up into another cirque, before it climbs yet another loose rock ridge to the highest lake in the Wallowas, and in Oregon.

Below the lake lies the haunts of the Rocky Mountain sheep. Since it was now 2 o'clock, we started back down the trail. We ran right into a "pack" of grouse; yes, a pack. I always referred to more than two grouse as a covey, until I read page 102 of Patrick McManus' "The Grasshopper Trap." Now I use the proper term. How did I know it was a pack? Well, that's easy, because a few members appeared to be unshaven.

Dan Warnock, of Imnaha, won the bull riding at the Joseph Junior Rodeo. He is shown here just finishing the ride. Rodeo clown J.D. Nobles diverts the bull's attention so Dan can bail off.

Returning to the trailhead, we came upon three fellows preparing to pack into a high camp to hunt the mountain sheep. Two of the party held hard-to-come-by tags that had been in the drawing.

Later, we picked corn at a friend's on Alder Slope in the rain.

Doing chores amid thunder and lightning, I thought about the sheep hunters way up in their high camp tonight.

Doug had been rained out of swathing on this Saturday, and couldn't believe our "short" hike had turned into an adventure.

September 15—The phone rang this morning, and when I answered, a small voice at the other end asked "Grandma, are you coming to watch Chad, Rowdy and me in the Junior Rodeo today?" On this bitter, cold day, I hadn't really planned on going outside at all, except to chore, but granddaughter Chelsie's invitation was pretty important, so grandma attended the rodeo.

A cold wind blew through the grandstands at the Joseph Rodeo arena, as proud relatives braved the elements to watch their offspring perform.

My three grandchildren participated in the Pee Wee events, which included sheep riding. This was hilarious, and the sheep quickly dumped the children, except for one little girl who hung on for dear life and made the whistle. Other events such as dummy steer roping, goat tying and cowhide races kept the crowd entertained way into the late afternoon.

Rowdy Nash of Alder Slope, "dabs one on" the dummy steer during pee-wee roping at the Joseph Junior Rodeo.

A record, being played over the loudspeaker in the announcer's stand, blared out over the rodeo in progress: "Mammas, don't let your babies grow up to be cowboys." Many here today will become cowboys, I thought, and a good thing too. Wallowa County is cowboy country.

Chad and his partner won second in the cowhide race and Rowdy won second in the dummy steer roping. Little Chelsie competed in the pole bending, barrels and goat tying events.

It began to rain but the rodeo continued. There were many adult volunteers working to make the rodeo a success. It seemed every back yard horse was there, a small one on his back. I was especially proud of one of my former Sourdough Shutterbug 4-H members, Tony Yost, who did a fine job as rodeo announcer.

After returning home, I froze the corn we had picked on Alder Slope yesterday.

September 16—A frosty 30 degrees this morning. A clear, beautiful day. Welcome, after days of rainy and cloudy weather.

Picked the green beans, as they are living on borrowed time. So clear, we can see the snowfields on the Wallowas; looks like winter up there.

We are trying to line up a crew for the potato harvest, which begins next week. The phone rings off the hook as I accept applications for working on the digger or driving truck.

Making "leather britches" beans, by stringing and hanging them behind the wood stove to dry. I froze the remainder of the green beans. Clouding up again.

September 17—Rain, rain, rain. The beautiful summer haystacks turning black with the prolonged moisture. Many ranchers still trying to get their second cutting up.

Wore my slicker out to chore as the rain poured down. The barometer has bottomed out. The wind tossed the clouds aside to reveal yet another snowfall on the mountains. I wonder about the sheep-hunting expedition away up in our mountains.

Blackbirds flock together this morning, lining the horse pasture fence. What kind of a fall will we have, maybe none at all, just early winter. Maybe we should ask the fuzzy caterpillars or the blackbirds.

September 18—Jack Frost painted the garden last night. The susceptible vegetables got nipped. From now on Jack will be a steady visitor, leaving his signature on every growing plant until it withers and dies.

Son Steve loaded up his pickup with furniture and clothes, then left for his third year at Blue Mountain Community College in Pendleton.

The crew busily readying the potato digging equipment and machinery for next week. I made a batch of old-fashioned molasses cookies, using a very old recipe. It was fun baking them and they were delicious.

Attended 4-H Family Appreciation Night at Cloverleaf Hall tonight. Since it was a potluck affair, I picked a cabbage from the garden, shredded a small head of red cabbage and some carrots (also from my garden) and made a great, fresh coleslaw.

A new moon appears in a clear sky brilliantly alive with stars.

September 19—Beautiful morning, with a heavy frost. The yellow crookneck squashes lay exposed amid their blackened vines.

September 20—Had visitors this morning. James and Betty Jo Paulson from Maupin, Oregon. Avid readers of Agri-Times and fans of this column, they had called, wanting to meet me and visit. James told me he has been coming to Wallowa County to elk hunt since 1948. They were interested in many places that were mentioned in my journal, so I gave them a tour. Wonderful people, it was my pleasure to meet them and I was honored by their visit.

Daughter Lori and granddaughter Lacey will arrive on the bus in Spokane tonight. Son Steve drove to Spokane to pick up some air pipe for the potato cellar, and will be there to pick up our Wyoming visitors.

I must do some shifting of my office, since I use the spare bedroom to do my writing. For two weeks my office will "float" between downstairs and upstairs. The clutter on my desk will be moved and I shall be lucky to ever find it again. Such is the life of a writer, grandmother, mother, wife and whatever the moment demands.

Helped serve sauerkraut and sausage at the annual Alpenfest at Wallowa Lake. Lori, Lacey and Steve arrived safely sometime in the middle of the night.

September 21—Attended the Wallowa County Hereford Tour today. A most interesting tour of Wallowa County ranches.

In addition to little Lacey, we had the three Alder Slope grandchildren this evening. We all attended the Alpenfest activities. We all got such a kick out of watching 3-year-old Lacey dance with her grandpa. The rustic log building that housed the Alpenfest was decorated in a very festive way, and seeing the dancers in their authentic Bavarian dress and listening to the music was like being transported to the Alps.

This year's Alpenfest featured the world's largest Alpenhorn, a beautiful piece of craftsmanship, made entirely of wooden sections. We left early, as the four grandchildren were weary, not to mention us.

September 22—A little one underfoot and accompanying me on my round of chores. Lacey's eyes got as big as saucers when she went to gather the eggs and a hen flew out of the nest, dropping her egg practically in her hand.

A nice clear day, Doug is raking hay.

Doug's brother Jack and wife Blanche stopped by with friends to visit on their way to attend the Alpenfest.

All over the valley the harvesting of the grain crops is in full swing. Huge monster harvesters moving down the fields, with clouds of grain dust billowing up like smoke from them. Some of the big machines operate far into the night, trying to get the crop in, before it should rain again.

My garden looks sad.

September 23—Our two big potato diggers take up the machinery yard, as the crew carefully cleans and greases all the parts in preparation for the harvest of the seed potatoes.

We are still enjoying the sweet corn from the garden, even though the stalks show the effects of the killing frost.

September 24—A golden, fall haze drifts over the valley, and as of the 22nd, another equinox has passed. Summer is officially over.

September 23—As autumn begins, the willows show the first tinge of yellow, the air will have a sharpness, a tang born of ripening apples and elderberries. The wine-bright days, my favorite time of year, a time when the vagabond and wanderlust comes out in autumn's children.

We have spent summer's end putting food by for the winter, gathering wood, making the nest secure for the cold months ahead.

September 24—No frost; a balmy, partly cloudy day. Doug still baling hay. Our new cellar ready to accept the harvest of seed potatoes.

Lacey helped me peel apples for pie and applesauce.

Gathered plums from a tree in Joseph on the way to attend a dinner for volunteers who helped with Alpenfest. Left a roast beef dinner in the oven for my family. The appreciation dinner was served in the rustic dining room of the Wallowa Lake Lodge. The old lodge is officially closed now for the winter season.

September 26—Started digging potatoes today. From our perch on the digger we can see the tamarack trees turning gold, high on the slopes of the mountains. As we get into the swing of working, our muscles will protest, until they become accustomed to standing for long periods of slinging rocks, dirt clods and vines into the trash eliminator. The screeching noise of the clanging, banging digger hammers in our ears. By day's end we will be covered with dirt and grime.

Every so often, a piece of rusty, antique machinery passes before us on the moving chain. We save these odd bits and pieces of old farm machinery that have been abandoned to the soil.

Jennifer calls them "white man's artifacts," an apt term for our growing collection of work-horseshoes, parts of horse-drawn farming equipment, and mower teeth.

It seems we are forever reminded of the past here in Wallowa County. A past that wasn't very long ago, as the first white settlers didn't arrive until the early 1870s. Wallowa County will celebrate its centennial in 1987.

After eight hours on the digger, we were ready to quit. The sun had long since gone behind the mountains, bringing an evening chill to Prairie Creek.

September 27—A 10-hour day on the digger, then home to chore and fix supper. Too tired to write much else.

September 28—Fifteen degrees! The coldest day we've had since March 26, when it was 10 degrees. Opening day of mule deer season. Just one crew working in the field today.

Scotty, a 4-H'er, Becky Jones, and I decide to hike up Hurricane Creek on this crisp, clear, fall day. The colors are indescribable, especially those of the aspen trees near Slick Rock. The tamarack wearing their golden needles contrast sharply against the evergreens.

Slick Rock Creek spilled over a frozen bed of ice, cascading down over the huge rock face that gives it its name. We climbed higher, photographing the fall color and absorbing the beauty and quiet.

We came upon waterfalls frozen in their tracks. The creeks we stepped over where laced with ice crystals. We hiked to within five miles of the Lake Basin and stood underneath the massive Matterhorn Peak.

Around 1:30 we found a camping spot along the creek, built a fire and brewed tea and soup.

Refreshed, we decided to head on home as we had hiked up the Hurricane Canyon for seven miles, and had that many more to return. It was already becoming very cold at 2:30, and we donned mittens and caps to keep warm.

Later at home, I chored, cooked a fried chicken dinner, did dishes and took a hot bath and sank into bed. The beautiful moon glows in a cold autumn sky; in the deer camps tonight it is the "Hunter's Moon."

As I fall asleep, I think about the moon shining on the frozen waters above Slick Rock Creek.

September 29—Doug took this Sunday off and went deer hunting. Came back a few hours later with his buck, just like he planned to.

It is crunchy-cold this morning. Am a bit stiff from my hike, can feel it in my bones. My work piles up here at home. I look up to the mountains, longing again for their peace, beauty and solitude, from whence I draw my strength.

We took Lori and Lacey to Imnaha this Sunday afternoon to visit daughter Jackie and family. We also stopped to wish birthday congratulations to old-timer Jim Dorrance at the Riverside cafe. He was 85 yesterday. It was a lovely day on the Imnaha; the sumac was on fire, its brilliant red leaves fairly glowing in the sunlight.

We enjoyed eating crisp, sweet apples from the tree in Jackie's yard.

September 30—Digging spuds again; I am so far behind, trying to catch up at home, so didn't join the digger crew today. A long day. We didn't eat supper until 8 p.m.

October 1—Warmed up a bit and cloudy today. The recent hard frosts and cold temperatures have frozen the fall colors, just like last year. The green leaves are now purple and black. The leaves that had already turned, are still colorful, but the slightest breeze sends them drifting downward.

The days are noticeably shorter. Our neighbors, the Houghs, are baling their second cutting of "bread loaf" haystacks. Lois was out raking hay all day yesterday.

We had deer liver and heart for supper, a treat for us. Picked the last surviving zucchini and made two loaves of zucchini bread.

October 3—Too busy digging spuds to write much. Doug took Lori and Lacey to catch the bus in Lewiston by 9 tonight. It will seem quiet around here without little Lacey Jo.

October 5—Indian Summer days. The potato digging goes on, as truck load after truck load goes rumbling out of the fields to the cellars.

October 6—Each day the tamaracks turn a deeper shade of gold. Scotty and I decide to take one last hike before the cold weather sets in. We drive to Alder Slope and hike up to TV Ridge. This long, high ridge is so named because the TV translator for our area is located on its top.

It is coolish and cloudy with brief periods of sunshine. We followed an old road that began near an abandoned apple orchard, and as we climbed higher, views of the valley unfolded below. Checkerboard patterns of farmland spread out over the fertile valley.

We finally made it to the top of the ridge. The weather was changing quickly for the worst, so we decided to hike farther up to have an even better view while we ate our lunch. Sitting on a log with the valley at our feet, we had just taken the first bite when it began to hail. As we looked across at the Freezeout saddle, the Seven Devils in Idaho, and over to the Findley Buttes, a big, dark cloud appeared, coming over the mountains at our back. Through Murray Gap spilled the misty cloud layer. The wind began to rise, accompanied by more hail. Since we were on such a high perch, we decided to vacate the premises before being engulfed in the fast moving storm.

We slipped and slid down the slippery ridge to the safety of the old road. Hail covered the ground like snow, but our exertion kept us warm. As we dropped in altitude, the hail turned to rain. We stopped in a thick copse of trees and built a fire in a streambed to dry off a bit. The beautiful golden tamaracks were losing their needles in the wind and the forest floor was soon covered by a yellow carpet. These lovely trees were losing their color right before our eyes. We looked back up on top and saw that the entire ridge was obscured by swirling mists.

We ran into two brush pheasants (ruffed grouse). As we emerged from the timber, we surprised a mule deer doe, standing on her hind legs feeding on the last of the apples clinging to the trees.

Back to our car and home to the warmth of the wood stove. Soon the mountains will be covered with snow. Today may have been our last fall hike.

This is what is so special about this country. One minute eating lunch on a high ridge top, the next by the comfort of the home fire.

Returned home to find that Star became a grandmother, her daughter Startch calved this morning. Threatening to really storm tonight. He better be a hardy little fellow.

October 7—Woke up to a full-scale blizzard. Wind whipping the snow around and the white world of winter upon us. I can envision the spot high on Sheep Ridge where we ate lunch yesterday.

All potato harvest activities halted until the storm passes. Spent most of morning answering the phone, our potato workers wanting to know if we were digging. With over 20 people on the payroll, it makes for lots of phone communication.

Treated my barn cats to left-over sourdough waffles and bits of venison scraps left from cutting up Doug's buck.

My garden looks so forlorn. Wind-driven snow swirls around the withered corn stalks.

October 8—My son Todd has accepted a job on a Northern California ranch. I must find renters for the Alder Slope house. Jackie and children here this morning.

We all drive to Alder Slope where Jackie and Buck help Todd drive his yearlings into a corral to be loaded into a truck and sold. It is bitterly cold with icicles hanging on the buildings and the snow-covered ground frozen.

Picked some frozen apples from a friend's tree, and made delicious apple dumplings.

October 9—10 degrees! It cleared off last night, but we had to wait until afternoon to dig spuds, as the ground was frozen. The layer of snow saved the potatoes and they are coming up just fine. It is still very cold, but the sunshine is welcome. We worked until 6:30 p.m. After the sun went over the mountain, we women on the machinery added more layers of clothing.

We covered our faces with scarves and old shirts. We joked about having a fashion show to model what the modern 1985 potato sorter considers high fashion. Our noses began to drip and turn red, and we jumped up and down to keep our circulation going.

We could see smoke curling up from the sheepherder's wagon in an adjacent field, and envied the sheep their warm coats.

Home after dark to chore in the cold 20-degree evening. Started a fire in the woodstove and began supper. Soon the house's warmth seeped into our bodies and the food made us drowsy. By 9:30 we had cashed in.

We are only half through digging the potatoes and the cattle are demanding attention. We must move some to different pastures soon. The snow-covered mountains were gleaming white today.

October 10—The pink blush of sunrise, reflected in clouds in the dawn sky, spills onto the mountain peaks...always a treat for the early riser. The pink glow soon fades away.

Todd left for his new job. A parent tries to raise children to be independent and that is good, but it is hard on mothers when they move so far away.

Attended a CowBelle meeting at C. Belle Probert's this afternoon. I took the minutes. Secretary Doris is on our digging crew and needed there. Much warmer today and the field crew making progress. We ate late tonight, as the potato workers didn't quit until well after dark.

October 11—Cloudy and the threat of another storm looms. Started digging spuds at 9 and it started to rain around 1 p.m. The rain didn't amount to much and the crew put in a full day.

October 12—Up early to breakfast, chore and be in my "cowgirl duds" by 7 to haul the horses to Alder Slope.

A crisp fall morning, with a little color still hanging on the trees. We gathered up the yearling heifers in a hayed-over alfalfa field. Had quite a time cutting out the neighbor's Longhorn bull. My horse was afraid of those long horns.

Doug finally chased him into a fence corner as we hurriedly drove the heifers out. Bud and Ben took the lead, while Doug and I brought up the rear. Ben's horse shied at the llamas, who were curious as we passed by. The mare side-stepped for quite a while. We drove the cattle onto the Hurricane Creek road, past the Joseph Airport, the Boise-Cascade mill, and in fact right across Main Street in Joseph.

To keep the cattle from trodding on lawns or entering businesses on Main Street, we took them across the intersection at a dead run. Joseph is definitely a "cow town," and the sight isn't all that uncommon. All went well as we "stampeded" the herd east onto the Imnaha highway. About two miles out, we turned them into another rented pasture. The heifers, in good shape, will continue to be on good feed.

The men drove back to pick up the cattle truck, while I rode my mare, leading the other saddled horses toward home. They got busy checking the fence line and so I ended up riding all the way back to the ranch.

It was well past noon when I finished unsaddling the horses and began lunch. I watched grandchildren all afternoon. They helped me dig the red potatoes out of my garden. We had venison, carrots and potatoes for supper. Clearing off and cold again tonight, as a new moon appears in the sky.

October 14—Time is slipping away, so we dig potatoes on this Sunday. The crew us in the field by 10 and working all day. I got the day off, so cooked a big venison stew in the dutch oven and made a mincemeat pie.

I also took some potatoes to Lawrence and Ilene Potter down on Little Sheep Creek. This fine, older couple continue to live on their small ranch, although it is increasingly harder for them to do some of the things they have always done. I enjoyed helping and they were so appreciative of my efforts.

Our potato "dome" is filling up with potatoes. Beautiful day today, although the fall color is all but gone.

Indian Summer days enabled seed potato growers to harvest their crop. This field is located on Prairie Creek in Wallowa County.

October 15—An Indian Summer heat wave this morning: 34 degrees.

October 16—Cellar crew working by 8; potato crew digging by 9. Up early to chore, load the saddle horses in the truck and drive to Wallowa Lake. We ride the moraine to gather the fall calvers and their calves.

The lake hill is steep, but we finally get them over the top. A cold wind blows as I ride the high ridge that affords a view of the valley, the lake and the mountains. I gather some cows and calves at the far end of the second moraine and around the ponds. Picked up a few in the timber and drove the whole lot down the road on the eastern side.

Doug, who had been riding the timbered areas up toward Mt. Howard, appeared just as I had them in one bunch. I took them down the road, while Doug brought a few strays out of the brush.

It had begun to rain lightly and the cold wind continued. We drove the cattle down into a fresh pasture. After riding back up over the top and down the lake hill to the truck, we loaded up the horses and headed for Joseph.

Doug treated his "cowgirl" to lunch at the Burger Barn. Home to change clothes, then back up to the lake where I had a photography assignment before attending our history group meeting tonight at the Bookloft.

Grace Bartlett, local historian and writer, read an interesting manuscript that she had written 30 years ago while living on Powwatka Ridge. Her writing had an immediacy that transported us back to that time. Her descriptions of people who lived there, the weather and the surrounding countryside were wonderful. We had a most enjoyable evening.

October 18—The crew began digging at 11. It is clear and cold again this morning.

Some of us Wallowa County CowBelles served the senior citizen dinner at noon today at the new Joseph Civic Center. I always enjoy visiting with some of our pioneers.

Warmed up and feels like a summer day. The potato digging is going smoothly and the end is in sight.

Doug home late from the field. A call from where our heifers are pastured: they are out in the road. So on this warm, windy evening, by the light of the moon, we round up the errant heifers and drive them back where they belong. A late supper tonight.

October 19—Thirty four degrees on Imnaha this morning, and a 50-degree reading here. What a switch.

Drove to Wallowa, then 13 miles out to where Ruth Baremore and her family were driving the cattle from their summer range to winter headquarters in the Lower Valley. Found them on the road, near the old townsite of Maxville.

Ruth's grandchildren were all mounted on horses, including a baby who rode on the front of the saddle. They had all spent the night in their cow camp, so as to be on the trail early. Ruth is quite a gal, Wallowa County's number one cowgirl.

The scene here is being repeated all over the valley these days as the cattle are being driven to wintering ranches, where they will be fed hay for many months.

Home to do some housework, then attend a most unusual "tea," and in the potato field yet! Scotty (of our digger crew) had prepared a tea, complete with lace tablecloth, fresh baked cookies and tea. She served it aboard the digger to celebrate finishing up the digging.

Scotty, originally from Scotland. always kids everyone on the digger about stopping for tea time, when in fact we work straight through the American coffee breaks, which are non-existent during harvest. Even lunch breaks are short when the crop needs to get in and winter approaches. God willing and the creek don't rise, we'll finish the harvest tomorrow.

Scotty Doyle prepares "tea time" on the potato digger to celebrate the end of seed potato harvest.

October 20—On this Sunday, the big monster-like machine came to a lurching halt. The chains and belts kept potatoes moving along in front of us, and the last of the potatoes spilled off into the truck alongside. A fierce wind had blown dirt at us all day. Us gals were covered with grime. *Yeah!* We were finished on digger number 1, and digger number 2 only had two more truck loads before the harvesting of 151 acres of seed spuds will have been completed. We beat the storm that had been building up and now the potatoes are stored for the winter in cellars.

Home to wash off the dirt. A howling wind and the skies are leaden. What are we in store for now?

A phone call at 11:30 tonight, a concerned neighbor wanting to know if we still had cattle up on the moraine: some logging slash piles, being fanned by the high winds, were burning out of control. The blazes could be seen from here. Doug dressed and called the loggers, who quickly hauled up a cat to contain the fires. Such a wind was howling, and the sky above the lake hill was lit up with an eerie glow. Our electricity went out in the high wind around midnight and didn't come on until morning.

Rain began this morning before noon. The fires on the moraine property under control. The rain turned to snow before afternoon. Everything turned white as a blizzard swept across Prairie Creek.

The snow melted off later and the skies are partially clear. The snow-line remains steadfast on upper Prairie Creek, however.

Watched the grandchildren tonight, while their mom attended a church meeting. They so love being here. After their baths, they snuggled up on either side of me in bed while I read the old fairy tales: Goldilocks, 3 Little Pigs, and Hansel and Gretel. During the reading of Hansel and Gretel, I was rather shocked at the horrifying story of children being left in the forest, because their parents couldn't afford to keep them. The mean stepmother's idea!

I didn't want my little sleepy heads to drift off into dreamland with such a story on their minds, so as I went along, I changed the plot, rearranging a few words here and there, making sure the children in the story were safe and sound. I guess my own little dumplings were bored, or contented, because they were fast asleep. I carefully unwound myself from between the sleeping children and went into our bed. A moon glows cold and white during this beginning of autumn.

October 22—The wind howling again, leaden skies overhead and a mix of rain and snow.

The little family left and I baked two loaves of sourdough bread for the harvest party, which we will have in our shop Thursday night.

Wearing gifts, the old, well-worn hats, Doug and Janie Tippett enjoy the Harvest Party in the Tippett Farm Shop. Yes, the pipe is a prop.

Must get myself organized for this yearly event to thank our digging crew. There are usually around 50 people to cook for.

The high winds have stripped the trees of any lingering leaves. Even though the calendar says fall is just beginning, we in the valley are saying goodbye to the season, and are ready for winter.

October 23—My kitchen smells good today; am baking sourdough bread and apple pies for tomorrow night's Harvest party. Having set a precedent over the past few years by preparing this home-cooked meal, I can't quit now; everyone looks forward to it. Even though it is work, I feel gratified because we have such good, faithful workers.

Jennifer Isley is now working for us as we move cattle. She is a good hand and has her own horse and saddle.

The men are bringing the big diggers to the ranch today, so they can be cleaned and stored for the winter.

Rain showers on and off all day. Doug attending the local livestock auction.

At 7:30 I drove to Enterprise to our local radio station, where they taped an interview of me for a series of radio airings that will be released next week. It is on Wallowa County Women of Achievement. It was fun doing the tape; everyone at the station put me at ease, so I wasn't too nervous! All I could think about was that I should be back in my kitchen preparing for the Harvest dinner.

October 24—Baked three pumpkin pies and a plum cobbler. Started the roast beef in a roaster oven. A huge kettle of beans and ham hocks on the wood stove. Jennifer helped me make a potato salad by peeling all the cooked potatoes. The crew here is cleaning out the shop, a big undertaking.

The party was a success as usual, with long tables set up and decorated with Indian corn, pumpkins and odd shaped potatoes.

Scotty presented her traditional gifts: a special cake for Ben; two old, well-used hats to Doug and me; and a corn cob pipe of my own. We had to wear the hats during the festivities. It was Jennifer's birthday, so we lit the candles on her cake and sang "Happy Birthday."

After everyone left, we carted the left-overs back to the house and cleaned up most of the mess. I had almost forgotten to do chores; just before dinner Star let me know by bawling loudly at the barn door. I managed to sneak away and tend to her and the calves.

October 26—The cowboys and cowgirl finished working the new calves down at the chutes on this mild day.

Doug, up in Washington looking at our feedlot cattle, called to say they were fat and would soon be ready to sell.

I took advantage of the lull to catch up on my photo journalism.

October 27—Remembered to set the clock back this morning, but my "body clock" got me up at the usual time. Star's clock also on daylight saving time. Her alarm of moos sounded as usual. Beautiful morning, with the sun bursting over the hills illuminating white snowfields on the Wallowas. It was so warm, I left the doors open to air out the house today. It is a rare thing for me to be alone on the ranch on a Sunday morning. A far cry from last Sunday, when we were all frantically digging the last of the seed potatoes.

I decided to let my laying hens out to scratch and pick…they are in heaven! A soft wind ruffles their feathers as they sing away.

Traded one of my fans a loaf of sourdough bread for some winter keeping squash. Frank McCorkle had called me up recently to compliment me on this column and said he "sure would like a loaf of sourdough bread." So I set up the trade for some of his acorn squash. Frank had set up a vegetable stand near Enterprise, but when delivering the bread and picking up my squash, I found that Frank was sick. Gave the bread to the fellow operating the stand to deliver it to Frank.

The wind makes a lonely sound today on Prairie Creek. I drove up on the side of Chief Joseph Mountain this morning to pick up some fire bricks for the wood furnace in the slope house. The view of the valley was something else. One could look over to the Buttes and the Seven Devils Range in Idaho.

The house where I picked up the bricks, was located on an old burn, where a recent planting of small trees were making a comeback. The house was a solar type. A lovely spot on this warm, sunny morning. The road up to the place was very steep. but I managed to negotiate the mountain side in the small pickup.

Elk hunters are arriving in droves. We are being invaded. Horses, camping gear, piled on and into all manner of four-wheel drive rigs. Most of them pulling small house trailers. All heading for Wallowa County's outback hunting areas.

October 28—Cold again, with the winter chill back in the air. The mountains showing off in snowlight.

My chicken house got a lift today. It sports a new tin roof. The cowboy crew hauling cattle to Enterprise this morning, so they can be shipped to C&B in Hermiston.

We enjoy Jennifer, she is always cheerful and such a good worker.

A full moon tonight and down to 15 degrees. Decided to cut the last of the red cabbage in the garden and finished digging the red potatoes.

Son Todd called tonight from California. Nice to hear from him. He is making a living far away from here, but misses Wallowa County.

October 29—At 6 a.m., the moon glows high in the sky. The long contrail of a jet hangs above the moon, forming an exclamation point over the mountains on this clear, frosty, zero degree morning.

The crew still shipping and working cattle.

October 30—Had the PCA man here working all day on the operating budget, so had him for lunch. Doug's sister Barbara here to photograph my animals so she can use the pictures for subjects in her painting projects. Star was bewildered when I had her come into the barn at 2:30. All for the sake of photography, I told her.

Our neighbors, the Houghs, are weaning calves; we can hear the chorus of their bawling from here. A taste of snow in the wind tonight.

Jennifer, Kirk and Ben not in from the hills until 7 p.m. after a long day of branding and working their cattle.

Carved a jack-o-lantern from a large pumpkin for Halloween. I did this for the grandchildren, but the child in me lit the candle, so I could enjoy the grinning pumpkin.

October 31—The wind this morning has a breath that is sharpened by blowing over snowfields.

The usual rush to get breakfast over with, lunches made, chores done, vaccinating equipment rounded up. Ben, Jennifer and I finally leave in one of the cattle trucks. Out the long road to Salmon Creek where we catch up our horses and saddle them. The air is frosty cold and snow clouds are moving in with the sharp, cold wind.

Doug arrives as we are bringing in a bunch of cows and calves. We sort a few that got mixed up yesterday, then drive in another bunch to be vaccinated.

While that is going on, I ride out to where Doug is bringing in the spring calvers and their calves. Since these pastures are around 1,000 acres in size, it takes a lot of riding to cover them. There are so many draws and hills to ride over. Somehow I missed Doug's bunch and rode, obscured by a hill, right past them.

It was freezing cold, my feet were numb, and my hands felt like sticks. My mare and I covered the area as we were told. No cattle, no Doug. Finally, we turned around, and by this time it had begun to snow. Stinging flakes hit my face as the sky darkened. An icy breeze continued. Finally far ahead I could see moving shapes, like ants, the cattle being driven by Doug, Jennifer and Ben.

I felt foolish, to say the least, to have completely missed them in that large pasture. One has to see the immensity of the country to understand how this could happen, but it did.

I put my mare into a trot and we quickly joined the moving herd. By this time it was really snowing. Since it was now near noon, we sat our frozen selves in the trucks and ate lunch. Doug then loaded up a sick calf and headed to town to the vet's.

Calves were sorted from cows; my job was to run the calves up the wooden chute to be worked. It continued to snow, the inside of the chute becoming slippery, the Salmon Creek soil turning to clay-like gumbo. Hard to keep my footing in the mix of muddy ooze, manure and snow. The exertion of driving unwilling calves, some of which weighed around 800 pounds, warmed me up.

As Jennifer and Ben were busy vaccinating and working the chute gate, the snow continued to fall thicker and began to stick. It covered my hat. All of us were wet, sloppy wet, and in a general mess. The wind mercifully died down as the world around us was transformed into a winter wilderness.

The cows bawled for their calves, their breath hanging in the air. I ran the last bunch of calves up the chute and finally the last calf was turned free.

We climbed aboard our wet, cold saddles and herded the cattle back to their range. As dusk descended in that lonely white hill country, we loaded up the horses and each of us drove a rig home. It continued to snow. When we arrived back at the valley ranch, the chores were waiting: Star bawling, eggs to gather, a fire to start and a hot shower. Doug and I attended a dinner on this Halloween night in honor of a newly married couple. We took the grinning jack-o-lantern with us.

November 1—Woke up to a snow-covered world. Out to chore, before catching up on housework.

We are saddened here in the valley to hear of the death of a fellow rancher. George Ketscher apparently had a heart attack while he was on the top of a haystack.

The Ketscher family recently won the Wallowa County Grassman of the Year award. George was such a vital, hard working man, who now leaves to his sons a well-run ranching operation.

The snow melted by noon, the skies gray and cold. 28 degrees. Fixed a casserole to take to the Ketscher family on Alder Slope.

November 2—Jennifer and Ben started trailing the heifers to the hills this morning. They will go halfway today. Would have gone along to help, but wanted to attend George Ketscher's funeral.

It was a brief service, attended mostly by local ranching families. Gloomy, cloudy day as we drove up to the Enterprise Cemetery. The spot is located high on a hillside overlooking Alder Slope and the Wallowas.

As the funeral procession drove down the cemetery hill, a huge shaft of sunlight streamed down upon Alder Slope and George Ketscher's Ranch. His fields were bathed in a golden glow. The sight lasted for only minutes before being replaced by the dark clouds once more.

Meanwhile, life on Alder Slope goes on. Just up the road from the Ketschers, a new baby boy is born in his parent's home. Welcome to the valley, Nathan Slinker. Life and death, all part of the total scheme of things.

Jim Blankenship of Alder Slope in Wallowa County displays some of the leather tack he makes. He's a rural mail carrier for the Imnaha canyon country and a former Snake River rancher. His handmade hackamores, hobbies and packsaddle equipment are sturdy and well-made.

It is after dark when Doug goes out to bring in Jennifer, who has been trailing cattle by herself. We invite her to dinner after her long day in the saddle. She is quite a cowgirl and almost like our own daughter. Son Steve and a college chum arrive bearing the usual dirty laundry. My supper for two turned into one for five. Luckily I had made a loaf of sourdough bread and taken steaks from the freezer. We had a merry meal with our young people.

November 3—Like a summer day as we trail the cattle up Dorrance Grade; so warm in fact, we had to stop and let the fleshy heifers rest. When most of the local ranchers are trailing their cattle in to the valley for winter, we are taking some of ours out.

Our destination is Butte Creek, where the water remains open and, if a mild winter should ensue, they can stay out all season.

From the time my feet hit the floor this morning at 5 a.m., I had been in motion. Breakfast of sourdough waffles, making lunches, chores, and by the time the boys were up to eat, Jennifer, Doug and I were leaving for the old Dorrance place. The golden bunch grass with a tinge of green beneath, the snow of a few days ago now gone made the work pleasant.

Doug went on ahead to put out salt, while Jennifer and I took the herd up the grade. I never tire of the view climbing up this road, as one can look back and see the snow-covered Wallowas in the distance, and the trailing cattle make a pretty picture.

At the top, we stopped to eat our lunches in the sunshine. Doug back to say he was heading for the valley, had a tire going flat. Jennifer and I were almost to the pasture at Butte Creek when he appeared again. The cattle were turned into good feed that will sustain them for awhile and hopefully all winter. Every little bit we can save on feeding hay counts these days.

We were home by 4. Darkness comes early now, so did chores before taking a hot bath. Relaxed and felt good. The quiet hill country has a calming effect on me. I wouldn't have missed this day for the world. Steve, having raided the freezer, left for college with his friend.

November 4—Cloudy, but mild. Watched grandchildren Buck and Mona Lee all day. Spent most of the time down at the chutes where Jennifer and Ben were branding the fall calves. Little five-year-old Buck helped poke calves up the chute.

It began to rain, so the children reluctantly came back to the house with me. Jennifer and Ben finished just as a big storm moved in. Wind-driven rain and early darkness. The children left with their mom for

Imnaha and I did my chores in the storm. Soon a hush fell over Prairie Creek as snowflakes replaced raindrops and swirled around in the wind.

The first elk season is over, many large antlers going out of the county, some tied grotesquely onto the front of hunting rigs. How undignified for the elk, leaving their home mounted on the front of mud-covered four-wheel drives, as they emerge from our vast back country.

We saw a large herd of elk yesterday while we were in the hills, as well as two bunches of deer.

Jackie's family brought us a puppy. We seem always to have a happy, tail-wagging border collie puppy around. Hopefully, one of these cute little balls of fur will grow up to be a cow dog worth keeping.

November 5—Snow on the ground with the solid white line remaining on upper Prairie Creek. The puddles of yesterday have frozen and become chocolate covered glass under foot.

The puppy at my heels as I walk to the barn to chore, ready to terrify the barn cats and lap up their milk. The cats form a disgusted ring around the hungry puppy, who is "inhaling" their milk. Finally having gotten his fill, he exits through the hole in the old barn door. How could anyone be sad with a puppy around? They are always happy to see you and have such unlimited energy.

Today I keep the fire fed, do some writing, and bake a custard using my fresh eggs and milk.

We took delivery on 80 head of weaned calves that Doug purchased locally. The sound of bawling calves comes from the lot below the house.

Had a journalism assignment at the lake; so quiet and peaceful this time of year. The resident deer, including a couple of five-point bucks, were wandering around in search of browse or a free handout.

November 6—A raw wind blowing this morning. Jennifer and Ben branding and working the newly purchased calves down at the chutes.

Doug is optimistic about the cattle market. He is at the auction purchasing more calves today.

I keep the syringes washed and in working order. Seems like my washing machine top is always covered with their parts these days.

Fixed mountain oysters for supper, then off to a 4-H recruitment meeting at Joseph High School. Picked up more new members for the Sourdough Shutterbugs 4-H Club.

November 7—CowBelles meeting today at the Pizza Emporium in Enterprise. A cold rain turned to snow by afternoon. A real white-out. Had a good meeting in the "Country Room" of the Pizza Emporium.

We drove home in a swirling snowstorm. A soft blanket of white covers Prairie Creek as early darkness descends and it turns very cold.

Heard a cute one at CowBelles today. Martha Jane Jacobs, a Baker County CowBelle, says she is going to breed a new strain of cattle. By crossing a Scotch Highlander with a Grizzly Bear, she figures we wouldn't have to calve them out, they would hibernate all winter. We wouldn't need cowboys, just Den Mothers.

November 8—Cloudy, cold and 20 degrees. Snow piled on everything. The sun comes out and a little melting takes place by mid-morning.

We trailed the cows and fall calves to the home ranch this morning. The forecasts are for continued cold and more snow. We had at least two more weeks of good feed in the pasture joining the lake hill, but mother nature isn't cooperating.

The cows and their calves headed down to the ranch on a dead run. They must have smelled the hay. It was a problem to slow them down; they set a track record getting here.

Home to stoke the fire in the wood cookstove and bake a batch of sourdough cinnamon rolls. The second season of elk hunting begins tomorrow. The hunters better be prepared for cold weather.

November 9—Elk hunters up early this morning, full of excited talk in the kitchen. I had made lunches the night before, so let the men have their time together. Besides, I wasn't joining them this year. Somehow, milking Star at 4 a.m. didn't appeal to me on this zero degree morning. The hunters got away long before daylight.

Scotty called and we worked up a short hike, combined with some errands on Alder Slope. As we walked up a snowy road to a friend's cabin, we jumped two cock pheasants feeding on corn left in a garden. The walk was invigorating.

Back at the ranch, I began to cook for the returning hunters. They appeared late in the afternoon, triumphant—typical elk hunters, covered with blood, gore and mud, wearing grins and excited as kids. The temperature dropped 10 degrees while they skinned out their elk. A howling wind materialized and continued to blow into the night. The ground froze solid.

November 10—Wind-driven snow on this freezing cold Sunday morning. Later in the morning, son Steve went out hunting again, as he hadn't been among the successful hunters yesterday. Doug feeding cattle on Ben's day off. I bundle up to chore, the stinging snow blowing against my face.

Lena Turner's barn on upper Prairie Creek in Wallowa County endures another harsh winter. Built long ago, the barn has withstood many winters.

Star is plastered with white as she walks into the barn to be locked into her stanchion, eat her grain and be milked. As I milk, big blobs of snow slide off her flank and onto me. A regular blizzard; a good day to stay inside and feed the fire. The cookie jars were empty, so baked a batch of monster cookies. Experimented with a recipe, making up my own version. Sent some cookies with Steve when he left for college.

While choring, I heard the wild clamoring of hundreds of snow geese. Bands of them flew around as though confused in the storm. As I looked upward, soft fat flakes of snow lit on my face, like feathers from the snow geese. Some of the geese flew so low, I could hear their fluttering wings. As I locked up the chickens for the night, I heard the cries of the Canadian honkers, a completely different sound than that of the snow geese. Their darker bodies showed up better against the snowy sky.

Darkness by 4:30. I feel sorry for the geese, not knowing where to land and perhaps blinded by the storm. By dark, the skies were filled with hundreds of them. Later when I stepped out into the frozen stillness to feed the puppy some table scraps, I could hear the geese again, still blinded by the snow, looking for a place to land for the night. It seems incredible that a week ago today Jennifer and I trailed cattle to the hills and it was in the 70s. Only in Wallowa County!

November 11—The sun rose over a snow-covered landscape, burning off low-lying mists on the creek. Frozen fog crystals floated in the cold air. Occasional bursts of sunlight created a rainbow. Unlike the usual arc or bow, this spectacle was simply a bar—a snowbow!

At least three more inches of snow had fallen during the night. The sounds of bawling cattle, wanting their hay, replaced the cries of last night's geese. The cold created problems. Some of the tractors won't start. Winter is here.

Drove to Joseph and the "Spindle Shanks" antique shop to borrow vintage clothing for the 1800s fashion show that CowBelles are putting on for the cattlemen's convention.

To bed early…on these cold nights, it is easy to fall into a lazy, "hibernating" sleep. We can pretend we are bears in our dens, sleeping a long deep sleep. Would be nice to wake up and find spring!

November 12—Many elk hunters are leaving as the bitter cold makes hunting dangerous in these below zero temperatures.

We shipped a semi-load of calves to Hermiston today. Soon they will be eating turnips before going into a feedlot at Bryan Wolfe's. We also hauled in the cows and fall calves from the hills so they can be fed hay.

November 13—We left the zero degree valley this morning, heading for Portland and the state cattlemen's convention.

We crossed the Blue Mountains and headed down into Pendleton, where it was much warmer. Visited briefly with Virgil Rupp and Jim Eardley at the Agri-Times office. Was pleasantly surprised to be nominated to the Agri-Times Pie Hall of Fame. Found out that Virgil's favorite pie is mincemeat. Will have to bake one for him now in order to live up to the nomination.

That evening, as we prepared to unload our car at the Red Lion Lloyd Center in Portland, we discovered that we had left the garment bag containing our clothes on our bed at home.

For the next three days, we were to find out what little significance clothes really played in our lives. I was wearing a pair of red cotton pants and a wool sweater. Traveling wear over the Blue Mountains in snow conditions should be something you wouldn't freeze to death in if you had car trouble. So there I stood in the plush surroundings of the Red Lion, clad in the only thing I had at the moment.

Doug had packed extra pants in his suitcase, but no shirts. Luckily Meier and Frank in Lloyd Center stayed open until 9 p.m.

November 14—Enjoyed listening to JoAnn Smith, the first woman president of the National Cattlemen's Association. She spoke with authority, grace and style, a very capable lady.

The fashion show at Western Fun Night was a hilarious success with some of our eminent cattlemen modeling the Jantzen collection of old bathing suits. I do not know how the Red Lion survived the good times experienced by our Wallowa County cowboys turned loose in the big city, but it did. Last I knew some of them were still trying to ear down Mack Birkmaier and put a saddle on him.

November 15—The Wallowa County delegation to the cattlemen's convention much quieter this morning.

I attended the 7:15 prayer breakfast. Ron Baker was the master of ceremonies and Gary Randall, the "Apostle of the Airways," gave an impressive talk. The theme centered on food and moral fibre—America's greatest assets.

Prior to the industry workshops, we viewed Nancy Kelly's excellent film, "Cowgirls, Women of the American West." It, for once, portrays the western cowgirl more like she really is, rather than the glamorized Hollywood version.

Our annual CowBelle luncheon was hosted this year by the Jackson County CowBelles. Luscious fresh pears were displayed in handmade horseshoe fruit bowls for the table centerpieces. We were served lime-thyme beef, Sally Vogt's winning Beef Cookoff recipe. Sally was present at our luncheon and turned out to be a delightful gal, as well as a winning cook.

A banquet this evening, followed by dancing to a '50s band. At one point, Don Ostensoe of the Oregon Beef Council proved he could play the trumpet. I won a door prize, an original sketch by none other than Jerry Palen. The Wallowa County delegation folded early tonight.

November 16—Was busy all during convention taking pictures, part of my job as state CowBelle publicity chairman. A tedious job, but one I do enjoy. Attended the CowBelle meeting chaired by our new state president, Kay Markgraf of Baker County. Many new projects and ideas coming from many Oregon counties.

A salute to Oregon CowBelles everywhere, many of whom can never make it to convention. We pledge our support to Kay as we begin a new year.

We left the comforts of the Red Lion and headed home in the afternoon. Much warmer as we travel up the Gorge, but recent snowy conditions await us.

November 18—We arrived back in the valley yesterday to a "winter wonderland." Snowing heavily as we feed the animals. Visibility limited to zero and early darkness on Prairie Creek. The snow is being blown into drifts by a sharp wind. The weather doesn't stop our crew from going to the hills to wean and haul in the spring calves. I fix a lunch for Doug and they leave. The frigid temperatures and howling wind continuing. Periods of sunshine brighten up the snowy landscape by afternoon, but black snow clouds wait in the wings.

My livestock glad to see me back at the barn. This is where I belong, feeling much more at ease here than in the Red Lion. It is nice to enjoy the comforts and be waited on for a while, but then somehow, something seems wrong. Perhaps all of us humans were meant to struggle a bit with life.

Oftentimes I've heard people say how they would like things easier, the ultimate goal being to "Live on Easy Street" so to speak. But when the goal is reached, something is missing. Methinks it is the struggle, the challenge to meet and overcome each new day's problems.

Phone calls from family, glad of our safe return. Catching up on our large family's lives during our absence.

November 19—Eight degrees, with a bitterly cold wind blowing, cloudy with more snow in the forecast. The cowboys and cowgirl off to the hills to haul in more calves to wean.

The first truckload of calves arrives around 12:30. Now the bawling begins, the calves separated by miles from their mammas and their warm milk, and on such a cold day. Poor babies. The mamma cows out on Salmon Creek will be bawling just as loudly tonight.

November 20—The crew, home after dark, finally finish hauling in the big spring calves. The bawling is intense.

I go from kitchen to barn to kitchen to darkroom to typewriter, trying to catch up.

Feeding cattle is now the number one priority. Doug attending the auction on this freezing cold day.

I baked a loaf of sourdough bread and made a beef-vegetable soup on the wood stove. Also baked a pumpkin pie. Doug called and said we had reservations to attend the annual Wallowa County Chamber of Commerce dinner in Enterprise. So I put everything away for tomorrow's meal and we braved the cold, snowy night.

What a complete surprise to find I was the recipient of the Chamber's Civic Leader of the year award. No wonder Doug insisted we attend. The hamber singers, a group of local people from all walks of life here in the valley, under the professional direction of Katch Hobbs, sang some beautiful Christmas carols to get us in the holiday mood. One cannot help but feel a strong sense of community pride when surrounded by Wallowa County people, all unique in their own special way.

November 22—Cold arctic air swirling around the buildings and creating more drifts everywhere. Around zero again this morning. I feel sorry for the cattle, dark shapes huddled against the storm, appearing and disappearing from sight in the blowing snow. The eggs freeze in the chicken house if I don't gather them in time.

Clearing tonight with a moon shining over the still, frozen world that is Prairie Creek. It is 10 below by 8 p.m.

November 23—Out in the frozen stillness of the vast Zumwalt Country, a rifle cracked. My friend Doris had downed her anterless elk. Doug and Calvin helped gut out the animal while I ran for my camera to record her first kill.

Long before daylight, Doug fixed sourdough hot cakes on the wood stove and I chored in the dark. I glanced at the thermometer by our clothesline on the way to the barn...20 below!

Bundled to the teeth, I managed to keep warm while milking Star. We were late leaving the ranch because of problems caused by the severe cold. The diesel fuel had jelled in the pickup, for one thing. Just after sun-up, we left, the crunchy cold, the sharp crack'in cold all around us.

Cattle huddled and standing still to catch the sun's first weak rays. We saw very few elk tracks near Butte Creek, and didn't spot any through the binoculars. I'm thinking an elk in his right mind would have fled to the warmer canyons during this cold.

We passed by some hunters huddled over a fire. In a draw, just beneath them, was a single elk calf, pawing through the frozen snow to feed on some mature grasses. We parked our rigs and Doris stalked her elk. When she was in firing range, she squeezed off a shot and down went her meat. It was now only 9:30 on this opening morning of cow elk season. After loading up the elk, we drove to the Wet Salmon Creek Ranch and built a fire near the salt house to warm ourselves and eat our lunches. Doug checked the stock water and saw that the cows still had sufficient grass.

The roads out in the hill country starting to drift, making it hard to negotiate without a four-wheel drive. One more good storm and that area will be plugged for the winter. If this weather keeps up we will be trailing all of our remaining cattle in the hills, to the valley.

Doris' smile warmed up the cold Zumwalt country after she shot her first elk. The temperature was 20 below zero for the opening of antlerless elk season in Wallowa County.

Meanwhile, back at the ranch, Doris skinned out her elk in the warmth of our shop. A fun day in unbelievable cold weather. Today's high was 10 below! Longjohn weather for sure.

November 24—Although it is 10 degrees warmer than yesterday, that means 10 below here on the ranch. The sunshine is bright, but not warm. The cattle have frozen breath wreathing their noses.

Doug carried in a frozen front quarter of his bull elk and laid it on the kitchen table to thaw! He laid another quarter on a bed sheet near the wood stove. Our house resembles an early-day homestead, with these great hunks of meat reposing around.

There is always plenty to do, even though outside work is mostly limited to tending to the animals and carrying wood in to feed the voracious appetites of our wood cookstove and fireplace.

I bake a sourdough chocolate cake while the wood cook stove oven is hot. The elk thaws enough to be cut up and Doug works on that. I put the neck meat in a large kettle of water and simmer it on the wood stove. When the meat is tender, I will grind it with a food grinder and use it to make a batch of mincemeat.

I must start thinking of Thanksgiving. Over 20 of us this year. My oldest daughter, Ramona, and her family will be visiting. They will bring my mother up with them from California. Always a worry for their safe arrival during this time of year. Many miles of icy roads separate us. This present cold wave has broken records all over the Northwest for November. Ten below again tonight.

November 25—Eight above, with frozen fog filling the air like fine snow that sifts down from everything. I went grocery shopping for the traditional Thanksgiving turkey dinner fix'uns. Home to grind up the elk neck meat, then peel and cut up bowls of apples in preparation for making the mincemeat. Hours later, the house is filled with the aroma of the mincemeat cooking on the wood cookstove.

The vet came out this afternoon to vaccinate our heifers. Doug took some protein blocks out to the cattle in the hills this afternoon, as it had begun to snow again.

We just found out that neighbors, Tip and Ruth Proctor, lost their house and most of its contents in an early morning fire Sunday. Some of us neighbors on the phone planning a fire shower potluck for the couple. They are living temporarily in a small trailer next to their burned down house. Since they have so many rabbits, plus other livestock to tend to, they are planning to spend the winter there.

Son-in-law Charley Phillips enjoys the warmth of the wood cookstove. He is assistant manager of the Lucky Hereford Ranch in Loyalton, California.

November 26—Above zero, and it got to 15 above by 7 a.m. What a relief, it feels positively warm after the past few days.

Shipped a load of feeders to Bryan Wolfe's feedlot in Hermiston today. Froze the mincemeat, made 15 quarts.

November 27—Spent this day before Thanksgiving preparing for the big meal tomorrow. Our California relatives due to arrive this evening. The pies are baking; mincemeat, pumpkin and wild blackberry cobbler. Have been making up extra beds, the downstairs resembles a dormitory. The cooking goes on...cranberries bubbling away, a 24-hour fruit salad is assembled. The refrigerator bulges, the tops of the freezers on the porch groan with pies.

After a 13-hour drive, the California relatives arrive. So good to see all of them. Granddaughters Tammy, Carrie, grandsons Shawn and Bart are all growing and changing so much. Can't believe my eyes when I look at 15-year-old Tammy; can it really be that this lovely, young lady is my oldest grandchild? When only a few years ago, or so it seems, I was her age, not to mention her mother. It will be a special Thanksgiving this year with so much family around.

November 28—Thanksgiving Day dawns cold and it is snowing lightly, a 10-degree reading on the porch thermometer. The smell of roasting turkey escapes from the wood cookstove oven. The rest of the family converges: Alder Slope son Ken, and his family. Daughter Jackie and her family from the Imnaha Canyon and another friend of the family from Alder Slope. Most all of our seven children and their children present with the exception of Lori, Linda and Todd who couldn't make it.

The excitement of little cousins meeting each other after long absences and the "catching up talk" of the older children (now young adults) makes for a jolly time.

November 29—Visiting, eating left-overs, enjoying family, and feeding livestock.

December 1—Amid tearful goodbyes, the California family leaves. What a letdown. Scotty appeared at the door to kidnap me, and we went cross-country skiing here on the ranch. A great boost to my lagging weariness from the Thanksgiving reunion. It felt so good to be out in the clean, crisp air skiing along in the stride and glide fashion of the cross-country skier. For an hour I forgot about all else and enjoyed the exercise.

December 2—My mother and I are sitting here in the kitchen, having made the decision not to go to Portland for the wheat growers convention. The worst storm of the season is blowing its full fury up the Columbia Gorge and Portland itself is a mess.

Couldn't get an answer from Amtrak to see if it was still running, and we didn't want to risk driving clear to La Grande (60 miles) only to find we couldn't get any farther.

So, I wasn't even packed. Did my chores, then Doug offered to drive us to La Grande in the hopes Amtrak would get through somehow.

The sun came out as we drove through the Minam Canyon, exposing a brilliant blue sky between the clouds. In La Grande, we found that we could board Amtrak. Doug left for home and the train pulled into the station a little late, but pretty much on schedule. Much warmer in La Grande.

Amtrak had a passenger load. We rode on the upper level, which afforded a splendid view of the Blue Mountains as we passed through. Big blobs of snow hung from the trees and created interesting shapes on fallen limbs. The ride was pleasant, the personnel courteous and the seats comfortable. I hadn't ridden on a train since I was a young girl. A 17-year-old mother, in fact, with an infant daughter in my arms. Now my daughter has her own 15-year-old daughter.

As the train rolls along through the mountains, I think about the ranch crew moving the cows in from the hills. Due to the severe cold and new storm, we are bringing them in before the roads drift shut.

The train rumbled along in the early darkness. As we stopped at various stations we could see through the lights that we were in a snow-storm. Nearing Portland, we were delayed numerous times while a crew cleared the switches of ice and snow. A necessary chore, as we could have derailed otherwise.

At 5:30, our scheduled arrival time in Portland, we were stopped just out of Hood River waiting for an emergency section crew from The Dalles to clear the switches again.

The train appeared to be stopped on a tilt. It became fascinating to watch the snow pile higher on the windows outside. Around 7, we were able to slowly resume our way down the Columbia Gorge.

At last we could see the far-off lights of Portland and soon we were going over the bridge to the huge Union Station. It was now 8 and we alighted from the train onto a melting, thawing pavement.

We eventually made it to the Red Lion at Lloyd Center. My mother, a terrific sport, thought the whole thing was an adventure, as indeed it had been.

December 3—Twinkling lights of a big city coming to life greeted us as we looked down upon Portland from the 14th floor of the Red Lion. Quite a contrast to the pink Alpenglow touching the high peaks of the Wallowa Mountain range, or the frozen stillness of Prairie Creek; but beautiful in its own way.

Spent most of the night tossing and turning, thinking about my speech. Remembering younger years as a 4-H member helped a lot: recalling standing before audiences, speaking or giving dairy cattle demonstrations. After all, these were farm and ranch people, just like myself...why worry?

At 7 a.m., the leadership breakfast began. There had been many cancellations due to the storm, but about 70 people attended.

I met Alice Ward, who was as pleasant as I had imagined from her letters and talks on the phone. In fact, everyone I met was warm and friendly...all my butterflies suddenly disappeared! I really enjoyed talking to these people and presenting my simple speech entitled "Agriculture: A Way of Life in Oregon."

Managed to get in a little photojournalism and listened to Senator Packwood's talk before Alice Ward drove us to Union Station.

Reflecting on this experience, I realized the highlight for me had been meeting so many of the interesting people who read this column.

After Alice left us off, we were soon to find out that our planned return to La Grande via Amtrak was not to be. We were told that unless we had tickets purchased a month in advance we couldn't board the train due to the storm and returning Thanksgiving traffic. No seats available.

We walked a block to the bus station only to find out that the gorge was still closed. However, a bus might leave around 4:30, going part way up the gorge on the Washington side. We purchased tickets in the hopes that the bus would indeed run.

The bus terminal is a gigantic new building with comfortable facilities, so we spent the rest of the time there. Was surprised to run into a Wallowa County person, Cal Long, returning from a Thanksgiving trip to the Willamette Valley.

Visiting with Cal helped close the hours. Also made the acquaintance of a woman who lived at the top of Minam Grade.

So waiting in this bus terminal, in a city clear across the state from our homes we were destined to ride together through the coming night and hopefully arrive safely in La Grande.

I called home to alert Doug about our uncertain arrival in La Grande, and for him not to pick us up. We'd stay in La Grande tonight.

At 4:30, an announcement…the gorge had just been opened. Our bus appeared shortly. We appeared to be traveling smoothly until we approached Cascade Locks, then the bus slowed to a crawl. Looking out the windows, we could see that we were sandwiched in a convoy of hundreds of trucks. Stalled and delayed in Portland by the storm, they were understandably anxious to be on their way again. Ice had formed on the highway as cold had come with the darkness. We continued to travel at a snail's pace.

We stopped in Arlington around midnight, where our driver talked the closing restaurant into fixing us some dinner. Once more we crossed the Blue Mountains, skimming over solid ice with a new driver who had taken over in Pendleton. At 3:20 a.m., the bus depot in La Grande looked forlorn and lonely. We got off, along with Cal Long and the woman from Minam Hill, who kindly gave us a ride to a motel to spen the rest of the night.

December 4—Called Doug, deciding rather than have him come all the way out, we would ride the Wallowa Valley Stage into Joseph. The stage left at noon and we were on it. No, this isn't a horse drawn stage, but a daily stage that delivers freight and a limited number of passengers to the valley. After making numerous stops, we arrived around 3 p.m. in Joseph. Our small town never looked so good. Now if we just had a saddle horse to ride to Prairie Creek.

As my mother and I were trudging along, carrying our suitcases toward a phone booth, we spotted Doug, who had come to meet us.

Home at last; must get back to work. Organizing the potluck for the family whose home burned. We decide to have the affair in our shop. Phoned various neighbors who will help with everything.

The cowboys finish branding the fall calves and bring in mountain oysters to clean and syringes to wash. A neighbor called from Alder Slope, saying that a herd of elk were coming in every night to feed on our hay stack up there.

Meanwhile, Doug had left to attend a growers' seminar in Hermiston. Welcome home! The ranch life goes on; never a dull moment!

December 5—Feels like a summer day, thawing and sun shining over the valley. We were finally able to get a truck to ship a load of cattle to Umatilla County today. Due to the recent bad road conditions, trucks have been at a standstill.

The kitchen is filled with the fragrance of baking cookies. Grandma is making a big batch of cookies from some persimmons she brought up from California.

My first chore this morning is to drive to Alder Slope and check on the elk damage to our haystack. Found bales lying around in disarray and droppings in the snow from a sizable herd of elk.

I feel sorry for them, as the severe cold brings them down to an easier existence, rather than foraging around the snowy slopes of the Mountains, where the snow lies deep and the food is scarce. However, it is a loss to us ranchers too. A continuing problem, trying to live with wildlife and continue to ranch.

December 6—Continuing to warm up, cloudy. Grandma and I into town to run errands. In return for a handmade ornament taken from the "Tree of Giving" in our Wallowa Valley Mall, I purchased a gift for a little boy, whose name and age appeared on the ornament. A wonderful tradition carried on by valley people each year to make less fortunate children's Christmases a bit merrier. The true spirit of Christmas which has always characterized Wallowa County people.

We treated ourselves to lunch at the Country Place. The nearby pond was almost frozen over, with the Canadian Honkers, swans and ducks either sitting on the ice or swimming about in the water. It was a sight to behold. We enjoyed homemade clam chowder and a salad in the quaint, relaxing atmosphere of Marvel Peterson's unique eatery.

Home to bake sourdough bread for the fire shower in our shop tomorrow.

Doug home safely from Hermiston.

Gathering up my collection of Patrick McManus's books, I attended an autograph session at the Bookloft for this celebrated author of such books as "The Grasshopper Trap," "A Fine and Pleasant Misery," etc. I have all of his books to date, gifts from a friend. They have been a great source of joy.

December 7—Cleaning out our shop for the fire shower here tonight. Cooking a pot of beans and baking more bread. By nightfall the shop was transformed into a mock-up of a Grange hall, complete with Christmas decorations including a Christmas money tree. Friends and neighbors from as far away as the upper Imnaha showed up. Snow fell softly, with many roads covered. Our shop, warmed by the wood stove and "good will" of our great Wallowa County people, warmed the night as well. It also warmed the hearts of the Proctors, who had lost their house, but not their reason for living in the valley.

December 8—Cleaned up the remains of last night's do'ins in the shop; carried all the chairs back to the house and bunk house.

Grandma and I attended the Imnaha Fellowship Church service, braving the icy roads for 30 miles to arrive safely, only a few minutes late.

Son-in-law Bill presented the sermon, and Mona Lee and Buck wiggled around on my lap. Very enjoyable listening to Bill, who talked so sincerely about what he had to share.

December 9—Awoke at 4 a.m. The electricity out most of the night. It is 10 degrees outside. Started up the stove and lit candles in the bathroom and kitchen. We must bring the remaining cattle in from the hills. Another subzero cold snap on its way, and the roads on Salmon Creek are all but drifted in.

I opted to stay home as am nursing a nasty sinus infection. Jennifer, Ben and Doug leave with the saddled horses in a truck. I can't help but think about them all morning in this bitter cold. Can they even get to the ranch to unload the horses?

Grandma and I keep the home fires burning and I catch up on my writing. Temperature is falling. Doug returned around 1:45 to report the cattle were out of the pasture and headed toward the Dorrance Place. They will spend the night at our holding pasture on the Crow Creek road. Doug takes a load of hay out to feed the trailing herd.

December 10—Below zero as Jennifer leaves early to drive the cows the rest of the way to the valley. It was so cold, she drove the pickup most of the way with the saddled horse riding in the back. The cows could smell the hay pile here at the ranch for miles and made good time.

We took grandma to La Grande to catch the bus. In the Minam Canyon we saw many deer pawing through the snow to find forage. A herd of elk was feeding on the grass seed fields near Elgin.

Zero degrees when we arrived back at the ranch. The house seems empty without grandma.

December 12—Wallowa Valley citizens alarmed at the proposed Wilderness Bill, which would add 300,000 acres to our existing wilderness and have a domino effect on the livelihoods of many valley people. Especially hard-hit would be the ranchers and timber-related industries. Many of us writing to our senators. A plea to preserve our way of life here in the valley, a way of life that could be threatened if this bill passes.

Baked mincemeat tarts for treats at our yearly CowBelle Christmas meeting-party. Also baked a large loaf of sourdough bread to give away at our gift exchange. The meeting was held on this cold day in the charming atmosphere of Gladys Yost's Prairie Creek ranch home.

I have been traveling to the Slope daily to start a fire in the wood furnace at the house there. The occupants are down in the Snake River country hoping to fill out a cow elk tag.

December 13—I seem to be falling behind these days, but managing to somehow get the important things done. Livestock fed, husband fed, keeping track of our large family. Doug cut us a nice Christmas tree and it is now up and decorated. I especially like to go outside at night and look from our snowy road to the brightly glowing Christmas tree in the window.

Doug has put out firecrackers that are attached to a slow-burning rope that will hopefully frighten the elk away from our haystack. This prevention procedure is supplied by our Fish and Wildlife people, but really doesn't deter a hungry elk, just makes a loud crack in the frozen stillness of Alder Slope's winter night. The elk, very adaptable creatures, soon figure out that they will not be harmed by the sound. We are hauling the hay to Prairie Creek as fast as we can. Hopefully, we can keep the damage to a minimum.

December 14—Same clear, cold days going on seemingly without end. Doris and I attended a home tour sponsored by the Centennial Committee.

It began with a benefit brunch at the Pizza Emporium in Enterprise. Very interesting tour and we so enjoyed seeing older, restored homes displaying their antiques and country charm amid the gaily decorated theme of the Christmas season. Most interesting was the Barklow home that had been converted into a lovely home from a stable! Beautiful handmade quilts decorated the house, lending a colorful note to the furnishings.

A small herd of resident White Tail deer were "caretaking" my property on Alder Slope for me today. How lovely they are, graceful and bounding away in their peculiar fashion, their white tails flashing in the sunlight.

Jackie and her family out for the night. Buck does chores with me in the gathering darkness. Shuffling along beside me in his snow boots: "Are you going to milk Star?" he asks.

"No," I reply. "Grandma is starting to dry her up."

A worried frown on the face of this five-year-old grandson. "What does drying up mean, grandma?"

So I went on to explain to little Buck that Star would calve in March and she needed a rest from milking before she became a mommy again, and I explained how a first-calf heifer is springing when she is due to calve and when she calves, she freshens. Just as I learned from my father so long ago.

Maybe in the year 2000-whatever, a grown-up Buck will be explaining these same "cow terms" to his own progeny. One thing for sure, these little minds absorb it all. Whatever we feed into their small computers, they will grow up to reflect. It is an awesome responsibility we parents and grandparents have.

December 15—Steve home from college for the holidays, must increase my cooking.

Drove to upper Prairie Creek for a photography assignment for our local museum. Enjoyed visiting with Norma Hope. This interesting lady, born on Imnaha, still raises a herd of cows and lives alone on her lovely little ranch.

December 16—Frozen trickles of milk form on the side of the milk pail as I milk Star, every other day now, trying to dry her up. Packing warm water to the chickens an everyday chore.

We are locked in a deep freeze. Ben chopping ice for the cattle's drinking water. Some of our pastures have automatic water heaters in the troughs, but others require constant chopping.

December 18—Around zero again, takes 10 minutes to get into and out of warm clothes to chore these days.

Sold beef certificates at the bank in Joseph for the CowBelles today.

The sun disappears over Chief Joseph Mountain at 3:15 p.m., and the cold settles in for another night.

December 19—An inversion has settled over the valley. It is actually warmer higher up on the mountains.

We enjoyed dinner at the lake tonight with friends. Good food and good friends amid the cheeriness of the Christmas season. As we drove home, we could see the cold, white light of the December moon reflected in Wallowa Lake.

December 20—Frozen fog crystals float down from trees, fences, telephone lines and sparkle and glitter in the rising sun.

Four teams of horses are pulling wagon loads of Christmas carolers around Enterprise this afternoon. The old-fashioned small-town Christmas is enjoying a revival here in Wallowa County, and it is nice.

December 21—The frozen filigree laced on everything again, as the fog freezes each night. Today is the shortest day of the year. The winter solstice begins.

Invited the Proctors for dinner, so they could get out of their small trailer and stretch their legs. Fixed a big pot of beef vegetable soup on the wood stove and baked a loaf of sourdough bread. Made a "from scratch" lemon meringue pie for dessert. Zero degrees again tonight.

December 22—After the feeding was done this Sunday morning, we drove to Imnaha to visit Jim Dorrance at the Riverside Cafe. Less snow in the canyons, but river ice was forming along the Imnaha's banks.

The red Osier Dogwood along Little Sheep Creek contrasted with the ice jams, which the water to flow out around the channel of the creek and form huge masses of ice on the meadows. Frozen ice-falls cling to the crevices and cracks in the canyon walls.

December 23—Baking Christmas Stollens…a traditional Christmas fruit bread. While in town shopping for some items for Christmas dinner, I enjoyed seeing the teams of horses delivering the Christmas baskets to needy families. One wagon even had a wood stove going to keep the workers warm.

The harness bells rang in the frosty air and Christmas carols floated out over the town. In Joseph today a one-horse open sleigh traveled right down through Main Street. So nice to have these traditions kept alive. The spirit of Christmas prevails here at the northeastern tip of Oregon. Cut off from the large population centers, we create our own warmth and cheer during the cold, holiday season.

December 24—Actually warmed up to 30 degrees today. The sunshine felt so good. Spent the morning delivering Christmas breads. My favorite thing. It is the "giving" that brings the greatest joy. Brightening someone's day with a visit and home-baked bread.

Home to bake raspberry and gooseberry pies for Christmas dinner. We savor the summer-time berries during this cold season, thanks to our freezer.

The Imnaha family here for Christmas Eve. The other children have other commitments or are too far away tonight. Daughter Jackie makes pizzas and then we open our gifts. We are so lucky to have family, food, warmth and peace on Prairie Creek tonight. Outside the moon glows softly over snowy fields…Oh holy night!

December 25—Christmas Day dawned clear and cold…fingers of fog lay in pockets. The rising sun burned the mists away by late morning, leaving the lacy effect of frozen fog on everything. This frosty white coating even covers the animals, right down to the whiskers on the cats and a "frosted" puppy.

The children sleeping on the living room floor in their new sleeping bags. The firelight from the fireplace glowing on their innocent faces. The stocking hung by the chimney held special "Santa" treats for us all.

Out to chore in my Christmas present...a new pair of insulated overalls.

December 26—Doug off to La Grande early to pick up daughter Linda who will spend a couple of days with us. She had to work Christmas Day.

December 27—It is snowing frozen flakes of fog this morning. When the sun burns it away, a fairyland of frozen lacy filigree covers the huge old willow trees along the ditch in the barn lot. By noon the frozen fog relaxes its grip and the sun's warmth causes it to sift silently downward.

Floating prisms of light crystals, sparkling in the sunlight, like millions of tiny diamonds. The snow on the ground sparkles with layers of crystals.

Doug called Turner Excavating to dig out our frozen ditch. Each day the water spills out onto a wider area, refreezing at night until our bull lot is like a skating rink.

Baked a mincemeat pie for Virgil Rupp. Doug will deliver it when he drives Linda back to Pendleton. Must live up to that Pie Hall of Fame nomination.

The winter moon, the December moon, is full tonight as it illumines the snowy, cold landscape. The mountains are aglow with white light.

December 28—The lovely moon still high in the sky at 6 a.m. As dawn light breaks over the fields, a repeat of yesterday's fairyland emerges.

December 30—Clear and sunny, the day begins with the pink plush of Alpenglow, touching the high peaks of the Wallowas, a sight so familiar, so dear to all of us who are fortunate enough to live here.

Left off some photographs for Grace Bartlett this morning. Enjoyed visiting this great lady in her modest home in the woods. Grace is a local historian, writer, curator of the local museum and an authority on the Nez Perce Indians. An inspiration to all of us. She is so interested in her life and surroundings, a truly fine person.

December 31—Very nice to spend a quiet New Year's Eve at home, for a change.

The Matthews family of Imnaha, Mona Lee, Jackie, Bill and Buck. The
puppy is a member of the family, too.

1986

January 1—Happy New Year! As this brand new year begins here on Prairie Creek, it is much warmer, a soft wind blows, blue sky appears and bursts of sunlight melt the snowfall of last night. Then by 9 a.m. it begins to snow heavily, a blizzard in fact. Took down the Christmas tree and watched the beautiful Parade of Roses in sunny Pasadena, Calif.

January 2—It was noon before we left Wallowa County; our destination: Nevada, to attend son Todd's wedding.

In the course of our lives circumstances sometimes work out like they were all part of a plan. Todd and Liza's wedding was just such a circumstance. I had called ahead to daughter Ramona's to say we were leaving for our yearly trip to California, when she informed me that Todd and Liza would be there just ahead of us to get married in Reno!

Big sister then intervened. In one day she would plan a "special" wedding for her brother and future sis-in-law. Due to our previously planned arrival, we too would attend. Needless to say I was most pleased with this turn of events.

As we passed through the Minam Canyon, we noticed that the Wallowa River was completely frozen over in places. Quite a sight. When we arrived at Farewell Bend, we were amazed at the great jagged chunks of ice that were causing an ice jam that backed up 40 miles of the Snake River.

It was 6:30 when we pulled into Jordan Valley and enjoyed dinner at a Basque restaurant. As we drove out of the town, I looked back to see a star and a cross high on a hill overlooking the small town. We sped on through the dark toward Winnemucca, where we would spend the night.

January 3—Awoke to a beautiful, clear, warm, sunny day, the first day without fog Winnemucca has had in days.

The drive to Lovelock was gorgeous, with clouds floating overhead, creating lovely shadows over the desert. Onto Reno where we would spend the night at Circus Circus. Gaudy-garish, brightly lit Reno! With high-rise casinos towering above the bustling city.

We wait in line to secure a room, wait for an elevator. We marvel at the people...young people carrying skis and clad in ski garb...families with small children, one child carrying a birdcage with a parakeet! Another dwarfed by a life-size teddy bear.

Since Circus Circus is one of the economical places to stay, this brightly lit hotel casino is always busy.

At the Reno airport, plane after plane deposits more "week-enders." While we watch this cross-section of humanity, an elevator door opens to reveal a full-house! Blank stares of occupants greet you! A lady in a wheelchair, with an oxygen tank, older senior citizens, cowboys, gamblers, the very rich, the very poor; they were all there.

Called daughter Ramona to see how the wedding plans were progressing. Everything was go!

January 4—Once more we waited in line...this time to check out. Leaving Reno behind, we drove out of town on 395, heading for Loyalton, which is located in the 5,000-foot Sierra Valley.

We crossed over Beckwourth Pass, elevation 5,222 feet, and thence down into Chilcoot, California. We passed Vinton, a town smaller than Imnaha, and shortly arrived at daughter Ramona's. We found ourselves in an immense valley that stretched for miles, surrounded by mountains and hills. The valley itself was one big meadow, used mainly for the grazing of livestock and the production of many tons of hay during spring, summer and fall months.

After turning into the headquarters of the 27,000-acre Lucky Hereford Ranch, we located the house where Ramona, her husband, Charley, and their children lived.

With much anticipation, I had been looking forward to a first meeting with Liza, my soon-to-be daughter-in-law, as well as seeing son Todd.

Not much time to visit because we were leaving presently to drive to Virginia City, Nevada, an old mining town that remains much the same as in the days when Samuel Clemens worked for the Territorial Enterprise.

It was raining when we stopped at the Vinton General Store to pick up the flowers. This remarkable store not only houses the town's post office, but provides for the town's groceries, hardware, clothing, gas, and is also the florist. Son Todd broke another record by purchasing a tie (a bit dust-covered) that proved to be the first tie sold in over a year!

It continued to rain as we climbed Geiger Grade to the old mining town of Virginia City.

The wedding, Ramona informed us, was to be held in the Silver Queen, one of the elegant old buildings that features a most fascinating attraction, the Silver Queen herself, a 15-foot painting, clothed in 3,261 silver dollars.

Entering the Silver Queen was like stepping back into the 1800s.

We located the quaint little chapel through a door that opened just to the right of the richly clad Silver Queen. A large "westerner-type fellow" entered the Silver Queen accompanied by an enormous black dog and proceeded to make everyone's acquaintance, shaking hands all around. While the bride changed into her wedding dress, grandson Shawn and I went shopping for a rattlesnake hatband for his hat! A promised gift for his 12th birthday.

Meanwhile, Ramona put a quarter in a nearby slot machine and proceeded to win first a $5 jackpot, followed by a $75 one! Granddaughter Tammy and cousin Libby went out to look in the shops and came back with a newspaper, "Virginia City Headliner." Printed on the front page was Todd and Liza Tie the Knot 1-4-86.

By some miracle the wedding party and guests were rounded up from the aforementioned activities and assembled in the chapel for the ceremony.

Liza was radiant, looking lovely in her pretty white dress, Todd proud and grownup beside her as they repeated the age-old vows. Ramona and I cried, the groom kissed the bride, and they were married!

January 4, later—After the wedding, we drove up an incredibly steep incline to another street that led to the Palmer House. This wonderful 1856 house escaped the disastrous 1875 fire that destroyed 2,000 of Virginia City's buildings, after a drunken man in Crazy Kate's lodging house tried to light his pipe from a kerosene lamp, which he upset. Fanned by the Washoe winds, flamed leaped from roof to roof of the miners' cabins and engulfed the town.

The Palmer House was perfect for a wedding reception: a warm, glowing fire crackled in the immense stone fireplace, a trestle table was laden with food, and on a separate table reposed the wedding cake. A local resident had been persuaded to bake it.

The interior of the house was remarkable, like stepping back into 1865.

As we wound down Geiger Grade, in and out of misty clouds, we could see the bright lights of Reno light up the desert sky. We spent the night in the guest house of the Lucky Hereford Ranch.

Todd Nash and Liza McAlister were married in Virginia City, Nevada.

January 5—We awoke to a splendid view of the Sierra Valley. A rainbow arched across the sagebrush hills, as sunshine shot through fine rain off in the distance. We could see for miles from the guest house...a vast, grass-covered valley, devoid of snow here at 5,000 feet.

Had packed my sourdough along, so was soon fixing sourdough pancakes for the grandchildren.

Rain showers chase each other over the valley. A few cattle across the road being fed hay, the bulk of the cattle wintering in the warmer grass-land ranges of the Sacramento Valley.

Truck after truck of hay leaves the ranch daily, a lot of it going to dairies and ranches in the lower elevation areas of California. Son-in-law Charley busy as usual helping to manage this large operation.

Enjoying being with family. The newlyweds stopped by on their way to Corvallis where Liza is a pre-veterinary student at Oregon State University and son Todd is employed at the Faxon Simmental Ranch at Philomath.

January 6—The school bus stops by to pick up Tammy, Shawn and Carrie. They attend school in Loyalton, about five miles down the road.

Charley took Doug and me on a tour of the ranch. This huge operation is owned by a corporation. Charley pointed out where early-day German and Italian Swiss settlers came into the valley and ran very successful dairies. Many old buildings remain to remind us of Sierra Valley's historic past.

We came upon a "graveyard" of old farm equipment, some of the first horse-drawn farming implements, most of them sinking into the sandy, sagebrush terrain. The early days have gone by the wayside, and the huge meadows that used to graze hundreds of cattle are now fenced. Fields of hay are raised under center pivots — 8,800 tons on this ranch alone.

The summer grazing for the 3,000 cows is located on BLM land in the Red Rock area. Numerous creeks run through the ranch. Irrigation is done with flood irrigating in addition to wells. While Charley kept things going via his CB radio, we continued our tour; the cowboys' cookhouse, cow camps, hay sheds, and field after field of hay ground. The day was clear, warm and lovely. So enjoyed the sunshine. We saw two coyotes running across the frosted, grass-covered meadows.

Home-grown beef steaks for supper...nothing finer.

January 7—Awoke to enjoy the early pink light reflected on Sugar Loaf Mountain. Fifteen miles from here, up a dirt road to a place named Sardine Valley, my great-grandmother, Electa DeWolf, spent the year of

1874 tutoring four children of the Parsons family, who were engaged in early-day logging.

Electa, like myself, kept a journal. Several years ago those journals and other writings were discovered in an old trunk back East. They have since been handed down to relatives. My sister, Mary Ann, is having the letters and journals published in book form.

What a coincidence: here, in 1986, Electa's great-granddaughter writes in her own daily journal. Snow made winter travel to Sardine Valley impossible, so we could not visit the area. Locals say it hasn't changed much.

On July 8, 1874, Electa described a ride she took on her horse, Prince— *A lady must, I suppose, attempt such an adventure under all the disadvantages of modern fashionable dress. A side saddle of course, a contrivance for riding which any gentleman would pronounce an unmitigated nuisance if compelled by law to ride in it, a long riding skirt ready to entangle you at any minute, and a hat with a veil at which every twig is making a grab, leaving you in imminent danger of losing the bothering thing, or being yourself left behind.*

Electa wrote about the valley, rode horseback, hiked and explored every chance she had. Of summer 1874, she says, *The snow, except upon the higher mountains and on the hills with a northern exposure, disappeared as if by magic, and the beautiful green of resurrected nature covered the valley. At first, the valley was like a sea of gold with a wealth of buttercups, and there were banks of violets as large and rich in coloring as our cultivated pansies at home.*

She continued to write for Ohio newspapers after her marriage later to John E. Butler, a California gold miner and rancher.

She had written to her mother about him:

He is an Englishman aged forty-four. He neither smokes, chews, gambles nor drinks poor whiskey.

Electa lived an active and productive life and died at age 96.

Perhaps Electa's spirit is still alive, manifesting itself in the zest for life and love of nature and the love of writing in the soul of her great-granddaughter. Anyway, as we grow older our roots become intensely interesting and make us proud of our heritage.

The Sierra Valley hasn't built up much in all these years, but east of Beckwourth Pass lies the city of Reno, with its gambling casinos, places of sin and garish lights that lure the valley cowboys and take their paychecks. Leisure time for thousands of weekenders is spent in such places, and we call this progress.

Doug Tippett looks over an old-time hay rake in the Sierra Valley near Loyalton, California.

We explored some old, abandoned homestead shacks across from ranch headquarters. Run down, falling down remnants of the past slowly rotting into the earth from which their raw materials came, adding to the humus...the end of an era.

January 8—Heavy frost this morning, clear and sunny as we depart for the Sacramento Valley. We left daughter Ramona's and drove to Portola, then onto Quincy and down the beautiful Feather River Highway. No snow, no traffic, no people nor habitation, just the beautiful river and canyon views.

We passed by old gold-mining communities and presently came to the vast hydroelectric project owned by P.G.E. and the beginning of the urban sprawl that stretches clear to Los Angeles.

Ate lunch in Oroville. Onto Marysville, Wheatland, and finally my hometown, Lincoln. The warm, sunny Sacramento Valley with highs in the 50s, lows in the 40s! Green grass, can you imagine?

Gone, however, was the incredible blue sky of the Sierra. The mark of civilization, the valley haze from the exhaust of the state's thousands of vehicles and industry, has taken away the blue skies. Drove out in the country to the Mt. Pleasant area and into the oak woods to Grandma's.

January 9—The familiar oak woods, sights and smells of my youth—tree frogs, leaf mold; the smell of winter in the Placer County foothills.

We awoke to a sunny day. Doug panning for bits of gold dust in the creek back of the house, I going for long walks and reliving the solitary wanderings of my childhood; a yearly ritual. How I love these oak woods which are home to the coon, red fox, blacktail deer, hawk and Blue Jay. Down by the old dredger digging ponds, the wild mallards and wood ducks hide out, and in the tall, brown grasses and scrub oak lives the valley quail.

On foggy, winter days, the deer can often be seen wandering around eating acorns that have fallen to the ground. There are many large rocks, some of which contain ancient holes, where Digger Indians, using rock pestles, ground their acorn meal.

Few of these special, wild places remain after the 30 years since I grew up on the original 240-acre ranch. Fifteen homes cover other parts of the property today.

Daddy's beautiful garden, his handmade cement creations; still so lovely. It is like visiting him to see this peaceful place he spent so many happy hours creating.

My three sisters and I hiked to the top of Mt. Pleasant today. We celebrated sister Kathryn's 40th birthday. What fun we had! We also visited old ranching friends who were branding their December calves. Sure seemed funny to be watching and not participating. We drove to the old Manzanita Cemetery and laid freshly picked narcissuses on daddy's grave. We four sisters, ages 40, 42, 50 and 52, will remember this day together for always.

We came home to a dinner grandma had put together using some of my Oregon sauerkraut with German sausage, a potato salad, and a mincemeat pie I had made yesterday.

January 12—Mary Ann, Caroline and I head for more "roots" as we drive to the Folsom, White Rock area where our pioneer relatives settled. Ranching families are still here, though threatened by the ever-widening urban sprawl.

We visited the Pioneer Cemetery at Clarksville. The hills around this spot used to be devoid of habitation as far as the eye could see. Now the freeway goes by and the huge El Dorado Hills Estates, golf course, and civilization creeps ever closer to the old cemetery hill. My grandmother and grandfather are buried here, as well as my great-grandfather, who came to California with the westward movement in a covered wagon.

Visited cousins in White Rock, still ranching even though they are all in their 70s and 80s. Edna Smith, a great lady, was recently awarded the 1984 California Cattleman of the year award. She has been actively engaged in cattle ranching all of her life.

These great people treated us to lunch, a hearty beef soup, homemade whole wheat bread, and homemade ice-cream and cookies.

We visit French Creek and an old homesite of more relatives, the home gone now except for the crumbling foundation and patches of blooming narcissuses. We had a most pleasant time hiking where Canyon Creek flows into French Creek. Blackberry vines, growing in wild profusion, threaten to choke the creek in places, and we find evidence of more early day gold mining.

Home to find the coon that had been raiding the cat food in mom's garage.

January 14—We drive to Grass Valley and visit some former Wallowa County friends who live at Lake Wildwood estates in Penn Valley. Another place that has built up with homes. We also visited Rough and Ready, a small community that is still in existence.

We ate lunch in the National Hotel, the oldest continuously operating hotel west of the Rocky Mountains. The hotel was furnished with antiques of the Gold Rush era. It was fun to walk around and look at this 130-year old hotel that has had such guests as Herbert Hoover, Lola Montez, and the bandit-poet, Black Bart.

Began to rain in Nevada City and poured all the way back to Auburn, where we had dinner with sister Mary Ann, who lives on a hill overlooking the American River canyon.

January 15—Lunch with more relatives in Sacramento. Very enjoyable being able to visit aunts and uncles.

January 16—Made potato candy today to take to the Potato Conference in Portland. Also made a loaf of sourdough bread. An old schoolmate stopped by to visit while I was baking. Hadn't seen him in 34 years.

Had dinner with more friends, then to Roseville to see Jennifer and Jeanette, my twin nieces, then on to more old friends, the Oakes.

January 17—Left the foothills and headed for the Sierras again, over Donner Pass to Truckee. Warm morning, no snow to speak of over the pass, the skiing resorts not too happy.

In Sparks, Nevada, we found granddaughter Mona Lee's new purple tennis shoes. Just what she had requested for her upcoming fourth birthday.

Over to the Sierra Valley once more where I fixed a chicken dinner for all our family. We listened to the "Coyotes in Stereo," as Ramona refers to them, their plaintive wails echoing around the valley tonight.

January 18—A blanket of fog lays over the valley. After sourdough hotcakes, Doug, granddaughter Carrie and grandson Shawn and I drive to an abandoned homestead where we scout up a draw above the fog.

The children and I decided to hike to the top of the highest point around. We startled deer that bounded off through the sagebrush and rocks at our approach. It was so warm and sunny as we climbed higher, and soon shed our jackets.

The sagebrush gave off a sweet odor, the alpine birds sang to us and finally we reached the top, where we could see the entire Sierra Valley at our feet, covered with the ocean of fog. A slight breeze sprang up and began to sweep the fog away. It was a wonderful feeling, high up on our rock promontory, watching the fog swirl around and dissipate.

Attended a money-raising Mexican dinner at the Loyalton High School for Tammy's sophomore class. Even met some people who used to vacation in Wallowa County. They even knew how to pronounce Imnaha. Small world.

January 19—Off to points north and our eventual destination, the Oregon Potato Conference in Portland. Beautiful day, a few clouds and plenty of sunshine. We head up toward Long Valley, Susanville, Alturas, Likely and Tulelake where we visit my nephew. Then on to Klamath Falls, taking Route 66 for 61 miles through two snow-covered passes. We crossed the Pacific Crest Trail, then descended a beautiful canyon through a layer of misty cloud. We glimpsed a beautiful, red-sky sunset as we drove down into Ashland. We had dinner in Medford, then drove to Roseburg where we stayed with Bill and Carolee Matthews.

January 20—Foggy morning, lambs being born on this small ranch, lush green grass everywhere. Carolee fixed biscuits and gravy for breakfast, before we drove to the small town of Oakland where we visited a harness and buggy shop. They restore horse-drawn buggies and wagons.

At Corvallis, stopped to visit with new daughter-in-law Liza. Son Todd at work on the nearby Faxon Simmental Ranch at Philomath. We left Liza off at OSU where she had a beef production class. Doug picked up the results of our seed potato trials while we were on campus.

Next stop was Woodburn to visit Aunt Amey and take her to dinner, then on to Portland to spend a few days. The lights of the big city were colorful and bright this clear night.

We've been gone so long from the ranch, I am anxious to be home. The Potato Convention begins tomorrow.

January 21—Woke to a splendid view of Mount Hood, bathed in sunlight on a crystal clear morning. The potato conference opens with meetings geared mainly for men, so Donna Butterfield, Eileen Theil and I fled to the Sellwood area and lost ourselves in the world of antiques, where I found a "Golden Guernsey" milk bottle. A rare item now. Golden Guernsey milk hasn't been bottled for years. This bottle holds a special significance for me. In 1949, I was the Golden Guernsey Queen at the California State Fair—at the tender age of 15!

Like the last year, we ate lunch at Jerry's Gable. Little did we know that this "dining experience" would last all afternoon.

Jerry himself ushered us in. He then took down from the door a large blackboard that had the menu written on it. We were all in a happy mood, talking a mile a minute. The choices on the menu were all so good, we had a hard time deciding. Finally I settled on rigatoni, since Jerry's cuisine was decidedly Italian.

While we enjoyed our soup, Donna mentioned to Jerry that I wrote a column for a newspaper. From then on we were treated royally. While Strauz waltzes played on the stereo, we were wined and dined like never before. Jerry even introduced "Roberto," the German cook who came out of the kitchen to entertain us with his jokes.

Our food was served on large silver platters. The wine, served in stemware from Czechoslovakia was very good. The rigatoni was heavenly, the coffee freshly ground. The procession of delicacies kept coming and so did the dialogue. We were the only people in the place, except for one other couple. After dining, we were served an after dinner drink, a white wine made with Cassis fruit (pomegranate), that was excellent.

The grand finale, chocolate applesauce cake, served with more gourmet coffee. You would have thought I was a writer for Bon Appetite instead of Agri-Times. We had a hilarious time, capped off when a Portland piano player celebrity walked in to further entertain us. Ironically, we had been listening to an album of his music at the time he appeared.

Donna told Jerry that I did outdoor catering, so he was interested in my outdoor dutch oven cookery and wondered if I'd be willing to conduct a demonstration at a cooking school in Portland.

We continued to laugh at Roberto's jokes, as he kept coming out of the kitchen to add his two bits worth to the lively conversation. We laughed until our sides ached, while devouring this procession of food and drink.

It wasn't until after we finished that we found out Jerry's isn't really open now to the public, just to members of a local gourmet club. We "Country Bumkins" had innocently stumbled in and sat down waiting to order. Jerry and Roberto got such a kick out of us Wallowa County gals, and we looked so sincere, they decided to serve us.

Stuffed full as ticks, we headed back to the Red Lion where we related our tale to incredulous husbands.

So, now I write about this and send it to Jerry's Gable, so he will, in fact, believe that there is an Agri-Times newspaper and this writer does have a column.

Back at the Red Lion and the potato conference, I found I had won a door prize—a 30 pound box of instant mashed potatoes.

January 22—Raining this morning and colder.

Did some photo-journalism for Agri-Times. Doug and I lunched with Don Ostensoe of the Oregon Beef Council.

January 23—Doug's meeting with the Seed Advisory Board lasted until 5:30, so it was late when we left the Red Lion. I passed the time visiting with Mary Ann Greenlund at the Oregon Wheat Commission office. While there, I had the opportunity to look at the controversial textbook "Get Oregonized."

I was impressed with the text and bewildered at all the fuss.

Seems to me it is about time students learn the real facts about agriculture. The book is put together so youngsters could be proud of their heritage and also appreciate the wonderful resources we have here in Oregon. The photography was outstanding.

Waiting for Doug's meeting to end, I continued reading Mark Twain's "Roughing It." While all around me flowed life in 1986, I read about life in 1886. Mining camp men in juxtaposition to the clean-shaven, suited men walking around with brief cases in the lobby of the Red Lion. How rapidly our culture has changed, in less than a heartbeat in eternity. Taming the environment in Twain's day, preserving it in our own.

I contemplate how bewildering it must seem to our children; many of whom carry dreams of settling a new land. No more frontiers to conquer, but that same pioneer blood runs in their veins and the drive to realize these dreams is very much alive. They meet a new world of challenges. These days, compared to grizzly bears and untamed, unconquered wilderness, man-made laws present a more formidable obstacle. I believe the pioneer spirit in these strong sons and daughters will triumph and that they will carry on, taking pride in their heritage and learning from our mistakes.

I continued to think about these things as we were swept away by the flow of rush hour traffic, caught in the exodus from city to suburbs.

We made it to Corvallis where we spent the night with the newlyweds. Fun getting to know my sweet, new, daughter-in-law. Since "Mom" was the official photographer at the wedding and had pictures developed while in Portland, we enjoyed looking at them.

We found out that Liza's roots were in the Wallowa Valley. Her great grandfather settled there years ago.

January 24—After a delicious breakfast prepared by new daughter-in-law, Liza, we headed north, stopping briefly at our State Capitol in Salem.

I love the cement sculptures that grace the entrance to this beautiful building. Beneath one I read the inscription, "Westward the course of empire takes its way." One of my father's favorite quotations.

Inside, I enjoyed gazing upward at the enormous murals of Lewis and Clark and Sacajawea, and the one depicting our pioneer heritage. Couldn't help but feel a sense of pride, knowing that agriculture had played such an important role in the founding of our great state.

As we travel up I-5, the living artery that connects the states, we notice pussy willows out along the freeway! The huge Willamette Valley is ready to burst forth into spring!

We headed home, stopping in Hermiston long enough to look at our calves at Bryan Wolfe's. They looked good, running and kicking up their heels. Good feed, turnips to chew on and plenty of space to exercise; ideal conditions to background calves.

A full moon followed us home and into the welcoming arms of the Wallowa Valley. We could see that the rivers were still iced over and the moonlight cast its silvery sheen upon their frozen surfaces.

Arrived home to a sleeping ranch, looking not much different than when we left. Some of the snow had melted and an enormous stack of mail awaited us. So good to be home!

January 25—Spent most of the day going through an accumulation of mail. Everything in order on the ranch, thanks to Ben and Kirk, our dependable help.

January 26—A cold, clear Sunday, back in the swing of ranch life.

Attended a birthday celebration for granddaughter Mona Lee today at her Imnaha home, her 4th.

Before we left on our trip, I had asked Mona Lee (over the phone) what she wanted for her birthday. She replied "tennis shoes." I asked what color, and she said "Purple." Then I asked this sweet little dumplin what size, to which she replied without a moment's hesitation, "The size that fits my foot, grandma!"

Doug spotted them first in a store in Sparks, Nevada, but we could only guess at the size. As Mona Lee opened up the shoe box that held the purple tennis shoes her eyes fairly shone. She was ecstatic and immediately put them on. A perfect fit.

The gathering of Imnaha's little children for Mona Lee's party was wonderful. The canyon children, isolated from "town," are in ways much luckier than their city cousins. They were so wide-eyed, staring at the lighted candles on the birthday cake.

The wonderful world of innocent children, so enraptured by a simple birthday party. These are little ones who have no televisions in their homes; only the canyons will mold their characters and make them strong to face the outside world. They will enjoy childhood and the outdoors that is all around them. Lucky children indeed.

Doug watching football on this Super Bowl Sunday. On my round-trip to Imnaha, 60 miles, I passed but two vehicles. Would guess most inhabitants of the valley also watching the Super Bowl.

I hear the hoot-hooing of our two resident owls from the willow.

January 29—Income tax time. Every year brings more forms and more paper work.

The space shuttle Challenger exploded minutes into its flight this morning. A tragic event that will go down in history as part of our continuing space exploration. Is the price we pay really worth it? Guess I'm old-fashioned, but am content to gaze in awe at the heavens, the stars, the moon, the inverted bowl of a blue sky or a flaming sunset, and simply let it remain a beautiful mystery.

Attended the 4-H Leaders banquet tonight at Cloverleaf Hall. We listened to a report about the projected 1990s 4-H program. Many changes will have taken place by then. As the age of computers dawns, 4-H records will be stored on floppy discs and the record book will be a thing of the past. I can't help but remember my own 4-H record keeping and how much fun they were to keep, how simple and uncomplicated the books were then. Even the leaders could understand them in those days.

At the age of 12, due in part to the program offered in 4-H, I unknowingly began a photo journalism education. By writing about my 4-H projects and taking pictures with a simple box camera in order to record activities like tours, field trips, fairs, demonstrations and the like,

I learned skills that have served me well. It was the best training a young person could have.

Today, we in 4-H need to keep alive the ideals of 4-H. Many times, as in the past, 4-H work has enabled a member to find his life's work. In this age of computers, we must not lose sight of building better citizens through the 4-H program. Children need to be rewarded for hard work and a job well done. 4-H provides for these things.

January 30—A low of 36. Everything is thawed and melting. Feels like spring. Even the hens think so and have begun laying again. The Banty rooster flew to the top of the chicken pen this morning, leaned back his head and crowed!

More thick fog as the warm air meets the cold ground. Drove very slowly to attend an advanced photography class in Joseph tonight. Could barely make out the road coming home.

January 31—Out again this fog-filled evening, this time to have dinner in Joseph with Bud and Ruby Zollman. A delicious meal served in their comfortable home.

February 1—Our photography class assembled in Joseph at 7:30 this morning. We tried photographing before the fog rolled in. Not much luck, so we headed out toward Sheep Creek Hill, getting in some good shots of sunlight on the mountains contrasting with the fog that lay like a blanket in the valley. A real challenge for us photographers today.

Although a chill wind blew, we had a good time, traipsing around with our tripods and cameras, learning more about depth of field, F stops and shutter speeds. Cameras these days are wonderful, provided you know how to use them! Our instructor, Doris, is very patient with us. Good thing! We definitely need help.

Home to some serious house cleaning as fog once more envelopes Prairie Creek. Baked a batch of mincemeat bar cookies to fill up the cookie jar.

February 2—Cloudy and it appears to be snowing over the mountains. Fed the horses their hay and, after breakfast, Scotty and I set out to take a hike and complete more of my photography assignments. Wallowa County is quiet and peaceful this morning; no one about except for the ranchers feeding their cattle. Continuing to melt, bare ground the rule now rather than the exception.

We walked up a snow-filled road to visit a friend. So good to be out walking. Occasional sunlight spread across the valley. Puddles of water everywhere that reflected the fence posts and wheel lines.

Home to put an elk roast in the oven. Our horse pasture is a lake.

The ground hog didn't see his shadow today. An early spring? Sure would be nice.

February 3—Judith and I cleaned house today. We chatted and visited about our different worlds. Judith is here visiting from the Netherlands. The dust flew as we took everything out of the front room and gave it a good cleaning. Since Doug was attending the livestock auction, we even cleaned his desk.

The weather was warm and balmy, so we opened windows and let fresh air circulate through the house.

I learned a lot about customs in Holland while we dusted, mopped and scrubbed. Judith, only 21, has done a lot of living in her young life.

My hens are beginning to lay again as we enter into a "false spring."

February 4—Doug off to the Washington Potato Conference in Moses Lake. It snowed during the night, a soft, wet, spring-like snow that covers everything. I drove one of the ranch pickups into town to be serviced and brought another one home that had been repaired.

Ben and Kirk hauling hay from Alder Slope. The county's haystacks are dwindling, with many more feeding days left this winter.

Returned from town to find our electricity out. After it was restored, I made a batch of date bars.

February 5—A wind blowing snow against the bedroom window awakened me at 3 a.m. Everything white this morning. Winter again!

Started a fire in the woodstove and fixed myself some breakfast before venturing out to tend the chickens, my only chores these days as the milk cows haven't calved yet. Ben has been feeding them as well as the horses. Really getting soft this winter. May as well enjoy the rest. Pretty soon all heck will break loose with the advent of spring.

I had the two Imnaha grandchildren today. We drove to Wallowa Lake State Park to see the frozen-over lake and feed the deer. Several six-point bucks came close and the children were thrilled, being able to feed crackers to them from the car. One big, old buck was chewing his cud while around 15 head of does, fawns and young bucks bedded down nearby.

My 21-member Sourdough Shutterbugs 4-H Club held its first meeting of the year tonight, electing officers and planning activities such as hikes and trips to our mountains and canyons.

Let "Faye," our cow dog, sleep on the porch tonight.

Snowing lightly outside.

Snow melted rapidly as unseasonably warm temperatures invaded Alder Slope in Wallowa County. This view shows the barn on the Kenneth Kooch ranch, which sits under Ruby Peak.

February 6—Went skiing with Grace Bartlett and Scotty at the new Ferguson Ridge ski area, located in the timber above upper Prairie Creek. It was completed recently with the help of local ranchers and volunteer help. A new T-barn as just been installed.

Some sad news from daughter Ramona: grandson Bart is in the Washoe Medical Center in Reno.

February 7—Nine above zero. Better to have this frozen cold than thawing conditions or feeding cattle. At least they clean up their hay and don't tromp a lot of it in the ground.

Called the hospital in Reno and talked to Ramona. Bart is improving.

February 8—Made a sour cream raisin pie from an Agri-Times recipe. Turned out delicious.

Doris came over this afternoon and began organizing my negative file. She is trying to "Organize Janie," an impossible job.

I made "Happy Family" for dinner tonight, a Chinese dish that consists of beef, chicken, shrimp, scallops and vegetables all stir-fried. The beef and chicken were our homegrown products, but had to purchase the shrimp and scallops. It was indeed a happy family that ate it. Doris and her daughter stayed to enjoy the meal with us.

February 9—The sun rose this morning in a clear, blue sky. The snow fields are blinding white, the air crisp and pure. What a day. The ground frozen again. Ben and Kirk faithfully feed long lines of cattle, a never ending daily job that lasts for months.

Scotty came by and we drove to Ferguson Ridge to ski again today.

Home to bake sourdough bread and fry chicken for supper. Into Enterprise tonight to hear Joe Lutz, Republican primary candidate for Senate.

February 10—Son Ken hauling hay again today, replenishing the many hay stacks required to feed all these cattle. The first of May seems a long way off, traditional "turnout" time for our cattle, moving them from hay to grass.

Judith over again to help me clean house. We tackled the downstairs this time. Organizing boxes from the Dug Bar Ranch, stuff stored down there since that ranch was sold. We carted some of it to the bunk house. Mentally, I planned a yard sale.

February 11—So nice having large, brown eggs again.

Had an eye checkup this morning. Was amazed at the many different tests given these days for eyes. As Dr. Peterson wrote down the optical jargon that described my present "seeing status," I was amused, especially when I was measured for width between the eyes. Although amiss in some categories, I left the office clutching a note that the doctor had written to Doug: "Jane is perfect between the eyes!" Perhaps this will soften the blow when Doug sees the bill.

February 12—Windy last night and the ground is frozen this morning. Beginning to snow lightly.

A used potato piler that Doug purchased in Rexburg, Idaho, arrived this morning.

I watch the Lockes feeding hay to their cows from my kitchen window. The same hay I watched them put up loose into an enormous stack this summer; the stack is shrinking as winter wears on. The loose hay is fed with a farmhand and tractor, much the same way most valley ranchers have fed for years. It continues to be a low-overhead way of preserving hay.

Daughter Lori called from Wyoming. Seems husband Tom is competing in the cutter races in Jackson Hole, and they want us to come back and join them for the meet. Doug says we can probably combine business and pleasure, as he needs to investigate a two-row potato planter near Twin Falls.

Son Ken and his helper hauling more hay today. They finish off the elk stew and sour cream raisin pie.

February 13—Doug and I left for Twin Falls, where we ate dinner. We spent the night in Jackpot, Nevada, as Doug decided we would drive there to see Cactus Pete's and Horseshu casinos.

Quite a place. This relatively new facility stands out in the middle of lonely sagebrush country.

It features top quality entertainment and, sure enough, many farmers, mostly from Southern Idaho, were in attendance. A different atmosphere here than in Reno. Cleaner, with the people more "countrified." Struck up a conversation with a woman who lived south of Calgary in Alberta, Canada. She said they raised Red Angus and had a huge trout pond where tourists could fish.

Later, she and her husband invited us to visit them and attend the Calgary Stampede. Only a dream as it will be "busy time" on the ranch. Maybe someday.

February 14—Woke up in the "Buffalo Wing" of the motel next to Cactus Pete's. We ate breakfast in Cactus Pete's surrounded by huge dried cactus plants. Purchased a wind-up fuzzy chicken toy for granddaughter

Lacey's birthday. Since her last visit to the ranch, all she can talk about is grandma's chickens.

In daylight we could now see the miles of sagebrush hills that surround Jackpot, Nevada. As we drove away, I noticed a sign near a young stand of evergreen trees: "Jackpot National Forest."

The snow melted as we sped toward Twin Falls, whereupon it began to rain. Rain showers followed us east across the state of Idaho and it was pouring by the time we reached Pocatello. We made it to Idaho Falls, then turned and followed the Snake River to Jackson Hole.

Gradually, bare brown fields gave way to snow covered farms and lonely, remote ranches stilled in a world of white. Numerous slopes, covered with leafless aspen, appeared in a dusky, misty afternoon light.

The Snake, free of ice except for what clung to the banks, was a deep turquoise color. Rising sap was beginning to turn the leafless brush along its route into a collage of deep reds, browns and rusts.

We noticed scattered herds of cattle being fed hay in areas of deep snow. After traveling miles on a snow and ice-covered road, we pulled into Jackson Hole. Imagine being in Jackson Hole in winter.

Jackson Hole and the town of Jackson were barely visible through misty clouds that continued to empty a mix of rain and snow. Darkness settled in at our arrival. We checked into a motel where we had reservations and met Lori and Tom, who had preceded us.

The town of Jackson was filled with Shriners, cowboys, cutter racers, their wives, Miss Teenage America contestants and the usual skiers.

Cutter-race enthusiasts drove in from all over, pulling horse-trailers, their chariots tied on top or in back of pickups.

We ate dinner at "Sadie's," where an enormous American flag bravely tried to wave. Its sodden ripples, weighted down with rain, were creating a flop-flap sound in the warm chinook wind.

The flag was spotlighted from below and we gazed upward into the lighted undulating motion of red, white and blue, to see the sky above backlit by the sifting down of snow. Very impressive. We soaked up "local color" until 1:30 a.m. by dancing to live western music; fiddles, banjos, guitars. No amplifiers, just good ol' foot stompin' music. The hilarity and spirit of fun that is synonymous with Wyoming cowboys was contagious; refreshing and real. Cowboys from all over, here to have a good time.

Headquarters for the cutter races were in "The Virginian." We waded through crowds of Shriners (who sponsor the event) and cowboys to watch the spirited bidding on selling the teams for the races tomorrow. Ten percent of the money goes to the Crippled Children's Hospital.

Tom Seely of Thermopolis, Wyoming, crosses the finish line in a winning time of 24.4 seconds at the Jackson Hole cutter races. Note the air-borne team in second place.

February 15—The heater in our room snapped, crackled and popped all night. Then blew a fuse. It turned out the melting snow and dripping water had shorted the element from outside.

"One of those heating systems designed for Arizona, not Jackson Hole," remarked the repair man.

On our way to breakfast, we noted the ski resorts had closed down.

We enjoyed a biscuits and gravy, eggs, ham and hot cakes breakfast; all you could eat, for $4.

We walked up and down the boardwalks and slushy streets, looking at the many tourist shops. The water simply poured off the roof tops and ran down the streets in torrents.

The cutter races began at noon, taking place three miles out of town on the Melody Hereford Ranch.

As the first teams came charging out of the starting gate, they were clocked at speeds in excess of 42 miles an hour. They came pounding down the slushy track, spewing mud and splattering the faces of the drivers, who stand in the small chariots.

The horses, usually seven-eighths thoroughbred and quarter horse, are high-spirited and conditioned to run; no stop, just run.

They came flying down the 440 track, pounding to the finish line, whereupon they had to negotiate a dangerous turn before they ran out of sight of the spectators. On this turn, we saw some pretty hairy spills…upset chariots and drivers hurled out upon the snow banks that lined the track.

After the teams cross the finish line, three outriders mounted on horses attempt to slow down the fleeing horses. The driver has the option to ride it out or be picked up, like a pickup man in a rodeo. Most opted to stick with their teams; others catapulted into the air. A potentially dangerous situation as they rounded the turn and the outriders tried to grab bridles and slow down the teams. If that failed they would be stopped by a huge snow bank where the track dead-ended.

Cutter racing is a popular winter sport in Wyoming and Idaho, and is gaining in popularity in other western states. Son-in-law Tom won his race in 24.40 seconds.

At intervals, the meet was bombarded with blizzard conditions, followed by periods of sunshine. It was never very cold. Spectators, colorful in yellow slickers, insulated overalls and hats, waded through the slosh eating barbecued beef sandwiches and hot dogs and drinking beer. Everyone was having a great time.

I was amused at the faces of the drivers after the race. Splattered with mud and spitting gravel, they continued to smile.

After the races we drove out to the National Elk Refuge. Over 6,000 head of elk winter on these meadows...an unreal sight. Elk wandered about or lay down for us as far as our eyes could see. Teams of horses, hitched to sleighs, were taking people out to view the herds. We found out later that 30 tons of hay pellets are fed daily.

Called daughter Ramona and found out grandson Bart is home from the hospital. Much relieved to hear that.

We ate supper at Jedediah's Original House of Sourdough. Was fascinated with their huge sourdough crock. They use 15 gallons of sourdough a day.

Just heard that they've closed Teton and Togotee passes due to slides. If the Snake River route follows suit, we may be "holed up" in Jackson Hole.

February 16—Jackson Hole's unseasonal warm temperatures changed abruptly. A blizzard enveloped us as we drove the eight miles out to the National Elk Refuge.

Bundled to the teeth, we climbed aboard a horse-drawn sleigh wagon that took us out to the herd. We were told this herd numbered 6,400.

The elk previously had been fed their daily ration (approximately seven pounds per head) of hay pellets and most of them were lying down or chewing their cuds while standing around in this sea of cows, calves and bulls. Many of the bulls were playfully sparring with each other, their enormous antlers sometimes entangling.

Doug, daughter Lori and I were agape at all the seven- and eight-point bulls. The wind picked up and it began to snow quite heavily. Imagine being in the middle of the world's largest elk preserve in a blizzard. Stinging sleet and snow hit our faces. The driver stopped occasionally so

Two bull elk spar playfully during a snowstorm in the National Elk Refuge in Jackson Hole, Wyoming. There are 6,400 elk in this herd.

we photographers could get in some shots. It was interesting to watch the bulls, who continued to play despite the storm.

Occasionally we glimpsed coyotes slinking around the perimeter of the herd. We guessed they had been feeding on some of the snow-covered carcasses of dead elk.

We were told by our driver-guide that 15,000 elk winter here in Jackson Hole. Many migrate up to 65 miles to their summer ranges, come May.

After our tour of the elk, we walked into the small headquarters building for a slide presentation concerning the elk refuge.

This afternoon, we watched the cutter races again, in a snow storm. We noticed that the ski lifts were again in operation. Due to possible slide conditions on the Snake River Route we opted to spend another night rather than get caught in darkness on some lonely road with a slide problem. Both Teton and Togwotee passes are still closed.

February 17—A trucker just came into the motel and informed us that a slide, two city blocks long, just occurred ahead of him near the Hoback Junction.

The Snake River Route was open, so we left around 9 a.m.

As we were leaving the Jackson Valley, we saw two teams of horses pulling sleds of hay that the ranchers were feeding their cattle with. We drove by numerous elk that were foraging for feed near the banks of the Snake River. We made it safely out of the mountainous areas where loose rocks were falling across the road.

It simply poured from Idaho Falls to Boise, then slacked off a bit at Ontario. Bare pavement and mild temperatures accompanied us to the Wallowa Valley. A long drive today, home by 11 p.m. Much of the snow had melted and our three border collie dogs ran to greet us.

February 18—The chickens had laid big brown eggs in our absence. Made a cherry pie from some frozen cherries in the freezer.

Our fields and barn lots are a mess of ooze and mud, as the frost begins to go out of the ground.

It is so muddy and wet that it is difficult for Ben and Kirk to find a clean place to feed the hay.

Pussy willows, buttercups and baby lambs are out on Imnaha. Soon it will be "baby calf time" here on our ranch, and the potatoes must be sorted and cleaned ready for shipment. The spring rush is just around the corner.

February 20—Snow fell during the night and the ground is frozen again. Just as well, handier to feed cattle.

Helped our CowBelles serve "Beefy Chili" at the Les Schwab Tire Center promotion at noon, then delivered copies of our new CowBelle cookbooks to Joseph merchants who had purchased ads for the book.

Our first new baby calf came this morning.

Working on details for our annual bull sale; Doug on the phone arranging shipments of seed potatoes.

Attended our history group meeting tonight. We are presently working on some projects for Wallowa Country's centennial year, 1987.

February 21—Cold, a light sprinkle of new snow fell last night. Weatherwise, we feel lucky here in the valley compared to what we hear about in California, devastating floods and such.

The men hauled our bulls into the vet's to be semen-tested this morning. Jackie and the children spent the night.

February 22—Rented a pair of little skis and took grandchildren Buck and Mona Lee to Ferguson Ridge to ski today. Quite a time trying to get five-year-old Buck up the tow rope; pretty hard on grandma. Buck did great, however, after we exited the tow rope, and skied down the hill like a pro.

We joined Bud and Ruby Zollman for dinner at the Elks tonight.

February 23—Rained all night, flood warnings out along the Grande Ronde. Doug and I drove to Imnaha and found many of the creeks overflowing their banks. Water was coming down in torrents, carrying with it debris that in turn plugged up culverts under the highway.

The Imnaha was running chocolate colored and frothy; huge limbs, logs and debris swept by as we viewed the high water from the River-Side Cafe. All the little tributaries that comprise the Imnaha drainage were filling the river to capacity. The warm rain causing snowmelt up on the North Fork, Middle Fork and Big and Little Sheeps.

We didn't stay long at the bridge due to the impending road closure.

We made it out "on top" safely, just in time.

Before leaving for Imnaha, I had baked some sourdough brownies and made a salad for the 4-H potluck tonight at Joneses'. So we attended that at 6 p.m. Kurt Eherler showed slides of his recent Rotary Exchange trip to Australia.

February 24—Sixty-two degrees today! Cleared off. Our lawn is uncovered, exposing the brown greenish grass that has lain unmowed beneath winter's blanket of ice and snow. Only a few patches of the white stuff remain.

Judy came over and cleaned out my garden of corn stalks and sunflowers, and pulled up the stakes. We had a fun day baking bread, cleaning and opening all the windows to the balmy air.

Baby calves running all over the lower pasture.

February 25—Rhubarb peeking its little red leaves through the wet, black earth, tulips are appearing, primroses are blooming alongside the house and the first robin has appeared.

Spring must be close at hand.

I ordered my baby chicks today, for April delivery.

February 24—The road to Imnaha is still closed. The community and the people who live along the river are cut off from "on top," except for four-wheel drive travel.

The Prairie Creek landscape has a brown, dull-looking appearance. The snow at least had a clean look. Now the yard is laid bare to winter's refuse: bones, twine and the "Junk Yard Dog." I must go out and begin to pick up this unsightly mess!

A flurry of activity at the cellar as our crew begins to sort potatoes, readying them, we hope, for shipment.

February 27—The valley is beautiful today. A cobalt-blue sky and a 20-degree reading on the porch thermometer.

Son Ken here washing and clipping the bulls for our annual production sale.

Attended my photography class tonight. We were given a quiz, then critiqued each other's prints. We were allowed to exhibit only six prints. Frustrating, as I had taken so many that I wanted to enter.

February 28—Another gorgeous morning dawns as the sun paints the high peaks pink before spilling its soft light over Prairie Creek.

We drove over to Hermiston late this afternoon, stopping by our potato cellar on the way to check on our crew.

We joined Lou Ann and Bryan Wolfe in Hermiston for dinner. Enjoyed visiting these former Wallowa County friends. It seems Bryan has been doing a bit of birdwatching lately. He claims to have discovered a rare species in the Hermiston area. Claims they are called "Milamoor" birds. You will just have to check with Bryan as to the validity of this bird tail (tale).

March 1—Came in like a lamb, except for a damp, chilly breeze that blew clouds over Hermiston.

We attended the annual C&B Livestock production sale at Ron Baker's. There were the usual crowds of people, everyone enjoying Jane's famous steak, eggs, biscuits and honey brunch. Jane smiling and wearing a pretty, new dress made by daughter Sheila.

Doug purchased a black baldy crossbred bull and, after munching down on the delicious apples flown in just for the sale, we left for our valley.

March 2—Incredibly beautiful morning. The blackbirds are having a concert in the bare-limbed willow trees. Our sale bulls, clipped and scrubbed, lazily soak up the sunshine.

In the lower pasture, newborn calves doze in the warmth, while their mammas just nibble at their hay and begin to graze the first green grass. They are becoming tired of hay.

March 3—Heavy frost this morning. Bright sunshine and blue skies. Nary a cloud or a breath of wind to mar this feeling of false spring.

Today is our sale day. The bulls are hauled to the Enterprise Livestock Auction. They are a nice set of bulls and we are proud of them. Raising quality livestock always brings a satisfaction that is apart from any monetary value.

Son Ken did a good job of presenting the bulls, they were gentle and looked good.

Grandson Bart taking another turn for the worse. I feel for this family.

March 4—Sourdough waffles for breakfast. Another nice day, until around 1:30, when a wind came up, a drying wind blowing over the snow-less brown fields. The hills are beginning to show the first, faint tinge of green.

Still sorting potatoes in at the cellar. Baked a gooseberry pie. Does anyone know of an easy way to clean the ends from gooseberries? If so let me know. I froze the berries with the ends on last year and it is a tedious task to remove them. Actually, I baked this pie with most of the ends left on, and it got eaten just the same.

The busy season begins, the phone ringing constantly. Son Ken and Ben working cattle today. More new baby calves are appearing. Attended a wrestling match this afternoon at the Enterprise school. Grandsons Chad and Rowdy are wrestling these days. Can they be old enough for this already?

Home to bake a meat loaf and set the sourdough biscuits to rise.

March 5—Have been letting the fire die out in the mornings after breakfast, it has been so unseasonably warm. Opened all the windows and did some spring cleaning. Baked a batch of cookies and their smell mingles with the fresh air.

Spotted the first pair of returning robins from my kitchen window. Buttercup reporters have been informing me of the first, small, waxy, golden patches, harbingers of spring.

Doug drove to La Grande early this morning to pick up daughter Linda, who will be spending a few days with us. I fixed a special T-bone steak dinner to celebrate her arrival. Linda, who is a waitress, appreciated the good "country cookin'," she said.

March 6—Cloudy with rain showers in the forecast, just when our 4-H Sourdough Shutterbugs are planning a Saturday campout on Imnaha.

After doing chores, I drove Linda to Imnaha to visit daughter Jackie and family. We saw the effect of the recent, heavy, warm rains. Sheep Creek, racing headlongs, carried the contents of its swollen tributaries. The canyons were greening, apricot trees beginning to bloom, and in Jackie's yard, crocuses and violets.

Son Todd's mare, spending the winter on Imnaha, is due to foal next month, another sign of spring. The canyons were warm and balmy, with a few sprinkles of rain.

We walked up the road to meet grandson Buck as he got off his school bus from kindergarten, a big smile on his face and clutching a pile of school work. Home to cook supper around a pot roast that had been cooking slowly in a dutch oven during our absence.

March 7—A strong wind romped around all night, accompanied by a warm rain. As I look out the living room window this morning, I see the eastern hills are clear of snow. Unusual for this time of year. The warm rain will gradually turn the valley green; that is, unless it turns cold again.

One of our cows lost her newborn calf in a ditch last night. Son Ken had an extra calf, so the dead calf was skinned out and the hide was tied on the new calf. Hope mother falls for the ruse. This trick usually works, but not always.

Doug drove Linda back to La Grande so she could catch the bus to Pendleton. I stayed home to answer calls from my 4-H'ers, who hope (despite the rain) we can still camp out on Imnaha tomorrow.

March 8—Cloudy, no rain, no snow, no wind. We decide to go ahead with our plans. We leave from our place at 10 a.m. Sleeping bags, food, camping gear all loaded into our rigs.

Our first hike along the river was halted after the rain that began with a gentle shower turned into a deluge! We had built a fire and eaten our lunch under some trees. It wasn't cold, but we were soon pretty soaked and had to return to the warmth of Jackie's wood cook stove.

We were camping in a barn along the Imnaha River on the Benson ranch where daughter Jackie and family reside.

Sleeping bags were spread out on straw and hay bales, comfy and cozy. The sound of the river's turbulent waters was ever present as the rain continued. The upper reaches of the Imnaha were contributing heavy snow-melt to the already swollen river.

We barbecued hamburgers on an open fire out in the pouring rain, a real challenge. They were delicious, anyway, as we had a good hot fire going. Grandchildren Mona and Buck joined our group and we had a great time. We were fortunate to have the nice barn to take refuge in.

By 9, the rain still drummed steadily on the tin roof and the river's roar filled our ears. Todd's restless mare, heavy with foal, munched on her hay. Tired from the day's exertions, I fell asleep, my two small grandchildren beside me in their sleeping bags.

We were awakened at 3 by 4-H'er Michele: "The mare is having her foal!" As I sleepily put on my clothes and boots, I could see the other 4-H'ers, sleeping bags wrapped around them, standing on bales of hay with their chins resting on the top rail of the horse stall, rapt attention on the mare.

A closer inspection of the pregnant mare led me to believe she was nowhere near foaling. Apparently she had lain down for a brief rest and

"Hummer" an Appaloosa cow horse, walks up a trail along the flood-swollen Imnaha River in Wallowa County. Ranchers in this rugged country rely heavily on the horse. This photo was taken on the Benson Ranch.

Michele thought her time had come. The mare was by now chomping down more hay.

Lulled to sleep once more by the incessant roar of the river, we all drifted back into dreamland. The grandchildren hadn't budged through the episode.

March 9—We had mixed up an enormous bowl of sourdough last night; this morning we found it bubbling and working. We whipped up a batch of sourdough hotcakes, made syrup, and fried bacon and eggs on a large cast-iron griddle I had brought along. We made hot chocolate from a mix one of the 4-H'ers had made. It was a beautiful rain-washed morning.

Willie Zollman was up early, heading up the trail to spot some deer glimpsed yesterday. The sky was the purest blue and the dusting of snow on the high rims made us glad we were on the Imnaha, rather than "On Top," where it would be white.

We spent the morning hiking the canyon trails and taking pictures. It was a wonderful time, free of cares.

All children should have this freedom of enjoying the outdoors.

Reluctantly, we left for home around noon. Am a bit weary, guess it could be that I'm not as young as the 4-H'ers.

Doug busy checking calving cows on this day. Another one born in a ditch and a backward calf that had to be pulled.

I baked an apple pie and fed an orphan calf.

Doug had been to the hills and brought me back a little pan of buttercups. He reported that the horse and mule "Maud" had made it through the winter in good shape.

March 10—The ground is frozen again and it appears to be snowing over the mountains. Potato crew busy, still sorting at the cellars.

Ken a-horseback, sorting out cows and baby calves to be put into another pasture. The calves are so healthy this year.

March 11—Spend the day "Sourdough Shutterbugging." Juggled a schedule that included baking sourdough bread and rolls for 30 people, working in the darkroom, typing out my weekly column, cooking for the ranch crew and answering the phone.

By some miracle, I got all the aforementioned accomplished in time to attend a gathering of Wallowa County Artists who got together for a potluck to plan another Art Festival in April. As a result, I got the job of baking sourdough bread for 400 people.

Imnaha cowboy Bill Matthews pauses along the road while trailing cattle from the Benson Ranch to another canyon pasture near Basin Creek.

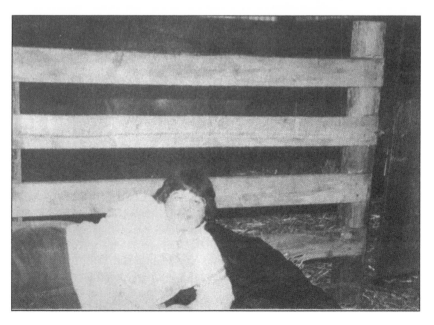

Sourdough Shutterbug member Becky Kunz, of Joseph, takes a break at a campout on the Benson Ranch. The mare in the stall behind Becky recently jumped the corral fence and foaled high up on a canyon rim.

Woke up to a fresh snowfall, still snowing. Just when we were used to a bare, brown landscape. Melted by afternoon, then more squalls. Typical March in Wallowa County. Baby calves are sprouting like mushrooms in the lower pasture.

Roast chicken and raspberry cobbler for supper tonight.

March 13—Listening to our local KWVR radio this morning, a taped phone call from Molly Murrill and Carolee Perkins in far-away New York.

After accepting the national award for the radio program "Women of Achievement in the Wallowa Country," KWVR's Molly broke down and cried.

Me too. As one of the women of achievement, I stood in my country kitchen, filled with emotion. Molly had accepted the award on behalf of all the 7,500 inhabitants of the Wallowa Country. At this point they had received a standing ovation from the prestigious dignitaries at the Waldorf Astoria in New York.

In a letter submitted by Lee Perkins, owner of KWVR, prior to the competition, he had described Wallowa County as comprised of some 7,500 human beings, 30,000 elk, 67,000 deer, uncountable coyotes, an overwhelming population of rock chucks and other varied wildlife that are unfortunately never counted in an Arbitron that rates listening audiences of TV and radio stations. Am sure all of us in the county felt a great sense of pride in our unique citizens. And to think of receiving recognition at the Waldorf Astoria! Even Phil Donahue knows about Wallowa County now.

Fed a newborn calf, which had experienced difficulty coming into the world, some thawed-out colostrum milk. This calf's legs are crippled somehow and the little fellow can't stand up. Such a big calf, too. Doug hopes to make a sling for him.

CowBelle meeting at noon today, held at Pam's Pastries in Joseph.

Home to feed the crippled calf and the other "mama cows" in the maternity ward.

Left-overs for supper and then off to a show for our advanced photography class. Master photographer Walt Klages, a Wallowa County resident, was our judge.

March 14—Up early to fix breakfast. The elder Matthews family returning from a week visiting on the Imnaha, stopped by on their way home to Roseburg. Grandchildren Mona Lee and Buck are very fortunate. They can boast more grand and great-grandparents than any children I know.

It breaks my heart to watch the crippled calf try to stand.

Liquid notes of blackbirds float down from the ancient willow trees. My primroses bloom profusely, not minding frosty mornings. I can feel and sense the earth awakening in so many ways. A pair of robins are busy building a nest in the gnarled old apple tree. Went for a walk down Tenderfoot Valley Road, noticed a field full of returning robins near Locke's Ranch.

Still waiting for the seed potato contracts. Normally we are shipping our good seed by now. Agriculture continues to have so many problems.

The crippled calf stood up on his own tonight, just after I had finished sewing him a sling.

March 15—A cold wind blows over a frozen landscape. Fed another newborn calf a bottle this morning. Attended a 4-H meeting at Cloverleaf Hall, missing the brunch that preceded the Centennial Home Tour. Was able to join the tour later at the Bane home in Enterprise. This 1920 house has the original red fir beams and window casings still intact. The front door is a beautiful oak and beveled glass work of art.

Next, we visited the Gile home high up on Alder Slope in the timber. This log home was built from Tamarack trees that grew on the property. A portable sawmill had been set up for the purpose of building the 2,700 square-foot, two-story log house.

This do-it-yourself project is only five years old but already has an interesting history. Large windows afford a view of the valley, the Wallowas and the Seven Devils in Idaho.

The owners brought a large oak ox yoke with them when they moved from Illinois. This yoke was from a farmer who used to haul his grain by ox cart to the Chicago market, a three-day trip, and it now hangs from the ceiling as a light fixture.

Next we visited a three-story barn, built in the late 1800s by a Mr. Roup. Most of the original barn is still intact, including the trolley in the loft. Where horse stalls once stood, a living and dining area now occupies the space. The former grain room is now the kitchen. The home is decorated in a country decor and the Purcells have enjoyed fixing up the barn.

Sis-in-law Barbara, Cousin Donna, and friend Marge and I had such a good time on the tour. Afterward, we stopped for tea and pie at Tony's in Joseph. We laughed until our sides ached at Barbara's tales.

Driving home by the calving pasture, I noticed four newly born, wet calves, standing wobbly legged for mammas to lick them off.

As I fed the crippled calf, Ben was busy pulling another calf from a first-calf heifer in the chute at the calving shed. It soon came into the world with a "swoosh" and slid to the barn floor.

March 16—Snowing, this morning our weather is "Marching." Typical for this time of year. The newly born calves must be hardy little fellows. Doug is doing the feeding today.

My wood cookstove pops merrily and warms the kitchen and front rooms. It is such fun to cook breakfast every morning on this faithful, old Monarch range that originally came up the Snake River by boat to Dug Bar.

The little orphan calf able to stand on her own now. She is such a big calf that I feed her a bottle three times a day!

I prepared a huge fresh fruit platter to take to the "Women of Achievement" reception at the Wallowa Valley Mall this afternoon. CowBelles provided the food for the affair. Molly Murrill and Carolee Perkins have returned from New York, where they attended the awards luncheon at the Waldorf Astoria for the winning Women in TV and Radio series that won a national award. It literally put the 7,500 inhabitants of Wallowa County on the map.

I enjoyed visiting other women of achievement. There are many more such women in Wallowa County who would qualify for the honor, I'm sure.

I left the reception early, so as to attend the annual Alder Slope Pipeline meeting. I always attend this meeting and look forward to visiting my Alder Slope neighbors. It is a once-a-year get-together of members of the ditch company. We elect officers and discuss the business of the pipeline, such as assessments, repairs and the like. The Pipeline Association's history goes way back and people like Wilmer Cook have been on the ditch for years.

Besides the Cooks, Guy and Reatha McCormack's roots go back to the Slope's early history. Guy McCormack's grandfather, William McCormack, was one of the first white men to build a cabin and spend the winter in the Wallowa Valley. He built a cabin on Scotch Creek near Hurricane Creek and Alder Slope areas.

After the meeting, home to feed the hungry baby calf and gather a basket of brown eggs from the hen house.

March 17—I got pinched first thing by my husband for not wearing green. Counted nearly 100 robins from my kitchen window.

Scattered snow showers all day.

Had fun juggling this morning. Made a lemon meringue pie from scratch, wrote in my journal, put together a slide show program for our history group. Doug had another orphan, so am thawing out colostrum milk to feed him. Fixed lunch for son Ken, as he is here working with the cattle today.

Another orphan, too chilled and small, died. Skinned the calf and Ken put the hide on my orphan heifer. Mother didn't like the idea; broke down the gate and fled down the road. Doug and I ran her into the pasture while my supper was held up until almost 8 p.m.

Doug off to a stockgrowers' meeting. I typed out some articles and crashed; just another typical "spring" day on the ranch.

March 18—A heavy frost lays over Prairie Creek this morning.

Ben drove the errant cow back in with the calf. She has decided this might be her calf...the hide anyway. After the calf got a taste of adopted mom's warm milk, she, too, decided the arrangement was OK.

Neighbor Steve Allison here early to use my darkroom. I instructed him on making proof sheets from negatives he has stored for 40 years! Film he exposed while in the service years ago.

Baked two loaves of sourdough bread and fixed lunch for the cowboys who are sorting and weaning our fall calving cows and calves in preparation for a cattle drive to the hills tomorrow.

Daughter Jackie here briefly to visit...her day in town. Gathering up some potato display material for our CowBelles' Ag Day project on Thursday. Also working on a program for our history group that night.

Attended a Centennial Committee meeting at Chandler's in Joseph. Our history group is hoping to put together a slide-tape program for our contribution to Wallowa County's 1987 centennial year celebration. It is a fun project, but one that will require lots of research and work.

Over to the Joseph School just in time to watch grandson Chad win his wrestling match.

Home to fix supper, gather eggs and catch up on household duties. Our front room is full of 4-H'ers' sleeping bags brought up by daughter Jackie from Imnaha (from our recent campout on the river). We didn't have room to bring them and the 4-H'ers out that day. To bed early, as must arise before dawn to get ready to trail the mamma cows to the hills tomorrow.

March 19—Muffled sounds of bawling had seeped into our bedroom. As I step outside this morning, the din is a solid wall of sound.

Ben, Ken and I saddle our horses and begin to drive the cows away from their calves, not an easy task; they keep running back toward their babies. We just about yelled ourselves hoarse, and succeeded, after a fashion, in heading the cows in the direction of the hills.

Bud, who is Wallowa County's "hardware cowboy," was good help. In addition to owning Bud's Hardware in Joseph, he is a top hand, always willing to help ranchers with moving cattle or on branding day.

We made it to the Dorrance place by 2 p.m. Ken had gone back to the ranch and hauled out a load of hay that he had scattered in the corral before our arrival. Unsaddled my mare and left her in a corral.

Was I sore! Soft after the winter, plus I had gotten thrown from my horse when she shied from a dead carcass along the road. Hadn't been prepared for such quick action and simply slipped off. My faithful mare waited patiently for me to gather up my composure and mount up again.

Daisy calved in our absence. A nice bull calf.

To bed at 7:30 for this cowgirl, after fixing dinner. Am 18 miles of saddle sore tonight.

March 20—Frost still lay in the meadows and draws as we drove out Crow Creek to our corraled cattle.

Caught my mare, saddled her up and carefully mounted up. OUCH!

The cows had ceased their bawling, and began running up Dorrance Gulch. Guess they could envision by now the hill land bunch grass.

I had noted in my 1985 journal entry, that it had been April 16 when we trailed these same cows to the hills last year. The grass is already good and there is considerable old grass left over. The snow banks are gone. Such a different year.

I rode behind the cows, bringing up a few footsore tail-enders. Doug went on ahead to repair more elk-damaged fences. Ben and Ken were still busy feeding cattle back at the valley ranch. I was alone with the herd. Beautiful day, enjoying the ride.

Ben and Ken showed up after the cattle had topped the grade. They drove onto the Johnson pasture, where they unloaded their saddle horses and would be ready to separate the herd: 40 head, three different pastures.

The lead was strung out ahead, so the men had two bunches counted out by the time I arrived with the stragglers. Ken took one bunch to the Red Barn pasture. Ben rode the fence at the Johnson pasture and I took my cows to Butte Creek.

Still sore, so got off and led my mare for quite a ways. Just as I approached the gate to the Butte Creek pasture, who should be driving out of our property but the Editor Emeritus of the Wallowa County Chieftain, Gwen Coffin.

"Did all right, didn't we?" this cow pony might be asking, near the end of a 30-mile drive to the spring bunch grass range on Butte Creek.

He opened the gate for me while I drove the cows in. We visited briefly and he said he had been trying to spot some game. After he left, I began the long ride back to the truck.

Doug appeared shortly and pointed out 200 head of elk across from where we were riding. The editor hadn't even seen them.

By the time I arrived at the Johnson corrals I had ridden over 30 miles in two days. It was beginning to tell on grandma. One more day, says Doug, and I would be in shape!

The fresh air was a tonic to my soul, however, and it was filled with birdsong. A pretty pair of bluebirds made my day.

Home to take potato pamphlets into the Wallowa Valley Mall where our busy CowBelles had set up a display for Ag Day. Then back to the ranch to let Daisy's calf in to nurse. The orphan unable to get up at all. Fed him some milk from the kitty dish.

Attended our history group meeting tonight, as I was in charge of the program. Showed slides of our last year's trip to the Maxwell, Grossman areas.

Son Ken and his family had picked up our motor home this afternoon. They will take it to Utah to attend a funeral…a death in daughter-in-law Annie's family.

March 21—Up early again, out to the barn to let Daisy's calf in to nurse. The orphan worsening. Poor little thing, he had more problems than we first realized.

Picked up Becky Hostetter in Enterprise, and we headed for Imbler and the Oregon Beef Pre-Cook-Off, a CowBelle- and Beef Council-sponsored affair. The five finalists selected here today will compete in the state cook-off in Portland.

The Imbler High School home economics room was a buzz of activity as the Union County CowBelles prepared various recipes. We could smell the wonderful aromas as we got out of our car in the parking lot.

Becky, who is a correspondent for the La Grande Observer, and I had eaten a skimpy breakfast, because we knew we would be allowed to sample the dishes at the cookoff. So by the time we got to taste the dishes, we were starved.

At last we were invited to sample the delicious recipes.

On the drive home, we spotted a quaint old home in Elgin. Like two kids out of school, Becky and I had to stop to photograph it.

Back to Wallowa County to fix supper and do chores.

Todd and Liza drive in from Corvallis, here to spend a week during spring break. Liza handed me a beautiful bouquet of daffodils. She had picked them from their yard in Corvallis. I put them in an antique fruit jar and placed them on the kitchen table. Fixed a nice supper of ham, fruit salad, asparagus and sourdough bread.

To bed early for all of us.

March 22—Gorgeous morning... frosty, 32 degrees. Fixed sourdough hot cakes, bacon and eggs on the wood cookstove. Liza and Todd did the actual cooking; enjoying the good ranch breakfast, especially the freezer raspberry jam and fresh eggs.

Doug did away with the orphan this morning. It was the only sensible thing to do; now she won't suffer anymore.

Baby calves are running around in the sunshine in the lower pasture. They are healthy and so far no scours have appeared.

Todd and Liza off to Imnaha to visit Jackie and family. Liza has yet to meet all of our large family. Doug left for Imnaha, too, steelhead fishing. I stayed home to hold down the fort and get caught up after three days of cattle drivin' and CowBelle'in.

Developed film, hung four loads of wash on the line, baked a peach cobbler, using some of our frozen Imnaha peaches. Cleaned house and enjoyed being a homemaker. House all to myself.

The days noticeably longer now, able to accomplish more. Prepared a fried chicken dinner for Todd and Liza, just back from Imnaha.

Fun, watching these two young marrieds, as they looked through family scrapbooks as Todd introduced Liza to our "extended family" via photographs.

March 23—Milked Daisy, keeping a gallon for house use.

The barn cat population has reduced itself to one very pregnant female, who shows up regularly for milk.

Doug built a hot bed, complete with glass door. He has placed it near the south side of our house and planted it to radishes and Walla Walla onions.

Liza and Todd up to the Slope house, which will be their future home.

March 24—After milking Daisy, spent the morning instructing daughter-in-law in the art of making pies and baking sourdough bread. What a fun time we had. Liza's raspberry pie and golden loaf of sourdough bread attested to the fact that she is already a good cook.

Typical March weather. Snowing one minute, sunshine the next.

More baby calves born this morning.

Liza and Todd at the Slope place, working in the yard.

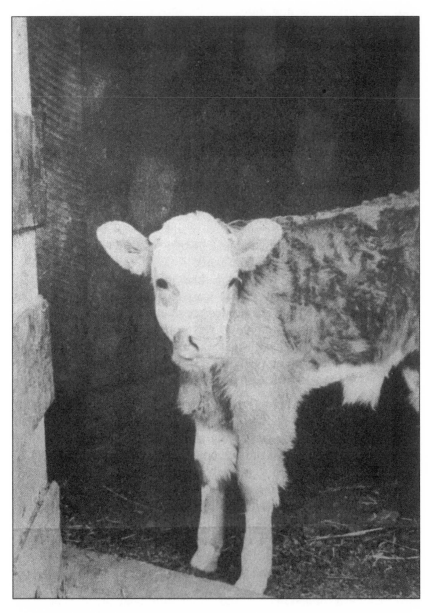

*Waiting for his breakfast, Daisy's half-Simmental bull calf peers around
the corner of the barn. This calf must share Daisy with an adopted orphan.*

Gave Liza her first cow milking lesson tonight. She practiced on Daisy. She is hoping for a Jersey milk cow when they move back to Wallowa County.

It is fun having the young people around again. Son Steve showed up late tonight from college. We were beginning to wonder if he'd be home for spring break. Mixed up the sourdough for one more mouth in the morning.

March 25—Up at 5:30 to fix breakfast. Added some frozen huckleberries to the sourdough hotcakes. Yummmmmmm!

Judith here to help me clean up the yard and wash windows. Liza and Todd up to son Ken's place to check on their animals while they are gone to Utah. One of their sows has five little pigs.

The young couple arrived home later, armed with two small "Easter bunnies" from the Proctors (an Easter surprise for Mona and Buck).

Attended a centennial meeting in Joseph, voted, and then grocery shopped in Enterprise.

The bunnies happily munch rabbit pellets in a cage on our back porch.

Doug left for Hermiston, to be there when our feedlot calves are shipped.

Everyone gone. Let Daisy's calf in to nurse, then milked her out for the dogs and the one pregnant cat.

Set a loaf of sourdough bread to rise, gathered eggs, checked the calving heifers and fixed an elk steak supper for whoever arrives by mealtime.

Todd and Liza back from the hills, where they reported seeing 80 head of elk, a few deer and one coyote.

March 26—Liza tending to the bunnies. I milked the cow at 6:30, then in to fix breakfast. Liza lined my laying hen's nest with clean straw this morning. Did four loads of son Steve's wash. Hung them on the line, as it was such a nice day.

Two of our hired men have the flu, which is making the rounds.

Todd and Liza are staging a "lasagne marathon" in my kitchen. I have strict orders to stay out. They are making enough for an army.

Came in from choring to find them laughing hysterically over quantities of sauce, noodles and shredded cheese. They filled every pan I had in the kitchen with lasagne. One pan went in the freezer and two will go to Imnaha tomorrow. Steve and I enjoyed the last small dish for our supper.

A new "kitty" has appeared at the barn, a black and white, striped affair. It drinks milk from the cat's dish, then leaves, trailing a musky odor. I glimpsed the intruder this morning, as its tail disappeared under the box stall. "Mr. Skunk" is free-loading on Daisy's milk!

Doug home late from Hermiston. The yearlings have been safely shipped to McGregor's Feedlot in Washington.

March 27—What a day! Doris, Becky Hostetter and I spent most of it "creating" two 16x20 black and white prints in my darkroom. Under the supervision of our instructor, Doris, it was quite an undertaking. Tonight, I am physically and emotionally drained.

After letting my two calves in to nurse Daisy, I was presented another rejected calf, so out to feed him a bottle.

Todd and Liza fled to Imnaha, armed with hard boiled eggs to color, sourdough bread, the two Easter bunnies and the two pans of lasagne.

Meanwhile we three camera freaks had spent until 5 in the darkroom. Doris and Becky left for home, leaving me with the clean up. The time spent was worth the effort, as Becky and I emerged with some pretty impressive prints, due in no small part to Doris.

March 28—Baked an angel food cake for daughter-in-law Liza's birthday today. Planned a nice dinner and invited friends over for tonight.

Liza and Todd up to the Slope house. It will be nice to have them living there soon.

Spent most of the day cooking…roast chicken, sourdough bread, creamed new potatoes and peas, home canned pickled beets and the birthday cake to be served with strawberries and cream. Doris will bring one of her good salads. It is wonderful to have Daisy's cream to make the cream sauce for the potatoes and peas and also for the whipped cream.

The men are either burning the old grass in the barrow pits or harrowing our fields today.

We enjoyed a great birthday dinner for Liza.

March 29—Up at the crack of dawn on this lovely spring day. Baked a raspberry pie and had it out of the oven before the sun was up. Fixed breakfast, milked the cow, packed a lunch and left with Grace Bartlett for the Tully Creek Ranch in Canyon country.

Todd and Liza left to visit Liza's mom for Easter Sunday in Vancouver, Washington, so off Grace and I went, she driving her four-wheel-drive station wagon. Grace at 75 is younger at heart and looks than many of her younger counterparts. She's a writer, historian and in charge of the Wallowa County Museum in Joseph. As we drove to Imnaha River, gardeners were out working the earth, readying it for planting.

The Imnaha is famous for its wonderful gardens. The Imnaha was running swiftly, with white, frothy snow melt tumbling by.

As we drove downriver, met son-in-law Bill on horseback, driving a herd of cows and calves to Basin Creek. Mona Lee and Buck ran up to meet us as we stopped to visit their daddy. They are just recovering from a bad flu bug.

We continued down past Fence Creek, then up the narrow, steep, winding dirt road that would literally follow the rims to our destination. We so enjoyed the sweeping view of canyon after canyon rolling off into the distance. The Imnaha River wound around below us like a twisted blue ribbon. Many pink varieties of wildflowers began to appear, as well as the bright splash of yellow balsamroot.

We passed Kettle, Little Basin and Packsaddle Creeks, then wound down a twisting, switchback stretch of road to Horse Creek Ranch.

We drove by the two Stubblefield graves encircled by a fence, then on down to the Corral Creek Ranch. Finally, we arrived at the Cow Creek Bridge.

We opened a gate and drove up a steep, rough, rock-strewn road that appeared to have been recently bladed. Earlier we had happened upon Sam Loftus and his granddaughter on horseback near Corral Creek. Sam had informed us that the road was passable from Cow Creek to the Tully Creek Ranch. but we would have to watch for a spring seepage, boggy area and go to the left. This we did and made it to the ranch without mishap.

We had intended to drive up Corral Creek, but recent heavy rainstorms had washed out the road there. This was the only access (by vehicle) to this remote ranch.

We came over a hill and there it was. Originally it was an early-day homestead nestled in a draw. The gurgling sounds of Tully Creek, some raucous crows, a sagging, creaking gate, swinging on a corral fence in the breeze, were the only sounds; otherwise absolute stillness... wonderful.

We were nearly 30 miles from the town of Imnaha, on the lower reaches of the Canyon country. Tully Creek Ranch (now deserted) commands an awesome view of towering rimrocks, unusual rock formations and bunchgrass-covered benches.

The old, original homestead had hand-hewn shakes on the roof. Hand-crafted rock in the fireplace chimney... an old screen porch, weathered wooden siding, a yard, withering daffodils.

The falling-down yard fence and screened porch entrance to the historic Tully Creek ranch house, site of an early day homestead. Situated under towering rimrock country, it is still used for a cow camp in Wallowa County.

The yard fence falling down and the outhouse, minus the front door, stood brazenly out in the sunshine. Pack rats nibbled, chewed and scurried around upstairs. Their holes appearing everywhere.

Daughter Jackie, her husband Bill, and their children lived here for a while while Bill was employed at the Corral Creek Ranch. Little Mona Lee was born during that time. What a remote place to bring a baby.

Grace and I ate our lunches in the shade of the screened porch and enjoyed the sweeping views in all directions. This place is so full of early Wallowa County history!

I drove back, so Grace could enjoy the views of deep gorges and chasms. Canyon drivers must pay attention, one mistake and you could end up over a steep embankment.

Before there was ever a road built from Cow Creek to Dug Bar, teams of horses and packstrings of mules freighted material into remote canyon ranches. What a time to have been alive! Now we can only reconstruct in our mind's eye the way it must have been. Being here today has helped us understand a little more of how the land lays.

The remains of an old flume can be seen. The flume was connected to an old ditch that a fellow had tried to bring water around to irrigate a small section of river bottom. Such an ambitious project! Canyon people must have been an independent, tough breed to survive in that rugged country. Nowhere is our present "time of change" so obvious as it is on our Imnaha ranches.

As it became increasingly difficult to operate these old, established ranches, we see a wave of new owners. Some manage to hang in there, while others are forced to leave. The Corral Creek Ranch is a prime example. A succession of owners, all with ambitious plans, have given time, money, and energy to realize their dreams.

Horrendous purchase prices, high interest rates and low cattle prices have forced many to sell. It breaks my heart to see these outstanding cattle operations broken up...and divided. This once proud Corral Creek Ranch consisted of the main headquarters at Corral Creek, the place at Horse Creek, the Tully Creek Ranch and Cow Creek.

These winter ranges provided the cattle milder weather to winter on and calve in the spring. The cattle were trailed up the old trails "On Top" in time to utilize the higher country grass at the Steen Ranch. Canyon cowboys performed the rides in the fall and spring. There are still cowboys left, but the old-timers are dwindling.

One such cowboy, Sam Loftus, remembers these ranches as they were in their heyday. Sam perhaps knows the country about as well as anyone (from the back of a cow pony, that is).

I recall, with nostalgia, the way these ranches were just a short time ago in the '60s.

A lump comes to my throat when I think of my husband's ranch on the Snake River. I think of the work that went into the Dug Bar Ranch, and what a great cattle setup it was. It is now a part of the National Recreation Area.

Hopefully, cattle will always be a part of this area...after all, it is livestock country, with wonderful grass that provided forage for hundreds of cattle and sheep, as well as a way of life that is fast becoming a way of the past.

We made it home by 5 and I did chores. Steve had departed for college. Just us two chickens here tonight. Quiet.

What a perfect day Grace and I have had.

March 30—Nursed three calves on Daisy, washed clothes, dug horseradish and ground it (outside to avoid the tears).

Colder air moving in. Plans for an Imnaha picnic fading fast.

We did drive to Imnaha. The fresh, warm rain is turning the canyons to technicolor. Blossoms everywhere. One neat little lawn in the small settlement of Imnaha had a carpet of purple violets.

The children ecstatic over the chocolate bunnies, and the live bunnies are running around the yard.

Rather than a picnic, we spent a pleasant afternoon visiting A.L. Duckett and Jim Dorrance at the Riverside Cafe. Listening to these two relate past Wallowa County history was a special treat that will be a treasured memory for years to come.

What an inspiration these two fine old gentlemen are to our county. They have survived hard times, emerging richer for it. Perhaps we need to listen to A.L. and Jim's philosophy a little closer these days. Maybe a dose of this old-fashioned thinking could be our salvation.

As we drove down Sheep Creek Hill, a burst of golden light swept over the valley. A nice ending to a perfect Easter Sunday.

March 31—As March leaves us here on Prairie Creek, the thermometer registers 20 degrees this morning.

We are shipping our first semi-load of seed potatoes. Hurrah! They will go out of the county and into Washington State. We were becoming a bit nervous, waiting on growers' contracts, who, in turn, had waited on bankers and processors. Hopefully, our top quality seed, stored all winter, will now start to move.

Arose early, cooked breakfast on the wood stove, did chores, dark-room work, then to potato cellar to help sort potatoes prior to loading a semi.

After driving into the cellar, I found that there was plenty of crew, so didn't have to work after all.

Guess Doug had tried to head me off, but made the wrong connections. So, I went home, got out of my dirty overalls and continued my domestic chores instead.

April 1—Ken and Ben working the weaned fall calves at the chutes. Buck walked down to "help." About an hour later this five-year-old grandson appeared at the kitchen doorway holding a pan overflowing with "mountain oysters." Blood all over his coat, his little hands covered with dirt and blood. By the looks of the oysters they had spilled onto the ground several times.

Mona Lee and I baked a pineapple upside down cake in a cast iron skillet and fixed a hot dinner for the menfolk. Doug to the hills to check fences. We are loading another semi of potatoes today.

Ben and Ken hauling bulls to the hills this afternoon.

Jackie doing her once-a-month shopping, will spend the night here before heading back to the canyons.

I read to the children. They took long naps. Snow predicted here in the valley tonight. Poked wood in the wood stove all day.

The children "helped" me chore this evening. They are wondering when mamma kitty will produce kittens from her greatly swollen belly. She can barely get around these days.

April 2—Sourdough waffles for breakfast, a request from Mona Lee. Jackie's family left for Imnaha.

Shipping more seed spuds today.

Did my grocery shopping, loading up on staples.

We had mountain oysters for supper and fresh sourdough bread.

Went into Bud's Hardware in Joseph today to purchase my fishing license. I not only got my license, but free advice on what to do in the event I actually caught a steelhead.

The fellow who offered the information, said I should tie the steelhead up for three days, this would cause all the oil to go out. He says you can simply tether the fish to the boat. Not a semblance of a smile crossed this customer's face, nor did the proprietor of that hardware store disagree.

However, me-thinks I've been duped. All doubt of this was removed when I related the free advice to my husband, who broke into hysterical laughter.

Bud's Hardware is famous for its small-town country atmosphere, its great line of items, ranging from fishing tackle to nuts and bolts.

One should take the free advice with a grain of salt. And whoever heard of halter-breaking a fish!

April 3—My mama kitty was nervous last evening; while I chored she kept jumping into Daisy's feed box! This morning she had given birth to seven kittens, right there in the manger. So I had to switch Daisy to the other stanchion.

Mamma kitty was obviously contented in her maternity ward. She simply looked proudly up at me and purred with contentment. She lapped up a bowl of Daisy's warm milk and once more settled in around her brood. The three calves nursed happily on Daisy, tails a-wagging. May is due to calve any day now; she will be followed by Star, my faithful, old Holstein. Since Doug sold Liza last winter, I am reduced to three milk cows this spring.

Made some fresh butter from Daisy's cream. The blender works great for small batches. Utilized some sour cream to bake sour cream raisin pie bars. Nice to have the whole milk to cook with again.

Robins are building nests everywhere. One pair of birds is building one behind the tail light of one of our stock trucks.

Ben fixing fence and harrowing the fields. The radishes are up in Doug's new little hot box beside the house.

April 4—Fixed sourdough hotcakes, milked the cow, tended chickens, drove up to Gorsline's where I was supposed to give Doug a ride home, as he is doing some plowing for Max.

Visited briefly with Norma Hope, who has been getting up nights to check her calving cows. She said she has 20 calves so far.

Drove to Enterprise, photographed Claire Casey, and her riding mule for an article. Also Dennis Brennan shoeing horses while at the fairgrounds. Then out to Creighton Kooch's to photograph Wallowa County's newest attractions, two Clydesdale foals.

Next stop, Bornsteds, to photograph our local veterinarian, who is also a cowboy poet, composer of local ballads, guitar player and a singer. We also did the picture out among his longhorn cows and calves. One cow, protective of her calf, made me keep my distance from those long horns. A pygmy goat ran out and joined the menagerie, which included a welcoming committee of dogs.

Took one of my black and white photographs to Futuristic Photography to be framed for the Art Festival. Home just in time to help May deliver a big bull calf that otherwise would have been born in the ditch.

Mama Kitty curls around her just-born brood of kittens in Daisy's manger.

This peaceful, pastoral scene is on the ranch owned by Norma Hope on upper Prairie Creek. Norma was born on the Imnaha and continues to raise cattle and operate her ranch, with the help of a neighbor. Although getting along in years, Norma still gets up at night to check her calving cows.

May cleans her newborn calf. The photographer came along just in time to keep the bull calf from being born in an irrigation ditch.

Baked sourdough bread. Attended a Grain Growers annual meeting and dinner with Doug at Cloverleaf Hall in Enterprise. The meeting was depressing, as is all farm news these days. Arleigh Isley, our extension agent, says this is the "pivotal year" for agriculture.

Doug and I doctored a sick calf after we got home from the meeting.

April 5—Up early to start the day. Baked two loaves of sourdough bread and let Daisy's calves into nurse, then May's. Called Grace Bartlett, packed a lunch, drove into Enterprise to trade the two loaves of bread for hazelnuts, raisins and apples at Frank McCorkle's produce stand.

Grace and I, in her four-wheel drive jeep, drove to the Downey Lakes area. We visited old homesteads and early historical places. The buttercups were everywhere, as were bluebirds and many deer.

Presently we came to the old Downey cabin, which stood near the shores of Downey Lake. The lake consisted of a water-filled, marshy area, filled with high, rank grasses. It contained many unusual water birds and some wild mallards. There were snowbanks nearby, the air fresh and pure, and the Seven Devils Mountain range brilliantly illumined by sunshine.

We never saw another soul on this Saturday. Billowy clouds floated above in an incredible, blue sky as we ate our lunches near the lake. We continued to happily bounce along in Grace's faithful Jeep to more interesting places before turning around for home.

Home to chores. Bill, Jackie and the children stopped by for a visit. The grandchildren immediately ran out to investigate the new kittens.

Meanwhile, here on the ranch, projects of increasing numbers loom around the corner. Grace and I spent a precious day really living. Residing here in our county has many advantages, one of which is the accessibility of such places as we visited today.

April 6—Up at daylight. Breakfast, milk cows, feed calves, pack a lunch and on this Sunday Grace and I will take 87-year-old Opal Tippett (Doug's aunt) out to visit her old home on Pine Creek. Opal expressed the desire to revisit her home where she and her late husband, Charley, raised a family, farmed and lived for 50 years.

This spot, situated way out in Wallowa County's Chesnimnus country, is where Opal reared her seven children. On the way out she related to us how one time she went for 19 months before coming to town!

We drove down Crow Creek past Birkmaier's and turned up Chesnimnus Creek. As we traveled this narrow road, Opal pointed out old homesteads along the way. We passed the Lewis School. It has since been moved from its original site further up the creek. Also the Hinton Homestead, where Effie and Sylvester Tippett lived. She showed us Tippett Flat, where her husband, Charley had been born.

Presently, we came to a dirt road that crossed Chesnimnus Creek. We could see that a nearby bridge had washed out and that the high water, caused by the snowmelt and spring run-off would make it impossible to ford the stream on this day.

Disappointed, we turned around and headed back up a draw toward Butte Creek where we met Jeannie Lathrop of the B. and H. Cattle Company, who let us follow her into a field where she was picking up an animal in a corral and putting out salt.

We drove as far as we dared, going around boggy areas, to a point that was still a hill and a draw away from Opal's house.

While Grace and Opal stretched their legs and enjoyed the wildflowers, I hiked to within a quarter of a mile of the buildings. What a peaceful spot; I could see why Opal wanted to revisit it.

On the way home Opal continued to relate incidents of her life on Pine Creek. We ate our lunch under the shade of a ponderosa pine tree, near Butte Creek. Opal told how she used to accompany her husband on horseback to cook for crews of cowboys in the canyons of the Snake River. She also cooked for the sheep camps.

After leaving Grace and Opal, I made it to my appointment to photograph the 1986 Chief Joseph Days court in Joseph.

Doug fed the cattle today, as the hired man isn't here. Did my chores, fixed supper and crashed. Another day well spent.

April 7—Another warm day, not a cloud in the sky. My two cows, Daisy and May, are bawling at the barn door ready to be milked and let in so their four calves can nurse.

Sourdough hot cakes on the wood stove. So much writing and darkroom work to do today, not to mention the ever-present ranch work. The days just aren't long enough to accomplish all I want to do.

Rolled up my sleeves to milk Daisy and do the chores. May's big half-Simmental bull calf is really something. May herself is Guernsey with a bit of Jersey thrown in. Her black nose belies her Jersey lineage.

Loading and shipping seed potatoes at the cellar today. Our seed sales are lagging due to last year's glut on the market, coupled with "signs of the times" factors beyond our control. The cattle market continues downward. So much of what is happening is beyond the ranchers' control, very frustrating. When will it end?

A happy note: the daffodils and crocuses are blooming. The primroses have been a show of color for weeks. I actually had to water plants along the house today. Everything is so dry. We need rain.

Doug to the auction in Enterprise.

Baked sourdough bread and made an apricot cobbler in between the darkroom and typewriter.

On this night I stepped outside to see all the twinkling stars as they glimmered in a cloudless sky. I noticed an especially bright star on the western horizon. It gleamed with red, green and yellow lights. What caused this phenomenon, I do not know, but it was startling. Maybe atmospheric dust. I won't try to analyze it, just enjoy.

April 8—Had a confrontation with "Mamma Kitty" at the barn this morning. "You simply must move your kittens," says I, explaining to her that I need both stanchion spaces so the two milk cows can come into the barn at once!

I proceeded to then move her family, lock, stock and cardboard box, to an adjacent horse stall. After milking a dish of warm milk for her, she happily settled into her new quarters.

By chore time this evening we will know if this arrangement is permanent. Daisy and May were then locked into the only two stanchions

I have in this limited milking parlor and the four calves began nursing happily. My chore time is shortened considerably.

Doug turned the water on under the trailer and after a long winter of packing buckets of water to my chicken pen, I now have running water from a hose. Pure luxury!

We are finding a few buyers for our seed potatoes, but we are having to take a considerable cut in price. A real blow to our operation. Better than going to cow feed, which would be the next alternative.

Many of our fellow ranchers are in serious financial difficulty these days. Wonderful, hard-working people, caught in a squeeze that is not of their making. Our world is changing so fast.

Competition is fierce. Record-keeping essential. Knowing where you are at all times becomes an absolute necessity. The paper work is staggering, leaving little time to do the actual ranch work. Government restrictions and intervention at every turn. 1986 will be a year of challenge for all of us engaged in "feeding the world."

April 9—Cloudy, a few sprinkles of rain, didn't amount to much.

Our neighbors, the Lockes, are farming. Dust clouds boil up from their field. Many farmers beginning to work their ground, seems early, but the ground appears ready.

Tended to the two Guernsey cows and four calves. Fed and watered the chickens. Baby kittens and mamma kitty content in the horse manger, kittens as fat as butterballs due to their mom's daily ration of fresh milk.

Two semis to load at the cellar. It will be a long day for the crew.

Put a chicken to roast in the dutch oven. Around 4:30, sat down for the first time all day.

Granddaughter Mona Lee called to say that their surviving Easter bunny had "ranned away."

"Or else the coyotes ate him up," she said.

Spent the evening trying to get organized for the career job fair at Enterprise High School tomorrow. I am to put up a booth in the cottage industry section and represent freelance photo-journalism.

I must offer the advice that to manage such a cottage industry, one needs unlimited energy and stamina, especially when one is a rancher's wife, grandmother and 4-H leader, to mention only a few other roles.

The phone rang all day. I directed truck drivers to our cellars and answered myriad questions associated with running a ranch. The spring rush is on.

April 10—Gathered up material and visual aids to take to the high school career fair.

At noon, I lugged all my stuff to the car, then met some CowBelles at Safeway parking lot where we carpooled to Marilyn Johnson's in Wallowa for our monthly CowBelle meeting. Marilyn's flowers were blooming and their ranch looked so nice. Guess most CowBelles were busy, as attendance was down.

April 11—Cold this morning, ice had formed in the hose and when I watered the chickens, little pieces of it sputtered out onto the ground. Cloudy and windy.

Took granddaughter Chelsie to lunch at the Country Place today, a promised, belated birthday present from grandma. She really enjoyed herself, as did I.

When I took her home, she and her two brothers, Chad and Rowdy, showed me one of their sows who had recently delivered a litter of baby pigs. They were all colors and delightfully entertaining. Lucky are the children who can grow up on a ranch and learn to raise livestock. A lesson that lasts all through their lifetimes.

April 12—My mind is still boggled by what we saw today. Arising early, I had baked one of those old-fashioned rice puddings, the kind that bakes three hours in a slow oven. Since I have an abundance of whole milk and fresh eggs, this dessert is a real treat.

After fixing breakfast and tending to my Daisy and May in the barn, I packed a lunch, grabbed my camera and backpack, then headed over to Grace Bartlett's where we met Scotty. It was snowing.

The road to the trail head up Hurricane Creek washed out, so we parked our car below and walked up onto the trail from there. We soon came to the fork in the trail, taking the route to Fall's Creek.

About half way there, we ran into the first avalanche. For as far as we could see up toward the falls, lay this enormous mixture of snow, ice, trees, limbs, pine boughs, splinters of tree trunks, rocks, gravel and packed snow. The falls at the top disappeared into a crevasse, reappearing far below, after it ran underneath the slide area. We walked on top of the packed snow down across Falls Creek. Here we had to detour in order to gain the trail. Hurricane Creek, living up to its name.

Historically, many slides have shaped this area in the past. However, we were not really prepared for what we were about to see.

Continuing up the trail everything appeared normal again. No snow in the trail, and despite the ever-increasing snowfall, the woods were almost dry. In fact we even stirred up dust in the trail! As we climbed up a rather steep part of the Hurricane Creek Trail, we could see that numerous trees had fallen across the creek. Mini-slides were present in every chute on the opposite side of the creek.

We crossed a steep, splashing stream that originated high above before crossing the trail to join Hurricane Creek.

Suddenly, at this point, before us lay a scene of devastation that is beyond any description of my pen.

For as far as we could see, lay fallen timber, big trees and little trees, lying cross-wise and tangled in a maze of splintered trunks.

This enormous slide area, covered with packed snow, broken limbs, rocks and loose dirt, completely obliterated the trail.

At this spot we met Stanlynn Daugherty and friend, who informed us they were also there to survey the damage. She said there had already been talk of clearing the trail (a monstrous undertaking) as 800 fallen trees had been counted in the trail alone, from Falls Creek to Slick Rock!

Decided to take some pictures. As I led the way up through the maze of fallen trees and snow, the snowfall increased and a blizzard enveloped us. Grace, 75, gamely kept up; this woman is in great shape. She was followed by Scotty, 65, who thought I was finally flipping my lid to go through this mess just to take a photograph.

We made it to a good vantage point where Grace and Scotty posed by a tree that had been sheared off at an angle.

Since it was close to noon, we climbed over more downed trees, ice and snow to the safety of "standing" timber. Along the bank of the aforementioned stream, we built a fire next to a rock. We were soon warming our wet selves. We three musketeers enjoyed our meager repast perched along the steep side of a very rushing, cold stream.

Snow continued to fall as we hiked out to the safety of Grace's jeep.

April 13—Spent this day catching up on darkroom work. A new snowfall melted by noon.

Becky and Doris were here and we "collaborated" on printing a picture for the art show. We joke about this lovely black and white print of an old house in Elgin. Becky had snapped the picture with my camera. I developed the film and printed up an 8x10 working copy. Doris enlarged the print to 16x20 on special paper I had here. I had done the dirty work of mixing chemicals, lugging trays up and down stairs to my darkroom, setting up and cleaning up.

Today, Doris Selenium-toned the print, which by now is a work of art. Next step will be to take it to be mounted and framed. The valuable print now reposes in a blotter book here in my bedroom.

Scotty Doyle and Grace Bartlett pose by a sheared off tree in a snow squall. The downed trees in the background covered a large area and resulted from an avalanche in the Wallowa Mountains. Hurricane Creek is in the bottom of this canyon.

Bill and Jackie were here and left the kiddies, so I fell into a chair and read to the children. Fixed a late supper after doing chores. The children's parents returned, picked up the sleepy youngsters and headed to Imnaha. Grandma crashed!

April 14—Judith here to help me get started on baking bread for 400 people for the Art Festival's buffalo dinner. Carol Borgerding of Imnaha will also help by baking some in her kitchen.

Doug off to Pasco to pick up a critical part for our potato loading equipment. Many shipments of seed to get out this week and we can't wait for the mail delivery. Need it now.

Jackie calls from Imnaha to report Todd's mare has finally foaled. The overdue mare had jumped over a corral enclosure and climbed high onto a canyon rim to have her baby.

Ate my supper of beans and ham hocks alone. Doug not back from Pasco until late with the part.

April 15—Winds continue to howl around Prairie Creek; the skies are black and gray. Raspberry canes beginning to leaf out more each day. Need moisture badly. Calves at the barn healthy; got them through a slight bout of scours by "pilling" them.

Judith came over and we had a fun, busy time. Into town to pick up my 75-day-old chicks, which now happily eat and drink under their cozy heat lamp.

We then began another bread-baking session.

Semis loading at the potato cellars today.

A new orphan for me at the barn this evening. This makes five calves on two cows. Star is close to freshening.

Doug and I enjoyed the beans and hamhocks and sourdough bread for supper, then off to an Art Festival planning meeting for me in Enterprise. Picked up Eileen and Donna in Joseph. They have been putting in long hours readying a new art supply shop they hope to open soon.

It began to rain this evening and it poured...hurrah! A gift from heaven, we so needed the moisture to make the grass grow.

April 16—Awoke early to a beautiful sight: clear, blue, rain-washed skies, nary a cloud, sunshine gleaming over a snow covered landscape with green grass poking through! Even on the high slopes of the mountains, the snow had melted off by mid-morning.

From now on, the valley will turn a brilliant green; how we have looked forward to this time of "new beginnings."

Daffodils and primroses are bright this morning, and the tulips just beginning to open.

The baby chicks are peeping happily, growing and eating.

Semis to load at the potato cellars again today. Our crews very busy. Our horses and cattle nibble more and more on grass these days, leaving part of their hay. They have had it with hay, especially now that the grass is beginning to appear.

Baking more bread today.

Attended a meeting in Joseph this afternoon for our Centennial Committee project. Am supposed to write the script for a slide tape presentation our local history group is contributing to the centennial year celebration, a sort of permanent record to be used by the schools and museum for future generations.

Home to start more bread to rise, do chores. Daisy kicked me above the kneecap this evening. She must be coming in heat. I hobbled around while baking cookies to fill the empty cookie jar. Took the last loaf of bread from the oven at 10 p.m.

April 17—Still baking sourdough bread for the Art Festival dinner.

Since I must always bake one for our family too, it makes for lots of baking.

Grocery shopping, visiting friends at the store. It is almost a social occasion in our small community to go to the store. Here is where we keep in contact with our neighbors.

Enjoyed visiting briefly with Marge McClaran, a ranch wife who manages an incredible schedule that includes maintaining households on Cow Creek (lower Imnaha), Pine Creek (Chesnimnus Creek), as well as the home in Enterprise. Not an easy job, and one that demands that a wife be extremely flexible.

Betty Tippett (Mrs. Biden) is another ranch wife who must set up housekeeping on the Snake River (Jim Creek), where the family lives while calving out the cows. Then when the cattle come out "on top" in the Zumwalt country, she must close up that home in the canyon and come out to the house in Enterprise. Every year she adapts to this life and soon has her yard looking like someone lived there all year.

Jackie and Bill stop by. Buck and Mona Lee "help" me chore this evening. They adore the baby chicks, kittens and calves.

April 18—After baking more sourdough bread and finishing chores, I picked up Grace Bartlett and we visited Guy and Reatha McCormack on Alder Slope. We are doing some research on early Wallowa County history.

Guy's family is especially interesting, because his grandfather, William McCormack, was one of the first white settlers in Wallowa County. He and a Mr. Keith built a cabin on Scotch Creek and spent that first winter in the valley. They were friendly with the Nez Perce Indians and put up wild meadow hay for their cattle. The cattle were eventually driven to the Joseph Creek area in later years and wintered there. The winters were so much milder. Guy's grandfather and father are both buried in the Alder Slope Pioneer Cemetery, which is situated on a plot of ground not too far from the McCormack ranch today.

Reatha's roots go deep in early Wallowa Valley history also.

Had baked a loaf of sourdough bread for the McCormacks. They have been good Alder Slope neighbors over the years and have done many favors for me.

Home to bake more bread: two for the freezer, one for us. Doug and I seem to consume as much of this bread as anybody. Maybe it's the sourdough that keeps us going!

We are still shipping seed spuds, having to take a cut in price this year in order to market them. A real blow to our operation.

Beef cattle prices continue to fall and the dairy buyoff program and other factors beyond our control make the situation very frustrating.

April 19—Off to the hills with Guy and Reatha McCormack and Grace Bartlett. We are taking Guy back to visit the old place where he lived as a boy, on Pine Creek. Guy showed us the old barn and told tales of how hard times were then, how bad luck befell the family one summer when his father broke his leg. The neighbors came in and put up the hay and got in the crops. It is hard to envision how life must have been then.

It is intensely interesting to Grace and me to research and study these early settlers and find out about their lives.

We also identified wildflowers and watched hawks and different species of birds. We visited an old pioneer cemetery on a lonely, windswept knoll, and found the gravestones still legible among the wildflowers and early spring grasses.

We stopped to look at the old Dorrance barn on Crow Creek. We were amazed at the workmanship and pride that went into such a wonderful barn. The enormous stalls for the big draft horses, the neat milking parlor, the huge loft and grain bins, all built so substantial, with beautiful timbers that remain in perfect shape, even to this day.

A wonderful time well spent with friends.

April 20—Up early to chore, then 12 Sourdough Shutterbugs converge, armed with cameras and sack lunches. Once more I head out to

Grace Bartlett and Reatha and Guy McCormack stand on the porch of the old Steen ranch house. About 100 years old, the log house is used for a summer and fall cow camp along Chesnimnus Creek, and is surrounded by Forest Service grazing permits in the Chesnimnus allotment. Cattle are driven up from the steep canyon winter range via old trails that top out near Buckhorn, or come up Corral Creek.

Clyde and Helen Stonebrink travel in style, parking their 1924 Model T Ford at Cloverleaf Hall while they attended a family reunion. Cressie Green snapped this picture of Janie Tippett at the wheel.

Two baby great horned owls peer up at the camera from their new "nest," a wooden box provided by the photographer after the babies' nest was destroyed in a windstorm on Prairie Creek in Wallowa County.

Crow Creek with my brood. First stop: a branding at the Dorrance place. Cowboys, cowgirls, horses, dogs and now my 4-H'ers! We did some photography using the lively, colorful event as our subject. The kids jumped back into the truck and we headed on down Crow Creek Road.

We stopped to visit Mack Birkmaier, who was horseback checking his cattle. "Sure need a good rain," stated Mack. I agreed.

Where Crow Creek joins Chesnimnus Creek and becomes Joseph Creek, we turned and drove up a narrow road that follows the creek. Passing the Lewis School, Hinton Homestead, B&H Cattle Company…stopping to eat our sack lunches where Pine Creek joins Chesnimnus Creek.

After lunch, we waded the creek and walked along the road that follows Pine Creek. The afternoon was very warm and the 4-H'ers were soon in the creek again. Becky discovered the water to be alive with fish. Suckers, hundreds of them, spawning.

What a sight the children made, chasing the fish on this hot afternoon.

We eventually made it to the Charley Tippett ranch. On the way in we had met Steve and Katie Combes and children driving out in their cattle truck. They had a horse they were hauling out to town. It had porcupine quills embedded in its nose.

At the house we took pictures, drank from the cold well water, rested a bit, then began the long hike out. We drove home by way of Gooseberry and Butte Creek, coming out near our summer range, and returned with the first sunburn of the season and the memory of a great day.

April 21—It is 50 degrees at 6 a.m. The full blush of spring is upon the valley, and two Great Horned owls that have been nesting in a giant cottonwood along our creek have lost their babies. Ben reported to me that the two little owlets had apparently fallen from their nest during a wind storm. I walked over to the spot, camera in hand, to photograph the fluffy, little fellows, and was greeted with two pairs of big, yellow eyes, two snapping beaks and parent owls hoot-hooing at me. Mamma and daddy took turns dive-bombing to distract me from their offspring.

Walking back through our hayfield, I noticed that Star's udder is tight and bulging. She just looked at me in a matronly sort of way, blades of grass protruding unglamorously from her mouth, as if to say, "Sure be glad to get this over with, I look udderly ridiculous."

After chores I drove to Cloverleaf Hall to set up our seed potato booth for the Food Fair tonight. The place was bustling with activity. Seems like Wallowa County can't stand to let a single weekend go by without scheduling something. Really keeps us in agriculture hopping; so many of these events involve us.

Star, the grand old Holstein matron, looks udderly ridiculous the day before she calved. She is now in her eighth lactation and has raised many orphan calves besides her own, and has provided house milk for many years.

Huge thunderheads build up over the mountains as temperatures soar into the 80s today. I listened to the rain drum down on the tin roof of the calving shed while I tended my baby chicks. Star nervous in the storm; I think her time is near.

Doug and I made the Food Fair by 6:30. A trim and pretty little Miss Homemaker, hired by various food companies, demonstrated different dishes. The preparation, pre-measuring and cleanup was all being done back stage by our CowBelles.

Our local radio station KWVR helped sponsor the event. Lee Perkins brought down the house when he donned a "blue bonnet" used for the margarine commercial. He then led the audience with "Everything's better with Blue Bonnet on it."

April 22—Up early. Warm, cloudy, wet. Fresh "earth smell" perme-ated Prairie Creek. Everything is growing frantically. Out at 5:30 to check on Star. Underneath an old willow tree, beside a ditch she lay. Stretched out in front of her was the calf. It was dead! I felt so badly, as a closer inspection revealed that this grand, old cow hadn't licked the sack from around the little heifer's head and she had suffocated.

Poor Star, 10 years old, a matron of so many unassisted births, had not taken care of her baby properly. She had licked off the part she could reach while lying down, but her tongue couldn't reach the head. Maybe she was just too tired to get up. Perhaps this will be her last year here. She is becoming a bit arthritic and the long, cold Wallowa County winters have taken their toll.

Doug says hamburger cows are bringing 12 cents. Somehow she is worth more. Besides, says I, she has earned a home here. Think of all the orphans she has raised, not to mention the milk she has provided our family. Felt badly all day. If I had only gone out a little earlier, maybe the little heifer could have lived.

We need to haul more cattle to the hills tomorrow; the valley is now verdant green.

I'm worried about the two little owls. Walked over after chores to their tree. The parents hooted a hello and this time didn't dive bomb me. I am sure this pair of owls are the same ones that have been in residence here on the ranch for the past few years. Looking in the nest box, I could see evidence that the parent owls had continued to feed their young.

Made a gooseberry pie. Began hauling cows and calves to the hills today. Raining again, which is good. I have the two Imnaha grandchildren this afternoon. Mom and dad at a meeting in Portland. Windy and cold. Built a fire. Yesterday it was 80, today we need a fire. Typical Wallowa County weather.

Baked more sourdough bread. The children accompanied me on my round of chores. It began to snow and blow. Mona and Buck entertained by the baby chicks and watching grandma milk over two gallons of milk from Star.

Took the grandchildren with me tonight to see a showing of the National Theatre Express, "Showing up for Work." Two actors on stage, two high stools their only props, provided excellent live theater.

The children fell asleep in the OK Theatre, one on my lap, the other leaning against me. I had to deal with their weight until a friend helped me put on their coats. I carried Mona and guided sleepy Buck to the car. At home I tucked the little ones into bed, mixed the sourdough, and crashed.

April 23—Cold, 20 degrees, ice on the chicken's water pan. Fixed sourdough waffles at the request of Mona Lee. Buck slept until 9. Milked Star and Daisy, let calves nurse, tended chicks.

After Buck woke up, I loaded the children into a little red wagon and pulled them through the hay field to the "Owl Tree." The parents didn't give a hoot, and the children were delighted with the baby owls.

Fixed lunch, then off to town with the children to run errands. Up to Alder Slope to check on my house.

Home to find the children's parents back.

Doug purchased a calf at the sale today to put on Star. Need help with all this milk.

Took a yummy pan of lasagna from the freezer to bake for supper. Thanks to Liza and Todd's previous cooking, we enjoyed a good meal.

April 24—Sourdough waffles for breakfast, then milked Star. Her udder is so huge! The new calf is most welcome. Turned May's two calves out with her. Six calves on three cows now. Tended to my growing baby chicks and the laying hens.

Back in the kitchen, I begin to bake more bread for the Art Festival dinner. Made an extra loaf for Joy Klages, who has framed my print for the Art Show.

Doris and Becky here this morning to photograph my baby owls.

Phone calls all morning...Grand Central Station as usual.

Warmed up left-over lasagne, fixed a salad and garlic sourdough bread. Becky, her son, Doris and I enjoyed the spring day by eating our meal out on the lawn. We all drove to Joseph, where we picked up our art work for the show. Into Enterprise to enter it. Hectic, but fun.

Doug discing a rented field near Enterprise. We will plant our fava bean seed there. He left later on to attend a Federal Land Bank meeting in Baker. He'll spend the night and drive on to Boise in the morning to pick up our fava bean seed.

Meanwhile, back at the ranch, I do chores and hold down the fort.

Back into Enterprise to attend the annual FFA banquet. Left before it was over to make it to the Walter Brennan Documentary at the OK Theatre; part of our Art Festival Week festivities. A showing of the Western film classic "Red River" followed the documentary, but even John Wayne couldn't keep me awake; I simply couldn't keep my eyes open, so left for home and rest. Must be up early to answer the phone for potato truck drivers.

Clouding up, looks like rain.

As I fall asleep, I reflect on the FFA banquet; am always so impressed with this chapter. I have had three children belong to it through the years, and hope that my grandchildren will also benefit from the program.

These young people are fine representatives of our agricultural community, and how we need them. They are building blocks of our future.

A full moon sails between clouds tonight.

April 25—Awoke early, peering outside in the dawn light, I see a world of white...wind blowing dark clouds across the sky. Doug called from Ontario around 6 a.m., on his way to Boise.

Built a cozy fire in the wood stove, enjoyed a cup of Postum and a grapefruit...did some writing, phoning and reading. A rare treat to be able to relax a bit before starting the day.

On my way out to the barn, orange-breasted robins contrasted with the white snow.

Many women are taking aerobics these days to stay in shape. I simply continue with the cow barn routine. Milking a cow, wrestling calves around, pitching hay, carrying water buckets, and horseback riding are my aerobic exercises. Add to this my role as grandmother, which demands that I must keep fit to keep up.

"Bag Balmed" Daisy and Star's teats; this icy wind would surely chap them otherwise. A necessary precaution to avoid getting kicked.

Baking more bread. Hope to finish today, my freezer groaning with huge loaves of bread.

Snow melted by noon, cold wind still blowing. Things look so green!

Clouded up and began to hail. A "mini-blizzard" occurred. This weather pattern continued all evening.

Son Ken and family here to get some boots for the junior rodeo. I gave grandson Chad a pair of mule-hide boots that were a bit too tight for me. Can it be this child can already wear grandma's boots?

To town for my weekly grocery shopping. Returned to find Doug safely home. On to chores—the baby chicks are feathering out and turning into the usual mouths! Will soon outgrow their present quarters.

Doug and I went to the Artists Reception and Buyer's Preview at Cloverleaf Hall. The quality of art from Eastern Oregon artists is up from last year. There are so many talented people living east of the Cascades!

Such a varied show...beautiful rawhide braiding, horse hair ropes, leather work, hackamores, handmade saddles, and bridles...created by our canyon cowboys. Pen and ink sketches express the lives of more local cowboys.

Carol McLaughlin of Alder Slope with her woodburning, water color creations, bronze sculptures, oils, water colors, and photography. Artists continue to appear out of the brush in our county...and it is gratifying to see it all here. Enjoyed visiting with other artists and nibbling on refreshments, our supper.

By 7:30, we joined a sell-out crowd at the OK Theatre to enjoy a "gathering" of cowboy poets. Most performers were from out of the county and state, but several were our own locals.

A memorable evening. These down-to-earth cowhands recited poetry, sang songs and performed on stage to a very receptive audience. The M.C., Val Geisler, brought down the house with his rendition of Robert Service's "Cremation of Sam McGree." Geisler ran up and down the aisles trailing a microphone cord after him. He gave the performance his all. Even had audience participation with sound effects. Warren Glaus of Imnaha has a marvelous wolf howl. Perspiration dripped from Val's brow as his reciting came to an end.

We were equally entertained by Blackie Black and Jack Miller, author of the book "Tough and Tender."

Wallowa County's own Fred Bornstead sang songs he had composed himself, songs like "Canyons and Trees"...words that came from Fred's heart, written when he was buckarooing on Snake River.

Once a canyon cowboy, always a canyon cowboy. His songs tugged at the heart strings of those of us who understand the canyons.

Sarah Miller from Prairie Creek, recited her own original poem, which described the Imnaha canyon country. Inspiration flows from these people, inspired as we all are by our love for the valley, mountains, canyons and hills.

Val led the grand finale. The audience joined in with the singing of Edd Arnold's "Cattle Call," "You are My Sunshine," and other favorite Western songs.

We drove home under a dark canopy of clouds that broke away momentarily to reveal a bright moon. I could picture the great horned owl swooping down to catch a field mouse, then flying back to feed the little owlets in their box in the tree.

April 26—Cloudy, with blue "petticoats" peeking through.

Brilliant sunshine lays in patches over an incredibly green landscape. The air here on Prairie Creek is filled with birdsong...happy, bursting with life, birdsong! Robins, crows, mallard ducks (nesting along the creek), killdeers, swallows, blackbirds and Jenny Wren celebrating this beautiful April morn.

Ralph Mun, 82, of Baker, recites his own poetry at the Cowboy Poetry Gathering in Enterprise, Oregon. Holding the microphone is Jack Miller of Kuna, Idaho, author of the new book, "Tough and Tender." Munn was born at Unity, Oregon, the son of a stagecoach driver and homesteader. Munn raised cattle, worked as a saddlemaker and freighter, and for the State Highway Department. His four children are encouraging him to recite his poetry as often as possible. He was the hit of the show at Enterprise.

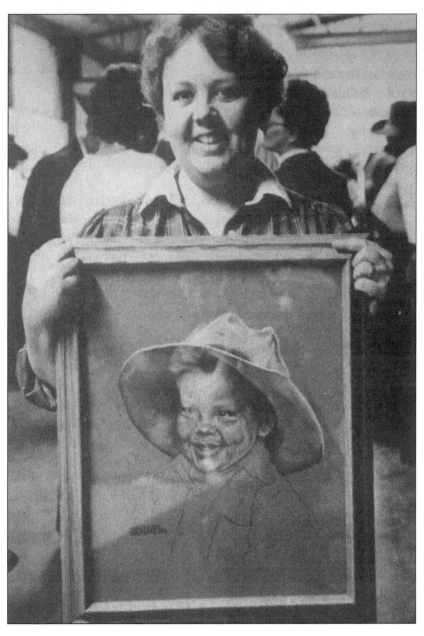

Linda Davies of Jordan Valley, Oregon, won first place and People's Choice Award with this work, "Cause it's m'dad's," at the Art Festival.

April 26, continued—Finished all my chores in just one hour. Doug doing the feeding, as two hired men are taking the day off. One to get married and Ben to attend the Asotin County Fair. Kurt here to feed a load of potatoes to the cattle.

Not a single vehicle passes by on Tenderfoot Valley Road on this peaceful Saturday morning.

I love the fact that we live on a road that is seldom traveled. Generally, the only traffic is someone who lives on a neighboring ranch, or perhaps someone on their way to Imnaha.

Baking the last three loaves of bread for the crowd expected tonight for the buffalo dinner, art show and dance. A very busy day ahead.

The cowboy poets, staying at the Buhler Ranch near Joseph, have surely fallen under the spell of Wallowa County after a morning such as this!

Daisy and Star aren't impressed with Art Festival Week. Their already disrupted schedule really went amuck today. At 3:30 I had driven them in from their pasture to the barn so the calves could nurse and they could be milked out. Star looked at me like I'd lost my senses. I tried to no avail to explain the necessity of this decision. I was supposed to be at Cloverleaf Hall by 4:30 with my enormous cargo of bread, I said.

She couldn't care less, but submitted to being milked out hours earlier, perhaps knowing it would be a long time before morning.

Arrived at the appointed time to meet Carol Borgerding, who was adding her bread to the growing pile. Because we may never attempt this again, I took a picture for posterity. Pretty impressive stack of homemade bread.

CowBelles and Art Council members had been cooking all day…many stayed to help serve. I was so proud of our CowBelles. We served two lines of people, around 400, in a half-hour. Roast buffalo, corn casserole, homemade beans, sourdough bread, salad and rhubarb and apple crisp. Quite a feat. It had required careful planning and hard work. As usual CowBelles came through and the meal was memorable.

The "Quick Draw," accomplished in an hour, was later sold in a silent auction. Very impressive, watching these artists work. Anderson Bennally, an American Indian artist, completed a painting, as did Eve Slinker, who was working with a live model, dressed as an Indian girl.

The crowd was fascinated watching artists in different media complete their work in that short time.

Carol and I got raves on our bread and the buffalo was consumed. The cowboy poets performed again and the successful affair ended with dancing to western music.

Son-in-law, Bill, won a merit award on his pen, ink and pencil sketch of Red's Horse Ranch Barn" and I sold one of my entries, a black and white print entitled "Canyon Cow Pony."

Doug and I danced a few before leaving for home. The quality of art was up this year, and the crowd most enthusiastic. Our county has come a long way in art appreciation.

April 27—Between Daylight Savings Time and the Art Festival, my cows really gave me the "moo" this morning. Hungry calves relieved full udders and I milked the usual gallon of house milk.

Relaxing this morning, I walked across our fields to visit the "owl tree." At my approach, one of the parent owls that had-been hunting nearby, flew to the box nest with some sort of rodent. The great horned owl watched me carefully, making a "woof, woof" sound alternated with who-whoop's. As I climbed up to peer in at the babies, the great owl flew farther up and lit on a branch high in the old tree.

She continued to "talk" to me as I watched her babies. They were hungrily feeding on a gopher but, at the sight of me, began backing into the corner of their nest. How they had grown, staring at me now with those big, yellow eyes.

I managed to snap a couple of pictures and left them to finish their meal.

Doug drove a tractor from the fava bean field to the potato cellars. I followed in the pickup to give him a ride home.

More potatoes to ship tomorrow. The cows with their spring calves will be started to summer range in the hills.

Baked a Boston cream pie, developed some film and fixed a fried chicken supper.

It began to rain around 5 p.m. and just simply poured. Did chores amid a cloudburst. Shortly after the storm, a huge rainbow appeared, arching itself across the fresh, green fields, as the sun burst through a layer of clouds. 'Tis the season for rainbows!

April 28—Up early. Doug fixes breakfast while I chore. Milk Star, strain milk and make lunches for Doug, Dan and me.

We mount our horses and ride to the pasture, where a few cattle are sorted out and started up the road. Another bunch is soon turned out. I was told to keep the herd from going back into the pasture. One bunch of cows and calves simply would not leave. We had a terrible time driving them out with their calves.

While heading off some critters that insisted on going into the Liberty Grange parking lot, my horse decided to buck, for what reason, I'll never know. I was tossed around on top of her like a bag of spuds and in the melee, my left foot got banged by a loose stirrup. It immediately began to swell and I suspected some small bones might be broken. The foot hurt for awhile, then blissfully turned numb.

Because all available hands were needed to keep the cattle going, I elected to stay on with the drive.

Finally, we were able to begin the long day of driving cows and newborn calves out to our summer range. It had been an ordeal; for some reason, they didn't want to leave the valley. After much yelling and pushing, we succeeded in at least getting them out of sight of the ranch.

Doug had come along in the pickup to remove my boot. I wasn't in any pain, other than the pain of pulling the boot off. I figured as long as I stayed in the saddle, I could make it all right.

I discovered later that my mare was in heat, which I suppose didn't help her disposition all day. At least she hadn't dumped me. Things could have been worse.

"Hey girls, hey cows, come on babies," we yelled ourselves hoarse. And our long day of "cow punchin'" was just beginning. Many miles separated us from the holding pasture on East Crow.

Right off, a baby calf developed a belly ache; so we left him tied to a fence, to picked up later in the truck. Doug went back to feed the remaining cattle their hay and potatoes.

Traffic on the Crow Creek road was bad today. Huge rock crushing equipment that has been working on the Zumwalt road was being moved to somewhere via this normally quiet road. A puzzle to us, imagining the money being spent on these remote roads that lead to where? Progress? Those of us on horse back, pushing cattle all day, could hardly believe our eyes as this parade of costly equipment rumbled through our herd.

Needless to say, these monstrous pieces of earth-moving equipment being hauled on incredibly long trailers disrupted our cattle drive considerably.

Unable to dismount due to my banged up foot, I was to be in the saddle for over 10 hours. Along the way, Dan's horse had developed azateria, severe muscle cramps, and was hauled back to town with fellow ranchers Paul and Gladys Yost, who happened along pulling a horse trailer. That left just Ben and me. Doug was on ahead repairing fence in the holding pasture where whole sections had washed out during a recent flooding of Crow Creek. He was gone two or three hours.

Meanwhile, it had turned cold, but we weren't too uncomfortable. Keeping so many cows and calves going warmed us. I sure wanted off that horse!

Around 6:30 or 7, Doug finally finished repairing the fence. The hours had dragged by. Meanwhile, Mack Birkmaier happened along and helped us push cows and calves for over an hour. Dan drove back out and helped also, on foot.

After Doug drove Mack to his parked truck, he came back and lifted me from my horse. Dan was able then to ride my mare. I hobbled to the pickup and was so glad to be out of that saddle.

It was after dark, around 9, when the last of the herd filed into the holding pasture. A long day that still wasn't over! We drove home in a cold rain and the air had a certain chill to it. Methinks it will be white by morning. For now, Star and Daisy bawling at the barn door, baby chicks, eggs to gather, and something to eat. Doug did all of this and then made late night phone calls to replace me in the morning. Mike McFetridge will help us.

Meanwhile, at our cellars, the crew had loaded two semis of potatoes today. A neighbor called late to say a calf we had lost along the way had wandered into his place and he had it corraled. Our cowdog "Faye" had gotten stepped on by my mare today. All in all, we were a pretty crippled outfit. I wrapped an ace bandage around my swollen foot and fell into bed. At least the cattle are halfway to Salmon Creek.

April 29—Slept fitfully, tossing and turning all night, my injured foot throbbing.

Awoke at 5 a.m., looked out the window to see a good five inches of soft, wet, spring snow piled on everything! The worst storm all spring. No wonder the cattle didn't want to leave the valley. They must have known.

I hobbled about the kitchen making biscuits, bacon and eggs for Doug. Boiled up some eggs to make sandwiches for three cowboys, did yesterday's dishes.

Ben and Mike left for East Crow to begin trailing the herd to Salmon Creek.

Snow lays on the trees and fence rows. Patches of green grass begin to appear and by noon the warm sun burns high in the sky and every-thing melts. The snow only a memory. Steam rises from plowed fields. Moisture, just what we needed!

A neighboring rancher called. It seems one of our cows (mother to the calf left behind) had jumped the fence and trailed all the way back to her calf. Rod had both cow and calf in his corral.

Doug brought more help for my surplus milk…another calf…wild and,big. I milked a little of Star's milk into a bucket, straddled the calf in a corner, stuck his head in the bucket. He got a taste and immediately began nursing Star. Just what I had hoped would happen.

Another cow had high-tailed it home…Mamma to the calf we'd left tied to the fence with a bellyache.

All is quiet here now on the ranch, except for the incessant ringing of our phone! More potatoes being loaded at our cellars today.

Spent the morning resting. Hope the cowboys have better luck today.

Fixed a cast iron dutch oven full of beef vegetable soup for supper to go with left-over biscuits. The cowboys had returned late in the afternoon, the ride smoother going today. In fact, they reported that the cattle had made it to the top of Dorrance Grade by 12:30.

The new calf nursed Star readily tonight and everything is back on schedule at the barn.

Good feeling, knowing our cattle are in the hills for the summer. Now our fields can recover.

April 30—As April leaves us, the temperature gauge under the clothesline reads a mere 20 degrees. One of the coldest recorded temperatures in the nation. Clear skies and a heavy frost this morning.

Our apple tree is just beginning to bud. Hope this cold snap doesn't damage the Imnaha fruit crop.

Unable to ship some of our seed potatoes. They are suffering from last fall's early frost damage. Hopefully, we will utilize them for cattle feed.

Turned Daisy out with her two calves. Just have the three on Star to contend with now. Seven calves on three cows; missing Liza this year. Doug sold her last fall because two of her teats were too big to be nursed out sufficiently.

Hung clothes on the line. My foot much improved, still very sore from over 10 hours in the saddle.

Spent three hours working in the darkroom.

Clouding up, much warmer tonight.

May 1—Beautiful morning. Warm. Snowfields gleam in the early sunshine. The valley is so green. Rain predicted. We are so busy. So many things to do. Planting fava beans today, harrowing fields, cleaning out the potato cellars. We are through shipping seed. Quite a loss this year due to a poor market and other factors beyond our control.

The wind blows incessantly over Prairie Creek. It hinders the seeding of the fava beans.

Gave a presentation this afternoon to the Joseph High School creative writing class. A very receptive young audience, extremely fortunate to have Betty Husted as their teacher.

Home to bake a loaf of sourdough bread, first one since the Art Festival. Fixed chicken fried steak smothered in some frozen morel mushrooms.

The gnarled old apple tree in our yard split in half during today's windstorm. The ancient tree, probably planted by an early day Prairie Creek homesteader, was almost hollow inside, having been eaten by some sort of insects over the years. The heavy limbs were covered with buds just beginning to blossom.

A robin's nest, remaining intact, had fallen with the huge severed section of the trunk. If this tree could talk, I mused, perhaps it would tell us of all the women folk down through the years, who had picked up the windfalls in autumn to make applesauce and delicious apple pies.

Doug home late from the bean field. The lonely wind blows over Prairie Creek tonight.

May 2—My baby chicks have outgrown their quarters.

Purchased my bedding plants today. How can one resist the wonderful array of flowers, tomatoes, cabbages and pepper plants? It got up to 67 degrees this afternoon, but I will wait a few more days to set them out.

Left supper on the stove for Doug, who would be in late from the fields. Attended a history group meeting at Chandler's in Joseph. Enjoyed viewing the slide narrative presentation given by Lloyd Coffman on early Wallowa County history. A good turnout of history enthusiasts.

May 3—Slept in 'til 6. A warm, fine misty rain fell all night and continued all day.

Doug cleaned out the chicken house, laid down fresh straw and then helped me move my chicks into their new quarters. They are now happily running around their large chicken house.

Spaded up my flower beds and incorporated cow manure into the soil. More rain. Doug resting up, the only way a farmer will rest, when it rains and keeps him out of the fields.

Doug and I enjoyed pizza tonight in Enterprise and then walked across the street to the OK Theatre to attend a performance of classical guitarist Neill Archer Roan. Wonderful evening made possible by the efforts of our Wallowa Valley Arts Council.

May 4—Big, fat flakes of snow falling from above on this Sunday morning. Doug and I to our separate chores after breakfast, just he and I alone on the ranch today.

The apple tree is now a cloud of pink and white blossoms.

Doug and I drove to Imnaha around noon. The canyons are wearing a green blanket and are much warmer than Prairie Creek. We ordered lunch at the Riverside Cafe and enjoyed visiting Jim Dorrance and A.L. Duckett while we ate.

Down river to daughter Jackie's to take pictures of Todd's colt. Is there anything so lovely as springtime on the Imnaha? Or anything that says spring like a newborn colt?

On the way back we visited again with A.L. Duckett at his pretty home. This 91-year-old cares for his huge yard and garden that is one of Imnaha's show places. His lilacs were in full bloom and I picked an armload to bring home.

A.L. reminisced about his early days as a stage driver. He told us about some of his experiences driving up Trail Creek. He said his place was once just a rock pile and he had spent years making it into what it is today. During the Great Depression, A.L. operated a blacksmith shop at Imnaha.

Today he is a widower, a man of many talents that include the building of his famous Duckett Wood Stoves. We could have visited A.L. all day, but evening was upon us and our chores beckoned. Homeward we went, loaded with apple butter and lilacs that A.L. had given us. We left the balmy air of the canyons and drove out "On Top" to our snowy mountains and the familiar, cold wind blowing over Prairie Creek.

May 5—Clear skies, a heavy frost, beautiful light on the mountains by 5:30. Huckleberry muffins, sausage and eggs for breakfast.

Up to Alder Slope to photograph the McLaughlin family for some articles I am doing. Incredible view from their ranch, snow-clad Wallowas, fields of newly seeded grain, and the town of Enterprise below.

Son-in-law Bill here to worm and vaccinate the fall calves. He and Ben then hauled them to a rented pasture on Upper Prairie Creek.

Because I hadn't visited my owl family for a while, I walked over and found they had flown the coop!

Turned windy and cloudy tonight. The fava beans are planted.

May 6—More than three inches of snow covers the ground, still snowing by 9 a.m. Sloshed out through the soft, wet stuff to chore. My calves had ravenous appetites this morning. Forked extra hay to the milk cows.

A robin flew to the pole fence in the yard, but couldn't get a foothold due to the snow piled there and fell off. Such is spring in Wallowa County. Only consolation is that when the snow melts, and it does very quickly, the grass will be a brilliant green and the wildflowers will turn the hills to color. Bluebells and a succession of other wildings will bloom on into the summer. The dandelions are out in full force. As the snow melts, they show up like light bulbs in the grass.

Son-in-law Bill arrives to help castrate and work a few more calves, then move some bulls up to another pasture. The fire in our woodstove feels good today.

May 7—Raining, the barnlot muddy, a bad time at the barn this morning. Star decided to "steal" one of Daisy's calves.

She was partially nursed out and therefore would have nothing to do with going into the barn. Had a time figuring this out, but finally did. I got my boot stuck in the mud and pulled out a stockinged foot, which fell into the ooze, then sucked down into the manury mire. I was muddy to my knees! I finally won out when I herded Star's "mothered up" calf into the barn and she followed at my heels.

Somehow my four hungry calves got fed; I had coaxed Daisy into help too. Even got a gallon of house milk and fed mamma kitty.

I was ready for the shower and smelled of Corral #5!

Another 4-H'er here to practice her demonstration.

Bill and Ben hauled some late calvers to the hills this morning. They reported the roads were extremely muddy. Doug repaired some fence on one of our rented pastures.

May 8—Doug, Ben and Bill headed for the hills to sort cattle preparatory to branding tomorrow.

Things much calmer at the barn this morning. Prepared a salad for the CowBelles' potluck.

Ran some errands for the ranch in Enterprise, picked up Doris, and drove to Imnaha. Jackie and the children rode up river with us to Barbara Warnock's. It was warm, green and lovely on the upper Imnaha and the balsamroot was blooming on the canyon sides.

The river was high and Barbara's yard was lovely as usual with her newly planted garden and flower beds. We were greeted by the smell of freshly baked rolls and bread as we entered her country kitchen.

Jackie's family must move...they recently received notice that new owners will soon be taking over the Benson Ranch. Many changes occurring on our ranches lately. California people buying up some of the properties along the river.

May 9—Up at dawn to chore, frosty, clear and cold. Doug fixed breakfast on the wood stove while I tended to my menagerie. After making lunches, we headed for our summer range on Salmon Creek. A coyote slinked over a rise as we approached one of our pastures. A few clouds formed and a slight breeze began to blow over the bunch grass ranges.

Caught and saddled our horses, then drove in the large herd of cows, calves and a few drys.

The wind turned colder and picked up speed as we gathered the scattered cattle in the vast rolling hills.

Wildflowers nodded their bright heads, hawks circled above, and numerous meadow larks sang as we drove the cattle into the big main corral. The calves, soon separated from their mammas, began to bawl. Likewise the mammas. Many bovine voices broke the silence of the Salmon Creek hills.

By the time we finished sorting, it was 11:30, so we ate lunch on a grassy spot in a patch of sunshine.

By 2:30, we had finished 100 head. A good crew! It had begun to rain by this time...a cold rain. We continued on, the rain let up, but a persistent cold wind continued. Smoke from the branding fire mingled with the smell of scorched hair...a typical branding day. Finished by 5:30, then ran all the cows through to be sprayed. We headed home, tired and cold.

The chores awaited us in the valley; then we cleaned up and attended Landfest at Cloverleaf Hall.

Gladys Yost and her CowBelles committee had prepared a delicious barbecued hamburger meal...our supper! The Wallowa County Cow-Belles booth won first place. Betty and Van Van Blaricom did a nice job on the display, which depicted one continuous "circle of conservation."

May 10—Cold, snowing on and off...the snow level on upper Prairie Creek. Where has spring gone? Ben, Kirk, Doug and Bill to the hills to finish up branding 25 more calves in a different pasture.

After making lunches for the men, I drove into the fairgrounds accompanied by two of my 4-H'ers, Jenny and Amy. They did a good job on their demonstrations.

Stopped at the Enterprise Flower Shop to pick up a beautiful growing arrangement, a Mother's Day remembrance from daughter Jackie and her family.

Made a blackberry cobbler and put a stewing hen on the woodstove to simmer for supper.

Jackie's little family moving today. They will be living near Imnaha along Sheep Creek.

Hurriedly did chores so we could attend the junior rodeo in Joseph this evening. I have four grandchildren competing this year! Son Steve home for the weekend from Blue Mountain Community College. Cowboys back from the hills and we actually make the rodeo by 6 p.m.

It is freezing cold at the Harley Tucker Memorial Arena, with snow showers and a chilly wind blowing off the mountains.

Right off the bat the chute gate opens and little five-year-old Buck comes out riding a sheep! His dream come true. The big ewes dumped most of the kids in short order, but the event was a crowd pleaser.

Granddaughter Chelsie bit the dust next and Rowdy got kicked by his steer. Chad rode his steer and looked pretty good for a 12-year-old.

Meanwhile, in the stands, we parents, grandparents and spectators braved the cold to watch our little heroes perform. We were bundled to the teeth in insulated overalls and had blankets draped over us!

The hot chocolate concession stand did a land office business as people consumed the hot liquid to stay warm. We managed to stick it out until the last bull rider came out of the chutes, then headed back to Prairie Creek and our warm fire. Lots of tired little buckaroos tonight.

May 11—Mother's Day dawned sunny, with beautiful clouds. The snowline retreated to upper Prairie Creek again. The valley is a bright green.

The electricity had been off in the night, but the baby chicks were OK, all huddled in a corner...none had smothered.

Received Mother's Day calls from our children and Doug gave me a pretty, little gold necklace.

Celebrated this day by attending the second performance of the Joseph Junior Rodeo. We enjoyed a barbecued beef dinner prior. A cold wind blew, but much warmer than last night.

Little Buck made it out from Imnaha to ride his second go-round in the mutton riding. Chad, Rowdy and Chelsie were fun to watch in many events and Chad won the steer riding...was all smiles at winning his first belt buckle.

We took the children home with us, as mom and dad are finishing up the moving to Sheep Creek.

July 19—Fooled you, didn't I? Just today I read the letter to the editor written by Bernice Riley. She is right. I really don't have to be so chronological. So here goes.

"Help!" says a young goat, as Chelsie Nash, 7, of Alder Slope, ties a ribbon on its tail during a junior rodeo in Joseph.

Only what do I do with the notes I take day by day, especially those I write up in the trailer after the day's other work is done and my writing day has just begun? She is a fine writer and right about what she said. It is necessary to be objective about one's own work and writing is addictive.

I have written for years and even if it weren't published I would continue to write. Am sure all of us who have a "writer's heart" will agree with this.

Anyway, thank you Bernice, for bringing this to my attention in a way that is finally going to make me do it. I *have* received comment on being behind, but turned a deaf ear, thinking most of the readers didn't mind. Seeing your letter in print did the trick.

I miss your column and join Virgil in congratulating you on your long and successful career. Because I had my entire column typed before I read Bernice's letter, I must do some changing. So I'll jump up to July 19. How's that for skipping?

Warming up today. Son Ken and wife Annie leave their children here for the rest of the weekend. They will take a pickup and horse trailer over to Corvallis to help son Todd and his wife and new baby move to Wallowa County. And I will finally see my new grandson for the first time!

Already scheduled is a campout at Kinney Lake tonight with my 4-H Sourdough Shutterbugs. I will take the grandchildren along.

We spent the morning loading up the old sheepherder wagon and digging worms for fishing.

By 2:30 we were on our way, the sheepherder wagon jouncing along happily in tow.

We made it to the lake and I parked under the shade of an old cottonwood tree. Thirteen of us spill out along with sleeping bags, tents, fishing gear, cameras and marshmallows. The youngsters set up their camps along the shore of the lake.

A pink, flowering water plant adds a special touch of color to the lake in the afternoon light.

Evening descends on the lake, the smoke from our fire drifts out over the water...reflections deepen and the pink water plants take on a richer hue...and pick up the evening pinks in the mountains...a good time to photograph.

Doug and Susanne join us for dinner around the campfire. Because this lake is close to our ranch, I suggested they join us.

Son Steve, who is home for the summer, was also invited, but had other plans.

Susanne is from Switzerland and has been living on the ranch with us these past weeks. She loves riding horses and being around animals and ranch life in general. I first met her on a llama hike our 4-H'ers took up Bear Creek this June, but that is another story.

Chelsie and grandma bunked in the comfort of the sheepherder wagon and the 4-H'ers camped out all night. And what a beautiful night it was. A gorgeous full moon was rising over the Divide, a black line of timber bordering its appearance.

As the warm light of the moon bathed the open country, a chorus of coyotes let loose from the direction of the Three Lakes area, a yipping symphony of wild sounds. A warm breeze whispered across the dry hillsides and the withered wildflowers gave off a faint perfume in the July night.

A very special moment for all of us. Below lay the lake, gleaming in the moonlight, and the sheepherder wagon beckoning with its comfortable bed.

Susanne Godola of Zurich, Switzerland, pets Faye, the Tippett's cow dog on the Prairie Creek Ranch. Susan loves animals, especially dogs, cats and horses. She has made friends with many animals on this Eastern Oregon cattle ranch. Susan saved the money she earned in Switzerland to come to the United States and is staying with the Doug Tippett family.

However, as usual, this 4-H leader was not going to have a peaceful night to sleep, not with 12 lively youngsters beginning to get their second wind and developing moon-madness or whatever youth develops after the sun goes down.

After everyone finally went to dreamland, I had to deal with the comings and goings of Saturday night necking parties that kept me up until 3:30 a.m. The moon was disappearing over the mountains when I finally got to sleep.

I managed to get in around 40 winks before awakening at 5:30 to a brilliant, clear morning.

The lake's reflections were perfectly clear and the water plants at their deepest pink yet.

We left reluctantly after breakfast and a hike or two to some deserted log cabins. The 4-H'ers dispersed along with their gear and I drove Rowdy and Chad up to Alder Slope to do their chores. Rowdy fed his hogs and Chad his 4-H steer.

Home to prepare lunch for seven. Cleaned up the mess left from camping and tidied up the sheepherder wagon for the next trip.

Fixed a big pot of spaghetti for supper, made sure all the children had bathed, and began to fade fast. A long day and a short night.

As I write tonight, I watch our neighbors, the Houghs, haying the field across from us. Lois is raking. She stands up occasionally to rest from the continual bump, bump of the tractor seat.

The field is becoming dotted with the huge "bread loaf" haystacks. The large compactor roars down the rows of hay with clouds of dust boiling up ever so often as the big machine clanks and bangs to give birth to another "loaf" of hay.

Peaceful and calm on Prairie Creek...the horses graze along the ditch, backgrounded by the haystacks in the soft, evening light.

Anxiously awaiting the arrival of my newest grandchild. It was after dark when I heard the pickups drive in. I had been writing in the trailer (my new writing studio since son Steve moved home for the summer; it used to be in his bedroom).

As I ran out to greet them, I noticed the golden full moon just coming over the hill. Precious little James arrived in the valley during such a moon. He was born one month ago during a June moon that brought the lowest tide in 20 years to the Oregon Coast.

I had him in my arms and took him into the house for my first look. Can there be anything to equal a sweet baby? Dark hair, perfect features...so big and filled out...such a handsome boy. His grandfather

James came to the Wallowa Valley years ago and now little new James has made the pilgrimage to the same spot years later.

So good to see Todd and Liza and welcome them. They were both tired from the moving, and hot from the long drive, but safely home.

Two great horned owls hooted at the moon off and on all night, but James slept on.

July 21—A clear, hot day on Prairie Creek and my new baby grandson is still asleep in his old wooden cradle.

After breakfast and chores, Susanne and I drive over to the Slope house to help Liza and Todd unload their belongings. Liza's horse is already grazing down the high grasses that have grown since the property has been vacant. Little James sleeps through it all. He is already in love with Alder Slope!

The mountain we call Ruby Peak looks down serenely on the busy goings on. The mountain has seen many families come and go through the years. The Juves, the Kisers, the Nashes, two of my sons, one with a family, and now my youngest son has returned complete with a family.

Perhaps Liza, too, will fall under the spell of the mountain. While she works in her kitchen, she will look out on its beauty, becoming familiar with its morning light, the bright pink glow on its summit that surely gave it the name Ruby Peak.

She will be there to see the slopes covered with golden tamarack in autumn and, as Indian Summer progresses, the first snowfall that will leave a dusting of snow on the high places. She will be friends a long time with it in winter, when the frozen stillness lasts and lasts and the pink alpenglow on the snow is another kind of beauty. Then in spring the snowfields will gleam and the sky above will be the purest blue ever.

Until once again, the summer thunderheads will build and sweep their shadows across the peak's snowless ramparts, and the red rocks will display yet another face, always changing, never two days alike. A panorama of light, shadow and color in motion on this special mountain, only a part of the Wallowa chain. The peak's slopes are home to many elk and deer, who find sanctuary on its timbered slopes, alder-strewn draws and spring-fed creeks.

We nibbled on fresh fruit, crackers and cheese, then finished unloading the remainder of their belongings.

Back at the ranch, we rested up, then baked bread and prepared a fried chicken dinner for the returning new family. They will spend another night here, and I will get to hold my new grandson again.

Jackie and her family stopped by; their day in town.

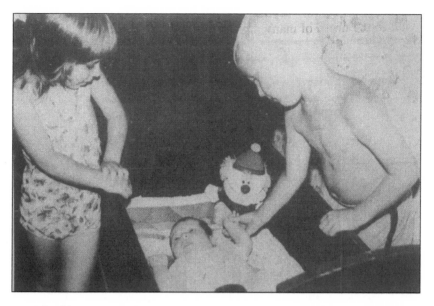

Month-old James Nash is welcomed to Wallowa County by cousins Mona Lee and Buck. The old wooden cradle has been used by little James's cousins before him.

Ben, Doug and Steve are moving yearlings to the ranch from one of our rented pastures. Very hot this afternoon.

The Houghs have finished putting up their "bread loaf" haystacks. As a few afternoon clouds form over the valley, it cools off a bit. Our lawn and yard are so pleasant on these long summer evenings. The petunias, snapdragons, cosmos, geraniums are a riot of color, especially my pretty"Happiness" petunias. They truly do bring happiness to all who view them. They provide a continuous show of color all summer, even into the fall...all shades of vibrant, pink hues.

Our normally quiet valley will change this weekend. The annual Chief Joseph Days celebration is gearing up for another run. Many people descending from all around, to camp everywhere, stay with relatives or just drive for the day.

July 22—Cooler today. Todd's little family left for their home on the Slope. Doug, Steve and Ben changing sprinkler pipes in our hayfields and pastures. Purchased some peaches from a roadside stand in Enterprise. The Imnaha fruit mostly got wiped out with frost, hail, or other weather-related problems this year. Such a pity, as normally we buy our fruit in the canyon country.

These days begin to shorten and darkness comes faster when the sun slips over the western ridges. Even my pet rooster "Chester" flies up to his perch in the willow tree earlier each evening.

The pipe changers in for supper around 7. I do chores, while Susanne lets the chickens out to run and eat green grass. This keeps their yolks a pretty yellow color...and that's no yolk!

July 23—Cooler again, pure heaven hoeing in my pretty vegetable garden this morning. How I love my garden, being in the fresh air, seeing the mountains and the wide open spaces of Prairie Creek on a perfect summer morning.

Not work at all...a privilege. Indeed it is, and this was brought home to me again when recently I was visited by a senior editor of National Geographic magazine. As he drove up, I was working in my garden and he commented on how lucky I was. He had flown to Pendleton from Los Angeles for an assignment here and said it was like coming to a completely different universe.

When not on an assignment, he makes his home in Washington, D.C., and spends most of the time in a stuffy office. I can very well see how he would feel this way.

Sy Fishbein and I had a most interesting conversation in my sheepherder's wagon. We discussed word processors, which he and I both don't like, and the modern ways of journalism versus the old Underwood Standard that I use, which had the case stepped on by a cow when it was stored in the barn on Alder Slope.

Anyway, we would like to leave the new-fangled aids to the younger generation, who are more adapted to them. We both agreed that we like to "feel" the words beneath our fingers, and have the typewriter say what comes from us, not shortened into some uninteresting, correct, straight to the point sentence that perhaps has all the adjectives removed and is DEAD.

Enough of this. That is another story, which I have voluminous notes on. Perhaps when things get dull. Ha. I will dig out the notes and tell you more about Mr. Fishbein and our trip to Imnaha.

Susanne and I froze peaches this morning, made raspberry jam and picked gooseberries. 'Tis the season of plenty.

Doug hauling some newly purchased heifers to the ranch. The daily pipe changing goes on and on. I wonder how the Alder Slope family is making it. Suspect they will be living out of boxes for quite a while. The baby's needs are primary now. How I remember those times. It always amazes me how such a small bit of humanity can dictate their parents' actions, but they do, and they are worth the effort.

Susanne is baking cookies. The cookie bear has been empty for quite some time. I put an elk roast in the oven, then Susanne and I ran errands in Joseph. Our small town is beginning to take on a festive air; banners wave over main street and western music drifts out over the town.

After supper and chores, I hoed in the garden until dark. Finished removing every last weed. The vegetables look so nice. They are a great source of pride to me, even if the rows are a bit crooked.

July 24—Nice having Susanne here to help. She does the breakfast dishes while I milk the cow and chore, and she peeled the peaches so I could make a fresh cobbler. Also baked sourdough bread. The smells from the kitchen are "Wonderful," says our Swiss Miss, Susanne.

As we wash the clothes and do housework, we listen to the music of Rodgers and Hammerstein's musical "Oklahoma" on our stereo. Susanne has never heard this before, but is familiar with classical works such as Mozart and Brahms. She plays the flute beautifully and comes from a musical family in Switzerland. It is indeed a beautiful morning as we look across at Hough's haystacks in the soft morning light.

Susanne has named my new little calico kitten "Pasta." This colorful little ball of fur has been winning her way into our hearts.

July 25—Another beautiful morning. Doug was up early picking raspberries. I fixed sausage, eggs, toast and fresh raspberry jam for breakfast.

Some of the grandchildren calling, needing rides for their assorted animals to the Kiddie Parade! Uncle Todd came to the rescue and offered his pickup.

Susan and I arrived in Joseph, and were soon surrounded by all manner of children and animals of every description.

I managed to do some photographing prior to the parade and especially enjoyed visiting with three charming Indian children. I gave each of them a quarter for posing for a picture; those smiles were worth it.

The Kiddie Parade has grown. A good crowd lined the main street of Joseph to watch Wallowa County's young people in review.

My grandchildren actually got there, Chad leading "Friendly," the family's pet calf; Chelsie pushing a doll buggy overflowing with cats, wearing bonnets; and Rowdy opted to carry his new puppy instead of bringing his pig to the parade. It seems the pig had other ideas about being led before he left home.

Willie Zollman's young jersey heifer wears a bonnet for the Chief Joseph Days Kiddie Parade. A member of the Sourdough Shutterbugs 4-H club, Willie keeps busy with a 4-H dairy project and took part in the Wallowa County Fair.

I was impressed with the Nez Perce Riders, a local 4-H club. Their riding group was comprised of many young people, all ages, riding horses, all sizes, all breeds that had been painted up like Indian ponies.

Clouding up, windy and dry. Home to fix lunch.

Thunderheads form over the mountains. Spent the afternoon preparing food for tomorrow's family picnic here after the big parade. Made a pasta salad, an apple pie and a wacky cake.

It was cold for the opening performance of the rodeo tonight. Doug and I didn't attend, but we did drive into Joseph for a while.

Things were not quite the same this year, due to the absence of the carnival. We missed seeing the lights of the ferris wheel and I have always enjoyed riding the merry-go-round. Grandmas can get by with this, by accompanying a grandchild.

Gaudy souvenirs were being sold by vendors that lined the street. There was the usual cotton candy, hamburger concessions and all the store windows were painted with clever drawings that depicted the Chief Joseph Days theme. Since most of the people were attending the rodeo it was rather quiet on Main Street. We drove up to the lake to check on our cows and were home in bed by 9.

July 26—Up to oven-fry some of my fresh frozen fryers...a big day ahead.

After changing pipes, Doug left for the steak 'n eggs cowboy breakfast in Joseph. While I chored and milked the cow, Susan saddled my horse for the parade. I gathered up props for the Sourdough Shutterbugs 4-H float and the CowBelle banner, and we were off to the big parade.

There we met Steve, who had driven one of our small tractors in towing a long flat-bed trailer, upon which the 4-H'ers were in the process of constructing their float.

Meanwhile, CowBelle Robin Ganos and I began to "practice" riding our horses while carrying the new banner. It soon became apparent that Robin's mare didn't want any part of this, and almost succeeded in unseating her rider, so we enlisted Paula Boston, whose mount wasn't too receptive either, but soon decided the "thing" wouldn't bite and settled down. Just in time, too, as we began riding down Main Street. The team and wagon, owned by Wayne and Joann Lathrop, comprised our float.

Helen Jones, holding her baby grandson, and Meleese Cook portrayed the 1886 ranch wives, while at the rear of the wagon, Amy Johnson and Leah Simmons demonstrated some of the roles played by 1986 CowBelles.

The Lathrop grandchildren added the final touch as they rode beside their grandparents on the seat of the wagon.

Our CowBelle entry was among the first in the parade line-up, so I was able to view the remainder of the parade. My Sourdough Shutterbugs went by and I could see by the time they reached the judges' stand they would be engaged in a full scale flour fight!

Members attired with backpacking equipment, taking pictures, tripods set up, roasting marshmallows over a simulated fire, fishing from a wash-tub, mixing sourdough all got into the act! They ended up winning first place, despite the fact that they were covered with flour to the point of being unrecognizable!

A sort of camaraderie exists among the members of my 4-H club, which is hard to put into words. Perhaps the closeness of shared outdoor experiences, their sense of unbridled fun, contributes to this. Maybe our excursions into the mountains, hills and canyons are an "escape' from a world gone mad. As I watch each child grow, each his own person, it makes me feel good to know that perhaps these times they now share will somehow help them, in a positive way, to meet some of their future challenges.

I contemplated these things as I watched other youth groups pass in review.

It is always a thrill to watch the big parade at Chief Joseph Days, as it boasts one of the largest concentrations of horses in the Northwest. I love seeing the big draft horses like the Kooch Clydesdales, all harnessed and decked out in their parade finery.

A mounted group of riders had ridden all the way from Milton-Freewater, through the mountains, to join the parade!

Averaging around 20 miles per day, they had camped along the way.

Home to put food on the picnic table for our family gathering. The menfolk got into a game of horseshoes that lasted all afternoon.

A beautiful sunset flamed and died as another day ended on Prairie Creek.

July 27—A succession of perfect days, not too cold, not too hot. Doug and I awoke to see two young men sprawled in sleeping bags on our living room floor. A note by the phone written by son Steve read: "Please do not feed the BEARs." He explained they were just friends who needed a place to bed for the night.

"Chester," our pet Banty rooster...another story...greeted me as I went out to chore. He joined the cat family and they all tagged after me to the barn. I notice our cow dog Kit is licking flour off the bed of the flatbed wagon of our leftover Sourdough Shutterbug float!

The valley is peaceful this Sunday morning. I can imagine the night-time crowds are still in deep slumber, like the two reposing on our floor. Wallowa County's visitors play hard for three days and by Sunday have slowed down to a crawl.

As the mountains look down on yet another Chief Joseph Days celebration they see the tepee village that is set up along the river. Wallowa County is proud of its Indian heritage and welcomes their return each year.

I enjoy sitting in our pretty yard and contemplating sunlight as it spills down on the pink cosmos this morning.

We attended the final performance of the rodeo this afternoon. It was a good show, featuring a fantastic trained buffalo act.

As people leave the valley, Joseph is buried under litter and refuse that will be cleaned up by the same volunteers that help make this annual event such a yearly success.

July 28—Another beautiful morning, almost a "fallish" feeling in the air already. Back to the routine of ranch living after the big weekend...pipe changing, cleaning house, picking raspberries. Doug finished picking all the gooseberries this evening. Cleaned and frozen, they repose in the freezer for winter pies.

July 29—Cut some of my fresh lettuce to take into the Country Place this morning. I have such an abundance, it is good to have it used up.

Doug left for Imnaha this hot afternoon to find his yearly trout, blackberry and rattlesnake!

I attended a 4-H leaders meeting; we are finalizing Fair plans.

Returning home, I stepped into the kitchen to see a dead rattlesnake reposing on the table, two enormous boxes of the prettiest blackberries you ever saw, and trout cleaned, in the fridge. Doug had been successful as usual. The dead rattlesnake, meant to be a practical joke (to the cook), evoked the desired reaction, which will satisfy the practical joker for another year! Susan will take the rattles back to Switzerland and tell her people the story.

July 30—Another hot day in a succession of hot days. Ben and Steve to the hill ranch to repair a bridge. Meanwhile, I gloried in blackberries...made two cobblers, freezer jam and froze some whole for winter.

The smells coming from the oven and the sight of the red juicy cobblers as they came from the oven made us all look forward to mealtime. These are the biggest, plumpest, wild blackberries I've seen in years. Two years ago the blackberry vines froze out on Imnaha, but they are back better than ever this year.

Around 5 p.m. Doug decided we should all go down to Packsaddle Creek and pick blackberries. So he, Susan and I took off for the lower Imnaha. We arrived, armed with berry buckets, and began to pick. Wary of snakes at first, we soon became braver and tromped right into where the biggest berries hung. After an hour or so, we had two more boxes of berries.

On the way home, we stopped at the Imnaha Store for a pizza, walking into the small country store, covered with blackberry stains. Meanwhile, back at the ranch, Star was bawling at the barn door and glad to see me.

July 31—Up early to make more freezer jam. While preserving these wild blackberries, I was also preserving the "feeling" of an Imnaha evening...memories tucked away of berry picking in that quiet, far-away canyon...remembering the cool fresh breeze floating down the draws. The smell of blackberries, ripened in the sun. The dusty road and dry grasses of July, the call of the canyon birds, attracted to Packsaddle Creek to drink in the cool.

The deer quietly appearing on the lower benches to feed in the evening light. And mostly I will remember the beautiful stillness of unpeopled places, which is synonymous with the Imnaha. As I stir the jam, then, I am preserving these sights, sounds and feelings in my mind's canning cupboard.

In the middle of the blackberry jam making, Doug presented me with two buckets of raspberries. What does he think this is, Knott's Berry Farm?

The cobblers were inhaled, so made another one for Susan's 19th birthday, which we will celebrate with a birthday dinner tonight. Also made a sourdough chocolate cake for the occasion. We will have 21 people for supper, if we count baby James.

Baked sourdough bread, roasted three chickens, made an enormous garden salad with corn on the cob, beets, zucchini and a large platter of fruit.

The food that took all day to fix was inhaled in a matter of minutes, including a freezer of hand-cranked ice cream. Yours truly forgot to put the dasher in and the poor grandchildren and daddies turned and cranked until they were blue in the face, before we discovered the error! (I'll never live this one down.) The dasher was inserted and the ice cream was the best ever.

Needless to say, Susan was overjoyed. An American birthday party!

She was on cloud nine when we sang happy birthday to her and she blew out all her candles.

I spent the night in the sheepherder wagon with Mona and Buck; this seems to be the highlight of all the grandchildren's stays here on the ranch.

August 1—Up early to clean after the party. Was pleased last evening when the Grays from North Powder stopped by to visit. I had given them a slice of sourdough bread and invited them for supper. They had been staying at the lake and just wanted to meet me and see the places I'd written about. Such nice people, ranchers like ourselves.

Picked the first ripe cherry tomatoes off the vines tonight. Just turned the calendar to August and see that it is completely covered with events: reunions, county fair, Stockgrowers, CowBelles meetings, 4-H, and birthdays.

Susan plays a silver flute...the beautiful notes of Mozart drift out over the valley. Perched on a stump of wood in the chicken pen, she plays to my chickens! Perhaps these birds will absorb a bit of culture...or be inspired to lay more eggs.

We are all enjoying the bounty of the garden: beets, lettuce, new, red potatoes, carrots and chard.

After pipe changing, and supper, Doug and I headed for our special huckleberry patch. As we drove up Salt Creek Summit, a mule deer doe jumped across in front of us with twin fawns in tow.

In the cool creek bottom, we picked huckleberries. They are few and far between this year, but we did manage to pick enough for hot cakes in the morning. We did notice that a bear had been feeding in our huckleberry patch before us!

August 2—Another hot day ahead. The huckleberry pancakes were wonderful.

My pet rooster Chester is becoming tame enough to eat crumbs from my hand. He wanders around mumbling to himself; such a character. He and the little Calico kitten, Pasta, play together while I milk Star. Chester can't quite make up his mind whether he is a cat or a people.

We attended the Ray Hunt Horse Clinic in Enterprise this morning. Ray started 13 head today, including one mule. It was fascinating to watch this master horse trainer work.

He watches the horse's every move and senses every change that occurs, be it ever so slight. He "reads" a horse's mind. Every horse is different, says Hunt, and when you figure him out, you can act accordingly.

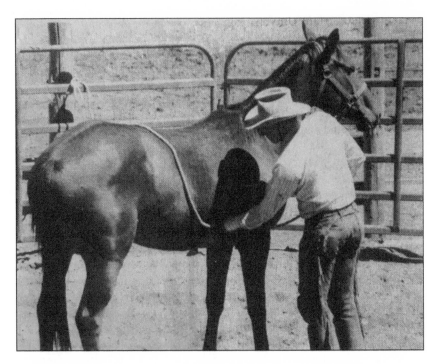

Ray Hunt with a young, unbroken horse at the County Fairgrounds.

Shortly after this picture was taken, Ray Hunt saddled this mule for the first time. A day later, the owner was riding the mule around the arena.

By late afternoon, Hunt had saddled all the animals and had their owners saddling them when a terrific wind storm came up. Blowing dirt and dust almost obscured the horses and people in the arena. The parched hills surrounding Enterprise have never looked so dry. We could use some rain.

August 3—Up at 5:30 to chore before breakfast, so Susan and I could hike up the mountain before the sun got too hot. We met another friend and drove up toward the trailhead.

However, partway up the road, a large truck was parked across the road and we had to turn around. For years we have used this access to climb up through Murray Gap and into the Silver Creek Country. Now signs proclaim, NO TRESPASSING! KEEP OUT! This, on a road we have traveled for nearly 20 years.

New people have moved into the area and obviously have different ideas. Nothing to do but turn around and approach our trail from another, longer direction! Later, as we trudged up an old logging road, the day began to heat up; we had hoped to get an early start and make the top before the intense heat arrived.

Welcome shady areas protected us from the direct sun, and the many green, ferny places that followed the spring-fed streams were havens in the heat.

We made our way to a familiar landmark, a sort of bald knob or knoll, that is visible from the valley below. This high point commanded a wonderful view of the valley and afforded a coolish breeze that blew over the parched vegetation. Never have I seen the country so dry.

Below we could see the checkered farmlands in shades of green and brown. The parched hills rolling off into the horizon shimmered in the August heat.

A smoky haze covered the distant Snake River breaks as well as the Seven Devils Range in Idaho. Freezeout Saddle, almost always visible from here, was obscured by smoky haze. A fire on Brushy last evening, put out during the night, left tell-tale wisps of smoke lingering over the canyon.

Sitting down to rest, we saw fresh indentations in the dry grass and other signs that indicated a herd of elk had bedded only hours ago at this same spot.

As we gazed up the long circuitous route that would take us to our destination, we opted instead to make a long half circle around the mountainside, staying in the shade as much as possible.

The exposed rocky area above lost its appeal as the heat became even more intense and draining. We scrambled around on a maze of mostly grown-over logging roads, pausing by old cabin sites; belonging to miners, I suppose.

Stumbled into an abandoned orchard where the deer had been feeding on the apples. We savored the cool of natural springs. Finally, back at Bill's cabin, we ate our lunches.

As we stepped out of the cabin, we startled a big, mule deer doe that had been feeding in Bill's garden. She had nibbled on the strawberry plants and nipped some young fruit trees. Bill gave us an armful of bright red rhubarb stalks and we headed home to rest up.

Son Ken and family returned our mule and horses after packing into Francis Lake. They had a grand time and caught enough fish for supper every night.

Since I had made a fried chicken dinner, a loaf of sourdough bread and a juicy rhubarb pie, they stayed for supper.

August 4—Hot...all night.

There is a green pepper forming on one of my pepper plants. A first on Prairie Creek for me! And the zucchini is ripening. Hurrah! "Oh no!" says Doug!

Did chores, then a huge washing. The hills are so dry looking. We need a rain. Clouds form every day, only to dissipate by evening.

Four-H'er Jenny here to print pictures in my darkroom for the fair, which is nearly upon us.

Fixed porcupines for supper...not real ones. They consist of hamburger, rice and onions, made into a meat ball, then baked in a tomato sauce. The result is this pretty little meatball, with rice sticking out...like porcupine quills! It is a recipe that Ellie Hanks gave me, a good cook who lives down along Little Sheep Creek. I picked the rest of supper from the garden.

August 5—Doug, Ben and Steve to the hills to haul in some heifers we will ship to a feedlot in Washington.

Lately it seems I am walking around carrying my typewriter. The house trailer studio is too hot during the day, the lawn too cold at night, the house too noisy, and the kitchen table always feeding someone. So my writing studio floats from place to place. I must make do the best I can. Watering takes precedence these days...the lawns, flowers, garden, hayfields and pastures.

The smoke from many fires blows over the mountains this evening. We hear on the radio that Baker County has some bad fires burning;

lightning-caused. A few burning in our Wilderness, being let go, as they will eventually burn out on the high, rocky terrain.

The mountains have lost all traces of snow, except for a small patch, visible from our ranch, on Chief Joseph Mountain.

Doug to a stockgrowers scholarship award meeting, I worked in the darkroom until late.

August 6—Warm, clear and dry. Busy. After doing chores, into Enterprise to pick up 80 frozen fruit pies at Food City. I will bake some and others will be distributed to Sourdough Shutterbug members to be baked for the Food Booth at the Fair. Worked on photography exhibit for the fair. Doug attended the final day of the Ray Hunt Horse Clinic.

Baked a fresh peach cobbler for supper. Susan does the dishes while I chore. All of us attended the Royal Lipizzaner Stallion Show at the fairgrounds tonight.

What a contrast! On the same ground Ray Hunt started Wallowa County cow horses, now parade the fancy Lipizzaners. Under lights and accompanied by loud music such as Blue Danube and other Straus waltzes, these stallions leaped into the air and performed intricate lead changes; all the while immaculately groomed, with silver manes and tails shining under the lights.

A large crowd turned out to view such a sight in Wallowa County. It was a perfect evening for the performance, warm and mild. As the sun disappeared over the western hills and the show began, the master of ceremonies stepped out in our dusty arena, decked out in tie and tux and beard. In an adjacent corral, the Ray Hunt Clinic cow ponies, their ears pricked toward the goings-on, wondered "What in the world!"

Perhaps the Royal Lipizzaner stallions looked at the cow ponies and wondered how it would be to be off across the Wallowa County hills, racing along, tails and manes flowing free in the wind, rather than be under the beck and call of their trainers.

We rather guessed that every cough and sneeze was recorded, as some of these horses were valued as high as $250,000.

The polished voice of the M.C! "For over 400 years, the six bloodlines of the Lipizzaner breed has been carefully maintained with tradition and marked control!"

I helped keep small James under control when things got a bit loud by waltzing up and down the aisles and "dancing" to the Blue Danube. Little month-old James has attended the Ray Hunt Clinic and now attends the Royal Lipizzaner Show. His education has begun.

August 7—The first pullet laid an egg today, and I picked the first zucchini this morning.

Fair-time weather, another cloudless, hot day. Up early to have breakfast on the table by 6. Cattle being shipped to their feedlot in Washington.

Off to the fair, loaded with pies and photography.

A long, busy day readying the 4-H photography entries. I am always impressed by the many volunteers who work so many long hours at the fair, mostly for the 4-H program. Susan and I ate a good hamburger at the fair food booth. I noticed that a few leaders and parents are beginning to wilt in the heat.

Grocery shopped for items I will use to help prepare a meal for 40 people at the lake tomorrow night. Home to chores, supper and writing. Sat out on the cool of our lawn this evening and enjoyed the quiet. A breeze sprang up and chased most of the smoke away.

The hills are as dry as Doug can remember. Sure hope we don't get any lightning starts!

August 9—Awoke to loud moos and answering bawls from the barn…in all the activities last evening, I had forgotten to do my chores! I had been feeding people and forgotten my animals! Even Chester, the banty rooster, mumbled disgustedly, as he fell in line behind the procession of cats that followed me and the milk bucket to the barn.

He has been spoiled lately by free handouts of barley that I snitch from Star's ration.

As I walked back to the house with my pail-full of milk, Maud, the mule, began to bray! Have you ever felt like the world depends on you to feed them? Well, I did this morning.

Since the people I had to feed were mostly still in bed, I drove over to Ben's to feed Zack's 4-H hogs, as they are gone for a couple of days.

Back to my "people kitchen" where I prepared a gig ranch-style breakfast for our house guests (how they love the berry jams, fresh eggs and homemade bread).

Susan home in time to do breakfast dishes, while I baked two black-berry cobblers and put eight more frozen pies into the oven for the fair food booth. The children went fishing in the creek, just as Jackie's family arrived to visit…children everywhere! Some playing the piano, some riding the three-wheeler, others simply running around the awn and chasing cats.

I corralled them all for lunch. Jackie's family had left for her class reunion picnic at the Enterprise City Park. Naps for some, so took advantage of the lull to bake bread and put a big pot roast to bake in the dutch oven for supper.

The men and boys left for the moraine pasture to check on the cattle.

The zucchini is on a binge! And the cherry tomatoes are ripening more every day. Another phone call...more company for supper.

Susan fed the orphan calf. It is still alive, but had a rough beginning to life. By the time more company from the Tri-Cities arrived, Jackie was back, so they loaded up all the loose children and took them to Wallowa Lake to swim.

Eventually everyone returned to the ranch (like homing pigeons) to cool off in the shade of our lawn. An uncleaned fish, caught earlier by Josh, expired in the back porch washtray. A succession of children have washed their hands over it and it is now a soap-soaked trout!

We enjoyed a supper of pot roast, baked potatoes, garden salad, fresh beets, sourdough bread, gallons of milk, and iced sun tea, eaten out on the big picnic table on the lawn. Guessed there must have been around 20 of us.

People kept coming and going; I didn't try to keep track. Merilee did dishes, while Fern and the tribe of children followed me out to chore. Star, alarmed at the approaching army, fled to the far corner of the pasture. After driving her in, she wouldn't let down her milk, even to fill the kitty dish.

After loading all the children up in the pickup, we headed over to feed Zack's pigs.

Todd and Liza came to borrow our motor home for a few days. They will spend a quiet time camping up near Indian Crossing with the baby.

After everyone helped themselves to blackberry cobbler, they went to bed. A long day, not over yet. I ended up in the sheepherder wagon with Mona and Buck. Members of our family kept arriving all night long, as I lay against the wall of the old wagon, scrunched beside two warm, little bodies. The open window permitted a cool breeze to blow over us and I could look up at the stars that were brilliant, and I could also see a new moon hanging in the sky.

Some time in the night, the daddy picked up the sleeping children and I had the whole bed to myself...heaven.

August 10—Slept in 'til 7; awakened by Chester crowing. Another hot day. Fixed sourdough waffles for the crew. Enjoyed visiting Bob Tippett, Doug's nephew, while cooking breakfast. He kindly did my dishes while I chored.

Shawn Ray Hook poses with her sheep in the Ladies' Lead Sheep contest at the Wallowa County Fair. The wool outfits worn by Shawn Ray and her lamb are made from the same material.

Ryan Hook, 12, son of Jerry and Nancy Hook of Prairie Creek, shot his first antelope, near Whitehorse in Southeastern Oregon. Ryan is a member of the Sourdough Shutterbugs 4-H club and a good outdoorsman.

Later on in the morning, I loaded the pies into the car and delivered them to the fair. I met Doug at the Country Place, where we had a gathering of the Jidge Tippett clan. We all enjoyed visiting and I especially appreciated the catered lunch, which consisted of chicken salad, stuffed tomatoes, homemade bread, fresh fruit and blackberry pie.

During the afternoon meetings we consumed gallons of iced tea and pink lemonade. A very hot afternoon, with enormous thunderheads building up in the skies.

The company has all left for home. It was fun to see everyone. Too bad it's only a once-a-year gathering.

August 11—Couldn't sleep well last night…lightning flashes lit up the sky, accompanied by claps of thunder that rolled off into the distance. Only a few sprinkles of rain fell. Dry lightning…what we have all been fearing. I could almost envision each strike starting a fire.

Doug and Steve left for the hills to bring in our dry cows to the sale today.

Susan cleaned house while I baked more pies for the fair.

The smoke from many lightning-caused fires billows up in many directions. We hear scattered reports about one in Imnaha, near Grouse Creek, and another on Joseph Creek Canyon.

A busy day at the fair…4-H'er Jenny Hanson and I photographed all the market animals for the buyers' cards. Jenny began with the fat lambs, while I tackled the hogs.

Have you ever tried to photograph a hog during a class? Well, let me tell you, it won't work.

Our extension agent suggested I photograph them after they were driven back to their pens. This worked fairly well and I did manage to zero in on the 4-H'er and FFA member and actually got a snout, back of a pig, or at least a few hairs into the picture.

The main problem was getting the porker to stand still long enough. I tried snapping off a few shots in the alley and found myself moving down the aisle at a rapid rate, holding my camera aloft, riding the back of the hog. The rascal simply saw his escape, right through my legs. I tried telling myself, women of my age shouldn't be put in these situations. Why me?

During this time, I missed seeing my grandson, Chad, show his first steer. I found out that he had gotten a blue ribbon choice on Ralph.

Arrived home just in time to find Doug and Steve leaving for the hills to check on the fire situation. They had our cattle sprayer filled with water and thermoses of coffee and some donuts.

They returned later with news that the fires are still a ways north of our range, but wind conditions could change or new starts could be discovered.

The smell of smoke fills the air tonight. Little did we know that our once clear, pure air would be polluted by the smoke of 127 fires and burn for days, or that more than 5,000 firefighters would invade us in the hours to come.

August 12—Clear, except for the smoke that hangs over the big fires.

Twenty-five additional crews have been brought in from all over to fight fires here in our county. Firefighters wait around for assignments as to what fire they will be sent to. We hear on the radio that presently 13 crews are manning spot fires that are among 2,500 lightning strikes that occurred Sunday night.

Planes landing continuously with infra-red pictures that enable the pinpointing of the fires. Meanwhile, Rogge mill workers are on strike over wage negotiations and the Boise Cascade crew is threatening too. Our peaceful valley is in a turmoil. Here on the ranch, as on other Wallowa County ranches and farms, life goes on... the daily work must be done. I feed the pipe changers their breakfast. Doug's back is better, but son Steve's is now injured. Ben has the week off for a deserved vacation.

Driving to Joseph this morning to pick up 4-H'er Jenny, I saw that the Joseph Rodeo arena had become a fire camp headquarters, with buses, Army trucks and tents everywhere.

Spent the day at the fair. Grandson Chad won the 4-H junior beef showmanship contest. Such a remarkable resemblance to his dad at that age.

While the fair continues, we see smoke from many fires burning out north. We find out that there is a big one on Starvation Ridge near Joseph Creek, another one on Kuhn Ridge. The Horse Creek fire on Imnaha is still burning.

While we watched the round robin showmanship class (where the winners of the beef, sheep and swine events compete for all-around showman), the fire planes continued to fly overhead. Borate planes and helicopters heading out north.

It was amusing to watch the competition between the 4-H'ers. Grandson Chad did fine handling his steer Ralph and managed to keep the hog under control, but had quite a time with the lamb. As he took hold of the woolly animal, it headed out the door, pursued by the leaders and members, and leading them on a chase before finally being captured.

Ralph, a 1,168-pound Simmental-cross steer owned by Chad Nash of Alder Slope, brought 80 cents a pound for a total of $934.40 at the Wallowa County Fair youth livestock auction. Purchaser was Mick Courtney of Enterprise. Nash expects to miss Ralph. Many young people shed a tear or two during the auction.

The competition was won by the two members who owned the lambs, as they were the only ones who could control them!

Driving home, we noticed a wind blowing smoke from the fires and soon the valley was filled with smoke.

We had been invited to a barbecue at Wallowa Lake and arrived to enjoy a nice meal cooked by Patsy and Janet.

August 13—We listen to our local radio station for updated reports on the fires. It is expected that 1,900 people will be on the fire lines today. Some hot shot firefighters flown in from Arizona are among them.

Fire camps are set up all over our county: Sled Springs, Imnaha, Joseph. The Imnaha School has been turned into a headquarters for the big canyon blazes.

We fear for our range land, which for the time being remains out of danger. The Starvation Ridge fire has joined another fire and now has a 2,800-foot front.

It is sad to think about the range and forest land going up in smoke.

Fixed breakfast and baked 14 more frozen pies for the last day of the fair. Much cooler this morning and the smoke has cleared somewhat, but a haze hangs out north over the fires.

Day after day of hot, dry weather hampers fire suppression and the governor flew over our county today and declared it a disaster area.

I think about the fences being burned, range lands that will take three years to completely recover, and the many other hardships to our county's ranchers.

At the fair yesterday, we met Rune Neeri, the International Farm Youth Exchange student from Norway. We gave him a ride home from the fair to the Lockes', where he is staying while in our county.

Rune is a very nice young man who is extremely interested in our area. This morning he is here riding horses with Susan.

Sent a birthday card to my oldest granddaughter, Tammy, who will be 16 tomorrow. Can this be? Where are the years going so fast?

Recent hot nights have caused the zucchini and crookneck squashes to go mad. The raspberries need picking and the lawn needs mowing. Help!

Delivered the last of the pies to the food booth at the fair and picked up my photography entries at Cloverleaf Hall.

Then Rune, Susan and I watched the 4-H sheep leading contest, which was followed by the 4-H style revue. So impressed with the talent displayed by our young people.

The FFA members served a barbecued beef dinner and then we watched the fat stock auction, where I watched my grandson, Chad, sell Ralph. With a grandma's eye, I noticed the sad look in my boy's face as he parted with his friend. The steer was such a pet and so trusting of his owner. Many tears were shed in that auction ring, dampening the necks of lambs and smearing the faces of the animals' owners.

Home by 10 p.m. to let Star in to nurse the two calves.

August 14—Son Todd's 24th birthday. Am planning a dinner in his honor this evening. Made an apple pie and a sourdough chocolate cake.

After lunch Susan and I went swimming in the Lockes' pool. Refreshing on this very hot day.

The fires continue to rage, over 27,000 acres having already been consumed. Cold statistics, but in reality it means our forest lands and ranges going up in smoke. So hot the days, so rugged the terrain, most of the fires simply burn on despite the efforts of so many firefighters. The total population of our county is only 6,000 and before the fires can be extinguished, perhaps the total number of inhabitants will almost double.

Refreshed by the swim, I baked a batch of sourdough bread sticks, fried chicken, and picked garden vegetables to complete the birthday dinner for Todd, who soon arrived with wife, Liza, and son James. My new grandson is such a healthy, happy baby. Already smiling and responding.

We ate out in our pretty yard, enjoying the warm evenings while we can. Fall will soon be upon us.

Called granddaughter Tammy to wish her a happy birthday. She had just sold her champion 4-H market lamb at the Quincy fair in California for $6 per pound!

August 15—Another hot, dry day. A busy weekend ahead, our stockgrowers' and CowBelles' annual meetings, the Wilson family reunion, and always the fires, which have affected all our lives here in the county.

This afternoon, Doug, Susan and I drove out the Zumwalt road to check on conditions there. We could see billowing clouds of smoke exploding from the big Pumpkin Creek fire on the long ridge that divides the Imnaha and Snake River canyons.

A very frightening sight on this hot afternoon as the wind blew, fanning fires that were now fueled by dry timber.

We could also see the Middlepoint fire on Imnaha as we drove farther out toward Zumwalt. We turned toward Pine Creek and drove by our cattle grazing the dry grasses.

Driving down Crow Creek, we saw fires burning on Mack Birkmaier's range, snags and stumps smoldering in the burned over areas. Turning up the Charlois Road, we eventually came out on the north highway to Lewiston. Beyond Snow Hollow Hill we were held up by road construction. Convoys of fire-fighting rigs lined up behind us.

We stopped at the Joseph Canyon viewpoint to watch the fires. Huge, billowing clouds of smoke exploded as they traveled up the timbered draws, creating their own fierce winds in the intense heat. Pitchy flames crept from tree to tree, licking up the dry canyon sides.

The once peaceful Joseph Creek Canyon is now an inferno.

We stopped at the Rimrock Inn for a cold drink of pop and watched more fires as a steady stream of pumper trucks came up from the road below. Helpless to do much in the intense heat, firefighters, both men and women, stood around waiting for orders. Borate planes, and helicopters, carrying huge containers of water dipped from the river, bombarded the flames. The sky was yellow hot, the air acrid with smoke.

Home to chores, then fixed a fruit platter for a get-together at Wortman's for CowBelles and Stockgrowers. A half-moon hangs in the sky and the talk is mainly of the fires.

Van Van Blaricom, Wallowa County's grassman of the year, and his wife, Betty, stand beside a display they put together earlier this year. It focused on soil conservation and won first place for CowBelles in the Landfest event.

August 16—Seem to be lagging behind in my journal. Guess these summer days are just too full. Will try to do a little "catching up," skipping a few days here and there.

On this hot day, with many fires continuing to rage over our county, the CowBelles and Stockgrowers had a busy time. The morning began with a Stockgrowers' annual meeting and breakfast at the VFW Hall in Enterprise, a CowBelle annual meeting and luncheon at Tomas Restaurant, and ended with a dinner-dance at Cloverleaf Hall. Yours truly attended them all and, by dance time, this CowBelle began to fade fast.

The 1986 Cattleman of the Year award went to our neighbor on Prairie Creek, Harold Klages, and the Grassman of the Year award was won by another neighbor, Van Van Blaricom, who ranches on upper Prairie Creek.

We drove home under a hazy moonglow, the smell of smoke ever-present in the air. I fall asleep thinking of the Pumpkin Creek fire and wondering if the cow camp and corrals at Cayuse Flat will escape the flames.

August 17—The hot, dry days continued, and so did the fires. The planes and helicopters flying overhead became a daily part of our lives, as did the smoky skies.

Grandson Buck turned six and we celebrated with a birthday dinner complete with the traditional sourdough chocolate cake.

On a Sunday morning we attended a Wilson family reunion at Wallowa Lake State Park, a breakfast get-together in the picnic area. Even the lake campgrounds are unusually dry this year. We were entertained by some of the mule deer that inhabit the park.

A steady stream of company arrived and departed, mostly relatives that we rarely see except for summer. Some of them take off across the hill to our creek to fish and enjoy the restful??? atmosphere of our ranch.

Perhaps, to a visitor, the pace does seem much slower than city life.

While son-in-law Bill barbecued steaks this evening for Buck's birthday dinner, a cyclonic wind came up and a fast-moving storm swept over us, bringing sprinkles of rain accompanied by claps of thunder and flashes of lightning, and our electricity went off. The wind blew away the smoke temporarily until the fires flared up again with renewed vigor.

To bed in the sheepherder wagon with Buck and Mona. Didn't sleep very well...the kitten "Pasta" spent the night with us and her motor didn't shut off all night!

August 18—I fixed sourdough hotcakes for breakfast and looked outside to see that the smoke filled our whole world.

Invisible mountains loomed behind a smoky curtain. Worst conditions yet. Almost 5,000 firefighters are on the lines now. New starts and old fires continue to eat up Wallowa County's range and timber lands.

We prayed for rain, even though none was in the forecast.

The men are readying our ag bagging equipment to begin harvesting the fava beans for silage.

Took Buck fishing up the irrigation ditch that flows from Wallowa Lake. His second cast landed him a 13-inch rainbow! Mona Lee meanwhile amused herself by picking me a bouquet of wild daisies that grew alongside the water.

Susan, our "Swiss Miss," is still with us, and she peeled apples for me to can for winter pies. I developed three rolls of film.

Spent hours at the typewriter preparing an article on the Stockgrowers' and CowBelles' annual meetings for our local newspaper, the Wallowa County Chieftain.

Invited Aunt Amey Wilson for supper, fixed a big pot roast, creamed new potatoes and peas, pickled beets, crookneck squash, cherry tomatoes, lettuce, all from the garden.

Baked sourdough bread. We ate out on the picnic table near the blooming cosmos. It is always such fun to prepare a meal in the good ol' summer time with all the wonderful produce of our garden. Our company always says it brings back memories of how their mothers used to cook on the farm. Guess times haven't changed that much around the supper tables in Wallowa County anyway.

Pipe changing goes on, a daily chore.

August 19—We began to cut the fava beans and make silage for winter cattle feed. The weather continued hot and dry, day after day of no rain. The cold statistics kept on too: 11,800 acres consumed to date on the Pumpkin Creek fire, 27,600 on Joseph Creek. Millions of dollars being spent…unreal!

Our local grocery stores worked night and day to keep the shelves stocked with food, and out-of-state catering trucks drove in daily with meals to serve at the fire camps. Local people worked long hours making sandwiches at the Joseph Civic Center and the Imnaha School.

It was mind-boggling trying to imagine the food it took to feed 5,000!

Our county soon resembled a war zone, with National Guard trucks and fire encampments located in remote areas like Corral Creek, Hat Point and Sled Springs. Evidence everywhere of organized attack against the fires.

One hot afternoon, we watched from the valley as a gigantic cloud of smoke billowed up out north. The Starvation Ridge and Brushy fires had merged!

A friend who had visited the huge fire camp at Sled Springs said it reminded him of an early-day Confederate Army camp.

The setting sun glowed an eerie red as the fading light filtered through the trees, making a striking backdrop to the bustling activity of a forest fire camp.

Smoke-smudged firefighters covered the once quiet forested area, some sleeping on the ground, others going out to the lines, others eating. The scene contained all the trappings of a battle area, and indeed it was, with tents pitched everywhere.

Of course, there was the absence of horses. Certainly, no caterer's trucks loaded with delicious salads, cooked meats, potatoes, gravy and desserts would have spoiled our soldiers of yesteryear.

Many of Wallowa County's early ranchers were appalled at firefighting methods today as opposed to those they knew.

One old-timer recalled: "You had a can of beans, some bread and you stayed with the fire until it was out! We fought fires mainly at night, and that is when we usually got them out. Sometimes we went without sleep for three days, grabbed a wink whenever we could."

Times have changed, but I'm willing to bet those fellows could still put out a fire! And reports around substantiate that indeed some of them did, to protect their lands.

Doug checks every day on our dry range, and we, too, were prepared to fight fire to save our grass lands. The daily hot, dry winds materialize every afternoon, fanning the flames.

Son Ken, a logger, is on the fires with his equipment and getting very little sleep, as are other Wallowa County men in that profession.

A 4-H meeting here to plan our annual trip to Red's Horse Ranch.

August 20—The town is swarming with firefighters. A smoky haze hangs over the entire county. Hot and dry, with no relief. Thunderheads build over the mountains.

Still no rain falls, and the air is so thick with smoke, it is hard to breathe. Clouds, obscured by layers of smoke, hang over the valley in a hushed stillness. Almost feels like it could rain. My outdoor person's sixth sense says it will rain. Our weatherman disagrees, but something about the air is different tonight.

August 21—I awoke at 2 a.m. to the steady drip, drip outside our bedroom window. Rain! Wonderful, blessed rain! The drops increased as the night progressed and by 4:30, when "Chester" the banty rooster crowed to awaken the ranch, I detected a slight dampness in his cockle-doodle-do! Our local radio reported that only Wallowa County had received the moisture. No rain had fallen anywhere else in the state!

In due time, the air over the valley turned fresh and clear and the skies returned to blue. Mop-up operations began and finally the last firefighter left the county.

It seems ironic that Mother Nature started the fire, and despite $6.2 million being spent by man, Mother Nature put out the fire!

The valley gradually returned to normal, and its hardy inhabitants picked up where they left off. However, summer 1986 will leave scars and memories for years to come.

August 21, late—Susan wanted to do my barn chores by herself this evening, so I stayed at the house.

After what seemed like an eternity, she returned...covered with manure! Perhaps Star had gotten a bit nervous with her new "milk maid" and...well I don't have to go into detail; anyway the cow's swishing tail had really done a number on poor Susan.

She commented that in Switzerland, the dairy farmers tie their cows' switches to a hook that is suspended from the ceiling. Not a bad idea, especially in fly season. Maybe I could rig up such a contraption in my milking parlor.

August 22—Beautiful day! After chores, spent the morning catching up on stacks of correspondence.

Sy Fishbein, from National Geographic magazine, sent me a marvelous bird book in the mail.

Made two loaves of zucchini bread. Entered three photos in the Joseph Chamber of Commerce photo contest today.

Made a batch of applesauce from the apples on our tree.

Doug in from fava bean field, tired. Fixed steak, corn on cob, and new potatoes for supper.

Grand Central Station here today. Family coming and going at all hours. Doug in late from irrigating.

August 23—Woke up to a wet curtain flapping at the bedroom window...raining, then a terrific clap of thunder followed by others until daylight, when a hot sun appeared...steaming up the dripping landscape.

Doug to the fava bean field. I took the rusty stove pipe out of my sheepherder wagon this morning. Will purchase a replacement for it at Bud's Hardware.

Salted the mule, "Maud," and my mare, "Cal." After having bag balmed Star's teats earlier, this mixture of salve, salt and soot made my hands appear quite the opposite of the TV lotion ads!

Susan left for Wallowa Lake, where she will help out during the Labor Day tourist rush at the Matterhorn Swiss Village.

The bean field too wet yet to work.

Wrote in trailer studio: my calico kitten "Pasta" kept walking on the typewriter keys, then decided to curl up on the sofa in a shaft of sunlight. How I envy the kitten, able to curl up and sleep.

I hear the steady jet, jet, jet of our sprinklers in the adjacent hayfield, the drone of a fly buzzing around the trailer, the noisy sparrows in the apple tree, swallows in the chicken house and the occasional hawk scream in the cottonwood by the creek.

Thunderheads build in the moist air…it is warm and humid. I can see the sunflowers in the garden, higher than my head and still growing. Dark purple clouds form in the west. Helicopters, airlifting mop-up crews, whirly overhead, coming from the inaccessible breaks of the Imnaha and Snake drainages.

I drove to the fava bean field this afternoon to photograph, and while walking up a row of swatched beans that bordered the uncut portion of the field. I came face to face with a mule deer fawn. Its spots were beginning to fade and he looked at me wide eyed!

The silage makers would soon destroy his bed.

Here we stood, the civilized one and the wild one, each trying to live with the other. I caught a glimpse into his world for one brief instant; did he too, I wondered, read anything in my eyes? Bow season opened this morning.

Lovely clouds hang over the valley today, swimming in blue skies, washed clean by the rains. So welcome after the past, nightmarish, smoke-filled days.

Had a big kettle of corn chowder ready for supper when Doug got in late from the bean field.

August 24—A long, peaceful Sunday afternoon. I indulged in a nap.

After another long day in the field, I treated my husband to a hamburger. fries and chocolate cake at the lake this evening.

Russell's is famous for its hamburgers and it was pleasant eating outside under the pine trees.

We sorta felt like tourists.

August 25—Amid ranch chores, I am finalizing plans to leave in the morning with my Sourdough Shutterbug 4-H Club for Red's Horse

Ranch. There will be 15 of us this year. Included will be Susan from Switzerland, Rune from Norway, and Scotty from Scotland... quite an international group.

August 26—We left Enterprise around 6 a.m. I drove the Enterprise school's suburban, followed by another van full of 4-H'ers.

We drove to Cove and then up the long, steep road to Moss Springs, our jumping off place.

Presently we were shouldering our packs and heading into the vastness of the Minam Wilderness. The trail to Red's Horse Ranch drops steeply down toward the Little Minam River. Here we stopped to rest, except for my herd of 12-year-old boys, who brought out their fishing poles and proceeded to catch some nice trout.

We stopped farther on along the little river and ate our lunches. The eight miles was accomplished and I brought up the rear with one straggler... thank goodness for him. I can't keep up with the 12-year-olds, my grandson Chad included.

The Horse Ranch, as it is sometimes referred to, is accessible only by plane, foot or horseback. It is always a relief to gain the ridge above the ranch and begin the long descent to the big meadow-landing strip. The elevation drops exactly one mile from Moss Springs to Red's.

We were greeted at the front porch by Kathy, the cook, and presently, the ramrod of the outfit. Other guides and hands were on a pack trip with some dudes into the back country. That left Kathy and the wrangler "Pete" in charge.

Since the hike in had been a hot one, all of us immediately jumped into the cool waters of the Minam River to wash off the trail dust and refresh ourselves. The children were delighted seeing a few spawning salmon going upstream.

Kathy rang the dinner bell and we trooped into the log dining room to partake of a feast that consisted of pork chops (from hogs grown on the ranch), carrot salad (fresh from the garden), noodles, relishes, bread, applesauce and green beans. Never had food tasted so good, and the young boys put that chow away in a rather frightening manner!

Like last year, we made our beds in the barn's haymow. As we settled in for the night, the generator was turned off by Pete... no lights, total darkness.

Then Kurt, bedded high in the loft... "Goodnight John Boy!" This brought down the house... er barn, and immediately all of the 4-H'ers chimed in... "Goodnight Becky Sue, Amy Lou, Jane girl." My 12-and-under herd of young boys joined in and hilarity reigned.

Morning sunlight spills across a meadow to lighten up the old log cabins at Red's Wallowa Horse Ranch, which is located in the heart of the Minam Wilderness Area. The Sourdough Shutterbug 4-H Club slept in the barn at far left during a visit to Red's.

Rune, bedded somewhere in the melee, never uttered a sound. Perhaps he thought his American counterparts were plumb daffy.

Around 2:30 a.m., the early morning stillness was broken by Scotty, who suddenly came to life. Somehow, she couldn't get situated in her lumpy manger, so with great aplomb, she had gotten up to shake out her sleeping bag.

Grunting, groaning and generally causing a loud disturbance, she finally settled back down in the manger.

A glimmer of moon shone through the old barn's logs and I was just beginning to drift back into dreamland when..."Landon, it's 5 o'clock!" This from Scotty. She had been told to wake up the boy for an early morning horseback ride!

This brought on an outburst of giggles that erupted from all over the haymow. The rooster in the chicken pen began to crow, the cow just outside the barn window began to moo, and her calf, stalled nearby, bawled back!

Presently, the wrangler appeared to drive in a "herd" of horses that came thundering in off the meadow next to us and into a corral. In an adjacent pen, the hogs began to grunt and, as the wrangler, Pete, emptied the slop pail into their trough, we could hear very plainly the slurpings and chompings of their breakfast!

What a riot! Everyone up trying to find their clothes in the hay.

The first wave of 4-H'ers left for the lodge and I got up to face the day, which had begun just a little too soon for this tired 4-H leader.

It was a change hearing someone else feeding the animals and milking the cow...and cooking. All I had to do was get myself to the dining room and partake of Kathy's wonderful breakfast, which, you guessed it, consisted of sourdough hot cakes.

August 27—After breakfast and a game of horseshoes, twelve of us took a walk up toward Minam Lodge. Hiking along a path that wound in and around some old, dead trees, we spotted a pair of pileated woodpeckers...these birds are almost as big as a small chicken and the male is very colorful.

The old lodge was deserted, and we could hear laughter and children's voices coming from the direction of the river.

It was our Shutterbugs, playing in the water. As the day began to warm up, they evidently took to the Minam again. They were about a quarter-mile downstream from the Horse Ranch in a wide stretch of river.

Because we, too, had on bathing suits under our clothes, we decided to cross the hayfield and join in the fun!

We swam and splashed in the cool waters before walking back on the trail to the dining room, where we picked up our sack lunches to eat in the shade near the river.

The searing heat bore down on the ranch; not a breath of air. Ninety-five in the shade! We sat around in our wet suits trying to keep cool.

The temperature soared to well over 100 by afternoon, so we hiked up river and found a secluded pool, fringed on both sides by willows and brush. We swam and savored the coolness. A little water ouzel, who lived there, put on a show for us, ducking under the water to catch whatever he could, then perching on the rock to fluff his feathers. Having approached the pool by way of a large gravel bar, we noticed a big elk track coming from a wet sandy beach, which led directly into the woods on the opposite bank. We kept expecting to see a bull elk emerge from the trees any minute.

Reluctant to leave this beautiful place, we swam until the sun lost some of its power and began to sink behind the rimrocks that tower above the ranch. Again we put our clothes on over our wet suits and waded the river down to the ranch. I shall always remember that wild place, and the blue-green pool we shared with the ouzel.

Refreshed from our swim, Scotty, Rune and I decided to hike down toward the end of the landing strip to see if we could catch a glimpse of the bear. He had been seen that morning near the garbage pit. No bear, but his sign was everywhere. Rune found where Bruin had dragged a bag of garbage into the woods, so he began tracking the animal in hopes of photographing him. We elected not to follow, but continued on around a trail that led back to the river. In the woods, we saw many blue grouse and numerous deer tracks...and luckily no bear.

After a vigorous two-mile hike, we returned to the dining lodge and joined the 4-H'ers for supper, which consisted of barbecued spareribs, homemade bread, coleslaw, vegetables and pumpkin pie.

The youngsters really put away the chow.

I offered to do all of the supper dishes again, as I knew Kathy would enjoy a rest from the kitchen. It was dark when I finished the last of the pots and pans.

Much quieter in the haymow tonight; we are all tired.

August 28—Awoke at 7 after a refreshing sleep. Scotty had gotten up earlier, making sure the young boys would be up and have their packs ready before breakfast. Good old Scotty, she keeps us all in line, bandages all the "owies," and is mother hen to us all.

A few clouds formed, making it decidedly cooler. We partook of another of Kathy's famous breakfasts. I swept the front porch, gathered up our scattered gear, and prepared to take off up the steep trail that leads to the high ridge above the ranch.

Rune decided to take off early so he could climb straight up to a high rim to get a good shot of the ranch below. The faster hikers left and I didn't see them again until Moss Springs. I stayed back to make sure all were ahead of me. Landon lagged behind again, but by promising him he could fish farther up the trail, we made it...although we were almost two hours behind the troops. On the last leg of the hike, where the trail follows a steep, open hillside, it was slow going.

Very hot and it seemed we never would reach the top.

But we did, and the crew was waiting at our rig.

Landon showed off the trout he had caught in the Little Minam, and we loaded up the suburban and headed down the long, winding road to Cove.

Below lay the Grande Ronde valley, hazy with heat and smoke. We stopped in Elgin for a cold drink and were back in Enterprise by 6. After delivering the 4-H'ers, I drove Rune back to Lockes. Through dark clouds, a beautiful burst of sunlight spilled down on Prairie Creek. Hundreds of blackbirds lined the telephone lines and flew in great, black waves over the hayfields.

A feeling of fall in the air.

Home to the ranch to chore, gather eggs and be welcomed by the barn cats and "Chester."

No one home, they were eating out; missed the cook!

Although it is a big responsibility to make sure so many young people return safely from such an adventure, and as the years go by, it becomes more exhausting, in retrospect I wouldn't miss these experiences for the world. In the weeks and months to come, I will remember the quiet, little pool where we swam with the water ouzel and my mind was at complete peace with the world.

Perhaps that is the purpose for wilderness...we humans need, that once in a while. Recognizing that need may be man's salvation.

August 30—The weather turned cooler and we had a thunderstorm which cleared the air and left beautiful, white clouds floating around in a fresh sky.

The garden continued to produce and we consumed as much as we could and I gave away zucchini by the wheelbarrow full.

On the opening morning of grouse season, it was cloudy, cool and threatening rain, but I talked Doug into hiking a ways up Hurricane Creek and onto the trail to the LeGore Mine.

I remembered seeing blue grouse in the area last fall. After chores, I packed a lunch and we took off. Not much evidence that anyone had traveled the trail much this year and no grouse sign, so after hiking up to the mountain mahogany trees, we turned around and headed back.

It was so misty and cloudy we couldn't see the mountain "Sacajawea," or in fact any view! Back at the pickup we ate our lunches and were joined by two friendly chipmunks who shared a few crumbs with us.

The hike had been refreshing and the warmth of the wood stove felt comfy and warm when we returned. Raining.

I washed the kitchen curtains, made apple sauce, swept and mopped the floors and made a batch of marshmallow treats.

The outdoor exercise had my blood circulating.

Imagine, a fire in our wood cookstove on this 30th day of August!

That's Wallowa County.

August 31—After doing chores, we were invited to a pig barbecue at Imnaha. Because it was a potluck affair, I made a zucchini-crookneck squash casserole to take along.

Down at the Bridge School we enjoyed a get-together of friends and such a meal...a 250-pound hog had been roasting on a spit, tended by his former owner, for more than 24 hours. A bright, red apple had been placed in his mouth. Even though the weather was on the damp side we enjoyed it all...delicious food and friendly people. And a great way to say goodbye to August...and summer.

Daughter Lori, her husband, Tom, and granddaughter Lacey arrived this evening. We were glad they had made the long journey from Wyoming safely.

September 1—Today is Labor Day and we CowBelles are busy! We helped make coleslaw this morning for our annual steak feed where we expect to serve meals to more than 500 people.

The feeder sale was a success and a mild sprinkle of rain didn't deter the usual crowds that converged on the auction grounds for the CowBelles' traditional dinner. A chill in the air tonight.

September 2—Gorgeous day. Enjoying little Lacey and visiting our family. Doug is swathing hay, our second cutting.

Ordered a 30-pound beef roast for a meal I am planning to cook for Mark and Anne Butterfield's rehearsal dinner at Wallowa Lake Lodge Friday night.

September 3—Another beautiful day, clear and warm...still no frost. The garden continues to bear, uninterrupted. Baked bread, made applesauce, and played with Lacey while her parents went grouse hunting up on Dead Horse.

September 4—Beautiful fall day, warming up in the afternoon. Scotty and I picked corn up on Alder Slope. Susan is back again and we have a busy day coming up tomorrow, cooking for 75 people. Grandson Buck called from Imnaha, so proud, he had lost his first tooth. Buck is now one of 14 pupils, grades 1-8, at the Imnaha school.

September 5—Up early to tackle this long day.

Scotty and Susan peel apples while I make three deep dish pies and a blackberry cobbler. Also baked a pie for our family.

Doug is checking out our boat, so we can leave on a camping trip to the Snake River tomorrow. Can't believe this is happening.

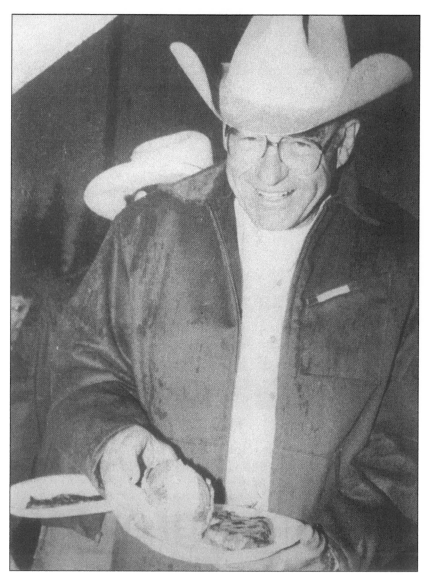

Imnaha rancher Howard Borgerding goes through the chow line at the Labor Day steak feed served by Wallowa County CowBelles. The potatoes, donated again by J.R. Simplot, were a hit with the more than 500 people served.

My crew and I work all day on the food. By 4:30 we load the car and drive to Wallowa Lake where we will finish the meal and serve the dinner. It is a lovely evening at the lake as we shuck the corn outside and two mule deer fawns jump up behind some garbage cans!

Shortly thereafter, delicious smells wafted out from the lodge kitchen as we cooked the mashed potatoes, made gravy, heated the rolls and cooked the corn on the cob. The meal was a success and I had plenty of food. Earlier I had picked some of my pretty, pink cosmos and arranged them in my blue granite-ware pots. They added just the right touch to the old lodge's rustic decor.

A fire glowed softly in the rock fireplace and the polished log interior shone with warmth as many wild animal trophy heads stared down from above.

Most of these mounted heads were bagged years ago by Doug's father, the late Jidge Tippett. If this old lodge could talk, it would have many stories to tell of a very colorful past.

Home late to unload the car and crash.

September 6—Up early to finish cleaning and storing my cooking kettles, then fixed breakfast for our household and did my chores. Just finished when Doug announced we would be leaving soon for the Snake River. So, I made new lists and began to plan meals and assemble camping gear and put the pack boxes in order.

Hell's Canyon Mule Days today, but we would be missing this year's event and heading for the canyons instead.

After a rather eventful trip on canyon roads, we arrived at Doug's former ranch at Dug Bar. About five miles short of our destination, our trailer tire went flat and we had no spare. So we limped along, pulling the boat, on a tire that held together even on the final, steep descent to the Snake. Quite a time launching the boat at Dug Bar, but we managed and soon were on our way upriver, little Lacey's red hair blowing in the wind.

Doug selected as our camping spot a sheltered white sandy beach at the mouth of Bob Creek. It was a perfect spot with sweeping views of canyon and river, a picnic table situated under some Hackberry trees and even a two-sided, roofless outhouse that afforded a view of rimrock and sky.

By the time we had camp set up, the sun had long since made its exit over the rims. After cooking a light meal of hamburgers, we fished a little and hit the hay... er boat.

The Jordan family's "Home below Hell's Canyon," as it looks today. Grace Jordan wrote a book by that name about her life at this place on Kirkwood Bar of the Snake River. A museum, open in the summer, is located near the storied house. Grace Jordan's husband, Len, became a governor of Idaho.

Doug and I slept on the padded seats that lined the sides of the boat. The night was brilliant and we gazed upward, enthralled at shooting stars, orbiting satellites, and the path of the Milky Way as it spanned the heavens.

Since construction of dams on the upper reaches of the Snake, the water level fluctuates without warning. During the night, I slid off my boat seat bed onto the floor...kerplunk!

This woke up Doug, who discovered we were about to be beached!

The boat was partly out of the water and tilted; I was on the high side. Nothing to do but jump out of the boat and begin pushing our bedroom back into the nighttime river waters. After much pushing, shoving and prying we were once again afloat. Doug dropped anchor and we were lulled to sleep by the swirling, sucking noise of the Snake as it sped toward Roland Bar.

September 7—As daylight broke over golden canyon rims, a flock of wild mallards flew downriver. Some sort of shore bird sounded various throaty cries near the Hackberry thicket. I had mixed the sourdough last night, and Doug was up fixing hotcakes on this beautiful canyon morning.

Since it was so warm, Lori, Lacey and I swam in the river before breakfast.

Later, we boated upriver past Copper Creek and Sommers Creek. As we sped by many historic places, my former river guide husband launched into the old routine...Pittsburg Landing, used to be a fine fishing area, used over the years by the Indians, once a townsite, a good boat landing, where the mail boat docked to bring mail to ranchers living in the canyon. We passed the Lem Wilson place, the Bud Wilson ranch on the Idaho side, and Upper China Creek Rapids, named for Chinese gold miners who frequented the area in early days.

We docked the boat at Kirkwood Bar and visited the Jordan Museum. Grace Jordan, author of "Home Below Hell's Canyon," lived here with her husband, Len, who was to become governor of Idaho. At the home, still here at Kirkwood, the couple raised three children and operated a large sheep ranch.

We enjoyed visiting with Hazel, who was raised upriver at Saddle Creek and is caretaking the museum and living in the old Jordan home. It is a very interesting part of the canyon.

I took numerous pictures and could almost "feel" how it must have been living there. Lovely clouds floated overhead in an incredibly blue sky and the air was fresh and clean.

Back in the boat, we headed up toward Suicide Point, a narrow trail carved out of solid rock, that lays high above the roiling waters of the Snake.

This trail was used by the Jordans and other ranchers to pack supplies into the canyon or to get from one ranch to the other. It is said many a pack mule or horse has lost its footing during icy conditions and plunged to death below.

As we passed the former Kenneth Johnson Ranch on the Oregon side, we thought about life as it was...the wonderful big sheep ranches, before instant wilderness changed the canyon's way of life. Recreation is the name of the game now...and here we were, ourselves, having changed our cattle operation due to the National Recreation Area, boating and recreating!

We stopped at the end of navigation and gazed far above to the tree line...we could just barely see the fire tower at Hat Point.

Turned around and headed downriver to Bob Creek and lunch.

September 7—We headed downriver after lunch to the mouth of the Imnaha to try some steelhead fishing. No luck, but we did observe a family of otters sunning themselves on a nearby rock. Without any warning, they dove into the wild, swirling waters of the river and swam toward our boat, their curious little faces looking at us, then disappeared under the water.

They looked for all the world like they were playing a game of peek-a-boo!

As our well-seasoned river boat pilot guided his outboard motor boat through some exhilarating swells of white water, we were quite often sprayed by the blue-green froth of some rapids.

The mighty Snake roared through its awesome gorge, consisting of gigantic rock formations that reach to the sky on either side of the river.

Millions of newly hatched gnats flew around in the balmy canyon air.

We gazed upward at paint on the rocks that marked the former, controversial High Mountain Sheep Dam site and soon the boat negotiated Warm Springs Rapids and the alfalfa field at Dug Bar came into view. Nostalgic memories came flooding back.

It seemed funny to go on by; it used to be home.

On the river, one notices a sense of timelessness, a lazy sort of feeling, a moment in time. Yet, one must respect the terrible forces of the Snake, for its waters can be treacherous to those who do not understand the river.

The mood of the canyon is constantly changing, one minute quiet and serene, the next in the middle of a storm.

Tonight was to be no exception. We had finished supper when a terrific fall storm materialized, seemingly out of nowhere.

It had been breathlessly hot, and we could see lightning zig-zags playing on the highest rims. Quite suddenly it turned very dark and Doug lit our Coleman lantern, the light of which attracted thousands of moth millars, who began cremating themselves inside the burning mantel.

We had enjoyed roasting ears, steak, potatoes and fresh tomatoes for supper when this hot stillness prevailed, followed by a rushing wind and drum rolls of thunder that reverberated back and forth across the canyon.

Suddenly all heck broke loose, and amid all this, it began to rain!

Since we had no tent, Lori, Tom and Lacey, who had been sleeping on shore, made a makeshift shelter, using our only tarp.

Doug, going to bed in the boat, was trying to cover up our sleeping bags with a poncho, which wasn't able to cover everything. I tried sticking it out in the boat for a while, but was getting soaked, so between lightning flashes I fled up to the hackberry trees and the picnic table.

*Evening shadows steal down the walls of Hells Canyon near Bob Creek on
the Snake River. Roland Bar is in the distance, and the Blankenship Ranch
is on the left.*

By this time it was pouring and the wind was so strong in that dark
night, I could scarcely stand. In my haste to find cover, I got wedged in
between the picnic table and the bench, but finally managed to crawl
underneath and crouch there until the rain slackened.

Over as quickly as it had begun, the storm rumbled off down the
canyon and I extricated myself from the table and began picking up pots
and pans that had blown off the table. Not a sound from Doug in the
boat. He had wrapped himself in the poncho and was reasonably dry.

Before fleeing the boat, I had shoved my sleeping bag under the bow
of the boat and it was still dry. I wiped the water off my mattress seat
and climbed into bed beside a wet-looking lump that was my husband!

Presently, stars appeared and it was as if the storm had never been!
We went to sleep smelling the scent of rain-dampened grasses.

September 8—Awoke to the sound made by a Shidepoke, or heron.
Since it was still so warm and mild, I simply slid off the side of the boat
for an early morning swim.

"Happy Birthday Grandpa"…this from little Lacey who came crawling out of her nest, none the worse for last night's adventure!

Today is my husband's 55th birthday and he is again cooking breakfast. Some chukars began calling from the opposite side of the river as the sun suddenly burst over the canyon wall amid some apricot-colored clouds.

After breakfast it began to sprinkle, so we began to break camp, load the boat, and head for Dug Bar. When we reached the spot where we had launched our boat, the weather improved somewhat, so we left our gear in the pickup and headed downriver again for more steelhead fishing.

This time Doug caught a nice one. I opted to investigate and photograph the old stamp mill foundation. This is all that remains of much early activity that centered around Eureka Bar years ago. Near here the Imnaha conflues with the Snake. An old mine tunnels through rock from the Snake side and reappears on the Imnaha.

Leaving Eureka Bar, we boated down to the mouth of the Salmon, then traveled upstream toward the River of No Return until we were forced to return due to some rather large rocks in midstream. Heading back to Dug Bar, we spotted a bald eagle perched on a rock, and a mule deer doe and her twin fawns standing in their own private canyon on the Idaho side.

Back safely at Dug Bar, we had quite a time pulling the boat out of the river due to the injured trailer, but managed to pull it up to the alfalfa field.

Since it was noon, we picnicked in the ranch house yard. Remembering…how it was.

Leaving the boat parked in the field, we began the long, steep, twisting, dirt road that would take us the many miles to Imnaha. We stopped briefly at the Riverside Cafe for ice cream and to visit Jim Dorrance, who used to lived on Snake River years ago.

Home at last…Doug opening presents left by our children.

What a wonderful trip we have had. Tom and Lori went to the show in Enterprise while we watched Lacey, or rather, she watched us! We were both so tired we couldn't keep our eyes open.

September 9—

September's child has a purpose true, important things to see and do.
Up at 6 to begin my 53rd year!

Clouds during the night kept Jack Frost away and the garden continues to flourish. Much attention from our children in the form of phone calls, presents and dinner invitations. Nice.

In our absence, Susan had done my chores and taken care of my animals. Picked cherry tomatoes and bell peppers beside the house.

Doug to the moraine to check our fall calving cows.

Doorbell rings…a lovely dish garden delivered by our local florist, a note from my three sisters in far-away California…and a tear or two. Thank you Mary Ann, Caroline and Kathryn.

Busy all day, catching up.

Our children treated us to pizza at the Pizza Emporium in Enterprise tonight…even little James was there. A fun time with family.

September 10—Washing clothes, made lunches for Doug and Tom who are leaving for Dug Bar to repair the boat trailer.

Steve in Walla Walla where he had a doctor appointment for his back problem.

Jennifer Isley stopped by to visit. Invited her to stay for dinner; also invited Wayne Tippett who is in the county working on a road construction job. Doug and Tom returned, so had nine of us around the supper table tonight. Fried fresh liver, heart and onions, new potatoes, biscuits and coleslaw.

September 11—Cooked a big sourdough waffle breakfast for Tom, Lori and Lacey before they departed for the Pendleton Round-Up. From there they will head back to Wyoming.

Doug, Steve and Ben ag bagging at our neighbors', the Klages, all day.

Susan is on a camping trip with our neighbors, the Lockes.

Scotty and I had a busy day. We picked corn on Alder Slope, then butchered six old stewing hens. I hacked the heads off and Scotty plucked feathers while I dressed them. Made a pan of sourdough rolls, then husked corn, blanched it and took it off the cob to freeze.

Got up at midnight to turn the sprinkler on in the garden. Old Jack Frost will be foiled one more time.

September 12—While sausage and eggs sizzled atop the Monarch wood range, I dashed out to read the thermometer by the clothesline…30 degrees!

Back to the insulated overalls for choring.

The men still hard at the "ag-bagging" at our neighbors', the Klages.

I walked through my garden this morning…quite an experience. Ice had formed over the large squash plant's leaves and as I touched them, "ice fossils" slid off into my hands.

Carefully, I picked one up, looking at the delicate tracery of the leafs imprint…a lovely piece of Mother Nature's crystal. As I brushed against the row of beets, they did an ice dance, tinkling in tune to my steps and shattering upon the ground.

Sunflowers dropped under the weight of their enormous blooms, carrot tops lay flat under a sheath of ice, the rows of com, only days from harvest, with their promise of delicious, sweet ears, remain unharmed. The dill, in full bloom, is fragrant in the crisp, morning air. Turning the sprinkler on at midnight had saved the garden. But winter looms, and its days are numbered. Hopefully, we'll have a long Indian Summer.

It won't be long until the flaming sumac will emblazon the canyons with its red color. And frosty nights will turn trembling aspen leaves to gold. The fire snaps and the clock ticks, and I can hear these sounds for a change! So peaceful after so many days of BUSY!

Picked a wheelbarrow full of giant zucchini and bright, yellow crookneck. Hung some of the large yellow squash on the garden fence.

Went to work on the pile of correspondence that has been stacking up on my desk.

Fixed fried trout, corn on the cob and sourdough rolls for lunch.

Picked beet greens, swiss chard, carrots, parsley, Walla Walla onions, three kinds of lettuce, bell peppers, cherry tomatoes, green beans, zucchini, crookneck squash and turned it all into a big salad!

What a treat! We had grilled steaks, linguine with clam sauce, my vegetable salad and french bread. Cherry cheesecake for dessert. The dinner, cooked by Doris, was to celebrate three birthdays!

September 13—Cloudy and warm, a few sprinkles of rain fell during the night. A new snowfall on Chief Joseph Mountain, the fall's first. Dark clouds roll over Prairie Creek, warm here at 4,000 feet, but the snow level expected to be around 5,000 feet by tonight. The garden is still green and luxuriant.

Ben is driving in our bulls and will vaccinate them for warts.

To town to grocery shop, and home again to bake an apple pie for a friend who gave me some cooking apples. Last night's snow mostly melted, periods of sunlight and lovely clouds today.

The men are plagued with "end of season" breakdowns on the ag-bagging equipment.

Another birthday dinner, this time at Todd and Liza's on Alder Slope. The children had contrived this get-together and fixed a great Mexican dinner. Liza had cooked all day. How we enjoyed the enchiladas, tacos and two birthday cakes. One for Doug and one for me.

Lots of warm, family fun. After all, we are all children again when it comes to birthdays. I let the grandchildren blow out the candles, but I made the wish.

September 14—Up early, cloudy and cold. Packed a lunch, did chores and after breakfast, Grace Bartlett, Scotty and I drove with Grace out the Zumwalt Road to Buckhorn, where we parked and met more people. From here, we walked to a high ridge above Cemetery Ridge, where we saw the remains of an old fire tower. The icy breeze and overcast sky made the air crisp and cold, but we did enjoy looking far below to the huge Imnaha canyon and all of its drainages.

We could see the canyons of Horse Creek, Lightning Creek and Cow Creek. We hiked on over to another vantage point, where we could look down through the breaks to Eureka Creek and see a bright spot! The Snake River…far below.

On a clear day one can see the Bitterroot Range in Montana. Today we could see miles of hazy, mist-covered ridges that separated themselves with various shades of blue and purple for as far as our eyes could see.

Standing far above Eureka Bar on the Snake River, I looked at my watch. At the same hour, just a week ago to the day, I had sat in our boat down there jotting down some field notes in my journal.

We ate our lunches on the sheltered side of a ridge near some wind-swept pine trees. Later, we tromped around the grassy hillsides looking for early-day cabin sites. We noticed how big the wild rose hips were this year. The season's first frost had turned them a brilliant red color.

Returning home, we saw lots of wildlife, including two enormous mule deer bucks near the Steen Ranch, and six head of elk crossing the road in front of us…three cows had jumped the fence to the left of us, but their calves refused to follow. As we watched, the calves trotted back toward Pine Creek and the cows circled around, re-jumping two fences to join their calves. Good feed in the hills had made them fat and sleek.

Threatening to, and did, thunder, lightning and rain, so I had picked the strawberries and tomatoes before the storm hit. After supper on this Sunday evening, the clouds blew away, exposing a bright, new snowfall on Mt. Howard. Cold outside tonight.

Son Steve left for his new job today. Plans are to attend winter term in college to pick up some needed credits. Susan is still attending Expo '86. Just us two chickens here tonight.

To bed with Scott O'Dell's novel on Sacajawea. Bright moonlight in a clear sky…frosty in the morning!

September 15—Heavy frost, 28 degrees, more new snow shows up on the mountains. Saved the garden one more night by turning on the sprinkler. Since we didn't plant seed potatoes this year, we won't have to worry about hard frost in the ground this fall.

Horses graze the golden fall grasses against a backdrop of snow-covered mountains. The scene is on Prairie Creek in Wallowa County, where recent storms have brought the snow line closer to the valley each day.

Intermittent thunder storms rumbled about in the mountains all day; unusual for this time of year. Put up five pints of strawberry jam, picked all the green beans, covered the tomato and pepper plants. Picked up some windfall apples from the neighbor's yard to make applesauce. Cooked a hot meal for the ag baggers at noon.

Late this afternoon, Prairie Creek sprouted a rainbow! I like to think it was a way of saying "happy birthday" to my father, who would have been 83 today. The cottonwoods by the creek are turning yellow.

September 16—Gleaming snowfields peek through billowy, white clouds and the sunshine is warm... no frost! The air is fresh and the sky an incredible blue, with a wine-like clarity. Autumn skies.

My gorgeous sunflowers contrast golden against the snow-clad Wallowas. The garden as green as it was in August! Picked the first delicious corn today. Sold some of our young bulls to a neighbor, a repeat buyer from last year.

Susan is home, wearing an Expo '86 T-shirt and sporting a new short haircut. We got an armchair report of the Vancouver World's Fair, as Susan showed us her souvenirs and pictures.

An autumn wind blows dark clouds across the face of the moon tonight.

September 17—Awoke to Chester's crowing, as he announces a new day from his perch in the willow tree by the clothesline.

A brilliant sunrise this morning, with pink reflections making a watercolor wash on Ruby Peak's snowclad top. The colorful sky provides a backdrop for my sunflowers as they wave in a clumsy, yet graceful sort of way in the autumn wind.

While choring at the barn, I heard loud mews and traced the sound to a hole in the hay stack. Mamma Kitty, having babies…again! Susan is delighted!

Dark clouds roll along, swept by the wind, bringing with them a promise of rain.

Susan has moved from the trailer to the house, since the days are turning colder now. Once again, I carry my "moveable" office back to Steve's old room.

I begin to compose the first, rough outline of the slide-tape presentation that our history group is contributing to the centennial year. As I write, I tend the sourdough, answer the phone, feed the fire and conduct my "ranch wifely" duties at the same time.

September 18—Picked the first sweet, crisp cabbage today and made a coleslaw.

Doug is attending a cattlemen's meeting in Baker and Susan is helping the Lockes work cattle in the hills; Ben has come and gone in the pickup…I have the ranch to myself. It rained during the night and turned warmer, and now the sun is trying to peek through a layer of clouds.

Worked on the history script all day; taking a half hour for lunch. It poured down rain all afternoon.

Met with our history group tonight at the Bookloft, where I presented my outline for the project.

Doug was home when I returned. A beautiful harvest moon lights up Prairie Creek tonight.

September 19—Frost on the meadows, 30 degrees. Saved the garden again by turning on the sprinkler. Cooked breakfast on the wood stove. Susan gone again, this time to help out at the Matterhorn Swiss Village during Alpenfest weekend. When the "Whiskers on the mountains" part, we see more new snow has fallen.

Did some housework and picked strawberries, which have now decided to bear like mad! Leaving roast beef and apple pie for Doug, I drove to Grace Bartlett's where Rich, Chuck, Grace and I enjoyed a most delicious informal lunch provided by Grace, after which we discussed my script and went over a manuscript that Grace is putting finishing touches on. Grace's book on Wallowa County history will soon be ready for the printers. Very interesting and stimulating talk by interesting people.

Stopped at the Grain Growers on my way home to purchase chicken feed, and then to the Enterprise Library to check out reference material for my writing.

Meanwhile, back at the ranch, Calvin, Ben, Doug and Herb had finished ag bagging at the Klages'.

Cloudy and cold as I drive to Wallowa Lake and the opening of the 1986 Alpenfest, which is held in the old "Edelweiss Inn," an ancient log structure that used to be part of Wallowa County's first dude ranch.

As I climbed out of my car, which was parked near the gondola terminal, a six-point mule deer buck ambled along in front of me! Several tourists were taking his picture.

It was rather drafty and chilly in the old building, but things warmed up pretty soon, as the crew warmed up the steaming sauerkraut, German sausages and rolls. Wonderful smells emanated from the kitchen as we prepared to serve the food.

I was on the sausage detail and had three kettles going to keep up with opening night dinners. Coffee was more popular than beer at first, but as people warmed to the Bavarian music and dancers, things got considerably "merrier" and the beer began to flow.

The old log building, decorated with colorful posters and taking on an air of the Swiss Alps, transported us to another culture. A land of alpenhorns, Swiss yodelers, Bavarian dancing and mountain merriment. Soon young and old alike were on the floor dancing to waltzes and polkas; many were dressed in authentic costume.

It was very colorful and I tapped my feet to the happy music as I tended to the steaming sausages. The new shift came on and I headed for home. It had been a long day, but worth it. I have helped serve for 12 consecutive Alpenfests and watched it grow from the first idea.

September 20—A steady rain fell all night; still raining this morning. What a contrast to the hot, dry conditions we experienced earlier. Now we live in a misty, cloudy, dream world. So many activities are affected by this weather. Alpenfest, the Centennial Home Tour, football games, not to mention the second cuttings of hay and the grain harvest that is now under way here in our county.

Stewing left-over roast and bones for soup stock; will add garden vegetable later. Set sourdough to rise.

Expecting company from California today.

As I was pulling carrots from my soaked garden, I heard, far above gray clouds, the first honking of wild geese beginning their southward migration. The blackbirds have been having "conventions" for weeks, deciding on when to head out. So cold, it almost feels like snow. As I pick the lovely, yellow crookneck, I know this may be its last day. The cabbage waits to be made into kraut...just needs time. The sunflowers, so large they cannot turn their golden heads to follow the sun.

Soup simmers on the wood stove and I keep adding vegetables...new potatoes, cabbage, carrots, corn on the cob, tomatoes, onions...even zucchini. Doug won't notice.

...End of Garden Soup!

Stewed up a kettle of fresh applesauce. We enjoyed the soup at dinner, then son-in-law Bill stopped by, so pushed the soup onto the hotter section of the Monarch and served him some.

Our company arrived, just as I was taking a large apple pie from the oven; Steve Dorrance, wife, Leslie, and sons Drew and Clifton from Toro Mountain in California. Steve's father, Bill Dorrance, was raised out on Crow Creek, a son of the Church Dorrances, early-day settlers.

The Dorrances were excellent horsemen and raised fine cattle. Their old "pink" barn and handhewn log cabins can still be seen today, 30 miles out along the Crow Creek Road.

Little two-year-old Drew did chores with me and succeeded in producing a few squirts of milk from one of Star's teats. Patiently, this grand old cow waits, while little hands squeeze and attempt their first experience at milking. She is the major attraction at our barn!

Our house is quickly transformed into a nursery: high chair, walker, diapers...and delightful children's voices.

A large, cold moon appeared over the hill as I let Maud, the mule, and my mare out to eat grass in the machinery yard. The visiting family to bed early as they were tired from traveling.

September 21—Fixed sourdough waffles with strawberries and cream, served for breakfast with my pullet's brown eggs and bacon.

The Dorrances left reluctantly. Drew especially didn't want to go. He loved the ranch and freedom from the car. Steve wanted to show Leslie the old ranch out on Crow Creek, whereupon they planned to cut across country and end up at Imnaha to visit Uncle Jim.

Beautiful morning, sunshine and fall air. A cloud layer had formed during the night and my garden remains unfrozen on this 21st day of September!

Since it was such a nice Sunday, we, too, headed for Imnaha to fish the river. The drive was beautiful, punctuated by cranberry-colored ninebark and the first reddening of the sumac.

Doug soon caught a limit of trout. I caught two, then contented myself with reading my book in the sunshine.

Mother Nature has already healed the scars of the burn. New green grass lies like a carpet over the blackened areas.

Jackie and Bill and children stopped by this evening and Susan brought home sauerkraut, sausages and rolls from Alpenfest, so we enjoyed dinner with them.

The harvest moon glows in a bright, clear sky... "Frost on the pumpkin" by morning.

October 1—Another cloudy, drippy day.

It rained almost all night. Although October brings visions of cold, frosty mornings, our valley remains green and it almost feels like spring. Misty clouds hover over the area like a gray blanket. Occasionally, a peek of blue appears between showers that rain straight down, turned on and off like a faucet. Around 1:30 this afternoon it hailed on us here at Prairie Creek.

The ground is saturated and covered with water-logged night crawlers.

Spent the morning readying articles for deadlines.

Doug up on the moraine to check cows and calves. He is riding the three-wheeler. Hope he doesn't get stuck.

Baked a pear-custard concoction that I made up as I went along.

October 2—No frost. Cooked breakfast, then made a lunch for Doug, who left for the hills with a small tractor loaded onto one of our trucks, to do some work at the Salmon Creek ranch. Made a zucchini casserole to take to the Hurricane Creek Grange potluck tonight.

Picked up Grace Bartlett with some friends and attended a Grange open house. I love this wonderful old Grange hall. Near Hurricane Creek canyon, not too far from the wilderness, it has beautiful hardwood floors that shine under the good care they receive.

As we entered the hall from the brisk, cold outdoors, we were greeted with the smell of freshly brewed coffee and the warmth of a cozy fire in the old wood stove.

Many people soon converged on the two-room hall; mostly all neighbors who live in the valley. We sat on long benches and visited before partaking of a feast that is hard to describe. Wonderful, home cooked food...meat dishes, casseroles, vegetables, cream pies and rich dark chocolate cakes. After supper we participated in a program that mirrored a small community's pride, love, care, and neighborliness all tolled into one.

Not to mention devotion to God, friendship and patriotism. Americanism at its finest. Strong emphasis on family here, with children present as well as adults.

There was group singing, skits, poetry readings, piano solos, and duets, as well as solo singing. Muriel Cleveland sang "The Desert Song" and it brought back memories of the days when I first saw the movie by that name.

I couldn't help joining in... "Blue heaven, and you and I, the sand kissing a moonlit sky, the desert breeze calling, its voice enthralling to make you mine." The era of the '40s. I also remember, as a girl, hearing the above words rolling loud and clear from the milking barn... my father's favorite song.

Maxine Kooch was in charge of the program, which was so varied and entertaining we could not but be impressed. Maxine had a childhood chum who had driven to the Wallowa Valley to play a duet with her. They hadn't played together in 50 years, but their fingers and. hearts remembered the lovely chords.

Reena Freels and husband John presented a funny true-to-life skit that depicted a farmer abed with the flu.

He wouldn't stay down or take his medicine, and the hired man and his son kept coming in with news, like how the cow started a fire that almost burned down the barn, or the pesky pigs were out again. Farmer John kept rearing up in bed to get the ranch under control.

He said reading the newspaper was depressing, because all the news was of fire, pestilence and flood.

About that time, the wife burst in with "John, John, put on your pants, the bathroom is overflowing!" Between the barn fire, the pesky pigs, and now the bathroom problem, it seemed farmer John was having the same problems as had been reported in the newspaper!

We enjoyed watching all these "salt of the earth" folks participate in their meeting. These hard-working people of the land, with lines in their faces and work-worn hands to show for the years of struggling to make a living in a hard country.

This is their home and their children's home. A little year-old boy toddled out in the middle of the floor and sat down on a small rug. Admired by all! His grandpa and grandma were farmer John and wife in the skit. Presently, he wandered over and sat on my lap.

Arriving home, I was greeted by our house guests, Sandra and Fred Hubbard, who had just driven in from California for deer season.

Sandra is a childhood chum. We went all the way through school together. Much to catch up on.

October 3—My oldest daughter's 35th birthday today. Happy birthday to you, Ramona, in far off Chilcoot, California.

Fixed sourdough cornbread and honey with bacon and eggs for breakfast.

Watched grandson James while mom went to the dentist. He snuggled up to grandma and was a joy to care for.

Sent boxes of fresh vegetables from the garden back with Liza.

Treated Sandra and daughter Jackie and granddaughter Mona Lee to lunch at the Silver Lake Tea Room at McCully Junction in Joseph.

October 4—Up at 5 a.m. Pitch black outside, 40 degrees. Clear skies, with every star sparkling before dawn. Doug fixed breakfast while I chored. Ever try to find a black cow in a black pasture?

I called Star's name and presently discerned a dark hulk ambling toward me in the murk.

Then four white stocking legs appeared. Still no sign of daylight as I brought the milk in to be strained. Doug was cooking up a storm on the Monarch, frying ham and making sourdough hotcakes. Sandra and I whipped up a lunch and we left in the truck just as it was beginning to lighten up in the east. Out on the Crow Creek Road, near East Crow, we spotted two bucks sparring with their horns on the skyline at the top of a draw.

Doug quickly downed one as the other one fled. We climbed up the steep draw and began to trail the fleeing buck. Although we never saw hide nor hair of him again, we got an incredible view of the back country from the top: rolling, undulating hills, red thorn brush, and the rising sun as it broke over the breaks of the Snake and Imnaha.

Doug went back to take care of his buck and I continued on down past a thorn thicket to investigate a hawk, which merely blinked at me from his perch in a snag. He had watched the whole episode and acted as though nothing mattered except the warm sun, which was making him sleepy.

Doug dragged the two-point back to the pickup and we continued on up Dorrance Gulch, which was beautiful on this incredible Indian Summer morning. Welcome weather after days of it being cloudy and raining.

We drove to our Butte Creek place, where we saw more deer, two bunches, 13 head, no horns. Ran into more deer near Salmon Creek and looking through binoculars in the distance, we watched while two hunters approached and shot two bucks. We checked on our cattle, which look good. The Seven Devil Mountain range in Idaho was quite striking, all snow-covered, as were our own Wallowas off in the distance.

Back at the ranch, the deer is skinned and hung. Our company walks up on the hill to survey Prairie Creek and "ooh" and "aha" at the views.

Drive out Crow Creek for an evening hunt. No luck.

Home to feast on venison liver and heart, smothered in onions.

October 5-8—Our Indian Summer continues.

Son Todd and his wife, Liza, bagged their bucks. Small James accompanied his hunting parents.

One morning I took Sandra and Fred up to the Divide to hunt; no luck, but more million dollar views. We enjoyed a tailgate picnic at Downey Lake.

Doug and crew still ag bagging the rain-damaged hay for the neighbors.

One night we hunted the high timber country above the moraine. Saw one doe and her fawn just under Mt. Howard.

One day, armed with beans, hamhocks and sourdough biscuits, we visited daughter Jackie at Imnaha. Mere words are insufficient to describe the Imnaha during the fall we experienced. The reds, yellows and flashes of color marching up the draws, the sun glinting through the fiery, red sumac, the bright river moving along in its autumnal clarity. We stopped often to photograph.

We noticed many nice sets of horns going out on hunters' rigs.

The heads grotesquely mounted for all to see!

We stopped at the Imnaha Store with its wooden Indians guarding the entrance. At Jackie's home a breeze sprang up, fluttering the quaking aspen and sending golden leaves sailing onto the waters of Sheep Creek.

Our company left on the 7th. We so enjoyed them.

The perfect Indian Summer continues. It is almost too beautiful. All I want to do is take pictures and sit and stare at the scenery.

October 8—After our company left, I pounded out my column and fixed lunch for the ag baggers.

Then into town to sell nine dozen eggs! My pullets are outdoing themselves.

Drove up on Alder Slope to pick up some Ted Juve Pottery. The Slope resembles a watercolor painting, so lovely with fall color. The tamaracks, beginning to turn golden, show up on the mountain sides, contrasting with the evergreens.

Stopped to visit Liza and James and look in on the young pigs they are feeding out. One, by the name of Strawberry, is earmarked for our winter ham, bacon and pork chops.

On my way home through Joseph, I noted the brilliant yellow maple trees that line the far end of Main Street. Their color is striking this year.

Baked a brown-bag apple pie... yup, it really works. Found the recipe in the *Northwest Living* magazine.

Doris, Calvin and I decide to give deer hunting one last go before the short season ends. We headed out toward Lick Creek, then up past Jayne's Ridge, Mahogany Cow Camp, Marr Flat and Harl Butte. Another gorgeous day, impossible to describe.

Near Marr Flat Cow Camp, we parked and hunted. I jumped several deer, but they disappeared into the brush before I could look through my scope to see if there were any horns. Virtually every camp we drove by had meat hanging. One woman ran out toward us, very excited, indicating that her husband had just got one!

We walked down around the cow camp and up the road to see if any tracks criss-crossed anywhere.

Doris and I met Calvin walking back down the road in our direction. He had gotten the pickup high centered on a rock. He and Doris managed to jack up the rig and get free, while I tried, to no avail, to flag down a log truck or hunter.

We ate our lunches and watched a weasel sneak up behind a log in front of us to mooch a bit of our lunch!

On the way home, near Lick Creek, we drove alongside a hunter who, only minutes before, had bagged his buck. Right by the side of the road, covered with blood, he looked up and grinned at us!

Home to gather eggs, do chores and fix venison steaks from Doug's buck for supper.

October 9—Up early, as we have a semi-load of mine salt to unload for both Tippett ranches this morning. Milked the cow, tended to my chickens, then developed pictures in my darkroom.

Biden and son Casey Tippett arrived to help unload salt.

Made it to Enterprise by 11:30, so as to catch the van to attend the monthly CowBelle meeting held today at the Rimrock Inn out near the Flora Junction. Along the way, we picked up other CowBelles, Carol Wallace and then Marian Birkmaier, who met us at the foot of Snow Hollow Hill. Beautiful drive, with the fall colors continuing to put on a show. Bands of the Kreb sheep were grazing the meadows along the north highway, the herders on horseback checking the flock with their border collie dogs tagging along to help keep the band together.

After a delicious lunch at the Rimrock cafe, we had a most successful meeting.

Joseph Creek Canyon is sprouting a carpet of new, green grass over the burned areas. Charred trees remain to remind us of the inferno that engulfed the canyon last August.

Back in Enterprise, I head for Imnaha to attend a surprise spur-of-the-moment going-away for Imnaha residents Carol and Howard Borgerding.

The community, saddened to hear of their rather sudden plans to move, had rallied to put on a going-away party at the Imnaha Store and Tavern. A quaint, homey atmosphere prevailed, and there were small children everywhere, most of whom were Borgerding grandchildren.

We will miss the Borgerdings and wish them well in Minnesota. Hopefully, one day they will return to their beloved Courthouse Ranch.

On the way home I was a bit misty-eyed...how could anyone say goodbye to Imnaha in such a fall as we are having?

As I drove by their ranch entrance, the last rays of the setting sun glinted off the canyon of the Big Sheep. Like the flaming fall will fade, so does the sun, as it sinks early now over the canyon rims.

I also thought about Kid Marks, whom I haven't seen in more than a year. So sad to see my friend disabled and wrought with sickness.

Somehow, seeing friends leave and seeing more grow older, has made me wiser, albeit a little sadder this day. Life goes on and nothing is for sure, except that everything will someday change.

A happy note, as I pondered these things. The old will fade away, but the young are taking their places on Imnaha. The old store was full of happy children. Children who will grow up loving the canyons like their elders.

To bed early, as Doug says we will take horses and the mule, Maud, and ride up McCully Creek Basin tomorrow. The last day of deer season!

October 10—We did! What an experience. Up at 5 to chore, while Doug fixed breakfast. I noticed a few foreboding clouds as I chored, but didn't think much about it.

We saddled and loaded the horses and mule into the big cattle truck, and drove to Upper Prairie Creek. Lots of frost in the hollows, and very cold. Wearing longjohns and down clothing, we started up the trail on horseback. Up through the splendid fall color, with the fallen golden tamarack needles softening the sound of our horses' footfalls.

Up we rode, following the cold, ice-encrusted waters splashing down McCully Creek. We reached the trailhead sign, which read: McCully Basin, 5 miles. As we rode higher, we encountered an occasional patch of snow, until finally we were in solid snow. Our horses began to sweat and steam in the cold air and their sweat froze on their bodies.

We hadn't yet seen the sun peeking over the high ridge to the east, when suddenly we were engulfed in swirling, misty clouds.

The wind moaned and whispered in the tree tops and it turned very cold. My feet and hands turned to ice, and I covered my head with a parka. As we climbed higher, there were more than 10 inches of snow on either side of the trail. The sun made a brief, weak appearance before being swallowed up by a massive, swiftly moving cloud. The cloud passed through us like a ghostly, frozen veil.

As we climbed still higher, the horses scrambled for a foothold on the slippery, icy rock in the trail. Doug, who was in hopes of finding a "mossy-backed" buck for me to shoot, rode on, undaunted, but I was beginning to have my doubts about the hunt, as we hadn't seen a fresh track. Years ago, he had seen such a buck on a high ridge above the basin and the memory still lingered.

Reaching the basin, we found shelter and built a warming fire. We ate our lunches and thawed out a bit, before riding up on the very ridge he had remembered. Now, we were in deep snow and off the trail, our horses floundering around the side of the ridge.

All that we heard was the chattering of a pine squirrel. Down the steep ridge we slid, scrambled and sloshed, in deep snow to the bottom.

The basin, deserted, lay in stillness born of the cold. All wildlife had fled! A deserted deer camp lay near the headwaters of the creek where it gurgled between snow banks. At least I was seeing McCully Creek's birthplace!

Red huckleberry contrasted sharply with the snowy landscape, and yellowing willows bordered the stream.

Once more we struck the trail and rode back to the truck, which was about a six- or seven-mile ride.

The wind continued and we rode by creaking trees alongside the trail. A brilliant bluejay scolded us, and except for the lone pine squirrel in the basin, that was all the wildlife we encountered.

The wood stove at home never felt better. Started a big dutch oven of venison stew for supper.

The "mossy-backed" buck will just have to grow more moss… for next year.

October 11—Twenty degrees. The cosmos limply hang their heads, while the geraniums I forgot to put inside last night are blackened with frost. The water froze in the hose I use to water the chickens and the long season of packing water has begun. It is time.

We drove to Clarkston, Washington, this morning to visit Doug's sister, Betty, who has been ill.

The ride over was beautiful with the sumac spreading crimson up and down Buford Grade. We crossed over the Grande Ronde River and headed up Rattlesnake Grade through Anatone, then Asotin, until we came to the Snake River winding its way slowly through Clarkston and Lewiston.

Betty lives in the original Tippett home that once was occupied by Doug's parents, Jidge and Jesse. The house is above the river and from the kitchen window one can watch the boats go by and witness the ever-changing moods of the Snake.

We felt Betty was cheered, somewhat, by our visit and we so enjoyed seeing her smile again.

October 12—Cold, heavy frost again. Even the sunflowers have lost their zest for living, and stand stark and dark against the morning sky, their bright faces now dulled by the frost.

At 6 a.m. I was frying chicken for our picnic on the Divide today. After chores, Doug and I packed the lunch into our pickup and met various members of our local history group at the end of Tenderfoot Valley Road before proceeding to the high plateau country, southeast of us, known as "The Divide."

The air was crisp and wine bright on top. Clear, blue skies and green, gold forested areas had greeted us while driving up Rail Canyon.

The views from the Divide were breathtaking. We could see the Wallowa Range on one side and the Seven Devils range to the east. Both mountain ranges were crowned in the brightness of the season's first snowfalls.

Our first stop was at the old Isley place, where the Divide schoolhouse stands. This wasn't the original location of the school. Like so many in the county, the school has been moved to its present site. Old-timers accompanied us, including Jean Butler, Ed Quinn and Bill Cool, all of whom lived at one time on the Divide. We were told the building had been moved on skids, from near the head of Coyote Creek, near the Cat's Back.

Butler, who had attended the school, recalled that one time 42 pupils were enrolled there. He remembered a game the children made up during

Ed Quinn, 88, talks about growing up on Wallowa County's Divide. Their place was between the Quinn Buttes, named after the pioneer family.

An old barn, about to fall down any minute, sags. The hand-made shakes blow off in the winds that sweep the Divide. This is known as the old Rumble place. The Divide at one time had enough settlers to fill a one-room school with 42 pupils.

recess called "Fox and Goose." In those days the children rode horseback from miles around to school.

Our caravan of rigs proceeded across the top of the Divide to many more old homestead sites. Ed Quinn, who had been raised between what are known as the Quinn Buttes, named after his father, pointed out many old locations of homesteads.

Presently, we came to the spot where the school had stood. We got out and walked around the area, trying to envision how it must have been. "Here is where the fence was, and the gate opened here," Jean Butler said, as if it were only yesterday!

We continued on down what is known as the Cat's Back, a long, narrow ridge that runs down in the direction of Two Buck. We selected a sunny spot at the foot of the Cat's Back to spread our picnic baskets.

We were joined for lunch by Paul Beske and my good friend Ed Quinn, who is 88. While we ate, Ed reminisced about life on the Divide.

Bill Cool, who still owns property on the Divide and maintains a cow camp there, filled us in on interesting items. We met Hank Bird, another cattleman who has range and property in the area, and stopped to visit him. We got out at one spot to stare, in awe, from the Cat's Back down to the canyon of the Big Sheep.

From our viewpoint, we could see Harl Butte, Marr Flat and all drainages of Big Sheep. We were "between the Sheeps," so to speak. Little Sheep Canyon on the west and Big Sheep to the east.

We drove slowly by the Quinn place, between the buttes, where Ed was reared. Earlier, we had gone past the Wasson homestead, where a little girl named Caroline kept a diary in the late 1800s that describes vividly their life there. From a small, crippled girl's pen there emerges a story that gives the reader an idea of how it was, through the eyes of a little girl.

Presently we arrived at the Downey Lakes area, where the swamp grasses and water formed a large low area. Nearby, on the shore or edge of the lake, was the original Downey cabin. We continued around a corner of the lake to investigate other places of interest. The rough, rutty road here began a rather abrupt descent down into a timbered draw that ultimately ended at Bear Gulch.

If I were an Indian, I would camp here until the end of the golden Indian Summer. What a spot!

Ed Quinn, with his alert mind and perfect recall, was an asset to our group, answering questions and filling in many blank areas for us. As the sun began to sink over the western slopes of the Wallowas, we reluctantly headed home.

I think Max Gorsline and Doug could have talked all day, but I imagined I could hear Star bawling from the Divide.

After chores and supper, I canned seven quarts of sauerkraut. A bright, full moon flows softly over Prairie Creek tonight and I think of the sight it must have made as it rose over the Divide! Such fun we've had today. It was heartwarming to see the men, mostly neighbors and ranchers, all taking the time to visit and see the country. I ponder on how, in these times, we have all but lost this ability, this taking time out from life's demands, to spend a day visiting and learning about other times and lives. The thing we have lost is neighborliness. Like Ed Quinn said, "When things were hard on the Divide, we all pulled together, like at harvest or during someone's sickness. We celebrated the happy times, too, but no matter, we always had time to visit."

I would like to feel that today's excursion into this beautiful day and little known country brought together old neighbors and revived that illusive "something" that seems to be lacking in our modern day society.

To bed with the book "Don Coyote."

October 13—Up early, Doug checking cattle on the moraine.

I canned seven more quarts of sauerkraut.

Hung four loads of wash on the line, thinking of excuses to be outside on this one more perfect day.

Doug and Ben saddle the horses and drive the cattle home from the moraine pasture. The cattle trail home willingly, knowing good hayed-over pastures await them. We shipped a few drys to market.

I made a batch of carrot-cookie bars. Set sourdough to rise. Biscuits and venison for supper. Made lots so we can use them for sandwiches tomorrow when we head for the hills to brand the fall calves.

Grandson Chad shot his first buck at age 12. Good for you, Chad, you are growing up in the Wallowa County tradition.

Walked out to shut the chickens in. Have been letting them out during the day to eat grass and bugs.

The moon was up, and the lonesome wail of a coyote broke the silence of the evening. To bed early, a big day coming up tomorrow.

October 14—Not one single rig did we meet today, in a nearly 60-mile round trip to our Salmon Creek hill ranch! It was so quiet out there, with the deer hunters gone.

The deer seem to know when the last shot has been fired, and we saw several bunches. Along the Crow Creek road, we spotted a badger and a coyote hunting their breakfasts.

Dean Garrett, one of the "gather" crew, pauses for lunch on a sunny hillside during a cattle drive to the lower elevations for winter.

Jill Yost, daughter of James and Vicky Yost of Enterprise, was one of the cowgirls who helped gather cattle on Red Hill in Wallowa County's Chesnimnus country this fall. It's the lunch stop, for her horse and dog as well.

To begin with, we drove the purebred Simmentals, along with their new, fall calves, into the corral. I noticed a sprinkling of longhorn influence in the calves! A neighboring longhorn bull had been "neighborly" to our cows while they were pastured on Alder Slope. The calves looked a little strange following their Simmental mammas.

We branded and worked the calves, me pushing them up the narrow wooden chute, which is now filled with rocks instead of mud! The calves were large, having been born around August. I managed all but one, which I left till last. This particular bull calf insisted on chasing me to the top of the fence each time I attempted to start him up the chute. Blowing through his nose and looking at me bleary-eyed, this Simmental-longhorn cross convinced me I had no business in there with him. Ben exerted the proper "influence" and he unwillingly ran into the chute, where he tried to shake the thing apart.

It was a clear, beautiful day, so we enjoyed our sourdough rolls and venison sandwiches out on the grass in the sunshine. We finished by late afternoon and turned some bulls into the small pasture by the creek. Fell asleep in the pickup on the way home. Gathered eggs, and cleaned the mountain oysters. Out in the withering garden, I found some corn still hanging on the stalks and decided to invent a recipe to use it up. Using tomatoes, onion, bell pepper, eggs, milk, cracker crumbs and butter I came up with a great casserole accompaniment to the venison steaks.

Because the swiss chard was still bright and crisp, I cooked some of that with bacon.

A bright October moon grows fatter each night and the lovely fall color has peaked here in the valley.

October 15—Up very early to fix breakfast and make a lunch for Doug so he and Ben could leave for the hills to work more cattle. Meanwhile, I chored, then left for Imnaha, where I picked up granddaughter Mona Lee, who accompanied me upriver to interview Doris Goucher for Agri-Times' "Women in Agriculture" issue. The crisp, bright October sunshine glinted off the river. Doris greeted us, then gave us a tour of the ranch and the partially completed log home they are building.

Later, we visited over coffee and freshly baked ginger cookies.

On the way back to Mona's house, this little four-year-old told me "most amazing things"... we had a wonderful one-on-one conversation. Such a granddaughter!

Back "On Top," I had many errands to run in town. I realized it had been 20 days since I'd been grocery shopping. So much of our food is home-grown.

Thinking of new ways to fix venison, I prepared pasties for supper. A delicious way to fix meat, spuds and onions, all cooked in a flaky pastry crust.

Enjoyed the October moon when I went out to lock up my chickens.

October 16—Indian summer continues, enabling ranchers to wean calves, work cattle, and put up the last cuttings of hay, as well as finish the harvesting of the grain crops.

We are branding calves here today. These are the fall calves to our cows on the moraine pastures.

Fixed a hot meal at noon for the cowboys.

Attended a history group meeting at the Bookloft tonight. Very informative. Wallowa County history is addictive. The more you learn, the more you want to learn.

October 17—Doug and Ben to the hills to work cattle again, as the weather is so cooperative.

My poor babies at the barn! Branded, dehorned and castrated, they stand around looking so dejected. In a few days, they will have forgotten the trauma and only be concerned with mamma's warm milk.

We are preparing for another trip to Dug Bar; this time we will take friends Doris and Calvin with us.

Attended a junior high football game in Enterprise this afternoon. Grandson Chad played. I sat between my two lovely daughters-in-law, Liza and Annie, and held baby James... naturally. It was cold!

October 18—All in readiness, chores done and messages left for Ben, who will tend to my animals while we are down at the river. I drove our mini motorhome and Doug and Calvin took the lead in the diesel pickup.

Cloudy and a heavy frost this morning. Driving to Imnaha, we continued to enjoy the fall color that is everywhere.

Leaving the pavement at Fence Creek, we began the 25-mile trip to Dug Bar. The road follows a twisting, rough course that winds around rimrock canyons that command a spectacular view of the river below. We made it down to Horse Creek, then Corral Creek, noticing many deer grazing the fall grasses.

We crossed the Cow Creek bridge and began the ascent that eventually took us up near Lone Pine Saddle. This saddle was part of the Nee-me-poo trail, the retreat route taken by the Wallowa band of Nez Perce Indians led by Chief Joseph. The fleeing Nez Perce crossed the Snake in spring flood with their women, children, horses and cattle near our old ranch at Dug Bar. A remarkable feat, when you stop to consider how high and intimidating the water would be in the snowmelt season.

We wound around high rims before beginning the long, steep, narrow descent to the Snake. Dug Bar lay dreaming in the October haze. We drove into the ranch and met the men, who had shot some chukars on the way in. We parked our motor home near the alfalfa field in view of the river.

Since it was Idaho deer season, many boats were on the river. We soon packed a picnic and headed upriver in our boat, to hunt chukars and do some fishing. Near Roland Bar, we tied up the boat and walked around a bit. Near the old Jim Blankenship ranch, I got a shot at some chukars, but missed all of them.

Since fishing wasn't that hot, we headed downriver to the mouths of the Imnaha and Salmon rivers. Calvin caught a bass, but otherwise fishing seemed at the moment to be in the doldrums.

Back in camp by dark, where we barbecued hamburgers over an open fire and watched a magnificent full moon make its appearance over a high rim on the Idaho side. The moonlight created a shining, golden path across the swirling waters of the Snake. Doris couldn't resist trying out some night photography.

Later, we were lulled to sleep by the river's sound. The ranch was bathed in moonlight.

October 19—Up to fix sourdough hotcakes, bacon and eggs. A gorgeous morning, and the moon hung over a rim. A little chilly, but here at 1,000 feet nothing like our valley home. Doug caught a nice steelhead, while I walked up to investigate the foundation of the old stamp mill at Eureka Bar and did some photographing.

Later, we fished again, startling a band of wild Canadian honkers that had been feeding along shore. Such a sight they made.

Saw many great blue herons and were able to shoot more chukars. At one point, we simply let the boat drift downstream and shut off the motor...peaceful. We spotted a pair of eagles and some more deer.

Reluctantly, we left Dug Bar around 3 in the afternoon.

We stopped to fish for trout in the Imnaha and the men bagged a few more chukars. We capped our "perfect" trip with a chicken basket dinner served up by Phyllis at the Imnaha Cafe.

October 20—Took a walk today, away from the typewriter and the ranch duties. The cottonwood leaves float down our creek; the water in the creek is yellow with them.

These heavy steel rings were secured to the rocks that border the Snake River near Eureka Bar, to help in pulling the big boats upstream. The river boat "Imnaha" sank at Mountain Sheep Rapid in 1903, losing machinery intended for the mining venture at Eureka Bar.

The Dug Bar Ranch on the Snake River, formerly owned by Doug Tippett, now owned by the U.S. Forest Service, is leased by Duke Philips, who runs cattle in the canyons. The road ends here. Across the Snake River is Idaho.

A spray of red rose hips is bright in the sunlight against the leaf-covered water. This time of year brings out the vagabond, the wanderlust feeling in me; I want to be out and about! Perhaps it is the wild goose in some of us that calls.

Finished digging my red potatoes and will store them in a root cellar on Alder Slope. Doug and Ben are hauling our bulls in from the hills today.

October 21—After driving the cows down from a rented pasture on upper Prairie Creek, Ben, Calvin and Doug are branding their fall calves this afternoon.

October 22—Another beautiful, clear day. How long will this last? Breakfast was mountain oysters and scrambled eggs...yum! Milked the cow, then to Joseph to pick up "Strawberry." Our pork is ready.

Grace Bartlett and I drove to Imnaha where we had lunch with Kid and Mary Marks, and I took pictures for an article I will do for Agri-Times. We had such a nice visit with Mary while she prepared a delicious lunch of home-grown food. Kid and Mary are two of my very favorite people.

From upriver, on this gorgeous Indian Summer day, we drove down-river to Inez Meyer's garden, where we picked the golden winter (keeping) squash. Never have I seen such squash, one vine, having escaped the garden had climbed a nearby tree. The squash hung down from the limbs.

"A squash tree," Grace said.

Inez, in her 80s, still gardens and is as spry as a kitten. This remarkable lady has deep roots in Wallowa County. Her grandfather, William McCormack, was the first white man to come into the country in 1871. He and a fellow named Neil Keith built a cabin on Scotch Creek, near Alder Slope, and spent that first winter in a new land that heretofore had been occupied only by the Nez Perce Indians.

We loaded up the trunk of my car with the pretty orange squash, which will be used for the big centennial dinner on Feb. 14, 1987, a dinner I will help prepare, to honor Wallowa County's 100th birthday. The menu will include beef, sourdough bread, homemade noodles, salad and blueberry buckle, in addition to the squash.

I loved Inez's old-fashioned garden. It was a tangle of dahlias, mums and roses, growing in profusion. An enormous old black walnut tree was losing its leaves and the ground around where we weighed the squash was a golden carpet of them.

October 23—Moon still high in the sky at 6:30 — clear, cold and frosty.

After breakfast of fresh sausage and eggs, I did chores, then climbed aboard my saddled mare "Cal" and Doug rode "Hummer."

We rode out to drive some fall calvers and their calves out onto the road from the north pasture. From here we took them about five miles to the base of the moraine to a hayed-over pasture.

From a creek alongside the road, we startled some wild mallards. While waiting for the truck to come pick us up, I curled up in the sun near my mare and napped, it was so incredibly warm.

Delivered my eggs to town, drove to Alder Slope where I stored the squash until February. Back by way of Hurricane Creek, where I photographed fall color. Home to make a peanut butter chocolate cake, then cook pork chops, mashed potatoes, applesauce and carrot-raisin salad for supper. You can tell we have fall appetites!

October 24—The Great Pumpkin hunt is on! Everyone is wondering where the pumpkin is hidden, and listening KWVR, our local radio station, for the clues. We are preparing to leave for Snake River in the morning.

Spent the day cooking for the trip. Made a plum pie, combining some of those grown on Alder Slope with those given to me by a friend.

October 25—Up before dawn, readying for our departure to Snake River. Max and Dorothy Gorsline arrived, whereupon we left by 7. Stopped at daughter Jackie's on Sheep Creek to pick up some freshly pressed apple cider. Once more we set up camp on our former ranch at Dug Bar — who would have thought we would one day camp here?

Bud and Ruby Zollman joined us in the late afternoon.

Since the Snake River permit (limited entry) bull elk season was due to open on Wednesday, many rigs pulled in near us. They all brought horses and pack mules or donkeys and were preparing to ride into the back country. Some real trophies are usually taken during this three-point or better hunt in the breaks of the Snake.

On one of our excursions downriver to Eureka Bar, we once again spotted the mountain sheep; the full-curl rams looked down at our boat from their high, rocky perches. What a thrill for our guests.

Bud and Ruby pitched their tent near the river, complete with a sheepherder stove. We feasted on roast chicken, beans and ham hocks, potato salad, sourdough rolls and the plum pie, which, other than getting a little mashed on the rough roads, tasted plumb delicious!

Because we had missed the boat to Ragtown, we sat around the campfire on this Saturday night and reminisced and told tall tales.

It was a treat listening to Max Gorsline talk about early days, the days of miners, and long-ago stories, some of which made us glad we live today.

Far up on the rims, some chukars tantalized us with their calling.

October 26—Elk hunters continued to arrive all night. In the morning we were surrounded by pack animals of every description, being packed with gear for the trip into the back country. Some were going to Deep Creek and others to the Palace.

During the night, the sourdough had done its thing and we had hot cakes plus all the goodies to go with, including wild blackberry jam that Ruby had made. Our breakfast, cooked outdoors, was seasoned with scenery and flavored with the canyon air.

At Eureka Bar, while Bud and Doug did some steelhead fishing, Max took us gals for a walk up past the old stamp mill. Our guide then led us to another historic site, the foundation of the old hotel that once stood there during Eureka's heyday. It was easy to envision the activity around this early-day camp...the big boats coming up to deliver supplies, some of which would be loaded onto horse-drawn wagon or mule pack-trains, and freighted up the incredibly steep road to Buckhorn and thence out to the Wallowa Valley...or down Spain Saddle to Imnaha. Max pointed out where the saloon used to stand, and the fact that it was a good distance away from the hotel. "So the fellers could sober up before returning," Max said.

Today, Mother Nature is fast erasing the effects of man's early activities at this once-booming settlement.

The brilliant red sumac is spreading everywhere, and the tall, golden grasses whisper secrets of long ago.

What a Sunday afternoon — followed by more chukar hunting.

Back in camp, I hiked up Birch Gulch (one of my favorite old haunts) on the pretense of hunting chukars. I came upon the seedling apricot tree, the golden leaves contrasting against the dry canyon grasses and rimrocks. What a sight in the evening light!

I scrambled up over a steep embankment to look down on the slender waterfall that makes wild music in Birch Gulch. A lone grouse flew up ahead of me. I had intruded on his private domain. Walking back down to the river, I followed a well-worn elk trail that afforded a magnificent view of the ranch.

Barbecued trout for supper and Ruby made biscuits in the sheep-herder stove. We sat around the fire, feeding it driftwood we had gathered during the day, staring into the glowing embers, listening to the river sound and remembering to set our watches back.

It would have been nicer, still, remain at Dug Bar and stop the marching of time entirely

October 28—Here they come, in all shapes and sizes, driving rigs of every description, wearing red hats, camouflaged hats, western hats, hiking boots and armed with enough ammunition to start a war.

They walk the streets and line the checkout stands in our grocery stores or purchase hay and straw for bedding and horse feed.

They have horses, mules, donkeys, and most have left their wives at home. "They" are the elk hunters, making their yearly pilgrimage to our country's rugged outback, in search of the elusive wapiti.

Tomorrow morning, as day breaks, the first shot will signal the beginning of that phenomenon known as "elk season."

By nightfall many of these big game animals will hang in camps scattered around our vast country.

October 29—Doug up long before daylight, preparing to go to the hills to mend fences—and check on elk hunters, who might mistake our cattle for elk, or leave a gate open. Actually, we have had very little trouble with hunters and find them to be a courteous lot.

If they ask permission to hunt our lands, it is granted provided they follow the simple common-sense rules. For most out-of-county hunters, we find that the reason for going to all this trouble in the first place is to temporarily escape the pressures of our 1980s world, and we can't blame them for this.

Hunting and harvesting the elk is a way of reducing herd numbers to a manageable level.

Since we, the ranchers and farmers donate our salt, range, and time mending fences for these animals, we appreciate the hunters. If it weren't for them, we would be overrun in some areas with these wild animals.

We enjoy seeing these big elk and watching the little calves in the spring, listening to the spine-tingling bugling of the bulls in the fall—as long as they aren't eating our precious range!

Cloudy, frosty, cold—feels like it could snow.

Zumwalt cow elk tag holders Ben and Calvin drive in with huge grins and two elk! Such enormous creatures, they fill the back of Ben's pickup.

A wind materializes, gusting to a steady roar by late afternoon.

My sons, Ken and Todd, and grandson Chad, hiked with cousin Terry up through Murrary Gap into the Silver Creek country, over Traverse Ridge, then down the Lostine, without bagging a single elk. It had begun to snow and was very cold. Dedicated hunters!

October 30—October is leaving, the fall color fading away. Last night's storm swept the last yellow leaves from the trees. The landscape has been replaced by brown November. The snowline is halfway down the mountain. The rain has ceased, dark clouds on the horizon and out north.

Milked the cow and tended to housework and writing.

Cleaning up the garden — dug the remainder of my red potatoes, fed the spoiled corn to the chickens, picked the sunflowers. Beets simmer on the wood stove to make pickled beets, sunflowers dry on newspapers on the floor, sage hangs to dry in back of the stove and carrots cook for supper.

Doug is attending a weed control meeting at Cloverleaf Hall, while I catch up on my writing. Stormy and cold tonight.

October 31—A bright new snowfall on this last day of October and Halloween. Delivered eggs to town, and also a loaf of freshly baked sourdough bread to a newly married couple.

Met my friend Doris at the Silver Lake Tea Room at McCully Junction in Joseph. I treated her to a belated birthday lunch. Fun! We had quiche, salad, English tea and Nainamo bars.

Son Tod and nephew Terry both shot their bull elk today while driving along a road out north. And after all that hiking yesterday.

Carved a pumpkin and placed a lighted candle inside his grinning face. Our only trick or treaters way out here on Prairie Creek were grandchildren Buck and Mona, who stopped by with their parents on their way to Enterprise to have supper with us.

November 1—The fallen leaves are edged with frost, giving them another chance at beauty before going into the soil.

Clearing off, beautiful views of the mountains appear to swim in a sea of clouds, surfacing once in awhile to reveal brilliant snowfields, then disappearing once more into the billowy froth.

Doug is hauling firewood from the moraine.

We enjoyed a fine dinner at the lake tonight with friends. The tourist season is over and the lake is quiet and deserted except for the year-around inhabitants.

November 2—Doug up early fixing sourdough hotcakes. He and Dwayne Wiggins will spend the day on Snake River steelhead fishing. It is a welcome change of pace not to have the responsibility of the seed potato crop this year. It has given us much more free time to do some of the things we enjoy.

Grace Bartlett, Guy and Reatha McCormack, and I packed our lunches and headed out Crow Creek to track down some early history of the area for a project I am working on. It was a beautiful day, crisp cold in the morning, but warming up with the sun.

We visited many old homestead sites and drove past the old Poulson place, Birkmaiers', then came to Chesnimnus Creek, where it conflues with Crow Creek and Joseph Creek heads.

Beyond this point, we investigated an old school house and log buildings nearby that are all that remain of a very old homestead.

We back-tracked and wound up Red Hill, passing by a group of cowboys and cowgirls. I stopped to photograph them as they rested the cattle and ate their lunches on the sunny hillside. Their view was of the Wallowas to the south and beneath them lay the sprawling Chesnimnus country — what a sight!

We continued on up to the Red Hill Lookout, where we ate our lunches. We could see the Seven Devil Range in Idaho and look out over the vast, forested areas toward Cold Spring. Looking through binoculars, we could spot the Findley Buttes and the big Zumwalt, Pine Creek and Salmon Creek country—and our hill pastures.

We drove back toward the old Dorrance place and up Dorrance Gulch, then out across the Pine Creek road to Zumwalt; where we walked in on a road to look at the old Stubblefield homestead.

The old house, barn, well and corrals were situated in a fold of the lonely hills. We were greeted by several saddle horses who came running up to us as though in need of companionship. As evening descended, we walked back to the car and drove home under a pink sky, as the sunset in flame over the Wallowas.

An autumnal chill set in and the warm day was only a memory by the time we reached the valley.

Aside from the cowboys, we saw few people on this Sunday, although we had driven many miles.

Meanwhile, back at the ranch—my cow was bawling, eggs to gather, daughter Jackie and children here, Janet Tippet was waiting—I had invited her for supper! Son Steve popped in with a friend, located his skis, and left.

I fried some venison for supper and put the children to bed. By that time Dwayne and Doug appeared, triumphant, bearing two huge steelhead, and more chukars. Enjoyed visiting sis-in-law Janet, then crashed; what a day!

November 3—Jackie and I drove Buck to his school at Imnaha on this lovely morning. Heavy frost, but clear and sunny.

Scotty appeared on schedule and I had a kettle of water boiling. I chopped the heads off the five remaining old hens and had them in the freezer by noon.

November 4—Election Day, and my—so many and varied measures to vote on. Had to spend a long time studying before deciding how to vote.

November 4—Spent most of this day cooking a special "Snake River dinner." We have invited the friends we took camping with us on Dug Bar.

Doug's specialty is the steelhead, which he barbecues outside. I prepared "Chukar a'la Dug Bar," using an old recipe given to me by one of Doug's former hunters, who year after year came to hunt when Doug ran his guide service. After the boned chukar meat is browned in butter, it is allowed to cook slowly in a sauce made of sautéed mushrooms, onions, white wine and drippings. Yum!

We had a wonderful dinner while reliving our adventures and enjoying our Snake River fare.

November 5—A brilliant salmon-colored sunrise reflected itself in dark, purple clouds that hovered over the mountains. A wind is rising, the weather changing.

Milked the cow. The wind nearly blew me and my pail away!

Ben and Doug working cattle down at the chutes all morning.

Daughter-in-law Liza called wanting instructions on how to cook a goose that her husband had shot. Of course, Doug had to "get her goose" by telling her that "First, you get some sawdust and put the goose in and roast it, then throw the goose away and eat the sawdust."

Baked a gooseberry pie and worked in the darkroom, printing for a few hours.

Doug is on duty at the hay station manned by local stockgrowers near the Minam grade just inside the Wallowa County line. This is a hay exchange program to prevent outside hunters from bringing in hay that might contain tansy ragwort or other noxious weed seed.

Black clouds darkened the skies all day and by chore time this evening, stinging flakes of snow driven by the wind hit me in the face. The weather is reminding us that it is, after all, November. We've been lulled into thinking the beautiful days would last forever.

November 6—Just a skift of snow left, but the snowline is just above us. It poured down while Doug sat in his shelter at the check station last evening, and news comes to us that there were eight inches of snow out at Buckhorn.

Did chores under steel-gray skies. We are having some backhoe work done at the potato cellar this morning.

To town to deliver eggs, run errands and purchase groceries. Also picked up my elk tag at Bud's Hardware.

Home to find my niece, Jeanette, and her boyfriend, Don, had made it here safely. Don plans to be here for the second bull elk season.

The Matthews from Roseburg stopped by on their way to Dug Bar to join daughter Jackie and family. They are also elk hunting and had their mule loaded in the truck.

Treated our guests to more chukars, Imnaha squash, sourdough biscuits and gooseberry pie! More snow predicted tonight.

November 7—Sourdough cooking on the wood range, much to the delight of our guests. Snow falling softly outside as we breakfasted. Our world is silently transforming to winter white. The horses are white, the cattle wear frosted coats and Chester the rooster, who still roosts in the bare-limbed willow tree, is dusted with snow.

After breakfast, Jeanette and I walked out to chore. Chester followed, making small chicken tracks. The orange cats contrasted sharply against the snow.

My frosted cow comes into the barn and soon blobs of the white stuff slide off her back onto my head while I milk. Jeanette thinks the snow is a novelty and takes many pictures.

Thinking all day about my oldest daughter's family, which is on the road traveling here for elk season. The family left Chilcoot, California, at 4 this morning.

Had a nice visit this morning with my friends, Marge and Joe Onaidia, who used to own and operate the Cherry Creek Sheep Company near Snake River. These wonderful Basque people have contributed much to our country. Joe gave me some of his good garlic to plant in my garden.

Ramona, Charley, Carrie and Shawn arrived safely. With them in a separate rig were Chris and Gary from Loyalton, who would also hunt elk. We have a full house.

Fun having such fun people here. Fried a huge pan of pork chops, made rolls, carrot salad, potatoes, relishes and applesauce. The food disappeared like magic.

Everyone is in a good mood, anticipating a good elk hunt, which would be accompanied by winter weather.

Every bed in the house is taken and Gary and Chris are bedded down in sleeping bags on the living room floor.

November 8—Up at 4:30 to fix sourdough waffles and bacon and eggs for the army, while Ramona made lunches. Twenty degrees, clear and cold. Elk hunters scattered, all with high hopes and bundled up in warm clothing.

It was dark and cold out tonight, with only a glimmer of a moon, and our hunters still hadn't returned. Around 9 p.m. Gary and Chris appeared, covered with blood and hungry as bears. The fellows were jubilant, having bagged an elk out on Elk Mountain! They had packed the quartered elk for about two miles on their backs to the pickup.

We had the entire family here for dinner and ate in shifts. By the time the meat was skinned and hung it was 11:30. A long day.

November 9—Heavy snowfall last night, still snowing. A repeat of yesterday, getting the hunters off.

Aunt Liza helped the children make a snowman today. He looks happy in our yard sporting a red scarf and a carrot nose.

I roasted three chickens, baked bread and a sourdough chocolate cake.

Icicles form on the eaves of the house and it is crunchy cold out tonight. I think about Chester perched on his cold limb.

The hunters returned late again, having tracked the "Big One" for miles in the snow. The roast chicken was reduced to bones and the cake to crumbs.

Grandsons Chad and Shawn are having a ball, racing around in the cold, moonlighted, snowy pastures on the three-wheeler. It is hard to believe these two grandsons are nearly 13.

I went to bed, leaving the hunters still talking around the wood stove. The temperature is dropping fast.

An Imnaha cowboy, Sam Loftus, called to tell us that son-in-law Bill had arrived safely with the 500 cattle at Somers Creek, 20 miles upriver from Dug Bar. He had several messages to deliver, in the event we would be going down.

November 10—Up early again.

Five below zero. Ice forming inside our windows. Doug helped me fix breakfast on the wood stove for the tribe. All the hunters except Jeanette and Don are preparing to leave for home.

I hadn't heard Chester's morning crow and looked outside to see him still in his tree — too cold to move, perhaps? I called and the banty rooster turned his head around to look at me, but didn't even try to fly down. Finally, around 8:30, when the sun warmed up his legs, he flew down. He looked so cold, and it took him awhile to get in gear. Soon he was running around like his old self again.

All too soon, it was time for my family to leave. I hugged my oldest daughter and grandchildren and they were gone!

The snowman, leaning slightly forward, is frozen to the picnic table.

Baked the "Herman Cake," which turned out delicious, since I "spiked" it with my sourdough.

A pink sky at 5:30, a lemon-colored moon, and a snowscape as bright as day greeted me as I chored tonight.

Slept in peace, as the California family arrived home safely, having called around 10.

November 11—We are leaving in a couple of hours for Dug Bar on the Snake River again, this time to take butane down for my son-in-law and daughter, who are staying in the house down there.

Bill helped trail 500 head of cattle down from "on top." They will be staying there for a week.

A returning cowboy reported they were out of butane and were cooking in a Dutch oven in the fireplace. Fun!

The wood cookstove that used to be down there is now in my kitchen.

We have had a houseful of elk hunters and visiting family, have been running a boarding house, and haven't had time to get out my column, so here are some timely pictures.

November 11—The wind came up during the night, sifting snow around the carport. Warmer this morning—20 degrees.

While Jeanette tended to my chickens, I milked Star.

By noon we had gathered up the supplies needed and were on our way to Dug Bar. As we drove out of our snowy world down into the canyons, dark clouds hovered over Imnaha's rims. Before long, it began to rain.

On top we could see it was snowing.

Splashing through ice-encrusted puddles, we traveled the long, winding road to Dug Bar. At last we could see the blue-green Snake winding in its canyon.

On a nearby hillside we spotted a covey of chukars, and Doug was able to shoot three birds. Misty rain continued to fall all the way to Dug Bar. The mists lay so thickly over the distant rim, visibility was limited.

Little Mona Lee and Buck ran out to welcome us. The children immediately took me by the hand and led me to the barn where they proudly showed me their cowdog, Maggie, curled up with her new puppies.

In the old house, a cozy fire crackled merrily and we soon warmed up.

Bill's dad had shot his three-point bull elk up near Dug Creek the day before, and Jackie and Carolee were frying the heart and liver with onions for supper.

We enjoyed a great meal in our former home and all engaged in a game of Scrabble before going to bed.

November 12—The rain ceased during the night, but misty vapors clung to and veiled the snow-clad rims. We enjoyed breakfast with our extended family in this remote ranch setting.

Jeanette, who had been more than a little dubious over the road on the way in, was wondering if she would ever return safely to civilization. Although she was having a good time, she kept thinking about going out; her first experience on canyon roads. She and Don left after breakfast to drive back to California.

The rest of us, children included, piled into the boat and headed down to Eureka Bar to fish. Once again we saw the mountain sheep and two bald eagles. We then headed upriver to Somers Creek, where a tent camp had been set up. This was the cow camp that Bill has been staying in and will return to. He and Dave Glaus will ride herd on 500 head of cows while they graze the good dry feed in the nearby canyons.

November 12, continued—Our last boat ride for this year. Doug loaded the boat onto its trailer to haul it out "On Top" tomorrow.

Jackie had put a turkey in the oven before we departed for Somers Creek in the boat. Upon returning, we were greeted with a mini Thanksgiving dinner and the smells emanating from the kitchen whetted our outdoor appetites. Jackie baked a pan of her famous sourdough rolls and we feasted.

Earlier this morning, I had taken a walk up the trail to the wilderness boundary where I had come face to face with a beautiful mule deer buck

Church Dorrance, Wallowa County livestock raiser, in this photo from the files of the Wallowa County Chieftain, poses beside his purebred Hereford bull. Early-day cattlemen like Dorrance established Wallowa County's reputation for quality livestock.

Snow falls softly outside and the sourdoughs bake on the cast iron griddle on the Monarch. The old wood cookstove is perfect for feeding hungry elk hunters.

A group of elk hunters from Portland head out. These fellows will set up camp near Deep Creek in the rugged Snake River country. They have been coming to this same area for years.

Chris, left, and Gary grin broadly as they pose beside the unusually large spike bull elk they bagged near Elk Mountain in Wallowa County during the second season. Heavy snow and below-freezing temperatures made hunting only for the hardy. Chris and Gary are from Loyalton, California. They were impressed by Wallowa County's scenery, people and hospitality.

and his two does. Although the trail was somewhat muddy, the view of canyons, rims and winding river was terrific.

Forty degrees tonight, much warmer. Darkness came at 4 p.m. as the sinking sun slipped behind the high rims. We played Scrabble again, until time for bed.

Sleep came easily in the silence of the Snake River Canyon. Nothing could be heard, save the sound of embers cracking softly in the old rock fireplace.

November 13—The sunlight burst through the clouds this morning. A gorgeous day.

After breakfast, the grandchildren, accompanied by their grandmothers, took a walk up the trail above the ranch buildings. We could look down on the famous Nez Perce crossing and I was able to get some nice shots with my camera.

All too soon, it was time for us to leave. Doug and Bill loaded the mule, "Cougar Johnson," into our truck and we left, pulling our boat.

Snow lay on the high rims, contrasting sharply against the brown grasses of the canyons.

Stopped at the Riverside Cafe in Imnaha to visit Jim Dorrance and eat a bite. Hunters coming and going, some reported that high winds had drifted the road to Hat Point.

We unloaded "Cougar" and led him into his pasture near Sheep Creek, and a pretty moon guided us home to the valley.

November 14—The alarm went off at 4:30! I made biscuits and sausage gravy before doing chores and leaving before daylight to go elk hunting.

Drizzly, misty rain accompanied us as we headed out toward Pine Creek. A large fog bank rolled up out of the canyons in the direction of Buckhorn. We spotted a small band of elk, no horns. We drove down past Chesnimnus Creek and joined the Crow Creek road, then turned up the Charlois Road.

Here we took another side road that wound up into thick timber. The road was covered with deep snow and we had to travel in four-wheel drive. We passed two hunters' camps, looking miserable and wet in the cold. Most of the hunters had pulled out with last week's storm and sub-zero temperatures.

Soon we came to a high ridge that looked down on Swamp Creek. Fingers of fog lay in the bottoms and curled up the sides of the timbered draws. A very quiet, lonely place in winter. We drove by "Little Elk Spring" and "Robert's Spring," and I wondered who "Robert" was. Fog-

A recent snowstorm brought below zero temperatures to Prairie Creek in Wallowa County. But this happy snowman likes the cold and is happy that Carrie and Chelsie created him.

shrouded Elk Mountain loomed ahead, and we glassed the area hoping to see an elk.

Once again we gained the Charlois Road and took yet another side road that led us past the old Weaver place and near the old Elk Mountain school house, still standing in a meadow. We continued on past many old homesteads, silent in the misty rain, which was now mixed with snow. In this lonely setting we pulled off alongside the road to eat our lunches.

By the time we gained the main road near the Pratt school house, it was beginning to snow pretty good.

I thought about daughter Jackie at Dug Bar and her husband, Bill, who will have ridden the 20 miles, horseback, to Somers Creek and his tent home.

November 15—Doug and I headed for the hills and a last chance at elk hunting. A brilliant sunrise greeted us as we drove out the Crow Creek road. The rising sun burned the mists away, exposing bright apricot-colored clouds. Out near Butte Creek, we could see the dark, purple Seven Devil range outlined against the orange sky. But no elk.

Looking off in the direction of Pine Creek, I scanned the horizon with my binoculars, and spotted the old Zumwalt school house with its empty bell tower. I could imagine hearing the ringing of that bell and how it must have broken the silence of these lonely hills.

Before we backtracked down the winding road toward Pine Creek, I took a picture of the view before us—the forlorn tombstone on the knoll above Maynard Gulch, the weathered barn and house on Biden Tippett's ranch, the cabin and pond on Ketcher's place, and the zig-zagging road winding up to the sky.

Down on Chesnimnus Creek, the red osier dogwood was brilliant in the morning sunshine. Mist was rising from the creek and made a pretty picture.

We drove home by way of the North Highway where I photographed the sheepherder near his wagon tending to hundreds of sheep.

Although we shot nary an elk, we did enjoy being out and about in this beautiful county of ours.

November 16—Awoke at 1 a.m. to gaze out at Prairie Creek's moonscape. The moonlight was shining across the snow; the wail of a coyote had awakened me. From the opposite hill he was singing his tune.

Was he hungry? Perhaps, like me, he was moonstruck!

Scotty and I hiked up past Clarice Southwick's to TV Ridge this morning. I went on the pretext of hunting a bull elk on this last day of the season.

Soft flakes of snow fell all during our hike and it was beautiful, except we couldn't see a thing from the top of the ridge due to the snowstorm.

The elk were relatively safe because Scotty and I talked and laughed as we tromped through the snow, giving the animals plenty of warning. We did see fresh tracks as we climbed up the trail, but they were filled with snow on our return.

November 17—A howling wind materialized in the middle of the night. I was up early, couldn't sleep. The exceptionally bright moon appeared to be tossing about.

Could hardly stand upright as I walked out to chore and the wind slid me along on the ice-covered path between the shop and the barn.

Jackie stopped by with the children. Buck and his cousin, Rowdy, had been riding Rowdy's pigs. They were filthy! "Having pig races," said Buck, grinning at the memory.

Organizing my 4-H Sourdough Shutterbugs for a new year. Twenty-seven members enrolled now!

November 18—Doug, Ben and Todd headed out to Salmon Creek with the cattle trucks to haul in the spring calves. They will be weaned away from their mothers.

Electricity was off this morning, due to the wind. Visited with our neighbors, the Allisons, over the phone about the power outage.

I asked if they had gotten their elk yet. Steve replied that they were eating "track soup," because all they had to show for hunting were tracks. I asked for the recipe, but guess it is a family secret!

As truckload after truckload of calves is unloaded into our corrals here on Prairie Creek, the bawling begins: Mammmmma. Out on Salmon Creek, I can imagine the answering back, over the miles that separate mama cows from their calves.

November 19—I cleaned house, made the dust fly!

CowBelle meeting here tomorrow.

November 20—I awoke at 4:30. The Prairie Creek wind is howling again, heralding an approaching storm. With increasing fury the force of the wind shakes the house as it comes sweeping down off the mountain.

An early breakfast so the men can be gone, still hauling the calves in from the hills. Baked a "Herman cake" and two pumpkin pies.

"Chester," the banty rooster, has moved from his willow tree perch to a gunny sack atop our outside freezer on the carport.

Guess the wind was the deciding factor, causing him to change bedrooms. Doug discouraged him with the broom and he was soon swaying in the wind out on his limb.

An overflow houseful of CowBelles converged and my two capable daughters-in-law were co-hostesses, with bouncing baby boy James the center of attention.

There is much discussion lately on the name change of the CowBelles. I will always have a soft spot in my heart for the name CowBelles; they have such a wonderful history in our county. Whatever happens in the final tally or vote, I feel that we in Wallowa County will always be known as CowBelles.

In my kitchen hangs a little cutting board that many of us CowBelles received at one of the state conventions. Printed on it are these words: *A CowBelle: Looks like a girl...acts like a lady...thinks like a man...and works like a horse!* Regardless of our name, we will always identify with this description.

One by one, our cattle trucks break down for one reason or another. Oddly enough the one that keeps going this time is the old '59 Chevy, one of those with the starter on the floorboard.

Luckily the sounds of the bawling calves are muffled by our bedroom walls or we wouldn't be getting much sleep these days.

The symphony of bawling goes on, a constant background of noise. Some are getting a little hoarse with time. Others have given up the idea of ever seeing mama again and are directing their energies to eating grain and hay. The fall calvers and their calves hear the silage truck approaching and run to meet it.

The ground is muddy and it is spitting snow. An unusual November.

Fred Bornstedt, our local veterinarian, will be out on Salmon Creek this afternoon to preg-test our cows.

In due time the bawling subsided and the swollen udders of the cows have begun to shrink to their dry state.

I began, in earnest, to work on the script for our slide-tape show concerning the past 100 years in Wallowa County. This project will take precedent over all I do in the coming weeks, until I am satisfied with it.

Chester is courting the pullets as they scratch around the yard. They resist his advances, but he remains undaunted...showing off, strutting his wings and sidling up to the red pullets in a sideways fashion.

Winterized the sheepherder wagon, washing the bedding and mouse-proofing everything. Received a letter from Susanne in Switzerland. She still misses us and the ranch and animals. She has pictures that she and I took pinned on her wall to remind her of last summer.

Skeins of wild geese, tossed around at twilight in the November wind, weave in and out of the gray skies. Their irregular V's waver in the wind. As the early darkness descends, I only hear the ghostly honking! Such a sad, melancholy sound.

A warm chinook blew all night.

The mornings are lovely, with the early pink sunlight touching the high peaks and illuminating the snow banners that swirl around up there, as the wind blows the snow off the highest places.

Had our first 4-H meeting tonight for the new 4-H year. It was held in the library of Enterprise High School.

I have noticed that many birds that normally fly south have decided to stay this year. They can be heard singing, as though it were spring, in the bare-limbed willows by the creek.

Undressed now, the trees stand stark against the landscape. Recent winds have blown their clothes away! Their leaves add to the earth's humus. The tree is a wondrous thing, taking sustenance from the earth and giving something in return. It spends its long life in one place, witnessing the season's changes, providing shade for livestock, and beauty for the beholder, not to mention a resting and nesting place for hawks, owls and other birds.

Last year, on Nov. 25, 1985, it was 13 below zero. This day this year it was so mild I hung my wash on the line!

Went up to lock the chickens in for the night, and lo and behold, there was Chester, sandwiched cozily between two young pullets!

Happy, content…and warm. I asked Doug what happened to the older rooster, who had banned Chester from the henhouse, and he simply replied, "He is gone." I didn't ask any more questions, and now Chester reigns supreme in the hen house. The undisputed head of the household…and 25 pullets!

November 26—Cranberries pop their skins, bubbling in red juice as they cook on the wood stove. Pumpkin pies, made from Imnaha squash, and elk mincemeat pies cool on the kitchen table.

The wind howls outside and it is snowing over the mountains. All is in readiness for the big Thanksgiving meal here tomorrow.

November 27—Thanksgiving was great. Plenty of good food, lots of family and our friend Bill here to share with us.

November 28—Up at 4 a.m., packed turkey sandwiches and left with friends to attend a horse race in Yakima, Wash. An exciting day. Even though it rained and the track was muddy, we enjoyed watching the thoroughbreds run. As the horses rounded the final turn we cheered for the Wallowa County horse. But the muddy track slowed him down and he didn't win like he was favored to do.

November 29—Our world is white again…a soft, bright, clean white. Around noon, blue, crystalline skies appeared and the warm sunshine melted the snow. It slid off the roof tops in big blobs.

Made turkey soup using the Thanksgiving carcass.

November 30—November is leaving and it has just barely begun! Our snow is hard and crusted now.

Long lines of hungry, bawling cows and calves follow the yellow silage truck, anticipating the palatable feed that will be augered out on the snow for them to eat.

Our house seems solar-heated today due to the sun shining off the snow through the window panes. Doug is braiding reins; Christmas presents for all the cowboys in the family.

December 1—Beautiful sunrise. Clouds were trimmed in pink lace. Ruby Peak was "ruby colored" for about five minutes! Seed potato growers' meeting here tonight. I baked the Herman Cake for refreshments.

December 30—December was spent working on the script for our history group's centennial project, baby-sitting grandchildren, cooking, feeding cattle in addition to the daily chores of milking the cow, gathering eggs, attending meetings and all the myriad of chores associated with the running of a ranch household. Not to mention getting ready for Christmas.

Our 4-H Sourdough Shutterbugs staged a fun, money-making community service project. It consisted of members taking pictures of local children sitting on Santa Claus's lap. We rented a Santa suit, purchased film and enlisted a great Santa, who also goes by the name of Jim Blankenship. We set up shop with Santa near the Christmas tree at the holiday crafts fair in Cloverleaf Hall. For two days my 4-H'ers snapped pictures of children with all manner of reactions toward Santa.

I was so proud of them. Even young ones, taking their time, using a tripod and flash, got excellent results. Santa proved popular with grandmas and moms as well and we got in a few extra photos.

Santa, wearing long-johns under his bulky suit, became a bit too warm at times and had to go outside to cool off.

Grace Bartlett, Scotty and I went cross-country skiing one morning. We drove up to the Ferguson Ridge ski area and were soon out of the fog. We had been plagued with fog for days, but knew the higher elevations were clear. We got our exercise tramping uphill next to the motionless tow rope, then skiing downhill. Fun. We were the only souls up there.

On the way home, Scotty and I hiked into the forest and cut a Christmas tree and dragged it out to the pickup. We also gathered pine boughs for decorations.

Christmas arrived and December flew by, so busy with everything I scarcely knew what day it was.

Broke tradition this year and purchased a delicious prime rib roast for our Christmas dinner. It was a hit, and we felt good about supporting our industry. The tree I decorated with homemade Christmas cookies including gingerbread men decorated with the names of all the grandchildren. I kept visiting children busy stringing popcorn and cranberries, which also were hung on our old-fashioned tree. I believe it was the prettiest one we ever had, and the most fun. Especially when it came time to undecorate.

In spite of Christmas, the script began to take shape and the hours of researching early Wallowa County history, rewriting and rewriting was paying off. It is fascinating and exciting work and our committee is anxious for the final presentation.

Wallowa County farmer's wife Hope McLaughlin sets up her booth at the Arts and Crafts Christmas Bazaar in Cloverleaf Hall. Hope makes quilts, such as the "Lone Star" pattern shown here, that sell for $200 and up. She also makes vests—she's wearing one—and handwoven rugs. Her husband, Harold, and son, Erl, are grain growers.

Winter weather finally arrived. The stock water froze and had to be chopped daily. We are now feeding 70 bales of hay a day to our livestock.

Grace Bartlett, Steve Roundy and I met at the museum this morning. Grace had gone in earlier to start a fire in the big barrel wood stove. We selected many old pictures to use for the slide show, and Steve began doing some of the copy work. My darkroom has now been moved to the basement of the Art Angle in Joseph. I hope it will work out better for me at that location. At least I'll be away from the phone.

Our cattle are heading in from the hills today. They are on the second day of traveling. We were able to leave them out there on Salmon Creek longer than usual due to the mildness of the winter, thus far, and the availability of feed. Just in time, too, as the thermometer begins to plunge.

December 31—As 1986 enters its final hours, we in Wallowa County feel fortunate, as compared to a lot of the outside world.

Our riches are counted in mountains, canyons, high grassy plateaus, clear rushing streams, miles of unpeopled places, fresh air... and a special breed of people. Those who came before and those who now inhabit the Wallowa country.

We brought the new year in with our neighbors, Max and Dorothy Gorsline, Jim and Lois Blankenship, and Doris and Calvin. After a potluck dinner at our house, the men sat around the wood cook stove and told tales, long tales, about mining, prospecting and old-timers in Wallowa County. Meanwhile, we women engaged in a lively game of Scrabble. Doris won.

Max and Dorothy, Doug and I stayed up to watch the new year come in. We turned on the TV and watched the festivities at Times Square in New York...and were so thankful to be here! 1986 is now history.

In March, the winter is over and these cows are headed to the bunch grass hill country range in Wallowa County. Ben Tippett leads the way up Dorrance Gulch into the Salmon Creek country. At the rear of the cattle drive is Herb Owens of Joseph. Much as in the late 1800s, cattle are trailed to summer range and back to winter headquarters. The role played by the horse in the history of Wallowa County was significant and horses continue to be a necessary part of the cattle industry in Northeastern Oregon.

1987

January 1—It began to snow at nine, and soon blizzard conditions prevailed. After feeding all the animals their New Year's morning breakfast, we watched the Rose Bowl parade on TV in sunny Pasadena. Meanwhile, our horses run around the field outside, feeling good, their manes and tails flying in the wind, and their heads held high, tasting the storm.

Shuffled through the snow to chore this evening. Chopped ice in the ditch so Star's calf could drink. During the night a soft wind had created pretty drifts under our living room window.

We welcome 1987, whatever the new year holds in store for us.

January 2—A brilliant display of stars glitters in a dark sky.

Clear and 13 degrees this morning. Three inches of snow fell during the night. Soon the clear skies gave way to dark, purple clouds...snow clouds. Good thing our cows are in from the hills, because wind could drift the roads shut any day.

Shuffled out through the fresh snow to chore. The occasional burst of sunlight made the landscape glitter with diamonds. Chopped the ice in the ditch for Star's calf to drink. Doug out to La Grande, attending the livestock auction. Our local auction is closed and La Grande is now the closest market for Wallowa County stockgrowers. The snow plow goes by here on Tenderfoot Valley Road, as the wind blows and drifts cross Prairie Creek.

Studded with garlic, a pork roast sizzles in the wood stove oven.

January 3—Wind moaned and howled all night. Could imagine the shapes being created outside, the snow sculpted by the wind. Baked a batch of whole wheat oatmeal scones for breakfast.

At daylight, we saw the drifts...a large interesting one by the burning barrel, another by the chicken pen and the raspberry patch. It is amazing that the drifts always form at the same locations each year. The frozen whirls and swirls made pretty sculptures. Mother Nature's soft, lovely contours, shaped lovingly by the wind.

It is 40 degrees on our carport! The wind almost a chinook and the snow is melting between the large drifts, exposing the dry frozen grasses.

Doug called the ditch walker because there is no water in the farmer's ditch. Turned out there was an ice jam above our ranch. Todd's family over for supper. Had a nice meal and got to visit with Liza's mother, who is visiting. She is a most welcome addition to our extended family, and another doting grandmother for precious James.

January 4—Clear and cold on this Sunday morning. Ben's day off, so Doug and I fed the cattle. I drove the big truck loaded with hay, which pulled another trailerload of hay behind it. I had a time avoiding the frozen irrigation ditches. I tried approaching them from an angle, so as not to get stuck in one.

The hungry cattle ran up to the truck, anticipating their daily ration of hay, their breath hanging in the frosty air. Doug took an axe and chopped the frozen layer of ice off the drinking hole in the creek, a daily chore.

Around 11, Liza, her mom and baby James came by to pick me up to go cross-country skiing. We drove to Wallowa Lake and watched the park deer wander around. One six-point buck came right up to us and ate an apple from Liza's hand. Later, we skied. I took turns watching James, who enjoyed the outing considerably. We had the head of the lake to ourselves, and the clear blue skies, snow, and fresh breeze blowing off the water were heavenly.

Later in the day, while Doug fed the silage to the cows, I skied around our ranch. So wonderful to be out in the fresh air and such great exercise.

January 5—I am beginning to dry Star up. She needs a much deserved rest until her March calving date. The winter, being milder this year, has been easier than usual on her.

Doug taking delivery on 30 calves he has purchased locally. Our veterinarian out this afternoon to vaccinate our heifers. It is partly sunny, turning cold and cloudy later in the day. Printed some photos in the darkroom in Joseph. Home to bake sourdough bread.

January 6—Busy morning. Had arranged meeting my friends, all of whom are either early settlers or descendants of Wallowa County pioneers, at our local radio station. With cooperation from KWVR's Lee Perkins, we taped these people, who will play a major part in our history group project honoring the centennial. These wonderful men and women were a pleasure to work with and it was a fun time for all of us.

Later we drove to the Wallowa County museum in Joseph, where Steve Roundy took colored slides of all of them. Grace Bartlett had kindly gone in earlier and started a fire in the wood stove to warm up the museum.

Lots of early history represented by these fine folks who help make our county what it is today.

This afternoon I visited Jim Weaver and his wife, Faye. Jim is the oldest living resident on Alder Slope. He and his wife live in a house that is all that remains of the original town of Alder, except for the school house, which has now been converted into a barn. At one time Alder was the only town, and was in existence before the county seat of Enterprise.

Also dropped by the nursing home to tape and photograph Wallowa County's oldest citizen, Josie Hays, who will be 102 this month. An amazing lady, who said, "The Zumwalt post office was named after me!" Today the settlement of Zumwalt is melting into the lonely, bunchgrass hills that surround it. The gray, weathered building that once housed the post office where Josie was postmaster is all that is left.

Up the road a ways, the falling-down Zumwalt school keeps its lonely vigil, and provides a landmark for travelers on their way to the Steen Ranch, Cherry Creek, or perhaps Buckhorn. Josie's maiden name was Zumwalt.

Stopped by to purchase a frame for one of my pictures at Harold McLaughlin's home on Alder Slope. Harold is rebuilding an old kitchen cabinet for me and doing an excellent job. His wife, Hope, was busy as usual, working on her beautiful handmade quilts that are gaining in popularity all over the Northwest.

It is always a pleasure visiting these folks in their home, situated high on the slope of the mountains. The views from up there are really something! Also purchased one of Harold's handmade stools for granddaughter Mona Lee's upcoming birthday.

Dark when I reached home. A long day, but much accomplished.

January 8—Working madly on the script, trying to finish before we leave for California to visit relatives. A cold, frozen fog lays over the valley and it was 15 this morning.

A CowBelle meeting today at Toma's restaurant in Enterprise. We enjoyed lunch there prior to our meeting. I went to the courthouse afterward to have copies made of the script, then paid a visit to Ed and Gladys Quinn. Two more Wallowa County natives.

Ed was reared out on the Divide and Gladys was a school marm for many years and taught at small country schools scattered all over the county. I taped and photographed them for our project. All of us in our local history group are very excited about our slide-tape presentation, and it is a labor of love for me. Working with these fine people is much a pleasure and has enriched my life.

January 9—We enjoyed a delicious supper last night with our neighbors, Max and Dorothy Gorsline. As we drove out of the thick fog in the valley on our way to upper Prairie Creek, we left the layer of cold stuff behind. Up in that slightly higher elevation, the stars were out and the temperature hovered around zero.

We partook of good roast beef and all the trimmings, after which we looked at old photos that Max had produced for our enjoyment. Included were scenes of sawmills, early towns, old cars and other interesting subjects. Max and Dorothy's roots go way back in Wallowa County history, Max's grandfather having settled here in the 1880s. Dorothy jokingly remarked that she was born in the museum in Joseph, which used to serve as a hospital for that area.

The thermometer under the clothesline registered 10 degrees when I came in from choring this morning. Hoarfrost covers everything; very beautiful, but bitterly cold to be out in. Wisps of hair that escaped from under my scarf and my eyelashes are all covered with frost.

It is fascinating to watch the telephone lines as they quiver under the weight of the frost. A slight breeze sends frozen crystals floating down. The air is alive with them. Above us, we know it is clear and sunny, but the fog persists, hanging like a frozen shroud over the valley. The temperature staying right around zero.

Baked a recipe of corn yeast bread and continued to poke wood into the hungry wood stove.

January 10—Made toast using the corn yeast bread, to go with breakfast. Temperature slightly above zero. The fragile beauty of our hoarfrost-covered world still in evidence.

Grace Bartlett accompanied me to Imnaha, where I taped, photographed and interviewed more old-timers for our centennial project. Crossing over Sheep Creek Hill, we drove out of the fog into the beautiful sunshine! Only a few wisps of clouds in an otherwise blue sky. Ice bordered Little Sheep Creek and wherever moisture seeped from the rocks was a frozen waterfall.

At daughter Jackie's we enjoyed homemade soup and sourdough rolls fresh from the oven. Our first stop was to meet with Jim Dorrance at the Riverside Cafe. The place was closed for remodeling, but we were let in by Jim's daughter, Phylis, who was painting the kitchen. The old cafe will soon look pretty spiffy, with new floor tiles and new paint. We were glad to see Jim looking so good. He is a 90-year-old native, reared on Crow Creek, who also ranched along the Snake River.

Across the street and next door to the small Imnaha post office, we visited Hazel Warnock in her home. Hazel was a postmaster of this remote post office for 20 years. She is the widow of Jesse Warnock, the son of pioneer William P. Warnock. Hazel's lovely, spic and span home had a spacious kitchen that commanded a view, through many windows, of the downriver canyons. She commented that she continues to cook on the same electric stove that she's had all through the years.

The sun began to dip over the rims of the Imnaha as we stopped at A.L. Duckett's. At 94, A.L. remains extremely healthy and well versed on just about any subject. Quite a man, informed and up-to-date and adept at many trades, including horseshoeing, building his own brand of camp stoves, boiler making, gardening, carpentry, and carrying the mail with a team of horses. He can talk politics and country philosophy all day, and speaks with the experience gained through a lifetime of seeing dramatic changes; some of them good, and some not so good.

A.L. has spent nearly all of his life on his beloved Imnaha, and in that time never strayed away for long. We could see why. His lovely garden spot, yard, view and quality of life would be hard to duplicate elsewhere.

A three-quarter moon, not yet illumined by darkness, hung over the rimrocks as we headed back "on top." Going down Sheep Creek Hill, the lovely valley, rimmed in by the mountains, was settling in for the night. The fog, which had retreated to the west, hung in the setting sun.

January 11—Clear skies, stars bright in the morning sky at 6 o'clock.

Milked Star for the last time; she is all but dried up now. Drove the hay truck and trailer while Doug fed the cattle. Made homemade noodles to go with chicken broth and giblets for supper.

The moon out in a clear sky. It is 10 degrees.

January 12—Star's adopted calf is most unhappy. He misses coming in to nurse, but he was getting so big he could scarcely squeeze through the small gate into the milking parlor.

Scotty and I drove to Alder Slope, where we loaded the Imnaha squash into the trunk of our car. The good root cellar has kept it well, but some was beginning to show signs of over-ripeness and I didn't want any to spoil.

At home, she and I peeled and cut up the bright yellow squash, and soon every kettle I had held the stuff. We carried the seeds and rinds up to the chicken pen, whereupon Chester and his harem had a feast.

Leaving the squash simmering on the wood stove, Scotty and I loaded up our cross country skis and headed for the lake. Gray skies began spitting snow as we parked near the picnic area and skied across the shoreline. A cold wind blew off the lake and little wavelets caused the moorings of the marina to creak and groan.

The deserted lake's silence was broken also by some resident honkers feeding along the shore. Park deer wandered around looking for hand-outs.

Meanwhile, back at the ranch house kitchen, the squash was done. I drained, cooled and froze it in plastic bags. For a while we were living in a world of enough steaming squash to feed 250 people at our big, upcoming centennial dinner. Couldn't believe, after dealing with all that squash, we could enjoy some for supper, but we did and it was delicious.

January 13—I have granddaughter Mona Lee with me for a few days. Her mom is on her way to Dug Bar with another cowhand's wife, each driving pickups loaded with supplies. They will spend tonight at the Dug Bar ranch house, then wait in the morning to board the mail boat, whereupon they, and the supplies, will head upriver to spend a night with their husbands, who are camping in a tent.

It will be a surprise—Bill and Dave have the job of riding herd on 500 cows for Duke Phillips, and they don't know their wives will be on the boat.

Appears to be a storm moving in. It is cold and windy. Mona Lee helped me get through the day and enjoyed watching Sesam Street on TV, as her family doesn't get such things in the canyons. Doug taking delivery on some bulls he has purchased locally.

January 14—It began to snow after breakfast. My thoughts were with Jackie and Mona Glaus, riding the mail boat up the Snake River this morning, and how surprised Bill and Dave would be to see their wives.

January 15—Five above zero this morning. More snow fell during the night and it is still snowing lightly, with a faint band of clearing beginning to appear in the west. Doug off to Hermiston with local seed growers and our county extension agent, Arleigh Isley, to attend a potato meeting.

Bundled up Mona Lee, taking her with me in the big cattle truck while I drove and Ben fed hay to the cattle. Later, Mona and I drove to Alder Slope where we watched grandson James, while mom did some shopping. By the time we returned to Prairie Creek, our thermometer registered a chilly zero degrees. No word from daughter Jackie, and by

Kid Marks is mounted on Janie Tippett's mare, Calamity Jane, near Tenderfoot Pass in the Imnaha-Snake country. Marks broke this good cowhorse. His dog, Patty, is with him. The photo was taken about ten years ago.

5 p.m. I was becoming a bit anxious. I knew they would be driving the long road out from Dug Bar, and it was so cold!

At 5:30 the phone rang. It was Jackie; she and Mona Glaus had arrived safely at Imnaha. Due to the fact that it was late and so cold, she would spend the night with friends who had been keeping son Buck.

Meanwhile, the temperature continued to slide downward. A gorgeous full moon climbed into the sky, making it seem even colder on this frigid, still night.

Jackie had reported that they had spent a memorable night in a tent at Christmas Creek on the Snake River. After the fire in the sheepherder stove went out, it was very cold, even in that milder, lower elevation. The wind blew all night long. The returning mail boat hadn't arrived at Dug Bar until 3 p.m., therefore I had worried for naught, as usual.

Trying to tell a mother not to worry is fruitless. We do it anyway. The husbands, Bill and Dave, were very surprised to see their wives get off the boat with their calving supplies that day! Jackie reported that the cows are beginning to calve and a busy season lies ahead for the Snake River cowboys.

This weathered cabin at Dug Bar dates back to the early 1920s.

This is how the Dug Bar Ranch looks today—the cabin, house, and an alfalfa field on the bank of the winding Snake River. Towering rimrocks guard the grassy benches that stretch as far as the eye can see.

I wrote down these lines during January of 1980, the last year Doug and I operated the Dug Bar Ranch.

January morning on Dug Bar

Shimmering bubbles float and gleam,
current slides by ebony rocks,
chukars call above river sound,
cold breeze rustles locust leaves.

Snow-dusted rimrock way up high,
frames sunburst over canyon wall.
Rattlesnakes sleep in rocky lairs,
alfalfa field dormant and brown,
waiting for spring...

Cured haystacks will stave mother cow's
hunger, when little calves come to
play on grassy knolls.
An eagle flies upriver.

Empty corral, weed-strewn, rustles,
as gate swings in the breeze.
Deer drinks at water's edge.
Skeletal clouds, resembling
Nez Perce band at famous crossing.

Listen closely, you will hear,
ghosts of those here in years past,
when work-worn hands held the plowshare
that stands forlorn in the weeds.

A buckrake, a mower, a hay wagon;
mute evidence of a bygone era.
Only the river remembers and the
Snake rolls on with eternity.

January 16—Fifteen below! Very still and cold, with the bright moon still shining in the sky at 6 a.m. Today is only the third time this winter that the temperature has dropped below zero—once November 10, then again December 18.

Doug arrived home safely late last night. Mona Lee went with me to Steve Roundy's in Joseph, where I discussed our slide tape program, after which I drove her home to Imnaha. The warmer waters of Little Sheep Creek sent trails of vapor into the cold air.

Everything appeared affected by the cold. Cattle stood around, waiting to catch the first rays of sunshine as it appeared over the canyon walls.

We found Jackie attempting to warm up their mobile home, which had frozen in her absence. Warmed to 10 above by noon. Long icicles hung from the eaves of the buildings. It was incredibly beautiful and intensely cold.

My mother's mind was worrying again—granddaughter Chelsie in La Grande having her tonsils removed—and Jackie's frozen pipes. With seven children and 11 grandchildren, there seems to be something to be concerned about all the time.

Cleaned out my refrigerator in preparation for leaving on our trip Sunday. Attended a meeting at Jim and Ethel Chandlers' to go over our centennial slide-tape show. It will be hard for me to leave, just when we must work on this project. We watched a previewed edition of the work our committee has done thus far—we are far from being finished, but the final presentation will be good, of this I am sure.

Warmed up to 20 degrees by nightfall. I miss my cheerful little Mona Lee around the house. My friend, Mary Marks of Imnaha, called tonight to tell me that her husband, Kid, had passed away. She sounded so alone. My heart went out to her. She wanted to know if I would write Kid's obituary as well as a tribute to Kid's life to be read at his funeral, which would be held Monday.

Although we plan to leave Sunday morning and won't be here for the services, I promised to do this final favor for my friend Kid. It was hard to write the obituary and tribute to Kid's life, because my eyes dimmed with tears, but I finished and felt my efforts were worthwhile.

Kid didn't quite make his 75th birthday, but lived a life that is fast disappearing from the West. It was a good life, with wife, Mary, ever by his side, as they rode the trails together; trails that wound up and down the Imnaha and followed the breaks of the Snake. Kid knew every landmark in that vast, rugged range, and it was there he was at his happiest, riding for cattle, mounted on a good horse.

Returning to cow camp at day's end, he would mix up a batch of sourdough biscuits and bake them in a wood stove. At this he was an artist. He always made a few extra to give to his faithful dog.

January 17—Up early, tying up last minute details in readiness for tomorrow's departure.

Little Mona Lee called, "Grandma, something exciting happened at our house! Our water is running again!" It seemed kindly neighbors had thawed out the pipes and luckily no damage had been done.

Checked on Chelsie and found her progressing, minus tonsils, satisfactorily. CowBelle president Judy Wortman stopped by with a large box of CowBelle nightshirts we would be delivering to the National Cattlemen-CattleWomen convention in Reno.

A gorgeous day, the sunshine gleaming off the snowy mountains. The nearby Ferguson Ridge ski area is now officially open, just when we are leaving. Fixed a fried chicken dinner, worked on my column and crashed.

January 18—Arising early, I was able to finish typing my column before 7. Fixed breakfast, tended to my chickens, bidding them goodbye for more than two weeks. Liza will come over to gather the eggs and sell them while Ben would care for Chester and his harem, in my absence.

We began packing clothes and odds and ends needed for our trip. I tried to concentrate on appropriate wear for the potato conference and Gerda Hyde's reception at the Bally Hotel in Reno, not to mention all the places we will need different clothes for our stay with relatives while in California.

While I packed, Doug drove the hay truck for Kane Maasdam, who will help with the Sunday feeding while we were gone. It was nearly 10 a.m. before we could leave, and snowing heavily, the roads icy and slick.

We stopped at Fred's Market in Joseph to pick up some locker beef to take to daughter Linda and son Steve in Pendleton. At long last, we were on our way. We stopped in Elgin for lunch, and again briefly in La Grande.

Driving through the Blue Mountains, bare pavement suddenly gave way to solid ice and it began to snow heavily again. Slowed down by a truck bearing a sign "Be prepared to stop," we took our place in a long line of cars near Deadman's Pass. Little did we Know that we would remain, stalled here, in a snowstorm, for two hours! Due to a wreck on Cabbage Hill, all westbound traffic through the Blues was halted.

To pass the time, I read a book I had with me, entitled One Woman's West, a true account of a family traveling the Oregon Trail. At least they were able to plod steadily westward by ox team, while we here in 1987 were at a virtual standstill. Here we sat in our modern car with all the luxuries, while mother nature held sway. After two hours of watching the caravan grow behind us and restless people walking to and fro, we were allowed to creep along slowly for a quarter mile, only to be pulled over because we didn't have studded tires.

Finally we pulled out and followed other cars until we began the descent of Cabbage Hill. At the top we observed the cause of our dilemma—two overturned trailer-truck rigs, which had been moved to one side of the road. Sandwiched between trucks that spewed us with snow, we made our way slowly down the long, winding hill to Pendleton, where ice gave way to slush. Visiting briefly with daughter Linda and son Steve, we proceeded west to Boardman where we secured lodging for the night.

A long day...many adventures lay ahead of us, but I already missed Wallowa County.

January 19—We were awake by 5 a.m. and walked to a nearby truck stop in Boardman for breakfast before hitting the road again. A layer of fog hovered over the Columbia River and the freeway was mostly all ours. The road was a bit icy, but we made it safely to Biggs Junction and turned south, heading down 97. We traveled through the silent, misty-veiled towns of Moro and Grass Valley.

Peering through the fog, we spotted the high desert ghost town of Shaniko. Presently the fog lifted. We were treated to breathtaking views of Mt. Hood and Mt. Jefferson. While their summits swam in a clear, blue sky, their skirts swirled in fog. The beautiful snow-covered peaks-glinted in the morning sun. Frozen fog clung to desert sagebrush and juniper.

We pulled into Madras for a hot cup of tea and, later, ate lunch in Bend. On the outskirts of Bend, we stopped at the Oregon High Desert Museum. A fascinating place. We took about an hour to walk around and look at exhibits that told the story of the Oregon desert. Outside, a sheepherder wagon exhibit drew my attention...the wagon looked just like mine!

Inside the museum, a young man made arrowheads. He used an antler to chip obsidian into points. All manner of aboriginal skills were demonstrated. A rotating display depicted the changing flora and fauna of the Oregon desert—wonderful visual contact with all the lovely wild things, such as wildflowers, sagebrushes, rocks, rabbits, and coyotes. A continuous bird show was staged in a small darkened theater. Wall displays explained the Oregon Trail and the route taken by the pioneers. In a gift shop there was a marvelous selection of Northwest books and I

Garth Carman, Wallowa County Stockgrowers president, and Judy Wort-man, Wallowa CowBelles president, pose by a poster that explains how checkoff dollars are used to promote beef. The Stockgrowers and CowBelles got together recently for a potluck in Cloverleaf Hall in Enterprise, along with other members of the community. A videotape showed outtakes of the filming of the beef industry's TV ads featuring James Garner and Cybill Shepherd.

purchased a copy of "Tracking Down Oregon" by Ralph Friedman.

Lo and behold, the first page describes our own Hell's Canyon and mentions our county's highest peak, Sacajawea. Just reading it makes me want to turn around and head back home. Although we will see many sights, none will capture my heart like my own Wallowa Country.

We continued on down 97 through Central Oregon and into Southern Oregon. The high desert gave way to pine trees that lined both sides of a road that lay straight ahead for miles and miles. We passed through places like La Pine, Gilchrist and Chiloquin; until we finally arrived near the outskirts of Klamath Falls. The pink light of evening was reflected on ice-covered Klamath Lake. It was a pretty sight, seeing the "pink-colored ice" bordered by blue-green sagebrush. The city of Klamath Falls, large and sprawling, was a busy place, with traffic going every which way. We in Wallowa County don't have a single stop light and the shock we experience upon entering a city is always a little frightening.

We spotted the fairgrounds from the freeway and were able to drive right to the Thunderbird where we had reservations. The motel was conveniently situated across from the fairgrounds, which was the headquarters for the Potato Conference we had come to attend.

We walked to "The Chuckwagon" for supper and enjoyed a delicious buffet before returning to the motel for a much-needed rest. Our Wallowa County neighbors, Tom and Donna Butterfield, called saying they had arrived safely, having left Wallowa County early this morning. They reported that five inches of new snow had fallen during our absence.

January 20—While Tom and Doug attended opening sessions of the Oregon Potato Conference, Donna and I "did" the town of Klamath Falls. We found a shop called "Jean's Antiques," an immense place, where we spent over an hour just browsing through the many interesting items.

As we were driving along, a yard caught our eye in the middle of town: an old house, hidden by unpruned shrubbery, situated next to a falling-down shop of some sort. But the yard drew our attention. We parked nearby and walked around the outside of an old ornate fence to peer inside.

As I was about to take a picture, a tattered old man emerged from the shop. He was no doubt wondering what we were up to. An enormous orange-colored cat followed him and curled around his feet, purring loudly as we visited. We learned that his wife had passed away some years ago and he had lived in this very place for 40 years. He had watched the city grow around him. He appeared to be a lonely soul and, champion of the underdog that I am, my heart went out to him. He said, "Thievery is rampant in the city and everything must be locked up."

His yard was cluttered with everything from old Indian totem poles to wagon wheels. Plastic flowers stuck out of all manner of containers he used for flower pots. Junk lay everywhere amid the brush that all but concealed his old house from busy main street.

"The world has changed so much," he said, and we agreed, leaving him still holding his cat. I photographed him that way. I can still see him standing there in his old torn clothes, clinging to his old ways and pride, surrounded by a city of newcomers, people he could no longer trust.

We visited two more lesser antique shops, full of clutter, but fascinating places to poke around in while visiting with the proprietors, who were always willing to talk. Later, around 2 p.m., realizing we hadn't had lunch, we enjoyed a bowl of soup in the big Shasta Shopping Mall.

Back at the fairgrounds, we found Doug and Tom and attended a social hour put on for the Potato Conference delegates and their wives. We walked around the Trade Show before returning to the motel. A beautiful day; crisp and cold and clear.

That evening, we drove to Grandpa Bailey's, which was an interesting restaurant in old-time decor, featuring homemade pies and bread. We ordered "Build-Your-Own sandwiches" and sampled the pies. Good, but not quite like Wallowa County home cooking.

It had turned very cold outside and we guessed it was well below zero at home!

January 21—A heavy frost covered everything in Klamath Falls. Another bright, sunshiney day ensued. Tom and Donna joined us for breakfast at the nearby Kopper Kitchen. While Donna was off to visit an art-framing shop, I attended the Potato Conference to do some photojournalism. I was one of two women present for the second day's opening session. At 10:30, I met Donna. We drove to the Oregon Institute of Technology where we found our way to the Mt. Shasta Room.

Here we attended a program that centered around the importance of holding farm and ranch family-type meetings. All of us "Potato Wives" participated in the discussions, which brought to the forefront the need to have good communication and sharing of responsibilities when running a ranch operation. This was followed by a delicious luncheon and fashion show. The ultra skinny models were wearing modern clothing, looking skinnier as we ate chocolate parfaits for dessert.

Somehow, I couldn't picture myself wearing a $300 creation, let alone paying that much for one. It was entertaining, but most impractical, at least for this potato grower's wife. Once again, Donna and I were loose in Klamath Falls. We spent the rest of the afternoon walking around a huge shopping mall, wandering in and out of shops. We had a ball trying on clothes, but I never purchased any. Some were the "Mod" styles and outrageous!

We had such a good time, even the sales ladies got a kick out of us "Country Bumpkins." We ambled into a book store, candy store, shoe store…our minds boggled by all there was to buy.

Later, we met our husbands and attended the annual Potato banquet held at the Elks Lodge, high on a hill overlooking the city. We were served steak and baked potato (natch!) while massive mounted elk heads stared down at us from the walls.

At the banquet I had the pleasure of meeting Steve James, who said he was a fan of my column. Steve, who works for the Powell Butte Experiment Station in Bend, had an exhibit at the Trade Show. I was honored and flattered to learn that Steve's office staff enjoys reading this column.

Donna and I went into hysterics as we listened to a substitute speaker, who introduced himself as having earned a Ph.D in…manure! "Shud," he called it. He said he had numerous titles associated with the study, disposal and analysis of manure.

We danced a few dances to a western band and enjoyed visiting with Luther Fitch and his wife, Joyce, before driving back to the Thunderbird. Tomorrow we cross the border into California.

January 22—The Butterfields, Tom and Donna, accompanied us to the Favell Museum. Everyone we met said we must visit this place before leaving Klamath Falls. We were soon to find out why.

To describe this collection of western art and Indian artifacts would be impossible. The museum was founded by the Favell family, who for years collected Indian artifacts. Later they added wonderful works of western art to their fabulous collection. The museum, then, is a realization of their dream, and now preserves and shares these artifacts with interested people…like us.

The Favell philosophy, carved in redwood, hangs over the entrance: "This museum is dedicated to the Indians who roamed and loved this land before the coming of the white man, and to those artists who truly portray the inherited beauty which surrounds us. Their artifacts and art are an important part of the heritage of the West."

One of the finest collections of contemporary western art in the world was on display in wonderfully lighted areas; works of more than 300 western artists, including many famous Oregon artists, and in all forms:

bronze, woodcarving, photography, watercolor, oil and even taxidermy. Never had we seen so many arrowheads, spears, tools, baskets and pottery, not to mention all the beautiful bead work. Sixty thousand mounted arrowheads were wonderfully displayed, including the world-famous fire opal arrowhead. This arrowhead was found in a Nevada desert. After two hours, our eyes were tired. It was almost too much to absorb fully in one visit.

In the gift shop, I purchased a Charles Russell book for son-in-law Bill's birthday. Then, Tom and Donna headed home to Prairie Creek, while we drove southwest and into California. In the small logging town of Doris, near the Oregon-California border, we ate lunch at a cafe called "Malfunction Junction." The door to the place stuck, and the malfunctions continued through the whole experience. It appeared to be a truck stop, and the waitress, who said she was hungry and hadn't had her lunch, was grumpy. There must have been 20 trucks go by while we ate, but not one stopped at the Malfunction. Aside from one other couple, we were the only customers. I must say the hamburger was good. The cook must have been functioning.

As we drove west, the magnificent view of Mt. Shasta was partially obscured by a layer of snow clouds. At Weed, we headed south on I-5, speeding past the Mt. Shasta resort area and enjoying the Northern California Siskiyou Mountains. Evergreens soon gave way to oaks and manzanita, and the mountains to rolling foothill country as we stopped to rest in Redding.

Finally, we arrived safely in Red Bluff, which I remember as a Northern California town, but which is now a sprawling city. It still caters to cowboys and cattlemen, as the outlying areas are still mostly big cattle ranches. Red Bluff's "cow-town" atmosphere was in evidence everywhere because the famous Red Bluff Bull Sale was on. Motels displayed signs "Welcome Bull Shippers," and Stetson-Levi-boot-clad men and women were walking around everywhere. I vaguely remembered where the Tehama County Fairgrounds were located, and we found our way there, after a fashion. It is now called the Sun Country Fair.

Across from the fairgrounds stood a "Cow-Town" Shopping Center, complete with store fronts that resembled a western movie set. After securing a motel for the night, we walked to a place called "Perkos" to eat supper. We felt right at home. "Bull shippers" were filling the place up, and the food was good. It was raining when we returned to our motel. I found it hard to sleep, listening to the constant roar of hundreds of vehicles speeding by on rain-splattered streets, an experience so far removed from our quiet, Prairie Creek home.

January 23—Up early and walked to Perkos again, to breakfast with more early-rising cattlemen. We followed pickups, all with dogs in the back, to the fairgrounds. We got in out of the rain under a large, metal pavilion where the working cowhorse geldings were performing, and watched these two- and three-year-old colts work cattle.

One catty young gelding kept right on cutting cattle, even after his rider reached down and removed his bridle. He merely hung on for dear life. We enjoyed seeing the cutting mules, most of which needed considerably more work, followed by the working stock horses.

Finally, we were able to see what most interested us: the working stock dogs. To start with, the owner of a three-legged border collie put on an exhibition with his dog. Being minus one leg didn't seem to affect his performance. All of the dogs had their work cut out for them, as they had to gather several yearlings into one bunch and drive them into a very small enclosure in the center of the arena. The dogs, geldings, mules, working stock horses, and bulls would all be sold in the sale.

It was nearing 1 p.m. when we followed the crowds to a nearby cafeteria where the Tehama County CowBelles (they have chosen to remain CowBelles) were serving up a barbecued beef lunch. It was delicious. Those cowgals had cooked more than 800 pounds of prime rib. It was their biggest money-making event of the year. These Red Bluff area ranch women really knew how to put on a feed. Our meal was eaten on clever brand placemats that gave the history of the cattle industry in Tehama County.

Our schedule didn't include being able to stay for the sales, so we continued on down south on I-5, before turning off onto 65 and taking 99 to my old home town of Lincoln. The California of my childhood is gone now; the small town of Lincoln hasn't changed much, at least not on Main Street, but the wide-open spaces, rolling foothills, oak trees and miles of ranching country are now only a memory.

The names of the former ranchers themselves are now the names given to the roads and subdivisions. This bedroom community to Sacramento has spread like a crawling giant, engulfing everything in its path. People tried to save many of the wonderful, old oak trees, and they stand forlornly in their concrete shopping centers. I remember the fields of golden California poppies and purple lupine, the new, fresh green leaves on the oaks, and the acres of green grass in the magic month of April.

Around my father's grave, the area remains unchanged. Cattle graze nearby, but only a short distance beyond are the lavish new homes of the one-horse, one-cow country gentleman rancher, the instant rancher, who commutes to his office in Sacramento to support the luxury of living in the country. Gone are the small dairies, like the one I grew up on, and the wonderful fruit orchards that provided summer employment for the young people. I can still taste the sun-ripened peaches, pears, and different varieties of plums; see the orchards in pink and white clouds of bloom in the spring; smell the fresh earth after a spring rain; and listen to the croaking of the bull frogs in the old dredger ponds, left from early-day mining activity.

I thought of these things as we drove up the winding Lincoln-Newcastle road to my sister Mary Ann's home in Auburn. Mists from the American River rose over the city as evening descended. Good to be with family again and relax.

January 24—My column seems to be falling behind again...too many experiences to write about. I shall skip here and there, and at least attempt to return us to Wallowa County. After visiting my friend, Pete Hawkins, in Placer County, California, we drove to Newcastle and found the old fruit packing sheds that Pete had spoken of. These long sheds used to be a beehive of summer activity, as workers packed the bounty of Placer County fruit into boxes that were shipped East. The sheds today house a row of antique shops.

Later we visited Lower Auburn, which is also transformed into an area of quaint shops that cater to the tourist. I can still remember the Chinese laundries, restaurants, bars and the old firehouse from when I was a girl. The beautiful courthouse sits atop the hill overlooking the area, and an immense form, made of concrete, a California 49'er panning for gold, squats in the center of the old town. All around grows the new Auburn—shopping centers, subdivisions and businesses lining a freeway that carries streams of humanity to playgrounds in the Sierra and Reno from the vast population centers in the Bay area and Sacramento.

In an antique shop I spotted an old rusted sign, a sign like the one that used to hang outside the entrance to our ranch. A color picture of a Guernsey bull and cow, only under our sign it read "Oakcrest Ranch." The sign had a $95 price tag. I wondered if the tourist who purchased the sign would ever know the story behind it, or even really care.

I wondered also what would become of Pete Hawkins's sign when he was gone. Would it, too, end up in a place such as this?

February 3—I will merely touch the highlights of the remainder of our stay in California. We enjoyed a get-together with my large family. On my mother's side, this family springs from California pioneers. We are no different from other families in that we are proud of our heritage and attempt to maintain a closeness. The trunk of this family tree is rooted in California, but the branch that grew me must have stirred the pioneer blood, as I sought new frontiers and, even in childhood, dreamed of Oregon.

In time, though, everything changes, and change we must accept. We visited my mother's home, a place that holds fond memories, but that too is soon to change. My mother, widowed and 75, will be marrying soon and changing her lifestyle. They will live in an apartment in Auburn. The home place will remain in my brother's family, but somehow the coming home will never be the same. My father is gone and my mother will have companionship in her final years.

I walked through my father's garden, around the ivy-choked trees and his concrete monuments. The woods are gradually taking control again. This beautiful area he so lovingly tended—what will happen to it? Perhaps some grandchild will someday care for it.

Doug panned for gold in Doty's Ravine and added more precious bits of color to his small bottle of gold. I took my yearly walks through oak woods. Spring was just around the corner in Placer County, and the birds and crows were singing their hearts out. After the rain, it cleared, warm and beautiful.

On a bright Sunday, my sisters and I took a hike up through the rolling hills to Coon Creek, a lovely, secluded, quiet creek where the Digger Indians camped years ago to grind acorns into meal. The holes in the rocks remain and the pestles are displayed in local museums. On the evening before we left, Doug was panning for gold when two owls in the deep woods began hooting to each other. I tried to catch a glimpse of them, but the dusk obscured my vision.

The weather will change, hooted the owls.

The next morning, we had a race with a storm headed over the Sierra. We made it over Donner Pass before it hit. As we pulled into Boomtown for lunch, we could see swirling snow clouds over the Sierra summits. A fierce, cold wind swept off the mountains down across the Nevada side.

We found the Convention Center in Reno, where the National Cattlemen's convention was in full swing. The wind continued to blow as we delivered CowBelle nightshirts for the Oregon delegation.

We headed west out of Reno into California again, and at the foot of Beckwourth Pass came down into Chilcoot, where we were greeted by daughter Ramona, in the middle of a 4-H cooking meeting.

Chilcoot, population 200, is situated at the eastern end of the big Sierra Valley. It was great fun seeing my grandchildren again. The next night, daughter Ramona and son-in-law Charley accompanied us to Gerda Hyde's reception at the Bally Hotel in Reno. Gerda looked great, surrounded by 170 delegates from Oregon. Visited with Gerda's husband, Hawk, about his successful book "Don Coyote." We all enjoyed dinner afterward, amid the glitter and finery of this swan Reno hotel, formerly known as the MGM.

It was snowing the next morning as grandchildren Tammy, Shawn and Carrie caught the bus. My daughter, who has her hands full, manages their home in Chilcoot, where the children are bused to the only school around, which is Loyalton.

Meanwhile, Charley spends most of his time managing the huge Fish Springs Ranch, which lies northeast of Doyle in the Nevada desert. On weekends, Ramona and the children join Charley where they maintain another house. One night we attended a basketball game in Loyalton. The Loyalton Grizzlies were playing Greenville. My 16-year-old granddaughter Tammy is a Grizzly cheerleader, so we yelled along with the crowd, and the Grizzlies won. Tammy was off to a school ski club trip to Tahoe, and Ramona and I gathered supplies to take out to Fish Springs.

Before we left we visited with Alvin Lombardi, who lives in Loyalton. It seems this fine gentleman had been receiving Ramona's copy of Agri-Times in his mail. He enjoyed reading about life here in Wallowa County, and looked forward each week to this column. Then he found out Ramona was my daughter. One day Mr. Lombardi's Agri-Times ended up in my daughter's mail (he had, by this time, subscribed), so I personally delivered the paper to Alvin.

We had a most pleasant visit with Alvin and his wife, who have lived all their lives in the Sierra Valley. For years they operated a dairy, then when margarine (that other spread) appeared on the market, the Lombardis sold out. Alvin went to work for the lumber mill and was injured. Today he spends his time in a wheelchair. Never have I met a man with such a good outlook on life. Meeting people like the Lombardis renews my faith and is one reason I shall keep writing.

We spent two marvelous days and nights at Fish Springs Ranch, which is located at the end of miles of dusty desert roads that wind through sagebrush and sand to this place, an early-day stage-stop. The old buildings and hotel have been replaced by modern buildings that resemble a condominium in the desert. A generator supplies electricity for the houses. A grand, old barn remains intact, and old corrals, made of railroad ties, give one a glimpse into the history of the place.

The view from the main ranch buildings is of sweeping desert bordered by snow-dusted mountains. A meadow with a pond attracts flocks of Canadian honkers. Out on the vast ranges that cover thousands of acres roam wild horses, antelope, deer and the Fish Springs cattle.

Among them is a feral steer—10-year-old "Henry," who Charley says is a landmark of sorts. He weighs a ton and has long horns. A loner that wandered in from a neighboring ranch years ago, he now ranges with the Fish Springs brand.

I enjoyed rambling around the desert with my grandchildren. We accompanied Charley on his rounds of checking stock water and salting the cattle. On the way back, we drove onto the Paiute Indian Reservation and near the shoreline of Pyramid Lake, all that remains of ancient Lake Lahontan, where rock formations resemble ghostly ships in the blue waters of the lake.

Back in Chilcoot I cooked a special meal for grandson Shawn's 13th birthday, before we left for home.

The trip north was gorgeous, and clouds formed in a sky containing three shades of blue. Suddenly, between the clouds, the snow-covered Steens Mountain appeared, shot with sunlight, gleaming in the distance like a fantasy. We drove through Rome, Jordan Valley, through the Owyhees, and finally the Wallowas. Our two border collie dogs welcomed us back with much tail-wagging. So good to be back home.

February 6—The sun rose over Prairie Creek into a brilliant blue sky. Began work immediately on the forthcoming centennial dinner, making lists and baking sourdough bread. Bread that would be stored in the freezer until 50 loaves were made.

So much to catch up on after being gone. Ordered 90 pounds of round steak for the big dinner, delivered flour and eggs to my "noodle maker" friend, Doris, and made more lists of things to do. Very mild for this time of year. Most of the pastures are free of snow. Several large, frozen drifts remain, but the ground is bare in between. Sourdough bread making now a daily chore.

Called Harold McLaughlin on Alder Slope; he agreed to make round bread boards for each of the 33 tables at the dinner. On each one will be printed "Wallowa County—1887-1987." They will be sold after the meal as souvenirs. For days, my kitchen smelled of baking bread. Some days I made as many as eight loaves of the round sheepherder loaves.

One night we drove up snowy Alder Slope to Jim and Lois Blankenships' for dinner. Lois cooked us up a fine meal, topped off with homemade chocolate pie. Afterward we went to the basement, where we peeked at Jim's rawhide and leather projects. He showed us reins, hobbles, tack bags, chaps and all kinds of horse gear. Jim and his family used to live on the Snake River at Roland Bar, where they operated a ranch. Jim, who has worked with mules and pack animals most of his life, has

Jim Blankenship of Alder Slope in Wallowa County displays some of the leather tack he makes. He's a rural mail carrier for the Imnaha canyon country and a former Snake River rancher. His handmade hackamores, hobbies and packsaddle equipment are sturdy and well-made.

many tales to tell. He is also the rural mail carrier to Imnaha, making three runs weekly to the "River."

Meanwhile, out at the barn, Star, Daisy, May and Startch are pleasingly pregnant, waiting for their calving dates. The barn cat population has dwindled to one female: the cat Susan had named "Nerma." She is lonesome and wishing one of the cows would freshen so she can have warm milk again.

The "back" of winter has broken, the bitter cold bite gone. Spring is only weeks away. On weekends I often go skiing with friends Grace, Cressie and Scotty. The nearby Ferguson Ridge ski area, maintained and developed by a local ski club, is an excellent facility and great family fun. The snow was wonderful, the exercise great, and the view from on top terrific. The fresh air and camaraderie of friends provided a much needed diversion from my kitchen.

Doug hired another hand today. There is so much feeding to do and calving is just around the corner. Somehow I managed to type up my column between kneading bread.

February 9—Doug and I, dressed in centennial pioneer wear, attended a potluck honoring the city of Joseph's 100th birthday. WHAT A POTLUCK! The tables groaned with food. All had outdone themselves preparing their best home-cooked specialties for the occasion.

An overflow crowd of 300 people converged on the new Joseph Community Center. At the head table there was a huge birthday cake, complete with 100 candles. Emcee Dave Turner commented that this new facility stood on the site of the old Mitchell Hotel, which burned down years ago. When it came time for lighting all those candles, he remarked that perhaps we should be careful to not let history repeat itself. The candles were quickly blown out.

The local citizenry sang Happy Birthday to their little town, which by modern standards is still very young. Wanda Sorweide played the organ using 1890s sheet music. Frank McCully was present as guest of honor with his wife, Ann. Frank's father, F.D. McCully, is known as the "Father of Wallowa County." He helped found the town of Joseph in 1880. He single-handedly pushed a bill through the Oregon Legislature that resulted in the organization of Wallowa County on February 11, 1887, and he is the only white man buried in the Nez Perce Cemetery at the foot of Wallowa Lake.

Along with other "pioneers," Doug and I enjoyed dancing the Virginia Reel. Herb Owens, 1986 Chief Joseph Days grand marshal, was my partner for the next dance, which was a square dance. Fun.

February 10—I have 41 loaves baked. Doris gaining on the noodles!

My daughter-in-law Liza is now the proud owner of a little Jersey milk cow. Her name is "Jenny" and she seems right at home on Alder Slope, having crossed the mountain from her former home in Milton-Freewater.

Doug acquired a new border collie pup from Jim Blankenship. His name, of course, is "Jim." Many locals working late each night as the big centennial ball draws closer.

On Prairie Creek it was like spring. Hardly needed a fire on some days. The birds in the willows began to sing. Seemingly overnight Christy Tsiatsos and her committee transformed the Community Center into an 1890s parlour.

February 12—I attended our monthly CowBelle meeting at the home of Pat Murrill, where I read the minutes in the absence of our secretary, Doris, who was home (you guessed it) making noodles! I gave a quick report on Gerda Hyde's reception in Reno, then left to deliver cooking utensils and supplies to the Community Center. I stopped on the way to take daughter-in-law Liza and grandson James with me, so Liza could see the way things were decorated. It was unreal.

Antique kerosene lanterns graced 33 blue-checkered table-clothed tables. A wood cook stove and a hoosier sat against one wall. Old-time photos hung on the walls, country curtains hung at the windows; there were rocking chairs and an antique bear collection. Everywhere nostalgia, like stepping back in time. The entire atmosphere was of early-day elegance, yet there was that special "homey" touch. The "social event of the century," as it was already being referred to, was nearly here. Thursday night I met with Christy and my servers, going over plans to serve 300 people at a sit-down dinner.

The mounting excitement gave me butterflies. So much to do. That night I lay staring into the dark, like an owl, with visions of the centennial ball dinner going through my head. Lists of things to be done were intermingled throughout it all. By morning I had it pretty well straightened out, and didn't seem to need the sleep.

February 13—Began this Friday the 13th at 5 a.m.

Finished chores and breakfast, and by 8 we were at the Community Center, where a day began that wouldn't end for many of us until 8 that night. While Doug cut the 90 pounds of round steak into strips, I started browning it in my big dutch ovens. Scotty began making enough sauce to go over the meat for 300 people. The sauce, which contained onion, garlic, rosemary, beef bouillon, carrots, celery and burgundy wine, was mixed in a blender. Carefully, to control quality, we made this in small batches until we had used up all the ingredients.

The sauce was then poured over the meat and allowed to cook slowly in cast iron dutch ovens. Jim Chandler, official quality control tester, said you could smell the delicious concoction clear down Joseph's main street. Jim appeared regularly to check out the cooking. The cooked meat was allowed to cool before being refrigerated. Scotty and I cooked all day, non-stop, washed up all the kettles and tidied up the kitchen.

At 8 Christy and I took one last look around the beautifully decorated hall, smiled at each other, and wearily left. The kitchen had been in high gear all day, with newspaper reporters coming and going, taking pictures, interviews on the radio, and us trying to cook. As I stepped outside it was snowing huge flakes and they were sticking to the ground. A blizzard obscured a Friday the 13th full moon. I had to drive very slowly as visibility was limited to a few feet.

February 14—Valentine's Day, the state of Oregon's birthday, and the date of Wallowa County's centennial ball. Up at at 'em, the big day is at hand. As I drove to Joseph on snowy roads, sunlight streamed through breaks in the storm clouds and illuminated the snowy ramparts of our beautiful Wallowas.

Scotty cut up and diced more than 100 apples for the salad while I made the dressing. Soon, Hope McLaughlin and Grace Bartlett arrived to help. Later, "Noodle Lady" Doris appeared. Harold showed up with the bread boards. At 11, I paused in my frantic meal prepartion to think about my 75-year-old mother, who at that moment was to be married in California!

Excitement continued to mount all afternoon as we put the huge meal together. My crew was in good spirits. At 6 o'clock the beautifully attired servers, 33 of them, arrived and donned their pretty white cotton aprons and listened to my last-minute instructions. Cars lined up clear down Main Street. Ladies and gents, wearing 1800s garb, began filling up the place. The gala evening was about to begin...and we were ready.

The men arrive attired in long tails, 1800s hats and ties, and some sporting fancy mustaches and long beards. They escorted their ladies, who were equally showy. Many had made dresses for the occasion, while others wore original early creations, some of which were family heirlooms. Everywhere, bustles, frills, lace, elaborate hats with pink and black plumes, billowy, frothy dresses, black dresses and red velvet ones, some with buttons lining the sleeves and fastening the bodices. There were high-topped buttoned shoes and lace petticoats. Never had we seen such finery. It was wonderful seeing everyone capturing the spirit of the thing.

Earlier, I had slipped into the restroom to change into my simple cotton patchwork print dress, feeling a little like Cinderella before the ball, surrounded by so much elegance. I left my comfortable shoes on. I knew from experience that my feet would be called beyond the call of duty before the evening was over. My kitchen crew donned prairie dresses and looked very much in style. We all wore the pretty lace cutwork cotton aprons.

Doug appeared, looking positively dashing in black pants, black high-topped western boots, with pants tucked in, and white shirt with garters on his shirt sleeves which he had made himself. His centennial beard was beginning to grow and he was going to help serve the heavy kettles of meat for me. The 33 pretty servers looked the part in their crisp white aprons as they gathered around me to receive their last-minute instructions. Each server had been assigned a table.

The lemon slices were in the water glasses, the butter balls and homemade jams and jellies were on the tables. The hall filled up rapidly. Guests, their costumed presence adding to the nostalgic atmosphere, were agape when they entered.

Right on schedule, the invocation was given at 7 o'clock, then our signal to begin. Each server, armed with a bread board and a loaf of sourdough, began to cut the bread at the 33 tables. Then they returned to the kitchen to pick up 33 bowls of centennial apple salad, waited for it to be passed around the table, and returned with the bowls to the kitchen, where this procedure was repeated until the squash, homemade noodles and meat were all served. It went like clockwork.

In the kitchen, we worked frantically to fill the bowls, trying to keep up. People clamored for more butter. They were putting it on the squash as well as the bread. We were kept busy refilling the supply. The dining area was beautiful. A gorgeous fresh flower arrangement sat in the center on a small table; candles lit in the kerosene lanterns, the lights turned low, and violin music played by the Chamber Maids Plus One provided a pleasant atmosphere.

We in the kitchen didn't absorb this dining experience, however, as the real work was just beginning. Grace and Hope dished up blueberry buckle with whipped cream and the servers took the dessert out on huge trays. The coffee disappeared and we made more. Just when we caught our breath, the 33 bowls of each dish on the menu began arriving, and soon were were surrounded by paper plates. Silverware, crystal ware and just plain ware! Never had I seen so much stem ware. There were the cast-iron cooking kettles, the squash pans and noodles, noodles, noodles. The kitchen overflowed and we had no place to put things.

Several ticket-holders came in late and had to be fed. A local basketball game was also in progress, and later one of Joseph's locals ran in the back kitchen door announcing, "Joseph won!" KWVR's Lee Perkins, who had been covering the game, appeared for his dinner, eating it in the kitchen.

The kitchen by this time was pure bedlam. Rick Swart, editor of the Chieftain, showed up later also, and the fellow who was doing the video-taping still had to eat. The servers sat on the sidelines, finally getting their own plates. After looking at all that food for what seemed like weeks, I could only try a bit of salad and blueberry buckle, which I never got to finish.

A.L. Duckett of Imnaha recited a poem and a few local histories were read. Gerval Ward, descendant of local pioneers, provided an account of an early Wilson family picnic. Emcee Mike Kurtz announced that the bread boards were for sale, along with a few loaves of leftover bread, and they sold out in a matter of minutes. People autographed their boards, passing them around to friends for souvenirs.

Meanwhile, out in the kitchen we couldn't clang and bang pots and pans or clink glasses during the program, so we did the best we could under the circumstances, doing what was most pressing and deciding to come back in the morning to face the "mess of the century." Besides, my help was fading fast, and so were my feet. I sank into a chair near a display of antique teddy bears, put my feet up, and relaxed for the first time in days.

I caught a glimpse of daughter Jackie and husband, Bill, who had arrived from the canyons in time for the dance. They were accompanied by Dave Glaus and wife, Mona. The two Snake River cowboys added to the colorful crowd. Such a far cry from their river-tent cow camps.

At 10 o'clock we all trooped outside to watch a spectacular fireworks display. Men and women clad in their finery stood out in the cold gazing up at a moon sailing in the night sky, waiting for the action to begin.

Pow! Zoom!

Rockets were launched between two sizzling, popping poles. Some exploded into reds, blues, yellows while others cascaded down in a white shower of stars. Several of the big rockets burst from the heavens and filled the air with a meteorite shower of sparkles, causing *oohs* and *aahs*, clapping and cheering. Wallowa County celebrated its 100th birthday in grand style.

At the perimeter of the Joseph Grade School playground, a group of children and teenagers had gathered to watch the spectacle. They, too, cheered at each burst of sparkles. A real treat for Wallowa County. And all the while, the grand old mountain known as Chief Joseph Mountain loomed above the little town, also of that name. It was as if Chief Joseph himself and the ghosts of pioneer ancestors were joining in the celebration. If only the mountain could talk, the stories it could tell. The past 100 years will be written about by many historians, but only the mountain will know what really happened. Time has a way of obliterating the true story.

The last spark died out of the night and everyone filed back into the hall to resume dancing until 2 in the morning. Doug and I danced until 1:30 and wearily went home. Earlier, I noticed Frank McCully waltzing by with Ethel Chandler. He was wearing Ethel's black-plumed hat! He was floating on cloud nine because he had been presented with a special gift: a beautifully framed photograph of his famous father, F.D. McCully, better known as "the father of Wallowa County."

February 15—It snows sometime during the early morning hours. Slept in until 7. Sure felt good.

Later, I returned to the mess at the Civic Center, where Mary Hays, bless her, was already in the process of washing stem ware. I sorted silverware three ways for more than an hour. Hope, Harold, Grace and Scotty showed up to help. Soon we completed the task of restoring order to the place. I was afraid my crew would mutiny if we did all those iron pots, so I loaded them into my car to finish at home.

Fixed a chicken dinner for two; what a switch. Late at night before I finished all those kettles and put everything away.

February 16—Snowed again during the night. By 8 a.m. it began to melt. Our barnlots going through their muddy-mess-time, a conditon that will continue until the frost goes out of the ground.

Scotty arrived around 10:30 and we went downhill skiing at Ferguson Ridge until 1:30. Owing to all that fresh, new snow, skiing was wonderful.

Spent rest of the day catching up on backlog of housework that had been accumulating because of preparations. Our supper of pot roast, cooked in a dutch oven in the wood stove, tasted so good after a vigorous day.

February 17—The days are so full and pass so quickly. I scarcely know what month it is.

We had our first baby calf, an early one, yesterday. The canyons are greening up. But it is snowing through the sunshine here on Prairie Creek this morning. Typical for this time of year. Looking out across the hills, I see just a few small patches of snow remain in the draws. It is a time when the refuse of winter is laid bare. The clean, white, protective blanket of snow is gone. The pastures are once more littered with cow-pies.

My hens are laying well. I let them out of their pen to run around and scratch and peck for a few hours each day. Chester, the banty rooster, flies to the top of the picnic table near the kitchen and crows loudly. If I tap on the window while I am working at the sink, he cocks his head at me in recognition, and we talk. Chester understands people talk better than poultry talk.

The new puppy, Jim, has scattered bones from heck to breakfast over our yard. By 11 it began to snow steadily. Oh well, good for us skiers. Ben and Tom feeding cattle, an all-day job. I finished typing my column while Doug attended a stockgrowers meeting in Enterprise tonight. Five-year-old granddaughter Mona Lee brought me two nice paintings she did for grandma, to decorate our kitchen.

February 19—Baked a loaf of sourdough bread to take to Ted and Leigh Juve. They are now the proud parents of a new baby girl. Welcome to Alder Slope, little Logan.

Decided to make some tapioca pudding using an 1880s recipe. I soaked the tapioca in water, made a custard and folded in egg whites. It was worth all the effort.

February 20—Ten degrees, clear and cold. A new snowfall covers everything. Beautiful morning. Did some photographing.

Doug pitted some frozen Imnaha pie cherries and I made a pie. After all, this is cherry pie month. Also made a lemon meringue pie "from scratch" as I have invited my centennial dinner-kitchen crew over for a "thank you" dinner.

Developed film and ran errands in town. Home to put together a turkey dinner with all the trimmings. Doug hauled my young unbroken mare in from the hills today. She has spent the winter on Salmon Creek. Her name is Soxy Kid, named for Kid Marks. My son-in-law Bill will start her for me in the Snake River canyons, and she will learn early about working cattle.

My "crew" arrived: Harold, Hope, Calvin, Doris, Scotty and Grace. We all had such a good time and enjoyed the food. Can you believe I even made two loaves of sourdough bread?

February 21—A beautiful morning, clear and cold. Cooked breakfast on the wood stove, watered chickens, and packed a lunch, whereupon Scotty and I were off skiing again on Ferguson Ridge. We were joined by Grace, Cressie and Bill. We enjoyed turkey sandwiches in the warming shack and skied until the afternoon. Fun.

Doug back from the hills bearing the season's first buttercups. Wore my white muslin wedding dress to the Sweetheart Ball at the Elks Lodge tonight. Still in the centennial spirit of things, old-style dress encouraged. We met Bud and Ruby Zollman there and danced 'til midnight to the music of "Muddy Creek."

February 22—Received a letter in today's mail from our Swiss Miss, Susan in Switzerland. She is working at a big resort hotel in the mountains. Says she misses us and all the animals.

Went skiing again today. Must make the most of these good snow conditions because they will end all too soon. At noon we all clomped into the warming shack, where we warmed ourselves by "Old Ferg," the barrel wood stove. By the time we left, it was snowing pretty good.

Doug and I attended a CowBelle-Stockgrowers potluck at Cloverleaf Hall tonight.

February 23—Snowing and cold all day. Twelve degrees this morning. Another calf born during the storm. Increased the cows' daily ration of hay because of the cold.

Son-in-law Bill hauled my mare to Snake River today. Spent from 2 to 4:30 in the darkroom at the Art Angle at Joseph, printing pictures. Tonight Christy Tsiatos treated the centennial ball committee to dinner at the Pizza Emporium. Doug and I enjoyed the treat. Afterward, I attended a meeting to plan yet another Wallowa County event, the big annual Festival of the Arts and Cowboy Poetry gathering.

You guessed it: I got put in charge of the dinner.

February 24—Five above zero. Grocery shopped, then up to Alder Slope where I met son Todd on the road. He pointed down to a neighboring field where 60 head of elk were feeding! Recent cold weather had brought them down out of the timber to feed on round bales of hay left in the field.

February 25—The buttercups Doug brought me from the hills are blooming in an old blue granite-ware pan. Sunshine spills down on their yellow, waxy faces, brightening the room. Found an old recipe for ranger cookies and made a batch to fill the cookie jar. More baby calves appearing in the lower field.

February 26—The chickens' drinking water is frozen every morning, so I take the tea kettle full of boiling water up to thaw it out. Our CowBelles served beefy chili at a Les Schwab tire promotion in Enterprise today. Baby lambs and calves all over the county now.

February 27—Rented skis for all my grandchildren. Tomorrow we will all go skiing at Ferguson Ridge.

February 28—What a day! I had all of my Oregon grandchildren and three of my four children up on the ski slopes today. The grandchildren so excited they could scarcely sleep last night. Spent the day helping little ones on the tow rope and toting skis, boots, poles and picnic lunches, not to mention keeping track of mittens, hats and jackets.

Six-year-old Buck made so many trips up the tow rope I couldn't believe it. Rowdy twisted his knee, and 12-year-old Chad was zooming down the slopes like an old pro. They had such a great time. It was worth the effort. Even six-month-old James watched his cousins from the inside of the warming shack.

Tonight, Doug and I took Bud and Ruby Zollman over to La Grande, a 60-mile drive, to watch the Joseph basketball team play Pilot Rock. Joseph won, and Ruby and I slept all the way home.

March 1—March came in more like the proverbial lamb than a lion, with mild temperatures. Partly sunny and extremely warm this morning. Everything is melting. Jackie and the children, who had spent the night, left mid-morning. Everyone is sore from skiing.

The baby calves are coming thick and fast now, and we have our first orphan. Thawed out the colostrum milk and used warm water to rub the little fellow down. I soon had him revived enough to drink the bottle. Pretty soon he staggered to his feet. I named him March. This afternoon I noticed feathers in the yard. They resembled Chester's! They were! Doug had acquired another border collie pup, which decided to eat the little rooster for lunch, or so it appeared.

While gathering eggs, I spied Chester, his pride and tail feathers gone. He looked just terrible, poor fellow. Having gone into hiding, he only came out when he saw me. Although stripped of his former dignity, he was still very much alive.

A cold rain began to fall and it appears to be snowing in the mountains. Wouldn't be at all surprised to see Prairie Creek white by morning. The little bull calf March was standing up waiting for his bottle tonight, and Tom and Ben presented me with the prostrate form of a chilled-down calf. On the back porch, we tube feed it and try to warm the poor thing. Just a typical March day on a cattle ranch.

March 2—A warm wind blew all night. Looks like it is snowing in the mountains. And here: mud, mud, mud!

The little bull calf following me around now, much different than the chilled-down baby of two days ago. It is chinooking today. All the snow is gone from Prairie Creek, except where the drifts were. Everything appears brown and muddy. The two pups are forever busy and into trouble, such as pulling clothes off the line or dragging the most ungodly things into the yard. Our old cow dog Faye is becoming pretty crippled with arthritis. She sometimes gets so stiff, she can scarcely get up.

Went out to chore and saw that Startch had calved. She was in the far corner of the pasture on a clean patch of old grass, licking off her nice big heifer calf.

March 3—A storm came racing down off the mountains in the middle of the night, accompanied by a south wind and rain. Can just imagine avalanches beginning in the mountains now. It is 45 degrees. I try not to think of Startch's new little calf out in storm.

Up early to fix breakfast on the wood stove; no electricity. Put Startch and her calf in the barn and spread out some clean straw for them. Now my busy time begins. I let the orphan into nurse. He soon got the hang of it...no more bottle baby.

The warm wind reduced the remaining snow drifts to glistening patches of ice. As I type my column the wind continues to roar. Electricity off all morning. Some tin blew off one of our sheds. Attended a 4-H leaders meeting tonight at Cloverleaf Hall.

March 5—Wind still with us. Its ceaseless roar continued all night. Yesterday's high set a record, 60 degrees. Let the three calves nurse Startch. I'll have another baby to put on May when she calves now.

This afternoon May decided to go into labor. Using binoculars, I watched her progress from the house. After a while she wandered over to a ditch and laid down. I sneaked up behind her, grabbed two legs and pulled with each contraction. The calf's tongue was blue, the head big and the eyes bulged. A big calf for this second-calf heifer. I kept pulling at an angle, until bit by bit the calf emerged. On the final pull, it slithered out, a big brown and white bull calf, covered with yellowish amniotic fluid.

I dragged the calf away from the ditch and left mom to lick off her baby.

Startch, a second-calf heifer, cleans her newly born calf. Startch is a Holstein-Simmental cross, the offspring of Star, sired by Polled Stretch—hence the name Startch.

March 6—The wind ceased altogether around 9 last night. The silence was wonderful.

Put May's big bull calf in the dry barn, cleaned out the milking parlor, shook out fresh straw. All babies and mammas doing fine. Soon it began to snow great big flakes which stuck to the ground.

Doug left for Hermiston to attend the C&B sale. I didn't go, as had my "herd" to tend to. Another Guernsey due to calve soon; Daisy is making up real fast. Ben and Tom have their hands full with the calving cows in the lower field. We seem to get a batch of new calves with each new storm…naturally. Worked on updating our Simmental cow cards.

Walked out to get the mail in the slushy snow, which all melted by nightfall. We've been experiencing it all: wind, mud, rain, snow. Around the feeders it is very sloppy, a condition we just have to live with for a while each year. Two calves on each of my cows now. Nermal, the surviving barn cat, is happy; she has fresh, warm milk twice a day again.

The snow-line has retreated to the timber on the slopes of the Wallowas. Read a book of essays tonight entitled "Having Everything Right," by Kim Stafford. The Kwakiutl Indians Boas transcription, He'lade, meaning "Having everything right, a place where people gather abundant berries and make good life." A nice thought to fall asleep on. Slept well.

Dallas Williamson, shown here with his wife, Charlene, will be grand marshal of the Chief Joseph Days celebration the last weekend in July in Joseph.

March 7—Awoke early. Not raining, not snowing, nor is the wind blowing. In the pre-dawn light, I see all is frozen and cold. Ice has formed on the chocolate-colored puddles. I fix a cup of postum and start a fire, savoring the quiet.

Out in the barn, hungry calves nursing, the barn floor foam-flecked as the calves slurp and swallow until their distended bellies bulge. One by one I drag them off, pushing them through a small gate where they contentedly bed down in fresh straw. What a life. The gargantuan form of Startch, the Holstein-Simmental cow, fills the milking parlor, leaving little room for the Guernsey-Jersey, May.

Talked to daughter Jackie on the Imnaha phone line; the children, Mona and Buck, watching their mother cat give birth to a batch of kittens. Spring has sprung.

March 8—I noticed the first pair of returning robins perched in the old apple tree on this beautiful morning. The mud puddles are covered with ice, and the day is mostly clear.

After chores, Grace, Scotty and I drove to Imnaha for a hike. On the way down, we noticed the old burn areas were greening up. Baby calves and lambs frolicked in the sunshine. Arriving at Dick and Gerry Waller's place, we walked along the river, crossed the bridge near Kriley's, then explored the canyons across the river. We had a lovely walk and enjoyed seeing a few yellow bells and buttercups along the way. We ate our lunches high up in an old abandoned apricot orchard which was just about to burst into bloom. Above us in the rimrocks, Dick Waller was fixing a rockjack fence. Beautiful clouds floated overhead creating shadow patterns on the high benches and rock formations.

On our return, we followed a river trail. It was so good for our spirits to be out in the fresh canyon air and to witness the first signs of spring. Home to develop film and do chores. A twin calf got separated from his family and no one seems to be able to get him mothered up...so I have another baby. I let him nurse Startch; three calves on her tonight.

Clouding up and beginning to rain, a good, warm rain.

March 9—Beautiful golden light, turning to shades of pink, flooded the snowfields of the mountains at daybreak. The ground isn't frozen this morning! Worked in the darkroom at the Art Angle, then organized a 4-H meeting at Cloverleaf Hall for my Sourdough Shutterbugs.

After our meeting tonight, for the benefit of our many new members, we viewed slides of last year's llama trip to Bear Creek and our trek to Red's Horse Ranch. We have 30 4-H'ers this year. Afterwards, we participated in a community service project, stuffing plastic bags for the Food Fair.

March 10—An apricot twig I'd brought home from Imnaha has burst into bloom in a fruit jar full of water on my kitchen table. Mild, spring-like...and muddy!

Doug and I drove to Butterfields', then to Theils', where we picked up potatoes for the potato bar that the 4-H'ers are organizing for a moneymaking project at the Food Fair. Later, Doug and I scrubbed the spuds. Busy all morning, organizing volunteers to bake potatoes and make toppings for the potato bar.

Watched my 12-year-old grandson, Chad, wrestle at the Enterprise high school gym. He won both matches.

March 11—Another gorgeous day! Clouds hang in layers, encircling brilliant snowfields. A meadow lark, perched on a fence in the cow pasture, burst forth into trills and song while I chored.

Had to "pill" 2 of my calves this morning, was a mess by the time I returned to the house...so much mud in the barnlots these days. It was so mild, I let the fire die out in the wood stove.

Daughter Lori called from Wyoming, reported it had been 80 degrees one day, then snowed the next.

March 12—Windy and cloudy today. One of my calves is pretty sick; am doctoring him daily, feeding him karo syrup and water to keep him from dehydrating.

Wrapped 100 potatoes in foil for baking, prepared a topping, multiplying the recipe five times. It was called Spinach Spud Supreme, a delicious concoction of chicken broth gravy, sauteed mushrooms, bacon bits, spinach and swiss cheese.

Attended a CowBelle meeting at Cloverleaf Hall. I will chairman the annual Grain Growers dinner, which will be a CowBelle money-making project. After the meeting I put up a potato booth for the Wallowa County Seed potato growers for the Food Fair tonight. CowBelles will work back stage, as they have in years past, preparing food for the event.

Such a busy time; home to take baked potatoes from my oven and do chores before returning to Cloverleaf Hall for the Food Fair. The Prairie Creek wind was really whipping it up while I chored. It began to rain later on. Our cows, sensing the approaching storm, began to calve. Before the night would end, they would have shelled out 15 calves!

Our 4-H Potato Bar was a success. The crowds were considerably less this year, as half the county was across the Blues attending the state basketball tournament in Pendleton. The Joseph Eagles were in the running for the championship.

March 13—Raining and windy. Out to chore, my sick calf still alive, but just barely. Snow line back on upper Prairie Creek. Watched grandson James today while mom painted their kitchen. We enjoyed seeing a beautiful rainbow this afternoon on Alder Slope.

March 14—Partially clear, a skift of snow on the frozen ground. Out to chore, expecting my sick calf to be dead. Instead, he was waiting at the gate, eager to nurse a cow.

Doug ground up some of our freshly dug horseradish. It goes so good on our roast beef.

Grace and I drove to Imnaha where I made a tape recording of Inez Meyers. Inez's grandfather, William McCormack, was one of the two first permanent white settlers in the Wallowa Country. I also took a colored slide of Inez for our history project. Violets, fragrant with the smell of spring, were running loosein Inez's lawn. What a pretty sight! The golden shower of forsythia brightened up the yard with its yellow light. As always, we enjoyed visiting with Inez, a wonderful lady.

We drove up-river to Mary Mark's, where I also made a tape of her, in her neat and tidy house. Mary's crocuses were blooming, and the sound of the Imnaha rushing by was pleasant. I photographed Mary standing beside an interesting log barn, which had served as an early-day homesteader's cabin. It had been moved from its original location. The dovetailed corners of the old building were fascinating. These wonderful hand-hewn structures stand to remind us of the splendid craftsmanship employed by Wallowa County's first settlers. When many newer barns have tumbled down, these old, log ones continue to stand the test of time.

Mary walked with us to the car: "Let's make plans to take a horse back trip to the cow camp this spring," she said. We made a promise to do so and left.

Doug home from the hills, where he spotted a large herd of elk. In the dusky light of evening, I could see a small, dark form lying close to Daisy. She had calved. Walking out in the pasture, I found she had a little heifer calf. The sick calf much improved tonight.

Read a book, entitled "Red Heroines of the Northwest." Very interesting reading, about Sacajawea, the Dorian woman and Jan Silcott. When you read about these women, you realize how little we use of our potential selves. These women met the challenges they faced with a calm acceptance. It wasn't until years after their deaths, that historians realized the significance of their deeds.

A watercolor moon, edged in dark clouds, swims about in the sky tonight.

March 15—Startch had such a overflow of milk this morning, I treated the chickens to some. Milked out some of Daisy's fresh colostrum milk to put in the freezer for future weak calves.

March 16—Five inches of spring snow. Opening the barn door, a big blob of snow slid off the roof and down my neck. Daisy kicked me in the thigh this morning. My fault. I was bag-balming her teats and took the hobbles off too soon. Am saving Startch's milk for house milk now.

Daughter Jackie left granddaughter Mona with us this morning. She will be spending a few days with us while her parents travel to Portland. Mona and I watched a gathering of birds at the bird house in the apple tree. We can't figure out what is going on. It appears that a northern flicker, four robins, numerous sparrows and Jenny Wren are checking out the house for future occupancy.

At noon, I read to Mona and we both took a long nap. So much fun having this cheerful little one around. Being a grandmother, I think, is one of life's greatest pleasures.

March 17—Up early on this St. Patrick's Day. It is snowing. Mona Lee had reminded me to mix the sourdough last night... she wanted waffles this morning. As I was choring, her little, dark curly head appeared through the barn door. She informed me that she already had gathered some eggs from under my protesting hens! All bundled up in her coat and gloves, Mona patiently waited while I milked and let the calves in to nurse. As the calves finished, they began to run around, bucking and playing, much to Mona's delight.

Instead of working on my column, I spent the morning cutting out paper dolls from old newspapers with Mona Lee. This afternoon we attended another wrestling match to watch grandson Chad perform. He pinned his opponents in a matter of minutes. Viewing it from this grandmother's point of view, I am just glad when neither boy is hurt.

Mona "helped" me make pudding, then poured it into little custard cups. She especially enjoyed eating it.

March 18—Worked on my column early this morning while Mona Lee was still in bed. Then, taking her piggy-back out to chore, I milked the cow and let the calves nurse May. A brand new snowfall covers everything. It is cold and windy. I warmed up a bottle of colostrum milk for another chilled baby calf.

Baked a wild blackberry cobbler this afternoon. Nothing is as lovin' from the oven as this, says Doug. When Mona and I chored this evening, the snow had melted into the mud. Much to her delight, Mona will spend one more night at grandma's house. It is 25 degrees outside.

March 19—Everything is frozen again, and there is ice on the chicken's water. Fixed breakfast on the wood stove. Nermal, the barn cat, spends a great deal of time among the rafters in the barn. This hiding place serves as an escape from the pups, who harrass her constantly.

Just learned today of the death of a dear friend, Ed Quinn. He died on the 13th. I will always remember Ed for his ready smile and respect for hard work. He and wife, Gladys, used to own a ranch on Alder Slope, before they moved into Enterprise. Ed spent his later years fixing up the small house and yard, which was to serve as a home for their final years. In the front yard he planted a tulip bed. It has been a joy to drive by and see the brilliant red tulips blooming there. Ed lovingly cared for his wife, who he had been married to for many years. Gladys taught at many of Wallowa County's one-room schools in the early years. Ed jokingly had said, "I married the school marm."

Ed was extremely talented at creating things from wood. He once made me a beautiful napkin holder, a boot jack and a plant hanger, with little hearts, all lovingly hand carved from cherry wood. He used small wooden dowels to hold his pieces together, and was an artist in the true sense. The wood he used was grown on his ranch...juniper, cherry and apple.

I shall always cherish these mementos made by a very special man. One of Ed's many fine qualities was patience, whether it was working with his horses, woodworking, gardening or whatever. He was a perfectionist.

Ed requested that he be cremated and the ashes scattered in his yard. Perhaps this spring, Ed's tulips will bloom with renewed vigor, nurtured by Ed himself, whose soul resembles the beauty of the flowers. He was a kind and gentle man.

Rest in peace, Ed. You will forever remain in the hearts of those who had the pleasure of knowing you.

Dagobert Runes once wrote: "Great is not the man who has taken from life and from the people a thousandfold share. Great is the man who has given to life and to the people. The greatest of all may be those no one knows." This was true of both my father and Ed Quinn.

My granddaughter is cleaning house for me! Daughter Jackie finally arrived around 1 p.m. to pick up Mona. Already I miss her cheerful presence. Mona and Buck are looking forward to joining their father on the Snake River for spring vacation. The whole family will enjoy a week together at Dug Bar.

Having an absentee cowboy father and husband is hard on all concerned, but that is a part of canyon life. It is nothing new for families of school age children who are separated for long periods, while cattle are tended to in the remote sections of Wallowa County.

Doug attending the livestock auction in La Grande today. Attended a history group meeting at the Bookloft. A cold wind blew down off the snowy mountains as we talked about Ed Quinn, and how glad we were that he had been able to accompany us on our trip to the Divide last fall, a day which he had enjoyed to the fullest.

March 20—The first day of spring. Just a skift of snow on the ground this morning on Prairie Creek. Patches of blue sky occasionally let sunshine spill down from above. The Vernal Equinox nears. Life goes on, and we inhabit the Earth, give or take from it, and pass on into eternity, just like spring, which serves to remind us that happiness follows sorrow.

The primroses and crocuses are blooming. The green shoots of the tulips have surfaced and the rhubarb is up! Drove to Alder Slope this afternoon to visit Alma Beaudoin. Her father-in-law was Pete Beaudoin, an early-day sheepman who at one time ran 40,000 head of sheep in Wallowa County.

I did a taped interview of Alma and took her picture for our slide-tape presentation. Alma remembered lots of Wallowa County history. She herself moved here in 1916, and was one of ten children reared in a family who dairied for a living in Minnesota. Today, Alma lives with her son, Bill, and his wife, Betty, on Alder Slope. From her downstairs apartment she can look up on the slopes of Ruby Peak, gaze eastward to the Seven Devils, down toward Enterprise and Joseph or out to the rolling hill land out north. She is a most interesting lady.

Ran into my friend Ruth Baremore in the grocery store. She is recovering nicely from being kicked in the face by her milk cow. We compared notes on being kicked by our charges, and agreed that we had been mighty careless. From now on we'll leave those hobbles on longer.

Came home after a meeting tonight to find five burros in our yard. The headlights shone right on the little rascals as they proceeded to feast on our hay stack. Neighbor Ardis Klages informed us earlier that a small band of donkeys had been roving around in the vicinity of Prairie Creek all week. Happy to report the burros were returned to their own pasture.

March 21—Doug is attending an Angus bull sale in Hermiston.

After doing all my chores on this absolutely gorgeous morning, some members of our history group and I all piled into Grace's yellow Jeep and headed for Horse Creek on the lower Imnaha. This "touring car" negotiates the most incredible roads with seemingly little effort. We stopped briefly at Imnaha, where I mailed a letter in the Imnaha Post Office. We also visited Ferm Warnock, and I photographed him for our history project.

Apricot orchards have transformed into clouds of white blooms. The sarvis berry bloomed in the lower canyons. Large billowy, white clouds floated in an incredibly blue sky. Imnaha residents were out in their gardens working the soil. After traveling the winding dirt road to the mouth of Horse Creek, we ate our lunches near the bridge that spans the Imnaha River. Such a beautiful day for a picnic.

After lunch, we drove up the narrow, muddy road that follows Horse

Creek, looking for the old double log cabin. What would it look like after the 16 years since last seen it? We were soon to find out.

The road followed the musical little creek called Horse Creek as it flowed down the center of the canyon. Bright patches of buttercups shone in the sunlight. The air was fragrant with the scent of pine trees that grew close to the road. We soon came to a clearing and there stood what was left of the double log cabin.

This place is steeped in early Imnaha history. The Stubblefields and Hasses were some of the families who lived here. Hass Ridge looms above the Horse Creek canyon, and the name Stubblefield is synonomous with the area. Cressie Green said she had an uncle who homesteaded at the mouth of Pumpkin Creek farther up Horse Creek.

The old log cabin had a "breezeway" between the cabins that were connected by a roof made of hand-hewn shakes. The roof sagged, but the wonderful art work of the logs, which had been chinked with mortar of some sort, was still strong and true. Crude windows had been cut to admit light, and doorways faced each other. It was a wonderful sight. The cabin, partially hidden by trees, was situated at the edge of the clearing. Green grass formed a meadow walled in on both sides by steep canyons. Cattle grazed nearby and, farther up the draw, some horses inhabited an enclosed pasture. It appeared they had wintered there.

We camera bugs went wild taking pictures. Everything was perfect for photographing: clear air, showy clouds and canyon scenery at its finest. We hiked around the spot before returning to Grace's Jeep. Before heading back, we stopped to photograph the old Horse Creek Ranch headquarter house, where blooming fruit trees added a pretty appearance to the river scene. This is where Kid and Mary Marks lived years ago.

On the way back up the winding road to Imnaha, we passed an area known locally as Maggie Beecher. I had always wondered who "Maggie" was, and learned that a woman by that name had homesteaded there long ago. The high grassy bench called "School Marin Flat" above Horse Creek has always fascinated me. I always hoped that perhaps Maggie Beecher could have been a school marm, but not so.

Like so much lower-Imnaha history and lore, the truth is written on the wind and will be repeated to future generations. As each year passes and the ones who remember are gone, the stories will vary, until one day perhaps no one will remember Maggie Beecher.

We stopped to rest at the Imnaha store and enjoy a cool drink before driving out "On Top." Doug had returned from Hermiston, having purchased three Angus bulls. We will use them for "Heifer bulls."

March 22—Up early on this Sunday morning. Ground frozen; skies partially clear, lovely clouds forming over the mountains and valley. Tonight, Doug and I attended Crocodile Dundee at our local OK Theater. Great entertainment.

March 26—To town to pick up meat and other ingredients for Friday's Grain Growers dinner that the CowBelles are preparing. I'll need all my energy for the days ahead.

Made out all the registration applications for our 1986 Simmental heifers and bulls. Delivered potatoes for CowBelles to bake, along with apples for making deep dish apple pies for the dinner. Arranged for some of the Imnaha CowBelles to send out some forsythia and daffodils for table decorations. Nothing like Imnaha's first spring flowers to cheer us valley people up.

Watched James tonight while mom and dad attended Crocodile Dundee.

March 27—At 6 a.m. everything is frozen hard—15 degrees.

Made two deep dish apple pies, worked on a history project scrapbook, and attended a history committee meeting on our slide-tape show in Joseph. Just when we thought spring had sprung, it turns cold and appears to be snowing over the mountains.

Put all the roasts for the dinner tonight in three ovens: one in the kitchen, one in the trailer, and even used the wood stove oven for baking all that meat. Loaded the car with cooking utensils, made all the gravy, loaded up pies and meat, and headed into Enterprise. My committee and I worked from 2 o'clock until after the meal was served in Cloverleaf Hall.

I returned to the ranch at 5 to do chores and pick up some antique fruit jars to put the fresh flowers in. The meal was a success, both from the point of tasting good and helping build up our CowBelles' treasury. It was midnight before I finished putting things away and fell into bed.

March 28—Cold, heavy frost, windy, with snow showers off and on all day. The Alaska fish truck was in Joseph, so I purchased some fresh scallops and crab for a special birthday dinner I will prepare for daughter-in-law Liza tonight.

I made a huge chiffon cake from scratch, using eight egg yolks and whites from my fresh-from-under-the-hens eggs. We had a fun family time and enjoyed the fish dinner topped off with fresh orange chiffon cake, real whipped cream and strawberries from our freezer.

March 29—Scotty and I wanted to go for a hike up on TV Ridge on this Sunday. I called Grace and she called Stanlynn; the hike was on. We began walking from Clarice Southwick's place at the edge of the timber on Alder Slope. The view in all directions was wonderful. We trudged up through patches of deep snow that had a crust on it, so the walking was fairly easy. The morning air was crisp and bracing. Sudden breezes caused big blobs of snow to fall from the heavily laden branches of the evergreens. The branches rebounded with a swish when their burden was released.

The smell of spring is everywhere; the earth oozing and melting and warming. A hawk screamed at our intrusion into his domain. We spotted pussy willows high on a sunshiney hillside, also buttercups and new green moss. So many varieties of trees: Engelmann spruce, sub-alpine fir, and pine. The tamarack's new needles had not yet appeared.

The snow became deeper and deeper as we worked our way slowly to the top. Delicate prints of coyote, snowshoe rabbit and squirrels told tales in the snow. The view of the valley when we finally reached the top was breathtaking. We built a small fire in a clearing, and boiled snow to make tea and chicken soup. On our lonely ridge top we felt like we owned the world on this March day. We enjoyed our "burnt tea" and agreed no restaurant in the world could rival our view.

We thought about those unfortunate souls who were, at this moment, propped in front of the tube instead of out enjoying the world around them. A cold wind suddenly sprang up and caused the snow in the firs to sift downward, resembling diamond crystals in the sunlight. The clouds hovering over the ridge thickened and we could taste the taste snow in the air. We began our descent, still enjoying the view. Fairly flying down the mountain, slipping and sliding in the deep snow, laughing and falling down, like children, we made it down in less than a half-hour.

Upon returning to the ranch, I fixed a chicken dinner with all the trimmings, as I had invited aunt Opal Tippett to dinner. We so enjoyed aunt Opal's company tonight. When she was a little girl, her parents had moved from California to take up a homestead on Chesnimnus. She remembers moving from all of her friends in a populated area to that wilderness in Wallowa County. At age 16, she met and married Charley Tippett.

"Everyone said it wouldn't work," recalled Opal, but it did, and she and Charley lived long enough for the couple to celebrate their 50th wedding anniversary. Today at 87, widowed, Opal lives alone in Enterprise. Her 22 grandchildren, 35 great-grandchildren and one great-great-grandchild comfort her a great deal. She recalls how, at 18, she accompanied her husband to sheep camps on horseback, leading a pack string of mules as they made their way from camp to camp, stretched over rugged terrain from Horse Creek (near Cold Springs) to Cache Creek on the Snake, to Dug Bar and Miley Creek. Opal did all the cooking and cleaning in the sheep camps. Sometimes the trails were so steep, Opal would have to get off and lead her horse. Her husband worked for early-day sheepmen Dobbin and Huffman at the time.

"All those wonderful years that we lived on Pine Creek," Opal said. "How I loved it out there. The Chinook salmon swimming up the creeks, the beavers playing, my children growing up in a wonderful environment. I remember the Nez Perce Indians traveling through and camping at our place. We would trade them hides for moccasins." She remembered that the cattle in those days roamed one vast range. The calves were weaned in the fall and driven to Imnaha. It was such a treat to listen to Opal talk of those times. We could have listened all night.

March 29—Ten degrees, heavy frost, ground frozen again. After finishing my chores, I turned Daisy's and May's calves out with them.

Doug and I drove to Imnaha to deliver a used washing machine to daughter Jackie, who was on Snake River with her family. The frost had affected the lower elevations as well, and the apricot crop appears to have been ruined. Stopping at the Imnaha store, we learned that the electricity had been out since 4 p.m. the preceding day, due to a power outage in the Idaho Wilderness. Ken Stein and Paul Kriley were firing up a portable generator to keep the ice cream from melting. Sally and I joked, saying they had a "special" on milkshakes today.

A barrel wood stove was being used for warmth. Sally had made up a thermos of hot coffee on a butane stove and was serving the coffee to customers from behind the counter. It was still cold outside, down to 17 degrees earlier. The sole topic of conversation in this small community was the unseasonable cold.

We drove downriver aways to have a look-see before returning to the store for a cold ham sandwich. On the way home, we passed several rigs headed down with generators to keep the freezers from thawing. Returned to Prairie Creek, where Doug went out to the hills to bring in the horses, as we will trail 158 head of cows to the hills on Wednesday. Jackie called later; all had returned safely from Dug Bar. Their electricity had come on around 5:30. The children had spent a marvelous week in the Snake River canyon, riding horses and being with daddy.

Fixed chicken and homemade noodles for supper.

March 30—Breakfast over by 6:30, bull buyers here at 7. Clear, sunny and 25 degrees this morning. Snowy mountains gleam in bright sunlight. Washed clothes and began working on slide-tape script. We have revised and worked it over...again. Doug shoeing horses in readiness for our cattle drive. Pages of reference material cover my kitchen table, as I work on the script during my "spare" moments. Daisy isn't letting her adopted calf nurse! Baked squash and swiss steak for supper.

After supper, I picked up Grace Bartlett and Ann Hays and we attended the Montana repertoire theater musical "Harvest" at the OK Theater. It was a very good contemporary play, written by William Yellow Robe Jr., an Assiniboin Indian. The scene, set on a Montana ranch, featured a plot centered around the dilemma of a modern ranching family. Stars out and warm tonight.

March 31—A little frost, but otherwise clear, sunny and warm. Beautiful morning! Hung four loads of clothes on the line, did chores; necking together Daisy's calves, with two collars connected with a swivel-chain in the middle. That will solve that problem! Milked Startch for house milk.

Attended a meeting on our centennial project; we viewed slides and discussed changes. Voted in the school election. Drove up to Alder Slope where I met daughter-in-law Liza and Nancy Maasdam walking along the road, their babies in packs asleep on their backs. Two lucky little children, being raised on the Slope.

Visited briefly with son Todd, who was shoeing his horse. Continued on up the slope to Dave Nelson's, where I did some interviewing and picture taking for an article I am doing for Agri-Times' horse issue. Home to start supper and chore.

The men are sorting cows from calves down at the corrals. The fall calves are being weaned and their mamas will be started to the hills in the morning. The bawling begins. So warm today, it was almost hot. After supper I mixed the sourdough and hit the hay.

A big day ahead tomorrow. Goodbye, March.

April 1—Up at 5 and that's no April Fool's joke. Beautiful light on the mountain tops. Clear, nary a cloud, very little frost and warm. Mixed up the sourdough and left Doug to fix breakfast while I chored.

After breakfast, the horses were saddled and Herb Owens arrived to help us cowboy. We drove the bawling cows away from their calves, which were penned nearby. We got them going pretty good, keeping them at a trot until they were out of sight of their calves. All was well, until we came to the four corners at Klages'. Then some of the cows took off toward the Liberty Grange Hall. My job, to keep them from running back to their calves. The three men pursued the running cows and soon had them turned back.

After yelling ourselves hoarse, we finally got them lined out and going pretty good again. A gorgeous day. As the cattle climbed Crow Creek Pass, they got a little warm. Riding along, we so enjoyed seeing the many patches of buttercups. Not a single snowbank left. We drove the cows along the long, dusty, gravel road until we came to Circle M, where we ate our lunches and let the herd rest a while before continuing on. Since the cows had wintered so well and were pretty fleshy, we had to travel slower so they wouldn't heat up.

Riding along, Herb told me about running wild horses in the Horse Heaven Hills when he was just a young cowboy. He told how they made wing-shaped corrals and rounded up the herds of inbred wild horses that used to run free there. He said they were small and very wild, not good for saddle horses. They were driven to a railhead, loaded and shipped in boxcars, and sold in Portland for hog feed for $5 per head. Herb's job was to ride in the lead of a wild band and let them follow his horse. This he accomplished on a dead run, and had to get a fresh horse often.

Once his flying mount hit a badger hole tunnel that had been hidden on the surface. The horse fell, pitching Herb off into space. The horse lay, quivering a while, before jumping to his feet. Whereupon Herb mounted up and went on. Those wild horse roundups were pretty hairy, Herb remembered.

An enormous barred owl flew from her thornbrush thicket near East Crow, and mallard ducks were beginning to pair up. Doug had long since left us to scare off marauding elk and check fences on Wet Salmon Creek. Making good time, we arrived at the "Pink" barn corrals by 2:30, where we unsaddled and fed our horses. Doug hadn't returned yet so we loaded up our saddles and drove the pickup back to the valley. My 53-year-old body was protesting; hadn't been in the saddle all winter.

Rested up, gathered eggs. The weaned calves very noisy while mamas had all but forgotten motherhood, and were now more concerned about reaching grassy hill pastures...no more feedings of hay. Doug treated this cowgirl to dinner at "Tony's Corner," a gas station-restaurant in Joseph. To bed, after a hot tub bath. Am 15 miles sore tonight.

April 2—Up at 5 again, and out to chore while Doug fixed pork chops, eggs and toast. The six calves all doing nicely on the three cows now. In house to make lunches before leaving with the men for Crow Creek.

Another beautiful morning. Caught up and saddled our horses before turning the cows out and heading up Dorrance gulch. This has got to be the "year of the buttercup." They were everywhere. Halfway up the grade, I dismounted, letting my horse follow along behind Ben, while I ran ahead on foot to photograph. Out of breath trying to stay ahead of the herd, I succeeded in scrambling up onto a rock for a good shot.

We soon made it to the top, then drove the cattle past the site of the Dry Salmon Creek school house. Ran on ahead again to deliver a note to Ben on just how many cows were to be turned into what pasture. When we reached the Johnson corrals, I counted out my 30 head and drove them to Butte Creek. Meanwhile, Ben and Herb drove the remainder of the herd to the Redbarn, Johnson and Deadman pastures. As we neared the Butte Creek place, I rode ahead and opened the "wire" gate. This one yielded to my tugging. Sometimes we gals have a time with these so-called "gates."

Rode my mare back to the Johnson corrals and took a nap in the grass until my ride showed up. Peaceful, listening to the "sound" of silence.

April 3—A pair of honkers flew over while I chored this morning. They must be nesting close by. Busy day; worked two interview and picture-taking sessions into my regular schedule. Beautiful, warm and sunny.

Grace Bartlet accompanied me to Enterprise where I interviewed Bob Masterson. We found him out back in his saddle shop. Like so many old timers, Bob has had an interesting life and his story weaves itself into Wallowa County's history.

This afternoon I drove to Alder Slope. There I spent two hours talking to Max Walker. Max is another packer-guide; a man of many talents. Among other projects, he is restoring an old bobsled. Every detail is perfect. I think it is wonderful that people like Max are preserving these old farm implements. Years ago, these bobsleds were necessary to haul hay to livestock during the long, cold snowy winters. Remnants of them lay all over the back country of Wallowa County, rotting slowly into the ground. Oftentimes they repose where they were last used.

Max and wife Marcel have purchased the old Lee Cook place, and the views from their house are pretty neat. Ruby Peak looms, literally in their back yard. In a nearby barn lot, placidly chewing her cud, stood a nice-looking Dutch Belted milk cow. She was obviously due to calve any time. On a nearby slope pasture, Max's mules came running down toward Max for attention and affection. Max had many tales to tell about his years as an outfitter, and when he worked for Len Jordan on the

Snake River. In spite of a steel pin in his hip; a result of a self-inflictd, accidental gunshot wound, Max continues to shoe horses and mules at age 72.

All of our fields are harrowed now. They look neat and tidy now that the manure is spread around.

April 4—After chores, I got busy typing three articles for Agri-Times's horse issue. Developed film and printed photos to go with them. Cloudy and cool; the wood stove feels good.

April 6—Awoke in the middle of the night and looked out to see everything frosty cold. The day dawned clear and beautiful. Milked Startch and let the calves nurse. All calves are growing like bad weeds. The mountains, defined sharply against blue sky and snowfields, blinding white, dazzle us this morning all over the Wallowa Valley.

Drove to Grace Bartlett's, where we worked all morning on the slide-tape script. It was very pleasant working there with the sounds of birds singing in the nearby woods and a stream close by. This afternoon Sarah Hale brought over the information I'll need to do publicity articles on the Cowboy Poets. Our annual Wallowa Valley Festival of the Arts looms, and I must attend to this job. My days are so filled! It seems everyone has a job for me to do.

April 7—Don't know how long I can keep up this pace, but here goes.

Up at 6; made breakfast, milked cow, typed column, housework, and off to Joseph to print photos for Art Festival publicity. Then, while at the Art Angle, I framed one of my photo entries for the Art Show. Back at the ranch, I worked on my column some more, fixed lunch, and picked up Grace for another taped interview for our history project.

We visited Donald Davis and his wife at their house at the mouth of Trout Creek, where it joins the Wallowa River. Donald was born in this very house, although it has been moved from its present location due to the highway construction. He is the son of Eckley and Mertie (Beecher) Davis. Mertie, by the way, was a sister to "Maggie Beecher", of whom I wrote a few weeks ago. It is fascinating to me how the history of the county begins to fit together like a giant puzzle.

Donald could remember when the Indians used to camp in the meadow on their place. He said at one time the Lapwai and Umatilla Indians camped there along the creek. During the Depression, he said, there was quite a demand for eggs in the area and they sold for 40 cents per dozen. A good price for the times. Donald built a chicken house over their milking barn and his wife raised laying hens and sold the eggs. This venture enabled them to make it through. Donald and his wife are good citizens, typical of the majority of Wallow County's natives.

A sad day today. Our cowdog Faye had to be put to sleep. She was run over by a car....and I was the driver. Crippled and lame with arthritis, she had been lying under the back of the car and I had failed to see her there until it was too late. Faye was a wonderful cow dog, and deserves a special place in "Dog Heaven." In her younger years, she accomplished the work of four cowboys; she knew what would be asked of her before she was told. The past few months, however, she has been too crippled to work.

Did chores with tears in my eyes. Fixed supper, finished my column and began working on cowboy poetry publicity. So very busy, crashed at 10:30. Another long day.

April 8—Took the collars off May's two calves this morning, as it appears she is permitting both to nurse now. My 4-H Sourdough Shutterbugs called about our proposed campout at Dug Bar this weekend. If it rains, we will cancel.

To Art Angle in Joseph, where I finish framing my two prints for the Art Festival's Art show. Cold and windy, with a few mini-blizzards all day long.

Met with Wallowa Valley Arts Council members for a no-host dinner meeting at the "Country Place on Pete's Pond." This unique dining establishment in Enterprise has recently been remodeled and enlarged. It is wonderful. Spacious and well planned, it is now able to accommodate large groups. We enjoyed a wonderful pasta dinner while gazing out across the water, and looking up toward the slope and the Wallowa Mountains. Flocks of Canadian honkers, two black swans, and numerous mallard ducks entertained us with their antics on the pond.

I gave a brief report on the dinner, which I will chairman. We expect in excess of 300 people at our annual "Western Art in Eastern Oregon" Art Festival, an event that grows more popular each year.

April 9—Cold, frosty, clear and sunny. Doug and Max Gorsline left at 7 this morning for Montana, where Doug will visit a seed potato operation. Busy time for me.

After choring I wrote cutlines for cowboy poetry publicity photos for the local Chieftain newspaper. Went grocery shopping, then drove to the Grain Growers feed department where my 75 peeping baby chicks were awaiting me. While at the feed store, I purchased my vegetable garden seeds. All too soon it will be time to plant the garden.

Back at the ranch, I scrubbed out the chick waterers and feeders with soapy clorox water, plugged in the heat lamp, and put the chicks in their cozy, straw-filled, large wooden box. They went directly to eating....a pastime they will continue, non-stop, until they reach butchering size. Twenty-five are pullets that I will raise for replacement laying hens.

Attended a CowBelle luncheon meeting at Pam's Pastries in Joseph. We enjoyed eating in their new expanded dining area, which is decorated with quality antiques. The salad bar resembled a chuck wagon. Busy times ahead for CowBelles, and many were absent due to conflicting dates. Region V will soon be here, and I haven't had time to concentrate on a presentation that I've been asked to prepare for the banquet. The event will be held at the Red Lion in Pasco, Washington.

Now I must concentrate on my 4-H'ers campout.

April 10—Up early. Cloudy and cold. Built a fire in woodstove. Called my 4-H'ers and canceled our trip to Dug Bar. The children were so disappointed, I decided to let them camp here on the ranch tonight. The weather, meanwhile, went from bad to worse and a fierce wind began to blow.

Worked on the script and completed five pages before concentrating on the arrival of the 16 4-H'ers. Loaded the pickup with a grill and grate, some wood, kindling and other items for our camp-out. By then, ominous-looking storm clouds began building up over the mountains. At 4 o'clock the 4-H'ers began arriving, until all 16 had loaded their camping gear into the pickup.

First, we all trooped down to the calving shed, where I tended to the new baby chicks. The chicks had survived their first night well, and the shutterbugs enjoyed taking their pictures. After finishing my other barn chores, I drove the pickup-load of camping equipment over the hill to set up camp along our creek. The children set out on foot, feeling great and anticipating having fun.

We started a cooking fire near some cottonwood trees, and soon members were preparing their camp-out meals. Just as we finished eating, it began to rain. The wind blew furiously while we loaded up everything and headed for the calving shed, where sleeping bags were laid out in the straw. Eric Johnson and Bryan Freels decided to sleep in the sheepherder wagon, which was cozy and safe from the storm. Rain continued to beat down on the tin roof as we prepared to "camp out" in the calving shed.

The baby chicks began peeping loudly, due to all the commotion, I guess. Because it was too early to go to bed, most of the 4-H'ers went up to the house and played Scrabble or visited in the living room. Suddenly, it turned quite cold and the wind increased. The rain came down in sheets. Then silence. The rain had been replaced by snow and a full-scale blizzard soon developed.

Snow blew so thickly we could scarcely see the road as we returned to the calving shed. The shed felt cold and damp and wind-driven snow whipped through a broken window. So, in that terrible storm, we carried all the sleeping bags to the pickup and transported all to the house. Huge flakes of snow, borne on the wind, hurled toward us as we flung our gear into the back of the pickup. After all the bedding was safely in the house, I built a fire in the stove and everyone was warm and out of the weather. What an experience.

Taking a flashlight, I peeked in on Bryan and Eric, who were snug, warm and nearly asleep in the sheepherder wagon; in the house, meanwhile, it was wall-to-wall children, sleeping bags spread out on the living room floor as well as downstairs. Wet tennis shoes, straw, mud, coats and camping gear strewn everywhere. My two grandsons, Chad and Rowdy, were having a great time, as were all of them. I made a huge pot of hot chocolate for everyone, which helped warm us up.

They were a great bunch of kids, even if they did talk until nearly 1:30 in the morning. The storm continued and I awoke at 3 a.m. to check on everyone. Found all of them sawing logs. The snow by this time had ceased, but it had turned very cold.

April 11—Doug called at 6 from Montana. He and Max had visited the seed potato outfit and even attended a Montana State college rodeo while in Bozeman, the same rodeo Doug rode in when he was a member of the college rodeo team way back when. They would head back to Wallowa County this morning.

The sound of snoozing children filled my house. Sleeping innocence. One by one they crawled out of their sleeping bags and came to life. I built a fire in the stove, went out to chore and came back in to find the 4-H'ers fixing their breakfasts on the cook stove. It was a novelty for them to cook on a wood cook stove. What an assortment of food: hotcakes, scrambled eggs, oatmeal.

The two boys in the sheepherder wagon were the last to get up. By 11, the last parent picked up their offspring. Chad and Matt went directly to Enterprise, where they worked on the 4-H radio auction already in progress. That meant I had to get busy and bake a loaf of sourdough bread, which I had donated as an item to be auctioned off. Setting the bread dough to rise, I tackled my upside-down house, which by now resembled a war zone. Beating rugs, sweeping, mopping, waxing, washing.

By afternoon I was fading fast. All day, snow showers; flakes of snow tossed about in three directions by the wind. This would be followed by snowflakes shot with sunshine. Fickle April in Wallowa County. A sort of phenomenon is taking place. The country is greening. My daffodils are blooming and the white, yellow and pink primroses are brilliant.

Finished vacuuming the downstairs, baked the bread, started a batch of sourdough biscuits…for us. Don't think my house has ever been this dirty, or this clean, in the same day. Ate my supper alone while watching the passing storms sweep across Prairie Creek. Swirling, airy white snowflakes tossed in the wind, shot with "Ross Light," that golden ethereal light born between clouds at sunset.

Doug arrived home safely around 9:30. Slept like a log.

April 12—Beautiful morning; heavy frost, with a few lingering clouds, but mostly sunny.

After chores, Grace Bartlett and I drove down toward Imnaha, turning up Big Sheep canyon. Our first stop was to leave off baking sheets for Susie Borgerding, who will bake more than 400 rolls for the Art Festival dinner. We enjoyed visiting Susie and her small son, and sipped a cup of hot tea while enjoying the canyon atmosphere. The creek splashes its merry way down past Susie's house on its way to conflue with Little Sheep.

We drove on up the greening canyon past the Courthouse Ranch. This place brought back wonderful memories of 4th of July celebrations at Howard and Carol Borgerding's. We continued through gates and drove by a herd of colorful longhorn cattle, which made a striking picture against the rugged canyon setting. Wild flowers were scattered everywhere. The blue sky, towering rims and passing white clouds held our attention.

Soon we passed the falling-down lamb and sheep shed that had been built by Wilson Wilde many years ago. At one time, thousands of sheep inhabited the canyon. Chukars flew at our approach. We drove through the Big Sheep ranch and finally arrived at the home of Mary and Steve Soderblom, after six miles of rocky, rutty, muddy road. Diapers fluttered on the clothesline, chickens scratched happily in the yard and the modest little house looked a bit lonely in that wild setting.

Mary and Steve invited us in to visit and we learned that Mary hadn't been on the "outside" in a month. Their charming little baby girl, Lindsey, was just learning to walk; a healthy, happy, pink-cheeked child. We asked about rattlesnakes and Steve informed us that he had killed 30 on the place last year! He wore a pistol on his belt for obvious reasons. Despite the lack of comforts such as electricity, the Soderbloms wouldn't trade their lifestyles for anything. They are modern-day pioneers; they left secure jobs back East and moved to this remote canyon, having purchased the 10 acres sight unseen.

When they first saw the property they knew they had come home. Hawks sailed lazily in the sky, and the rimrocks changed color under the moving clouds. I thought about Big Sheep Creek, joining Little Sheep before confluing with the Imnaha at the bridge. The Imnaha would rush on to join the Snake at Eureka Bar, which would, in turn, flow into the mighty Columbia before mingling with the salty Pacific.

Briefly we visited A.L. Duckett in his beautiful home near Imnaha. We always enjoy listening to A.L., who at one time owned a store and blacksmith shop at Imnaha. At 93, he is still going strong. Guess that's what the good life on Imnaha does for you.

April 14—Had the most marvelous afternoon. Took care of grandson James while his mom attended a meeting. Placed my little pal in his backpack and we walked forth into this beautiful day.

We visited the Alder Slope puppies, goats, horses, cows and new calves. Every once in a while, I would bend down so James could touch the animals, at which he squealed with delight.

Moving colors on the mountainsides created a display of lights and darks as pretty clouds swept by overhead. Above us, the brilliant snow-covered peaks played hide and seek with the moving clouds. As we walked down the country road, we could see Enterprise below, look eastward to the snowy-blue Seven Devils range in Idaho, or look just above us to the protecting influence of Ruby Peak. Everything was in the process of turning into spring green.

Later, after arriving home on Prairie Creek, I called grandson Buck and granddaughter Mona Lee. I reminded them to build their Easter nests, as the Easter Bunny would be down on Sunday to leave surprises.

Sold another bunch of yearling bulls to a local rancher today. Gorgeous moon out tonight.

April 15—Beautiful day. Out to chore, all the calves and baby chicks doing just fine. Spending much of my time working on the history script.

April 16—Cloudy and warm.

Grass is growing, but we still need rain.

Had my hair cut in Enterprise today. The hairdresser, Phylis, whose maiden name was Hafer, was reared out on Eden Bench. I always enjoy

Members of 1987 Chief Joseph Days court are, from left, Princess Roberta Garnett of Imnaha; Queen Tonya Pfeaster of Wallowa; and Princess Kim Rudger of Enterprise.

talking to her about her family, descendants of early homesteaders. Even though the Hafers have no electricity, no phone or other so-called modern conveniences, they are living the life they enjoy in the place they want to live. To me this is success. In a world so complex as the one we live in today, success should, after all, be reduced to these two things.

The Hafers and others like them have lived in harmony with Wallowa County's seasons, and continued the pioneeer spirit begun by their grandparents. Eden lies far out in the northwestern part of Wallowa County. The first settlers must have thought it was the Garden of Eden when they named the spot: to get to Eden, one must first travel to Troy.

Met tonight at the Bookloft in Enterprise, where our history group reviewed the slide tape program as completed thus far. When finished, this project will represent many hours of work and research.

April 17—We are having the Grain Growers co-op apply fertilizer to our fields today. The new green leaves beginning to appear on the willows by the creek are a sight for sore eyes. Our cows are nearly through calving. Just a few late ones left to go.

Received a letter from Rose Harris in Waitsburg, Washington, wanting to knew if I would, for sure, attend the Region V meeting for National CattleWomen in Pasco on May 2. I assured her I would be there for the Saturday night banquet, even if I had to crawl. That is, if there was anything left of me after the Art Festival dinner and moving cattle to the hills.

After supper tonight, I noticed an odd-looking black cloud racing toward us. The power lines began to sway to and fro due to high cyclonic winds that accompanied the cloud. It began to rain and the cloud quickly moved on toward the area known as the Divide. At bedtime, the wind continued to howl. It rained on and off all night.

April 18—Very cold. Still windy and ice had formed on the chickens' water. Milked the milk cow Startch and let the calves nurse.

Today is grandson Chad's 13th birthday. For his present, I will bake him a pie of his choice every month for a year. His father is especially happy about this gift. Today I made the first pie: apple.

Boiled eggs for the Imnaha grandchildren to color for Easter.

Drove to the Joseph Rodeo arena, where I photographed the 1987 Chief Joseph Days court. Daughter Jackie was helping judge the horsemanship trials. Bundled up beside me was Mona Lee, watching with great interest the proceedings. Perhaps one day this little miss will follow in her mom's footsteps and be a member of a court.

Back home in my kitchen, I baked another pie, for us, a blackberry one for Easter Sunday dinner on Little Sheep Creek. Called some of our CowBelles to bake deep dish apple pies for the Art Festival dinner.

Clouds were clinging to the sides of Chief Joseph Mountain as I drove to Joseph to attend the Chamber of Commerce coronation dinner tonight at the Community Center. A large crowd turned out for the evening, which began with a delicious meal catered by "Pam's Pastries" in Joseph: barbecued beef, beans, baked potatoes, three kinds of salad and chocolate cake. The program was emceed by Prairie Creek rancher Van Van Blaricom. A dance followed, with music by the "Hat Band."

At 9:30 the big moment had arrived, what everyone had been waiting for: the crowning of the 1987 Chief Joseph Days queen. During a very impressive ceremony, Tonja Pfeaster of Wallowa was crowned queen by former Queen Sandy Turner, a member of last year's honorary court.

Flanked by princesses Kim Rudger of Enterprise and Roberta Garnett of Imnaha, Tonja seemed a bit overwhelmed by it all. A lovely threesome.

Darlene Turner told the court, "You represent the greatest rodeo in the Northwest," and indeed they do. Darlene has worked hard to carry on the tradition begun by her late father, Harley Tucker, who was a well-known stock contractor.

Returning home I saw a spotlight's beam wavering in the calving pasture. Ben out checking the cows.

April 19—Easter Sunday dawned cold, around 15 degrees, as had been predicted. Baked a big home-grown ham, from Todd and Liza's hog, in the wood stove oven. The tulips droop under the weight of the frost, but revive later as the sun warms things up.

Loading up the ham, blackberry pie and fresh cream for making ice cream, we headed for the canyons. The sarvis berry in bloom higher up in the canyons now, as the season lengthens. New leaves on the cottonwoods; gooseberries, alder and willow flash in the sunlight along the creek. Great cloud shadows sweep across the rims.

Spring on the Imnaha is a magical time, Little Sheep Creek running pure and cold. When we arrived at Jackie's, I savored the smell of new cottonwood leaves and absorbed the peacefulness of the canyon's solitude. The grandchildren had made their Easter nests and lined them with apple blossoms. They even had a small nest made for James.

Todd and Bill cranked the ice cream while I played with the children. We had a luscious meal with the ham, Liza's fruit salad, asparagus, Jackie's sourdough, whole wheat rolls and crock-pot beans. We made short work of the blackberry pie and homemade ice cream. Best of all, grandma had her yearly fun being Easter Bunny.

It had warmed up by the time we arrived home to Prairie Creek. The baby chicks have begun to feather out. Daughter Lori called from Wyoming. She and granddaughter Lacey will arrive Wednesday for a two-week visit.

April 20—Beautiful, clear, warm morning; so dry, I had to water the tulips, daffodils, primroses, raspberries and rhubarb. Attended an Art Council meeting tonight at Cloverleaf Hall, where we completed plans for our big Art Festival. More busy times ahead.

April 21—Beautiful morning. Our potato seed arrived from Montana today. The truck driver, who had never traveled into our county before, was a little shook up over both Rattlesnake and Buford grades. He said the map showed it as a straight route from Lewiston!

From left, Fred Bornstedt, Blackie Black, Scott McClaran and Sam Loftus perform at the OK Theater during the Wallowa Valley Festival of Arts.

Picked Grace up and drove to the Alder Slope cemetery, where I did some photogrpahing for the slide presentation. Then we drove farther on up Alder Slope, where I photographed the old A.C. Smith house, which is now owned by the Juve family.

Back home, I baked a batch of cookies using a 125-year-old recipe from a California Grange centennial cookbook. Wonderful, big, fat cookies called Farm House Cookies. Made a scalloped potato and ham casserole for supper. The first tulip is blooming. Very warm and dry; we really need rain.

Doug attending a stockgrowers' meeting tonight in Enterprise.

April 22—Another clear, warm day. Milked a gallon of house milk from Startch before letting calves nurse her out. Doug turned the water on under the old house trailer today. No more packing water to chickens in the hen house. Hurrah! It's been a long winter.

Doug, Tom and Ben working yearlings at the chutes all day. Did some photojournalism for our local CowBelles, who are staging a beef education program at the three county grade schools this morning. They used a cleverly contrived "talking cow" as an effective teaching aid. By the end of each session, Amy Johnson and Betty Van, who propelled the cow, were glad to escape from under the burlap hide and breathe fresh air.

Came home and wrote up the article. Doug left for Lewiston to meet the bus when daughter Lori and granddaughter Lacey arrived. Continued working on plans for the Art Festival dinner.

Bright, red tulips are all in bloom alongside the house. Very hot and dry. Did some yard work, raking the lawn, cleaning out flower beds, and spaded the tulips, daffodils and primroses. The lawn needs mowing, and it is only April.

Doug arrived at 5 with our Wyoming family, who will spend two weeks visiting. Lacey was very glad to get out and run around. Did chores, Lacey tagging along. Answered a thousand questions by the four-year-old.

Attended the Enterprise FFA banquet tonight—A most impressive affair. The FBLA girls, prettily attired in dresses, served a great roast beef dinner. The FFA members all decked out in white shirts, ties and blue jackets. Such a great group of young Americans.

The Enterprise chapter is very fortunate to have such a dedicated advisor in Dick Boucher. Boucher had to admit this graduating class was a unique bunch of young people. They obviously were close-knit, and became a bit teary-eyed as they received their awards, saying goodbye to a special time in their young lives. Even a few parents brushed a tear or two away. These youngsters will continue to make our community proud and our world a bit better by their presence. Groups like FFA and 4-H help shape young lives and leave lasting impressions.

Was especially proud of one young man, Tony Yost, as he is a former member of my 4-H Sourdough Shutterbugs. Three of my own children participated in the Enterprise FFA chapter. Interestingly enough, all three, after college, have returned to live in Wallowa County, making their living in agriculture and related areas, including logging. Many more like them are making their own way here in Eastern Oregon, which is a continuing challenge. Am sure FFA and 4-H contributed much in preparing them for their futures.

An unusually loud clap of thunder, followed by a pouring rain, accompanied the awards program. Hope the rain amounts to something.

April 23—Awoke to the banter of four-year-old Lacey Jo. Fixed an early breakfast as Doug had to get to potato cellar to receive more potato seed. Lacey talked to me while I milked the cow, then trailed along behind while I tended to the young chicks.

Gathered up my big kettles and roaster pans in readiness for cooking beans for the big dinner. Going over lists that lay all over the house. Susie Borgerding called. She is almost through baking all those rolls. Mike Kurtz has ordered more than 100 pounds of fresh asparagus from Walla Walla. The cowboy poets are beginning to arrive.

The grass is growing and is a brilliant green color. Mowed the lawn after giving the lawn mower its usual spring cussing. It never starts after the long winter. Lori, Lacey and I visited Liza on Alder Slope this afternoon. Finished grocery shopping for the Art Festival dinner.

Another thunder and lightning storm, with very little moisture. Broiled big rib steaks for supper, a treat for Lori and Lacey. Clearing in the west.

April 24—Took Scotty with me to help load up the 200 pounds of beef and deliver it to Jim Probert's ranch, where he will pit-barbecue the meat. Back home, Scotty made 500 butterballs and Lori peeled apples while I turned out four big roaster pans of deep dish applie pies before noon. Naturally I had to bake a small one for us. Ben happened in and I gave him a warm helping fresh from the oven.

Scotty, at 65, said she needed more exercise, so walked home. Just 11 miles. She made it in two hours.

In reading Agri-Times, I see that I'm to speak at the Red Lion, Region V National CattleWomen meet, and I've nothing prepared! At 3 I attended a critique of art work at Cloverleaf Hall. My two photos made it into the juried show. We artists sat in a semi-circle around Nancy Lundberg, while she critiqued our art work. Very interesting. Art in many mediums, including watercolor, pastels, oils, pen and ink, bronze, basketry, fabric, leather, photography and pottery and sculpture filled the hail with a showcase of western art.

Home to chore, then all of us back into the artists' reception. A wonderful affair. We ate a pizza at the Pizza Emporium, so we could watch the line form across the street for the showdown at the OK Theater! Our local poets stole the show this year. Mike and Sarah did a great job of organizing the cowboy poetry gathering, as well as performing themselves.

Scott McClaran's poem that he wrote about the AUMs and grazing on public domain was one ranchers could identify with. Scott composes poetry as he rides the canyons of Imnaha. Jennifer Isley's rendition of the Swamp Creek Grange dance, and the poem about wire gates that gals must sometimes open, were also a hit with the crowd.

Imnaha cowboy Sam Loftus had the audience laughing while he recited a poem in a sing-song fashion. Val Giesler held the pages and

Cowboy poets enjoy breakfast, sponsored by the Wallowa Valley Arts Council and prepare at the Don Buhler home near Joseph.

underlined the words with his finger, then flung the finished pages over his shoulder. Sam shook so with fright, the whble stage quivered...but he done good!

Our local vet, Fred Borsted, was attired in a NEW vest and hat. He said his wife, Edna, had insisted he clean up his act. We all knew how Fred felt when he sang his song "Canyons and Trees." Then there was Owen Barton and, all the way up from Yosemite, Billy Fouts. Once again Val Geisler had everyone sitting on the edge of their seats as he recited the "Cremation of Sam McGee." Warren Glaus of Imnaha was on hand again to give the wolf howl at the appropriate time.

Blackie Black, cow boss at the big MC spread at Adel, Oregon, was back on stage, tipping his black hat and reciting poetry. A great evening and a packed house at the OK. Home under a star-studded sky to soak beans for 400.

April 25—Virtually every large kettle I own is full of cooking beans! The largest of these simmer on the Monarch. After chores, I drove up to the Buhler Ranch, where a breakfast was in progress for the cowboy poets. A gorgeous morning. Recorded the event in black and white film for the time capsule that the Centennial Committee is putting together for the 1987 year. This Art Festival is my assignment.

Rich Wandschneider was busy making hotcakes on a wood cookstove in the kitchen of the rustic log home owned by the Don Buhler family. An enormous old pine tree stood just outside the house. I learned from Allison Kurtz that this tree was known affectionately as "Pierre," named after a family pet dog by that name buried beneath the tree.

The Chandlers arrived bearing a wonderful breakfast casserole of eggs, chili and cheese. There was a long table on the wooden patio, laden with coffee cakes, fruit, ham, sourdough biscuits and sausage gravy. The smell of hot, steaming cowboy coffee mingled with the piney woods' smell. The visiting poets obviously were enjoying this breakfast, served up by members of the Wallowa Valley Arts Council amid the mountain scenery.

Jennifer Isley was there with her dog Smoky. Fred Bornstedt showed up wearing his old black hat, looking more like the Fred we were used to. He said it felt more comfortable. Bob Casey played the mandolin, much to the delight of a flock of children who gathered around him to listen. The relaxed, outdoor atmosphere was just what all the committee members needed for a little R. and R. before tonight's festivities. Home to stir the beans. Lori and Lacey gone visiting. The house smells like a beanery. Added onions and hamhocks.

At 1, Scotty arrived to help load both of our cars with beans, pies, paper plates and cooking utensils, plus all those butter balls. At Cloverleaf Hall, we unloaded and transferred the beans to the kitchen stoves, where they would continue cooking. We worked steadily all afternoon and by 5, people began to arrive.

First on the program was the "quick draw" contest, where artists, working in different media, had one hour to complete a piece. Always a popular event with the crowd. The art work later was sold at a silent auction.

Ted Juve created a piece of his wonderful pottery. Terri Barnett completed a painting of "Spot," the record bighorn sheep found recently in the Wallowa Mountains. All the while, background music provided by "The Chambermaids Plus One" created a most pleasing atmosphere.

At 6, Jim Probert arrived with the pit-barbecued beef, followed by Allison Kurtz carrying buckets of coleslaw, and her husband, Mike, lugging coolers full of pre-cooked asparagus on crushed ice. Susie Borgeding drove up from Imnaha with her 450 rolls. We set out C. Belle Probert's homemade salsa for the meat, and Allison's hollandaise sauce for the asparagus. The Imnaha Grange ladies arrived bearing deep-dish pies, as did the CowBelles.

The CowBelles and Grange ladies began dishing up the pies and setting up two lines to serve from. At 6:30 the beans were done, the rolls warmed, the coffee made and we began to feed the people. Doug cut up the meat at one table while Carol Wallace did the same at the other table. I ran thither and yon, keeping the servers supplied with food.

The crowd was fed quickly and we didn't run out of food, thank goodness. Finally, the crew ate and rested before cleaning up some of the mess. We were able to watch the show, which consisted of more cowboy poet entertainment. Later, still wearing my apron, I took more photos for the time capsule. The popular People's Choice award went to Dave Crawford for his excellent wood carving. Found out later that one of my photos had been sold. The subject had been my sheepherder wagon.

People continued to crowd the dance floor, which Doug and I left around 10, after dancing to a good western band. At home on Prairie Creek, I tended to only the most pressing things before falling into bed.

April 26—Very hot and dry. Desperately need rain. Breakfast, chores, then into Cloverleaf to finish the real cleaning. Returned home to wash up my kettles and put my catering equipment away. The unfun part of being in charge of a big meal.

Son Steve, girlfriend Jo and daughter Linda arrived from Pendleton to visit Lori and Lacey. Continued cleaning and storing; fixed lunch for everyone before collapsing for a nap.

Up and at it again, while Doug drove the "clan" up to the moraine to hunt squirrels and mushrooms. Very hot. Eighty degrees under the clothesline. Finished mowing the lawn. The grass very high and thick. Had to go slowly or the motor would quit.

Let everyone fix their own supper while I developed film. Finally finished, after everyone went to bed.

Frank McCorkle called. Said he'd be over first thing in the morning with a box of fresh-picked asparagus in return for two loaves of sourdough bread.

Stars all out, mild, windows open. Mixed sourdough and hit the hay.

April 27—Up early to fix sourdough waffles and set two loaves of bread to rise. Milked Startch, hayed cows, fed and watered chickens. Did a sinkful of dishes. Lori and Lacey out with Doug to hills to salt cattle. Nearly 80 degrees again. Frank showed up with the asparagus and traded for the hot-from-the-oven bread. Froze most of the asparagus and saved some to eat fresh.

Ben and Tom working cattle at the chutes. Baby chicks outgrowing their quarters in the calving shed. Returned coffee pots to the Chandlers in Joseph, then printed pictures in the darkroom at the Art Angle until after 4 o'clock.

Doug reported very dry conditions in the hills, with some ponds rapidly drying up. Fortunately, we have live water and springs in most of the pastures. Snow is melting at an alarming rate from the high mountain peaks. A dry wind isn't helping matters.

Went grocery shopping, folded clothes off the line, prepared supper. Lori and Lacey off to Wallowa Lake this evening. Doug to a potato meeting. Wrote until late, then out to bottle-feed an orphan calf (no bigger than a minute) born to one of our yearling heifers in the feedlot.

April 28—Up early. Didn't sleep too well, thinking about my upcoming speech at Pasco for the National CattleWomen. After chores, attended a meeting in Joseph on our slide-tape project. Session lasted through lunch.

This evening I attended the annual meeting of the Alder Slope Pipeline Association. Wouldn't miss this for the world. A yearly opportunity to visit my Alder Slope neighbors.

During the meeting, members report on such things as leaks in their pipeline, and this year we discussed the assessment fee and decided to lower it. Imagine, in an age of escalating costs, we voted to lower the fee from $4.50 per acre to $4. The meeting was adjourned and Erica Stein, secretary-treasurer, served delicious homemade cookies, tea and coffee. Little Logan Juve slept through the entire meeting, nestled in her daddy's arms.

Balmy evening, stars out, very unusual for this time of year. As I walked across the road to where my son Todd lived, I noticed in the eastern sky lightning flashes playing against a black curtain of clouds. Son Todd begins a new job tomorrow at Boise Cascade mill in Joseph.

April 29—Up to fix sausages and eggs, and milk the cows, Lacey ever at my side. I succeeded in getting the tiny calf to nurse Startch.

Doug, Lori and Lacey to hills with a load of cows and calves. Fixed supper, all the while answering a thousand questions posed by four-year-old Lacey. Doug scheduled a weed meeting here after supper, so made a gooseberry cobbler.

To bed early, as we'll trail cattle to the hills tomorrow. I promise to "catch up" on my column next time.

April 30—As April leaves, it finds us here on Prairie Creek arising at 5 a.m...Doug fixing breakfast, me choring at the barn. About half way, we encountered some rain, sleet and wind, followed by claps of thunder and flashes of lightning. We needed the moisture, so no complaining.

Herb Owens, Ben, Doug and I spent a long day in the saddle. At one point Lori showed up with Lacey who wanted to "help," so I boosted her up in the back of my saddle and away we went. She got a kick out of the "Tin Dog" that her grandpa kept throwing at the cattle to make them move faster. Along the way he had picked up an old garbage can lid, which he sailed, frisbee-fashion, through the air, whereupon it landed in the road with a marvelous clatter!

That first clatter caught my horse off guard, and yours truly had to grab leather in order to stay aboard. It was tricky, as I also had to hold onto Lacey. After some time, I didn't hear a sound from little Lacey and soon felt the nodding of her head bumping me on the the back. She was asleep. Presently, mom showed up to remove her sleeping child.

Herb and I, left at the end of the herd, ate our lunches on foot, in a rainstorm, all the while herding cattle, so they wouldn't turn back on us. Ben was in the lead. Doug and Lori and Lacey had gone to town.

At 5 p.m., we turned the cattle into the holding pasture at East Crow, Doug having returned to drive us home. A flat of bedding plants waited for me on the porch. A Mother's Day gift from daughter Jackie and family.

To bed at 8 p.m. as to be up by 5, to finish trailing the cattle to summer pastures.

May 1—I did the chores while Doug fixed lunches and breakfast. Ben and Herb left in one pickup, while Doug and I followed in another. Out on East Crow, we caught and saddled our horses.

It was a cold, misty morning, with an icy wind blowing as we headed the cattle out the Crow Creek road. The freezing wind continued. Even clad in down clothing and leather chaps, it was hard to keep warm. Arriving at last to the Dorrance corrals, we sorted out a stray calf that had joined us along the way, and left him in a corral.

As we wound up Dorrance grade, the sun came out and it warmed up some. Lori appeared again with Lacey, who was soon riding double with grandma. She is a real dyed-in-the-wool cowgirl.

Everywhere were birdsong, yellow blooming balsam root and fresh green grass. The ground is dry for the first of May, however, and we noticed that Dry Salmon creek, normally "wet" this time of year, was not even running.

We reached the Johnson corrals by 12:30 and ate lunch. By 2, we had the cattle turned into Deadman. Then Herb and I rode to Wet Salmon, where we unsaddled after moving some dries across the road, then loaded up the horses and headed home to the valley. We drove through a terrific hail storm on the Crow Creek road, the tires of the pickup crunching through the hailstones.

It rained the rest of the day. After doing chores, Doug treated all of us to dinner at Tony's Corner Cafe in Joseph. Then, a hot tub bath and blissful sleep.

May 2—Up early to chore, fix breakfast, pack my suitcase and head for Pasco where I was scheduled to appear at the Region V National Cattlewoman's meeting. Lori and Lacy rode with me as far as Waitsburg, Washington, where they would stay and visit relatives.

May 3—Slept till 7, heaven...what luxury!

Janet whipped up a great breakfast and we read the Tri-City Herald. Sure enough, there was the article, just like the young reporter had promised.

It was fun being with Janet. We visited and dawdled over breakfast, and I didn't have to go out to the barn to chore. Janet put a video-taped VCR cassette in the TV and we watched the taped-together old movies taken years ago of the Tippett family. We were transported back in time to when 4-year-old steers were being driven to the railhead in Enterprise, and when hay was being stacked, using a swing-pole derrick, powered by mules and horses.

Once in awhile a tow-headed boy would appear in branding or riding scenes...my husband. For over an hour, we watched the old movies showing ranch activities at Dug Bar, Cold Springs and Rogersburg. That era that has already gone, but the essence has been captured in these wonderful old films, mostly taken by Doug's mother, Jesse.

All too soon it was time to go. Janet guided me to the freeway and I was soon one with the stream of Sunday morning traffic, flowing along, until finally, I turned off at the Burbank cutoff.

When you consider that there is not one single stoplight in all of Wallowa County, and definitely no freeways, we locals have a hard time adjusting to traffic.

After picking up Lori and Lacey, we headed home over the Blues. My calves at the barn were moving slower than normal and appeared a bit sore...they had been branded and castrated in my absence! Doug had also cleaned out the chicken house and, after supper all of us, Lacey included, he moved the chicks to their roomier quarters. All too soon they will be ready to butcher.

May 4—Up at 5:30. Doug fixed breakfast while I milked the cow. We had the horses saddled and were on our way over the hill by 7 to move some yearlings to another pasture, Mike McFetridge helping us on this beautiful clear morning as we drove the cattle onto the Imnaha highway, before turning onto Tucker-Down road.

From there, we took them up the road a mile or so, then toward Kinney Lake. We turned the cattle into their summer pasture near a small creek and rode back to a waiting truck to load the horses. Lori and Lacey, asleep when we left, had appeared again to let Lacey ride behind grandma.

Am tired today from such a busy weekend. More potato seed arrived from Montana, so Doug ate a hurried lunch before leaving for our cellars. Purchased my bedding plants today. When will I have time to plant them? Doug's son Steve has decided to come back to Wallowa County and work on the ranch this summer. By some miracle, I typed my column and got it ready to mail.

May 5—Seventy-two degrees at 10 o'clock this morning! Doug and Ben moving more yearlings to the Marks pasture. Slowly but surely, we're getting all the cattle turned out on grass. Cleaned house, then planted six tomato plants on the south side of the house.

May 6—Worked all day cooking a nice birthday dinner for daughter Lori's 27th birthday. There will be 13 people here tonight! Made a "from scratch" orange chiffon cake and an apple pie. Am irrigating the raspberries and rhubarb, as everything is so dry. It was around 80 degrees today. Huge clouds form every afternoon, but produce no rain.

Our neighbors, the Lockes, have had their wheel line going all week. The dandelions are out in full force. Baked two loaves of sourdough bread. Phoned daughter Ramona in Chilcoot, California, this morning, as hadn't heard from her in a while. A busy time of year for them, too.

Doug and crew hot and tired, working cattle at the chutes all day. The old, gnarled apple tree is in full bloom, with bees buzzing around the blossoms in the sunshine. Fixed an early dinner for son Todd, who stopped by on his way to the mill, where he works the night shift. Friends and family arrived, and we ate out on the picnic table in the yard on this perfect May evening. We so enjoyed the barbecued steaks, sourdough bread, asparagus and salads that daughters-in-law Liza and Annie made.

Along with her salad, Doris brought fresh morel mushrooms, which she sauteed in butter. Afterward, we lit the candles on the birthday cake and sang "Happy Birthday" to Lori. Lacey blew out the candles. Birthdays are important occasions around our house. It is a time when we can make a family member feel special and loved. Left windows open in bedroom tonight. The warm air was bright with moonlight.

May 7—Lori and Lacey left this morning. Doug drove them to Lewiston, where they caught a bus to Wyoming. Quiet around here now with just the two of us. Typed all day, catching up.

Ben and Tom setting out our irrigation pipes. Hot, with dry wind blowing. Began irrigating our lawn. The wind sends down showers of white apple blossoms. They drift onto the lawn and swirl around my newly-planted tomato plants. It was so pleasant in the yard on these long evenings, I was able to plant the lobelia in my old, blue granite-ware, as well as the geraniums.

Hearing a flutter of wings, I looked up to see Chester roosting in the apple tree. Guess he preferred the apple blossom bedroom to the crowded roost in the hen house. As the snow continues to melt on the mountain near the head of McCully Creek, "Tucker's Mare" begins to take shape. With a little imagination, one can see a horse's outline in the snow. The "mare" is emerging earlier than normal this year. It is 80 degrees on our porch at 6 p.m.

May 8—Up early to fix breakfast for Doug, who is now changing pipes every morning, and finish my chores. We saddled our horses before driving the fall calves into the corral, sorting heifers from bulls and one water belly steer. While Ben and Tom trucked some calves to the Strickler place, Doug and I drove the rest of them about five miles up the road to a pasture south of the Imnaha highway. It was hot and muggy as we turned out the yearlings and rode the long way back to the ranch.

Showered and into Enterprise to meet granddaughter Chelsie at school by noon; took her to lunch at the "Country Place on Pete's Pond." A belated birthday present. As Chelsie and I ate, we could look out across the pond to the mountains and watch the thunderheads build or be amused by ducks, geese and swans upon the water. Chelsie got a kick out of feeding the huge trout that rise and leap in the air to receive their trout chow pellets.

Leaving Chelsie off on Alder Slope, I continued on around to visit Liza and James. New babies; Liza's cow Jenny had a new little calf, and the milk goat had a kid. Back home, I put a stewing hen in the pressure cooker and noticed a thunderstorm approaching. Hope we receive an appreciable amount of moisture.

Fixed chicken, dumplings and gravy for supper, after which I planted some petunias, strawflowers, forget-me-nots and more lobelia. A little rain fell, and it began to clear in the western sky after a brilliant sunset.

May 9—Up early to chore and make a lunch before Grace Bartlett and I departed for Horse Creek on the lower Imnaha. The canyon country had received quite a little moisture, but it was now quite warm. Near the mouth of Horse Creek, across the river in a big meadow, the branding was in full swing. While 400 head of Duke Phillips' cows and calves milled around, nearly 20 cowboys and cowgirls roped and dragged calves to a waiting crew at the branding fire, where they were castrated, branded, vaccinated, dehorned and ear-tagged.

What a colorful sight it was in that wild canyon setting, and what a gathering of Wallowa County cowboys and gals: Sam Loftus, Bill Matthews, Dave and Warren Glaus, Jim Steen, Roger Nedrow, Dave Yost, Jim Probert, Duke Phillips, Mona Glaus and even Bud Zollman.

The cattle had been trailed from Dug Bar the day before. Grandson Buck had "helped." Granddaughter Mona and her little friends were riding horses in the meadow. Cow dogs ran around or sat in pickups. Camera enthusiasts everywhere to record the action, me included. The last calf was branded by noon, and the cattle made a pretty picture as they were turned loose to drink at the river's edge.

We drove across the bridge to the ranch house and ate our lunches under the shade of some old locust trees in the yard. Many owners have occupied this house, among them Kid and Mary Marks. Soon cowboys arrived and headed for the river to wash off the dust. We left the crew to enjoy their potluck and drove back out on top, stopping briefly to visit the Wallers, who treated us to a glass of ice-cold lemonade. It was very enjoyable sitting on their wooden deck that overlooks the river. The sweet fragrance of locust blossoms filled the air and dramatic thunderheads were building up over the rims.

May 9—Evening found me sitting in the stands at the Harley Tucker Memorial arena, watching the Joseph Junior Rodeo. Like last year, I had grandchildren competing in events that ranged from pee wee goat tying to steer riding.

Am continually impressed with the volunteers who work so long and hard to put on this show. People like Char Williams, Peggy Brennan, Dave Yost, J.D. Nobles, John Bailey and the Dawson brothers, to name a few. These people keep the show going. A long rodeo, which lasted till 10:30.

May 10—Happy Mother's Day to all mothers. Spent most of the day watching the second go-round of the junior rodeo. My Mother's Day gifts included watching grandsons Chad and Rowdy and granddaughter Chelsie compete in many events. Chad won the belt tuckle in the cowhide race and Rowdy won two: for pee-wee roping and goat tying.

While at the rodeo, Doug and I enjoyed visiting our friend Jess Earl, who is 84. Jess has spent 34 years on Imnaha and was an early-day packer for the Forest Service.

Tonight, Doug and I drove to Russell's at the lake, where we ate hamburgers and watched a big moon appear above Mt. Howard.

May 11—Another clear, flawless, warm day, in a succession of them. Seems more like July than May. Began working the fields in preparation for planting seed potatoes. Irrigation in our hayfields and permanent pasture is in full swing. Calves in the hills need to be worked and it is time to trail the fall calving cows to the moraine pastures. All at once, everything needs to be done, now!

Another bull buyer here today. He purchased seven bulls.

So warm, we left the windows open all night.

May 12—Thunderstorms in the mountains and some rain here, thank goodness. Son Ken and wife, Annie, and children left me a flat of petunias for Mother's Day.

May 13—In addition to the men, Ben's sons, Zack and Seth, are changing pipes now. Cressie Green and Grace Bartlett came by this morning, and we began organizing slides to go with the slide-tape program.

Much cooler and cloudy, with periods of sunshine. Grass is growing at a furious rate. A gorgeous moon, of a deep golden color, appeared around 9:30 over Sheep Creek hill.

May 14—A perfect May morning. A few clouds swim in a blue sky. Meadow larks, sparrows and a pair of quail all being very vocal around the ranch this morning. My "Early Girl" tomato plants are beginning to bloom. The men are either in the potato field or changing irrigation water. An occasional hawk screams in the willow trees by the creek. My milk cow's udders are so full of milk, what with all this good grass, and the calves show it. They are "blooming." How I love these May mornings, when the scent of new grass mingled with clover blossom drifts over Prairie Creek, borne on warm zephyrs.

Made a large potato salad to take to the North End today. Our CowBelles will have a potluck, before the meeting, at the home of Joe and Patti Beach, who live a distance out on Paradise Ridge. We CowBelles carpooled from Cloverleaf Hall out the north highway, where we stopped to pick up Marian Birkmaier at Snow Hollow hill.

We drove by the Joseph Canyon viewpoint, then turned right and headed out on Paradise Ridge. We passed the old Paradise one-room school house and finally arrived at the Beaches'. I could see why the early settlers named this Paradise. What a beautiful spot, especially this time of year.

The Beach ranch, which sprawls along the ridge, is visible from Rattlesnake Grade when one is traveling from Lewiston south toward the Grande Ronde River. Perched on the edge of the ridge, the red barn and white corrals make a pleasing picture. From their yard, adorned with fruit trees, berry patches and a newly planted garden, one can look out over the breaks of the Grande Ronde. Views that are splendid in all directions greet the eyes.

Patti's yard, immaculate and full of blooming plants, mirrored her love of gardening. Already cherries, apples, pears and other fruits hung thickly from the branches. At the edge of some nearby woods wild roses bloomed and in the wide open fields on the ridge the grain fields waved in the breeze. This is a vast, dryland farming area, where many acres of grain are raised and cattle graze the benches.

We enjoyed such an array of salads that accompanied tasty meatballs prepared by the North End gals. Due to the absence of the secretary and treasurer, I filled in. When the meeting adjourned, I slipped outside to photograph the sights.

Coming home, we saw the large bands of sheep grazing the meadows along the north highway. A colorful sight: the herder, his dogs and the sheepherder's wagon. A herder's life has always fascinated me. Nomadic and free. Always had it in mind that if I had been born a boy, that would have been my occupation, in addition to writing.

I was out of film and frustrated, because the herder's dog was astride the horse, perched in back of his master, surveying the sheep. Doug, Ben, Herb and Tom sorted cattle in the hills this afternoon, for tomorrow is branding day. One of our Simmental cows died last night, leaving another calf, a two-month-old heifer, to put on Startch.

May 15—The big heifer calf wouldn't nurse. I milked some of Startch's milk into my hand, pushed the calf into a corner and put the milk in her mouth, then disappeared. Peeking through a knothole I saw the calf go right to nursing the cow. She was hungry.

We headed for the hills when the irrigating was done. The land is so dry. Some ponds have no water and others are very low and muddy. There were no late snowbanks to feed and fill these normally full watering places. It is reported some ranches are already hauling stock water. Our range looks good, but shows the effects of the prolonged dry spell.

We rode out in the pasture west of the corrals and gathered in the cows and calves, the same ones we'd driven out a few weeks ago. All day I worked the chute gate and got ear tags ready to apply. It was late when the last calf went through the chutes; then, all the cows had to be sprayed for flies, lice and ticks. The bawling gradually subsided after the calves were turned out with the cows.

Drove home tired, dusty, hungry and with chores awaiting. Doug, Ben and Tom changing irrigation water and pipes. Lovely sunset this evening. Fixed supper and crashed.

May 16—After chores and breakfast, we all headed to the hills again to finish working more spring calves. Along the Crow Creek road, we passed son Ken and grandsons Chad and Rowdy, moving their cattle to summer range. Another long day on Salmon Creek, after which I drove to Alder Slope to tend to Liza's chores, as she and Todd are out of town.

Milked Jenny, the Jersey cow, as well as the goat. The goat milking turned into a fiasco, with the goat on top of me and milk all over the place. But I got the job done. Washed out the syringes, warmed up leftovers for supper and did my chores at the barn.

Doug in from irrigating around 8:30.

May 17—Driving over to do the Alder Slope chores, I picked up Scotty along the way. She was race-walking. Things went easier this morning as I had Scotty hold the goat.

May 19—Looking outside this morning, I see the fence, where the sprinkler hits it, encased in ice! It is 22 degrees! Luckily I had covered my plants last night. Mike McFetridge and Ben are beginning a three-day drive that will take the fall calving cows to the high moraine pastures. Tom is changing irrigation pipes on our rented pasture at the Marks place. The remainder of the crew is cutting seed at the potato cellar. Meanwhile, Grace, Cressie and I worked more on the slides that will accompany our program for the centennial project. Later, we met with Dave Nelson, who will do the narrating of the script. The first of the seed potatoes, our nuclear seed, is now in the ground. Received a fan letter from Ben Flathers of Prescott, Washington, who had recognized old acquaintances in my column. Nice hearing from him.

May 20—Frost again, but warmer. The cold makes the land appear even drier. Our cows arrived here on Prairie Creek this afternoon. Cowboys Ben and Mike herded them into a corral. Finished the first irrigating of the fields today. My fryers and pullets are consuming vast amounts of feed.

Cheryl Cox of Imnaha made this tepee using a treadle sewing machine. It was used to show children how the Indians used to live on the Imnaha.

Visited Mr. and Mrs. Audas Bechtel this morning. A lovely couple. Audus, at 82, still gets out and does the irrigating on their ranch. He remembers when he worked as a lad on the building of the Minam Grade road. He also worked as a logger when the Splash Dam was in operation above Red's Horse Ranch on the Minam River. Audas' job was to help float the logs down the river as they made their way to the mill in Wallowa. A crew at the Splash Dam was out in the middle of the night with kerosene lanterns to release water that then races the logs toward their destination.

Audas' wife is a granddaughter of Wallowa County pioneer Henry Schaeffer, who came into the Wallowa when it was a virgin valley. He was single when he came to the area on November 4, 1871. After his first night, spent near Wallowa Lake, he awoke to four inches of snow on his bed and opted to spend the winter in Union County. He returned the next spring with several families, and established a claim on the Wallowa River bottom near the Powers family.

Henry married the eldest Powers daughter, thus becoming the first recorded marriage in Wallowa. Audes, who was born on Cricket Flat, remembers seeing the Lower Valley covered with large haystacks, which were put up with horse-powered derricks.

"It was quite a sight," he said as he showed me some early photos of those days.

Home to fix lunch for the crew. Herb Owens is on the tractor, working up another field to plant seed potatoes in.

May 21—Up early. Did a wash after breakfast and chores. Saddled our horses and rode off over the hill to begin trailing our cows to the moraine. Before starting the climb to the high pastures, we split the herd two ways. On top, Doug and I split our herd again, thus putting cattle in three pastures.

This evening, I attended the Imnaha "End of School" program. Using contributions from local pioneer families, the school children had put together a museum, an impressive exhibit that included Indian artifacts, guns, old family histories and photos, saddles, cooking utensils, rocking chairs, old glassware, portraits of the area's first settlers, old letters, and even a blueprint of the Eugene Pallette ranch.

It seemed as though the entire population of Imnaha, up and down-river, had turned out for the occasion, which began with a homemade chili dinner served outside on picnic tables.

While rimrocks formed a backdrop for the Bridge School, the peaceful scene was punctuated by the river flowing past and the neighborly chatter of young and old. Chairs had been placed outside, so the audience could view a program put on by grades one through eight of the one-room school. Due in no small part to the efforts of "school marm" Char Williams, a most successful centennial-theme play was presented. A skit featuring the Bronson twins, who played the role of Lewis and Clark, complete with Sacajawea holding an authentic cradle board and doll, started things off.

A handmade tepee, constructed by local resident Cheryl Cox, stood as the only prop. The stage was the Imnaha Canyon setting. Grandson Buck played the part of Chief Joseph's brother Ollokot, and his friend Luke played the great chief.

A.L. Duckett, 92, recited a poem about how his "get-up-and-go, got-up-and-went." Good to see Howard and Carol Borgerding again, visiting from Minnesota. Everyone joined the school children in the pledge of allegiance and the singing of "God Bless America." Overhead, a faded flag waved in the warm evening breeze.

To the tune of "Old Man River," a young woman sang a song composed by Marsha Oman entitled "Old Imnaha River." This was followed by the awarding of an eighth grade diploma to the graduating class—of one: Nicole Jones.

On the way home, I marveled at this great bit of Americana that I had just witnessed. Secluded from the rest of the world, I felt that perhaps this community has a message to share, a message being lived by this close-knit settlement about making our world a better place in which to live.

Driving out "On Top," my car radio gradually changed from static humming to music as I left the canyon behind. The Imnaha, cut off from radio and TV (except for satellite dish), didn't really need news from the "outside." This canyon community created much better news of its own. It was dark when I reached Prairie Creek and found Startch bawling at the barn door.

May 22—The three calves on Startch doing nicely. Separated and transplanted my strawberry bed today. Fifteen acres of seed potatoes planted. Took my Sourdough Shutterbugs on a hike up on the moraine. Beautiful clouds floated in the sky; light and shadows swept across the face of Chief Joseph Mountain. Our cattle made a pretty picture grazing their Switzerland-like pastures.

Far below us the turquoise waters of Wallowa Lake were filled with Memorial Day weekenders out in all kinds of boats, either kokanee fishing or sightseeing. Taking pictures, the children and I walked the high, ancient Indian trail, savoring the wildflower-scented air and marveling at the views in all directions. We were treated to the sight of mountain bluebirds flying to and fro with food to feed their young in birdhouses nailed to the old fence posts. After eating our lunches, we walked down a draw into a second moraine that formed a natural bowl.

Old weathered bucking chutes, gray and falling down, made good subjects. This was the site of a rodeo held in 1946 to celebrate the building of the Joseph airport. It was to be the forerunner of the now famous Chief Joseph Days rodeo. We could envision the spectators sitting on the hillsides to view the performance.

Back on top, we viewed the Seven Devils Range in Idaho, and looked out over the checkerboard green and brown farmlands of Prairie Creek. Out north, the rolling hills stretched before us, melting into more pale blue mountains. Chief Joseph's homeland. A land that creates, in all who enter, a feeling of having come home. The hillside was splashed with the golden color of the balsamroot. It seemed as though, in this moment, we owned the world.

May 24—Hin-mah-too-yah-lat-kekht, which means "Thunder-Rolling-In-The Mountains," is the Nez Perce name given to young Chief Joseph. A big black cloud hovered over Crow Creek and Chief Joseph spoke to all of us as the thunder rolled away off across the valley and into the hills.

Doug was curious if the cloud had dumped any rain on our rangeland, so we took a tour and found the thirsty hills drinking up the effects of a real gully washer. Hoorah!

May 25—It rained on this Memorial Day, a blessing for us farmers and ranchers. We enjoyed having dinner with Aunt Amey and Berniece at the lake cabin this evening. Flowing right beneath the living-room window, the rain-loosened snow-melt came tumbling down out of the mountains above, and rushed down toward the lake.

May 26—Rained on and off all day.

May 27—Worked with Grace on the slides all morning; today was her 76th birthday.

After lunch I put a kettle of water on to heat and soon had the heads lopped off six fryers. When I finished, they weighed, collectively, 25 pounds, dressed. Not bad for seven-week-old fryers.

Began planting the garden: onions, peas, pod peas, swiss chard and radishes.

Wallowa Lake, a spot well-known for its excellent kokanee fishing, also provides irrigation water for Wallowa Valley farmers.

May 28—Star is beginning to make up to calves. By 9:30, six more fryers in the freezer. Frank McCorkle appeared on my doorstep with a 10-pound bag of fresh asparagus.

Had my first experience today in operating a word processor. I am using the one at the Joseph Public Library. I will enter the script onto a disk. Actually, I managed quite well, thanks to the patience of instructor Bob Jackson. Couldn't believe my eyes when the thing spit out my typed words. It is, however, beyond my limited range of comprehension to understand what happens inside these complicated machines. Anyway, I had great fun with the McIntosh mouse.

Don't think I'll rush out and buy one, however.

May 29—As May rapidly comes to a close, the pace quickens. Take today, for instance. Made sourdough waffles for breakfast, milked cow, did three loads of wash, set two loaves of sourdough bread to rise, and tended to the chickens. Scotty soon arrived and together we butchered and dressed 12-fryers by 10 o'clock.

Doug needed help at the cellar, so we headed in there to cut seed potatoes until noon. Doug treated us to lunch, after which I hurried to meet Grace at the museum, before going to the library to finish entering the script into the McIntosh. Finished typing the 21 pages by 3:45.

Home to take clothes off the line, as it was threatening rain. Fixed supper, did chores, then drove to Enterprise library, where I listened to a presentation on the Nez Perce battle at White Bird.

Quite a full day and typical, it seems, of this time of year. One of our crews is ag bagging haylage on Alder Slope for Bob Stangel, while another is planting potatoes in one of our rented fields. Busy time for us all.

May 30—Acted as a "gopher" all morning. Ordered six tons of 16-16-16 to be picked up this afternoon at Grain Growers. Ran to town to pick up a v-belt, then to purchase chicken feed. Helped cut seed again at the cellar, non-stop, until 1 on this cold day. Worked until 9:30 tonight organizing slides for the script.

May 31—Rained hard during the night. This morning is beginning to clear a little. After chores, I put together a quick lunch and, taking my day-pack, headed to Alder Slope with Grace and Scotty for a hike. As the clouds lifted over the high country, we saw that a fresh, new snowfall had occurred during the night.

Everything rain-washed and fresh-smelling as we began our hike at Bob Jackson's Tree Farm. Clouds swirled overhead, shadows interspersed with patches of blue sky and bright sunlight. We walked up through beautiful stands of timber, glistening with new growth. We climbed to a meadow, where elk and deer grazed near an abandoned orchard. Nearby, the remains of an early-day sawmill caught our eyes.

Looking for mushrooms, we hiked higher and higher. We enjoyed the many different wildflowers, such as false Solomon's seal, and the lovely calypso, which grew in mossy, damp places. This delicate, pink beauty is of the orchid family, and known also as lady slipper. It was named for the sea nymph Calypso of Homer's Odyssey, who detained the willing Odysseus on his return from Troy. Like Calypso, the plant is beautiful and prefers secluded haunts.

In sunlight, Indian paintbrush made a splash of red-orange in contrast to the grassy green mountainside. We crossed over small, spring-fed creeks running clear and cold through moss and fern. Heavily-used elk trails led to watering places. Such a paradise for the wildlife.

Crossed an unnamed creek. Bill called it Farlow Creek, for a former owner of the property. We hiked in and out of the public lands, no fences, only boundary markers on the trees. In and out of all types of weather—sunshine warmed us, until swift-moving clouds brought down a misty, fine rain. Higher up on the mountain, it began to snow. Falling straight down, each flake quivered, melting on contact. Sunlight again, filtering through falling snow—a fairyland!

A breeze stirred the treetops and chased the clouds away, so that we could see the valley below. We were heading up and up to the headwaters of Spring Creek. Below us, dark clouds swept out across the northern plateau, or "hill" country. Wallowa Lake, with its perfect moraines, came at last into our line of vision.

Everywhere the shades of spring-green grass contrasted with plowed fields. The black loam, for which Alder Slope is famous, lay darkly against the base of the mountain. Spring in the forest; chipmunks, snowshoe rabbits, and many species of birds singing for joy. In some places there was a jungle of downed trees and huge ferns. We finally discovered morels, calf brains, cauliflower and puff ball mushrooms. We filled our bags with several kinds.

As we climbed higher, clouds obscured the sun and it turned very cold. Having eaten our lunches in a sunny clearing and picked more morels, we decided to head back to the car. It began to rain and we were a little wet when we got back home, but none the worse for wear.

Back at the ranch I baked a pan of sour cream gingerbread, and cooked a potato and steak supper. Mighty tasty after the refreshing hike. A late evening storm left a rainbow over Prairie Creek, an appropriate farewell to the magic month of May in the Wallowa Country.

June 1—Awoke to a bright, new day. June is busting out all over. The yellow roses alongside the bunkhouse are in full bloom, a good two or three weeks earlier than normal. Chicken feathers flew again today. Scotty and I put eight more birds in the freezer. Thirty-two out of 50 finished.

June 2—Bright, clear, cold, frost in the bottoms. Planted more garden, zuchinni, crookneck squashes, carrots, corn and beets. The soil is warm and friable. Made some delicious cream of asparagus soup for lunch, using the fresh asparagus. Baked sourdough bread. Our neighbor, Willie Locke, began swathing his hay today. Defrosted and cleaned out the freezer. Found some 1983 chukars and lamb chops. Fixed them for supper and found them to be just fine. What would we do without freezers?

June 3—Grandson Rowdy's birthday. His gift from grandma will be a fishing trip. Clear and warm; good growing weather. Nearly 80 degrees today. Planted more garden: three varieties of lettuce, sunflowers, sweet peas, nasturtiums and dill. We have a resident pair of quail. They especially like it near the gooseberry bushes in the garden.

June 4—My days are filled with hoeing, weeding and lawn mowing, but the place is starting to look nice. The men are still planting potatoes and ag bagging at Greg Wieck's. Began chopping heads off fryers. Got carried away and did 13. It was 5:30 p.m. when I finished.

June 5—Willie Locke raked his hay this morning and began baling this afternoon. The soft-looking round bales make a pleasing picture from my kitchen window. Eighty degrees again today.

June 6—Watched baby James while mom and dad went for a horse-back ride on the mountain this morning. He was such a good boy, and we both enjoyed ourselves. Baked a peach pie for son Ken's 34th birthday tomorrow.

Doug rented a small boat at Trouthaven this evening, and we went kokanee fishing on the lake. It was very peaceful and quiet up there, and the setting sun reflected itself in the water, pink ripples following in our wake.

When the sky darkened, a moon beam brightened and danced across the lake. Stopped in Joseph on the way home for a milkshake at Tony's.

June 7—After breakfast and chores, I joined Scotty, Stanlynn and Bill on Alder Slope for a day of hiking. We began our trek up near the old Weaver place. Shouldering our day packs on this overcast but warm morning, we began our climb at 8:30 a.m.

We crossed a spring and walked up through a meadow clearing where an old homestead once stood. A few more clouds formed overhead. Our destination: the Silver Creek country. We had to skirt private land to gain the high trail leading to the Gap. New owners recently closed an access road that has been open to the public for years.

We followed an old logging road, then turned off into a log-strewn gully and took another of Bill's famous "short-cuts." These detours off marked trails are only for the hardy and adventurous. They wind in and out among the timbered ridges and canyons of Ruby Peak. It was quiet in the forest, and we came upon some ripe wild strawberries, which we paused to eat.

Following a cluttered game trail that wound up through a maze of fallen timber, we began our ascent toward the old stock driveway. This trail was used as access to the Silver Creek Country in the old days when sheep were trailed to summer pastures. Before we reached the stock driveway, we climbed through jungle-like growth, fallen timber, broken limbs and mossy, ferny springs that flowed from under old rotten stumps. We couldn't see out of the canopy of trees, and the country all looked the same. At one point, to skirt a windfall of trees, we found ourselves climbing straight up out of a deep chute, grabbing a handhold wherever we cold.

Stopping to rest, our hearts beating furiously (good aerobics!), we made it onto a ridge and into a clearing with a spring-fed pond nearby. Soon we emerged on the upper end of the stock driveway. In the 1930s, many thousands of sheep, followed by the herder, his horse and pack animals, made their way over this very route. Old stumps remained to guide us on this old trail, but it was pretty much grown over now.

Shortly, we left the old trail and skirted the sheer talus wall near the uppermost reaches above timberline. Bill's trail. The valley below lay hazy but beautiful on this Sunday. We made our way slowly over loose scree where one misstep would send us falling. A few scraggly trees showed the effects of their hard existence. We stepped across a large rock slide into loose red dirt. Above us towered weathered spires and pinnacles carved by Wallowa County winters.

It was afternoon when, at last, we gained the trail to Murray Gap and climbed the final few feet through the Gap. Magnificent view of the valley below. To our surprise, there was hardly a snowbank left. The Silver Creek Basin, normally full of snow in early June, was green. Silver Creek, flashing and falling downward, lent a musical sound to the place. We wound our way through wildflower-strewn meadows and came to a spot high above the creek, where we ate lunch and held a meeting to decide which route we would take on our return. Because the trail up had been such a hard one, we decided to follow the old pack trail that follows Silver Creek to its confluence with the Lostine River. Little did we know how long this would take. This decision would cost us dearly in time and energy.

Looking for old blazes on the trees, we slowly made our way down the old pack trail, which appeared not to have been used since the 1930s. Elk, deer and bear signs everywhere. Unusual rock formations, created when lava flows went through rapid cooling, were visible from the trail.

The high divide across from us, Traverse Ridge, had many snow-fed waterfalls trickling down its steep chutes. Presently we entered a trembling aspen thicket and discovered carvings on the trees, left by early sheepherders. One carving had the date 1938 still legible on the scarred, old, white-barked tree. These trees told a story. We rested here and I took some pictures. We were dampened by occasional rain showers, but it was perfect hiking weather.

Startling a few elk from their beds, we broke out onto an old burn and onto a logging road. We were now on the site of the Lostine Burn, which occurred in the 1960s. Darkened tree stumps stood out in a sea of grass sprinkled with blue Alpine forget-me-nots and red Indian paint brush. A new crop of evergreens was making a comeback, and we wound in and out of these small trees that grew among downed logs in the old road. Suddenly, we turned a corner and far below we could see a large manmade lake and the valley of the Lostine. It was now 4 p.m.

Wearily, we kept on walking the rock-strewn road. It began raining again as we continued downward on the long switchback trail that lay ahead for miles. Five p.m....5:30...on we trudged, lower and lower through new stands of quaking aspen. The old burn appears to be recovering nicely and is a haven for wildlife, which abounds, including the mountain sheep. As evening descended, deer began to appear, feeding on the open hillsides. At once we approached a sheer cliff and wished we could be hawks or eagles and fly to the Lostine road, which lay so close but so far.

It was 6:30 when we did gain the main road. We had been hiking almost steadily for 10 hours! I walked on ahead to Old Pat's cabins and phoned son Todd, who came to our rescue. It continued to rain and the coolness revived us. A motorist gave us a ride until we spotted Todd, whereupon we transferred our soggy, tired selves to the back of his pickup. Grandson James waved his chubby little fist at us through the window.

Thinking I couldn't take another step, I had to walk out to the barn and chore. It was late and luckly Star hadn't calved in my absence. A long soaking tub bath and I felt good as new. Well, almost.

June 8—The warm rain has made the garden sprout. Hoed the strawberry patch so I wouldn't be stiff and sore. A rainbow grew over Prairie Creek this evening, followed by an apricot-colored sunset.

June 9—Star calved today. I had been watching her from the yard through binoculars all afternoon. When I saw her going into final labor, I walked down through the pasture and arrived just as she was giving birth to a big bull calf. The black and white Simmental-Holstein cross calf was soon up nursing. A lucky calf, born on a beautiful day to a loving mother with gobs of milk.

A gorgeous moon appeared over the hills tonight, flooding Prairie Creek with light. The corn and squash are up.

June 10—Bacon, eggs and birdsong for breakfast. All the windows in the house open to this beautiful morning. Son Ken here to borrow our motor home. The family will stay in it during the Eastern Oregon

Star's big bull calf looks at the camera, at four hours of age.

Livestock Show in Union, where Chad will show and sell his 4-H steer. His brother and sister, Chelsie, and Rowdy will stay with us.

After digging worms in the garden (almost as much fun as fishing), the children and I traipsed through the hayfield to the creek to try our luck. The fish weren't biting, but we enjoyed watching a northern flicker drumming above us in a huge, old cottonwood tree.

This evening the children helped me bring Star's calf into the barn. The old cow followed, and I milked a pail of milk from her to feed the dogs and chickens. After supper we decided to go fishing at Kinney Lake. Rowdy caught 20 toads, which appeared to outnumber the fish. They were everywhere. He hauled them up the hill to the pickup and placed them in back. When we got home I had to put everything but Rowdy in the washing machine.

Our irrigation ditch is now swarming with toads. Three of them occupy the "toad hole" by our front door. For years the grandchildren have kept toads here. They keep the insect population down and provide entertainment for the kids. The toads seem perfectly happy there and whenever the children visit they run to the toad hole to take out the toads, much to the horror of mamas, and have toad races. They become regular pets.

June 11—After breakfast and chores, I took Chelsie and Rowdy to Imnaha where they will spend the night with Aunt Jackie and cousins Mona and Buck. The wild sweetness of syringa filled the canyons with their wonderful mock orange fragrance. We saw many deer in the road as we traveled along Little Sheep Creek. The mule deer does are beginning to fawn.

Arriving at Jackie's, the children were delighted with Maggie's litter of six border collie puppies, a new kitten, and a cherry tree laden with bright red fruit. By the time I left, Chelsie and Mona had caught a trout in the creek.

Ran errands in town before meeting Doris at "The Country Place" on Pete's Pond for lunch in Enterprise. Swans, Canadian honkers and mallards, with their young trailing behind, amused us while we ate our lunch.

We then drove to Alder Slope to pick up Liza and James, then met Ilene Potter at Safeway before driving to Amy Johnson's in Wallowa to attend our monthly CowBelles meeting. The meeting was held outside in Amy's well-kept yard. For refreshments, we were served pink lemonade, freshly baked cookies and huge strawberries from Amy's garden. CowBelles are so busy this time of year. Our calendars are covered with beef promotion projects.

Grocery shopped on the way home. Doug had gone to the hills to check on the cattle. The orphan steer is nursing Star now. That makes four cows with eight calves; the grafting is accomplished for this season. The garden is all up now, and the golden light of a full moon floods Prairie Creek tonight.

June 12—Pitted cherries and made a cherry pie before Jackie arrived with the children. Had promised Chelsie I'd let her and Mona make cookies, so they made a big batch, which Rowdy and Doug began consuming. Buck is helping his dad move cattle to Camp Creek today.

Later, the children and I drove the pickup to Joseph to bring home a bookcase I'd purchased. The pickup sounded terrible, like the fan belt was about to break. We loaded the bookcase, then pulled over near the Burger Barn to have a cold drink, whereupon the rig simply went dead. Called Doris, who came to our rescue.

Later Doug and I drove back to replace the fan belt. Eighty degrees today. Made a rhubarb-strawberry pie to take on the grass tour tomorrow.

June 13—Up at 5 to chore, so as to take Rowdy and Chelsie to aunt Liza's and be at Toma's for a no-host breakfast prior to the tour. Very warm; feels like it will be a scorcher today.

Doug and I joined Jim and Jean Stubblefield at breakfast before boarding the bus at Cloverleaf Hall. Two busloads of assorted local people, including ranchers, extension people, and wildlife representatives, took off for a combination conservation, weed, grass and wildlife management tour. We were in for an adventure-filled day that would take us from the Lostine area up Parsnip Creek and into the Leap, with its picturesque old homesteads dotting every draw, to Elk Creek, Chesnimnus, Red Hill and finally Miller Ridge.

While we were viewing a hillside of leafy spurge in the Leap area, one of the ranchers' wives, who had brought her little dog along, noticed the dog taking off in hot pursuit of ground squirrels, which were abundant in the area. The dog was in heaven. It ran across a draw and up a hill. The young woman followed, all the while hollering for the dog to return. Meanwhile, all eyes were on the dog. Doug passed his hat, taking bets... on the dog. The dog continued to happily run from one fresh scent to another, oblivious to its mistress's commands. Finally the red-faced gal caught up to her pet and came carrying it up the hill. Everyone cheered.

It was very hot by the time we stopped at the Yost place on the Chesnim. Soon hamburgers were cooking on the grill and the women set out an array of salads and desserts on a long wooden table. Cold drinks were most welcome at this point.

After lunch, Mack Birkmaier suggested we take a side tour on the way back, which proved to be the beginning of an adventure for us all. Mack, a rancher in the Crow Creek area, wanted to show us a new grass seeding on the burn area at Miller Ridge. He said it was just "off the road a piece." So we turned up the Charlois Road and took the Miller Springs Road. Up and up we bumped on a steep gravel road. On top we turned right and looked off into Baker Canyon, before arriving at a high ridge. Evidence of last summer's fires were everywhere.

We drove out to the end of Miller Ridge to a helicopter log landing, where Columbia Helicopters had been conducting salvage logging operations in the burn areas. The re-seeding project had worked and lush green grass grew under scorched trees. Far below yawned the breaks of Davis, Swamp and Joseph creeks. We could look across to Starvation Ridge, where two big fires had merged. Because the road dead-ended at the landing, we turned around and headed back, where we found ourselves at a fork in the road.

Here the decision was made to take a short-cut. Thus we embarked on a safari through a forested ridge top that lay above Swamp Creek in the vicinity of Little Elk and Robert's springs. The rough, rutty road gradually narrowed to not much more than a cow trail. The yellow buses crept along at a snail's pace. Once in a while the men had to get out and hold back a tree limb so we could pass. All at once, within sight of the road we should have taken, the lead bus came to a halt. Everyone erupted from the buses to inspect this new obstacle. A rather precipitous grade lay before us, with a series of deep waterbars covering what was left of any semblance of a former road.

The immediate problem was a young tree that grew in our path. We were at a point of no return. The men scratched their heads and finally Ed Jones climbed the tree, which bent beneath his weight and split. Our extension agent took his pocket knife and, calling upon years of growing-up experience on Wallowa County's Divide, proceeded to cut off the sapling. This left a rather high protruding stump, but did remove the tree. The bus inched its way through, angling and backing up a few times, and somehow got through, with only inches to spare. The second bus proved more of a challenge because it was longer.

It is fitting in Wallowa County's centennial year that our "pioneer spirit" is still alive. We agreed that a team of horses would have been much easier than buses to travel this road. Everyone was in a good mood and had a good laugh. All aboard after the buses lurched and crawled down through the waterbars and made it to the safety of the main road.

"Forward," said Grace, and Cressie Green, reared on Elk Mountain, remembered riding these woods as a girl.

After chores and supper, Doug and I headed for Trouthaven, rented a boat and went kokanee fishing on the lake. Nice and cool there, and the fish began to bite after the sun went down. What a day!

June 15—Flash flood warnings in Eastern Oregon, reports our local radio station. Lostine received inch-size hailstones! The storm passed over and we on Prairie Creek were spared the hail.

Wouldn't you know it would rain the minute we began swathing hay?

Whiskers on the mountains and much cooler. Good weather for the transplanted strawberries.

June 16—Fire in the wood cookstove. Cloudy, cool and damp. Made a dutch oven stew. Helped Doug put a hose down a bloated steer, who then belched loudly and felt much better!

June 17—Varnished my unfinished bookcase. Transplanted petunias in some leftover space in the strawberry patch. Steam rises from the warm, wet ground, causing the garden to leap up.

Hurricane Creek trail winds through a meadow below Sacajawea Mountain, the highest peak in the Wallowas.

Doug and I invited Bud and Ruby to dine with us at Vali's Alpine Delicatessen at the lake tonight, as we celebrated our anniversary. The menu: Hungarian goulash and fried bread. Rum ice cream cake and Black Forest cake for dessert.

It simply poured down rain while we enjoyed our meal. Home to find one and one-half inches in the rain gauge.

June 18—Put the new bookcase in the living room, and it inspired me to clean house. Books, one of my favorite things, lay scattered all over. For once they would have a home. As I lovingly dusted each book and put it away, I remembered the wonderful words that lay between their pages and the hours of enjoyment these "friends" would continue to bring me. Wallowa County winters are good for the mind, if you have a good library.

Cooked supper on the wood cookstove, as the electricity was out this evening.

June 19—More housework, tackling Steve's old room, cleaning out closets and drawers; now have room for my office. After chores and supper tonight, Doug and I drove to Imnaha and picked cherries at daughter Jackie's.

June 20—Gorgeous morning, bright with sunshine. After breakfast and chores, I donned my L.L.Bean hiking boots and left in the pickup for the Hurricane Creek trailhead, where I was joined by other members of a group whose gear would be packed in by Stanlynn and her Hurricane Creek llamas to a site about six miles up the trail. I helped hold the llamas while they were packed.

The pack train took off to set up camp, while we followed along, slowly, taking photography lessons from our instructor, Jack Teece. This photography workshop, referred to as the "Wilderness Exposure," had been organized by local photographers for the purpose of taking pictures in a wilderness setting.

The only problem for me was that I kept seeing subjects to photograph and was not paying much attention to the instructor, whose familiarity with the camera was much more than mine. I was at home outdoors, however, and when just the right light fell on a cluster of red Indian paintbrush or a colorful burl on a tree, a distant waterfall, or shadows on the mountains, I was off taking shots. Am afraid I was a poor student. A pity, as I could have benefited from the lessons.

We made our leisurely way up the trail, which was refreshingly damp and cool due to recent rains. Dew-sprinkled trembling aspen leaves glittered in the sunlight. Wild columbine nodded alongside the trail. Penstemon crawled out of the rocky places.

Presently we arrived on the site of the great 1986 snow avalanche. A path had been cleared through the downed trees. Below us, the blue-green waters of Hurricane Creek meandered through sand and gravel bars. Above, we could hear the distant roar of falls that flung themselves downward from Deadman Creek.

Great clouds began to form, sending their shadows racing across the Hurricane Divide. At this point we decided to hike up through alder and willow to where Deadman Falls spills down over a series of rock terraces. It was around noon, a poor time to photograph, but we did anyway, before selecting a high, grassy hillside, sprinkled with wildflowers, on which to eat our lunches.

From our vantage point, we gazed at the beautiful face of Sacajawea Mountain, the highest peak in the Wallowa chain, a mountain whose bold beauty has been capturing my heart for years. We enjoyed the sound of the falls and the sight of the Hural Divide across from us. The last of the snowbanks glistened white against talus slopes. After lunch, we gathered up our tripods and day packs, and headed back down to join the main trail. The class would spend the night in the Eagle Cap Wilderness, but I was to return, and made haste to arrive in camp earlier than the class, so as to rest up before the return.

Hiking alone now, enjoying the peace and quiet and photographing (without lessons), I made my way to Slick Rock and took a shortcut trail that followed the deep gorge high above the falling water. Below me a wall of tumbling, rushing, white water roared through a solid rock cleft. Seeing this example of nature's inexhaustible vigor gives me strength and sets my soul free.

A huge grove of quivering aspen shimmered in sunlight below the falls. Gray talus slopes, which contained a reddish intrusion of rock, stood guard on the opposite side of the creek. Soon the trail crosses Slick Rock Creek, where water comes sifting and spraying off sheer rock. Hence the name Slick Rock: This veil of water makes its way downward to join Hurricane Creek. As I crossed the creek and continued up the trail, I could hear the roar of Hurricane Creek as it came rushing down into the rock gorge.

I entered a deep, green woodsy area before breaking out into a series of meadows. Some of these meadows gave off a sweet scent in the warm afternoon. The yellow bloom of the sage-like cinquefoil was very pleasant. I enjoyed the solitary walk, and I tracked the llamas as they crossed soft sandy places. At one point I lost the trail, but walking off the trail downstream of a small stream, I found where they had crossed. Quite suddenly, I came out upon a green meadow where the llamas were staked and grazing. It was very cloudy by this time, but a shot of sunlight illumined the Matterhorn, which loomed above camp in all its primeval beauty. Alpine forget-me-nots bordered the meadow and the stream wound through; occasional willows grew along the banks.

Met Stanlynn, who borrowed my tripod to mount her spotting scope so she could look for mountain goats that inhabit the high, rocky ridge above. After a brief rest and nibbling some crackers and cheese, I headed back down the trail, all the while wishing I could have spent the night, or at least enjoyed supper with the class, but I had six miles out and chores waiting at home. It had begun to rain, but was not cold or uncomfortable at this point.

Coming down the trail, I turned around for a last glimpse of Sacajawea. This beautiful mountain is named after the Shoshone Indian girl-mother who accompanied the Lewis and Clark Expedition. In the evening light I came upon two mule deer bucks, in the velvet, feeding on golden morel mushrooms.

Longfellow's poem came to mind, something like "When Daniel Boone rides by at night, the phantom deer arise, and all lost, wild America is shining in their eyes."

I hurried on past Slick Rock and arrived at the pickup by 7:45. Driving home, I remembered how my father, on frequent visits to our area, must have felt. He would disappear for all day sometimes and mother would worry about him. Most of the time he returned to Hurricane Creek, and suddenly now I knew where he had been and what he had seen. The trail must have kept calling for him to see what lay beyond the next bend. After all, that is what life is all about, taking each day like another bend in the trail.

June 21—First day of summer and Father's Day! Went to work on the cherries: baked a pie, canned 14 quarts and made a batch of preserves. Feels like the first day of fall instead of summer. Cloudy and cool, the mountains obscured by misty rain clouds. I wonder about the photography group. Bet they are a bit soggy. Our swathed hay is getting wetter and wetter. Built a fire in wood cookstove.

June 22—Beautiful morning. Great misty-veiled clouds play hide and seek with the mountains, revealing a new snowfall. All ag bagging and haying is halted by the weather. Our hired man, Tom, informed us his wife just gave birth to a 10-pound, 11-ounce boy.

Sylvanus Neal, 103, of Lostine, recently enjoyed a birthday party for centenarians in Enterprise.

June 23—Grandson James' first birthday. Finished ag bagging the haylage at Brinks today. James stole everyone's heart tonight at his birthday party, given in his home on Alder Slope. The birthday boy enjoyed the whole affair, especially his cake with blue frosting. His father, uncle and assorted cousins cranked the ice cream freezer for more than an hour and it just wouldn't get hard. Come to find out, the dasher wasn't rotating.

June 24—Ben, Doug and Steve haying again. The smell of newly mown hay drifts through the windows. The valley is so green now, because of recent moisture.

Our potatoes are up! Rode with Doug up to the moraine this evening while he salted the cattle. We glimpsed deer running through the trees, graceful and beautiful, their tawny bodies flashing color as they bounded away at our approach.

I went for a walk on top, while Doug loaded salt onto the Honda and took it down to the salt grounds. Far below, the lake shimmered in the evening light. The tall, soft green grasses moved gently, stirred by a warm breeze, while wildflowers nodded, their sweet scent filling the air. Huge pines stood stately tall, grouped as in a park.

Away to the east, the Seven Devils mountain range appeared dark blue in the distance. Freezeout Saddle etched itself against the evening sky. Bluebirds, swallows, meadowlarks, robins, all calling together in that sweet-throated sound of joy that only birds can convey. Two mule deer does walked gracefully by me, then stood in the last rays of the sinking sun, which cast a golden glow on their bodies. These, I suspected, were some of the park deer that had wandered up on the moraine for better pickings. They weren't afraid of me at all.

June 25—Supposed to get up around the 90-degree mark today. Finished hoeing the strawberry patch. Baked a cherry pie for grandson Chad's ongoing birthday present. Ran to Enterprise for baler parts.

June 26—Hot and dry. Good haying weather. Watched a re-enactment of the Great Joseph Bank Robbery this afternoon. A rope had been stretched across Main Street above the old bank building, which now houses the museum. Tourists were everywhere. Western music blared out onto the street from speakers in the museum, and soon four armed horsemen came riding up Main Street. Joseph looked, for all the world, on this hot afternoon, like it had stepped back in time.

The riders rode up to a vacant lot next to the old bank and tied their horses to a hitching rail. Meanwhile, across the street an old-timer was repairing a wagon wheel; a girl, clad in 1800s attire, strolled into the bank, followed by the saloon keeper down the street. The youngest of the four masked men, carrying a rifle and sporting a mustache and wearing chaps, spurs and an old hat, walked into the bank.

He turned around a moment later and walked out, removing his hat to scratch his head, a signal for the robbers to enter. This was followed in quick succession by screams from the girl, the robber running out the door with a bag full of money and a volley of gunshots. The girl was whisked off as a hostage, then left clinging to the wall of the bank, still screaming. The robber, Fitzhugh, escaped, leaping onto his horse and clattering at a full gallop down Main Street, past Bud's Hardware and the Chief Joseph Hotel; singing bullets followed in his wake.

Suddenly it was over. The crowd of onlookers loved it. It seems the Old West still lives in our hometown of Joseph. Yee-Haw! This drama will be played out every Wednesday, Friday and Saturday through Labor Day. It is interesting to note that Tucker, the young boy in the robbery, served his time in prison and returned to become a respected sheep rancher and later vice president of the bank he had helped rob!

On the way home I stopped to photograph Tom Butterfield's potato field. Very hot today. Thank goodness the evenings on Prairie Creek are cool. Then, how we enjoy eating outside on these long summer days.

June 27—Wallowa County's lovely June is all but gone. Up to Alder Slope to watch grandson James while his mom, dad and cousins Rowdy and Chad ride out to the hills to drive some errant bulls back in with son Ken's cows.

Son Todd had purchased a small mule by the name of Belle, who came complete with a pack saddle, halter, grain, hay and insect repellant. Today they put a small saddle on her and Rowdy rode her.

Doug putting in long hours, baling even until midnight. I could hear the echoing thump, thump of the baler from over the hill on this warm summer night.

June 28—Very warm. Hardly any dew on the hay. Began baling by 8:30 a.m.

The flies are bothering the cattle. Startch switches her tail continuously to rid herself of these pesky insects. She seemed very grateful when I sprinkled fly powder on her back this morning.

I wash the morning dishes, and from my kitchen window watch the rhythm of ranch life unfold here on Prairie Creek. Before me stretches the hayfield, with its long rows of raked hay. Before the tall grasses fell to the swather, I watched hummingbirds drink sweet nectar from the clover blossoms.

Tomorrow the loader-stacker will pick up the bales and haul them off. Soon the sprinklers will wet the field and the grasses will grow again. As fall approaches, the grasses will yellow with frost before being covered by a blanket of snow. My wintertime view will last longest of all and cattle will eat their hay, spread out in long lines on the snow-covered fields. A warm chinook will come out of the south in late February or March, and the ice and snow will melt. The dull brown grass will slowly change to green and the cycle is repeated.

I think of these things, my hands submerged in the hot, sudsy water. For this reason I am against dishwashers. It is a time to dream, plan and contemplate.

June 29—Enjoyed dinner on this Sunday evening at "The Country Place" on Pete's Pond in Enterprise. Max and Dorothy Gorsline joined us at this popular eatery and we sat out on the new-constructed deck and watched a small child feed the trout. Flocks of waterfowl entertained us as we ate. Large thunderheads built up over the mountains and put on a show for us.

We drove up on Alder Slope afterward, breathing in the sweet smell of freshly mown hay. Many colorful old barns added to the pastoral setting.

June 30—Haying continues, as does the irrigating of the potato fields. Answered the phone all morning in response to an ad we put in the paper advertising for women to rogue potatoes.

Voted in a special levy election today, before disappearing into the cool depths of the Art Angle darkroom to print some pictures. Purchased my controlled elk hunt application. Couldn't believe what it takes to fill one of these things out.

July 1—My days are spent irrigating the berries, garden, flower beds and lawns. Had an interview today with four Wallowa County youngsters: Josie Hays, 102; Odell Marr, 100; Sylvanus Neal, 103; and Hattie Fisher, 99.

Hattie taught schools in Wallowa County for 46 years. She lives alone and does her own housework. "Who needs to go to the nursing home when they don't have to?" she says. Hattie, who will be 100 soon, sleeps and eats well.

Sylvanus lives in Lostine, and Josie and Odell are residents of the nursing home. A birthday party was held in their honor today.

July 2—Cloudy and cool; large thunderheads build over the mountains. Attended a day-long class on "Introduction to Word Processing" at Enterprise High School. It was a day of intensive instruction. At the conclusion of the class, I was beginning to catch a faint glimpse of what could be accomplished with one of these modern things. Although impressed, I feel I would need to work every day using one to justify the expense of owning one. For the time being, my old-fashioned portable typewriter suffices.

Doug cultivating in the potato field until late this evening.

July 3—Sourdough hotcakes for breakfast at 6:30 a.m., so Doug could be off to cultivate again. The remainder of our crew is irrigating the hay, potato, and rented pasture fields. Milked my cow, then began writing articles for two newspapers. Hoed the entire strawberry patch before lunch. Beautiful day—white clouds float in a blue sky.

Ben raking hay in the lower field, and Tom building my chickens a new and larger pen. Doug was baling hay this evening while I weeded my vegetable garden, which is now growing at a fantastic rate. How I love my garden, treating it like my children, caring, nurturing and loving it before reaping the rewards. Weeding out the bad, training them to grow straight, strong, healthy and happy. In a garden, just like with children, one receives what one puts into it. Both are, in my opinion, worth the effort. Another plus: they keep re-seeding themselves. Grandchildren seem to sprout up all over the place. They are perennial.

As I weed and hoe, I can hear the rhythmic "thump, thump" of the baler. In the west glows the aftermath of a salmon sunset; the moon grows. I think of son Todd camping with a friend at Francis Lake. The fishing should be good.

In the western corner of the garden, the perennial patch of Sweet Williams rivals the sunset's colors. I kneel among my plants to weed, smelling the evening cool as it softly steals across the earth. A robin follows me, snatching worms I've unearthed. I reflect that when I grow too old to maintain a garden, perhaps I. will recall this time as one of my happiest. Being one with the soil, and the pulsating life I have created with my labor of love.

Doug baled on into the night.

July 4—A perfect morning for this 4th of July. Ben loading and stacking hay.

Doug and I drove to the small town of Lostine, where we found Main Street and all the side streets lined with vendors and their booths of every description. The gigantic 4th of July Lostine Flea Market was in high gear—the fleas were hopping! Antiques, collectibles plus wares of every kind were laid out on tables in the morning sunshine. Music from the "Possum Trotters" floated out over town. The smells of hamburgers, sauerkraut and hot dogs mingled with sourdough hotcakes, grange pies and popcorn. Folks had come to Lostine from the farthest corners of our vast county. It was hard to find a place to park.

Near the old Lostine school building, where the runners were assembled, a bus waited to transport the 10K runners to their starting point up the Lostine River. Because my friend Scotty, 65, was in Hawaii welcoming a new granddaughter, I was the only 50-and-over entrant in the mile run.

The gun fired and we were off. I had intended only to race walk, but felt so good that I decided to jog, and did an eight-minute mile! Wearing my new T-shirt with "Lostine River Run," I joined Doug to enjoy the flea market. For $5 I purchased an old, long-handled fry pan to use for camping. It would fit nicely on a pack mule. Doug found some bargains: an old brass hammer and a chukar call.

We wandered into a vacant lot where pioneer demonstrations were being performed under several large apple trees. Women, dressed in long calico dresses and wearing bonnets, were tatting lacy edgings. Anna Marie Swafford, one of the women, showed us her lovely work, which is almost a lost art these days. Another woman churned butter nearby, while next to her a young woman baked sourdough hotcakes on a hot griddle. The village smithy stood under the spreading apple tree, and there was Dennis Brennan, the hot coals of his forge glowing red, shaping a horseshoe on his anvil. Jim Blankenship demonstrated the art of working with rawhide and was scraping an old cowhide.

The apple trees provided shade for Luwana,the pretty Imnaha girl, making pine needle baskets, beautiful basketry woven in all shapes and designs. A homespun looking young woman, dressed in calico, her bare feet pedaling a spinning wheel, spun her carded sheep's wool into yarn. She made a pretty picture as she sat spinning at this ancient craft. A few wisps of dark hair fell from a coil atop her head and her strong bare arms and dextrous fingers fed the wool into the spinning wheel. Another girl, fashioning willow trellises, was as slender and supple as the willow she worked with. These young women are representative of Wallowa County's new pioneers. Many supplement incomes with their skills.

Near the blacksmith's anvil stood a stalwart young lad, clad in woodsman's clothes. His muscles tensed as he cut shakes from chunks of seasoned tamarack. His ancient tool sliced through the beautiful wood and one by one perfect shakes fell to the ground. Erl McLaughlin was there with an old McCormack Derring tractor he'd brought back from the grave and restored to its original dignity. Perched on an old hay wagon, the Possum Trotters fiddled and sang. Fred Bornstedt broke into a sweat while playing his guitar and singing a lively hoedown.

All up and down the street were the people, all kinds of people, who make up this northeastern corner of Oregon. Everyone being neighborly in this centennial year. Nostalgia of the past mingled with the present. Wallowa County, 100 years old and still maintaining the pioneer spirit.

Thunderheads continued to form and huge floating clouds sent their shadows sweeping over colorful Lostine. We watched the parade before returning to the ranch. I missed seeing Bill Steen and his elk horns, pack saddles, dog sleds, snowshoes, Indian artifacts, Mexican blankets and bearskin coats. Bill was killed in a car accident in California a few months ago. He always lent a colorful note to the annual affair. In his spot this year stood an old sheepherder wagon.

Fixed a chicken dinner with all the trimmings, including hand-cranked ice cream for visiting kids and grandkids who came to help us celebrate the 4th of July. After dark we had our own small fireworks display, much to the delight of oldsters and youngsters alike. After the first loud bang, our border collie pup, Stubby, fled over the nearest hill. No fireworks for him!

July 5—Rain doused the last sparkle of fireworks last night, and it is coolish this morning. By evening I wore a jacket to chore.

July 6—Thirty-eight degrees!
A 4-H meeting here tonight; we planned our float for Chief Joseph Days, and also backpack trips into the mountains.
The summer has just begun.

July 8—The ranch is a beehive of activity: irrigating, haying, cultivating. I keep food on the table, answer phone and run errands, like all ranch wives do during the course of a day. Made a batch of apricot-pineapple jam.
Herb Owens is breaking my mare to harness. She will soon be pulling an old-time buggy.

July 9—Spent the morning selecting just the right slides for our history project. Copies must be made, so we will have two sets. Attended a CowBelle meeting this evening at president Judy Wortman's charming home. It was decided to have a night meeting this month, so more of the working gals could attend. Rained a little, on everyone's hay. A big moon tries to escape the clouds tonight.

July 10—Cloudy, cool, raining off and on all day. Typed up minutes of CowBelle meeting, as had filled in for the absent secretary last night. The rain continues and the wind blows as I disappear into the darkroom downstairs at the Art Angle to print.

Home to wash clothes and put a roast in the oven for supper. Met with Grace Bartlett and Dave Nelson at our local radio station this afternoon. We listened to the taped script. Dave will make a good narrator. Hopefully, we will soon be through with this year-long project.

July 11—A gazebo, entirely constructed by volunteers of the community, will be dedicated today on the courthouse lawn in Enterprise. Another centennial project. Such a bandstand stood on the courthouse square once, during Wallowa County's early years. It was the site of many outdoor concerts, speeches and community get-togethers. Now, in our centennial year, a similar structure will be available for such functions. Except for the shakes on the roof, this very handsome edifice has finally been completed in time for the formal dedication.

Arriving at the courthouse lawn to organize a booth where my Sourdough Shutterbug 4-H members will be selling sun-tea and sourdough bread, I found the place already resembling an early 1900s scene. Old buggies and hacks were parked in the parking places instead of cars.

The morning festivities began with a parade down Main Street, which tied in with the Enterprise merchants' Crazy Daze event. Ladies and gents strolled around in early fashions of the day. Doug and I enjoyed lunch with Max and Dorothy Gorsline. We ate a sandwich on a sidewalk table outside the Cloud 9 Bakery.

Suddenly, a curious crowd of people began looking up to the sky. A bright, rainbow-colored sun-bar appeared to hover over Enterprise. Mother nature's contribution to the celebration?

Across the street from us, a team of mules and some saddle horses were tied to hitching posts near the courthouse lawn, while nearby stood large animal watering troughs. Old-time farm machinery also was on display.

Colorful booths dotted the lawn west of the gazebo—Ted Juve's pottery and Pam Royes's lovely dried flower bouquets—and there was pink lemonade and all sorts of crafts for sale. Our 4-H'ers had a silent auction going on two loaves of sourdough bread. Doug kept coming by and raising the bid, signing his name Chuck Adams!

At 1, the gazebo dedication began with speeches. Cliff and Pearl Collingsworth sang some nostalgic, lovely old songs. Everyone got goose bumps when the Wallowa County band played. Made up of local citizenry,

The Wallowa County band played in the new gazebo during its dedication at Enterprise. Shakes have been added to the roof to complete it.

Claire and Megan Casey won most original centennial dress.

Traveling all the way from upper Prairie Creek to attend Enterprise's gazebo dedication were Max and Dorothy Gorsline. Max is left holding the reins, but Dorothy wields the whip. The buggy is original and belonged to the Hass Ranch on Alder Slope many years ago. Max says this particular buggy could have been purchased through Sears and Roebuck for around $75.

under the talented direction of Bob Clegg, this band was inspired to its best performance yet.

Later, the gazebo bandstand rang with the music of the Possum Trotters and the Side Road Band, before the Alpine Twirlers performed some square dance routines. Jean Stubblefield called while the gents twirled their ladies across the floor. Recognition was given to Jim Stubblefield, Robert Stubblefield and Myrna (Stubblefield) Witherite, who are descendants of William Stubblefield, one of the founders of the city of Enterprise. Alice McCully looked the part as she was introduced and honored for being a granddaughter of another founder of the city, John Zurcher. Stubblefield and Zurcher donated lots from their homesteads to wealthy Island City merchants and thus began the city of Enterprise, which would eventually gain status as the county seat of Wallowa County.

The courthouse lawns were bright and colorful with blooming golden poppies and other flowers. The durable, locally quarried "Bowlby stone," of which the old courthouse was constructed, remains as beautiful today as when the courthouse was completed in 1909.

Rich Wandschneider related a brief history of Enterprise to the gathered crowd, assembled under a canopy, seated in chairs or sitting on the lawn. Bob Casey kept busy pulling a wagon-load of children and adults with his mule-drawn carriage. His pretty wife, Claire, and daughter Megan won the most appropriate centennial dress prize in the parade.

At 5, we CowBelles served nearly 400 people barbecued beef, calico beans, cucumbers and onions, bread, watermelon, lemonade and coffee. We served for 2-and-a-half hours non-stop. People ate at long picnic tables on the lawn while music floated out of the gazebo bandstand.

Did my chores late at the barn tonight. A great day.

July 12—Up at crack of dawn to fix breakfast, a lunch, did chores and took off for the South Fork of the Lostine. Another beautiful day. Arrived at the Lostine guard station by 8, where I met a group of people who would be clearing and marking an old trail that follows Lake Creek.

We began hiking, armed with axes, saws and pruning shears, at the trailhead near Hunter Falls. Here, Lake Creek, born in the high country near Sawtooth, splashes under a bridge to join the Lostine River. A small group of us had worked on this trail last year, and today we hoped to make further progress. Fallen lodge pole had to be cut and removed from across the trail and new growth brush pruned.

While working, we had the pleasant water sounds of Lake Creek in our ears. This water, an accumulated drainage from the last of the season's snowbanks, plus tributaries fed by springs and a stream that flows from Francis Lake, tumbles down through a series of rocky gorges. Green grass grew thickly on the hillsides and everything was fresh from the recent rain.

The warm sun released the pitchy smell of the ponderosa pines, and Indian paintbrush, delphinium, fireweed and dozens of other wildings greeted us along the trail. The dim, old trail climbed steadily upward. In some places it was very steep, while at other times it crossed boggy, spring-fed streams, all ferny and cool smelling. Brake fern, wild huckleberry, gooseberry, snow berry and mountain ash grew in profusion among the evergreens.

Groves of quaking aspen, white-barked against blue sky, as the trail wound in and out of checkered shade and sunshine. Sometimes we felt the spray of waterfall mists, where white water fell, swirling into blue-green pools, foaming and frothy, as we rolled rocks to one side of the trail or removed fallen limbs.

Noon found us on a high, cool perch amid the trees. The day was warming as we ate our lunches and relaxed before coming to the huge, fallen tree that blocked the trail. This obstacle had stopped us last year. We began marking a long detour around the tree, which was complicated by a rather long, rock-strewn gully. Up higher, near a grove of willows, we found a way across and continued marking and blazing a detour route back to the main trail.

Soon we came to a steep, rocky area and picked our way slowly upward. Following ancient blazes on the trees, we came up into the HIGH country. We breathed the rarified air, the very essence of the Wallowas. From our vantage point atop the ridge, we could look down hundreds of feet into a gorge carved over eons by Lake Creek. Through a copse of evergreens, we glimpsed a long waterfall, falling straight down the mountainside on the side of Traverse Ridge. Below, the stream flashed white in the sunlight and the roar of the waterfall could be heard from the distance. Looking southeast, we could see the sharp-pinnacled mountains that flank Francis Lake, as well as the divide that separated us from LeGore and Deadman lakes. I could envision these "jewels in the sky" as they lay hidden from view but a short distance away.

We walked farther on up the ridge and viewed the country we had just climbed. Took some photographs, but somehow photos can't capture the wildness of this place. As the crow flies, we were only a short distance from Francis Lake, but it was 5 and we opted to start back. Even so, the lure of going on was pretty tempting. Not a soul did we see, only tracks of elk and deer. Hawks spilled out of a high rim and floated lazily in air currents; butterflies, bright in sunlight, drank nectar from the wildflowers, and bluejays scolded us.

We reached the trailhead at 7 p.m. Drove home tired in body but refreshed in spirit.

July 13—Our potato roguers in the field by six this morning.

Fixed sourdough pancakes for breakfast, milked the cow, tended chickens. Eighty-six degrees today. The raspberries are ripening.

Doug baled late into the night.

July 14—HOT!

July 15—The lack of a sufficient snowpack in the mountains is being felt all over the county. There are water shortages and dried ponds everywher. A long, dry summer ahead.

July 16—Baked two batches of sourdough bread sticks and froze them for an upcoming catering job. Picked, cleaned and froze more gooseberries. Cooler today.

July 17—Dark clouds hover over the mountains, and a cool breeze blows. We hear on the news that there are bad fires in Spokane and Southern Oregon. Purchased a 25-pound baron of beef and other groceries I'll need for the dinner on Sunday at the Imnaha River Woods. At noon we CowBelles served senior citizens' dinner at Joseph Civic Center. Pouring rain as I left Joseph. The bank robbers got wet today.

Beverly Hansen from the McKenzie Valley, one of my fans, had stopped by in my absence and left two delicious-looking jars of homemade raspberry and blackberry jam. What a treat. Beverly and her family had come to Wallowa County on a vacation and were planning to re-visit the old Vance place on Chesnimnus. Beverly hadn't been there since she was a young girl. While starting a fire in the wood stove, I was startled when I lifted the stove lid and a small bird flew in my face. Apparently he had been in the stove and was getting smoked out. I opened the door and he flew outside.

Across Tenderfoot Valley road from our ranch, a pair of hawks alight on the tops of two "bread loaf" hay stacks. The rain has halted many ranch activities. Daughter Jackie safely home after a week-long pack trip to Brownie Basin in the Wallowas as a counselor for Wilderness Trails, which consists of young disadvantaged girls, who look forward to this annual experience. Her husband, Bill, leaves this week with the boys.

As wisps of misty clouds unfurled around the mountains, they revealed a new snowfall dusting the higher peaks. Attended a surprise anniversary party this evening at the Joseph Civic Center, for our neighbors, Gardener and Tappy Locke. A large crowd gathered and waited in the dark, before turning on the lights and yelling, "Surprise!"

The party, planned by the Lockes' children, was done up in grand style. Marvin Lovell had a whole hog turning on his homemade spit barbecue, which was powered by an electric motor. It was done to a mouth-watering goodness. The roast pork was served with buttered fresh corn-on-the-cob, whole wheat rolls, fruit and green salads and relishes.

Dinner music, provided by the Chamber Maids Plus One, was followed by a Mariachi-type band from San Francisco. The dance floor was soon crowded as the musicians played song after song of toe-tapping music. A woman sang, accompanied herself on the accordian, while a man, wearing a tin vest, tapped out rhythms while beating his chest with spoons. Other unusual instruments, plus a fiddle and guitar, completed this unique ensemble. It was fun watching the young people dance to the fast music.

There were balloons, flowers, and pictures on the wall of the honored couple when they were newlyweds. A large, decorated cake was cut and served during the evening's festivities. We danced until nearly 12:30.

It was clear and 40 degrees when we got back to Prairie Creek.

July 18—Clouded up and rained again during the night. Fire in wood stove. Partially clear, the air freshened by the rain. Picked up Cressie and Grace before heading out north to attend the Flora Flea Market.

It is fun to go to Flora. This small town is sometimes referred to as a ghost town, but isn't really. People live here and the community is part of an area known by Wallowa County residents as the "North End." Due to possible showers, the flea market was held in the Grange hall. While browsing through the many items, I found an old eight-cent milk bottle to add to my collection.

There were lovely handmade quilts, old books and tables of treasures (one person's junk is another's treasure). Elmo Curry was warming himself by a cozy fire burned in an old pot-bellied stove. From the kitchen wafted the smell of freshly brewed coffee and homemade pies.

After seeing all we could, we decided to take a stroll up Main Street. Many of the rustic, old buildings are abandoned and make good subjects for photos, not to mention the green, rolling hill land, dotted with timber, blue sky and pretty clouds. This scene was punctuated with the earth tones of summer fallow and the yellowing of the ripening grain fields. The North End is a great dryland farming area.

Walking up to an older house, we knocked on the door as several cats scurried into the high grass that grew nearly up to the windows. This was the home of Zelma Weatherman. I had known her husband years ago when he came into town to the Grain Growers, where I worked.

I had never met Zelma. Now 82, she lives with her cats and her numerous potted plants. Old lace curtains adorned her windows and brightly-colored geraniums bloomed profusely on the sills. Sunlight cascaded into the room through windows that framed a sweeping view of Flora's rolling hills. Exotic plants hung from the ceiling. I especially admired one, and as we left she gave me a small started one of the same variety. Zelma, her white hair contrasting with a pretty pink blouse, looked as spry as a kitten as we bade her goodbye.

Note: And now, as I type this column today, I hear that Zelma has passed away. We are so glad we stopped to pay her a visit.

We drove to the Flora Cemetery, where I took some pictures of pioneers' headstones. Wildflowers grew among the graves and the scene was one of tranquility.

A small, gray kitten, seemingly lost, was huddled beside the road. We took it with us, naming it "Flora," before discovering it was a male cat. We drove with the kitten, which had fallen asleep on Cressie's lap, to Lost Prairie, where I photographed the old school house. The same one my friend Spencer Bacon had attended as a boy. We walked around the Lost Prairie cemetery, enjoying views in every direction.

We drove by the Cannons'. This farm has been owned by the same family for 100 years. Past the Fordice place and Larry Bacon's, the road ended at Larry's dad's place, Spencer Bacon's. Another century farm owned continuously by the same family for more than 100 years. The farm house stood empty and looked lonely now, and tugged at my heart as I remembered the old gentleman who used to live there. The years pass so quickly and the Lost Prairie wind now carries much of the history written there.

Spencer and his beloved wife, Mabel, raised their children in this house where Spencer himself was born. An early death took Mabel when Spencer had many years left. And now he has joined her, and his many friends will always remember his friendly smile and fiddle-playing music. Spencer's parents were among the North End's first pioneers. Lost Prairie, a beautiful, haunting sort of land, stretches on out to the breaks of the Grand Ronde.

From Spencer's farm we could look over to Bartlett Bench, Eden, Grouse Flat and down to Troy. We were happy to see the farm being run by Spencer's son Larry. Dark, purple clouds created a moody backdrop to abandoned homesteads and old, falling-down buildings. Wild roses bloomed beside fences and acres of rolling grain land stretched before us.

Around noon we were seated in the dining room of the Rimrock Inn, enjoying the view of Joseph Canyon and eating lunch. Last summer's fire scars were now covered with a carpet of green grass. It began to pour rain as we traveled down Snow Hollow Hill.

Company here when I arrived home. After they left, I baked apple, raspberry and gooseberry deep-dish pies for the dinner tomorrow, before making more bread sticks and boiling potatoes for a salad. Fixed supper, did chores. Took the last batch of bread sticks from the oven at 8:45. Crashed.

July 19—After breakfast and chores, loaded up my car with fixin's for the catered dinner this evening. Scotty arrived and we were off for the Imnaha River Woods. We traveled by way of Salt Creek Summit, Lick Creek and down Gumboot to the Imnaha River. The drive was lovely.

Presently we arrived at the settlement known as the River Woods. After driving down and across a meadow, then over a bridge, following a road on the opposite side of the river to where a few houses were situated on adjacent lots, we arrived at Abigail Kawananakoa's place. This remote subdivision, far removed from civilization, is 30 miles upriver from the tiny settlement of Imnaha and 60 miles from Joseph. Secluded amid manicured yards, these homes reposed in a woodsy setting. To the west, billowing, white clouds floated over towering rim rocks.

A pit had been dug and a stack of alder wood lay nearby. Soon a fire was started and a bed of coals was ready. We introduced ourselves to Abigail and her friend SunBeam, who is a former Polynesian singer. Abigail (Kay) is a descendent of Hawaii's royal family, and is most interested in the restoration of the Iolani Palace. She is a very gracious lady and a pleasure to know.

While Scotty and I busied ourselves with meal preparations, Doug arrived in time to lower the marinated meat, which had been placed in my cast iron dutch ovens, into the pit. This was then covered with coals, a piece of tin, and lastly dirt. Doug disappeared upriver with his fishing pole and gold pan. Scotty and I busied ourselves making fruit salads, husking corn, and organizing the serving table. Doug returned around 5, just as the guests began arriving.

At 7, Doug unearthed the dutch ovens of meat, lifting them out with a long hook. The guests gathered around, curious about this method of cooking. *Ooh*'s and *aah*'s as the lids were removed. Done to perfection. I, meanwhile, gave a sigh of relief when the meat was done; all pits and fires are different. Our food was colorful and tasty and the guests devoured it with gusto.

Abigail's house-warming for her new Imnaha River Woods home was a success and everyone welcomed her to Wallowa County. She had purchased the property, sight unseen, 12 years ago. Like all newcomers to the country, she fell in love with the area. Although maintaining her residences in Hawaii and Palm Springs, she hopes to spend time here.

July 20—A beautiful morning as I scrub and season my big, heavy iron kettles. Ben and Tom are worming some heifers down at the chutes. Made a blackberry pie for grandson Chad's pie-a-month birthday present. Then had to make Doug a chocolate cake.

Picked the first raspberries today. Threatening rain this evening while I chored. Thunder rumbled off somewhere in the eastern sky. On phone organizing our 4-H float as well as the CowBelles' entry for the coming Chief Joseph Days parade.

July 21—Received a letter from 89-year-old Helga Travis of Prosser, Washington, a fan of this column. She sounds like a delightful lady. It was good to hear from her.

While purchasing a pair of tennis shoes at the Shoe Hut in Enterprise today, I visited with Leona Wagner. She mentioned that her husband, Dave, had been an avid fan of this column. We certainly all miss this friendly man, who was Wallowa County's brand inspector for many years. Made a batch of raspberry freezer jam.

July 22—Rained all night. One inch in the rain gauge! Luckily, all our hay is up. Our neighbors, the Houghs, worked until late last night in an effort to get their "bread loaf" hay stacks up.

Took grandchildren Mona and Buck into Joseph to watch the bank robbery re-enactment this afternoon. Buck's eyes got real big when the robbers entered the bank and the first shot was fired. Low, dark clouds formed a backdrop for the escaping robber, who fled down Main Street at a full gallop. Tourists were lined up six deep in back of the roped-off area near the museum. This drama is becoming quite an attraction.

July 23—Gorgeous morning. Did chores, then straightened up house, as we are expecting company from Texas this morning. After they arrived, we traveled in their Suburban on a quick tour of the area. We felt like tourists ourselves as we pointed out our potato fields, cattle pastures and the ranch. Doug decided to take them out to the hills, so still seated in the Suburban we headed out the Zumwalt road. Viewed through the filtered windows of that nice new van, the clouds were beautiful as we drove out through the high plateau country known by us locals as "The Hills."

We passed by Tippett Corrals, owned by brother Biden, noticing the rain puddles and the fresh new greenness of the grass. We drove on by the Steen Ranch before stopping at Buckhorn for a spectacular view of the canyon country. A perfect morning as we stared down into the hazy depths of the Imnaha drainages. So peaceful and calm. Hawks flew lazily over the canyons, and everywhere stillness, the kind you can hear.

July 24—Up at the crack of dawn, including grandchildren, who are excited about the Chief Joseph Days kiddie parade today. Fixed sourdough waffles and did chores before leaving for Joseph. The kiddie parade continues to grow each year and is becoming one of the highlights of Chief Joseph Days.

Daughter Jackie had organized an entry for the Imnaha children. They would march as a unit with a sign, held between willow sticks, that

The 'Imnaha Pioneers' took first place in the Chief Joseph Days junior parade.

read Imnaha Pioneers. The children were all dressed in keeping with the centennial theme. Little girls in calico dresses and bonnets, the boys dressed like early settlers.

Arriving in Joseph, we found a large crowd of children, mothers, dogs, horses, mules, calves, sheep, bicycles, motor bikes, wagons, Indian children, babies, balloons and bedlam. A sight to behold. People already lined the streets, waiting for the parade to begin. I especially look forward to this time to visit the wonderful Indian children, who come every year to be in the parade. They are encamped along a stream near the rodeo grounds in tepees. We welcome them and think they are a very important part of Chief Joseph Days.

It was a grand parade, and the Imnaha Pioneers won a first place. After the long parade ended, the children and I got lunch-to-go at the Burger Barn, then picnicked in the quiet of the Joseph park. Later, back at the ranch, I began cooking for tomorrow's family picnic here. Baked sourdough bread sticks, and bread, a rhubarb-strawberry deep-dish pie; roasted two chickens and made a large macaroni salad.

Doug and I attended the opening performance of the rodeo tonight. After all that cooking, it was a treat to eat a hamburger at the rodeo. It was an exciting performance, which lasted until nearly 10:30. A good crowd and a warm evening. Had a surprise at the rodeo from Maria Gadola, our Susanne's mom, from Switzerland—She was visiting friends at the lake and wanted to meet us.

July 25—Up early, Doug irrigating while I chored before gathering up all the props needed for the CowBelles' float. We ate outdoors at the cowboy breakfast served in Joseph. You could smell hotcakes, ham and eggs and steaks cooking all over town.

Located the parade formation where Wayne Lathrop waited with his team of horses and wagon. CowBelles arrived and the float soon took shape, as did a huge thunderhead, which formed before the parade over Chief Joseph Mountain. Lightning flashed and thunder rolled. We just knew we were in for a cloudburst.

Meanwhile, my 4-H'ers arrived: Chad on horseback and leading a mule, Bryan with his pack horse, and the others wearing backpacks, carrying fishing poles and wearing their cameras slung around their necks. I joined this group with my backpack, donning a slicker as the first drops of rain began to fall. The enormous, rain-filled black cloud continued to hover overhead, when all of a sudden the wind shifted and the cloud moved off in a westerly direction, and sunlight shone on our parade.

As we approached the old Chief Joseph Hotel, the Wallowa Mountain Boys began shooting it up and spooked Rowdy's horse, Apache. Rowdy dismounted and let older brother Chad lead his horse, while he led the little mule, Belle...or rather Belle led Rowdy. Children love this parade and line the route, scrambling for candy, which is tossed to them along the way.

Meanwhile, back at the ranch, we enjoyed our traditional picnic and a chance to get away from the crowds. All the little cousins ran around and played until they dropped from exhaustion. After evening chores and pipe-changing, Doug and I drove back into Joseph to watch a street dance near Jerry's Mainstreet Market.

The Sideroad Band played western music under an old apple tree in the parking lot. Soon, hearing the music, people began drifting in and started to dance under the stars, young and old alike. Our normally quiet hometown was ALIVE on this Saturday night. We peeked into all the Main Street establishments, seeing all types of people—cowboys, old sheepherders, visiting American Indians, tourists and locals—enjoying this yearly celebration, which is named after Hin-mah-too-yah-lat-kekht, Chief Joseph. And Thunder-rolling-in-the-mountains led the parade this morning!

July 26—"Come join us for the best breakfast in town," boomed a voice from the loudspeaker, as we made our way to a line forming for another cowboy breakfast. The town of Joseph is not as lively as last night. People visited as they ate at long tables in the morning sunshine. Almost everyone, it seemed, had come to town.

Walked through the tepee village, visiting some of the people camped along the river. The tepees looked right at home here and made a colorful picture backgrounded against the mountains. Later, joining daughter Jackie's family, I enjoyed listening to the King's Witnesses as their gospel songs of joy floated out into the rodeo arena. Seated with other members of our family, we took in the final performance of the Chief Joseph Days rodeo this hot afternoon.

Picked the first zucchini this evening.

July 27—Awoke to the honking of more than 100 Canadian geese landing in our meadow hay field.

The storm that preceded yesterday's parade created hail damage in the gardens that lay in its path. Luckily mine was spared.

Tom finished the new chicken pen today. Chester and his harem are living in pure luxury. Fixed a casserole of creamed new red potatoes with the first fresh garden peas for supper. Yum!

July 28—Hot. Irrigating. Cowmilking.
Cooking and making raspberry jam.

July 29—Same.

July 30—Susan's mother, Maria, from Switzerland, visited our ranch today. "I now understand," she said, "why my daughter enjoyed it here." Maria looked at her watch, which she kept on Swiss time, and said, "Now it is Susan's birthday; she is 20 years old."

July 31—It seems sad that July is leaving so soon. Almost feels like fall this morning; the thermometer reads 45 degrees. The crew finished putting up the ag bag haylage at O'Rourke's today.

Our cows on the moraine are beginning to calve. Somehow the elk fence gate was left open and a few elk have escaped onto Prairie Creek.

August 1—Thirty-two degrees! The squash and corn were nipped.
Up at 5:30 to fix breakfast, do chores and pack my gear before leaving for Enterprise to pick up 10 of my Sourdough Shutterbug 4-H'ers. We drove to Lostine, then up South Fork until we arrived at the Bowman trailhead. The kids, including two of my grandsons, shouldered their packs and took off up the trail. We were to meet at the first fork in the trail.

The Bowman trail follows Bowman Creek and the ascent is gradual at first, but soon begins a series of switchbacks that offer different views

Jim Chandler, Wallowa County centennial chairman, chats with Josie Hays, 102, of Enterprise. She was an honorary grand marshal of the Chief Joseph Days Parade in Joseph last week.

at every turn, looking downward to the Lostine or across at Twin Peaks and vicinity. Here and there glissading waterfalls were spilling over dark rocks and glistening in the morning sunlight. A turn in the high trail brought into view the breathtaking sight of Eagle Cap, the landmark this wilderness is named after. It was near here I finally caught up with the tail end of my group.

The morning, crisp and cool, was good for hiking. Hazy, high clouds formed and a refreshing breeze stirred the trees. Waterfalls tumbled down with increasing frequency, until we reached a fork in the trail that turned out to be near Brownie Basin. It was 11:30. We decided to camp there as it was such a beautiful spot. The vanguard of our group, who had arrived some time ago, agreed.

Before us stretched a high mountain meadow, rimmed in by forest and talus slopes. Meandering, clear, blue Bowman Creek wound its way over a sandy bottom and was fringed by wildflowers and low-growing willows. Several varieties of evergreens grew there, and large rock formations lay scattered about. High above, two snowbanks clung to the inside of the bowl-like mountains that cupped Brownie Basin. This was one of the prettiest places we'd seen yet.

As we set up camp near the stream, it appeared for the moment that we had the basin to ourselves. We ate our lunches before deciding to hike to Laverty Lake, which is about one mile on up the trail.

Relieved of my burdensome pack, I arrived at Laverty Lake to see the boys were already catching fish. Looking at my map, I saw that 7,600-foot Chimney Lake lay just above. Because I had always wanted to visit this lake, I continued up the trail until, rounding a bend, I came upon a blue-green lake tucked in the wilderness. This lake, named because of an unusual chimney-like rock formation nearby, lies in the heart of the Eagle Cap Wilderness.

A slight breeze rippled the surface of the lake and water lapped peacefully at the shore as I walked around a wooded bend in the trail and saw three horses. They jerked their heads in my direction. One horse was tethered and the other two were loose. I saw no camp. From here I could see a steep, loose rock, zig-zag trail that led up and over a pass. I supposed it to be the trail to Hobo Lake. By this time my 4-H'ers had arrived to fish this lake. I began the long, steep climb to Hobo, as the trail afforded a good view of Chimney below for photographing.

At the halfway mark, I decided to try for Hobo. It was 1:30. Climbing the final few feet through the high pass, I could look down on Chimney and see the Twin Peaks clear across the Lostine. A weathered sign that read "Wood Lake and Hobo Lake" stood in the pass.

I took the steep trail to Hobo. As the air thinned and my feet thought they could not take another step, I reached a high, rocky promontory and looked out over 7,800-foot Hobo Lake. Truly a high-country lake. Not a soul around. Water spilled out of the end of the lake near the trail I had ascended. After

a brief rest, I walked up through another rocky cleft to view the area around Bear Lake and the distances that unfolded for miles to the northwest of Wallowa. Looking down at Hobo, I wondered why it was so named. Perhaps up here, all by itself, alone and free, it led the life of a hobo. That beautiful afternoon I shared the lake with two shy rock rabbits, or pikas, a hawk and a mountain bluebird. I shall always remember Hobo Lake on August 1, 1987.

At 3 I left, one step taking me downward and out of sight of the lake. It disappeared as suddenly as it had appeared.

While descending the trail to Chimney, I could hear the boys' laughter far below. Lucky children. Reaching the lake I sat upon a log to watch the kids fish. The trout began to feed and did flip-flops all over the lake. One of the boys would occasionally catch one, but generally the fish won.

Arriving back in camp we gathered firewood and started a cooking fire. In our absence, a Boy Scout troop hiking through had decided to camp nearby for the night. Each 4-H'er cooked his own supper over the fire. Such a variety, and it all went down with gusto. A chill soon settled over the basin and we added wood to the fire. After we roasted marshmallows, darkness began to come on gradually until at 9 p.m. all light faded. A bright, lemon slice of moon shone briefly before disappearing over the mountains.

The children grouped around their fire, telling ghost stories while I attempted to sleep. Around midnight their voices diminished and all was quiet, save for the murmur of the stream. I looked out from under my space blanket, which was wrapped around a down mummy bag, to see a layer of frost already had formed. A brilliant, star-filled sky looked down on us. One side of me was always cold, and I peeked out at half-hour intervals all night, wishing for dawn. After what seemed like an eternity, the stars began to fade and the basin walls became faintly visible.

The pre-dawn sounds of Alpine birds were joined by a pair of friendly camp robbers waiting for our breakfast remains. I crawled stiffly from my cocoon and stoked to life last night's embers with some pine cones. Soon a steaming cup of hot cocoa warmed me, and the world looked brighter, although I could have done with some sleep. The 4-H'ers, evidently snug and warm, still snoozed as I fixed my breakfast.

Soon the sun spilled into the basin, firing the high places with golden light. One by one, my sleepy kids made their way to the fire, armed with breakfast fixin's. All appetites satisfied as the sun crept down the timbered slopes and across the meadow, which glistened with frosty sparkles. Ice bordered the creek and the ground was frozen hard. We guessed it to be around 15 degrees.

By 9:30 we cleaned up camp and packed our backpacks, and were headed down the trail when several pack trains on their way to North Minam Meadows passed us, along with a few scattered hikers. Arrived at the trailhead around 11:30, the kids having made it in far less time than their leader.

At home the garden had been nipped again. Doug soon arrived from Imnaha with freshly-picked wild blackberries. Must admit that as much as I like camping, a warm bed felt pretty good again.

Mildred Searcey stands beside the Wallowa County Centennial stage coach, which her grandfather, Billie Arnold, used to drive.

August 3—The wonderful smell of bubbling, juicy, blackberry cobbler fills my kitchen this morning. Heat waves shimmer across the ripening grain fields and many Wallowa County ranchers are putting up their second cuttings of hay.

August 4—A dry wind blows. No sooner do I finish irrigating the yard, garden and berries, than it is time to begin again. Potato field inspection took place today. Good news, they found 0 readings on our plants!

August 5—Day after day of clear, cloudless days, as summer progresses. The mountain snow pack is long gone and many irrigation ditches are running short of water, while others have run out entirely.

Steve began swathing our second cuttings, some of which will be used to fill an Ag Bag with haylage. Picked and froze two batches of pod peas. Made a rhubarb-strawberry pie for son Ken's "Pie-a-Month" birthday present. Attended an old-fashioned ice-cream social this afternoon, which was held on the courthouse lawn in Enterprise. Strains of music drifted from the newly dedicated gazebo, as Wanda Sorweide played the organ and Gail Swart, the piano. The Wallowa County Band performed again while the community socialized and ate ice cream.

The Soroptimist sponsored this social, which was another way of recognizing our Centennial. Ice cream cones were five cents and sundaes, 15 cents. This year has been good for the local citizenry. More people are taking pride in our communities and in simply being neighborly. Was having such a good time visiting, nearly forgot that a potato growers meeting was scheduled at our home this evening.

Back at the ranch I put a fresh peach upside-down cake in the oven and finished my chores. Doug, who had gone into the ice-cream social later, got to visiting and was the last one to arrive.

August 6—After chores, I gathered up two photos to enter in the Wallowa County Fair this morning. Leaving them at Cloverleaf Hall, I drove to the old mill site below Wallowa where I had an assignment to photograph the Centennial Stage Coach Run. Another project associated with the on-going Centennial recognition is a Time Capsule, being put together by local photographers, of this year's events.

The stage coach was hitched to a team of two horses and two mules. The beautifully restored coach was authentic, being the same one used on a stage line that made regular trips between Elgin and Joseph until January 1909. I was among the first to board the stage, which would first deliver mail to Wallowa, then pick up mail, freight and passengers all the way up the valley. With me were three children.

Soon we were off, clattering along highway 82 to Wallowa. The team walked briskly along, pulling the stagecoach as log trucks and tourists lined up behind us. We crossed the railroad tracks and creaked into town, stopping at the post office. Our outriders, Keith Waters and Leroy Granning, protected us from any hold ups. I got off here and had my ticket stamped, which will be a nice Centennial keepsake, since it was ticket number one!

While I photographed the mail being loaded and delivered, men brought out freight to be loaded on top. New passengers climbed aboard and the stage was off again. After being given a ride back to my car, I followed along for more picture-taking.

As we slowly wound up the valley, I thought about the advantages of stagecoach travel versus modern day means of transportation. Traffic sped by, always in a hurry. Everyone, it seemed was in a hurry in a modern vehicle. In a stagecoach…one speed. The passengers and driver accepted that, relaxed and enjoyed the scenery. Here they could see the Wallowa River, listen to the birdsong, feel the breezes, smell the fresh air and new-mown hay, or visit. No exhaust fumes or roaring motor, only the creaking of harness leather and wheels turning on the road.

How far civilization has come in such a short time. Today Los Angeles freeways are the scene of shootings, due, in part, to bumper to bumper frustrations. There is good and bad, however, as I mused about all the things we accomplish in a given day due to the car.

Back at Cloverleaf Hall (by car), I worked until afternoon accepting 4-H photography entries and setting up displays. Attended a Mule Days meeting tonight in Enterprise, as will be working on publicity for this growing event.

August 7—Sourdough huckleberry hotcakes for breakfast. Started a batch of sourdough bread sticks to rise. Milked the cow and strained milk. When the bread sticks came out of the oven, took them to enter in the fair before meeting the stage near Lostine for more photographing.

Purchased a box of fresh peaches, grown in Milton-Freewater, at a roadside stand. At noon joined the crowd near the OK Theatre and Circle T restaurant to wait for the stage to arrive in Enterprise. Soon it hove into view, right on schedule, rounding the corner by Harold's Women's Apparel. Reporters from other newspapers there during this hot noon hour. Locals, donned in Centennial dress, gathered to meet the stage. The old stagecoach looked like a scene from the past and everyone loved it. Ate a hamburger, prepared by the 4-H'ers at the fair food booth.

Later, I waited at Joseph for the stage's arrival. Traffic was heavy on that Friday as the different modern-day-vehicles whizzed by the team plodding steadily toward their final destination. Horses in pastures along the route ran to whinny their greetings. When the stage arrived at the Joseph Post Office, quite a crowd had assembled. As the team halted, all heck broke loose—masked bandits, on horseback, appeared from a side street and held up the stage.

The scene was made even more realistic by a frightened, small boy passenger, who began to wail in spite of mother's telling him it was only a game. The passengers were ordered, at gunpoint, out of the stage, hands up, and they obliged. There was gunfire and the team spooked before being brought under control by the driver. Presently, the sheriff and his deputies galloped onto the scene and to the rescue. The bad guys were caught and brought back to the Chief Joseph Hotel, where two hangman's nooses dangled from the porch. A passenger began to yell "Lynch 'em," and at this point the drama luckily ended! The little boy's cries subsided and he was persuaded everything was all in fun.

While this was going on, I met Mildred Searcey, who told me her grandfather, Billie Arnold, had driven this very stage for six years. He had been under the employ of Rumble and McCully of Joseph. The summer's activities are just now shifting into high gear.

August 8—Doug has been growing a beard for the Centennial, as have many men in the county. Today was the Centennial picnic at Wallowa Lake. It was a gorgeous day for a picnic and various organizations sold all kinds of mouth-watering foods like elephant ears, corn-on-the-cob, watermelon, home-cranked ice-cream and homemade pie. Our CowBelles served beef-on-a-stick. The marinated beef was skewered and barbecued. We gals were kept busy until we ran out at 8:30.

Activities, like tug-of-war, horse shoe pitching and sackraces, filled the afternoon. It was a colorful scene, with ballons escaping and floating up into the branches of the pine trees. The sparkling waters of the nearby lake and mountains made a nice setting. A large awning-covered stage was the center of festivities including music, a fellow reciting a history of the Oregon Trail, and the beard-growing contest. The beards were measured with much ceremony before winners were selected in different categories. The day's activities climaxed, after dark, in a display of fireworks that rained out over the lake.

Drove to Asotin on this hot morning, before turning up the Snake River to Heller Bar, where the annual meeting of the Tippetts was to take place. In spite of the oppressive heat, we enjoyed seeing relatives and the buffet lunch, served in the dining room overlooking the Snake.

We stopped in Clarkston to visit Doug's sister, Betty, who was in the hospital. Nephew Mike has been visiting and we always enjoy having him here.

August 17—Awoke to a beautiful, mountain morning. Max and Doug, looking a little strange with swollen chins and ears, suffered no further ill effects from their hornet episode. Doug was just turning the horses loose to graze, when he quietly motioned for me to look up from our camp…at a six-point bull elk! The bull stood in a clearing and soon we noticed another bull with five points standing with a group of cows. As sunlight spilled into the opening, they simply melted into the timber.

While I wrangled horses and began fixing breakfast, the men went fishing. As I mixed the sourdough hotcakes, I noticed that the horses and mule were trying to sneak off down the trail in search of greener grass. Running ahead of them, I caught the leader and brought them all back to camp, tying them so I could proceed with breakfast. Soon Max and Doug, looking like two small boys, returned with a string of bull trout, which I added to the breakfast menu. I made lunches for all of us and soon we were off up the trail for a day of exploring.

We rode up South Fork to Blue River where a trail takes off to Cornucopia. The signs read Blue Creek and Cliff Creek, but Max said they used to be called rivers. A light-colored mountain to the right of us had an unusual vein of dark red rock running through it.

"There used to be an old log cabin here somewhere," Max said, and sure enough we found it, partly hidden from the trail by a stand of evergreens. We rode up to have a look. Probably placed there by an early-day miner, the rough-hewn log walls appeared sturdy and held the cabin together. Max commented that this cabin was old in 1937! The roof was covered with rusted lard buckets, coffee cans and syrup cans, which had been flattened out and nailed over shakes. A small square opening had been crudely cut for a window.

Farther up the trail, Max poinied out a site where an early-day airplane had made a forced landing in a large cottonwood tree. The pilot, who had been dropping supplies to a fire crew, had walked away from the crash. Now nothing remained but the rotting trunk of a large tree. Nearby stood similar live cottonwoods. The fuselage had been taken apart and packed out of the wilderness.

Every so often Max would exclaim, "Isn't this just wonderful, to see all of this again after all these years!" The trail followed the Imnaha, which was so clear that every underwater rock was visible. On our right we gazed up to see steep mountains where little shelves of timber jutted out. Above timberline were many colorful rock formations and limestone deposits.

Another spot in the trail brought back to Max's memory the story of a fellow who had roped a deer from his horse. Then he pointed upward to the mountain and a high, gun-sight pass and said, "I'd sure like to ride up there again." So up we went, horseback, following game trails right into the heart of that steep mountain. We let our horses rest often before gaining a high, rocky point where a few scrub pine clung to a gravelly crevice. We tied our horses to the trees and ate our lunches. Far below wandered the South Fork, while across from us lay the Pine Valley country. Ahead loomed Hawkins Pass and Cusick Mountain, awesome views in all directions.

After lunch, we rode slowly under the crest of the mountain. Presently we crossed a boulder-strewn chute and a loose-rock face, leading our horses, and me wondering if I would meet my demise on this mountain. I soon spotted a little Alpine meadow far below and headed for it while Max and Doug explored farther up the high, rocky ridge. Arriving safely at the meadow, I rested my horse while waiting for the men to return. I also scouted the vicinity for another old cabin that Max said was near here. I watched as the men, skylined above, descended.

Failing to find any remains of the cabin, we made a scrambling retreat to the trail below. How I had missed that trail. It was nearing 4 o'clock when we decided to ride up toward Hawkins Pass. The beauty of this area is indescribable and my pen is helpless when it comes to painting a word picture of the wildflower-fringed meadows, the Imnaha narrowing as it approached its headwaters, clumps of willows, aspen and alder and the ever-present mountains that loomed up on both sides.

Soon the trail became steeper and we entered a high grassy basin rimmed by weathered, solid-rock mountain sides. An early, high-country frost had painted the grass a golden color. We were looking at the Imnaha's birthplace! Here, live springs created life for the river with the Indian name: Imnaha.

I wanted to ride up the steep trail that led through Hawkins Pass, but it was nearly 6 o'clock, so we headed back down the trail to camp. Arriving just before dark, we started a cooking fire and grilled steaks for supper. Again, our doe appeared. I saw that the leftover hotcakes were gone from the log near camp. She was looking forward to another handout.

Leaving the men to jaw around the fire, I hit the sack.

August 18—Arose early to put sourdough biscuits to rise in the dutch oven. Today we would ride to Bonner Flat. I knew there was a trail somewhere, but had been unable to locate it, so we headed up through a steep, grassy opening where we had seen the elk. We rode through what we now referred to as "Hornet Flat." Another mountain loomed and a repeat of yesterday's adventure appeared imminent as we rode our horses straight up that mountain and looked down from dizzying heights to the river below.

We were eventually halted by a formidable jumble of boulders that made further progress impossible. The view, however, was terrific. We could look out over the eastern horizon and see forever: the Seven Devils, Snake, Salmon and Bitteroot ranges, separated by hazy shades of blues and purples. We were looking clear over to Montana!

Doug immediately became fascinated with the rocks, which contained quartz. I watched the horses while Max scouted around below on foot to find a way out of that gigantic rock slide. He returned, having found a way through, and we pried Doug away from his rocks to slowly, leading our horses, make our way around the slide. We finally reached a grassy opening, above which appeared a loose-rock mountainside.

The men headed up, their horses scrambling for a foothold. Not me! I dismounted, tied the reins around the saddle horn and let my mare follow them. I crawled on all fours until I felt safe enough to stand. One slip in that loose scree would have sent us all sliding down the mountain. My horse carried my precious camera and made it safely to the top. I arrived shortly after and a great sight greeted me: Bonner Flat. To my right, in a saddle, was a trail, the one we should have come up on. Frosted golden-brown grasses waved in a late-summer breeze of a summer that had been hot and devoid of moisture. All the waterways appeared dry. Such a change from the last time I'd seen the area in the '70s.

Like a mirage, the distant Bitteroots shimmered in the distance. This high, grassy area is more rolling hills than a flat, and was named after an early-day sheepman named Bonner. At the edge of some trees, we found the remains of an old miner's cabin. Roofless, it lay nestled under a solid-rock mountain peak. We ate our lunches near the cabin, enjoying the solitude and sunshine. We talked about the miner. What was he prospecting for? Was he ever caught up there in a fall storm? Perhaps he was even buried there. We found one live spring, the only water, and let our horses drink. Nearby, in heavy grass, we saw imprints where elk had recently bedded down. We explored all around that grassy, high setting and looked over at the Tenderfoot and Middle Fork country.

We located the trail and soon we were riding down the steep switchbacks I'd remembered from 12 years ago, on the back of a horse named Bullet. Back in camp, we three were a bit weary after three days of hard riding. While I prepared supper, two women and two men with a pack string stopped and visited. They were headed for Cornucopia. I gave them coffee and cookies. The fellow in the lead said they'd make "Copia" by 9 that night. He mentioned that they had come upon a fresh cougar kill this morning, a doe that had been partly eaten, covered with brush and pine needles.

As the stars popped out, we enjoyed another perfect night in the mountains.

August 19—Strange noises in the night, which turned out to be a porcupine, had me a little spooked until we discovered the varmint had made off with Maud's saddle blanket. Max found it in the weeds with holes chewed in it. As we breakfasted on sourdough hotcakes, Canadian bacon and Max's fried potatoes, Doug said, "It just don't get any better than this!"

I made lunches and soon we began packing the horse and mule for the trip out. As we prepared to leave, Max commented, "This is kinder a tear-jerkin' moment." It was. None of us wanted to leave. There was still so much country to see. We hadn't gone to Cornucopia, Tenderfoot and the Middle Fork. As we left, a two-man Forest Service trail crew rode by, sporting new, modern packing equipment.

"Things have sure changed from 50 years ago," Max quipped.

We returned via the Lick Creek trail, eating our lunches on top of the high ridge. At home I watered my parched garden and again took up life on the ranch. This trip will be remembered for years, especially by Max. My pullets laid their first small, brown eggs during my absence.

August 20—Occasional lightning lit the sky last night, and I thought about Todd, Liza and baby James, who packed in with horses and their mule to Francis Lake this week. The clouds have disappeared and there is a "fallish" feeling in the air.

Trying to catch up after being gone; worked at the housework and my writing. Doug checked on cows calving on the moraine. Baby calves all over the place!

August 21—Milked Startch this morning. Had turned the calves out in the pasture with her in our absence.

Began organizing my 4-H club's annual trip to Red's Horse Ranch. The mountains seem brighter now, against the clarity of early autumn skies. As I worked downstairs in the Art Angle darkroom today, I could hear the commotion of another bank robbery re-enactment taking place on the street above.

Picked and froze more raspberries and pod peas. My pullets are all laying now. Fixed the first fresh pork chops for tonight's supper from the 4-H market hog. Was successful in persuading the orphan to nurse Startch this morning.

August 22—Sourdough hotcakes and sunshine for breakfast. Let the three calves nurse Startch. Typed out "CowBelle Corner" for our local newspaper. Still working on the final script and set of slides for our history project. After spending more than a year on the presentation, we will soon have it ready for public viewing.

Ben and his two sons rode through the cows and calves on the moraine this morning. The cows are mostly calved out now. While Doug and Max Gorsline took off for the Imnaha to do some gold panning, I stayed home to catch up on the work so as to be ready to leave Monday morning with my 4-H'ers for Red's Horse Ranch. Irrigated the lawn, hoed the strawberries, made a batch of sourdough cinnamon rolls, and got my weekly column ready to mail.

Had the ranch all to myself this Saturday afternoon, except for hundreds of starlings and blackbirds that are gathering for a convention here. Son Ken's family returned our motorhome, arriving just as I took the cinnamon rolls out of the oven. Well, that's what grandmas are supposed to do, isn't it? My quality control testers gave their approval. Thunderstorms on and off all night.

August 23—The pullets are laying mostly double yolk eggs. Doug swathing hay all morning, until thunderstorms put a halt to it. Baked sourdough bread, then began readying my backpack for our trip tomorrow.

August 24—Up to chore and ready to go by 5:30. Picked up some of my 4-H'ers and drove to Enterprise High School, where I traded my car for one of the school vans. Scotty arrived, as did the remainder of our group, and we all piled into the van, 14 of us and our backpacks. Beautiful morning as we drove to Cove in Union County, then headed up the long, steep gravel road to Moss Spring. Several groups of bow hunters were packing up to ride into the back country when we arrived at the trailhead.

Shouldering our packs, we took off down the steep, open hillside on a trail that would drop 1,000 feet in elevation in just eight miles. It was 9 a.m. My herd of strong, young boys, two grandsons included, took off in the lead as usual, followed by the three girls. Scotty and I brought up the rear. The now familiar sight of the vast Minam Wilderness stretched out before us, and we could look to the upper reaches of the Little Minam country with its green, forested slopes. As the morning warmed, the trail wound down over creeks and cool places, then followed the Little Minam River.

We were all in high spirits, and anticipating another adventure at Red's. Walking steadily, without pause, we crossed the wooden bridge that spans the Little Minam, then began another long hike to gain the ridge above the ranch. Reaching the ridge by noon, Scotty and I rested and ate our lunches. Far below, we could glimpse through the trees and see the landing strip, horse pasture and a cluster of log cabins.

Fifteen minutes later we were descending the long switchback trail to the meadow. Just as we approached the ranch, a plane swept down over the barn and landed in the meadow pasture. Some guests boarded the small plane before it taxied down the grass runway and took off over the barn and down the Minam River. It appeared we had the place to ourselves.

The boys, having long since arrived, were already in the river. We left our packs in the barn haymow which would serve as our bedroom, before heading for the river to wash off the trail dust. The water, unlike last year, was frigid. We got in above our waists, which refreshed us considerably. Later, over a hot cup of tea prepared by the cook, Lee, we relaxed on the porch of the dining lodge. Lee, a dark-haired, friendly girl, was stuffing a turkey for supper. Soon the delicious aroma of roasting turkey drifted to us.

Greg, a horse wrangler, and Lee were the present crew, as the boss, Cal Henry, and the remaining help had left that morning with 22 horses and mules to set up hunting camps farther up the Minam River trail. They would be gone two days. That evening, our ravenous group savored roast turkey, dressing, fruit salad, green beans, homemade whole wheat bread and brownies. Lee only had to ring the dinner bell once.

Scotty and I helped with the dishes while the children played tug of war and pitched horseshoes. At 8:30 Scotty and I attempted to hit the hay, literally. The 4-H'ers had, by this time, shifted into high gear, fueled by their dinner. At 9, the generator that supplies electricity for the ranch was turned off and all was dark.

Earlier, Greg, who was the relief milker in the absence of a girl cow-milker, had struggled with the milk cow, Daisy. After 15 minutes he had a pail full, some of which he mixed with ground barley and fed to two young hogs, who squealed in anticipation in a nearby pen.

We could hear far-off thunder rumble down the canyon and soon a roaring wind came sweeping down off the rims. It was a warm wind that rattled the tin roof and blew fine rain through the cracks in the barn walls. Suddenly, we were inundated with children, who scrambled around in the hay with flashlights to locate their sleeping bags. Then they began to talk all at once. Until 12:30.

Scotty and I managed to rest, not sleep. The wind continued and the rain ceased. It was very warm. A young bull had settled himself down for the night just opposite me, outside the barn wall. All night I was to hear the inner rumblings of his stomachs, until it got so I could tell just when he would finish chewing one cud and burp another. Just at daybreak, I managed to get a little sleep before the bull got up, stretched and bawled loudly.

August 25—Scotty and I walked to the main building, washed our faces and began the day. The children, who slept longer, were up in time to hear the breakfast bell. And what a breakfast. It would have satisfied a haying crew. hotcakes, bacon, eggs, melons, juice, milk, and hot cocoa. The children, looking none the worse from last night's late hours, relished their food.

Bow hunters, their faces painted and wearing camouflaged clothing, with bow and quiver of arrows hanging from their saddles, rode through the ranch on their way up the trail. Just looking at most of them, we figured the deer were pretty safe.

Lee made 14 sack lunches for us and some of us decided to hike upriver to the old Splash dam site, about five miles from the ranch. It was a lovely morning, and hiking up that trail brought back memories of when I was an elk camp cook for Red's and we packed 19 miles up to Elk Creek and spent nearly 20 days in a tent in November. By noon we had reached the meadow near the old Splash dam.

Sure enough, the old log timbers with enormous spikes holding them together were still intact on one side of the river. The water flowed through this spot over solid rock and splashed down into a series of foamy blue and gold pools. We did some photographing. This dam, to me, exemplifies the ingenuity of the early logger, who contrived this means of transporting logs to distant mills. Water from the dam was held back, then released to race the logs 30 miles downriver to the mill in Wallowa. Along their route, the logs would have to be prodded and broken up from jams, which required skill and daring.

We ate our lunches along the river bank and enjoyed the solitude of the Minam.

September 9—August faded into history and September arrived, with still no rain in sight. My garden matured and we gorged ourselves on its fresh bounty much longer this year, due to the mild weather. We finished putting up the second cutting of hay.

I kept very busy in the kitchen; making pickles, sauerkraut and canning whatever I could get my hands on for winter meals. Another Mule Days rolled around; a great show this year!

September 10—We gained another grandchild, a boy, Ryan Douglas, born in Wyoming.

September 16—We attempted to save the garden by turning on the sprinkler, and by morning it was 24 degrees. Everything was encased in ice! I watched as one by one the corn stalks fell with the weight of the ice. The corn continued to ripen, however, as it was still attached to the earth. We ate corn on the cob for two weeks!

September 20—Our history group traveled to Sumpter to ride on the Sumpter Valley Railroad. This old steam train features the former W.H. Eccles Lumber Company's gear-driven Heisler locomotive, two observation cars, and the former SVRR No. 5 caboose. We all rode on the nearly seven-mile run that passes through the old dredge piles above Phillips Reservoir, on a narrow-gauge track that even crossed a highway!

The entrances to several tunnels, carved through solid rock, can be found near the old Joe LeGore cabin. The early day miner built his home near the highest lake in Oregon—LeGore Lake, in the Wallowa Mountains. Janie Tippett holds a rock that contains quartz crystals and fractured garnets.

Along the route we were able to view wildlife, such as deer, beaver, and waterfowl. The train, affectionately known as the "Stump Dodger," has an interesting history that began back in 1890. It used to carry logs from the huge forests that lay south and west of Baker City, Oregon, to the saw mills.

We were enthralled as we watched the wood fire in the engine heat the water that produced steam to power the big locomotive. What a thrill it was to hear the first chuff, chuff start up, and then the lonely sound of the whistle. Before our ride got under way, we waited in the observation car while the engine took on more wood and water.

After visiting the old dredge at Sumpter and eating our lunches nearby, we visited the Oregon Trail Museum in Baker. We were most impressed by the large rock and mineral display. We returned home by way of Richland and Halfway, a long, scenic trip that we all enjoyed.

According to our calendar, summer ended on September 22; however, the warm, dry conditions continued day after day. On that last day of summer, we trailed 100 head of cows to another pasture in the hills to prevent overgrazing on our dry ranges.

September 24—The temperature ranged from 30 in the morning to 80 in the afternoon. It was nearly dark by 7:15 p.m.

September 25—We began digging our nuclear potato seed. It was also time for the annual Alpenfest at the lake. I again helped serve sauerkraut and German sausage.

September 26—The season's first snow fell in the mountains and a light rain dampened the ground here in the valley. I had managed to pull and dry my keeping onions from the garden before the rain.

September 27—We moved our steers from one rented pasture to another on upper Prairie Creek. Spent most of the day a-horseback. That night I discovered a skunk in the hen house. After almost touching it in the dark, thinking it was Chester the rooster, I pulled my hand back just in time. The chicken pen was aromatic with essence of skunk for days.

The rain didn't amount to much and we ended up having to irrigate our fields to soften the earth before digging potatoes.

October 1—Thirty days hath September and they are up! The Blue and Gold days of October have arrived, and I spent this day working on the potato digger. Home late from the field to wash off the dirt and prepare supper.

October 4—Doug, Herb Owens and I moved the fall-calving cows and their calves off the moraine to the Harris place. It was pretty exciting this morning, as deer season was in full swing. Three rifle shots whizzed over our heads before Doug hollered, "Hold your fire!"

Luckily we survived the day, which was long. Some of the calves managed to escape along the route into the neighbor's pastures. By the time we got them caught and loaded and returned to mothers, it was 9:30 p.m.

October 6—We moved the potato digger from Dawson's field to Brink's field and the two diggers, operating at once, made short work of the remainder of the harvest.

October 7—I spent another 10-hour day on my feet working on the digger. The potatoes came up clean and our yield is up considerably this year.

October 10—Scotty, Bill and I hiked to the LeGore mine and cabin today. A fire that had been burning for days near the head of Scotch Creek was visible from the road as we drove to the Hurricane Creek trailhead.

The blaze appears mostly contained. Pack strings of mules continue to carry water up a newly built pack trail to the fire crew. This fire flared up from a smoldering August lightning strike. We first noticed it while working on the digger, as the first puffs of smoke billowed up from the steep mountainside. The woods were tinder dry and the trail powdery with dust, until we turned onto the little-used Falls Creek trail.

We passed Falls Creek, whose waters fell perpendicular down a sheer rock face. A splash of golden color greeted us on the opposite mountainside: a grove of trembling aspen. Historically, this is a great slide area and evidence of previous action is all around. As we climbed higher, the great mountain, Sacajawea, came into view. Soon the trail wound through a patch of mountain mahogany, where we jumped a few grouse.

We reached a high aspen grove by noon and ate our lunches under an incredibly blue sky, framed by a canopy of golden leaves. Just when our legs were about to give out, we reached the old mine area and walked the final, steep steps to the old miner's cabin. I photographed before the sun sank behind the steep mountain above us. It was hard to imagine the work it must have taken to build such a cabin in such a place. Especially since all supplies had to be packed in via that trail. To me the place evokes a feeling of elusive mystery and a haunting loneliness.

We explored around the old tunnels and examined many interesting rocks. Due to the dry year, the stream that normally ran cold and clear near the mine entrance was completely dry! Around 3:30 the sun left us and a chill set in. But we soon warmed up, sliding and scrambling down that steep trail to Falls Creek. The last rays of the sun lingered a moment on the high peaks opposite us and it was nearly dark when we reached the pickup.

October 11—The fire on the mountain flared up again due to a sudden breeze and continued dry weather.

October 13—We finished digging the seed potatoes today! Hurrah! We had an excellent crew this year... around 25 men and women. The crop is stored in temperature controlled cellars, where it will remain all winter until time for spring shipment.

October 14—Doug up early to try his luck at bagging a buck on this last day of deer season. He rode up McCully Creek, leading the mule Maud on this 15-degree morning. I stayed home and began baking pumpkin pies for tomorrow's harvest dinner for our potato crew.

Doug returned at 8 with a buck. He said he and son Steve shot the animal at the same time. It was the only legal buck they saw all day. A big day tomorrow, as I must prepare food for 60 people! We've invited our potato digging crew and their families to a "Thank You" harvest dinner in our shop.

October 15—Frosty-cold and clear when I did my chores this morning. Scrubbed and cooked a large kettle of potatoes, and hard-boiled some eggs for a humongous potato salad. Peeled apples and baked deep-dish apple pies before Scotty showed up to help with the big meal for our harvest dinner tonight. Baked more pumpkin pies, washed mountains of dirty dishes and, amid the clutter, fixed lunch for Doug. The men, who spent most of the day cleaning out the shop, hauled tables and chairs and set them up.

By 3, the beef was buried in the ground, cooking in dutch ovens; a huge kettle of beans and hamhocks simmered slowly on the wood stove, and the last pumpkin pie came out of the oven. We had fun decorating the tables with Indian corn, yellow squash and fall leaves. I did my barn chores while Scotty gathered the eggs, and by 6 our potato crew and their families began arriving, until our yard resembled a used car lot!

The dinner was a big success and by 9:30 I was ready to fold for the night.

October 16—Sixteen degrees, and a heavy frost. Before sun-up all of my cast iron dutch ovens were scrubbed, seasoned and put away. The rest of the mess was cleaned up and by 10 I was on my way to serve the senior citizens' dinner at the Joseph Civic Center. I set the tables for 55 people in a sort of daze. Other CowBelles soon arrived and we made short work of the job. Will I ever be able to fix supper for two tonight?

Stopped by Jerry's Market and picked up the 60 pounds of sirloin tip roasts I'd ordered for the 4-H Appreciation Night. Joseph 4-H leaders are supposed to be in charge of the meal...and guess who got the job. Oh well, at least I'm in practice.

Very warm and dry today. Not a bit of moisture anywhere in sight. Finished typing my column in advance of the deadline, because we plan on leaving in a few days for a week's trip to Wyoming to visit new grandson Ryan.

October 17—Hardly enough moisture to make frost; another clear day. The veterinarian here, preg-testing our heifers.

Steve Roundy, Grace Bartlett and I met with Russell Ford at the OK Theater in Enterprise this morning to make sure the projector will work for the premier showing of our "Wallowa Story." If all goes according to plan, the event will take place November 17 at the OK Theater.

While we were there, Russell treated us to a tour of the projection room, which has been renovated. The theater's stage now features modern lighting and is used for performing arts. Russell, who says he should have been born in the last century, loved seeing the slides taken from old museum prints in our slide show.

Visited son Todd and family on Alder Slope. They were making jerky from a four-point white-tail buck Todd had bagged during deer season. The Bauers from Imnaha stopped by with some wonderful baking squash, which they traded us for potatoes.

Met with Prairie Creek neighbor Denny Dawson for picture-taking and interview for an article in the forthcoming Women in Agriculture issue of Agri-Times. Dug my carrots and stored them for winter. Began weaning one of Startch's big calves, so when we leave she will have only two nursing her.

October 18—We have had more than 50 continuous days with no rain! In addition to the usual work, I roasted 40 pounds of beef for the annual 4-H Appreciation Night, to be held at Cloverleaf this evening. Another 4-H leader, Louise Kunz, cooked 20 pounds for me. So here is me, alone, with roasting meat on this Sunday, while Doug is off to the Imnaha to try his luck at gold-panning.

Appreciation Night was a success and many awards were presented to 4-H members and leaders. I was honored to receive a national photography leader's award sponsored by Eastman Kodak Company.

October 19—Clear, cold and 19 degrees. The cowboys began moving our heifers from the ranch to the Harris place this morning. After chores, Doug and I headed for Pendleton to visit daughter Linda before my scheduled appearance this evening at the White Eagle Grange near Pilot Rock.

After seeing Linda, we located the Grange hall, where we were greeted by Betty Martin and her husband, Bill, who had invited me to show the "Wallowa Story" at the White Eagle Grange open house. The old Grange hall has been lovingly maintained since it was built in 1927. Hardwood floors were polished to a sheen and lace curtains adorned the windows. These folks, much like our Wallowa County people, were very hospitable and obviously excellent cooks. The potluck tables groaned with such delectibles, choices were hard to make.

Enjoyed visiting Virgil Rupp, of Agri-Times, and meeting people like Grace Harvey and Bertha Baker, with whom I visited during the meal. Was impressed with Grace, who is widowed and lives alone on her mountain ranch. An interesting gal, one who has certainly done a lot of living and continues to do so.

I presented the slide show of Wallowa County's past 100 years, which is similar, I suspect, to many rural areas in Eastern Oregon. It was well received, and as we left we were presented with several gifts that were most appreciated. We considered it our pleasure to be invited to their open house.

On the way home we stopped to pick up Linda, who would be traveling to Wyoming with us. It was nearly 2 in the morning before we went to bed.

October 20—Busy morning, trying to get off for our trip. Finally we were on our way. Made Ontario for lunch before heading east. It was clear, sunny and warm driving across Eastern Oregon.

October 21—Spent last night in Jackpot, Nevada, slightly off course, and now on this beautiful morning, we speed down the road to Twin Falls. Then on to Idaho Falls, where we left the freeway and took a route that follows the Snake River. Even though the fall color obviously had peaked and now lay on the ground, the aspen thickets that lined the hills created their own special beauty. The winding Snake was lovely in the brightness of fall.

Drove by Calamity Reservoir, where the bright blue waters contrasted sharply against the dry landscape. The water level was low and people had gathered the beached logs and sticks and stacked them in great piles all along the shoreline.

As we approached Jackson Hole we noticed the haystacks, put up with the beaver slides in the big meadows. Cattle grazed the hayed-over fields along the road. It was evening when we left Jackson Hole and headed up toward the Continental Divide. The great Teton range loomed stark and dark in the fading twilight. Devoid of snow, with only a few glaciers sunk into their massive crevices, they were a beautiful sight.

A huge cow moose, followed by her calf, appeared from the edge of the timber and walked toward the river. The elk winter-feeding grounds were vacant, waiting for the snows to drive the herds down from the high country. It was such a treat seeing the "Hole" without the usual crowds of tourists.

October 21—While climbing Togwotee Pass, darkness overtook us, and when we reached the Continental Divide, we could just barely see the light sprinkling of snow bordering the road. We drove down into the

Wind River country, where the dark shapes of wind- and weather-carved mountains loomed above, and the winding course of the Wind River glinted in starlight.

We pulled into Dubois, Wyoming, where we spent the night at a little log cabin motel by the name of "Trail's End." Wishing it were, we enjoyed a good night's rest before continuing our journey.

October 22—At 6,900 feet, Dubois had no frost this morning! Described as a rustic, western cowtown nestled in a valley between the Wind River and Absaroka Mountain ranges, Dubois is 30 miles east of the Continental Divide and boasts one of the largest herds of bighorn sheep in the U.S. We were thrilled to see these wild sheep from the road as we left town.

Many colorful and varied rock formations continued on into the Wind River Indian Reservation, the land where Sacajawea is buried. As we passed through Riverton, it appeared to be a thriving place with new building and activity going on everywhere. We approached Boysen Reservoir in Boysen State Park and saw the enormous body of blue water caused by the dam that holds back the Wind River.

Proceeding down the awesome Wind River Canyon, we read signs along the way that explained the formations of rocks and their ages. One sign stated that the bottom layer of rock was 600 million years old! Over the eons, the river had carved its way down the gorge. We stopped to look closely at what a 600 million-year-old rock looked like.

We were soon out of the canyon and entering Thermopolis, home of the world's largest mineral hot springs, according to a sign. There was a sulfur-like smell to the air, which we quickly adjusted to. Bubbling hot springs, with their halo of rising steam vapors, drew our eyes to the waters that ran down over a series of rocks to various public pools. Known to the Shoshone as "Bah-gue-wana" or "Smoking Waters," this mineral hot springs is still worshiped and used by the Indians.

The cone shape of the spring symbolizes the belief that the water comes from deep in the earth and brings to the surface health-giving elements, according to the local legend. People suffering from arthritis or other ills travel for miles to soak in the Thermopolis hot springs.

We finally arrived at our destination, a ranch that bordered the Big Horn River, where we soon were cuddling and cooing over little Ryan Douglas, who was quite accommodating and smiled back. Her long pigtails flying, four-year-old Lacey ran to meet us. Hugs for grandma, grandpa and auntie—what we had traveled all these miles for.

October 23—The weather was hot for October, even in Wyoming. Morning mists rose from the waters of the Big Horn River and the crows were raucous; there must have been hundreds of the noisy birds in all the surrounding meadows.

Later we drove up Kirby Creek, where we spotted several antelope feeding amid that vast land of sagebrush and rock. In the hazy distance we glimpsed the Big Horn Mountains.

This afternoon, Doug and I took Lacey with us and visited the old coal-mining townsite of Gebo, which was quite a place during its heyday

October 24—We enjoyed lunch today in Thermopolis at a place called Pumpernicks, which is decorated with artifacts from the old town of Gebo. We were amused to see horses tied out front of the town's saloons. Saddled, they waited patiently for their riders, who were participating in a "poker ride." Lori and Tom explained that the riders order a drink at the bar, receive a playing card, mount their horses, sometimes with drink in hand, and ride to the next saloon and repeat the process, until they have a poker hand.

Best hand at the end of the ride wins. That is, if they can still see and don't fall off their horses. Driving along the street later, we were held up by these men, and women, who took up the entire street, and no one seemed to mind! We also noticed a team of horses pulling a wagon load of very merry people, whom we guessed were part of the same ride.

Linda, Lacey and I went swimming in the Tee Pee Pool. Pure heaven. We first swam inside, then walked to the outside pool, which was wonderfully refreshing and relaxing. An experience I shall always dream about. While leaves swirled downward from some nearby trees, a cool October breeze sprang up. We remained warm and cozy, submerged in the natural hot springs water. Dark, purple clouds formed—wind clouds—and we luxuriated in the healing waters and fresh air of Wyoming.

We were hungry as bears when we returned to Lori and Tom's, where we enjoyed a special ham dinner that Lori had prepared to celebrate several birthdays. Even had birthday cake and a Halloween jack-o-lantern that grandpa and Lacey had carved.

October 25—I was up early, before sunup, to take color slides of a Wyoming sunrise. Frosty cold, but the effort was worth it on this beautiful October morn. We remembered to turn our watches back, but I was still on Oregon time, which is now set back, and Mountain Time is an hour later! Oh well, on this trip I'll go by when the sun comes up and sets.

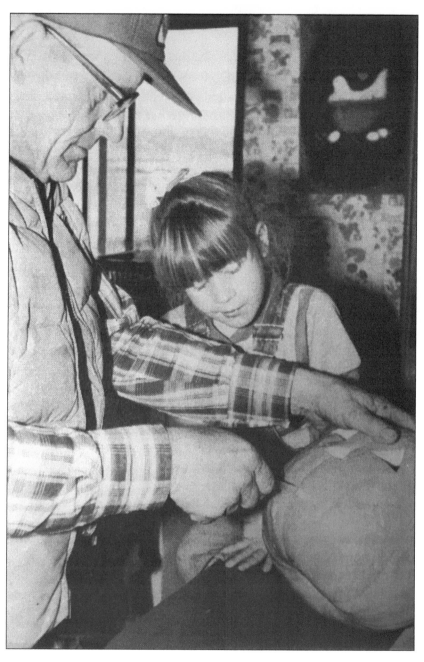

Doug Tippett and granddaughter Lacey carve a jack o' lantern.

We said our goodbyes to our Wyoming family and drove toward Metetsee and on to Cody, where we had a cup of tea at the Irma Hotel. Built in honor of Buffalo Bill's youngest daughter, Irma Cody, this hotel was opened to the public on November 1, 1902.

For many years the Irma has been the gathering place for local stockmen, woolgrowers and oilmen. Many thousands of dollars continue to change hands each year over a cup of coffee and a handshake. For 83 years the Irma has stood, with its historic heritage so rich with memories, it just had to be preserved. The old rooms had been redone, but the old flavor of that Victorian period prevails.

We enjoyed our visit there and sure enough the place was full of stockmen and several families eating a Sunday morning brunch. As we drove along the Shoshone River and up toward the east entrance to Yellowstone, we noticed a cloud of dust swirling down the canyon. A high wind was blowing the dirt, which appeared as thick as fog or smoke.

I guessed it was man-made, and was right! The inevitable road construction that seems to be going on all over these days. It seems someone is forever bent on tearing apart or rearranging what it has taken Mother Nature eons to create—and why? The money that is being spent is beyond my understanding.

It was a relief to enter the park, where the lack of tourists was evident and the quiet serenity of wildness contrasted with the furious activity going on outside. We were treated to the sight of hundreds of wild geese swimming or walking along the shores of Yellowstone Lake. High winds whipped the lake waters to a froth and the geese bobbed up and down like corks.

We saw many buffalo, their dark bodies appearing in the golden meadows. Autumn in Yellowstone...the best time to visit. The visitor centers and lodges all buttoned up for winter and virtually no traffic. We drove toward Canyon and the north entrance. Mammoth Hot Springs was quiet and I photographed the steaming waters that spilled down pretty, multi-colored rocks. Nearby we spotted a large herd of elk bedded down near some park service homes. Among them were several large bulls, which lay chewing their cuds, just under the windows of the houses.

We exited the park at Gardiner and found a place to eat lunch before heading up the Yellowstone River to Livingstone and Bozeman. Lovely, wind-swept clouds created shadows that floated across the vast Montana landscape.

Doug took us on a brief side trip to Manhattan and Amsterdam, where the Manhattan seed potato growers were located. We were very impressed with their neat, tidy and prosperous-looking farms. These Dutch descendants appeared to be a very industrious people. In the small town named Amsterdam were small wooden windmills in nearly every yard. It is from this area we purchased our potato seed last year.

It was dusk when we topped the Continental Divide and looked down on the hundreds of blinking lights in Butte. A slice of new moon stuck in a cloud and the weather was extremely mild. Down in that glitter of lights, we spent the night.

October 26—Up at 4:30. Many miles to go before we sleep. Drove in the dark toward Missoula and watched the darkness fade and the mountains take shape before a beautiful Montana sunrise ensued. We stopped to breakfast at Deer Lodge before heading to Missoula. The fall colors were gorgeous here; prettiest we'd seen on the trip thus far.

We stopped to rest at Lolo before heading up Lolo Pass, a beautiful drive with more fall color. Down the Locksa and Clearwater rivers, gleaming brighly in the autumn sunshine. Yellowing leaves and river for 193 miles!

It was 3 p.m. when we left Clarkston after a visit with aunt Betty, and drove to Pendleton. We said goodbye to Linda and began the long journey home to Wallowa County. Today we traveled in Montana, Idaho. Washington and Oregon.

Such is life in the great Northwest.

October 27—My milk cow Startch so glad to see me back this morning. She nearly pushed me off my feet in her haste to enter the barn. The fall colors are brilliant around the county, when normally most of the leaves would be long gone this time of year. The area is incredibly dry as the days continue without a drop of rain.

Son-in-law Charley and friend Scott drove in this afternoon from Fish Springs Ranch, Nevada, for the opening of elk season. Treated them to a Wallowa County meal tonight: blue grouse, sourdough biscuits, mashed potatoes, gravy, salad and blackberry pie. Those two really put away the chow.

October 28—Up at 4 a.m. fixing breakfast of sausage, eggs, more biscuits with raspberry jam, then lunches for the elk hunters.

Daughter-in-law Liza had a cow tag for the Zumwalt area, so she brought sleepy little James over for me to watch. James and I went back to bed to catch a little more shut-eye before going out to do the barn chores. With my little buddy sitting in his backpack on grandma's back, we managed to get everything done.

It was so warm today James and I went for a walk, which he loves. I had a time keeping up with him as he ran most of the way. The hunters returned this evening with the most incredible hunting stories...but no elk. Meanwhile, I had whipped up another big meal, using the good Imnaha squash and some pork chops. Everyone early to bed.

October 29—Doug up this morning fixing breakfast for the hunters, who left before daylight. Milked the cow, fed and watered chickens, then walked around our ranch on this beautiful morning, photographing the gorgeous fall colors.

Attended a meeting around 10 a.m. to complete plans to premier our "Wallowa Story" at the OK Theater on November 17.

The visiting hunters haven't bagged their bulls yet, but not because they haven't seen any. They are having a great time covering lots of country. Doug returned late, having filled his cow elk tag. The men went out to the shop after supper to skin the animal.

October 30—All of us up at 4:30. Doug fixing breakfast again...sourdough's on the wood stove.

Meanwhile, I went out in the dark to chore before leaving for Alder Slope to watch James for Liza, who had to leave by 6 to drive the 60 miles to La Grande and attend Eastern Oregon State College. She is taking courses there during the fall term to make up some missing credits. James and I had a great time and spent most of it outside, as it was warm and sunny all day.

Later, at home, I put a 20-pound ham to roast in the oven as most of our family will converge on us for supper tonight. Everyone wants one last visit with Charley before he leaves tomorrow. The little cousins, my grandchildren, who love an excuse to get together, especially enjoyed the evening. They seem to be growing up all of a sudden.

For entertainment we watched James and listened to more hunting stories. We lit the candle in the grinning pumpkin and turned out the lights. The Imnaha family spent the night and Tooth Fairy Grandma got up in the middle of the night to perform her duty.

October 31—Halloween dawns cloudy with the feel of snow in the air. Charley and Scott went for one last hunt this morning before leaving for home. Jackie's family left for Imnaha, Buck still clutching his dollar bill and flashing a toothless grin. The hunters returned, without their elk, but had tracked a big bull halfway up the mountain before they gave up. Doug and Ben to the hills all day fixing fence.

Received a letter from my three sisters. They will be here next week for a visit. Developed film and wrote articles for Agri-Times all afternoon, as it is very quiet with everyone suddenly gone. The willows and cottonwoods cast a golden glow, reflected in the waters of the creek. Soon a wind began to blow, and golden showers of leaves were tossed about in the early darkness when I went out to chore.

Boiled up the elk neck meat to make mincemeat. I lit the candle in the pumpkin, propped him in the high chair and placed him in front of our picture window. Tenderfoot Valley Road was so quiet tonight, however, that not one single car passed by.

Windy, cloudy and spooky outside. So long, October.

November 1—It is raining! The first appreciable moisture since August. Finally, the long drought is broken. Even if it only amounts to a few drizzles, at least the dust is settled. Red, yellow and brown leaves are softened by the warm rain. We seem to be a month behind.

Doug is smoking elk jerky and the cats and dogs are feasting on the meat scraps. I wandered around outside picking up pretty leaves to put in a basket. Pulled up the last of my huge sunflowers, carried it to the house and stood it by the front door, its drooping head full of seeds.

The constant running battle that I wage with the strawberry patch goes on. Right now the weeds are ahead, so I hoed, hoed, hoed until, finally, I won! I hope the cold weather will arrive and put a halt to further growth until spring, when the war will resume.

On this Sunday afternoon Doug and I drove to Imnaha, where we ordered chicken basket dinners at the Riverside Cafe. While we ate, we visited with 87-year-old Jim Dorrance, who is the official greeter and host of Imnaha, having been promoted from dishwasher. Elk hunters trooped in and out and we caught snatches of their conversations. It seems overall success was good this year.

Clouds obscure the moon tonight.

November 2—Rained off and on all night. Wonderful rain. The mountains hidden by misty clouds.

Peeled apples and combined all the ingredients for making mince-meat, the amounts of which are measured in bowls. So many bowls of cooked ground elk, apples, raisins, vinegar, apple cider... By noon the fragrant concoction simmered happily away on the stove.

The Halloween pumpkin is baking in the oven to make pies and my kitchen smells like fall. How sweet it is to breathe moist air and walk through puddles instead of dust. The veil of mist lifted over the mountains this morning, and shafts of sunlight filtered down between clouds to reveal the high peaks on Chief Joseph Mountain and Sacajawea, once again white with snow.

November 3—While Doug was looking at his rain gauge this morning, a spider crawled out of it. "Guess that spider drank what moisture was in there," he said. Many tall tales such as this are circulating around the Northwest during the dry fall we are experiencing.

After chores, I drove to Joseph, where I retreated to the basement darkroom to print photos. Worked steadily until after noon. Ran errands, then home to bake a pumpkin pie from the Halloween jack-o-lantern.

Watched grandchildren Buck and Mona Lee this evening while mom and dad attended a meeting in Enterprise. Seven-year-old Buck can sure put away the elk steak, potatoes and gravy, not to mention pie.

November 4—Twenty-eight degrees, heavy frost on this beautiful, bright, sunny morning. The last fall colors cling to the trees. Spent most of this day cleaning house and placing fresh sheets on the spare beds in anticipation of the arrival of my three sisters.

While washing the bathroom curtains, I noted that in places they simply disintegrated. I wondered why until I realized they were more than 20 years old. Patched them up and rehung them. After all they have antique value now. Besides, crisp, clean muslin is always in style.

My sisters, Mary Ann, Kathryn and Caroline, will leave from California in the morning. I can scarcely wait to see them. We have dreamed of meeting like this for years in Wallowa County. As I set a batch of sourdough biscuits to rise, a chill settled over Prairie Creek.

It was around 4 p.m. when the sun disappeared over the mountain. Just 15 minutes later, a large, fat November moon rose over the eastern hill. I finished choring at the barn and hurried to the warmth of my kitchen.

November 5—Prepared breakfast on the old Monarch wood range. Our weaned calves continue to bawl loudly down in the feedlot. Poor babies want their mamas. More colorful leaves fall to the ground on this 18-degree morning. While delivering eggs to one of my customers, I noticed the new dusting of snow on the mountain tops. It is almost a novelty to see the white stuff again after so many months.

Baked pumpkin and fresh mincemeat pies this afternoon, then invited Max and Dorothy Gorsline over for the evening to view slides I'd taken on our trip up the South Fork of the Imnaha. This would help pass the time while waiting for my sisters to arrive. I tried to imagine the three of them watching the full moon rise somewhere over the Owyhee mountains.

We enjoyed the slide show, Max and Dorothy's company, and the pies before the gals arrived safely around 11 p.m. And they had indeed seen the moon rise over the Owyhees!

November 6—So excited I could hardly sleep, and was up early fixing breakfast and planning our day. After chores we climbed into two pickups and headed for Imnaha on this perfect fall morning. Beautiful clouds floated in an azure sky, and fall colored leaves were brilliant in the canyon's draws and along Little Sheep Creek.

Visited daughter Jackie and children before driving down the Imnaha canyon to Cow Creek. This was a first for my sisters. They loved it as we skirted the high rims and looked down from dizzying heights to the river below. A patch of brilliant red sumac greeted us at Pack Saddle Creek, and on a high grassy bench we met son-in-law Bill on horseback. Nearby grazed a herd of cattle that were being trailed to the range at Dug Bar. What a picture they made, the cattle amid the golden fall grasses, the cowboys, their horses and dogs in that wild canyon setting.

Bill told us they would drive the herd to Horse Creek tonight, and on to the Snake River country the next day. We visited with Dave and Mona Glaus, who were riding along the road helping with the drive. Another cowboy, Dan Bronson, was sleeping on a sunny hillside, while next to him stood his horse and dog. Bill explained that this was lunch stop, as they had left before daylight this morning.

After a brief visit and a round of picture-taking, we continued on down past Horse Creek, Tulley Creek and the Corral Creek Ranch before parking near the Cow Creek bridge. Doug went on ahead, riding his Japanese quarter horse, Honda, to select a spot for our picnic, while the four of us walked along the Imnaha Gorge Trail.

We ate our lunch near the river in a sunny clearing, then took our time walking and photographing as there were new sights to be seen at every bend in the trail. The recent rain had calmed the dust and everything appeared fresh and the water-smell of the river itself was wonderful. There was an abundance of wildlife, including merganser and mallard ducks, water ouzels (dippers), chukars, and the evidence of several busy beavers. The trail was made colorful by the presence of red sumac and bright, yellow willows, not to mention the colorful canyon rock formations. We feasted our senses on the four-mile walk to the Snake River.

It was nearly 3 p.m. when we arrived at the Imnaha's mouth and found that Doug had already caught a steelhead. As darkness comes early to the canyon country in November, we were headed back up the trail by 4 o'clock.

About a quarter-mile from the old mine tunnel, we were treated to a rare sight: three full-curl rams, wild mountain sheep, looking at us from across the river on the opposite canyon side. As dusk enveloped the gorge, various shades of blues and purples appeared on the canyon sides and the brightly-colored sumac intensified and gave off a glow of light along the trail. While my two younger sisters took off in the lead, Mary Ann and I brought up the rear.

In the gathering darkness we were startled by a large owl that flew out ahead of us. By the time we reached the pickup, it was totally dark. As we slowly drove the long canyon miles to Imnaha, a gorgeous moon rose over the rim rocks that border the Snake River country. Far below, in the solitary house at Horse Creek, we could see the tiny glow of a kerosene lantern. Here Bill and the crew were spending the night. One single light in the night, surrounded by endless wild canyon and miles of unpeopled places. Large mule-like ears and glowing eyes of many deer feeding on the golden, moon-washed grasses shone in our headlights.

As we rounded the final high rim, we looked down to see the first lights of the settlement of Imnaha. We joined the first pickup load at the Imnaha Store for a glass of its famous dark beer before walking next door to order supper at the Riverside Cafe. Such a fun time, even though we were a bit weary from the eight-mile hike. A perfect day. The camaraderie of my sisters, Doug feeling good about catching his fish; a day to be remembered for always.

November 7—Cloudy, cold, yesterday only a dream.

Today was spent visiting family and friends, showing off my children and grandchildren. We met Doug for lunch at the Country Place on Pete's Pond in Enterprise.

November 8—After a hardy breakfast of sourdough waffles, my three sisters helped me with chores. It almost seemed as though time stood still, and we were growing up again on the small Placer County foothill dairy of our youth—until we looked at each other's gray hair!

The cow was milked and the chickens tended, we left to meet friend Bill at the Hurricane Creek Trailhead. Because this was one of our father's favorite trails, the area has always held a special significance.

Even though most of the fall color was gone from the high country, the air was crisp and cold, and views of mountains, forest and fall creek very refreshing. Sitting on a fallen log near Deadman meadow, we munched on granola bars and visited. We were surprised to see Deadman Creek completely dry. Leaving the meadow, we crossed the creek and hunted up an old log cabin hidden in the trees. Apparently built by an early-day sheepherder, the cabin is now inhabited by a family of packrats.

Suddenly, a fall wind sprang up as we climbed the steep trail to Slick Rock. Here the air was cooler and we gazed down at the creek, which flowed through a steep-sided, rocky gorge to form frothy pools in the narrow caverns carved by the gorge. We paused where Slick Rock Creek falls over a solid rock face to join Hurricane Creek, and rested a bit before heading back down the trail. We looked back to see Sacajawea Mountain lit with late afternoon sunlight and wearing a blanket of new snow.

Arriving back at the trailhead, we were followed by a fellow on horseback leading a string of mules that were packing out a five-point bull elk. Hurried home to get a loaf of sourdough bread to rise, while Kathryn tossed a big salad and Doug barbecued the steelhead. A feast to end another perfect day.

November 9—A pink sunrise preceded a cloudy, rainy day. Up early to put a three-hour rice pudding to bake on the oven, a favor for sister Kathryn. The chores and pudding done, we piled into Caroline's car and "did" the shops. What fun. I felt like a tourist in my own town. We visited Centennial House, Eagle Mountain Gallery, and the Art Angle.

By mid-morning it had begun to rain pretty good, and by noon we were seated in the Common Good Market Place on Enterprise's Main Street eating lunch: delicious homemade mushroom soup and sandwiches. We drove back to the ranch for rice pudding.

The cowboys branding our fall calves down at the chutes all day in the rain. All too soon it was time for good-bys. Bearing sourdough starter, homemade pickles, sauerkraut, granola, elk jerky and rolls of exposed film of Wallowa County, they left. A sad moment when they drove out of sight. The gloomy weather matched my melancholy mood.

Soon, though, I was again immersed in the preparation of our history project's meeting tonight in Enterprise. By 5:30, leaving Doug's supper in the oven, I was on my way to Enterprise, where Grace Bartlett, Steve Roundy, Dave Nelson and I worked on the "Wallowa Story" at radio station KWVR until 11 p.m.

We were all so tired by the time we finished, we could barely keep our eyes open. Dave will record the final narrative on the tape and Steve will synchronize the audio-visual, and it will be ready for the premier showing on the 17th. Hoorah!

November 10—Clear and frosty, until a fog bank rolled over Prairie Creek. The men finished working the fall calves today, and Doug presented me with a large panful of mountain oysters to clean. We sure had a lot of bull calves this year.

The fog, which didn't lift all day, limited visibility, and several of the calves had gotten away during the day and were wandering around the county roads.

November 11—The sun not having much luck attempting to peek through the fog. Am now feeding a bunch of peewee calves, in addition to Startch's big heifer, who towers over them. Our neighbors begin to call this morning, telling us the whereabouts of the missing calves.

Filled out forms for my new 4-H club members. Thirty of them again this year. I can tell these new-fangled forms are for computer use when they reach an office. In the meantime, the volunteer 4-H leader must amass all the info and codes at her kitchen table. With 30 members, this is no small task.

In between this, I typed my weekly column. A warm fire cracks and pops in the wood stove and is the only sound I hear. Outside, the ranch noises are muted in the fog. My world has shrunk to the circle of light on the kitchen table where I write.

Neighbor Ardis Klages called to report some of our missing calves are in with their cows. Made an apple pie for son Steve's birthday, and another one for us. The cowboys have finally succeeded in rounding up the runaway doggies.

Darkness comes early now and the evenings are long. I feel like a sleepy, hibernating bear and have the urge to curl up somewhere and sleep away the winter. The frantic pace of the past spring, summer and fall is finally catching up with me. To bed early.

November 12—The drippy drizzle of a warm rain on Prairie Creek this morning makes us feel like it is "September in the Rain" instead of November. Whipped up (from scratch) a lemon pie for son Ken's pie-a-month birthday present, before attending our monthly CowBelle meeting this afternoon at C. Belle Probert's on Prairie Creek.

Our busy CowBelles have so many projects planned, it makes me tired to think about them all. These gals have to eat plenty of beef to keep up their energy.

Doug home from the 120-mile round-trip to attend the La Grande Livestock auction today.

November 13—Misty rain falls on this Friday. Doug to the hills to check on our cattle while I attempted to catch up on backlog of letter writing. A new storm moves in as blustery winds, rain and dark clouds race across the sky. It is fascinating to watch these clouds boil up, change shapes and move on. The wind slackened somewhat before bedtime and the smell of snow is in the air.

November 14—Awoke around 2:30 a.m. to an unusual light: the moon shining brightly between clouds. With the coming of daylight, we looked outside to see snow covering everything. Even though only a light skift, it had transformed our dreary world!

Yesterday's winds had stripped the very last leaves from the trees. It was 29 degrees. Out in the snow to chore, then began typing "CowBelle Corner" for our local newspaper.

The snow melted by afternoon, so I planted two rows of garlic, pulled some beets and picked the remaining two heads of cabbage.

We ate our last meal fresh from the garden tonight: coleslaw, beets, swiss chard, accompanied by fried chicken, buttermilk biscuits and milk gravy. A good, hot meal on a cold, snowy night.

November 15—The ground white with frost; 20 degrees. The wood stove gulped wood all day. What an appetite.

Daughter-in-law Liza, baby James, Liza's mom, Wanda, and I drove in the four-wheel-drive up on the moraine this morning to gather pine cones for Christmas wreaths. Later, we drove toward Imnaha to pick red rose hips, juniper berries and elderberries. We saw many deer, including a small herd of whitetails, grazing in a hayfield. When we drove "On Top" of Sheep Creek Hill, we watched as another herd of mule deer ran, jumped and played in the early darkness.

Very cold tonight. Winter is here in Wallowa County.

November 16—Cloudy and cold; snowing in the mountains. After chores, I drove through a mini-snow squall to Joseph, where I met with our history committee to complete plans for the premier showing of "The Wallowa Story."

Doug, Ben and Steve to the hills, hauling in more calves to be weaned. Baked a blueberry buckle and started an elk stew simmering on the wood range. By mid-afternoon, a real blizzard materialized and the snow began to stick.

Dark by 4 when I did chores and the men returned with more bawling calves. The wind died down after supper and the storm blew over, leaving Prairie Creek wrapped in frigid silence and a winter-white blanket.

November 17—Clear and 9 degrees! Bundled up to chore, I stepped outside to the din in the feedlot, a wall of sound produced by our bawling calves.

Tonight is the BIG night. The premier of our "Wallowa Story." The culmination of more than a year's worth of work. Throughout the day lines from the script ran through my mind...will it be accepted? Will people like it and really come to see it on this cold night?

Doug and I drove into Enterprise on this clear, cold evening. There it was on the OK Theater's marquee: "The Wallowa Story." Grace, Chuck, Steve, Dave and I felt like playwrights on opening night.

People began to arrive before 7. By 7:30, they continued to pour into the old theater. People from Paradise, Flora, Imnaha, Wallowa, Lostine, Alder Slope, Prairie Creek, Joseph and Enterprise, even a few from out of the county. The seating capacity at the OK is 400 and it filled up. Still they came, and chairs were set up in every available space.

Grace, Dave, Doug and I stood in the aisle, so others could have seats. A few were turned away or chose to go home and see it another time, as there simply was nowhere left to sit.

Then the opening lines could be heard, along wjth the projecting of the slides of our beautiful county. It was for real! A very exciting moment for those of us who had labored for months over this project.

After the 45-minute presentation was over, I showed slides of Wallowa County pioneer descendants accompanied by their taped interviews. The program was well received and all the hours spent seemed worthwhile. What a relief.

The people spilled out of the theater into the cold Wallowa County night and went home to continue living their daily lives, lives that will write the next 100 years of "The Wallowa Story." As we drove home I wondered just what our county would be like 100 years from now.

November 18—Another clear, nine-degree morning. Doug off to a 7 a.m. potato meeting in Enterprise. I did chores, turning Startch's calf out with her, as we will be leaving for Portland today to attend the Oregon cattlemen's convention. Packed what we needed for the trip; then our car wouldn't start. It was 12:30 before we finally got away from the ranch.

We stopped in Lostine to eat lunch before heading out of the county. Doug got sleepy at the top of Minam Hill, so I drove through La Grande and on to Pendleton. The roads, which were free of ice and snow, made traveling pleasant.

I pulled into Arlington to rest before continuing on along the Columbia River. The sun began to sink into the western horizon and the river's water was being tossed about by a wind, causing little wavelets to slap against the shoreline.

Hundreds of Canadian honkers, some flying low over the water, some swimming, while others flew in large wavering V's upriver. Mount Hood loomed in the dusky, pink twilight. The colorful sky reflected in the Columbia's waters near Hood River. Darkness, and with it we could see hundreds of blinking lights gleam along the shoreline as we sped along the freeway. The speeds at which people drove seemed to accelerate as we approached Portland.

Alongside of us I noticed the drivers hunched over their steering wheels, grimly trying to outmaneuver their counterparts. Some began weaving in and out, while others maintained frightening speeds in the fast lane. We were soon swept along in a vast stream of light, heading into the city like lemmings rushing to the sea.

My Wallowa County cowboy husband drives in Portland just as though he were still in the saddle or driving a four-wheel-drive vehicle over our back country. He gets his bearings, oblivious to freeway signs, by heading "over a hill" or "down that draw." Anything goes to arrive at a given destination. So, thinking we should be close to Lloyd Center, he zoomed onto an off ramp that deposited us into the middle of the Hollywood district.

At this point, the horse, 'er, car, must be made to stop at stop signs, which appear at every block, turn the right way on a one-way street, and avoid pedestrians, all the while heading in the direction of a glowing Red Lion leering at us from afar.

We actually made it and came galloping into the rear entrance, made a fancy U-turn, and reined up in front of the hotel. From then on, our world was transformed from the work-a-day world of ranch life to one of catered ease. A valet loaded our luggage onto a cart as we stepped into the luxurious confines of the Red Lion Motor Inn.

Life becomes very uncomplicated as far as creature comforts, but much more complicated by other standards. By pressing a button, a glass elevator sweeps us to the 11th floor. The valet, a young boy, carries our luggage into the room, holds out his hand for a tip, and vanishes with "Have a good day." It is night.

In our room above the city, huge sliding glass doors open to reveal a high balcony that overlooks east Portland. I look down on hundreds of lights that form a steady stream of motion, flowing into the city. Thus ensconced in our room, with two queen-size beds, thick carpet, bath, dressing room, two toilet paper holders, two sinks, color TV, wake-up-to-the-music radio, and lights everywhere, we take the elevator down to the coffee shop and order dinner.

A far cry from coming into the house after evening chores and smelling supper cooking on the wood stove. Seated next to us are two charming little ladies from Prineville, Oregon. We become acquainted and learn they both know people we know. Even in a big city, it is a small world. Soon we met the large delegation beginning to arrive from Wallowa County, one that would number nearly 50, counting children, who would be present for Bill Wolfe's president's banquet.

It was like old home week when we saw our neighbors, Willie and Nancy Locke, Trudy and Steve Allison, Rod and Linda Childers, the Birkmaiers from way out on Crow Creek, Hazel Johnson, Pat and Judy Wortman, Duke and Rhea Lathrop, Melvin and Mary Lou Brink, Marilyn and Reid Johnson, the Rex Zieglers, and more, traveling to the western side of the state to attend the 74th annual cattlemen's convention.

To bed early, the first good sleep I've had in two days.

November 19—Up at 6:30 to look out on the city. A thin slice of moon hung over the eastern horizon and the snowy hulk of Mount Hood was outlined in a salmon sky full of high cirrus clouds edged in pink lace.

Commuter traffic, already flowing into the city, formed a wavering line of lights. From atop Meier and Frank, a large American flag waved gently in the morning breeze. The city was awakening. Or did it ever go to sleep?

Several pigeons flew past the window and I could hear the far-off scream of a siren fading into the dull traffic's roar. Western Oregon viewed by an Eastern Oregonian. Prairie Creek seemed non-existent.

Opening ceremonies began at 9 with an address by Oregon Governor Neil Goldschmidt. From 1:30 to 5, the CattleWomen met in the exhibit hall across the street.

That night we all attended Western Fun Night and participated in the silent auction to raise money for the 1989 National Beef Cook-Off, which will be in Portland. Ron Baker, C&B Livestock, supervised the carving of huge "Light Beef" roasts that were served with thin slices of french bread, horseradish and hot mustard.

Beef producers partook of their nutritious product and it was indeed delicious.

Nov. 20—By 8 a.m. a few of us CowBelles and CattleWomen were already sitting in on planning sessions involving the 1989 National Beef

Cookoff, which will be held here in Portland. I spent most of the day there, as I will be working with the press during this gigantic undertaking.

I did manage to walk across the street to Lloyd Center and purchase some photography supplies. I enjoyed being outside for a change, on this pretty fall day. Some skaters were twirling and gliding around a huge ice-skating rink, situated in the middle of the shopping center.

Christmas decorations were already up, including a huge Christmas tree that had been "created" by sticking branches strung with hundreds of tiny lights into holes that had been drilled into the trunk of the mighty tree. Meier and Frank was very festive with old wooden carousel horses decorated with greenery and ribbon. It is always fun to ride the escalators, even though I have quite a time finding stairs that go up and ones that go down.

At a joint CattleWomen-Cattlemen luncheon, we enjoyed visiting with Agri-Times's Virgil Rupp. John Huston from Chicago, the "Head Cat," as described by Polly Owen of the National Livestock and Meat Board, was an impressive spokesman for the industry. He expounded on the benefits of the National Beef Cook-off and lauded Oregon's Polly Owen, who holds a prestigious position on the Meat Board.

Huston, who is a former farmboy-4-H'er, also mentioned the excellent job done by another Oregon CattleWoman, Gerda Hyde, outgoing president of the National CattleWomen. I spent the remainder of the day sitting in on further cook-off planning meetings conducted by chairman Ann Tracy and new Oregon CattleWoman President, Bonnie Thornburg.

These gals spent most of the convention hammering out the multitude of details hosting the 1989 National Beef Cook-off. The project is pulling together Oregon CowBelles and CattleWomen in a gigantic effort to make this the best cook-off ever!

Tonight was the president's banquet. Before going down to the banquet room, Martha Jane Jacobs from Baker County told us this story:

It seems this Brahma-cross calf, weighing close to 650 pounds, escaped while their crew was working calves, and ran down the road to a neighbor's rather elegant house, cowboys and gals in hot pursuit. The calf disappeared around the back of the house and pretty soon they heard glass breaking.

The calf, seeing daylight through solid glass windows, had simply broken through. He continued through the living room before busting out another set of windows near the front entrance!

"He tipped over a Jade plant, missed the baby grand piano and left a few tracks on the white carpet, before fleeing down the road in the

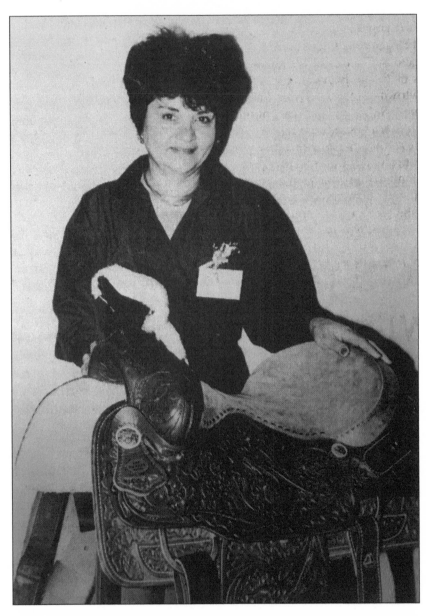

Mary Lou Brink of Enterprise took home this $1,500 custom-made saddle from the Oregon beef industry convention. She is the wife of farmer and stockman Melvin Brink.

Susan Evans of Heppner, 1987 president of Oregon CattleWomen, unwrapped this gift as one of her last official acts at the state convention.

direction from whence he came!" Leaving chaos in his wake, and this story for Martha Jane to tell at convention.

We once again had the pleasure of being seated next to Virgil Rupp and becoming more aquainted with the editor of Agri-Times, as we partook of a sirloin steak dinner. Wallowa County delegates were just plain lucky. Mary Lou Brink, Enterprise, won a $1,500 custom-made saddle. Then our extension agent, Arleigh Isly, won a pair of his-and-her boots for himself and wife, Glenna.

Pat Wortman LOST his boots somewhere when they walked away from the elevator entrance, only to re-appear at the end of the Convention! Bill Wolfe, newly installed Oregon Cattlemen president, won the big, beautiful Simmental bell. Dave Parker of Alder Slope won a hatful of silk flowers, and several of us CowBelles won sorting sticks. I plan on using mine often.

What is a sorting stick, you ask? Well, most of you gals can relate to being asked to stand by a swing corral gate and let "ins" in and "bys" by. However...if most of you are like me, you figure out beforehand what is being sorted...heifers, steers, different colored ear tags or culls; so YOU can determine if it is an "in" or a "by". That way, you don't have to make a quick change when the critter approaches the gate as an "in" and hubby suddenly changes his mind and says "by".

This is when the sorting stick will come in handy! To hit husband? Of course not, BUT to persuade the animal to change its mind.

The large Wallowa County delegation gave their own Bill Wolfe a rousing cheer when he was introduced at the banquet. Between Bill's family and the rest of us, we made an impressive cheering section.

November 21—Attended the CattleWomen's general session presided over by new president, Bonnie Thornburg, after which Diane Byrne and Janet Lund, of the Oregon Beef Council, put on a Beef-in-the-Microwave demo. Bob Skinner of Jordan Valley, out-going president, served as master of ceremonies at the last joint luncheon as the convention ended.

This year's meetings were a "hype" for the cattle producer, so to speak, a nudge we all needed to return to our ranches and continue raising beef. Now, as never before, producers need to be involved, not only with raising beef, but promoting and marketing as well. We all agreed that we had gained a lot from attending this 1987 convention.

Next year the convention will be held in Baker to commemorate its 75th year, as the first convention was held there. We hope Martha Jane keeps that run-a-way calf under control!

It was nearly 2 p.m. when we left on a cloudy afternoon and entered the freeway to be swept away in an exodus from the city. The fall colors in the gorge were lovely and it began to rain at Cascade Locks. The rain subsided and, by the time we rested at Boardman, the temperature was a balmy 40 degrees. Climbing up Cabbage Hill, we looked back to see the lights of Pendleton below. Over the Blues to LaGrande where we stopped to eat a Chinese dinner at Fong's.

Home around 9:30, the big city and freeways all behind us. Quiet, cold and still on Prairie Creek.

November 22—Back into the routine of ranch living, beginning the day by fixing breakfast on the wood cook stove. Windy, frosty and clear. Snow all melted except for the mountains. The milk cows glad to see me, as were the barn cats, waiting for their bowl of warm milk. Even Chester the rooster mumbled something about wondering where I had been!

Developed a roll of film I had taken at convention, and wrote some articles. Attended a Chamber of Commerce dinner meeting on this Sunday evening at the Joseph Civic Center. It was spitting snow when I picked up Wanda McAlister, James's other grandma, in Joseph. We enjoyed a delicious meal featuring Cornish game hen, after which Gerald Perren conducted a short meeting and awarded the civic leader, educator, and business leader awards.

November 24—Our cattle, pastured out in the hill country, were trailed to the valley while Doug and I attended the cattlemen's convention. They are now grazing a rented pasture on upper Prairie Creek. The fall calvers, hearing the sound of the silage truck, run to meet it each afternoon. Having cleaned up their daily ration of hay, they look forward to this treat.

It began to snow heavily while I chored this evening. A wind blew all day, warning of the approaching storm. Naturally, I began to worry about daughter Ramona's family, on their way up from Chilcoot, California, to spend Thanksgiving with us. Much relieved when they arrived safe and sound around 6:30.

November 25—Fixed a hearty breakfast of ham and eggs and sourdough cinnamon rolls. Thirteen-year-old grandson Shawn helped me chore on this snowy, 27-degree morning. Ramona washed the breakfast dishes while I strained the milk, then she, Charley and the children were off to Imnaha to visit daughter Jackie's family.

I completed some photojournalism assignments before beginning to cook for the big Thanksgiving meal here tomorrow. A kettle of cranberries soon began popping red skins on top of the wood range, and the fragrance of mincemeat and pumpkin pies filled my country kitchen. I cleaned house while the pies baked, and made up a panful of spaghetti sauce for supper.

The family returned with big appetites and we enjoyed a cozy supper around our kitchen table. It stopped snowing and the radio announced that the temperature is supposed to dip to seven degrees by morning.

November 26—A beautiful Thanksgiving Day, not as cold as predicted. Ramona fixed breakfast for the crew while I chored. The children are all excited about visiting more of their cousins.

Shawn, who had spent the night on Little Sheep Creek with cousin Buck, was last seen climbing a steep canyon with his cousin, looking for deer. They'll have a great time. My oldest grandchild, Tammy, is very much grown up at 17 and is a delightful young lady who now talks about college!

Because there would be 21 of us for dinner, Doug and Charley set up two sawhorses with plywood for another table. We added tablecloths, and the grandchildren decorated the tables with Indian corn, fall leaves and nuts. Out came the pretty desert rose Franciscan-ware plates, and the place began to look festive indeed.

I had it pretty soft this year, as daughters-in-law Annie and Liza each brought a cooked turkey, and Liza's mom made the dressing. Jackie arrived earlier, bearing a large pan of whole-wheat roll dough, which she proceeded to turn into tempting hot rolls, fresh from the oven to the table. Annie brought a large salad, so all I had to do was prepare mashed potatoes and gravy.

I mixed up a fruit punch in an earthen ware crock and the food was ready to eat by 1:30. It was pretty overwhelming with everyone seated, holding hands in our Thanksgiving tradition, while Jackie said the blessing. How truly thankful we were, all together on this Thanksgiving.

After dinner, the young wives took charge of clean-up and dishes, and shooed we oldsters out of the kitchen. Glad for an excuse to visit among themselves, they made short work of the dishes, and without the aid of a dishwasher. They had a great time, laughing, joking and reminiscing about their growing-up years.

While some of us retired to the living room to be entertained by 17-month-old James, the "herd" of young "country cousins" ran around outside on this pretty day.

By late afternoon the crowd began to thin somehwat, after several pies were consumed. The young families returned to their homes to stoke home fires and do chores. What a wonderful, happy, family time.

November 27—Twelve degrees! The household awoke by stages and we staggered breakfasts, then piled into Ramona and Charley's Bronco and drove to Alder Slope, where I remained with Mona and James while the gals did the shops.

By 1 we were all together for lunch at The Common Good Market Place in Enterprise. Fun being with my daughters. Young people seem to rejuvenate me.

Everyone returned to our house tonight, making turkey sandwiches, talking, laughing, and later on getting into a rousing game of hearts. The little children and I watched a Walt Disney circus on TV before they fell asleep on the living room floor, snuggled in sleeping bags.

November 28—It was still very dark when I tiptoed past the sleeping children, fixed a breakfast of sourdough waffles, and ventured out in the cold to milk the cow and chore.

The day dawned with blue skies, sunshine, and bright snowfields gleaming on the mountains. It was 27 degrees. Two Portland hunter friends stopped by to visit on their way home. They had spent Thanksgiving down at Dug Bar, and were pretty proud of the five-point bull elk they had bagged in the Snake River unit.

Doug picked one last frozen tomato from the vines beside the house today. I fixed a fried chicken-apple pie supper for the family, one last get-together before they all leave in the morning. Twelve of us around the table tonight, as we demolished the food I'd spent all day preparing. Hugs and tears of parting when the Wallowa County families said goodbye to the Chilcoot family.

November 29—The Phillips family left on this 10-degree morning. Filled them up with sourdough hotcakes for the long trip home. As they pulled out of the driveway, still waving, a great emptiness washed over me.

Thankful for my upside-down house, I began cleaning and was then able to take my mind off the departing family. Swept, mopped, did three loads of towels and sheets, made beds, put away blankets, and soon the house was in order. But still I missed the friendly banter of my children and grandchildren.

Doug doing all the feeding today, as it is the hired men's day off. As the sun disappeared over the mountain around 3:30 p.m., a bitterly cold stillness settled over the valley.

This evening Doug and I attended an open house at Jim and Ethel Chandler's in Joseph, a thank you get-together for those who worked on the past year's centennial projects. Grace Bartlett accompanied us and we were treated to the warm hospitality of the Chandlers, who operate a bed and breakfast known as Trail's End.

The warm, wood tones of the peeled log interior glowed in candlelight, which also cast a soft glow on pine and fir boughs. Bowls of punch and trays of goodies tempted us as we visited friends and recalled all the happy events of our centennial year. What a year it has been!

When we returned to our warm house, glittering, frosty stars sparkled in the night sky, and two great horned owls hooted at each other from the old willow trees.

November 30—Nine degrees as November leaves us. The flaming, flamingo-colored sunrise brightened the eastern horizon on Prairie Creek this morning, backlighting the dark shapes of the cattle. Dark blue clouds hover over the mountains.

While I walked from the barn to the house, a fierce wind out of the south sent dry leaves swirling in every direction. Loose hay, caught in a vortex, flew away from the cattle feeders. The dark clouds broke loose from the mountains and began to roll across the sky. The temperature rose from nine to 30 degrees in less than an hour. A chinook.

Baked a chocolate pie for grandson Chad's pie-a-month gift. Typed out "CowBelle Corner" for the local newspaper, ran errands in town, baked a pan of gingerbread, and fixed pork chops for supper. The wind continues to howl.

Tomorrow is December 1st and that means now we must all think Christmas.

December 1—Weatherwise, we are experiencing it all on this first day of December. The wind didn't let up all night and by morning freezing rain began to fall, before a 40-degree chinook swept away the remaining patches of snow.

The warm winds created a huge dust cloud that blew above a plowed field, the wind's fierce breath sucking up the little moisture left in the soil. Stepping outside to walk to the barn, I watched fascinated as a gust of wind picked up a bucket that had been lying near the shop, spun it around in the air, and deposited it near the bull corral. So strong were these gusts, I had trouble standing upright.

The snowline retreated to upper Prairie Creek again, and winter seems delayed—for the moment, anyway. In spite of the wind storm, our crew is working the weaned calves down at the corrals, and the vet came out to Bangs vaccinate more than 100 head of our heifers this afternoon.

Baked an old-fashioned rice pudding in the wood stove oven for the potato meeting here tonight. The high temperature today was 50

Snowy peaks provide a scenic backdrop for Wallowa County buckaroos.

degrees! By 9:30 p.m. the wind ceased, as did the rain.

December 2—Doug left early this morning to attend a farm fair in Hermiston. Forty degrees, cloudy and no wind while I chored at the barn and fed the horses. Began calling some of my 4-H photographers to take pictures of children on Santa Claus's lap, an annual community service project. Early darkness brought with it the return of the wind.

December 3—Wind continued all night, tearing at the house with furious gusts that fairly rattled the windows. At daylight, ragged black clouds, torn apart and borne across the dark skies, scattered in all directions.

One large black cloud loomed briefly on the eastern horizon before sailing over Prairie Creek to be ripped open by the fierceness of the wind. Fifty-one degrees on the clothesline thermometer! Spent the day catching up on a huge stack of correspondence. Our phone has been dead most of the day, no doubt due to the wind storm. The moon appears and disappears on this blustery December night.

December 4—Still no frost, and a 50-degree wind. The snow-capped Wallowa peaks stand out boldly against the stark, dark skies.

After chores, I assembled Santa suit, camera and tripod, and headed for Cloverleaf Hall, where the Hand Crafters were holding their annual Christmas bazaar. The entire hall was filled with beautiful handmade items including fudge, aprons, teddy bears, lovely decorator pillows, rawhide and leather craft, wooden toys, Hope McLaughlin's handmade quilts and rugs, art work, tole painting and Christmas ornaments.

The quality of the work was better than ever, making a very impressive display. Seated by a large Christmas tree was our Santa, Jim Blankenship, who had such a terrible cold that we sent him home at noon.

In just the nick of time we enlisted another Santa, alias Cub Begley, who kindly consented to fill in. The Santa suit was a tad too small and Cub's bare legs peeked through between the suit and his shoes, but no one seemed to mind except "Mrs. Claus."

Our 4-H'ers photographed all manner of children, from babes-in-arms to big kids. The ladies seemed to be especially popular with Santa. Cub made an excellent Santa Claus, and we closed shop at 3 and dropped the film off at Enterprise Photo Express.

Because Cub had other commitments for tomorrow, I spent the entire evening trying to enlist the services of yet another Santa Claus. Have you ever tried finding a Santa on short notice? I must have called at least 20 men and, for one reason or another, they simply couldn't do it. I never heard so many reasons.

December 5—This has been the most incredible day. Doug and I left at 5 a.m. to go hunting.

Earlier this year I had applied for, and received, an Alder Slope antlerless elk tag. And today, our calendar said, was opening day. Because it was too dark to see, we stopped at Tony's Shell in Joseph to wait for daylight. Somehow my heart wasn't with elk hunting, as I was still wondering who I would get to be today's Santa.

A warm, frostless morning dawned as we drove up on Alder Slope. I saw no sign of an elk, a hunter or much of anything—thank goodness, as I had been mentally figuring out how to fit in a successful hunt with what I had to do today.

The snowline had marched farther up the mountain, and with it, apparently all the elk. Returning to the ranch, I went out to the barn to milk my cow, who thought I'd deserted her for sure this time. Then on the phone again to locate a replacement Santa.

I called John Freels, Elmer Storm, Don Kooch and Max Walker. No one, it seemed, was free to portray the jolly old fellow with the big white beard. Arriving at Cloverleaf Hall, where I had about decided I would have to play Old Saint Nick, Cub Begley once more appeared to save me from such a fate. Bless him.

He'd been at John Freels' when I called. Cub was into the suit again, passing out candy canes and the 4-H'ers were snapping pictures right and left, when "Santa" was called to appear at the courthouse.

About that time my own little grandson, James, appeared to have his picture taken, whereupon grandma disappeared and reappeared as Santa. I had stuffed my jacket inside the suit to produce a big belly, donned the itching whiskers and hurried out to the Christmas tree. Even by lowering my voice, I couldn't fool 18-month-old James. He knew his grandma's eyes.

In my haste to dress, I had forgotten to put on Santa's black boots and all of a sudden I realized my white tenny runners were showing. Whoops! It was extremely warm under the suit and the whiskers itched so under my nose, that I stuck my nose through the mouth hole and became a very hairy Santa.

I took a brief break at noon and enjoyed partaking of the Imnaha Grange ladies' lunch of homemade soup, sandwiches and pies. Thus fortified, I returned to my station by the Christmas tree. After a while, I really got into the act and actually enjoyed it, especially seeing the children, who really believe in Santa and told me what they wanted for Christmas, and visited as if we were the best of friends. It turned out to be a very rewarding experience after all.

Mercifully, 3 p.m. arrived and the 4-H'ers had done very well. Did two weeks' grocery shopping on the way home. Fixed hot roast beef sandwiches for supper, then did two days' accumulation of dirty dishes in the sink. A very long and confusing day. Tonight, as Doug braids reins for Christmas presents, and I write, the wind still moans on Prairie Creek.

December 6—The wind blew so hard last night, it seemed as if our roof would surely blow away! Angry clouds rolled into the valley this morning, and the mountains became invisible as the clouds emptied themselves over Prairie Creek.

Wanda McAlister and I had planned to climb Sheep Ridge. Wanda showed up at 9, just as a burst of sunlight brought the mountains into focus. The slopes gleamed brightly under a blanket of new snow. It appeared, for the moment anyway, that it wasn't snowing on T.V. Ridge, so we donned raincoats and decided to go for it.

Driving to Alder Slope, we passed by a downed power line that had fallen victim to the wind. A PP&L crew was in the process of repairing it. We managed to barely miss a runaway wheel line rolling down the middle of the road.

Pulling into Clarice Southwick's yard, we parked a safe distance from several tall pine trees swaying in the wind. It didn't seem too cold, and a light sprinkle of rain began to fall as we visited briefly with Clarice, who thought we'd lost our senses. Warning us to watch for flying limbs or falling trees, she wished us luck.

Clarice's small herd of goats followed us up the hill to the old logging road, then abandoned us as we began the steep climb that proved easy walking due to the absence of any snow. Meanwhile, trees twisted and groaned all around us, limbs falling everywhere as the pine needles swished and swayed.

We hiked along at a pretty good pace, all the while enjoying the novelty of a December storm on the mountain. Looking out in the direction of Ruby Peak, we saw sheets of sleet being driven by the powerful wind.

Gasping as the wind tore our breath away, we finally reached the top, which consisted of a narrow hog's back that ran back to the end of the ridge. On the other side of the saddle we could look down toward the Lostine. Far out north, in the high plateau or "hill country," the sun was shining! As we walked past the big TV antennas the wind slackened.

Hiking still higher on the ridge, so Wanda could photograph the panorama below, the constantly changing weather sent dark clouds racing over us and it began to rain again. The temperature dropped dramatically and the rain turned to wind-driven sleet that stung our faces.

We hurried back down the mountain, arriving safely at the car by noon, though wet and cold, and by this time it was raining steadily. Driving to Grace Bartlett's, where we had been invited to dinner, we looked up at the mountain to see it snowing. Our timing had been just right.

We basked in the warmth of Grace's snug little home, and the wood stove soon warmed us, as did the delicious meal of chicken pot pie, mashed potatoes, Imnaha squash, homemade bread, peach preserves and hot tea. This repast ranked as one of the best we'd ever eaten.

Red geraniums bloomed on Grace's windowsill, while winter held sway outside. Later we accompanied Grace while she fed her thoroughbred horses. We must have seen close to 20 deer, wandering around in her woods in the storm.

Driving back to Prairie Creek we ran into a large bunch of cattle that were wandering around near the four corners. The cows belonging to our neighbors, the Klages, had pushed open a wooden gate and made their escape. At home I called to inform Ardis about the cattle.

Learning that she was the only one home today, Wanda and I drove back. The three of us "gals" rounded up the scattered cows and drove them back into their pasture. Gathered the eggs and fixed a big pot of clam chowder for supper.

The wind finally died down, but the rain continued on into the night. Curled up with a good book on this Sunday night.

December 7—A moon, still high in the sky at 6 a.m., reveals a new snowfall on Prairie Creek. After chores I began working on some journalism deadlines. A soup bone simmers in a kettle on the wood range, and I add something to the broth every time I walk by: cabbage, potatoes, carrots, onions, canned tomatoes. By noon the soup is just right.

As I drove to Wallowa this afternoon and interviewed the new Oregon Cattlemen's president, Bill Wolfe, a warm sun began to melt most of the snow. Tonight Doug and I attended a potluck put on by the Wallowa Lake tourists committee.

Pat and Ray Combes' lake home was festooned with lovely Christmas decorations and the roast beef and potluck dishes were most delicious. After showing "The Wallowa Story" slide-tape presentation to the members of the committee, we drove home.

A brilliant moon lit up the snowy mountains and shimmered across the lake.

December 8.—A gray, windy day, the puddles of water turning to ice.

Very busy, working on the details of many projects. Attended a centennial meeting at Chandler's this morning as we wind up Wallowa County's centennial year.

Doug returned from neighbor Max Gorsline's with a sackful of cats, which he turned loose in the barn. What will Mamma Kitty and Nermal think?

I attended a 4-H leaders meeting tonight at Cloverleaf Hall while Doug went to a stockgrowers meeting.

December 9—Thirty-two degrees, the chinook replaced by a freezing wind that goes right through you.

"Bag balmed" Startch's teats this morning, as the cold wind caused them to chap. The new barn cats are very shy, but appeared one by one as I poured warm milk into their dish. The wind evaporated the puddles and the ground is dry again.

I had been invited to show the "Wallowa Story" at the Wallowa Grange Hall tonight. As Grace and I drove to the lower valley, power lines swayed in the wind, and trees were down along the road. It was an effort to keep the pickup on the road. Herds of tumbleweed-like bushes skittered across in front of us like cattle.

Stars twinkled brightly in a clear dark sky, and it was unbelievably warm for December. Arriving at the Grange hall, we were greeted by Rae and Orie Mahanna, who assisted in setting up the projector. The old Grange hall, which used to be a theater, was a perfect place to project the slides. A fire had been started in a basement furnace and the place was warm and cozy.

Presently a good crowd assembled and I began the show, when all of a sudden the lights went out! The outage was short-lived and we continued on before they went out again, this time to stay out. We were all plunged into total darkness. The only light came from an occasional passing car on Main Street.

Everyone simply sat and waited and visited until someone appeared with a flashlight to report that the power outage had been caused by three downed trees over power lines between Lostine and Wallowa. Nothing to do but load up our equipment, by flashlight, and head home into the dark and windy night.

Driving back to Prairie Creek, I watched a bright, orange-colored moon emerge between ghostly-looking, black clouds on the eastern horizon. Just barely walked into our house when the electricity went out all over the area! The black clouds multiplied and the rain began. It will be a long night for the PP&L repair crew.

December 10—It is raining this morning and seems so quiet. After all the wind we've had, the stillness is absolute. The rain had turned into a tapioca-like sleet by the time I went out to chore. Baked a loaf of sourdough bread for a CowBelle gift-exchange today.

Lawrence Potter drove wife Ilene out from Little Sheep Creek, and she rode with me to CowBelles. The meeting was held at Childers' on Prairie Creek, and it began snowing as we drove over to Linda's. The big fat flakes began to stick to everything.

Linda's home was already decorated for Christmas with many pine boughs and colorful, country decorations. Cattle were feeding at long bunks in a nearby feedlot.

Met with my 4-H Sourdough Shutterbugs tonight, while they elected officers and planned the coming year. Such an ambitious group. Hope I can continue to keep up with them.

December 12—15 degrees, cloudy and cold. Began writing Christmas card letters.

December 13—Doug and I went Christmas tree hunting this afternoon. After looking at many kinds, we finally selected a red fir that was just right. Mounted in its stand, the little tree stood proudly in our living room, ready to be decorated.

I dug out the Christmas decorations and strung lights, then hung stockings from the fireplace mantel. There is something about a Christmas tree that makes a house feel cozy and warm on a cold winter's evening.

While I strung popcorn, Doug worked on a set of braided reins for a Christmas gift. So much to do getting ready for the holidays. More snow in the forecast.

December 14—Finished shooting the end of a roll of film, as per instructions from an assistant editor of Sunset Magazine, who is doing an article on sourdough and considering some of my recipes. She wanted to know how the lighting was in my kitchen, so had sent me a roll of film to take various shots. Naturally, I had fun taking shots of biscuits just out of the oven, wood stove and all.

In between typing my column and CowBelle Corner, I managed to get all the Christmas cards in the mail.

Very cold this morning, around 10 degrees. Ice is forming in the calf pen and it is becoming a daily chore to chop a hole for them to drink.

December 15—After chores on this cold morning, I mixed up a batch of gingerbread cookie dough. Just finished when an Alder Slope neighbor, Ted Juve, called, saying, "If you don't have your elk yet, better grab your rifle and get right up here. The elk have returned!" Ted said another permit holder already had one down, and a second elk was still in the swamp below his house.

So, I washed cookie dough from my hands, changed into my hiking boots, grabbed my .243, and Doug and I headed out the back door. I remembered to stuff my anterless December elk permit in my pocket, and we were off to Alder Slope.

When we arrived, Ted pointed to a nearby alder thicket and said the elk was still there. It was bitter cold and spitting snow as I climbed over a fence and cautiously approached the trees. I walked through an opening and spotted the lone, young elk. Taking a rest on the limb of a tree, I squeezed off a shot.

Unfortunately, I hadn't taken time to sight in my gun, and so shot low and missed. I fired again and hit the elk in the foot. By this time I was feeling sorry for the animal and wanted to get the whole thing over with.

The young elk stood his ground, not far from his downed comrade, seemingly reluctant to leave. For what seemed like an eternity, he stood, with his rump to me, so I waited for him to turn broadside. Since I was hidden from his view, he didn't know which way to make a getaway, and the injured foot discouraged his jumping over the fence.

Finally, he turned and I downed him. A fine, anterless bull. None of the meat was spoiled. The last shot had penetrated his heart. He lay near a frozen swampy area. I didn't get much of a thrill out of killing the animal, but the Alder Slope herd is growing too large and has been encroaching on rancher's lands. The elk are becoming an increasing problem as of late, and so the herd definitely needed to be thinned out.

Doug gutted the animal and we loaded it into the pickup. It was freezing and we stopped briefly to visit Wilmer and Mary Cook, and warm outselves by their cheery fire. Doug and Wilmer got to discussing their gold panning hobby, and it was hard to leave these good friends, whom I have known for many years. The couple raises a big garden every year with raspberries, horseradish and many varieties of fruit trees. They have a few milk cows and ducks, and have reared five children, and now have 14 grandchildren.

Home to stoke the fire and fix lunch, before Doug skinned, quarted and hung my elk. While grandchildren Buck and Mona Lee were here this afternoon, I kept them busy stringing popcorn for the tree, and then we baked the gingerbread men, one for each member of our large and extended family.

December 16—Still chopping a hole in the ice so the calves can drink. Blue sky and very cold today. I wrote the names of the family in frosting on the gingerbread men, and hung them on the tree.

Decorated the fireplace with pine boughs. It's beginning to look like Christmas.

December 17—Sixteen degrees and clear, sunny and mild for this time of year. Began Christmas shopping for 12 grandchildren. Met Doug for lunch at the Common Good Market Place in Enterprise. Seemed as though most of our neighbors were in town today, hustling around, shopping, cheerful and friendly in the holiday spirit.

While in town, I attended the Enterprise school Christmas program and watched granddaughter Chelsie's third grade class sing Christmas songs. What a crowd. Every mom, dad, aunt, uncle and grandparent must have been there. Chelsie looked very sweet in her little red dress.

Visited Gladys Quinn in the nursing home and took her an amaryllis bulb to grow in her room. It was so good to see her. After supper, Doug and I headed for Imnaha to watch their Christmas program, which consisted of an hour of plays, skits and songs, ending with the appearance of Santa Claus.

Grandchildren Buck and Mona played different roles, and the canyon children really outdid themselves with the help of school marm, Char

Williams, and several of the mothers. Using homemade props and performing plays they had written themselves, they brought down the house.

Santa appeared with his large sack full of oranges and candy. The little one-room school house was filled to overflowing and we were all treated to homemade cookies, Christmas goodies and punch. 'Tis the season to be jolly.

December 18—Twenty-six degrees, partly sunny and dry. The busy days continue, wrapping, Christmas baking, and mailing packages to out-of-state family.

We began cutting and wrapping my elk for the freezer today. The Sunset Magazine editor called and postponed their visit until after January.

December 19—Nearly 8 a.m. when the sunrise showed us clear blue skies, and only a skift of snow on the ground. It is 20 degrees this morning.

Watched grandchildren this afternoon. They were entertained by cutting up last year's Christmas cards and pasting them on long sheets of butcher paper to make murals. Also played Crazy 8's with Buck, who takes this game seriously, and usually wins.

December 20—Ten degrees when I chored this morning. It had gotten down to five for the low last night. Still working on Christmas. A lamb roast sizzles in the wood stove oven for supper.

Ben and Steve spend most of the day feeding the many cattle that we winter here, a routine chore that takes place at the same time each day. There is a good supply of hay in the valley this year.

December 21—Jackie's family spent the night last night, leaving around 5:30 this morning for Roseburg where they will spend the Christmas week with Bill's folks. Milked the cow, worked on my column, and did more Christmas baking before delivering it to friends and neighbors.

Relieved upon hearing of the safe arrival of the Imnaha family. One always worries these days when loved ones travel our modern freeways...at least, grandmas do!

December 22—A new snowfall on this first day of winter. Nineteen degrees, which feels mild for this time of year. Scotty showed up while I was baking, armed with her annual gift of Scottish shortbread, a real treat.

It began snowing again as I delivered more Christmas breads to friends, the mountains obscured by swirling snowflakes that drift downward from cloudy skies. Enjoyed watching grandson James this afternoon, while mom ran errands. It finally feels like winter is here, and I am ready for Christmas.

December 23—A large hay shed burned last night on the Buhler Ranch near Joseph.

Up before dawn, fixing breakfast for Doug and Max Gorsline before they left for Sunnyside, Washington, where Doug will pick up a part for our silage truck. It was still dark when they left, so I read a book by the fire and waited for daylight to make its way over Prairie Creek.

Out to do the usual chores, breaking ice for the calves to drink and hauling warm water to the laying hens. Made a batch of caramel corn and left some in the mailbox for our mail lady, Ella, who has been good to us this past year. Sometimes we are out of stamps, and she takes the change we leave and puts stamps on for us. This is time-consuming and we appreciate these things, so at Christmas time we say thanks to Ella.

Spent a quiet afternoon reading by the stove. Can't believe all the Christmas preparations are done and I seem to be a lady of leisure so close to the holidays. Walked out our snowy lane to get the mail and enjoyed reading the welcome Christmas cards. Filled up the empty wood box and gathered the eggs. It was nearly 10 p.m. and snowing again when Doug and Max returned with the part.

December 24—Doug left early this morning to drive to Elgin and pick up daughter Linda, who will be spending Christmas with us. Two great horned owls hoot-hooed at each other in the willow tree. It must be going to snow again; these owls are my weather forecasters.

Prairie Creek is locked in winter silence today. It is five below zero under the clothesline. Began weaning Startch's big heifer calf, as she has grown so large, she can scarcely squeeze through the small door to reach her mom stanchioned in the milking room. This moment is when all the big milk cow's calves get weaned.

Straining the milk when Doug drove in with Linda. After saying hello, she went directly to bed with a bad cold. I began baking blackberry and gooseberry pies for Christmas dinner tomorrow. To make Linda feel better, I cooked up a pot of clam chowder for supper. Just the three of us here on Christmas Eve.

Very cold outside; a good night to stay by the fire. We opened our gifts and enjoyed the quiet evening. Our tree, along with a bright red poinsetta plant and the many Christmas cards sent by friends, made the living room cheerful and warm. The lights from the tree were reflected on the snowy lawn...and it was a holy night on Prairie Creek.

December 25—Christmas Day dawned in a flawlessly clear sky that brought a five-above zero reading on the thermometer. Chores over with, I began cooking our traditional prime rib dinner, and the house was soon overflowing with children, grandchildren, and the wonderful aroma of roast beef.

Twelve of us around the table today. A wonderful meal, with contributions from daughters-in-law Liza and Annie, who also did all the dishes. The children played outside until the short daylight ended and darkness settled over the valley.

Everyone left and suddenly the house was quite again. I could hear our dog, Stubby, howling at a coyote, who answered from a nearby hill on this cold, still night.

December 26—Temperature hovered around 10 degrees and the early pink blush stole across Ruby Peak and Chief Joseph Mountain before the cold winter light brightened the valley.

My laying hens roost early during these short winter days. Chester the rooster, sandwiched in between, seems to accept his lot. Wonder what they find to talk about, perched on their roosts for all those long, dark and cold winter hours.

My 4-H'ers enjoyed an ice-skating party on a frozen pond near the Ed Jones ranch. They built a bonfire, roasted hot dogs and marshmallows and had a great time. Darkness came early and the cattle licked up the last stems of hay as a bitter cold settled over Prairie Creek with the disappearance of the sun.

December 28—It was four degrees and the daily chore of chopping ice so the cattle could drink became commonplace. All over the valley, livestock waited patiently for their daily ration of hay.

December 29—Our dog Stubby barked at a coyote that crossed the road in front of our house. A fog bank rolled in and locked us into a silent, cold stillness. It was 10 degrees when the fog lifted, leaving frozen filigree on every blade of grass, tree limb, fence and power line.

December 30—Awoke to see a good seven inches of snow had fallen during the night. Powdery, dry snow covered Prairie Creek on that 20-degree morning.

More snow came with the daylight. The fence posts looked like ice-cream cones. Broke a trail to the barn to chore, as the barn cats ran to meet me. I began drying Startch up; it was time to wean her big heifer. Grandchildren Buck and Mona Lee spent the night that it snowed; next day we bundled up and pulled the sleds to the top of a hill and sledded down.

We made "snow angels" by lying on our backs in the soft snow and making impressions with our bodies. The snow was so powdery and dry we didn't even get wet. We built a snowman in the front yard and used a carrot for his nose and put a bright red scarf around his neck.

Because of the snowstorm, Doug, Ben and Steve trailed the cows home from the Harris place on upper Prairie Creek. It was quite a sight seeing 300 head pass by on the snowy road. The snowfall had put a halt to their winter grazing. Hay will be on the menu from now on. The cows were in good shape, considering they had been on dry feed with molasses block supplement.

December 31—Five below zero on this last morning in December. While running errands in Enterprise, I was glad to see a two-mule open sleigh skimming around town. Bob, Claire and little Megan Casey were out exercising their mules! Hearing sleigh bells, people stopped and stared; it looked like so much fun.

As the day faded away and the light diminished, it was nearly dark by 4:45 p.m. The minutes ticked away and Wallowa County would soon enter its second 100 years.

A bright moon shed its light on the snowy valley and mountains as we drove to Bud and Ruby Zollmans' in Joseph to celebrate the coming of the new year. While we visited with friends, the temperature continued to fall outside. Inside there was the warmth of friendship, food and a fire in the fireplace. We all agreed that 1987 had been quite a year, what with the centennial celebrations and all.

After midnight when we drove home to the cold, frosty, moonlit world of Prairie Creek.

Index